1990

ARISTOTLE'S TWO SYSTEMS

ARISTOTLE'S TWO SYSTEMS

DANIEL W. GRAHAM

CLARENDON PRESS · OXFORD

Oxford University Press, Walton Street, Oxford OX2 6DP

Oxford New York Toronto
Delhi Bombay Calcutta Madras Karachi
Petaling Jaya Singapore Hong Kong Tokyo
Nairobi Dar es Salaam Cape Town
Melbourne Auckland
and associated companies in
Berlin Ibadan

OXFORD is a trade mark of Oxford University Press

Published in the United States
by Oxford University Press, New York

First published 1987
First issued in paperback 1990

British Library Cataloguing in Publication Data
Graham, Daniel W.
Aristotle's two systems.
1. Aristotle
I. Title
185   B485
ISBN 0–19–824315–4

Library of Congress Cataloging in Publication Data
Graham, Daniel W.
Aristotle's two systems.
Bibliography: p.
Includes index.
1. Aristotle.   I. Title.
B485.C584   1987   1985   87–7764
ISBN 0–19–824315–4

Printed and bound in
Great Britain by Biddles Ltd,
Guildford and King's Lynn

TO CAPTAIN ALDEN GERARD GRAHAM
ΠΑΤΡΙ ΚΥΒΕΡΝΗΤΗΙ ΤΕ ΣΑΟΦΡΟΝΑ ΘΥΜΟΝ ΕΧΟΝΤΙ
ΤΑΥΤ᾽ΑΝΕΘΗΚΑ

PREFACE

δίπλ' ἐρέω . . .
 . . . τοτὲ δ' αὖ διέφυ πλέον' ἐξ ἑνὸς εἶναι.

EMPEDOCLES

The idea for this study emerged while I was still working on my dissertation, which I wrote on a topic in Aristotle's philosophy of action. As I was researching the history of the potentiality–actuality distinction, I discovered that Aristotle did not use his word 'matter' anywhere in the logical works. The discovery was a discovery only to me; it had long been known. Yet it seemed amazing to me that a principle as important as that of matter should not appear in so large a body of work. Did this omission have important consequences for the interpretation of Aristotle? I found that interpreters saw the omission as at most a curiosity; after all, the subject-matter of the logical works was unique. Yet the same interpreters had long ago abandoned the assumption that the logical works were purely devoted to logic. In particular, the *Categories* is commonly taken to be a prime source of information about Aristotle's early metaphysical theory. But how could Aristotle have formulated anything like this mature metaphysical theory without the matter–form distinction? Was the unity of Aristotle's thought not really an illusion? Were there not really two sets of theories, two metaphysical conceptions, two philosophical systems?

I found that a few philosophers had asked these questions and had concluded that there was indeed a crucial development in Aristotle's thought such as I envisaged. I was especially impressed by a perceptive and provocative essay by Russell Dancy (1978), to which someone referred me when I read a paper of my own (a 1979 draft of Graham 1984) on the subject. Dancy's article stressed conceptual relations, whereas my paper concentrated on the developmental questions. Nevertheless, Dancy anticipated many of the major conclusions of both my article and this book, and I regard his essay as a major contribution to the two systems question. I also found that Alan Code held similar ideas about

Aristotle's development, some of which are expressed in his articles. Finally, I was encouraged in my project at a fairly early stage by the late G. E. L. Owen, to whom I showed a draft of what was to become my 1984 article. As he read the paper through in my presence he anticipated most of the conclusions and expressed agreement with them. I was pleased, since although his own published writings contain some hints of the two systems theory, they do not strongly support it.

Despite the authority that these scholars might lend to my project there has been surprisingly little done in the direction of a complete two systems theory. A few additional scholars have made passing claims to the effect that Aristotle developed his hylomorphic views after writing the logical works (see Chapter 4 n. 39). But effects of these combined pronouncements have been slight. Much scholarship still proceeds as if Aristotle's work were a seamless whole. And although it is popular to allow for some kind of development in Aristotle's thought, most developmental schemes in current studies are *ad hoc* constructs with no guiding principle to sustain them.

What I seemed to see as a I pursued my study of the relation between early and late Aristotelian theories was a great divide that separated all of Aristotle's thought into two separate watersheds, such that everything on one side of the divide behaved differently from everything on the other. Philologically the terminology was strikingly different from one system to another; philosophically the respective doctrines seemed almost directly contradictory in some cases. The differences appeared to be systematic and to persist right down to the bedrock of Aristotle's philosophy. To borrow another geological analogy, it was as if there were a fault line running right down the middle of Aristotle's philosophy; one could observe considerable continuity on each side, but a regular displacement of features occurred from one side of the rift to the other. Moreover, Aristotle's philosophical tremors always occurred right at the fault line, as if two plates were clashing at just that point.

One may well wonder how such a major division as I posit could go unnoticed and uncharted for so long. Perhaps like early geologists we have been looking at surface features too much and the underlying structure of the systems too little. To the challenge of credibility I think we should interpose a counter-query:

how could we possibly overlook these major differences so long? So pronounced are the differences that except for the strong tradition of manuscript transmission they would provide plausible grounds for attributing the *Organon* and the physical–metaphysical treatises to different authors. Indeed, it was for a long time the fate of the *Categories* to be excluded from the canon of Aristotle's writings on just such grounds. Having readmitted the work to the canon, modern scholars have not yet faced up to its implications. Here is a work which cannot be banished as spurious, cannot be explained away as merely logical in content, and cannot be reconciled with the metaphysics of the *Metaphysics*. Although the *Categories* is not by a different author, the work expresses a different philosophy.

In what follows I have tried to give my vision of Aristotle's two systems concrete expression in an argument with historical, philological, but above all philosophical dimensions. If the argument is right, a fact about Aristotle's development that has been relegated to asides and footnotes should have a central place in interpretations of Aristotle—should be a point of departure for many studies and provide a limit of inquiry for others. At present few scholars would agree with such claims. To be sure, many would grant that the metaphysical assumptions of the *Categories* are different from those of the *Metaphysics*; but this fact does not seem to have any far-reaching implications for their interpretations of Aristotle, and so I infer that they do not subscribe to a dualistic interpretative theory. A mere handful of scholars have advocated a two-systems theory in some form or other, and I believe that there is only one person who holds the Two Systems Theory with all its ramifications. However, as Socrates has taught us, it does not matter what the many think, but what the expert in truth has to say—that is, what the outcome of the argument is.

In this study all translations of works cited are my own except as noted. In quotations of modern sources all italics are those of the original text except as noted.

I am indebted to the National Endowment for the Humanities for several vital grants: I wrote most of the first draft of this study under an NEH fellowship in 1983–4; Chapter 2 was largely written with the aid of an NEH summer stipened in 1982: and I did important preliminary work while studying under Gregory Vlastos at the University of California, Berkeley, in an NEH summer seminar in 1981. Certain paragraphs of Chapter 1 are borrowed from an article of mine which is forthcoming in *Metaphilosophy*; I thank that journal for permission to reprint. I am grateful to colleagues and the administrations of the schools at which I have taught, namely Grinnell College, Rice University, and Brigham Young University, and the school at which I did my doctoral work and where the seeds for this study were sown, the University of Texas at Austin; they have all provided invaluable personal and institutional support for my studies. I am also grateful to Brian L. Merrill for preparing the indexes. I should like to thank three great scholars of ancient philosophy for their example, friendship, and continued support: Alexander Mourelatos, Paul Woodruff, and Gregory Vlastos. My wonderful father, to whom I dedicate this book, and my dear departed mother have been a source of inspiration and strength to me. To my wife and editorial adviser Diana and to my children Sarah and Joseph go my loving thanks for their encouragement, their faith in me, and their willingness to share me with a troublesome philosopher from Stagira.

D.G.

Brigham Young University
Provo, Utah, USA
August, 1986

CONTENTS

List of figures   xiv

Abbreviations   xv

1   The Two Systems Hypothesis   I
   1.1   The Developmentalist View   4
   1.2   The Unitarian View   7
   1.3   Reconciling the Two Points of View   10
   1.4   Overview of the Argument   14
   1.5   The Significance of TSH   17

2   S_1: Atomic Substantialism   20
   2.1   Ontology   20
   2.2   Logic and Language   38
   2.3   Philosophy of Science   46
   2.4   Conclusion   54

3   S_2: Hylomorphic Substantialism   57
   3.1   Ontology   57
   3.2   Logic and Language   62
   3.3   Philosophy of Science   72
   3.4   Profiles of S_1 and S_2 79

4   The Incommensurability of the Systems   84
   4.1   Hypotheses Concerning the Relation
       Between S_1 and S_2 85
   4.2   Evaluation of the Hypotheses   87
   4.3   The Incommensurability of S_1 and S_2 93
   4.4   The Genetic Relation of S_1 and S_2 112
   4.5   The Motivation for Development   116

5   The Hylomorphic Turn   119
   5.1   Concepts of Change in S_1 120
   5.2 S_1 and the Eleatic Problem of Change   123
   5.3   Aristotle's Options   128
   5.4   Models and the Schema of Change   131
   5.5   Conclusion   152

6   The Growth of S_2: The Four Causes   156
    6.1   The Development of the Four Cause
          Theory   156
    6.2   Explanation of the Development of FCT   172
    6.3   Conclusion   181

7   The Growth of S_2: Potentiality and
    Actuality   183
    7.1   'Ενέργεια-Α   185
    7.2   'Ενέργεια-S   192
    7.3   The Development of the Concept of
          Actuality   194
    7.4   Potentiality in *Met*. ix   199
    7.5   Conclusion   206

8   The Paradoxes of Substance: Matter   207
    8.1   Aristotle's Continued Acceptance of S_1 207
    8.2   The Problem of *Met*. vii   210
    8.3   The Conflict of S_1 and S_2 in *Met*. vii   221

9   The Paradoxes of Substance: Form   233
    9.1   Form as Substance   233
    9.2   Essence as Substance   239
    9.3   Problems of the Well-Tempered Substance   244
    9.4   The Incompatibility of the Systems   252
    9.5   Aristotle's Other Solutions   257
    9.6   Conclusion   261

10 S_2 Without S_1: What Aristotle Should
    Have Said   263
    10.1   The Claims of Form   263
    10.2   Problems with Aristotle's Platonism   268
    10.3   The Composite as Primary Substance   275
    10.4   Resolving the Antinomies of Substance   281
    10.5   Conclusion   288

11 The Two Systems Theory as an Interpreta-
    tion of Aristotle   290
    11.1   Recapitulation   290
    11.2   Towards a Consistent Aristotle   293
    11.3   Problems of Dating   297
    11.4   Contextual Advantages of TST   310
    11.5   Evidential Advantages of TST   314

11.6 TST and Other Interpretations   323
11.7 Conclusion   331

References   333

Index Locorum   347

Subject Index   354

LIST OF FIGURES

2.1. Categorial Ties 22
2.2. Basic Entities 22
2.3. Aristotle's Categorial Scheme 35
3.1. Profile of S_1 and S_2 80–1
3.2. Epistemological Profile 83
4.1. Types of ’Ενέργεια 98
4.2. Differences in the Meaning of Terms of S_1 and S_2 100
5.1. S_1 Schema of Change 140
5.2. Analogy between Changes 143
5.3. Craft Model I 150
5.4. Craft Model II 151
6.1. The Craftsman Situation 179
6.2. The Four Causes 180
7.1. Energy Levels (EA) 196
7.2. Curve of Becoming (ES) 197
7.3. Types of Potentiality–Actuality 201
8.1. Combinations of Powers 226

ABBREVIATIONS

Bonitz   Hermann Bonitz, *Index Aristotelicus* in Immanuel Bekker, ed., *Aristotelis Opera* vol. 5, G. Reimer, 1870; repr. in 2nd edn., Olof Gigon, ed., Berlin: W. de Gruyter, 1961.

DK   Hermann Diels, *Die Fragmente der Vorsokratiker*, 6th edn. rev. Walther Kranz, 3 vols., Dublin: Weidmann, 1951.

LSJ   H. J. Liddell and R. Scott, *A Greek–English Lexicon*, 9th edn. rev. H. S. Jones and R. McKenzie, Oxford: Clarendon Press, 1940.

WORKS OF ARISTOTLE

Cat.	*Categories*
DI	*De Interpretatione*
A.Pr.	*Prior Analytics*
A.Po.	*Posterior Analytics*
Top.	*Topics*
SE	*De Sophisticis Elenchis*
Ph.	*Physics*
DC	*De Caelo*
GC	*De Generatione et Corruptione*
Mtr.	*Meteorologica*
DA	*De Anima*
DS	*De Sensu*
PA	*De Partibus Animalium*
GA	*De Generatione Animalium*
Met.	*Metaphysics*
EN	*Nicomachean Ethics*
EE	*Eudemian Ethics*
Pol.	*Politics*
Rh.	*Rhetoric*
Poet.	*Poetics*

GREEK COMMENTARIES

Greek commentators are cited by page and line numbers from the appropriate volume of *Commentaria in Aristotelem Graeca*, 23 vols., Prussian Academy (Berlin: W. de Gruyter), 1882–1909.

I

The Two Systems Hypothesis

Consider two recent interpretations of Aristotle's *Categories*:

... the *Categories* is a carefully limited work—possibly an introductory one—which seems determined to contain the discussion at a metaphysical level that is, though in some ways sophisticated, still simple, and especially to block any descent from its own curtailed universe into the much deeper as well as wider universe of the *Metaphysics*. There is also evidence of a notable concern not to get involved in 'causes'—to set out some ontological phenomena ... without delving—here—into the underlying structure of the nature of things from which these phenomena eventuate. And a critical factor in maintaining that simplicity is the designation of the substantial individuals as ultimate objects, at the 'floor of the world' ... (Furth 1978: 629)

While Aristotle has spoken in the *Categories* as if the claim that substances underlie properties is totally unproblematic, in the *Metaphysics* he begins to draw consequences from this claim as to what really is the object or substance. As one can see in *Met* Z 3 he considers whether to say that substance, that which underlies everything else, is matter or form; by contrast in the *Categories* he had still spoken as if substances were the concrete things of our experience—tables, horses, trees, men—just as we are acquainted with them. How does it come about, we must ask, that Aristotle is no longer satisfied with the answer of the *Categories*? (Frede, 1978: 31 f.)

Although we would like to say that we have come a long way in interpreting Aristotle in the last half-century, it is an embarrassing fact that one cannot get past the first Bekker page of his text without coming face-to-face with a fundamental bifurcation in the path we must follow. In the first interpretation, by Montgomery Furth, the *Categories* is a propaedeutic which carefully avoids certain problems by limiting its principles and objectives; thus it prepares us for the *Metaphysics* account of substance by giving a simpler version of it. According to Michael Fede in the second passage, the difference of doctrine between the *Categories* and the *Metaphysics* is not anticipated in the prior work, and it is to be explained as a change in Aristotle's philosophy.

One might try simply to compare the two disparate viewpoints thus expressed with the evidence so as to make a straightforward decision between them. Unfortunately, both accounts are consistent with the evidence. Or rather, each view construes the immediate data so differently that there is no one set of evidence by which to decide between the views. For Frede the indivisibility of substance in the *Categories* account shows Aristotle has changed his views; for Furth the same fact shows Aristotle is limiting his account. Thus we arrive at an exegetical stalemate. Yet the situation demands a resolution as a precondition to further interpretation. For we have here a confrontation between two radically different and exclusive perspectives. Moreover, we cannot avoid the problem of choosing between views by saying the differences do not matter; for at stake is the theory of substance itself—the cornerstone of Aristotle's philosophy. The question is whether there is one theory of substance or two (or more), and hence whether there is one Aristotelian philosophy or two.

'Perhaps', we may console ourselves, 'the presence of such disparate viewpoints on a basic issue of interpretation is not so much an academic scandal as a manifestation of the pluralism of approach which makes contemporary research so rich.' But this will not do. For while it is desirable that we should have the alternatives presented for evaluation, we cannot rest content with a final stalemate between them. Furth's and Frede's views are incompatible, and both cannot be right; surely there must be some way to decide between them. It would be surprising, in fact, if in all the Aristotelian corpus we could not find convincing grounds for favouring one of the interpretations.

Indeed it is possible to have reasons to prefer one view to another. But in order to provide rational grounds for a decision, we must begin with higher-level questions than are usually addressed in studies of Aristotle. For typical studies of Aristotle *assume* the correctness of a methodology, and hence some prior principles about the nature of Aristotle's thought. But if we are to criticize the methodologies, the principles themselves must come under our scrutiny. We must, then, first identify the principles of different approaches. Fortunately, the standard approaches are easy to distinguish and their principles are not far to seek.

The two standard approaches represented above may be designated as the *unitarian* (Furth's) and the *developmentalist* (Frede's). The unitarian interpreter lays stress on the unity of Aristotle's thought and seeks to explain difficulties and apparent inconsistencies (of which there are many) by appealing to some distinction that will harmonize doctrines. The developmentalist recognizes developments in Aristotle's thought and allows himself the option of reconciling doctrines by isolating stages of thought and attributing conflicting views to different stages. For instance he may assign the conflicting doctrines of substance in the *Categories* and *Metaphysics* to different developmental strata.

Behind these two methodologies lie two different forms of explanation. The unitrian depends exclusively on a form we may call *systematic* explanation, in which what is at stake is the place of a doctrine, theory, or concept in a philosophical system. By positing a priori the unity of the system we leave open as the only path to explanation the detailed articulation of the system so as to accommodate all the theses which are assumed to be parts of that system. The developmentalist recognizes a form of *genetic* explanation, in which one item is identified as a precursor of another in that it is earlier in time and approximately identical in function. For instance the theories of substance of the *Categories* and *Metaphysics* occupy a similar functional space and the latter post-dates the former. By establishing these relationships the developmentalist may give a genetic account of the apparent inconsistency of the two theories of substance.

Now we should note that nothing in the two forms of explanation *per se* excludes the scholar from using both forms in conjunction,[1] although of course he cannot apply both to explain the same phenomenon in the same situation. Systematic explanation presupposes a unity of system, but it does not presuppose a *single* system—for there may be multiple systems or subsystems in a philosophy. Thus one might make use of systematic explanation in one domain while employing genetic explanations in another. Similarly, genetic explanation does not preclude systematic explanation; indeed, it presupposes a certain background of systematic

[1] In particular, the citation of Frede comes from an article that is largely an essay in systematic analysis.

explanation which is necessary to identify functionally similar units.

While nothing prohibits a circumspect use of both kinds of explanation, in fact there are doctrinaire proponents of the systematic and genetic modes of explanation. The proponents tend to promote the appropriate form of explanation to the detriment of the other. And indeed the unitarian and developmental approaches may aptly be taken as methodic applications of systematic or genetic explanations, respectively. The arguments proponents give in favour of their methods tend to be apologetic and polemical, and have often served to obscure rather than illuminate the advantages and disadvantages of the approaches. It will be helpful, therefore, to examine the approaches in a non-partisan way.

I.I   THE DEVELOPMENTALIST VIEW

Unlike Plato's dialogues, which were published individually and because of their publication and artistic form resisted revision, Aristotle's treatises formed an encyclopaedic series of lectures that remained in Aristotle's possession throughout his life and could be modified with changes in his thought. This fact, together with the systematic way in which the views in the several treatises interlock and complement each other, seemed to forestall any attempt to see a development in his philosophy. Accordingly, for many years developmental views were highly speculative and were put forth tentatively if at all. But in 1923, in what has proved to be the most influential book of the century on Aristotle, Werner Jaeger argued that there was an objective basis for the dating of certain of Aristotle's works. In *Aristoteles*, Jaeger began by showing that the fragments of Aristotle's lost dialogues, which leading scholars had rejected as spurious, were genuine. These dialogues had been rejected precisely because they seemed too Platonic. But Jaeger found evidence to confirm that various fragments were genuinely Aristotelian, and he pointed to the plausibility of Aristotle's having been a Platonist as a youth in the Academy. By noting shifts in Aristotle's manner of referring to Plato's school Jaeger was also able to establish that Books i, iii, and xiv of the *Metaphysics* were written shortly after Aristotle left the Academy in 348/7. He further found evidence that Aristotle's activity in collecting Greek constitutions and lists of Delphic victors was late, and he argued that such projects required the support of a research institution such as Aristotle did not have at his disposal until he founded his own school during his second stay at Athens. By putting together a few literary landmarks and the difference between the Platonism of the dialogues and the empirical researches Aristotle practised at the end of his career, Jaeger came up with a developmental theory: Aristotle progressed from Platonism to a practical empiricism. Thus if one kept in mind the direction of progress and the landmarks along the way, one could now hope to plot each work on a relative time line.

Jaeger's book opened new horizons for Aristotelian scholars, who at first often accepted his major results uncritically. However, further researches on the genesis of Aristotle's philosophy revealed serious problems in the Jaeger scheme. For instance, the available evidence pointed to the fact that some of Aristotle's metaphysical treatises were late while the strongly anti-idealist *Categories* was early (and genuine). Furthermore, it had been observed before Jaeger's book was published that Aristotle was already carrying on significant empirical researches in biology in his middle period. Thus Jaeger's simple scheme of progression from Platonizing idealism to scientific empiricism fell victim to an increased awareness of the complexity of his development. Nonetheless, Jaeger had opened the door to significant developmental studies and had recognized some of the landmarks that made progress in understanding Aristotle's development possible.

Subsequent developmental studies have gone a long way toward establishing a more satisfactory account of Aristotle's development on the basis of Jaeger's methods. But they do not in general address more basic objections to Jaeger's whole methodology. A fairly typical pattern for developmental studies consists of isolating some concept or theory that seems to involve an inconsistency, establishing a sequence of works in which versions of the theory appear, identifying some version as early and another as late, and exhibiting the versions as a sequence of dated theories which show a progression from early to late. For instance, in one of the more classic studies in this genre, Nuyens (1948[1939]) investigated doctrines of soul. He found that the early Aristotle saw soul as a substance, while the late Aristotle saw it as the form or actuality of a material body. The ideal result of such a study is the establishment of an independent criterion of dating based on a comparison to the concept studied; for instance, by knowing what Aristotle says about soul in a given work, we can expect to assign a relative date to it. Thus in general terms, a developmental study establishes that works W_1. W_2, W_3 can be assigned to times t_1, t_2, t_3; it then exhibits doctrines D_1, D_2, and D_3 from the respective works as instances of a progression; finally it invokes the discovered progression as a criterion for further ascertaining relative dates of other works which make reference to doctrine D.

In terms of this scheme we can see an objection to the method as a whole. In effect what the developmentalist does is to establish not D_1, D_2, and D_3, but D_1-at-t_1, D_2-at-t_2, and D_3-at-t_3. Ultimately what he is able to reveal is not Aristotle's thought as a whole, but Aristotle's thought-at-t_1, thought-at-t_2, and so on. Furthermore, there seems to be in principle no terminus to the successive subdivision of Aristotle. What the method seems to produce is a wholesale fragmentation of Aristotle. For it aims at and results in a relativizing of all doctrines with respect to time, while it offers no principle or prospect of reintegrating the pieces into a coherent whole. Thus although an extreme developmental approach seems useful for determining the relative dating of works, it proves disastrous for the criticism of Aristotle's philosophy.

There is a futher problem with the developmental approach to Aristotle. As developmentalists work out the progression of ideas in a given sequence, they almost invariably omit to give any *philosophical* reasons for the change. For instance Jaeger explains Aristotle's progress as a gradual weaning away from Platonic idealism to a scientific attitude. But he gives no philosophical reasons for the change as a whole, nor does he cite such reasons for individual episodes within the evolution. Yet if we reflect on this omission, we will see that it is inexcusable. It is a fact that philosophers change their views on issues. However, it does not seem to be the case that they do this capriciously; at least, good philosophers have good reasons for changing their views, and the only relevant good reasons are philosophical reasons. Kant was awakened from his dogmatic slumbers, but not by an internal clock: he was awakened by reading the philosophical arguments of a sceptic. Wittgenstein abandoned logical atomism, but not because it was unpopular or *passé*: rather he found that his early conception of language failed to capture all the functions of language. Similarly, it is plausible to believe, and charitable to assume, that Aristotle had philosophical reasons for changing his views.

It is not simply an oversight that leads Jaeger and other developmentalists to omit philosophical motives from their explanations. It is an outcome of their method itself. For to establish sequences of doctrines in the developmentalist way does not require philosophical analysis beyond a minimal recognition of difference and similarity. A genetic explanation can account for a change of doctrine by identifying its source. What is missing for an adequate philosophical account of the change is a final cause—not in the sense of a direction of change, but in the sense of a rational purpose for making the move.

Overall, the two objections we have examined, that the developmentalist approach fragments Aristotle and that it gives no philosophical account of change, come down to a basic deficiency: the method does not focus on the philosophical dimension of change. What it does do is to focus on the historical or temporal sequence. This is an important part of determining philosophical change, but it is not by itself sufficient to capture the whole story. It is not plausible to think that we can explain Aristotle's thought merely by tracking a concept or doctrine through time. If we are to approach Aristotle the philosopher, we must conjoin a perception of his temporal development with an increased awareness of the philosophical motives he had in developing his position. Such an awareness requires familiarity with the unity of Aristotle's thought.

I.2   THE UNITARIAN VIEW

Many students of Aristotle effectively ignore the alleged presence of different temporal strata in his works. Their method is to analyse philosophically the texts so as to identify distinctions that will harmonize conflicting doctrines. The systematic nature of Aristotle's philosophy itself offers a rationale for the method. Harold Cherniss (1935a: 270) observes:

. . . when the whole body of writings consists of lectures that were repeatedly delivered and bound together by backward and forward references which may have been added at various times, it is apparent that the author looked upon the whole corpus as forming a self-consistent, unified system, and philosophically his work must be judged as such, if it was such that he intended it to be.

Cherniss provides a strong case for the unitarian approach: since Aristotle himself does not seem to recognize a historical stratification, why should we? For does not the corpus represent Aristotle's mature thought?

However, the case for the unitarian approach is not so simple. In the first place, Aristotle's system is not obviously self-consistent. In fact, Cherniss admits the likelihood of inconsistencies, but curiously he uses this as an argument against Jaeger:

Jaeger tacitly assumes that at any given moment Aristotle's doctrine would not include contradictions and where contradictions are apparent there must be a chronological difference in composition. Such conditions not only fit no other philosophical system known but, as assumed, they make any real 'development' highly improbable, for development is the result of difficulties and contradictions felt by the philosopher in his current doctrine. (1935a: 265, cf. 270 f.)

Cherniss puts his finger on a weakness of developmentalist approaches, namely their hastiness in turning conflicts into evidence for temporal strata. As we have pointed out already, philosophical problems are the spur for systematic development. But there is a further difficulty that one cannot dismiss so lightly as Cherniss does. When the historian of philosophy discovers an apparent inconsistency, he cannot simply flag it and continue his survey. From inconsistent premises anything follows. The doxographer may leave off at this point, but the historian of philosophy is just beginning when he perceives such a difficulty. He must either show that the apparent inconsistency is not a real one because of some distinction that can be drawn—possibly a temporal distinction—or failing that, that one position is the philosopher's considered position while the other is to be abandoned because it is somehow wrong for the philosopher. Just how a decision between positions is to be reached is a matter for art and not a priori method to decide. But some decision must be reached, on pain of turning a philosophical position into logical chaos.

We thus see that in cases of perceived inconsistencies some sort of reconstruction is imperative. Need this reconstruction be genetic in character? There is no a priori reason why it should have to be so. Nevertheless, factual considerations point in the direction of a partially genetic solution for conflicts in Aristotle. If all difficulties in Aristotle were a matter of isolated claims conflicting there would be no need for genetic explanations. But some of the most serious problems arise out of the presence of more than one incompatible theory to explain the same phenomena. In such cases it cannot be argued that two apparently conflicting claims address different aspects of a problem, because the theory aims at providing a self-sufficient explanation of the problem. For instance, the *De Caelo* explains celestrial revolution as produced by the circular motion of the fifth element, whereas *Physics* viii and *Metaphysics* xii explain it by reference to an unmoved mover. Here we have a case of overdetermination in Aristotle's explanation. It is plausible to think that one of these explanations is a later one taking into account different causal factors. Similarly, Aristotle has two theories of ethics (assuming, as most scholars do today, that the *Eudemian Ethics* is a work of Aristotle's). Questions may be raised as to which work is earlier, which superior, and so on, but the presence of two works clearly suggests a temporal ordering inasmuch as their scope is so similar. In the case of the ethics we also note a situation in which three books are common to the two ethical treatises. This suggests that Aristotle may have been satisfied with the parts of his ethical theory discussed in those books but dissatisfied with other parts. What this shows is that Aristotle did *not* necessarily consider all of his treatises to contribute to his final mature position. One may infer that some of his later ethical theory superseded his earlier work.

In many cases it may not be obvious which theory superseded which, but we must raise the question of which took precedence wherever there is a plurality of conflicting theories. Moreover, the practical problem of determining relative dating is not so hopeless as Cherniss suggests: cross-references between the works are not promiscuous. In many cases only a narrow range of works is referred to by another work. Of course this may be the result of systematic connections between the works, but there may be reasons to argue for the presence of a temporal order based on references. Furthermore, it simply does not seem to be the case that Aristotle ever undertook a complete recension of his works; rather, certain sets of theories, vocabularies, and forms of argument tend to appear in certain works that can be dated together while other works with the same subject-matter take different points of view. Thus one can say that if Aristotle meant to revise his works so as to harmonize them, he failed. In fact, the very volume of Aristotle's output suggests that he did not have time to make extensive revisions to harmonize his doctrines—a task that later in his career would have been equivalent to revising an encyclopaedia.

I conclude, then, that while an appreciation of systematic connections in Aristotle's philosophy is essential to understanding his position, the developmentalist point of view is also valuable in some contexts and indeed is forced on us in some cases.

I.3   RECONCILING THE TWO POINTS OF VIEW

So far I have argued that we must accommodate both genetic and systematic points of view. One might wonder whether it is possible to employ both perspectives in a single interpretation. But a moment's reflection should convince us that there is nothing essentially incompatible between an explanation in terms of origins and one in terms of system. A system can have an origin and a collection of ideas can evolve towards a system. The question is whether an approach that makes use of both perspectives is practical for Aristotle scholarship.

That it is practical is best shown by noting previous examples of successful research employing the two perspectives. A notable example of such research is provided by the work of the late G. E. L. Owen. Beginning with a brief review of Jaeger's developmental theory, Owen (1960) suggests that the evidence points to a development towards rather than away from Platonism. He argues that Aristotle's theory of πρὸς ἕν equivocity or 'focal meaning' opens the way for Aristotle to overcome his initial rejection of a science of being qua being. Owen (1965a) further relates this development to Aristotle's evolving theory of predication, which is seen as in part a response to the Third Man Argument. Owen's theses are controversial, but they have triggered valuable research into the interconnections of various Aristotelian theories. What is significant for our purpose is the fact that Owen employs a method involving the use of both genetic and systematic points of view. In order to establish the direction of Aristotle's development, Owen considers his work as the application of new logical methods to shared problems. We see Aristotle as a philosopher working out the systematic implications of his methods, and, in the process, hammering out a philosophical system that has roots in an earlier and different position.

Thus genetic and systematic points of view have been combined in an effective way to increase our understanding of Aristotle's philosophy. This synthetic approach could be put on a secure foundation if we could do what so far has never been done: to move from an intuitive awareness of the approach's usefulness to a theoretical justification of it. Such a justification should define the roles of genetic and systematic modes of explanation in a synthetic approach that fuses both. Is this possible? It depends on what the relation between the two modes of explanation is. We can recognize that systematic analysis and genetic analysis must embody co-operative perspectives rather than exclusive alternatives because we can in principle view any event in time either as a state of affairs at one instant or as a process through time. But do the modes of analysis occur in free variation, or are they functionally interdependent? Clearly they must be interdependent in some way, since systematic analysis with its a-temporal perspective furnishes the terminal state of affairs for a genetic analysis. What we need is a model by which we can exhibit the two modes in a functional relationship.

We can, I believe, find the perfect model in a science in which temporal and systematic distinctions are essential preliminaries to successful inquiry. Ferdinand de Saussure (1915/1966: 79–100) founded his theory of linguistics on a typological distinction between what he called synchronic and diachronic linguistics. In synchronic linguistics we study a language as a system at a given time. Leaving aside all genetic questions, such as those of etymology, we can ask how the elements of the language function together. This is the point of view from which the grammar of a language operates. Diachronic linguistics, on the other hand, studies linguistic entities as they change through time.

According to Saussure, the distinction between synchronic and diachronic studies is made imperative by the nature of language. Language is a purely conventional means of communication, and accordingly elements gain their meaning only by their relation to other elements of the system at a given time. However, language does change through time, precipitating new networks of relations. Thus language is much like a chess game (pp. 88 f.), for the significance of the pieces changes with their changing configurations of the board. The move of a single piece can and does produce a new state of affairs. For instance, in Old High German the plural ending -*i* of *gast* 'guest' produced the umlauted plural form *gesti*, which later underwent another sound change in the ending to provide the modern *Gäste* (cf. pp. 83 f.). Now although the change from the earlier to the later form was mechanical, as we might say, it has important repercussions for the present state of the German language. For since the singular did not change significantly in form, the result was a new paradigm for forming the plural from the singular, namely by umlauting the vowel and adding -*e*. Thus the phonetic change that effects the plural of *Gast* has a significance that goes beyond its own occurrence: it creates the precedent for a new pattern of forming plurals of nouns and thus alters the morphology of the language. Accordingly, in language as in chess, one move can change the whole state of affairs.

There are some important analogies between language and philosophy that make Saussure's distinctions invaluable. Like language, philosophy is systematic in nature, or at least capable of being so. And as with language, a small change in some element of a philosophical system can have important implications for the system as a whole. Saussure (p. 89) notes one disanalogy between a move in a chess game and linguistic change: linguistic changes are not intentional acts. In this respect philosophical change is more like a move in a chess game than is linguistic change. But this does not mean that every consequence of a philosophical change is thereby intended, any more than is the case for a move in chess. It may escape the player, for instance, that by attacking one piece with his queen he is exposing her to attack in turn. Similarly, a philosopher may make adjustments to one theory in order to resolve one problem, only to find out that he has created new problems.

Saussure's model suggests one important point of priority. In linguistics the synchronic view is fundamental, the diachronic derivative (p. 90). For linguistic elements get their meaning only in the context of a system of arbitrary signs, and hence the changes, which though regular are accidental with respect to the system, can only be evaluated with respect to their impact on the system of relations. More precisely, it is only by comparing system S_1 at time t_1 and system S_2 at t_2, where a given change occurs between t_1 and t_2, that we can understand the significance of the change. Now if we think of a philosophy as a synchronic system and a change as a move from one synchronic system to another, we may understand the significance of the change in a similar way. Of course the philosophical change is also an intentional act, so that we can not only evaluate the effect of the change but also the success of the change relative to its intended effect. The synchronic system must take priority over the diachronic development in philosophy as in linguistics. The reason, however, is different for each. For philosophy it is not that the elements are meaningless by themselves but that they only acquire their full significance in the context of the system. And moreover the change itself is typically directed at a systematic outcome: one modifies a theory in order to make it more powerful or more harmonious with other theories or facts. One makes alterations for the sake of the system but one does not make the system for the sake of altering it.

The distinctions which Saussure makes might prove valuable if we could identify certain states of Aristotle's philosophy which are relatively coherent but which differ from one another. This raises a problem of individuation: how can we tell the boundaries between one state and another? To this there are no a priori answers, either in linguistics or in philosophy. A certain amount of experience and good sense are necessary to decide when a set of differences is significant enough to warrant identifying two states. Where do we draw the line between Middle English and Modern English? There is no answer that is not to some extent arbitrary, but at the same time some distinction must be made. For differences in vocabulary, pronunciation, and syntax make it evident that there are at least two states involved. On the other hand, one might argue that in principle any change, however slight, is grounds for identifying a new state. Thus any development threatens to dissolve into an infinite series of stages, a Heraclitean flux. However, since for us the synchronic–diachronic distinction is the basis for a tool of analysis and not a metaphysical dogma, it should suffice to invoke pragmatic criteria much as the linguist might: our identification of states will be adequate if it results in generally coherent systems with definable relations to each other.[2]

[2] I have developed applications of the Saussurean model further in Graham (1987a).

Now if the unitarians are right, there are no significantly different states of Aristotle's philosophy: all problems can be solved from a synchronic viewpoint, and no violence will be done to Aristotle's thought, which forms a single coherent system. On the other hand, if the developmentalists are right, there may be so many fragmentary stages that no coherent set of states emerges from Aristotle's thought. Or, if we take Jaeger's view seriously, the development may provide a continuum with no major breaking-points. In this case, some distinction will be possible, but there will be an element of arbitrariness in our divisions.

As I have indicated in my overviews of the unitarian and developmentalist positions, I think there are reasons for accepting certain features of both approaches and also reasons for rejecting the overall programmes of each. Thus we must employ both systematic and genetic analysis if we are to understand Aristotle, and we must refrain from a one-sided application of either. Now it seems to me that Saussure's typology of linguistics offers us a model for a joint application of systematic and genetic analysis. It will be our first task to identify systems, and our second task to explain the changes that transform the earlier to the later.

1.4   OVERVIEW OF THE ARGUMENT

Not only is a synthetic approach to Aristotle a plausible way to compromise between the extremes of unitarianism and developmentalism, but there is a very natural place to draw a distinction between systems. We can locate one major break which potentially serves as a fault line in Aristotle's work, such that doctrines and theories can be assigned to one system or another in a relatively straightforward way. There may be other discontinuities as well, but other lines of development that I have noted seem to be explainable as attempts to reintegrate elements into a new system after the break has occurred. I wish to suggest, then, that there are in fact two and only two major systems in Aristotle, which in fact stand to each other as successive states in a diachronic ordering.

1.4   The Two Systems

The great divide that I see in Aristotle's work is roughly coextensive with the distinction between the *Organon*, or collection of logical treatises, on the one hand and the physical–metaphysical treatises on the other. That these two sets of works differ in terminology, doctrine, and outlook has been recognized for as long as scholars have commented on Aristotle. However, commentators have generally accepted an explanation of these differences which excludes a developmental interpretation. They do in any case hold that the *Organon* is a system by itself, though not a full-fledged philosophical system. For their part, developmentalists have successfully applied genetic analyses to works within each of these groups of treatises, but their method generally commits them to following themes and ideas in works that are topically related. Thus there has been a general neglect of the relation of the logical to the physical works. Accordingly, although there are obvious incongruities between the two groups of works—and indeed their potential for genetic analysis has often been remarked—there has been almost no research specifically devoted to illuminating the relation of the logical to the nonlogical treatises.

1.4.2 *The Hypothesis*

The stratification that I am suggesting is thus an obvious place to begin in a search for systematic differences in Aristotle. It is coextensive with the doctrinal gap that Furth and Frede wish to bridge. Of course I cannot offer this distinction as anything more than a conjecture based on an insight at this point. But I do wish to subject the conjecture to the rigorous testing it deserves. In this book I shall argue for two theses:

(1) There are two incompatible philosophic systems in Aristotle, namely those expressed in the *Organon* and the physical–metaphysical treatises, respectively.

(2) These systems stand in a genetic relationship to one another: the latter is posterior in time and results from a transformation of the former.

The first thesis is a systematic claim; the second is genetic or developmental in character. By ordering the theses in this sequence we may observe the order of priority identified by Saussure, namely that synchronic analysis must take precedence over diachronic analysis. The theses may be taken in prospect as heuristic principles and thus regarded as hypotheses or as components of a comprehensive hypothesis. From this point of view I shall call the two theses, together with supporting hypotheses, the *Two Systems Hypothesis* (TSH). They may also be taken in retrospect as constituting an interpretation, which I shall call the *Two Systems Theory* (TST).[3]

For the sake of the argument it is important not to begin by assuming that my putative systems are related as theses (1) and (2) assert. Indeed, we should not even assume that there are two distinct systems. I shall attempt to minimize the assumptions by designating the set of doctrines and theories of the *Organon* as system S_1 and that of the remaining treatises as S_2. I do wish to make one qualification to this division: for reasons that will become apparent later, I regard the *Rhetoric* as belonging to the same system as the logical works, and I shall accordingly stipulate that this work is included in S_1.[4] As for my identification of S_1 and S_2 as systems, I wish to require only that they be viewed from a systematic point of view, that is, synchronically, leaving it as an open question just how coherent each is individually, that is, whether each ultimately constitutes a unified system. For the present they may be considered as states of affairs delimited arbitrarily. The value of the distinction will be determined pragmatically, by reference to its ultimate results. The colourless terms 'S_1' and 'S_2' are designed to discourage premature speculation about the relation between the systems. For I shall also leave it as an open question what the precise relation is, not excluding the possibility that S_1 and S_2 are identical. They may also be related as part to whole, as theories about different subject-matters and hence as not overlapping, or in any of a number of other ways. The important point is that the mere act of distinguishing two states of Aristotle's philosophy may be accomplished as a heuristic move— whether motivated by an insight or as an arbitrary exercise does not matter at this point—without begging any questions either as to the existence or the significance of the two potential systems expressed in those states.

---

[3] In fact one might conceive of a set of two systems theories which embody basic principles of the theory I shall develop. I do not wish to rule out a priori other types of two systems views, some of which have already been adumbrated. However, I aim at a kind of ideal two systems view that makes the most of the evidence available, and this is the view I shall designate as TST.

[4] See Ch. 11.3. Because of the different subject-matter of the *Rhetoric*, its contribution to an understanding of S_1 is small and can usually be ignored.

1.4.3   The Argument

I shall argue for TSH as follows. In Chapter 2 I shall consider S_1 from a synchronic point of view and argue for a specific characterization of it, at the same time showing that it does form a coherent system. In Chapter 3 I shall make a similar study of S_2. It will be evident by the end of Chapter 3 that S_1 and S_2 are not identical in doctrine, and Chapter 4 will show that they are logically incompatible, or more interestingly, incommensurable systems. At this point I shall have demonstrated thesis (1).

S_2 can be arrived at by performing a certain logical replacement on S_1. Chapter 5 will find an occasion on which Aristotle was compelled to introduce a new principle and hence to transform S_1, and thus it will reveal a motivation as well as an occasion for the development. We shall find confirmation for the developmental account in the transformations of the theory of the four causes (Chapter 6) and the theory of actuality (Chapter 7), which come to occupy central roles in S_2 which they did not enjoy in S_1.

Since I maintain that S_1 and S_2 are incompatible, it follows that the presence of principles from both in a theory would result in logical incoherence. I shall argue for important instances of such incoherence in Aristotle's theory of substance. Specifically, certain paradoxes in the theories of matter (Chapter 8) and form (Chapter 9) are traceable to his invoking what are for his philosophy obsolete principles.

If TST correctly diagnoses why the paradoxes of substance arise, it should indicate how to avoid them. In Chapter 10 I sketch a theory of substance appropriate to S_2 which, being uncontaminated by incompatible S_1 assumptions, avoids the paradoxes. Finally, Chapter 11 will recapitulate the argument and indicate the advantages of TST relative to other competing theories, and also use TST to reveal some weaknesses of influential approaches to Aristotle.

1.5   THE SIGNIFICANCE OF TSH

So far, in good Aristotelian form, I have presented only a rough sketch of an argument for a thesis that I have crudely stated. I expect that there will be two sorts of negative reaction at this point. The first reaction is one of incredulity; the following pages are written mainly to satisfy the sceptic. Indeed, since I claim that my position is not one that has been argued for or even explored in detail hitherto, a sceptical attitude seems to be appropriate for the reader, and I accept the burden of proof. As may be supposed from the general character of the theses, they will unavoidably issue in an overall interpretation or reinterpretation of Aristotle. It does not follow, however, that the details of the interpretation must be assumed in order to argue for its foundations. Rather, the argument I have outlined above is designed to avoid question-begging anticipations of the interpretation itself.

More difficult to deal with is another type of reaction, one which I have met with in conversations with colleagues. This is the reaction that the theses are true but obvious: everyone knows that there are two stages of Aristotle's thought that are characterized roughly as I have characterized them. In practice scholars recognize distinctions between the *Organon* and the physical–metaphysical treatises. There is no real value in pursuing the distinction any farther than so as to point out a more developed account in later works. I find this reaction puzzling. In the first place, while the distinction is noticed by many scholars, it is by no means universally acknowledged. Furthermore, even if it should be the case that some sort of distinction is widely accepted, there are divergent views as to its explanation, and hence as to its significance. I hold that the cause of the distinction is the presence of two incompatible philosophical systems; others hold that the distinction stems from the presence of theories with different subject-matters or from further articulations of an original system. These various explanations would entail profoundly different ways of reading Aristotle.

Yet perhaps the most telling failure of this objection from apathy can only emerge from my whole study itself. It is that although many insights on which the present interpretation is based have been expounded before, the radical implications of those insights have been totally ignored. If this study is successful, it will force us to see that we cannot hold to some commonly held views about Aristotle without abandoning certain widely accepted approaches to his work—without realizing that some of the questions we have been asking are the wrong questions. What is at stake, then, is not insignificant. The study of Aristotle's two systems raises fundamental problems concerning his philosophy: its unity, its development, its overall coherence. These are problems which confront us on page one of the *Categories* and which should vex us to page 1462 of the *Poetics*. To investigate the relationship between the *Organon* and the physical–metaphysical treatises is to begin at the beginning. And as Aristotle himself might counsel us, it is not unimportant how we begin—for it makes all the difference.

2

S₁: Atomic Substantialism

I have stipulated a distinction between S_1, the doctrines of the
Organon plus the *Rhetoric*, and S_2, those of the remaining
treatises. In this chapter I shall consider S_1 as a state of affairs,
without reference to S_2. I make no assertions here as to the
reasons for doing this, nor do I wish to presuppose any thesis
concerning the relationship of S_1 and S_2. What I do wish to argue
here is that S_1 embodies a philosophical system. This does not
mean that it embodies a complete system—that it addresses all
philosophical topics or contains all necessary theories to account
completely for the world. It may be the case that S_1 embodies only
part of a complete philosophical theory of the world. It may also
be the case that S_1 is identical with the system presented in S_2, or
that it is part of a larger theory of the world of which S_2 is another
part; and these parts may or may not overlap. Or it may prove
to be the case that S_1 and S_2 are incompatible systems. Such
possibilities must be considered, but only after the systems have
been considered independently.

If, as I assert, S_1 embodies a philosophical system, the various
theories that Aristotle puts forth in it must interrelate in some
organized way. It will not be necessary to summarize all the
contents of S_1, but we must extract salient theories and attempt to
synthesize them. In what follows I shall examine (1) ontology, (2)
logic and philosophy of language, and (3) philosophy of science,
using only evidence from the treatises of S_1 (except for incidental
observations from S_2). I shall attempt to show how these theories
are interrelated.

2.1 ONTOLOGY

An ontology is a theory of the basic items of reality. It consists not
merely of a list of those items, but also of an account of the way

they are related to each other.[1] The relations that hold between the items cannot themselves be items of the ontology, on pain of infinite regress. For instance, in an ontology like that of logical atomism, the connection between a location and a sensory quality cannot be a relation which is an item of the ontology, for then we might ask in what consisted the connection between the location, the sensory quality, and the relation. Presumably, we would have to produce another relation which itself was an item of the ontology, and then the question of what *its* connection was would arise in turn. This problem, a form of the Bradley regress,[2] can be avoided by simply recognizing that there are connections between items of the ontology which are primitive and are not of the same order as the items they connect.[3] Following W. E. Johnson (1921: 10)[4] I shall call these primitive connections ties. An ontology, then, will consist of basic items of reality, which I shall call entities, and ties which connect them. Furthermore there will be rules governing the way that ties connect entities.

One other distinction will help to clarify elements of Aristotle's ontology. There may be a *formal ontology* that consists of theoretical entities and ties considered in the abstract, which can be considered in a purely formal way, and an *interpretation* which assigns to those entities items of experience that are claimed to be instances of the entities or manifestations of their existence. Aristotle does not keep these aspects of ontology distinct, but it will be helpful to us to note what features are formal elements of the scheme and what are dictated by the intended application to experience.

2.1.1 Formal Ontology

Aristotle uses two ties to generate the classes of his formal ontology (*Cat.* 2). These are the Said-of and the In ties. Specifically, all entities are either Said-of a subject or not, and either In a subject or not. Each entity is assigned a place in a 2 × 2 matrix according to whether it possesses or lacks each of the ties in relation to a subject. Using ' + ' for presence and ' − ' for

---

[1] See Gaukroger (1978: 53–7), discussed below.
[2] F. H. Bradley (1897: 32 f.).
[3] Aristotle is aware of such a distinction in *Met.* vii. 17, 1041ᵇ11–34; the Third Man Argument raises similar difficulties in the Platonic tradition.
[4] It is not clear whether Johnson means for his ties to be logical or ontological in character. I intend them to be ontological. Cf. Strawson (1959: 169).

+ S	+ S, − I	+ S, + I
− S	− S, − I	− S, + I
	−I	+I

FIG. 2.1   Categorial Ties

absence, we have the scheme in Fig. 2.1. For convenience, I shall introduce arbitrary letters (unrelated to those of Fig. 2.1) for the classes having or lacking the ties as represented above (which I shall later give a mnemonic value). These are as found in Fig. 2.2. Aristotle's remarks indicate that items of *US* are Said-of items of *IS*, and items of *UA* are Said-of items of *IA*. Items of column *A* are In items of column *S* (although the precise relation between the rows with respect to the In tie is unclear). Now if *x* is Said-of *y* or is In *y*, Aristotle calls *y* a subject of *x*. Thus the *S* column provides subjects for the *A* column and the *I* row provides subjects for the *U* row.

U	US	UA
I	IS	IA
	S	A

FIG. 2.2.   Basic Entities

Aristotle gives a theoretical name to items of the *S* column: they are οὐσίαι. The basic meaning of the term οὐσία is 'being', 'entity', or 'reality', but the term is traditionally rendered 'substance'. It is just as well that we do not render οὐσία by its etymological meaning because it is not the only class of entity; however, we should note that the term does have a pregnant sense, and that the etymology indicates the pride of place Aristotle's theory assigns to this class.[5] There are two types of substance, primary and secondary, whose ordinal designations reveal their ontological rank (*Cat.* 5, 2ᵃ11–19). Aristotle identifies primary substances with members of *IS* and secondary substances with members of *US*. What is it that is so unique about *IS*? From its place in the formal scheme we can discern the answer: it is only

[5] On the pregnant sense, see Evans (1977: 15).

members of this class which are always *subjects* and never Said-of or In other subjects. In other words these entities are by nature subjects. Aristotle confirms this point:

It is because of their underlying all other things and all other things being predicates of them or in them that primary substances are especially called substances. (2^b15–17) Primary substances are called substances in the chief sense because of their underlying all other things. (2^b37–3^a1)

Members of other classes are in some sense subordinate because they are Said-of or In a subject—they are 'predicates'. Subjects are presumed to be prior to predicates. Thus we have a purely formal principle of ontological priority which serves to organize the whole ontology.

But why should ontological subjects be prior to ontological predicates? To this question there seems to be no answer except at the level of what we might call metaphysical intuition. Aristotle gives no arguments, and if he did they would probably beg the question anyway. The true reality (οὐσία) is the subject or substratum (ὑποκείμενον: what underlies) which in underlying *supports, sustains, upholds* predicates. For 'predicate' Aristotle uses a participial form of the corresponding verb κατηγορεῖσθαι 'be predicated', which in ordinary usage meant 'be accused'. The predicate 'follows' (ἕπεται, ἀκολουθεῖ) its subject and belongs to it (ὑπάρχει) (*A.Pr.* i. 27, 43^b3–5), that is, it is an attribute. An attribute is an entity which has an innate dependence on something else: it is an accessory, a possession, something that belongs to something else. By splitting reality into subjects and predicates or attributes Aristotle has introduced a duality of being into his ontology that promises to avoid problems the Eleatic tradition poses with its monolithic conception of being, as Ernst Tugendhat (1958: ch. 1) has shown. As against Plato's Eleaticism, according to which the primary realities are *toto caelo* different from the secondary realities, Aristotle is able to show the fundamental interconnectedness of entities by making one set depend upon the other. The substrate is a metaphysical foundation for reality; the attribute is a superstructure in need of a foundation.

All this remains metaphorical, but at an intuitive level it is difficult to be other than metaphorical. Indeed, philosophers have come to see that it is often in terms of models and metaphors that even rigorous scientific systems are elaborated.[6] One metaphysician, Stephen C. Pepper (1942), has even argued that all major philosophic theories are developed as articulations of what he calls a root metaphor. He points out that other possible sources of systematic philosophy fail to be suggestive enough to generate a theory that attempts to explain all phenomena—a theory of the type he calls a world hypothesis. I think Pepper's thesis is too simplistic to account for the diverse levels of explanation and complexity of structure of actual world hypotheses. In fact I hope to reveal a number of different kinds of formative influence that are operative at different levels of Aristotle's theory. However, I find the notion of a root metaphor—if understood in a restricted way, such that it is not supposed to generate the whole system—to be illuminating and suggestive. Aristotle has no argument for his root metaphor, but he conjures up quasi-explanations in the language of support and foundations which indicates the heuristic power of the metaphor in his thinking.[7]

Aristotle often repeats a charge against Plato's Forms that they are hopelessly sundered from the world. There is no need of 'one beside the many' or a 'one over many' such as the Forms are.[8] The last phrase shows Aristotle's awareness, still at an intuitive level, of a certain metaphysical orientation in Plato's philosophy that can best be expressed by a spatial metaphor. Against the background of Platonic metaphysics, it is evident that Aristotle appreciated his own orientation as a contrasting one. He finds the source of ontological stability in support or foundation. Against Plato's fundamental insight he places his own dissenting view. To coin a phrase in an Aristotelian mode, we may call his fundamental insight, his root metaphor, the *One Under Many*. This encapsulates his programme for a solution to the problem of the One and the Many that was the legacy of the Presocratics to the Academy. The One Under Many is the chief reality, πρώτη οὐσία or primary substance.

---

[6] Cf. Hesse (1966).

[7] Pepper (1942: 162 f.) assigns a different root metaphor to Aristotle. For criticism see Ch. 11.6.3.

[8] *A.Po.* i. 11, 77ᵃ5–7; 22, 83ᵃ33–5; cf. *Met.* i. 9, 990ᵇ7 f.; xiii. 4, 1079ᵃ9. However, at *A.Po.* i. 11, 77ᵃ9, Aristotle uses ἐν ἐπὶ πλειόνων of universals rather than Forms, and at ii. 19, 100ᵃ7 he uses ἐν παρὰ τὰ πολλά to designate universals.

2.1.2   Interpretation

But what precisely is primary substance? Aristotle characterizes it as indivisible (ἄτομον), unitary (ἓν ἀριθμῷ), and hence 'a This'—τόδε τι (3ᵇ10–13).[9] What Aristotle means by these terms is obscure—especially since he also characterizes members of IA as indivisible and unitary (1ᵇ6–9), though he never uses the term τόδε τι for them. The best method of approaching the problem is to go to the interpretation of the entities and consider the examples, since Aristotle is more generous with these than with explanations of his classes. Examples of primary substances are: a certain man, a certain horse (1ᵇ4 f., 2ᵃ13 f.). Secondary substances (members of US) consist of kinds to which the primary substances belong, such as Man and Animal (2ᵃ14–19). Although a secondary substance may seem to be τόδε τι because of the way we speak of it, it is not really so because it is not really unitary, applying as it does to many particulars. A secondary substance indicates what kind, differing from quality by indicating what kind of *thing* or substance a particular is (3ᵇ13–22). This account suggests that primary substances are indivisible and unitary because, in Quine's words, they do not 'divide their reference' (1960: 91).[10] Specifically, they are not said of anything else (3ᵇ16 f.), and so, presumably, they cannot be divided into a plurality of instances, but are individual and single. If this is correct, we see that being indivisible and unitary are purely formal properties of primary substances: the entities on the bottom row of the matrix are indivisible in the stated way by definition, that is, in virtue of their place in the scheme. I shall follow tradition in calling the entities that are indivisible and unitary *individuals*, using a term that has traditional ties to Aristotle's ἄτομον (Frede, 1978: 17 f.).

The term τόδε τι seems designed to emphasize the spatial location of an entity as well as its independent existence, such that it can be singled out by ostention. The closest English equivalent for such a term is 'particular'.[11] That primary substances are

---

[9] The γάρ in ᵇ12 seems to indicate that being indivisible and unitary is a sufficient condition for being τόδε τι; this cannot be, since non-substantial individuals fulfil the conditions (*Cat.*, 2, 1ᵇ6–9) but do not seem to qualify as instances of τόδε τι.

[10] Cf. Frede's approach (1978: 19–21) using a scholastic distinction.

[11] Strawson (1959: 10) makes location in space and time a key feature of particulars; J. A. Smith (1921) has argued that τόδε τι means 'anything which is both a this and a somewhat', i.e. 'this *F*'. However, his arguments are not

particular may be a consequence of their role in the system. If the technical term 'In' carries with it a primitive notion of location it follows that entities in column S of the matrix provide the primary locus for entities in column A. Thus entities in A can be located only derivatively, by reference to their respective subjects in S. I suspect that the term 'In' also trails with it historical associations the Greek preposition ἐν has with the concept of dependence.[12] It is of course a philosophical and grammatical commonplace (maligned by Plato) that existence is connected with location,[13] so that the existence of x in y amounts to a kind of derivative existence of x. The primary entity has both existential independence and primary location; subsidiary entities have location and (hence?) existence in a derivative way. Thus although there are unitary individuals in IA as well as in IS, only those of IS exist independently and are full-blooded particulars.

Aristotle seems to make some further tacit restrictions on primary substances—restrictions we could not have predicted from the formal character of the scheme alone. (1) They are uniformly 'middle-sized objects'; and (2) not just any middle-sized objects, but preferably biological ones. Thus from the interpretation of the ontology we catch a glimpse of another element present in Aristotle's thought: naturalism. From his examples we learn that primary substances like a certain horse, a certain man fall under genera and species, for instance, Horse and Man are species and Animal a genus. I take it that there is no *formal* need to differentiate US into genera and species, but rather what Aristotle recognizes as a factual constraint determines this differentiation. The species is the less comprehensive classification, the genus the more comprehensive. These designations seem to be relative in that one classification could be a genus relative to a lower species and a species relative to a higher genus. Aristotle conceives of the

convincing: see Ross's criticisms (1924, i. 247). Tugendhat (1958: 25 nn. 22, 31) stresses the independence of τόδε τι and argues further that τόδε τι is not sensible. Sokolowski (1970: 283 n. 33) rightly defends the possibility of ostention of what is τόδε τι. For a more extended discussion of the problem, see Ch. 9.1.

[12] See Mourelatos (1970: 171 f.).

[13] See *Tim.* 52 B. For Aristotle location is itself a category accidental to substance, so that it would be wrong to make location in any sense prior to existence for a substance. But it is true that location belongs primarily to substance and hence can be used as a criterion to distinguish the substance which directly exists somewhere from its accidents, which only indirectly exist there.

connection between *US* and *IS* not as a simple subordination of an element of *IS* to one of *US*, but as an inverted tree in which members of *IS* are grouped under a lowest species—a member of *US*—which in turn, together with other species, is grouped under a higher species and then a higher until all fall under a single class. Thus we have a stemma of substances within which each can be classified according to its place in the structure. Aristotle conceives of a complex formal structure at this level, but the actual form of it is indeterminate in that it is a matter of empirical fact exactly what classes there are. Perhaps the most important feature of this interpretation is that all classes of *US* are identified with natural kinds. Accordingly, all members of *IS* are members of natural kinds and are themselves natural objects. We can extract, then, a thesis to the effect that species and genera are natural kinds. I shall call this thesis Naturalism.

2.1.3 Accidents

Thus far we have dealt with the substance column of the ontological matrix. For the *A* column, not only the terms but even the examples are obscure. We have already noted that the In tie which joins members of *A* to members of *S* involves dependency of *A*s on *S*s. Examples of *UA* are knowledge and colour, and of *IA* 'a certain knowledge of letters' (ἡ τὶς γραμματική) and 'a certain white (τὸ τὶ λευκόν). In general, one can see that Aristotle intends column *A* to contain entities which characterize substances without constituting, containing, or otherwise being definitive of them. These entities we can call, following Aristotelian terminology (*Top.* i. 5, 102ᵇ4–9), accidents (συμβεβηκότα). Let '*A*' in Fig. 2.2 stand for 'accident'. The problem in interpreting Aristotle's theory of accidents is in understanding what *IA* stands for. Traditionally, individual accidents (*IA*) are taken to be particular instances of accidents, for example, Socrates' white colour or Socrates' knowledge of grammar. Although it is unclear what the last example amounts to, I suggest that it is, for instance, Socrates' recognition of this mark as an *A*.[14] On this

---

[14] Cf. *Met.* xiii. 10, 1087ᵃ16–21; *DA* ii. 5, 417ᵃ28 f. For the Greeks the science of grammar was not distinguished from the art of literacy, and grammatical knowledge was basically the knowledge of the letters of the alphabet and the rules of their combination. See Plato *Phil.* 17 B 6–9; Aristotle *Top.* vi. 5, 142ᵇ30 ff.; *Met.* iv. 2, 1003ᵇ20 f.

interpretation, white is in body because Socrates' white is in Socrates' body, and so on for a large number of instances of white. Recently, Michael Frede (1978) has revived a challenge to this interpretation,[15] arguing that individual accidents are not particular instances of universals but fully determinate universals; for instance, 'a certain white' would signify a certain determinate shade of white in a continuum of colour and would be individual or indivisible because there was no further division into kinds below it. When Aristotle says that white is in body (*Cat.* 2, 1ᵃ27 f.), he means in body in general, which is the proper substrate of colour, not in some particular body which is the subject of this instance of colour.[16]

It is difficult to decide between interpretations, especially since Aristotle says so little about individual accidents. However, certain remarks of his about knowledge of letters suggests that his model is one of acquaintance with letter tokens,[17] which would imply that the knowledge in question is a particular instance of general knowledge of letter types. He also calls white a simple colour in his theory of colour, which might imply that there are no subspecies of white.[18] These hints about the way Aristotle understands his examples tend to favour the traditional interpretation: ἡ τὶς γραμματική and τὸ τὶ λευκόν are particular instances of knowledge and colour rather than fully determinate types.

There is, moreover, one passage in *Cat.* 2 that itself seems to favour the traditional account. Aristotle observes:

Some things are neither in a subject nor said of a subject, such as a man [ὁ τὶς ἄνθρωπος] and a certain horse [ὁ τὶς ἵππος]; for none of the things like

---

[15] For a standard view, see Ackrill (1963: 74 ff.); Owen (1965b) attempted to argue that members of *IA* were universals, but his argument has drawn more criticism than support. See Moravcsik (1967c), Allen (1969), Matthews and Cohen (1968); Jones (1972) presents a view somewhat like Owen's.

[16] Heinaman (1981) offers an interesting defence of the traditional view. However, his case depends in part on a questionable reading of Aristotle's 'same in number' distinction. If to be the same in number entails being a particular, then there is much evidence for the traditional view. But in fact in its early exposition in *Top.* i. 7, being the same in number is compatible with being a universal; in any case in which there are two names for one thing (even when the 'thing' is a universal) we have sameness of number, e.g. 'cloak' and 'robe', 'man' and 'two-footed, footed animal'.

[17] See references in n. 14.

[18] See *Top.* iv. 6, 127ᵃ20–5; *Ph.* v. 4, 227ᵇ7–11; see Heinaman (1981: 297–300); *DS* 3, 439ᵇ19 ff. implies that white and black are elements of colour.

these are either in a subject or said of a subject. But in general the things that are indivisible and unitary are said of no subject, but nothing prevents some of them from being in a subject: for a certain knowledge of letters [ἡ . . . τὶς γραμματική] is one of the things that are in a subject, but it is said of no subject. (1ᵇ3–9)

Here Aristotle is asserting that things which are indivisible and unitary, that is, individuals, are not necessarily in the substance column, but they are necessarily on the lowest line—they are zero-level entities. But in the process he uses the same form of expression for both *IS*s and *IA*s: *ὁ τὶς F*, 'a certain *F*'. To suppose that Aristotle has a different account of '*ὁ τὶς F*' in each case is to make Aristotle guilty of a Rylean category mistake or an Aristotelian equivocation (which he has specified in Chapter I of the *Categories*). If the expression is not univocal, Aristotle is guilty of using a systematically misleading expression. But since the terminology is invented by Aristotle *ad hoc* it seems unlikely that he is either taken in by a linguistic ambiguity or unaware of the implications of using the same expression for both classes of entity.

I take it, then, that individual accidents are particular instances of accidents and that Aristotle does not call them indivisible and unitary in an equivocal sense relative to substances. Consequently, in Fig. 2.2 we can identify the *U* row with universals and the *I* row with individuals, understanding the individuals in question to be particulars or particular instances, while we identify the *S* column with substances and the *A* column with accidents. Already we have seen that the matrix in Fig. 2.2 is a simplification, because universal substances, that is, secondary substances, are distinguished into species and genera in an ascending tree. The same holds true of accidents. For example, this particular instance of white is white and white is a colour. Thus we have ascending trees of universals in both columns.

But there is not just a single tree in the class of accidents. Whereas Chapter 2 of the *Categories* offers a simple categorial distinction between substances and accidents, Chapter 4 gives a tenfold classification of entities. Besides substance there are nine categories of accidents: quantity, quality, relation, place, time, posture, possession, action, passion. In *Topics* i. 9 Aristotle presents a game for establishing the ten categories: one is shown a man and has to reply to the question, 'What is it?'; his answer

('Man', 'Animal') denotes (σημαίνει) a substance. When a white colour is presented, his answer denotes a quality, when a cubit length is presented a quantity, and so forth. The exposition is not without a touch of *naïveté*, since one cannot normally present a colour or a cubit without presenting a substance also—a fact of which Aristotle is usually well aware. Any item available for presentation (for example, a yardstick) would consist of a substance with a plurality of characters—colour, length, place, time, relations, and so on. In other words, the categories are never presented separately: only an act of analysis could distinguish such items, as Wittgenstein saw.[19]

Although the game is misconceived, it does allow us to appreciate Aristotle's attitude to the categories. Aristotle's term κατηγορία seems to mean 'predication' or 'predication type' rather than 'category' (Frede, 1981), and in the *Topics* what we see are different types of predication determined by asking 'What is it?' questions of different types of predicates. Aristotle conceives of the several predicates as falling under other predicates which in turn can be characterized as belonging to a certain ultimate class. In other words, he understands the predicates as forming inverted trees which ascend to one of ten trunks, each of which represents a predication type or correspondingly an ontological type. In general each tree is distinct from every other (although there are some branches that cross over) and every entity is classified by its place in the scheme.[20]

2.1.4   Vertical Ties

In accordance with the schematic account of Aristotle's ontology given above, we may designate the connections between universals and individuals and those between substances and accidents as vertical and horizontal ties, respectively. Although there are difficulties in understanding both horizontal and vertical ties, the accidental nature of the horizontal tie seems to preclude any precise determinations. On the other hand, the vertical tie proves to be the glue that holds the world together as an intelligible system of relationships. In order to understand

[19] *Philosophical Investigations*, secs. 28–36.
[20] e.g. Knowledge is a relation because it is *of* something (i.e. the expression is an incomplete predicate presupposing another term or subject), but its species Literacy is a quality: *Cat.* 8, 11ª20–38.

Aristotle's ontology, we must investigate the nature of his vertical ties.

Aristotle clearly distinguishes (in fact, invented the distinction) between universals and individuals:

By 'universal' [καθόλου] I mean what is characteristically predicated of more things, by 'individual' [καθ' ἕκαστον] what is not so predicated; e.g. Man is a universal, Callias an individual. (*DI* 7, 17ᵃ39–ᵇ1)

Although Aristotle makes individuals the foundation of his ontology, he is no nominalist. For he does not attempt to banish universals from his ontology. He merely grounds them in their particular instances. His goal seems to be to keep universals from a Platonic separation which will promote them to another world and in fact misconstrue them as individual members of that world. Thus he retains them as entities of a different type from individuals and ties them down to individuals.

Another move he avoids (or perhaps never considers) is a move to separate individuals from universals in an absolute way. He never entertains the possibility that any individual might not fall under some universal. In other words, there are no 'bare particulars' in his ontology. Although he does not state this fact, he shows it by the way he refers to individuals in *Cat.* 2: he uses the formula 'a certain *F*', where '*F*' is filled in with a general term signifying a universal. Thus every individual turns out to be an instance of a universal.

The most interesting category for Aristotle and for us is that of substance. Substantial individuals (primary substances) fall under substantial universals (secondary substances). We have already seen how Aristotle consistently construes substantial universals as natural kinds. For instance, Horse and Man are substantial universals of a lower level (species) which fall under a higher substantial universal (genus), Animal. But how precisely are genera and species understood? Are they classes or properties? To this Aristotle seems to give no clear or consistent answer. At times when he speaks of primary substances being in the species he seems to have in mind taking the secondary substances as classes (*Cat.* 5, 2ᵃ14–17). At other times he speaks of the secondary-substance term as specifiying a property—'a certain character [ποιόν τι]' of substance—finding it difficult to distinguish this from the category of quality (ποιόν) (3ᵇ13–21). Overall, Aristotle seems to have no clear concept of a formal semantics for his theory of substance which would specify secondary substances as either classes or properties.[21]

A related difficulty concerns the nature of the tie between the particular and the species compared with that between the species and the genus. Gregory Vlastos has criticized Aristotle for not distinguishing between class membership (between particular and species) and class inclusion (between species and genus).[22] It might be possible to defend Aristotle by pointing out that he seems to use a different locution for the particular-species tie ($\dot{v}\pi\acute{a}\rho\chi\epsilon\iota\nu$ $\dot{\epsilon}\nu\ F$) than for the species-genus tie ('genus of the species') when he is speaking as if secondary substances were classes ($2^{a}14–17$). On the other hand, he does not seem to make much of this hint of a distinction. In general, it seems to be true that Aristotle does not recognize the difference between class membership and class inclusion. However, the criticism seems question-begging in a curious way. For the criticism can only be made by assuming that the correct way to interpret Aristotle's secondary substance is on a model of classes. It is not clear that this is a valid assumption, nor is it clear that there is anything vicious in Aristotle's approach to predication at this point. We must be careful not to assume a formal semantics alien to Aristotle's theory of predication and then use it against him. One of the reasons for maintaining the class-membership/class-inclusion distinction is to enforce a type distinction between referents of proper names and of general terms. But Aristotle's ontology has that type distinction built in. He does tend to ignore the possibility of a different kind of tie between ontological types here (both are described by the term 'Said of'), but he is in no danger of taking particulars for universals or vice versa.

We have seen that secondary substances are natural kinds which can be differentiated into species and genera for the purposes of comparison. It is further the case that there are definable relationships between species and genera. For instance, Man can be defined as Two-Footed Animal. The definiendum consists of a species, the definiens of an adjective and a noun which signify the differentia and the genus, respectively. The differentia proves to

---

[21] Cf. Driscoll (1981: 142); *A.Pr.* i. 1, $24^{b}26–30$ suggests the interchangeability of talk about universals and classes.

[22] Vlastos (1973: 333 f. and n. 21). Cf. Ackrill (1963: 76).

be something of a categorial maverick, since it tells what a
substance is, but is not itself a secondary substance and seems to
give a quality.[23] However awkward this may be for a categorial
scheme, it clearly introduces an important new dimension into
Aristotle's ontology. Aristotle might have created an ontology
without the definition by differentia and genus, and in that case he
would have had a complex but less bold metaphysics. As it is, we
see that the primary substance not only falls under species and
genera, but is fully definable in terms of them. The scheme
suggests that particulars not only fall into natural kinds but do
so in an intelligible way: the world is articulated into rationally
determinable kinds.

For Aristotle, then, the following thesis holds:

> *Definability* (D): Every species is either identical to a
> primitive genus or is identical to the differentia of a genus.

Schematically, if S is a species, D a differentia, and G a genus,
$S = D(G)$. (In the limiting case that the species is identical to the
genus the differentia drops out.) On the basis of this scheme
Aristotle might have made a reductionistic move to eliminate the
species so defined from his ontology in favour of the defining
terms. But he shows no interest in making the move, and indeed
seems rather to think that the definition has conferred ontological
security on the species. To the reductionist this seems to be a
curious excess of tolerance. However, Aristotle has a rationale for
keeping the species in his ontology, in the One Under Many
principle: the lower-level universal is more basic than the higher-
level simply by virtue of its closer relation to the substantial
individual. Hence it cannot be eliminated in favour of higher-level
universals, even if these are more intelligible.

The verbal definition represents a structured complex feature
which constitutes the nature of the species. It is called an essence
(*Top.* i. 5, 101ᵇ39). The essence is Said-of the species, and the
Said-of tie is like a transitive relation—if A is Said-of B and B is
Said-of C, then A is Said-of C (*Cat.* 3)—so the essence is also Said-
of the primary substance (1ᵇ10–15, 3ᵇ2–7). In other words, not
only natural kinds, but also particular substances have essences.
Besides essences or essential properties, Aristotle also recognizes

[23] 3ᵃ21–ᵇ9; *Top.* iv. 2, 122ᵇ16 f.; ibid. 6, 128ᵃ26 f.; vi. 6, 144ᵃ18 ff.

ἴδια or Properties, which necessarily belong to a natural kind but which are not definitive of it (*Top.* i. 5, 102ᵃ18 f.).

2.1.5   *Ontological Principles*

At this point we can glimpse a subtle and highly intricate ontology in the *Organon*. If we return to the table of four ontological types which we took from *Categories* 2, we can understand the structure of his ontology by enriching it. Instead of just one class of accidents there are nine, and instead of just one row of universals, there are several—the number varies for different categories, but it is finite. Thus we have a scheme like that shown in Fig. 2.3. The picture is yet more complicated than the diagram because at each level within a single column there may be a plurality of nodes comprising a branching tree. Nevertheless, the diagram is sufficiently representative to show us the complexity of Aristotle's ontology. There are various philosophical and exegetical problems associated with it, as we have seen. But despite difficulties in the scheme, its architectonic elegance exercises an appeal of its own— one that is perhaps sufficient to account for Aristotle's failure to identify certain incongruities. The scheme could be likened to a grand edifice, whose foundation is individuals and whose cornerstone is primary substance. The well-founded edifice is reminiscent of the images that were so seductive to Descartes and Bacon.[24] Of course, while foundationalism for them was an epistemological enterprise, for Aristotle it is ontological and metaphysical. It should also be noted that Aristotle does not use foundational imagery himself. But the ideals of security, order, and intelligibility which his scheme embodies anticipate those of later foundationalists. And at least his own metaphorical orientation is the same as theirs: clearly primary substances *underlie* and *support* other entities and his ontology is meant to develop from the bottom up.

It is evident even from this brief synopsis of Aristotle's ontology in the *Organon* that he presents a complex scheme of entities. It will be useful for later comparison with S₂ to isolate from our analysis certain key ontological principles, some of which have

---

[24] Descartes, *Discourse on Method*, pt. ii, Haldane and Ross, i. 87 f., 89; cf. pt. i, p. 85; Bacon, *The Great Instauration*, proemium; *Novum Organum*, aphorism 31.

Category:	substance	quantity	quality	relation
	·	·	·	·
U	seconday substance		·	· ·
I	primary substance		·	·
	S	Accidents		

Category: (*cont.*)	place	time	posture	possession	action	passion
	·	·	·	·	·	·
U						
I	particular instances			·	·	·

Fig. 2.3. Aristotle's Categorial Scheme

already been identified. The ontological principles of S_1 are as follows:

Substantialism (S): Primary substances exist independently; for all other entities, to be is to be In a subject or Said-of a subject.

Substantial Atomism (SA): Primary substances are ontologically indivisible particulars.

Secondary Substantialism (SS): Every primary substance falls under a secondary substance, which is a species.

Definability (D): Every species is either identical to a primitive genus or is identical to the differentia of a genus.

Naturalism (N): Species and genera are natural kinds.

The last three principles may be considered to constitute a position called Essentialism (E) which determines the nature of primary substances.

Aristotle assumes that all classes referred to above are non-empty;[25] hence every universal statement about the members of a class carries existential import. The most important message of the ontological system is one that is a theme of Aristotle's exposition of the *Categories*: substantial individuals are the foundation of all

---

[25] I am considering the species and genera, etc., as classes from *our* point of view; as I have noted, Aristotle is unclear on the point.

reality. I shall designate the overall ontological position portrayed above as atomic substantialism (AS) to reflect this emphasis.

In just what does the superiority of substantial individuals consist? Above I have characterized the In tie as marking ontological dependence. I have used the independence–dependence contrast loosely thus far. Some distinctions that Stephen Gaukroger (1978) has made will be helpful to clarify the relationships. He argues that 'ontologies do not simply consist of kinds of entity— they consist of kinds of entity bearing certain complex relations to one another' (p. 57). One possible relationship is that of dependence, but there may be different sorts of dependence:

Dependence . . . is neither a simple nor even a univocal relation. In the Classical Atomist ontology for example, we can say that the three kinds of entity are matter, space and time. These each have an independent status in that none is reducible to the others. Nevertheless, while space and time are conceived of as requiring neither each other nor matter for their existence, matter cannot exist without the (logically) prior existence of space and time on this account. (pp. 56 f.)

I have tacitly followed Gaukroger in treating Aristotle's ontology as a set of entities having complex relationships to one another. Regarding the specific relationship of primary substances to other entities we may note that the relations are complex indeed. While Aristotle explicitly states that other entities cannot exist apart from primary substances (*Cat.* 5, 2^a34-^b6), it is also clear that he envisages no primary substances which do not also have accidental attributes and belong to natural kinds. The independence–dependence relation involved, then, must not be of an absolute kind, but must consist of a sort of relative ontological priority. Primary substances are the most important, most basic entities of the system, but they are not the only real beings.

2.1.6 S₁ as a System

In the remainder of this chapter I shall attempt to outline other areas of Aristotle's philosophy in the *Organon*. Gaukroger makes some further distinctions which will help to link these areas to Aristotle's ontology. Gaukroger's analysis aims at illuminating what he calls explanatory structures, with the ultimate goal of applying his account to explanations in the philosophy of science. However, his scheme, by its abstractness, is also suitable for application to a general philosophical system. I find that his theory clarifies relationships that are normally left obscure and at the same time begs no questions of concern to us. Accordingly, I turn to a brief exposition of his theory of theories and 'theoretical discourses' or systems of theories (1978: 13–16).

A theoretical discourse is constrained by an 'explanatory structure' which 'determines what counts as an explanation in the discourse' (p. 14). The elements of an explanatory structure include an ontology, which posits entities having an explanatory function in the discourse, and a 'domain of evidence' consisting of phenomena that can confirm or disconfirm explanations. The ontology must be connected to the domain of evidence in order to effect an explanation, and this connection is achieved by a 'system of concepts' unique to the discourse and a 'proof structure' giving constraints on the relations of proof and evidence between statements of the discourse. Roughly, the system of concepts is the interpretation assigned to the relatively abstract ontology, and the proof structure is the logic of explanation. (However, the proof structure is not merely a logic, since it may contain concepts of its own. For instance a given explanatory structure might contain a set of physical notions as its system of concepts but have a proof structure that introduced mathematical concepts.)

Among Aristotle's ontological principles, as I have outlined them above, we can note some elements from the system of concepts. In particular, thesis SS identifies secondary substances with species and thesis N identifies species and genera with individual natural creatures and secondary substances with natural kinds. It is already evident in Chapter 2 of the *Categories* that Aristotle wants us to identify primary substances with natural kinds. Further links between species and genera appear in thesis D. Thus in the opening statement of Aristotle's ontology we have not a pure ontology of abstract entities but an ontology-*cum*-interpretation, or, in Gaukroger's terms, an ontology with a system of concepts. Accordingly, Aristotle's ontology already contains the roots of an intended range of application which establishes it as a metaphysical interpretation of the world.

In what follows I shall examine the outlines of Aristotle's logical theory and his philosophy of science in S_1. These theories will provide information concerning Aristotle's proof theory and also the intended range of application of the set of theories that comprises S_1 as an explanatory structure.[26] The study of S_1 as an explanatory structure will accomplish two objectives: (1) if it is successful, it will provide evidence that S_1 is indeed a *system* of theories and not merely a collection; (2) by identifying what the elements of the system are, we shall gain a sort of definition of the system that will provide the basis for comparison with S_2. For it would appear that S_1 will be identical to S_2 just in case they constitute the same explanatory structure—that is, they have the same ontology, system of concepts, proof structure, and domain of evidence.

2.2 LOGIC AND LANGUAGE

2.2.1 Language

Aristotle begins *Cat.* 2 by observing, 'Of expressions,[27] some are said in combination, some without combination.' He recognizes the distinction between a sentence such as 'man walks' and uncombined words such as 'man', 'walks'. He goes on to treat ontology with a parallel remark: 'Of entities, some . . .' After discussing ontology, Aristotle returns to expressions: 'Of expressions not said in combination, each stands for either a substance or a quantity . . .' (4, 1ᵇ25 f.). Obviously, there is a parallelism between the domain of expressions and the domain of entities which allows Aristotle to switch back and forth between subjects without losing the train of his argument.

---

[26] Note that my project differs from Gaukroger's: he is interested primarily in Aristotle's philosophy of science alone, whereas I am interested in his philosophy as a whole. Furthermore Gaukroger makes what I claim is an unwarranted assumption in that he combines evidence from both S_1 and S_2 to produce his account; the result is an account that confounds the proof structure of S_1 (which he stresses) with concepts from S_2.

[27] τῶν λεγομένων: a more literal rendering is 'of things said'. However, this rendering is misleading in relation to the technical use of λέγεσθαι 'be Said-of' which is prominent in the chapter. I am tempted to render λεγόμενον by 'word'. Aristotle and his contemporaries had no word for 'word'. λόγος *never* means 'word' in the grammatical sense, and the closest available term was ὄνομα, which was used in this sense by Plato (e.g. *Crat.* 385 c), but which had already been specialized to mean 'noun' (Plato *Sph.* 261 E–2 A, cf. Aristotle *DI* 2; I am assuming the Platonic work is earlier, though there is no guarantee for this assumption). Yet although 'word' is a useful approximation of what Aristotle intends, it is not broad enough in extension. For expressions like 'in the Lyceum' and 'in the market-place' count as λεγόμενα without combination. The combination Aristotle refers to is the combination that makes sentences out of expressions. See Ackrill (1963: 73), Moravcsik (1967*b*: 126 f.).

Simple expressions stand for entities and classes of expressions stand for classes of entities, that is, categories.[28] In the *Categories* Aristotle does not point out that not all words have this signifying function, but elsewhere he acknowledges that there are 'syncategorematic' terms, as the medievals called them, which do not refer to categorial entities.[29] In general, Aristotle is aware of a semantic relation between words and things, even if he is sometimes careless in the distinctions he makes about them.[30] All nouns appear to be signifying terms which pick out items in one or other of the categories; adjectives, verb-forms, and other derivatives of nouns are used as predicates which do not directly signify but which presuppose signifying expressions.[31] The most important class of nouns is the class of substantives, for which the following relation obtains:

Substantival Reference (SR): Singular substantival terms refer to primary substances.

Thus proper names refer to individuals. General substantival terms such as 'man' and 'horse' appear to refer to individuals but rather signify secondary substances (*Cat.* 5, 3^{b}10–23).

In his concept of expressions said in combination, Aristotle tacitly makes use of the syntactical concept of a well-formed formula. He implies that a sentence must be composed of noun and verb, and he distinguishes these parts of speech (*DI* 1, 16^{a}13 ff.; 5, 17^{a}9–11). A sentence (λόγος) is a well-formed string meaningful in combination (4, 16^{b}26–8). Only sentences assert and deny, hence are true and false (*Cat.* 4, 2^{a}4–10), but not all sentences are assertions and denials—for instance, wishes are not (*DI* 4, 17^{a}2–5). Sentences that assert or deny are propositions,[32]

---

[28] I shall use the term in the traditional sense. Note, however, that Aristotle's κατηγορία has a more limited sense, and Aristotle does not even use the term here.

[29] *Poetics* 20, 1456^{b}20 ff., Ockham *Summa totius logicae* i. 4. Note, however, that there are some strong reasons for thinking that the *Poetics* passage is a post-Aristotelian interpolation: Maier (1900b: 46 ff.).

[30] See *DI* 1, 16^{a}3 ff. Irwin (1982) argues that we should not identify Aristotle's theory of signification with a theory of meaning. See ch. 3 n. 12.

[31] This seems to be the inference of *Cat.* 4, 1^{b}25 ff., which ascribes reference of expressions to entities in each of the categories, and 7, 6^{b}11–14, which states that e.g. lying, standing, and sitting are postures but that to lie, to stand, to sit are not, since they are paronyms of the aforesaid entities. On the theory of paronymy, see the second paragraph below and n. 34.

[32] These are not named in the early chapters of the *DI* but are called προτάσεις elsewhere. See *A.Pr.* i. 1, 24^{a}16 f.; cf. *DI* 5, 17^{a}8 ff.; *A.Po.* i. 2, 72^{a}8 f.; a presumably early use of the term is expounded in *Top.* i. 4, on which see Kapp (1931).

and logic deals mainly with these (*DI* 4, 17^{a}5–7). Propositions are true or false according to whether the fact that they assert obtains; moreover, they change their truth values as the fact comes to obtain or ceases to obtain (*Cat.* 5, 4^{a}23 ff.).[33] Propositions representing a single fact are simple, those representing a plurality of facts are compound (*DI* 5, 17^{a}15–22).

Aristotle tacitly recognizes a difference between surface structure and deep structure. The ontological difference between the Said-of tie and the In tie in the *Categories* generates distinct analyses of the sentence frame '—— is ——', such as the difference between 'Socrates is white' and 'Socrates is a man'. In fact, Aristotle recognizes at least ten possible analyses for the sentence frame '—— is ——' corresponding to the ten categories. He is aware of the differing function of subject and predicate in language—although his interest is usually in the ontological implications of a term's occupying that role rather than in the grammatical implications. Further, his theory of homonymy and synonymy (*Cat.* 1) shows that he is sensitive to the plurality of meanings that a word may have, and his theory of paronymy (ibid.) shows that he is aware of morphological relations between words.[34]

For the purposes of his logic, the most important syntactical distinction is that corresponding to the Said-of/In distinction in ontology. From a logico-linguistic point of view this may be called the difference between essential and accidental predication.[35] Aristotle's predication theory may be stated as follows:

---

[33] Aristotle's concept of a proposition is different from the modern one, since according to him propositions can change their truth value with time. Thus they are not timeless or dated assertions as in modern theory. See Hintikka (1967).

[34] However, the theory of synonymy–homonymy is not purely linguistic, since it is things rather than words that have these properties. Similarly the theory of paronymy is not a purely linguistic theory of morphology since for him e.g. λευκός 'white' is derived from λευκότης 'whiteness' and δίκαιος 'just' from δικαιοσύνη 'justice', i.e. the adjective from the abstract noun (*Cat.* 8, 10^{a}27–32; cf. 1, 1^{a}14 f.), whereas etymologically speaking the nouns in question are derived from the corresponding adjective. Aristotle's interpretation here seems to be strongly influenced by Plato's account of the individual *F* being *called after* the Form of *F*-ness (*Phd.* 102 B). Note that if Aristotle had made the adjective basic and the abstract noun derivative, he could have used paronymy as a criterion for picking out non-substantival nouns. Aristotle is aware of morphological relations in the inflection of nouns and verbs, *DI* 2, 16^{a}33–^{b}1; 3, 16^{b}16–18. He does not yet systematically distinguish the different kinds of inflection appropriate to different parts of speech: Trendelenburg (1846: 27–9).

[35] Of course this terminology is often used in the context of metaphysical analysis. I shall use it by preference for logico-linguistic analysis.

Predication (P): There are two forms of predication: *Essential Predication* (EP) is of the (logical) form *S* is *P* (where *S* and *P* are nouns); *Accidental Predication* (AP) is of the (logical) form *S* has *P*.[36]

Thus 'Socrates is a man' is analysed into 'Socrates is a man', but 'Socrates is white' is analysed into 'Socrates has Whiteness.'

2.2.2 *Logic*

Aristotle's syllogistic is a logical system designed to account for the logical properties of subject–predicate propositions. There is a subset of propositions for which an Aristotelian logical calculus is possible, composed of sentences in which the predicate is connected with the subject in one of four ways. Using capital letters as variables for terms (as Aristotle does), we may represent the four types of connection between terms as: (1) A belongs to all B; (2) A belongs to no B; (3) A belongs to some B; (4) A does not belong to some B. Aristotle prefers to give the predicate before the subject as I have—probably to indicate the asymmetry of predication—and this practice has important applications in his logic which will become apparent.[37] The connections between the predicates and subjects of these four kinds of propositions—traditionally known as categorical propositions—can best be understood as logical constants. I shall follow Patzig in designating the four constants by the letters used in syllogistic logic to characterize the four kinds of categorical proposition: a, e, i, o.[38] I shall represent 'A belongs to all B' with 'AaB', etc.

Distinguishing between premisses and conclusion, Aristotle defines a syllogism as 'an utterance in which some claims are advanced such that, if they are true, some statement other than those claims necessarily follows' (*A.Pr.* i. 1, 24^{b}18–20). In effect, a

[36] The 'is'/'has' contrast is not Aristotle's. He prefers the 'Said-of'/'In' terminology. (The discussion of 'have' in *Cat.* 15 suggests its potential value for an analysis of predication, but Aristotle does not capitalize on the suggestion.) I would rather reserve the latter pair for the ontological tie and the former for the linguistic relation. By retaining 'is' for the linguistic tie we capture the implications of the 'Said-of' terminology; while the 'has' expression blocks the transitivity of predication and requires a nominalization of the predicate, as does the 'In' formula.

[37] Cf. Łukasiewicz (1957: 17) following Alexander *in A.Pr.* 54.21 ff.

[38] Patzig (1968: 49). Traditional logic would give the subject first, e.g. 'A belongs to all B' would traditionally be rendered as 'BaA'. Note that Patzig (pp. 52 ff.) treats a, e, i, and o as non-logical constants, specifically relations, following Łukasiewicz (1957: 14 f.). Against this see the second paragraph below and n. 40.

syllogism is defined as a *valid* argument, and Aristotle refuses the appellation to invalid arguments (though he does use the term in a looser sense at times). What is most important is that he recognizes that an utterance is a syllogism *in virtue of its form.*[39] In specifying that form he ignores other valid argument forms, but he does give a correct characterization of aguments using pairs of uncompounded categorical propositions. He maintains that a syllogism is composed of three categorical propositions—two constituting premises and one being the conclusion. Longer arguments are analysed as strings of syllogisms, while shorter arguments tacitly assume a premiss. The argument-places of categorical propositions he calls terms (ὅροι). There must be exactly three terms in a syllogism.

With regard to evidence, there are two kinds of syllogism, the perfect and imperfect. A perfect syllogism is an argument whose validity is *self-evident* (*A.Pr.* i. 1, 24ᵇ22–4), while imperfect syllogisms are not obviously valid. Aristotle's method of establishing the validity of an imperfect syllogism is to 'reduce' it to a perfect syllogism. Recent studies have identified this method as a technique of natural deduction in which laws of conversion are used like rules of inference to deduce propositions which are the premisses of a perfect syllogism.[40] The perfect-syllogism form in turn is used as a rule of inference to draw a conclusion. Laws of conversion allow one to infer one kind of categorical propositon from another. For instance, from AaB it follows that BiA. Now it seems bizarre to us that Aristotle should say that all valid arguments have two premisses when he builds into his system argument forms such as the above conversion law that have only one premiss. However, Aristotle worked with a more restricted notion of argument than we do, and he simply did not recognize every valid inference as a valid argument—because not every inference is an argument. We may extract the following principle:

Syllogistic Theory of Arguments (STA): Arguments are syllogistic orderings of categorical statements.

---

[39] Alexander *in A.Pr.* 52.19–25, 53.28–31, 55.21 ff., Philoponus *in A.Pr.* 46.25 ff.; Ross (1949: 29); Łukasiewicz (1957: 7 f.) observes that modern commentators (except Ross) have never noticed this vital point.

[40] Smiley (1973) and Corcoran (1974b) given convincing arguments against the view defended by Łukasiewicz (1957, ch. 3) and Patzig (1968: 132). See also Corcoran (1974c), Lear (1980: 8–10).

By modern standards Aristotle's method of determining validity makes heavy demands on intuition: he takes the perfect syllogism as unproblematically valid without any justification, and then reduces other syllogisms to perfect syllogisms. In general, Aristotle has no formal semantics in the modern sense. This does not mean that his logical principles cannot be given justification in terms of formal semantics; it simply means that Aristotle does not make the attempt. Many of the features of Aristotle's logical system that were long regarded as idiosyncrasies have recently been shown to make good logical sense apart from any Aristotelian metaphysical background.[41] It is precisely by constructing a formal semantics for Aristotle's logic that logicians are able to justify various features of his system.[42]

This raises the question whether Aristotle's logic is in any way dependent on his philosophy. To this question the answer is that, while from a formal point of view Aristotle's logic need not be founded on his metaphysics, in fact Aristotle himself regards it as so founded. In *Prior Analytics* i. 27 Aristotle details the kinds of objects in the world and finds that some can be subjects but never predicates, some can be either subjects or predicates, and some can be only predicates. In order to reason well one must set out the subject and its attributes, whether essential, proper, or accidental, and see what follows from these appropriate propositions. Aristotle is thinking of his syllogistic as a calculus for deducing predications from other predications. He points out that there is a practical limit to predications, one set by the order of nature.[43] Furthermore, he uses his logic to criticize the method of Platonic division (*A.Pr.* i. 31). He considers that his method does what Plato's is supposed to do—to demonstrate classificatory definitions—and does so correctly, whereas the method of division merely begs the question as to what the definition of a thing is. Aristotle's references to the world show that although he does not have a formal model for his syllogistic, he does have an informal model. This model is the metaphysical picture of the world as made up of substances and attributes and hierarchically organized into genera, species, and individuals.

---

[41] This is a principle theme of Patzig (1968).
[42] e.g. Smiley (1973), Corcoran (1974b), Thom (1981).
[43] Cf. *A.Po.* i. 19–22, which makes free use of metaphysical and epistemological concepts.

We have seen that in Aristotle's ontology there are several inverted trees of entities which compose the realities of the world. The relation between an attribute and a substance is expressed in language as the relation between a predicate and a subject. Now the relations of subordination between attributes of different levels in the same tree can be captured by different predication statements—different categorical propositions—relating the several entities to one another. Sequences of propositions can represent chains of predicates. By noticing a common relation between the sequences of propositions and the chains of predicates, we can see how propositions can provide a calculus of predicates. What is common between logic and the world is a relation of *transitivity*: if aRb and bRc, then aRc for a transitive relation R. In the ontology, if a is over b and b is over c, then a is over c. In logic, if A belongs to all B and B belongs to all C, then A belongs to all C. But this last relationship is just a perfect syllogism. And now we can see why a perfect syllogism is perfect: because it allows the transitivity of essential predication to show itself.[44] The terms fit together like links in a chain that joins one extreme to another; the linking term is schematically in the middle. Hence Aristotle's technical terminology of extreme and middle terms.[45] The reordering of terms in traditional (that is, medieval) logic such that the subject is first and the predicate last destroys the perspicuity of the perfect syllogism, for it makes the order of statement 'All B is A, All C is B', transforming the middle term into an extreme term.[46] Furthermore, the listing of premisses and conclusion in a vertical column which has become traditional tends to obscure the transitivity which Aristotle's linear mode of expression emphasizes. All in all, the traditional syllogism tends to obscure the logical properties of transitivity which the Aristotelian syllogism is designed to reveal. And the logical properties which Aristotle's syllogism reveals are those inherent in ontological trees.

Wittgenstein said, 'There must be something identical in a

---

[44] Patzig (1968: 51 f., 57); Kneale and Kneale (1962: 73). Thus the four kinds of perfect syllogism are all first-figure syllogisms having the four kinds of categorical proposition, respectively, as their conclusions. See *A.Pr.* i. 4, 25ᵇ32–6ᵃ2; 26ᵃ17–28.

[45] Patzig (1968: 102 f.).

[46] See Patzig (1968: 57–61). On pp. 69–83 Patzig traces the history of the perfect–imperfect syllogism distinction through the centuries; he finds the key obfuscation in Boethius, whose method made it impossible to see how the perfect syllogism was syntactically perspicuous.

picture and what it depicts, to enable the one to be a picture of the other at all' (*Tractatus* 2. 161). And indeed there is an isomorphism between the world, structured as it is in a hierarchical fashion, and the syllogism, with its terms which can be linked together to form a chain of assertions leading from one predication to another. The isomorphism does not stop at the level of syllogism, but goes right down to that between a proposition and a fact, a term and an entity. To be sure, every description of a fact is not a perspicuous one—'*A* is *B*' may translate into '*B* is In *A*' or '*B* is Said-of *A*', and 'Pleasure is good' may mean 'All pleasure is good' or 'Some pleasure is good'—but when a proper analysis is made language is a transparent window to reality. Language and logic do not need an artificial formal model because they already have a model: the world itself.

However, this is perhaps a naïve way to put the relationship between language and the world. If instead of asking how logic or meaning is possible we ask how does Aristotle derive his system, we turn the tables. What is Aristotle's model of the world? I think the answer must be: language.[47] We have seen that what formally characterizes primary substance is subjecthood. To be fully real is to be an absolute subject. Secondarily, to be real is to be a predicate of a subject. Now there is no a priori reason why reality should resolve itself into substances and attributes. Plato certainly does not think of the world in this way. Furthermore, there is no a priori reason for entities to be hierarchically organized. However, language exhibits horizontal differentiations into subject and predicate and vertical differentiations into less comprehensive and more comprehensive terms. Aristotle uses the same term, ὑποκείμενον, for the subject of accidental and the subject of essential predications. Why does he conflate the two after distinguishing the logical form of the two types of predication? It must be that the two types of

---

[47] See Trendelenburg (1846: 11–33), Gillespie (1925), Ackrill (1963: 78–81). Moravcsik (1967b: 140–42) criticizes Ackrill's account of how the categories were derived. His most telling criticism is that on Ackrill's account Aristotle argues from language to the categories and then from the categories to the primacy of substance in a question-begging way. But if linguistic usage is taken as a datum, i.e. as a priori, one is perfectly justified in inferring the primacy of substance from the structure of the categories. Moravcsik's own solution appeals to the insight that 'Aristotle's list yields a survey of what is given in sense experience' (p. 143). His interpretation commits the anachronism of starting from sense experience rather than from the ἔνδοξα. Recent studies have tended to stress that Aristotle's starting-point for inquiry is more philosophical than empirical; see especially Owen (1961).

subject are expressed by the same grammatical function in both types of sentence.

Language is not merely a tool to get around in the world; it reveals the structure of the world. The surface structure, to be sure, can be deceptive, but the deep structure of language is isomorphic with the world. This claim may seem puzzling in the light of Aristotle's view that language is conventional. However, if the elements of language are conventional, there is no real problem. The specific words we use are language relative, but words stand for thoughts and thoughts belong to a mental life that is common to all human beings (*DI* i. 1, 16^{a}5–8). Thus the terms that we use to divide up and articulate the world, as these are suitably corrected in a scientific way, actually mirror the world. Furthermore the deep structure of language imitates the structure of the world. The world has, as it were, a syntax revealed in language. Aristotle envisages a 'λόγος-textured' world,[48] one whose elements are informed by λόγος—by language and reason —and hence one in which logical relationships obtain. In this world, logic can reveal connections between elements because language and the world have a form in common. This brings us to an examination of the principles of scientific explanation. Precisely how does Aristotle conceive of science in a λόγος-textured world?

2.3   PHILOSOPHY OF SCIENCE

2.3.1   Demonstration and Science

For Aristotle, scientific knowledge is demonstrated knowledge. To have scientific knowledge of a fact is to know its cause, to know that this cause is the cause of the fact in question, and to know that the fact cannot be otherwise than it is (*A.Po.* i. 2, 71^{b}9–12). This sort of knowledge is produced by a deduction in which the premisses are true and also ultimate, immediate, better known than, and explanatory of the conclusion—that is, they are first principles for the explanandum (^{b}20–23). Thus for S₁:

> *Scientific Knowledge* (SK): Scientific knowledge is demonstrative knowledge.

This account raises a problem: if scientific knowledge consists of a deduction from first principles to conclusions expressing the facts

---

[48] The expression is from Mourelatos (1973: 16).

to be explained, what is the status of the first principles? If they too are known by deduction, there must either be an infinite regress of principles (and hence no real *first* principles at all) or the principles must be justified by deducing them from the conclusions. In the first case there is no real deduction since there are no real principles, while in the second case explanation is circular (*A.Po.* i. 3). Aristotle rejects both these accounts; he holds that there must be a non-inferential kind of knowledge which knows first principles—they are, after all, immediate (ἄμεσα). This kind of knowledge must be intuitive and more reliable than scientific knowledge so as to form the foundation of science (i. 3, 72ᵇ18–25; ii. 19).

And indeed, scientific knowledge is foundational in nature. One begins from first principles, which must be necessary truths if they are to demonstrate how facts cannot be otherwise than they are (i. 4, 73ª21–4; 6, 74ᵇ5 f.). One then proceeds by a deduction process that preserves necessity to show that the facts follow necessarily and are necessary given the premises. A given science contains in its first principles 'axioms' which are presupposed by all the sciences (2, 72ª16 f.) and truths unique to the given science (10, 76ª37 f.), and proofs can only proceed according to principles appropriate to the subject (9, 75ᵇ37–40). Thus the explanatory structure of a science is like that of a mathematical axiomatic system in which one begins with axioms, definitions, and postulates and deduces theorems which in turn provide the justification for further theorems. Science is foundational and deductive in character. We have, then, a further thesis concerning philosophy of science:

Demonstrative Knowledge (DK): Demonstrative knowledge consists of theorems deduced from self-evident principles.

But what kind of deduction is appropriate to demonstration? Clearly the only kind of formal deduction Aristotle recognizes, the syllogism, must be the vehicle for proof. Thus the apodeictic of the *Posterior Analytics* presupposes the syllogistic of the *Prior Analytics*.[49] For instance, Aristotle makes a distinction between knowing a fact (ἐπίστασθαι τὸ ὅτι) and knowing the explanation

---

[49] See Ross (1949: 8–13), following Ross (1939a). Barnes (1981) has recently argued that Aristotle's apodeictic is independent of his syllogistic. For a discussion of this view see ch. 11.5.3.

(ἐπίστασθαι τὸ διότι) (*A.Po.* i. 13). Let *A* stand for 'being near', *B* for 'not twinkling' and *C* for 'planets'. Now we could argue that (1) What does not twinkle is near, (2) The planets do not twinkle, hence (3) The planets are near; i.e. *A–B*, *B–C*, hence *A–C*.[50] We might expect Aristotle to call this deduction a proof of the explanation, since in it we deduce the explanation for the second premiss. But Aristotle maintains that this is a mere proof of the fact. The proof of the explanation is given by taking the sequence (1*a*) What is near does not twinkle, (2*a*) The planets are near, hence (3*a*) the planets do not twinkle; i.e. B–A, A–C, hence B–C.[51] In this syllogism the phenomenon is expressed by the conclusion, and the explanation is given by the premisses, namely a general principle (1*a*) and a specific fact (2*a*) that connects with the principle. This is a proof of the explanation because it *shows* the explanation *as* an explanation, that is: occupying the premiss positions. It will be more natural in English to call the proof of explanation an explanatory proof.[52] Thus scientific proof seems to require a syllogism—even mere proof of the fact does. And although the reciprocal proofs are sometimes possible using the terms of a syllogism in different sequences, there is only one ordering of terms that displays the explanation as an explanation, and hence that formally explains the explanandum. Generalizing from the example, we thus have the following principle:

> *Scientific Explanation* (SE): Scientific explanation is the deduction of a description of phenomena from premisses exhibiting the cause.

In *A.Po.* i. 14 Aristotle explicitly invokes his syllogistic theory to support scientific proof.[53] He mentions the three figures of the *Prior Analytics* and points to the fact that the first is the most scientific, for three reasons: (1) most of the sciences use this figure,

[50] I omit the logical constants here, since they are not immediately relevant to the problem. I have changed the order in which Aristotle presents the premisses to allow the terms to show their connection.

[51] Aristotle reassigns the letters here, but for purposes of comparison I keep the same assignments.

[52] Patzig (1981: 143 f.) argues that the phrase συλλογισμὸς τοῦ διότι should be taken as employing a genitive of quality rather than an objective genitive; i.e. 'deduction *from* the because'.

[53] Cf. Hintikka (1972), who argues for the close connection between science and syllogistic on the grounds that the theory of syllogism accounts for Aristotle's views on the ingredients of scientific explanation.

(2) the explanatory proof generally relies on this figure, and (3) only the first figure can have conclusions which are both affirmative and universal. But this is just what science aims at in so far as it seeks *essence*, since essence will be predicated universally and positively of its subjects. Aristotle expands on the superiority of universal and affirmative modes of proof in Chapters 24 and 25. Here it is important to note the close connection between proof and essence. As with the isomorphism between language and reality, we see here a parallelism between proof structure and the order of nature. Aristotle does not conceive of apodeictic as a purely formal calculus of consequences from first principles. Rather, he sees it as securing the reliability of science inasmuch as it imitates the underlying structure of the world. This high-level isomorphism provides a further guarantee of the efficacy of Aristotelian scienific method. We see that despite the appearance of abstract formalism that pervades the first few chapter of the *Posterior Analytics*, Aristotle's philosophy of science has a strong metaphysical motivation.

In a number of other ways Aristotle's philosophy of science is dependent upon his ontology and logic. In the first place he holds that demonstration is only possible in the case of essences of properties which belong to a substance necessarily: 'Demonstration is of attributes that belong properly [καθ' αὐτὰ] to things' (*A.Po.* i. 22, 84ᵃ11 f.). There are two kinds of predication: proper and accidental; proper predication is the logical connection between *A* and *B* when either *A* is in the definiens of *B* or *B* is in the definiens of *A* (4, 73ᵃ34–ᵇ4). If neither of these cases obtains, the connection between them is accidental predication (ᵇ4 f.). Only proper attributes belong necessarily to their subjects, so only they can be demonstrated as belonging to them. Furthermore, the chain of deductions in a demonstration cannot be infinitely long, because the number of essential predicates in a tree is finite (22, 84ᵃ17–28). Thus Aristotle interprets demonstration as grounded in the ontological Said-of tie, the linguistic correlate of which is proper predication, and constrained by the dimensions of the ontological tree.

Aristotle gives an analysis of cause in the *Posterior Analytics* which connects his philosophy of science with his account of syllogistic deduction. He maintains that a cause is a *middle term* (ii. 2). What he means is that in an explanatory syllogism the middle term of the premisses expresses the cause. For example, if we wish to explain an eclipse of the moon, we can set up a syllogism as follows (ii. 8, 93^{a}29 ff.): (1) Eclipse is said of light being blocked by an intervening body; (2) Having its light blocked by an intervening body applies to the moon; therefore (3) Eclipse belongs to the moon. If we use the letter A for 'eclipse', B for 'having its light blocked by the intervening body', and C for 'moon', the syllogism exhibits the structure A–B, B–C, therefore A–C. The middle term, B, expresses the cause of the phenomenon: the blocking of light by an intervening body is the cause of an eclipse. Clearly this syntactic analysis of cause presupposes the syllogistic of the *Prior Analytics* with its apparatus of terms. Indeed, the definition of cause as middle term is meaningless apart from the principles of syllogistic. Against the background of syllogistic theory we have the following theory of cause:

> *Middle Term Theory of Cause* (MTC): A cause is the middle term of a scientific syllogism.

According to the middle-term analysis, a cause is identical with one term of a syllogism. The conclusion of the syllogism must be the description of a phenomenon and the premisses explanantia of the phenomenon. The term which represents the cause is intermediate between a higher-level universal and a universal which is identical with the subject of the phenomenon. For instance, Cloud is the subject of Thunder, a higher-level universal. The intermediate universal is Quenching-of-Fire. According to this analysis, the cause is a link in a chain of universals. To discover a cause is, as it were, to discover a *missing link* in a chain proceeding from the highest genus to the subject term. We understand why A belongs to C when we discover that A belongs to B and B belongs to C—that is, when we find the term that links, and preferably immediately links, the predicate to the subject in the description of a problematic phenomenon. I shall call the S_1 theory of cause the Missing Link Theory:

> *Missing Link Theory of Cause* (MLC): A cause is the missing link in a chain of universals exhibited by the terms of a sequence of syllogisms in a projected demonstrative proof.

MLC is a consequence of MTC and a certain understanding of the order of universals which the terms of syllogisms signify. This interpretation of cause makes it possible to view the construction of an explanatory proof as the concomitant discovery of a cause; it minimizes the distinction between the context of proof and the context of discovery.[54]

2.3.2   The Four Causes and Demonstration

In *A.Po*. ii. 11 Aristotle identifies four kinds of cause. They are (1) the essence (τὸ τί ἦν εἶναι) (2) the logical ground of a deduction (τὸ τίνων ὄντων ἀνάγκη τοῦτ' εἶναι), (3) the first cause of movement (ἤ τι πρῶτον ἐκίνησε), and (4) the final cause (τὸ τίνος ἕνεκα). He asserts that each kind fits the analysis of the cause as middle term. There are certain problems connected with his four cause theory in the *A.Po*., both concerning its relation to the four cause theory as expressed in the works of S₂ and concerning his argument that each constitutes a middle term. However, I shall postpone a discussion of these problems until we examine the four cause theory in detail in Chapter 6. This theory plays no significant role in S₁ since it rarely appears in the *A.Po*. But it is important to specify the four causes for later comparison with the S₂ version of the theory:

> *Four Cause Theory* (FCT): There are four kinds of cause, (1) the essential cause, (2) the logical ground, (3) the moving cause, (4) the final cause.

Aristotle emphasizes that the four causes can all be analysed as middle terms of a syllogism (94ᵃ20–4). Thus FCT is an instance of MTC and constitutes a specification of the syllogistic analysis of cause rather than an extension or a modification of it.

2.3.3   The Domain of Evidence of S₁

Earlier I discussed Gaukroger's analysis of explanatory structures into an ontology, a system of concepts, a proof structure, and a domain of evidence. At the beginning of this chapter we discussed the ontology and in part the system of concepts or the interpretation of the ontology. We are now in a position to make some general remarks about the proof structure. For Aristotle the form that a proof takes is a syllogism or series of syllogisms. Ultimately a scientific proof begins with first principles. It consists of a series of

---

[54] Consequently this interpretation contrasts strongly with the view defended in Barnes (1969) that syllogistic proof is an exercise in didactic exposition. For a discussion of Barnes's thesis see Ch. 11.5.3.

statements, each of which is a first principle or a theorem derived
from first principles by rules of inference.

The question is often asked what provided the inspiration for
Aristotle's apodeictic. An obvious candidate is the science of
geometry. Although we do not know in precisely what form
geometrical knowledge was organized in Aristotle's day, it seems
likely that Aristotle's contemporaries anticipated Euclid's system
in many respects.[55] Thus we might expect that the axiomatic
method of geometry provided a model for Aristotle's apodeictic.
There is, however, one serious obstacle: as Ian Mueller (1974) has
shown, Aristotle's syllogistic fails to provide a calculus powerful
enough to justify even elementary geometrical proofs. One needs
the propositional calculus and some first-order predicate calculus
to account for all the steps of a typical Euclidean proof. Aristotle's
own syllogistic proofs of geometrical theorems remain curiously
non-Euclidean.

What emerges from this is a somewhat complex picture of the
relation of Aristotle's theory of demonstration to mathematics. On
the one hand, he seems to think he is using a mathematical model;
on the other hand his own logic falls short of the logical power
exemplified in the model. In broad outlines he seems to have
grasped the elements of the mathematical method. The only likely
source of inspiration here is geometry. Yet Aristotle seems to have
grafted onto this trunk the details of a logic that is not
mathematical in origin or character. His own syllogistic seems to
be rooted in the dialectical tradition—as evidenced by the
Topics—and to have antecedents in the Socratic search for
essential definitions.[56] There are formal similarities between
syllogistic and set theory, but there is no indication that Aristotle is
interested in the abstract questions of set theory *per se*. Rather his
interest stems from a desire to codify essential biological relations.[57]
For this reason universal first-figure syllogisms are particularly
important to both his syllogistic and his apodeictic. Such syllogisms
are the most scientific because they have significant applications to
statements of definitions by reproducing the transitivity of real

[55] Cf. von Fritz (1961: 607), Mueller (1974: 35, Heath (1921: 216 f.)
[56] See Kapp (1931), *Met* i. 6, 987ᵇ1–4. On the origin of the syllogism, see Shorey
(1924), (1933), Ross (1939a), Solmsen (1941).
[57] Cf. Kullmann (1981), who suggests that the theory of demonstration is
designed to apply to natural science.

definitions.[58] Dialectical practice combines with a conception of mathematical organization and Aristotelian metaphysical assumptions to provide the inspiration for Aristotle's philosophy of science.[59]

One element of Gaukroger's analysis of explanatory structures that we have not discussed is the domain of evidence. To determine the domain of evidence for S_1 is a complicated matter, since there are a number of interconnected theories which must be examined. For instance, Aristotle's syllogistic deals with deductive arguments, while the domain of apodeictic is demonstrations from necessary principles. In both of these theories it appears that Aristotle was not as attentive to the domain of evidence as he might have been, for he overlooked many kinds of valid arguments and he failed to note that the geometrical demonstrations that formed his model did not conform to some of his strictures. Yet as interesting as such questions are, a more important problem concerns the intended domain of the whole set of theories comprising S_1. It should be evident by now that S_1 does constitute a system and not a mere assemblage of theories. Is the system embodied by S_1 merely an *organon*, that is: a logical tool? More specifically, is it a metaphysically neutral logic of science? Or is it the metaphysical foundation of a philosophical view of the world—a world hypothesis?

We should now be in a position to give a preliminary answer to this question. It appears from the evidence that we have seen that although much of S_1 could have been constructed as a theory-neutral logic of science, Aristotle did not conceive it that way. He saw the theories of the *Organon* as a system that was able to provide a foundation of science because it incorporated a true metaphysic. It was up to each science to characterize its subject-matter, but the guarantee for science as a whole was a metaphysical one. Although each science has a delimited domain of evidence,

---

[58] See *A.Po.* i. 24–6.

[59] It is tempting to go further and claim that Aristotle's perfect syllogism marks an attempt to capture the fundamental set-theoretical relation of class inclusion. (Hintikka 1972: 56 stresses that syllogisms work by class inclusion.) However, I have already noted that Aristotle's own remarks vacillate between treating predicates as expressing classes and as expressing properties. Thus I wish to avoid reducing syllogistic to a department of set theory or founding it on a set-theoretic semantics. Nevertheless, the transitivity that the perfect syllogism embodies is clearly found in class inclusion.

jointly the sciences range over all phenomena, at least of the physical world. Since the sciences consist in the application to specific contexts of metaphysical principles, they are in the last analysis the vehicle for a metaphysical interpretation of the world. Of course the sciences will determine their own specific interpretations of the phenomena in their domain. However, it will be predetermined by Aristotle's metaphysic that the sciences will be dealing with relationships between universals, and that the possible relationships will be finite in number. Overall, each scientific advance will be a concomitant advance in the explanatory scope of substance metaphysics. The method of scientific demonstration that Aristotle advocates is inextricably bound up with his metaphysical insights, and consequently a metaphysical view of the world is present in S_1

2.4 CONCLUSION

We have now briefly outlined the ontology, logic, and philosophy of science of S_1. What emerges is not a mere set of conceptual tools (as the traditional name *Organon* suggests), but a system of interrelated explanatory schemes. The ontology provides a foundation for the system. According to this ontology, the realities of which the world is composed are atomic objects which are to be identified with biological individuals; these are organized under universals which are to be identified with natural kinds. In general, natural kinds are analysable into differentiae and genera which uniquely define them and constitute their essence. In the first place the atomic objects and in the second place the kinds they fall under are called substances. Attributes are instantiated primarily in individual substances and secondarily in universal substances. These attributes, called accidents, characterize substances without belonging to them necessarily. The general metaphysical position to which Aristotle adheres I have called atomic substantialism (AS).

Language is conventional in its phonology, vocabulary, and surface structure, natural in content and form (deep structure). If one is careful in investigating the deep structure of the grammar, one can discern the underlying ontological ties, for language is isomorphic with reality. Language exhibits logical properties which justify inference in the form of arguments having premisses and conclusions. Arguments are analysable into 'syllogisms'—series of propositions having two premisses and a conclusion, the series containing three terms used twice each in propositions relating two terms in one of four standard ways. The logical properties of a syllogism are a function of the order of the terms and their relation to one another; the terms can function like links in a chain of logical relations leading to the assertion of relations between the first and last terms. Validity is determined by relation to logically perspicuous arguments called perfect syllogisms. Although Aristotle's syllogistic can be defended as a logical system independent of any particular metaphysics, Aristotle interprets his syllogistic as a calculus of universals which can be used to investigate the structure of reality. It is constrained by the ontological limits of predication. It is superior to the Platonic method of division in its power to justify its conclusions, which are definitory of the nature of things.

Aristotle's philosophy of science envisages an axiomatic deductive system which begins from necessary premisses known intuitively and demonstrates the necessity of conclusions drawn from these. The method of deduction Aristotle requires is syllogistic. Ontological constraints on the limits of predication determine that each science will be composed of a finite set of propositions. Demonstration reveals the cause of each phenomenon, which is exhibited as the middle term of the syllogism demonstrating the phenomenon in question. The cause is thus the missing link of a chain of universals organized in a tree.

Thus we see the ontological theory pervading and grounding the logical and scientific theory. Aristotle grounds his logic in turn on his theory of language and his philosophy of science on his logic. We have seen also that language provides a model for the construction of Aristotle's ontology and that geometry and dialectic co-operate at different levels to provide a model for his theory of scientific demonstration. The several theories of the *Organon* are closely interrelated and integrated such that they comprise a single outlook on the world. It follows that the *Organon* is not merely a set of tools for analysis that are topic neutral and devoid of metaphysical presuppositions. Aristotle's ontology is thoroughly and unabashedly metaphysical, and this ontology undergirds the whole collection of logical treatises.

Thus the fact that the *Categories* is preliminary to the *Analytics* does not so much mean that the former work is a merely logical treatise as that the latter are in part metaphysical treatises. This discovery makes a confrontation with the metaphysics of the rest of the corpus inevitable. We must turn now to what we traditionally call the physical and metaphysical treatises to examine the character of the philosophical system embodied in them.

3

S₂: Hylomorphic Substantialism

We turn now to S_2, the system embodied in the works outside the *Organon*. S_2 is generally considered to be Aristotle's philosophical system *par excellence*. It may seem otiose to rehearse his theories since they are so well known. However, current accounts of Aristotle often present S_2 theory contaminated by doctrines imported from S_1. In any case, the inquiry we are pursuing requires a more structured exposition of Aristotle than usual. For having gone through the salient doctrines of S_1, we must now examine their counterparts in S_2 as a preliminary to comparing and contrasting the two systems. Our choice of subjects has been guided in part by an analysis of the elements of a theoretical discourse. If we could establish identity between the corresponding elements of the two discourses in question, we could establish the identity of the systems; if we discern differences between the elements, we produce evidence for asserting that our hypothetical distinction between the systems has a foundation in reality. We shall, accordingly, examine in order the ontology, theory of logic and language, and philosophy of science of S_2.

3.1 ONTOLOGY

3.1.1 *Formal Ontology*

The ontology of S_2 emerges most clearly in the opening chapters of *Met.* vii, where Aristotle identifies the problem of determining what being is—that is, the central problem of ontology—as the problem of defining substance (1, 1028^{b}2–4). It is clear from his conception of the problem and his preliminary arguments that substance is the basic entity, and that all other kinds of being are to be explained by reference to substance and its fundamental characteristics. Thus we find that Aristotle's interest in substance in S_2 is no less intense than in S_1. However, the real question is to what extent the concepts of substance of S_1 and S_2 are identical.

The picture of substance is more complicated in S_2 than in S_1, for Aristotle makes a distinction between a composite substance and its components (3, 1029ᵃ2 f.). The components are matter (ὕλη) and form (μορφή or εἶδος). Matter he explicates as a subject of which all features are predicated, but which is not identical with them, or even with the denial of these features (ᵃ20–6). Thus matter appears as a substratum which is indeterminate *per se* and has determinations only incidentally. Form, on the other hand, is the principle of determination by which matter becomes something. It is separable and a This (τόδε τι, ᵃ27–9). Thus Aristotle seems to envisage a fundamental distinction between an indeterminate medium and a determining principle which complement each other in a substance compounded of both.

The analysis of the composite substance into form and matter brings with it a problem of priority. One of the functions of substance, in S_2 as in S_1, is to provide a foundation for every kind of being. As such, substance must be ontologically prior to every other kind of being. However, if substance itself is a manifold concept, it appears that we must ask which concept of substance is the fundamental one. Aristotle quickly dismisses matter because it is not separable or a This. But both composite substance and form satisfy the criteria. He resolves the problem with an argument: 'The substance composed of both elements, namely matter and form, may be dismissed; for it is posterior and obvious' (ᵃ30–2). The problem with composite substance is evidently that it is derivative. Hence it cannot fulfil the role of being a foundation for being. Only a simple entity can be really real.

Aristotle confirms the priority of form by giving it the name of primary substance: 'By primary [substance] I mean what does not imply one thing being in another, i.e. having a substratum that functions as its matter' (11, 1037ᵇ3 f.; cf. 4, 1030ᵃ10 f.). In other words, primary substance is not a composite of form and matter. Although both the composite and form are separable and a This, the composite is a derivative entity which owes its substantial characteristics to the element that is the chief bearer of them. What then are these characteristics? Unfortunately Aristotle does not explicate them. However, the very absence of an explanation seems to indicate that they are not to be understood as arcane or recondite. Rather, the distinction is meant to be self-evident. What is separable and a This seems to be what can be singled out for ostention. In philosophical terms, the criteria establish the particularity of substance.

3.1.2 Interpretation

What are the correlatives of the concrete substance, form, and matter in the world of experience? Aristotle consistently identifies the concrete substance with individual natural objects—individual human beings, animals, and plants are the paradigm instances (Met. vii. 7, 1032ª18 f.). He often uses artefacts for the sake of illustration. This is evidently because the correlates of form and matter are obvious in these cases: the form is the shape, the matter the material out of which the artefact is constructed. Nevertheless, Aristotle treats such objects as only quasi-substantial. The primary application of the ontology is to natural objects.

This leaves the question of what precisely are the correlates of form and matter in the natural object. To this there is no simple answer. Aristotle points out that 'to each form there is a different matter' (Ph. ii. 2, 194ᵇ9). The assignment is *relative* to the object under consideration. Thus the form and matter of a plant differ from the form and matter of an animal. But the relativity is not confined to such cases. Aristotle also holds that there are different *levels of composition*. The most simple things are the four traditional elements, earth, air, fire, and water; they combine to form chemical compounds; these in turn form homogeneous tissues, out of which are formed heterogeneous organs, out of which the organism as a whole is composed (PA i, 1, 646ª12 ff.). At each level one can distinguish a matter and a form. The matter at a given level of composition can serve as the composite substance for a further analysis into matter and form. Thus there are two kinds of relativity that we might distinguish: the form–matter interpretation is *object-relative* and *level-relative*. We must specify both the object of analysis and the level at which the analysis is to take place.

The relativity of form–matter analysis complicates the interpretation of the S₂ ontology. Nevertheless, if only the relevant object and level of analysis are determined, it would seem that the appropriate correlates can be identified in a given case. However, there seems to be a further source of indeterminacy. Even for a given object and level of composition, Aristotle gives various interpretations of form and matter. At times Aristotle treats the form–matter components of the individual animal as soul and body.[1] At other times he seems to hold that the matter is flesh and bones while the form is their organization.[2] In some situations he identifies the matter with the seed,[3] or even the menstrual fluid.[4] The presence of so much variation in what should be a straightforward assignment is perplexing. It is possible that Aristotle is himself uncertain as to what the appropriate assignment should be. On the other hand, the problem may be in the context of evaluation. It might be necessary to assign interpretations of form and matter not absolutely, even in the case of a determinate object at a determinate level of composition, but according to the context of analysis. In other words, perhaps different answers arise because different questions are being asked. If this is the case, the interpretation of form and matter is *context-relative* in addition to being relative in two other ways. In any event, the form–matter scheme is in itself indeterminate and requires specification for its application to a determinate situation.

We have already noted a problem of priority in the S$_2$ account of substance. Aristotle's considered response to the problem is that form is substance in the primary sense. However, we have just noted that the notion of form has many interpretations. Which interpretation gives the primary sense of form, the sense in which form is the foundation of all reality? In *Met.* vii Aristotle makes some identifications which reveal the chief sense of form. In order to explicate the notion of form (3, 1029ª32 f.), Aristotle turns to the concept of essence (τὸ τί ἦν εἶναι) (Chapter 4). He discovers that 'there will not be an essence of anything that is not the species of a genus, but only of species; for these things are not predicated by way of participation or attribution, nor accidentally' (4, 1030ª11–14). But he has already argued that there is essence only of what is primary, that is, what does not consist of one component predicated of another (ª6–11). And this must be the form.[5] Thus form must be identical with species and species must have an essence.

The species Aristotle has in mind is the natural species of a genus. Thus he espouses a principle of naturalism in S$_2$. Not only

[1] *DA* ii. 1, 412ª19–21.   [2] *Met.* vii. 8, 1034ª5–7.
[3] *Ph.* i. 7, 190ᵇ3–5.
[4] *Met.* viii. 4, 1044ª34 f.; *GA* i. 22, 730ª32–ᵇ24.
[5] Cf. *Met.* vii. 11, 1037ᵇ2 f.

are the paradigm correlates of composite substance natural objects, but the paradigm correlates of form are natural species. Since matter is in every case relative to a corresponding form, the paradigm correlate of matter must be whatever medium it is that species informs to create the individual.

Furthermore, since the form–matter analysis applies to all natural objects, and the form is identical with the species of a concrete substance, each substance must have a set of features such that they belong to it necessarily and by definition. And since species are definable in terms of differentia and genus—for it is they that are chiefly definable—the principle of definability also holds.

There is one further characteristic of substance that is central to the S$_2$ account. Substance, and in particular form, is associated with actuality (ἐνέργεια) while matter is associated with potentiality (δύναμις) (*Met.* viii. 2). In some contexts the form–matter and actuality–potentiality distinctions are used almost interchangeably. However, Aristotle clearly considers the latter to have some explanatory value the former does not. Although ἐνέργεια can have several meanings,[6] the one which is relevant to substance analysis is that in which it 'tends to mean ἐντελέχεια'.[7] The basic notion signified by ἐντελέχεια is completeness. Between the unformed matter which is possibly an *F* and the informed matter, which is an actual *F*, there are various stages of partial completeness. Actuality is a measure of reality based on the degree of completeness exhibited by a composite substance. Full actuality corresponds to the full realization of a form in a matter.

3.1.3 Summary

It will be helpful to formulate key principles of the ontology of S$_2$ as we did for S$_1$:

> *Substantialism** (S*)*: Primary substances exist independently; for all other entities, to be is to be the substratum of a concrete substance or to be an accident of a concrete substance.

> *Hylomorphism* (H): The concrete substance is composed of form and matter.

> *Formism* (F): Form is substance in the primary sense.

[6] *Met.* ix. 1, 1045^{b}32–6^{a}4; 6, 1048^{a}30 ff.   [7] Ibid. 3, 1047^{a}30 f.

> *Formal Substantialism* (FS): Every concrete substance falls under a species, which is identical with its form.
>
> *Definability* (D): Every species is either identical to a primitive genus or is identical to the differentia of a genus.
>
> *Naturalism* (N): Species and genera are natural kinds.
>
> *Actualism* (A): A concrete substance exhibits more reality to the degree that its form is more completely realized in its matter.

The feature that seems to be most distinctive of this ontology as contrasted with that of S_1 is the presence of a doctrine of hylomorphism. Although analogous theses hold in most cases, they differ to the extent that hylomorphic composition must be accommodated in S_2. For instance, we find form instead of secondary substance being identified with species. Furthermore, instead of the particular substance holding primacy, the formal component is designated as primary substance in S_2. Let us see if the principle of hylomorphism is reflected in the logic and philosophy of science of S_2.

3.2.   LOGIC AND PHILOSOPHY OF LANGUAGE

S_2 does not present a complete logic or philosophy of language. In this respect we cannot compare the logic of S_1 with that of S_2. However, S_2 does introduce some important theories in the realm of logic and philosophy of language which seem to have important implications for the construction of a general theory. I shall examine several instances in which Aristotle's analyses point to general positions in logic and the philosophy of language. As is the case with S_1, his logical theory is not clearly demarcated from his metaphysics. But as in S_1, the parallelism between language and reality makes it possible to read off logical insights from metaphysical assertions. A metaphysical theory of S_2 that has striking implications for logic is that of predication.

3.2.1   *Predication*

In Chapter 3.1 we examined some of the implications of *Met.* vii. 3 for Aristotle's ontology. The chapter also has important implications for the theory of predication. Aristotle's inquiry into the claim that substratum is substance leads to an analysis of the different senses of substratum, which are (1) matter, (2) form, and (3) the composite. First he evaluates the merits of (1). He defines matter as what is not a thing or a quantity or any of the other predicates (1029^{a}20 f.). If so, it must be the subject of all determinations, but totally indeterminate in itself. Accordingly, although it is the ultimate substratum of predication, it is not separable and τόδε τι, it cannot be substance in the primary sense. On the other hand, (3) is a compound and so reducible to its components, so that it cannot be substance in the primary sense. By elimination, (2) must be the primary sense of substance. Indeed, Aristotle prematurely reveals the key role of form when he says, before discussing (2):

The other attributes are predicated of *substance*, and this of matter. (^{a}23 f.)

Here 'substance' cannot mean matter, since it is predicated of matter, and it cannot mean the composite, since the matter of which substance is allegedly predicated is a component of the composite; 'substance' can only mean form.

The 30-odd lines of 1029^a provide a wealth of intriguing insights and difficult problems for an understanding of predication. What does Aristotle mean by matter, and precisely why does he reject it? What is the relation of form to matter? What is the criterion that discriminates against matter and favours form? The argument is compressed and in some respects seems to make unusual assumptions about the nature of matter and form. Yet the chapter seems to contain Aristotle's most direct statement about predication. As in S₁ metaphysical predication provides the basis for understanding linguistic predication. Let us then consider the relevant metaphysical claims of *Met*, vii. 3, examining first the role of matter in predication.

In Aristotle's analysis of matter he first considers what is left if we take away length, width, and depth from a thing. In other words, take away the three dimensions of body and what is left is matter. If this were all he had to say, we might conclude that matter is the resultant of a physical analysis of reality.[8] However, Aristotle then goes on to say that it is that of which the categories are predicated and which is not identical with any of them. This suddenly presupposes a logical or metaphysical analysis of matter.

---

[8] This general interpretation of matter is defended by Sokolowski (1970: 277 ff.) and Cohen (1984: esp. 179 f.).

Matter is the final substratum that is left after all defining predicates are abstracted from a thing. This raises a problem of reference: what is it that is referred to in such a way? I shall put off a discussion of reference until later. However, we should recognize that what such an analysis arrives at is an ultimate subject of predication, which I shall call, in light of some similar notions in recent philosophy, the logical subject. Apart from the problem of reference there remains the problem of the relation between the several predicates and this logical subject.

It is evident from Aristotle's remark at 1029^a23 f. that there is a difference in the way predicates attach to matter. Form must attach directly to matter. The accidents attach, says Aristotle, to the form. For now, let us just consider the relation of form to matter. The relation is not a physical one, for form and matter cannot be *parts* of a physical whole. They are principles on a different level of reality (cf. *Met.* vii. 17). They must be metaphysical components connected by a metaphysical tie. The tie will be *sui generis* and ultimately ineffable, since it is not mediated by any other relation, on pain of falling victim to Bradley's regress. But how is it to be reflected in language? It is difficult to find a translation. If we offer the proposition 'Socrates is a man' as a statement reflecting the form–matter tie, the predicate represents a form predicated of Socrates. But notice that 'Socrates' does not refer to anything identifiable as matter. If anything, Socrates is a composite of form and matter. Thus the sort of statement that in S_1 exhibited the fundamental metaphysical tie no longer suffices in S_2. Instead, it exhibits the relation between a composite and its form. The logical form of the sentence is more analytical than predicative.[9] We might suggest for consideration the statement 'This is a man.' But the pronoun subject is now an indexical that must be accompanied by a gesture of ostention, and the ostention seems to pick out a composite substance again rather than the matter.[10]

The problem begins to emerge that there is *no* possible way of directly capturing the matter–form predication in a subject–predicate

[9] I do not mean to imply that it is analytic in Kant's sense, although Kant's notion of analysis as conceptual containment is not too far removed from the present case.

[10] Stahl (1981) thinks this is the moral of *Met.* vii. 3. On the inscrutability of reference, see Wittgenstein, *Philosophical Investigations*, secs. 33–5, Quine (1960: 52 f.).

sentence. Anything that can stand as a subject will refer to something more concrete than the matter of a thing. Of course one can say 'This package of flesh and bones is a man', but the statement does not belong in ordinary discourse. It is already a theory-laden sentence. Moreover, the matter in question has to be individuated by some device such as 'package', which then reifies the material referred to. A more proper description of a matter–form relation than, for example, 'The bronze is a statue' is 'The statue is brazen', a fact that Aristotle recognizes, and which we shall discuss below. Thus language and reality seem to lose touch in an important area. Certain metaphysical relationships that are simple and direct in S$_1$ do not show themselves in S$_2$.

There is, however, still the problem of what Aristotle has in mind by abstracting from matter all predicates. Since the predicates have correlates in language (linguistic predicates), it seems possible to represent this abstraction process linguistically. The appropriate representation seems to be 'This is six foot tall and white and in place P and at time T and a man . . .' Here of course we are not dealing with an ordinary-language assertion, and the indexical subject cannot be accompanied by a deictic gesture. For all one would be pointing to is place P and time T and a man, etc. In our decription 'this' is a mere place-holder for a non-ostensible subject—the logical subject of predication. The metaphysical analysis does not illuminate ordinary-language predications, nor does it grow out of a linguistic model of reality. Rather it is the product of a metaphysical analysis whose motives are extraneous to language.

Thus form–matter predications are not represented in any direct way in language. What then of accidental predications? Aristotle has claimed that accidents are predicated of form. What sense can be made of this? Surely some modification must be made in this claim. It is not, for example, Socrates' form—his soul or his manhood or whatever his form is understood to be—that is pale or dark, tall or short (although his soul is wise and his manhood is an instance of animality). Nor is soul in general or manhood in general the subject of these attributes. If we are to save Aristotle from a major error, we must suppose that he means that the attributes are predicated of matter as qualified by form. Thus form is prior to the attributes in that it must first be predicated of matter for there to be something at all; only then is it possible for attributes to belong.[11] Thus, form is (logically) prior to the accidents. If this account is correct, it is possible to represent accidental predication in language: 'Socrates is white' says that whiteness belongs to a certain matter as informed by humanity.

Thus we find two predicative ties in S_2, the form–matter tie and the accident–composite tie. These ties are not equally represented in ordinary linguistic predications. The former has no direct representative at all while the latter does. Yet there is a kind of predication that at least indirectly corresponds to the form–matter tie. It is the predication exhibited in such a sentence as 'Socrates is a man.' Here the sentence has a logical form that could be represented as follows:

> Essential Predication* (EP*): m-F is F.

Here m stands for matter, F for form, and the hyphen represents the form–matter tie. This logical form is analytical in that it portrays an analysis of the composite substance into a component element. Although this formulation loses the isomorphism between metaphysical and linguistic predication of S_1, it seems to gain in explanatory power. For on this account, the necessity of essential predication shows itself in the property of analyticity. Of course Aristotle was not acquainted with the analytic–synthetic distinction, but he has the notion of identity, which is all that is needed to appreciate this analysis. Furthermore, he did not have the contemporary reflex of depreciating analytic claims on the grounds of their vacuousness. Indeed, his remarks in *Met.* vii. 6, where he argues that each substance is identical with its essence, seem to confirm his adherence to some principle like EP*.

By contrast to essential predications, sentences expressing the relation of attributes to composite substances show no analysis of the subject:

> Accidental Predication* (AP*): m-F is A

where *A* represents the accident. To put these theses together:

> Predication* (P*): There are two forms of predication: *Essential Predication* is of the form m-F is F, *Accidental Predication* of the form m-F is A.

As in S_1 there are two metaphysical ties and two forms of predication; however, the several relations are different in the two

---

[11]   Cf. *GC* i. 3, 317ᵇ8–11.

systems, and the correlation between ties and predication types in S$_2$ is not as close as in S$_1$: the high degree of isomorphism of S$_1$ is missing. For while accidental predication in language mirrors the tie by which accidents are connected to substances, essential predication does not mirror the tie connecting matter and form but rather presupposes it. Thus a gain in analytic power in S$_2$ corresponds to a loss in isomorphism.

3.2.2 Reference

Reference is the semantic relation between the linguistic term and the entity in the world.[12] In a sentence such as 'Socrates is a man' the subject refers to the thing in the world which goes by the name Socrates. As we have seen, however, such a sentence does not reveal the structure of the referent, which is really a compound of matter and form. Our sentence is accordingly, not logically perspicuous, and if we are concerned with maintaining the link between language and reality, some reconciliation must be made.

Aristotle's exercise in subtracting the predicates from the subject in *Met.* vii. 3 seems in part to be an attempt to give a linguistic interpretation to the analysis of the composite into form and matter. Since form constitutes the matter as a thing, and since all other determinations are posterior to form, matter must be what is left over after all predicates have been abstracted from the sensible substance. In the realm of language we are left with a pronoun subject, the logical subject, which is merely a syntactic place-holder in the sentence and refers to whatever it is that is the ontological subject of all determinations. Aristotle arrives at the logical subject through a process of philosophical analysis, not through an appeal to ordinary language intuitions. Here language is not a model for metaphysics: metaphysics autonomously determines a restructuring of language. Aristotle is generating a philosophical grammar that is grounded in a metaphysical theory.

The metaphysical theory seems to posit the existence of a subject that is completely indeterminate in respect to cognitive content but is the ground of all predications. The reference of the subject is something like the bare particular. Its role in the system

---

[12] Irwin (1982) wishes to distinguish Aristotle's theory of signification from our concept of meaning (including reference). I would rather use a broad notion of meaning in general and reference in particular that can apply to both Aristotle's and our theories.

is not to provide any content to the character of the sensible substance but only to provide an anchor to which all features can make fast. The bare particular is the One Under Many carried to the ultimate extreme. The presence of such an entity seems to raise difficulties for the interpretation of Aristotle's general metaphysical position. We cannot pursue these here, but we shall return to them in Chapter 8. What is important for now is that Aristotle must provide the beginnings of a philosophical grammar to accommodate certain features of his S_2 metaphysics.

One question can be raised about the significance of Aristotle's derivation of matter by abstraction here. Is this his own considered opinion about matter?[13] Typically he equates matter with high-level substrata such a bronze (as here in 1029ª4). And at ª26 f. he offers a disclaimer of the conclusion of his argument which seems to cast doubt on the whole method of abstraction ('substance turns out to be matter for those who take this approach'). Certainly Aristotle does not endorse the conclusion, and certainly he finds something wrong with the method. But it is not possible to attribute the method to any historical philosophers. For Aristotle's predecessors who did equate matter with substance did not view matter as a bare particular: matter was always air or water or fire or some set of such natural substances. Indeed, no one could have attacked the problem this way before Aristotle because no one had his unique concept of predication. Thus while we cannot attribute the method to Aristotle *in toto*, the analysis of substance he provides here could only grow out of a dialectic based on an Aristotelian theory of predication, and in particular a theory of predication informed by a hylomorphic metaphysics. If the analysis which yields the bare particular does not completely reflect Aristotle's own position, it nevertheless is the product of an Aristotelian inquiry. The bare particular is what could have been substance if Aristotle had chosen to make a certain move.

When Aristotle retreats from the matter-as-substance interpretation he gives a reason for preferring the composite and the form: they are separable and τόδε τι. Both terms he uses have metaphysical implications which we cannot pursue here. But they also seem to admit of a linguistic interpretation that can throw some light on Aristotle's semantic assumptions. To call something

---

[13] See the argument of Schofield (1972) that the view of matter set forth in *Met.* vii. 3 is a straw man.

separable and a This seems to suggest that that thing can be isolated from its environment and identified by a deictic gesture.[14] The fact that Aristotle does not take the trouble to explain the terms at this key point of the argument seems to suggest that he thinks the terms to be self-explanatory and hence invites us to take them in this obvious way. But to be able to isolate and pick out an object seems to be the main function of linguistic reference. Thus it appears that the reference of the subject, at least in ordinary language situations, is properly to the composite or the form. Now since the composite is itself analysable, the question arises whether reference picks out any component. Aristotle's argument indicates that it does—the referring term picks out the form. The potential conflict between the claims of the composite and the form as referent can be resolved if we say that the term refers to the composite in virtue of its having a form.[15] Implicitly the referring terms in question have been understood as substantives—whether proper or common nouns. Thus we may conclude:

> *Substantival Reference** (SR*): Singular substantival terms refer to the composite in virtue of its exhibiting a form.

We see that in S₂ linguistic reference is primarily to composite substance as mediated by form. The presence of a hylomorphic analysis seems to complicate the theory. It renders the logical subject immune to ordinary linguistic reference and makes the composite the object of reference only mediately.

3.2.3   The Logic of Mass Terms

Philosophers and linguists distinguish between mass terms and count terms.[16] The former refer to stuffs or massive bodies, while the latter distinguish discrete and countable objects. Thus 'gold', 'food', and 'water' are mass terms while 'man' and 'horse' are count terms. Actually, the distinctions are more subtle, since some nouns can be used either as mass or as count terms. For instance we can talk of 'pie' as a mass ('Give me some pie') or as a discrete object ('I bought two pies').[17] Mass and count terms behave

---

[14] See ch. 3.1.1.

[15] Thus a referring expression 'the *F*' is able to pick out the *F* because of its form *F*. Cf. *Met.*, vii. 11, 1037ᵃ5–10.   [16] Cf. Quine (1960: 91).

[17] Because of this flexibility of expression, it is better to speak of mass/count *predications*. There are comparable cases in Greek, e.g. ξύλον = 'wood' (mass predication) while ξύλον τι = 'a log' (count predication) (*A.Po.* i. 22, 83ᵃ2 ff.).

differently in language, so that it is possible to develop a logic of mass terms. In S_2 Aristotle shows a keen sensitivity to the logical properties of mass terms which is almost totally absent from S_1.[18]

Scattered throughout the works of S_2 are observations on the nature of mass terms. He makes the following points concerning nouns denoting masses (which I represent schematically as M in contrast to count terms [F]):

(1) We say F comes to be from M but not that M comes to be F.[19]

(2) We do not say that x is/comes-to-be M but that x is/comes-to-be M-en.[20]

(3) The expression 'M-en' is similar to 'F-en' (adjectival) expressions used for attributes and connotes indefiniteness.[21]

The overall result of Aristotle's linguistic researches seems to be that (a) mass terms can serve as grammatical subjects only in a qualified way,[22] (b) they cannot serve as predicates—for a denominative adjective must be found to replace them—and (c) they have properties in common with terms for attributes. Now it should be noted that (a) and (b) are results that apply in Greek but not in English. For we can say, for example, that the bronze became a statue and that the statue comes to be bronze. This only shows that the logic of mass terms is different in English and Greek. Result (c) is especially interesting because it shows an awareness on Aristotle's part that mass predications and attribute predications have similarities. Grammatically speaking, both are adjectival—a fact acknowledged by Aristotle in his use of the morphological feature -ινος '-en' for both. To make a mass predication is not to classify or sort something, but to describe its material nature. It is to tell what a thing is *made of*, not what it *is*. In this it is like an adjective predicating an attribute which characterizes a thing but does not tell what it *is*. By saying that mass predications are indefinite, Aristotle is making a point that is

---

[18] The only time he seems to recognize the possibility of a mass term is in the passage cited in the last note. See Graham (1984: 40–2) on his failure to recognize mass terms.

[19] *Ph*. i. 7, 190ª25 f. See ch. 5 n. 24 on a different interpretation of this statement.

[20] *Ph*. vii. 3, 245ᵇ9–12; *Met*. ix. 7, 1049ª18 ff.; vii. 7, 1033ª5 ff.

[21] *Met*. ix. 7, 1049ª30–ᵇ2.

[22] They can appear as grammatical subjects, but only in limited contexts: *Ph*. vii. 3, 245ª12–14.

made by modern linguists and logicians that such predications do not admit of counting. In order to individuate or to make definite a mass predication, we must add a count term to the expression. We can count piles of rock, cups of water, and shovelfuls of dirt, but not rock, water, and dirt. The case is similar with adjectives representing attributes—one cannot count white or tall by itself. In general then:

> *Mass Terms* (MT): There is a class of mass terms which consists of indeterminate nouns standing for massive bodies.

In every case Aristotle's consideration of mass terms occurs in the context of some potential application to metaphysics based on the relation between form and matter. The logic of mass terms is a means of getting at the obscure and sometimes intractable subject of matter. It appears, then, that the distinction between mass terms and count terms is a reflection at a linguistic level of the ontological distinction between matter and form. In pursuing the logic of mass terms it is clear that Aristotle still wants to uphold the close association between language and reality. Aristotle still looks for isomorphisms between the word and the world. But in the present case, as in the other cases of logical insight we have examined in S_2, the simple isomorphisms of surface structure and reality of S_1 have been complicated by layers of deep structure. The criterion for mass terms is a multifaceted set of linguistic tests described in (1)–(3) above. Mass terms appear outside the classification of predicates in the ten categories. They can be used in predication statements, but they are not like countable substantive terms nor quite like adjectives standing for attributes, though they have something in common with both. In short, the study of mass terms enforces a complication of the linguistic scheme that mirrors reality. The syntactic perspicuity of S_1 disappears beneath a haze of implicit transformation rules.

As in the case of predication and reference, the theory of mass terms in S_2 seems to owe its development to Aristotle's interest in the metaphysical distinction between form and matter. Mass terms are the correlates of matter, while count terms are the correlates of form, or of informed matter. In every passage in which Aristotle explores the characteristics of mass terms he does so in the context of a metaphysical inquiry concerning the relation of form and matter. Aristotle's fascination with the form–matter analysis evidently provides the occasion and the motivation for a development of the logic of mass terms. And indeed, it seems plausible to hypothesize that behind the overall difference of logico-linguistic theory between S_1 and S_2 lies the bifurcation of reality implicit in the S_2 thesis of hylomorphism.

3.3 PHILOSOPHY OF SCIENCE

Scientific studies occupy a considerable portion of S_2. These typically consist of specialized studies dedicated to some aspect or other of natural science, with the exception of the *Physics*, which deals with natural science as a whole. Although this work does not address questions of the structure of scientific explanations *per se* in the way that the *Posterior Analytics* does in S_1, it does provide a general inquiry into the conceptual foundations of science. As we shall see, this inquiry produces a framework that is central to the philosophy of science of S_2.

3.3.1   The Four Causes

In *Ph*. ii Aristotle introduces four causes, or more correctly, four kinds of cause. Numerous references to this work throughout the corpus make it clear that this is the *locus classicus* of the four cause theory (FCT), and that this theory is one of the foundations of Aristotelian science. We have already met with a version of FCT in S_1, but as we shall see, there are at least prima-facie differences between the S_1 and S_2 versions, so we cannot at this point make any inferences as to the relation between the versions.

The four causes of *Ph*. ii. 3 (which is closely followed by *Ph*. ii. 7 and repeated by *Met*. v. 2) are (1) 'the source from which something comes to be'[23] which is called matter in Chapter 7 (198ᵃ20 f.), and which is exemplified by bronze from which a statue is created; (2) 'the form and the paradigm [τὸ εἶδος καὶ τὸ παράδειγμα]', which consists of the essence and related features, for example, the cause of the octave is the ratio 2 : 1; (3) 'the first source of change or rest', such as the planner, the father of the

---

[23] A more liberal, but less comprehensible, translation would be: 'that which something comes to be *from* in the sense of persisting in the result'. The rather cryptic definition seems to be an allusion to the theory worked out in *Ph*. i. 7–9, culminating in a definition of matter at 192ᵃ31 f.. The *Ph*. ii definition is a condensed version of the *Ph*. i definition. For more on the argument of *Ph*. i, see ch. 5.

child, and the creator of the product; and finally (4) 'that for the sake of which' or the final cause, for instance health as the end for the sake of which we walk (194^b23-33). The present order of causes evidently does not matter, since in other lists other orders are given, presumably for the sake of convenience in fitting the causes to the context at hand.

3.3.2 *The Meaning of the Four Causes*

In early modern science many battles were fought over the question of whether any of the four causes except the efficient cause ([3] above) were really causes in the scientific sense. However, modern scholars have made major advances in explaining the four causes, advances which can show us how the early modern debate was mistaken. The Greek concept of αἴτιον or αἰτία is broader in scope than that of 'cause' in the scientific sense, and includes reasons as well as causes. The key to understanding Aristotle's notion of cause is found in Aristotle's preface to FCT in *Ph.* ii. 7: 'That there are causes, and that they are as many as we say is evident: for Why questions comprehend just as many types' (198^a14-16). The four 'causes' are four ways of answering a Why question. In other words, Why questions fall into four distinct logical types which in turn require four distinct logical types of answer. To prove that there are four causes is simply to exhibit the four different logical types of Why question with their corresponding answers. Thus the four causes are four Becauses,[24] not four alleged types of mechanistic causes.

For example, consider the following four questions:

Q1 Why is the statue heavy?
Q2 Why is this a triangle?
Q3 Why did the rock fall?
Q4 Why did Socrates go for a walk?

All are legitimate Why questions. But their answers show that each question has its own presuppositions:

A1 Because it is made of bronze.
A2 Because it has three angles.

[24] Wicksteed and Cornford (1929: 126 f., 165), Wieland (1962: 261 f.), Owen (1965c: 82), Vlastos (1969: 292 ff.), Charlton (1970: 99), Hocutt (1974), Moravcsik (1974), Barnes (1975: 96), Sorabji (1980: 40), Annas (1982). For a strikingly similar modern account, see van Fraassen (1980a: ch. 5), based in part on Bromberger (1966); van Fraassen (1980b) applies his account to Aristotle.

A3 Because someone pushed it.

A4 Because he wanted to digest his food.

A1 states an answer in terms of the material component, A2 in terms of the structure, A3 in terms of a source of change, and A4 in terms of a good or end to be achieved.[25] The surface structure of the four questions appears to be the same, or at least very similar (the only notable difference is that the first two questions use the verb 'to be' while the second two use an action verb). But the difference of answers reveals an underlying semantic difference in each question. Why questions seem to exhibit (at least) a fourfold ambiguity. This must reflect a difference in deep structure or logical form in the questions themselves. At this point we can look for less obvious differences of structure in the questions and notice some subtle but important variations: Q1 uses the copula, but Q2 the 'is' of identity; Q3 has a non-deliberating subject while Q4 a deliberating subject. Aristotle's insight into the nature of the four causes seems to be correct and illuminating.

Objections have been raised to the interpretation that makes the four causes four Becauses.[26] The interpretation seems to take what are for Aristotle real factors and turn them into mere explanations —that is, into linguistic items. It seems to me that a middle ground can be found between the mechanistic cause and the explanatory reason. For Aristotle there is no absolute barrier between the linguistic and the real. The 'efficient' or moving cause may be an agent—a substance. The 'material' cause (in A1) may be an instance of matter, the 'formal' cause (e.g. A2) may be an instance of form. The four αἰτίαι are four ways of answering Why questions, but the answers often refer to real items.[27] As Frede (1980: 223) has pointed out, the term αἴτιον tends to keep the sense of the adjective αἴτιος 'responsible'.[28] The causes are factors

---

[25] This can be brought out yet more clearly by the alternative formulation:

A4′ In order to digest his food.

I expressed A4 in terms of desire to show how this answer, too could be construed as a Because. But in the answer the object of the desire plays a more important explanatory role than the subject's desiring. Note that a single well-chosen question can elicit all four Becauses, as the example of Hocutt (1974: 392) shows: Why did Socrates die?

[26] Mure (1975) attacks Hocutt (1974) on grounds similar to those I cite.

[27] Cf. Moravcsik (1974: 6 f.).

[28] Frede (1980: 222 f.) finds that there is an original distinction between the αἴτιον or cause and the αἰτία or account of the cause; the latter is an explanation

which are *responsible* for a given situation. But they may be responsible in a variety of ways. They may be responsible as providing a substratum, a structure, an impetus, or a goal. The same entity may be responsible in several ways. For instance, the form of a plant may provide the structure, impetus, and end of its development. The mechanistic cause could only be responsible for a limited range of phenomena. It cannot be responsible for every aspect of a situation—it cannot answer every question. Hence we need several causes/becauses to account adequately for the world. On this account we can accept the causes as Becauses and still do justice to Aristotle's scientific realism. Thus we have a thesis of the philosophy of science of S₂

> *Because Theory of Causes* (BTC): A cause is an answer to the question Why.

3.3.3 Hylomorphism and the Four Causes

One salient difference between the four causes of S₁ and S₂ is that the latter include a notion of a material cause in place of the 'logical ground of a conclusion'. Not so obvious, perhaps, is another difference: the S₁ list does not have a *formal cause* either, but rather an essential cause.[29] The formal and essential causes are often equated, but the equation begs an important question that we must face. Thus there is an apparent difference between the two lists in that the S₂ list exhibits a hylomorphic interpretation of the causes which the S₁ list prima facie lacks.

But what precisely is the role of matter and form in the four causes of S₂? The traditional names 'material cause' and 'formal cause' tend to suggest that matter and form are coextensive with two of the causes. Aristotle himself seems to talk as if they were at times.[30] But a closer look at the *Ph.* ii account will show us that the relation is not so simple. At 195ª15 ff. Aristotle gives a more detailed list of the kinds of thing that count as members of each

---

and thus a linguistic item. Plato preserves the distinction between terms, but Aristotle does not.

[29] τὸ τί ἦν εἶναι, *A.Po.* ii. 11, 94ª21; cf. τὸ εἶδος καὶ τὸ παράδειγμα, *Ph.* ii. 3, 194ᵇ26; τὸ τί ἦν εἶναι, 195ª20.

[30] e.g. *Ph.* iv. 1, 209ª20 f.; *GA* i. 1, 715ª6 f.; *Met.* viii. 4, 1044ª34–6. Moreover, note that it is a mistake to confuse explanatory and ontological contexts: see ch. 6.2.

class of cause. For the material and formal causes he gives the following members:

material cause : formal cause
letters : syllable
material : artefact
elements : body
parts : whole
premisses : conclusion

Aristotle summarizes the relationship by saying 'some of these examples are causes in the sense of substratum, such as the parts, and some are causes in the sense of essence [τὸ τί ἦν εἶναι], for instance the whole, the compound, and the form' (^{a}19–21). Whereas in his initial statement of the four causes (194^{b}23 ff.) Aristotle seems to identify two of the causes with form and matter *simpliciter*, here he reduces form and matter to species of more comprehensive genera. Form and matter belong properly only to the analysis of artefacts. The genera are essence and substratum, respectively. Evidently form and matter stand for two of the causes by a sort of metonymy. They become *paradigmatic examples* of two causes. Ultimately, form and matter can serve as generic causes only by courtesy, or by the terms gaining a broader meaning than the original one. Since Aristotle has no technical terms in the modern sense for the four causes, there is no clear-cut choice between alternatives. It is clear, however, that 'form' and 'matter' become terms of art in S₂ such that their applications extend far beyond their own place in the original language game.

Thus hylomorphism does pervade the four causes of S₂, although it does so by extension: certain examples of essence-substratum relationship that are in fact ignored in S₁ appear as paradigms in S₂. As with the logic and philosophy of language of S₂, the ontological analysis into matter and form plays a prominent role in the aetiology of S₂. Accordingly we are justified in attributing to S₂ a modified version of FCT:

FCT*: There are four kinds of cause: (1) the formal cause, (2) the material cause, (3) the moving cause, and (4) the final cause.

3.3.4 The Importance of the Four Causes in S₂

The significance of the four cause theory for Aristotle's science in

S_2 is everywhere evident. One of the clearer examples of its pervasive influence can be found in the introductory remarks to the *Generation of Animals*. Aristotle points out that there are four causes which 'underlie' (ὑπόκεινται) everything. Three of the four causes have already been discussed. Aristotle presumably means to signify that the *De Anima* has dealt with the soul, which is alike the formal and the final cause of the animal. He specifically refers to his discussion of the parts of animals (in the eponymous work) as treating of the material cause of animals. And he announces that the present work will deal with the moving cause of animals, namely their reproductive systems (715^a4–18). Here we see that the four causes are so basic to Aristotle's scientific thought that they provide a conceptual scheme in terms of which he organizes whole groups of treatises. In fact the four cause theory seems to suggest to Aristotle a programme for organizing all biological research. Evidently the four causes form a kind of system within which the important questions that a scientist can ask are ordered. First in order of priority come questions of the final cause and the form; then the material cause may be dealt with in relation to the form; and finally the efficient cause may be sought.

A further instance of the pervasive role of FCT* in S_2 is found in the *De Anima*, where Aristotle makes a point of examining the senses in which the soul is a cause. He finds that it is not only the essence of the living thing, but also its final cause and efficient cause (ii, 4, 415^b7–28). This assessment arises in the context of a discussion of the definition of soul and how this relates to the various life processes. To state the causal properties of soul is closely linked to providing a definition of it. And in general, to give a causal account of anything is evidently to locate its role in the system of four causes.

Although examples can be multiplied from the scientific works, perhaps the clearest account of the role of the four causes and their importance comes in *Met*. i. After arguing that the wise man must have knowledge of causes, Aristotle identifies the causes that one must know as the four causes, alluding to his account in *Ph*. ii (*Met*. i. 3, 983^a24–$^b1$). Here knowledge of the four causes, which were introduced in the *Physics* as conditions for scientific knowledge, is equated with Wisdom, as a general goal for education and the life proper to a free man. Aristotle's commitment to the four cause scheme is more than a passing fancy in *Met*. i, for it informs the whole book, again providing a programme for investigation. This time Aristotle elaborates a schematic history of philosophy detailing the discovery of various of the four causes. He satisfies himself that no additional causes have been discovered, and indeed that some of the four have only been obscurely glimpsed. From Aristotle's point of view all previous philosophies embody partial or one-sided views of reality because they have comprehended only a subset of the kinds of causes. Hence their philosophies have consisted of only partial explanations of the phenomena. Here we see as nowhere else the fundamental importance of the four cause theory for Aristotelian philosophy. It is the distinguishing mark of Aristotelian philosophy, the goal of Wisdom, and the touchstone of adequacy for all systematic explanations. This point we may express as a thesis of S_2:

Wisdom (W): Wisdom is knowledge of the four causes.

3.3.5   The Structure of Scientific Explanation

No such extravagant claims are made for the four causes in S_1. Indeed, they seem to go almost unnoticed except for *A.Po*. ii. 11, where they serve as an illustration of what is evidently a more important theory, that of the middle term (MTC), and, by extension, the missing-link theory of causality (MLC). Now there is no direct conflict betwen S_2 and S_1 on this point, since S_2 does not deny this theory. However, there is a surprising discrepancy. And that is in the matter of the structure of scientific explanation. In S_1, as we have seen, scientific explanation requires—and indeed consists in—the deduction of an explanandum from prior premisses through the only deductive system Aristotle recognizes, the syllogism. In S_2, rich as it is in scientific explanations, the deductive mode of explanation plays no part.

No one has been able to produce anything that looks like a sustained demonstration, fitting the Aristotelian canons, of a scientific theorem, law, or phenomenon.[31] On the assumption that S_2 is an application of the logical principles laid down in S_1, this absence of deductive explanation is embarrassing at best. It is not merely a matter of Aristotle's sparing us technical details, it is a matter of his not giving anything that would count as a scientific

---

[31] Barnes (1969: 124).

explanation at all. Scholars have made a number of attempts to reconcile this apparent inconsistency.[32] We cannot go into these interpretations at this preliminary stage, except to note the difficulty. The fact is that the expectations the *A.Po.* account of science creates in us are not fulfilled in S$_2$.

Instead of a tight formal system, the scientific method of S$_2$ appears to support a more open-textured inquiry, in which surveys of received views stand on an equal footing with definitions, and the argument is more often dialectical in character than deductive.[33] Examples, analogies, indirect and *ad hominem* arguments are frequent elements of Aristotle's scientific explanations. If there is anything that seems to distinguish Aristotle's scientific discourses from his logical ones, it is the use of the four causes themselves as vehicles of explanation. I would like to suggest that it is the four cause theory itself which provides the logic of scientific explanation in S$_2$. This scheme alone provides a programme and a rationale for scientific inquiry. For instance, what seems to qualify the *Generation of Animals* as a scientific treatise is that it treats of the efficient cause with respect to animal life. The account of Wisdom in *Met.* i leads us to believe that the essence of Wisdom is the ability to grasp the four causes in any context of inquiry. We may thus formulate the S$_2$ attitude toward scientific explanations as follows:

> *Scientific Explanation** (SE*): Scientific explanation is the explication of phenomena by means of the four cause theory.

3.4   PROFILES OF S$_1$ AND S$_2$

Our brief overview of S$_2$ has revealed a distinct set of doctrines in the realms of ontology, logic, and philosophy of science. The objective of the present survey and that in Chapter 2 has been to provide the basis for a preliminary comparison of S$_1$ and S$_2$ as explanatory structures. A listing of the theses we have discovered in each system will constitute a profile of it as an explanatory structure. To juxtapose the two profiles will exhibit the ostensible similarities and contrasts of S$_1$ and S$_2$ (Fig. 3.1).

This schematic comparison reveals some prima-facie differences

---

[32] See Barnes (1969: 125–37) for criticisms of previous attempts.
[33] Cf. the findings of Owen (1961).

S_1	S_2

Ontology

S: Primary substances exist independently; for all other entities, to be is to be In a subject or Said-of a subject—i.e. to depend on a primary substance.

S*: Primary substances exist independently; for all other entities to be is to be a substratum of a concrete substance or an accident of a concrete substance.

F: Form is substance in the primary sense.

SA: Primary substances are ontologically indivisible particulars.

H: The concrete substance is composed of form and matter.

SS: Every primary substance falls under a secondary substance, which is a species.

FS: Every concrete substance falls under a species, which is identical with its form.

D: Every species is either identical to a primitive genus or is identical with the differentia of a genus

D obtains

N: Species and genera are natural kinds.

N obtains

A: A concrete substance exhibits more reality to the degree that its form is more completely realized in its matter.

Logic

P: There are two forms of predication: EP is of the form S is P, AP is of the form S has P.

P*: There are two forms of predication: EP* is of the form m-F is F, AP* is of the form m-F is A.

SR: Singular substantival terms refer to primary substances.

SR*: Singular substantival terms refer to the composite in virtue of its exhibiting a form.

MT: There is a class of mass terms which consists of indeterminate substantives standing for massive bodies

STA: Deductions are syllogistic orderings of categorical statements.

Science

SK: Scientific knowledge is demonstrative knowledge.

W: Wisdom is knowledge of the four causes.

DK: Demonstrative knowledge consists of theorems deduced from self-evident principles.

S$_1$	S$_2$
Science	
SE: Scientific explanation is the deduction of phenomena from premises exhibiting the cause.	SE*: Scientific explanation is explication of phenomena by means of the four causes.
MTC: A cause is the middle term of a scientific syllogism.	BTC: A cause is an answer to the question Why.
MLC: A cause is the missing link in a chain of universals exhibited by the terms of a sequence of syllogisms in a projected demonstration.	
FCT: There are four kinds of cause: (1) the essential cause, (2) the logical ground, (3) the moving cause, and (4) the final cause.	FCT*: There are four kinds of cause: (1) the formal cause, (2) the material cause, (3) the moving cause, and (4) the final cause.

FIG. 3.1   Profile of S$_1$ and S$_2$

between the present system and S$_1$. The ontologically simple entities of S$_1$ that Aristotle calls primary substances in S$_1$ have no counterpart in S$_2$. The sensible substances, which serve as paradigm cases of primary substances in S$_1$, are found to be ontological complexes in S$_2$. Decomposed into form and matter, the compound substance holds no intrinsic interest in S$_2$, but rather forfeits its ontological primacy to its components. Aristotle considers both form and matter for the role of primary substance and settles on form, although the argument is not clear. Other theses of S$_2$ seem similar to S$_1$, *mutatis mutandis*. However, a new dimension in Aristotelian metaphysics is created by the addition of a theory of actuality which correlates degree of completeness of an object with its degree of actuality.

Not only are there evident differences, whatever may be their explanation, between S$_1$ and S$_2$. There also seems to be a focal point for the difference. I characterized the ontology of S$_1$ as exemplifying the theses of atomic substantialism (AS). Where S$_2$ differs from S$_1$, we find in every case the presence of form and matter playing a part in the S$_2$ account which it did not play in S$_1$. In light of this fact, I would like to advance the hypothesis that the root difference beween S$_1$ and S$_2$ is the presence of a theory of form and matter in S$_2$. We can capture this essential difference by designating the overall ontological theory of S_2, hylomorphic substantialism (HS). Whereas sensible substances are atomic in S_1, they are hylomorphic in S_2. Theories of language and logic that show a close isomorphism between the logical and the grammatical subject in S_1 are amended or replaced in S_2 by theories in which an analysis of the logical subject corresponds to the exploration of deep structures differentiating mass and count nouns. Again the atomistic conception of S_1 contrasts with the analytic hylomorphism of S_2. Furthermore, while a four cause theory is found in both systems, the S_1 theory shows no recognition of a formal and material cause in the classical sense. The S_2 theory, on the other hand, makes prominent use of form and matter. The four cause theory also proves to be much more central to the project of science in S_2 than in S_1, while chains of formal demonstrations such as those recommended in S_1 play no noticeable role.

In the above characterizations of S_1 and S_2 I have concentrated on the elements of theoretical discourses in general and have brought in considerations of the scope of S_1 and S_2 only in a limited way. Yet it has become increasingly apparent that the scope of S_1 extends beyond the narrow confines of a logical theory. If we were to compare S_1 and S_2 not merely as theoretical discourses, but as world-views, we should include a comparison of their epistemological doctrines in addition to the others listed above. Although Aristotle's account of concept formation is found in a single chapter of the *A.Po.* (ii. 19), the contrast with S_2 doctrines is striking (Fig. 3.2).[34] For S_1 the important relation is that between the universal and the particular. For S_2 the particular–universal relation is mediated and explicated by the matter–form relation. Making use of a hylomorphic conception of substance S_2 replaces the vague notion of coalescing with a more precise account of abstraction.[35] Again we find that the differences between S_1 and S_2 correlate with the presence or absence of hylomorphism. The contrasts between S_1 and S_2 are persistent and systematic.

The differences we have found do not constitute an ending-place but rather a beginning-point for serious inquiry into the relation of

[34] See esp. *DA* ii. 12, iii. 4–5.
[35] Both the S_1 and S_2 accounts are somewhat metaphorical. But the *A.Po.* account offers only the curious image of soldiers making a stand after a rout in battle (100^a12 f.), whereas S_2 invokes the central craft model with its suggestive connections to the theory of substance.

S_1	S_2
Epistemology	
Universalism(U): Universals coalesce as a result of particular experiences; understanding arises from the synthesis of these universals into a system.	Abstractionism (Ab): The mind abstracts forms from particular experiences; understanding is the result of perceiving these forms in their proper conceptual configurations.

FIG. 3.2   Epistemological Profile

the two systems. A theory intended to reconcile S_1 and S_2 will at least have to account for these differences. It should also give a plausible explanation of the relation of S_1 to S_2 in the general context of Aristotle's thought. And it should be able to generate some new discoveries concerning the interconnections between various parts of his system as explained in the theory. Several hypotheses have been advanced to deal with this question. Some are based on systematic concerns, others on biographical development, and some attempt to synthesize the two. None has been so completely explored as to establish its claim against the others.

In the following chapters I shall attempt to work out a theory which will explain the differences in light of both systematic and historical considerations. I have already suggested that the essential difference between the two systems lies in the presence of a doctrine of hylomorphism in S_2. This raises two sets of questions, one systematic and one historical. (1) Is the presence of hylomorphism compatible with the atomism of S_1? If not, is it possible to make S_2 compatible with S_1? (2) Which is the earlier system? Is this time difference significant for understanding the theories, or is it merely an accident of composition? A negative answer to the first two questions makes the second two more urgent, for some way must be found out of a contradiction. In the following chapter I shall address the questions about compatibility and argue for the negative answer.

4

The Incommensurability of the Systems

Thus far we have divided Aristotle's works into two groups of treatises (Chapter 1), have found a system of theories in the first group, S_1 (Chapter 2), and have found another system of theories in the second group, S_2 (Chapter 3). Each system seems to manifest a metaphysical conception which acts as a unifying idea in the component theories of the system. In the case of S_1 the metaphysical conception is atomic substantialism: the basic entities are indivisible substances which fall under natural kinds and which enter into complex relationships of essence and accident. In the case of S_2 the dominant metaphysical notion is hylomorphic substantialism: substances are complexes of form and matter which participate in developmental processes. We have discovered a remarkable similarity in the scope of the two systems, along with some pervasive differences in content and emphasis. Moreover, the fact that we have tentatively been able to trace the differences in content to a difference in metaphysical principles indicates that the variations between S_1 and and S_2 are not fortuitous but rather systematic in character. Thus our findings create a presumption against interpretations which minimize the differences between S_1 and S_2.

Nevertheless, the study we have undertaken so far decides nothing. Thus far we have only been gathering comparative data for an analysis of the relation between the two systems. And although it is true that no data-gathering exercise is free of theoretical presuppositions, it is also true that such an exercise cannot in itself determine the significance of the data. All we have done so far is to locate some prima-facie differences between systems which indicate some prima-facie conflicts. The discovery of these potential conflicts puts constraints on what a satisfactory theory of the relation between S_1 and S_2 must accomplish, but it does not rule out any of the standard theories. Thus we can say that our study has served to focus more clearly on the challenges to be met by a theory which purports to explain the relation of the *Organon* to the rest of Aristotle's work. But we cannot say that any theory has been vindicated as against competing theories. It is time now to identify and evaluate the theories.

4.1 HYPOTHESES CONCERNING THE RELATION BETWEEN S_1 AND S_2

There are three major hypotheses which attempt to account for the relation between S_1 and S_2. I shall describe them in order in this section. In the following section we shall consider their relative merits.

According to the first hypothesis S_1 and S_2 deal with different domains of evidence. S_1 is a theory in the realm of logic; it deals with terms, propositions, arguments, and formal systems, as well as debate in informal contexts. But it is not a theory about the world as such. Accordingly, S_1 cannot conflict with S_2. S_2 is a theory or system of theories about the world, which makes use of the logical theory of S_1 as a *means* to elucidating a view of the world. Seen in this light, S_1 is a logical tool, in Greek an ὄργανον, for the furthering of our knowledge of the world; it is not a competing theory. Thus any apparent disagreement between S_1 and S_2 arises from a failure to appreciate the different context in which the two systems are proposed: S_1 is a theory of logical entities and relations while S_2 is a theory of real entities and relations. I shall call this hypothesis the *Organon* Hypothesis (OH).

A second hypothesis takes S_1 and S_2 as both dealing with the same domain of evidence, but treats S_1 as a simplification or preliminary approximation to S_2. On this view, there may be disagreements between the two systems, but they are not ultimately serious inconsistencies. There are at least two explanations of the presence to two distinct systems. According to the first, the order of exposition dictates that certain works be studied first. In the words of Montgomery Furth:

. . . the *Categories* is a carefully limited work—possibly an introductory one—which seems determined to contain the discussion at a metaphysical level that is, though in some ways sophisticated, still simple, and especially to block any descent from its own curtailed universe into the much deeper as well as wider universe of the *Metaphysics*. (1978: 629)

In other words the *Categories* is meant to introduce the student to the basic concepts of philosophy without bringing in the complicating factors of form and matter which would unduly burden the novice philosopher. On this view the concepts of form and matter are withheld until the *Physics*, in which they are necessary for an understanding of natural phenomena. A second explanation for the presence of two systems is a genetic one. Aristotle developed S_1 first. He later found that S_1 had to be supplemented by additional theories in order to account for all the phenomena of the world. Aristotle thus developed S_2, which is a theory elaborated out of S_1 and is, in its main lines, compatible with S_1 even if it is more powerful and detailed. What both the pedagogical and the developmental versions have in common is that they construe S_2 as comprehending S_1 but more powerful than it. That is, every consequence of S_1 is also a consequence of S_2, but S_2 has further consequences that are not consequences of S_1. Yet none of these further consequences is inconsistent with the statements of S_1. On this interpretation S_2 and S_1 have a determinate logical relation which is described by called S_2 a logical extension of S_1. Accordingly I shall call the present hypothesis the Extension Hypothesis (EH).

The third hypothesis takes S_1 and S_2 as dealing with the same domain of evidence but holds that they are inconsistent. I shall call this the Incompatibility Hypothesis (IH). IH differs from EH chiefly in that it takes the disagreements between S_1 and S_2 to be serious in nature. The differences cannot in general be reconciled by noting the similar core of axioms or principles exemplified by the two systems. Needless to say, this hypothesis is the most unfavourable to Aristotle, and it does raise questions about the continuity of his philosophy. Moreover, it seems to conflict with Aristotle's own attitude about the unity of his system, since he nowhere explicitly repudiates one part of his philosophy in favour of another. However important this consideration may be, I propose to leave it out of account for now, since the immediate question is the unity of Aristotle's thought, not Aristotle's opinion about the unity of his thought. I shall return to the latter question in due time. In any case, this hypothesis has the pragmatic disadvantage that it does not give as charitable an interpretation of Aristotle's position as do OH and EH. All things being equal, we should prefer the first two. However, our surveys of S_1 and S_2 have shown that the differences between them are deep and pervasive, and IH may turn out after all to be the most adequate explanation for the differences. I turn now to evaluating the three hypotheses.

4.2 EVALUATION OF THE HYPOTHESES

4.2.1 OH

OH is a venerable interpretation with roots in early commentaries on Aristotle. As Alexander of Aphrodisias puts it:

The method of logic occupies the place of an instrument [ὄργανον] in philosophy: whatever is pursued in logic is pursued insofar as it is useful for philosophy. (*in Top.* 74.29–31)

Simplicius calls logic the instrumental part of philosophy (τὸ ὀργανικόν ἐστι μέρος), likening it to the ruler used by carpenters and builders (*in Cat.* 20.11 f.). Ammonius explains the point of the distinction as indicating that logic is not even a part of philosophy, since an instrument is not essential to a whole as a part is (*in A.Pr.* 8.26 ff.). Modern scholars often pay lip service to OH, and sometimes strongly endorse it.[1] Unfortunately for OH there is no evidence in Aristotle's writings that the *Organon* is meant to be limited to logical theory. As Ingemar Düring (1966: 53) forcefully argues:

Aristotle himself never speaks of his so-called logical works as a unity. He never says that there is a discipline that is an instrument of scientific thought, nor does he say that logic does not belong to philosophy. These characterizations and arguments arose in the polemic against the Stoics and they are generally valid for the later commentators. But for an understanding of the writings that are collected under the title of the *Organon* it is vitally important not to be influenced by the knowledge of Stoic logic and the commentators of late antiquity, but to grasp the writings in their own historical context.

As impressive as is the unanimity among ancient commentators in favour of OH, a strong suspicion remains that Aristotle's logic is being viewed in light of the Stoic trichotomy of logic, physics, and ethics, and that OH is doing double duty as a hypothesis concerning the relation among Aristotle's treatises and a dialectical antithesis to Stoic theories of logic. For according to the Stoics,

---

[1] For lip-service, e.g. Lloyd (1968: 127): 'The philosopher as logician investigates the tools of thought.' For a major recent endorsement, see Guthrie (1981: 135 f.).

logic (understood to include elements of what we would now call
metaphysics and epistemology) is an integral part of philosophy.
Although there are some grounds for attributing the trichotomy to
Aristotle,[2] he makes no explicit pronouncements for excluding
logic from the purview of philosophy, so that the Stoic view of the
role of logic in philosophy is actually compatible with his stated
views.

Furthermore, it is a remarkable fact that the commentators do
not refer OH to Aristotle himself, but to the Peripatetics. In other
words, they seem to be aware of OH as originating in the
doxographical tradition. Alexander, writing in the late second
century, indicates that the view antedates his own commentary,
citing it as held by some unnamed ancients ($\dot{\alpha}\rho\chi\alpha\hat{\iota}o\iota$).[3] This may
take us back to Andronicus of Rhodes in the first century BC.[4]
Nevertheless, we are still far removed from Aristotle. We can
further trace the development of OH in the ancient commentators
so as to observe how Alexander's initial characterization (in the late
second century AD) of the method of logic ($\lambda o\gamma\iota\kappa\dot{\eta}$ $\pi\rho\alpha\gamma\mu\alpha\tau\epsilon\dot{\iota}\alpha$)
as an instrument is extended by other commentators until in the
sixth century the set of logical treatises themselves is termed an
organon.[5] Thus while OH is of unquestionably ancient origin, it is
nevertheless post-Aristotelian and consequently deserves the same
critical scrutiny as other posthumous interpretations of Aristotle.

There are, furthermore, compelling reasons to reject OH. The
chief problem with OH is that it delimits the theory of S_1 to the
realm of logic. Problems immediately surface for OH when we try

---

[2] *Top*. i. 14, 105^{b}19–25; *A.Po*. i. 33, 89^{b}7–9. Although Aristotle seems to have
only a rough-and-ready conception of what might constitute each class (see
105^{b}25–9), he at least recognizes the trichotomy. Düring (1966: 53) suggests that
the commentators' adherence to OH stems from a misreading of *Top*. i. 14. It
seems to me that the passage in question does provide evidence of an early
Aristotelian trichotomy. Nevertheless the trichotomy does not entail OH. In any
case, the commentators are quite capable of overinterpreting passages. For
instance, in the context of the passage quoted above Alexander surprisingly reads
the trichotomy into *Top*. i. 11, 104^{b}1–3. For the pervasive use of the trichotomy in
Hellenistic philosophy, see Moraux (1973: 77) with his references. He concludes,
'Man kann sie als einen Gemeinplatz betrachten, der zu Andronikos' Zeit fast
obligtorisch in einer Klassifizierung der Schriften des Aristoteles begegnen musste.

[3] *In A.Pr*. 3.2–4; see the elaborate discussion in ibid., 1.3–4.29, which suggests
the background of a major debate.

[4] Moraux (1973: 79); cf. Düring (1957: 447) on Elias *in Cat*. 118.20–119.12.
Moraux points out (p. 78) that there is no actual evidence that Andronicus used the
term $\dot{o}\rho\gamma\alpha\nu o\nu$, *pace* Düring (1957: 423).

[5] Cf. Ross (1923: 21), Robin (1944: 40).

to do more than merely pay lip-service to it. For OH implies a programme of interpreting or reinterpreting all statements of S_1 so as to involve no ontological commitment. This programme is rarely carried out, but occasionally some determined proponent of OH actually makes the necessary connections. For instance, David Sachs (1948) has claimed that both primary and secondary substances of S_1 are logical *terms* presupposing no extralogical entities. This interpretation seems immediately problematic—can it really be that Aristotle makes no ontological commitments in the *Categories*?[6]

Now, following Gaukroger's analysis of theories, we may say that any theory has an ontology proper to it. This does not entail that the ontology of the theory is an ontology in the absolute sense, that is, an account of the *ultimate* realities of the universe. However, our study of S_1 indicates that the ontology of the *Categories* is an ontology in the absolute sense. Aristotle sets out to identify the things that are. He calls them primary substances and discusses both their formal characteristics and the objects which instantiate them, and also the derivative entities of the world. The *Categories* expounds a theory that is every bit as metaphysical as it is logical in nature. In a similar way we have seen that his logic is a 'philosophical logic', a logic that reveals the nature of things in the world. Although his logical theory will stand alone as an independent formal theory, Aristotle never attempts to isolate it from its applications in the world. Aristotle's logic undergirds his philosophy of science, which in turn is no merely formal methodology of science, but an account of the nature of scientific explanation in light of metaphysical presuppositions about the world. Moreover, his logic is intimately associated with his epistemology, which in turn forms a background for his theory of science. In short, Aristotle simply does not invent a pristine logical theory which operates as a self-contained system in isolation from metaphysical and epistemological considerations. Presumably Aristotle was capable of conceiving alternative logical systems, but he would no doubt have rejected these as not the

---

[6] See the criticism of Sachs by Mure (1949). Against this view see also Randall (1960: 49–51) following Dewey (1933: 599). Randall finds OH in Łukasiewicz (1957); however, the latter does not seem to endorse the view (see Łukasiewicz's assessment of the debate over OH, 1957: 13).

right way to illuminate the relationships that really obtain in the world.

One further defence of something like OH considers the context of Aristotle's discussions in the *Categories* and elsewhere. According to this view, he is addressing problems of language and being, not problems of change. Since his theory appears in this context, it should not be applied to the physical or metaphysical works, in which other considerations and hence other analyses are relevant. It seems to me that this defence brings one perilously close to committing the genetic fallacy: the fact that we can locate the origin of the S_1 ontology in a certain context of discovery does not mean that it cannot be applied outside that context and so become part of a more extensive theory. It is not the *origin* of the theory of categories but the *use* to which it is put that must decide the issue. The central role the *Categories* theory plays in the network of theories constituting S_1 indicates that Aristotle is making some far-reaching ontological commitments. It therefore seems naïve to claim that the analysis of being in the *Categories* is of only limited relevance to physical and metaphysical analysis.

4.2.2   EH

EH takes S_1 and S_2 to have overlapping domains of evidence, and hence must take apparent conflicts between the system as serious and in need of elucidation. However, EH holds that ultimately these apparent conflicts can be resolved. We have already noted what appears to be a central and persistent difference between S_1 and S_2. S_1 conceives sensible substances to be simple and irreducible; S_2 takes them to be complex and reduces them to compounds of form and matter. The strategy of proponents of EH is to grant that S_1 does not analyse sensible substance into components as does S_2, but to maintain that the S_2 view is a natural extension of the S_1 view. Of course one can generate a contradiction by conjoining a statement derived from each system: 'Sensible substance is simple' and 'Sensible substance is not simple.' But S_1 is only a preliminary statement—either because it is simplified for the novice or because it does not yet take into account the full range of problems that a philosophy has to confront. Thus the conflict is not vicious. One has to appreciate the limited context in which S_1 is advanced.

Arguments in favour of EH are usually made at an intuitive

level, and the assumptions that underlie them are seldom attended to. I propose that we take seriously the claim that S_2 is an extension of S_1. In logical theory, one system is an extension of the other if it contains all the axioms of the other and at least one new axiom besides. For instance, let L_1 be an axiomatic system with axioms A_1, A_2, and A_3. Let L_2 be an axiomatic system with axioms A_1, A_2, A_3, and A_4, where A_4 is logically independent of A_1–A_3. Then L_2 is a logical extension of L_1. Every theorem of L_1 will also be a theory of L_2, but L_2 will generate theorems which are not theorems of L_1. However, no theorems of L_2 will contradict theorems of L_1. L_2 is thus compatible with L_1 but more powerful than it—indeed it entails L_1.

Is this the relationship that obtains between S_1 and S_2? I suggest that it is not, and that we can see that it is not from the limited profile we have before us of S_1 and S_2. Notice that SA and H are inconsistent propositions, on the assumption that 'primary substance' and 'concrete substance' have the same reference—which they do. (For example, Socrates is a primary substance for S_1 and a concrete substance for S_2). According to SA Socrates is metaphysically simple; according to H he is metaphysically divisible, namely into matter and form, hence he is not metaphysically simple. Thus SA and H entail p and not-p. Now, I would like to suggest that SA and H have a role as principles of their respective systems. Note, for instance, that the logic, epistemology, and philosophy of science of S_1 are predicated on the assumption that there are discrete, indivisible particulars. On the other hand, where S_2 differs from S_1, it is by the assumption that matter and form are intrinsic components of reality. Thus SA and H occupy a central place in their respective systems. Of course S_1 and S_2 are not really formal systems. But we can understand their structure by reference to formal systems, and this analogy seems to allow us to understand the several interpretations that are alleged to hold between S_1 and S_2. According to this analogy SA and H function as axioms of their respective systems.

If these assumptions are correct, we can prove that S_2 is not an extension of S_1. What results from adding H to the axiom-set of S_1 is an inconsistent set of propositions. For H and SA, an axiom of S_1, are inconsistent. Thus it is not possible to enrich S_1 by adding H as an axiom, and S_2 cannot be an extension of S_1.

But perhaps we could save EH or something like it by a

strategem. Let us drop SA and add H in its place. Then there is no inconsistency in the set of axioms, and S_2 can be seen as an extension, in a looser sense, of S_1.

This defence is doomed to failure. Consider an analogy from the realm of mathematics. Taking the set of five axioms of Euclidean geometry, one can replace the axiom that through a point external to a line a parallel line can be drawn with the axiom that through such a point no parallel can be drawn. The result is Riemannian geometry.[7] But it would be perverse to consider Riemannian geometry to be an extension of Euclidean geometry. For the meaning of terms shifts in a systematic way from one system to the other. Some truths of one system are truths of the other—after a manner of speaking—but it is only by courtesy that they can be called the same truths. For the same words do not mean the same things. For instance, it is true to say in both Euclidean and Riemannian geometry that the shortest distance between two points is a straight line. But 'straight line' does not mean the same thing in both systems. In Riemannian geometry a straight line is interpreted as a geodesic of curved space. Moreover, the two systems generate different theorems. For instance, the sum of interior angles of a triangle in Riemannian geometry is greater than 180 degrees and varies with the area of the triangle. Now one can object that since 'triangle', 'angle', etc. have different meanings, this theorem does not contradict the Euclidean theorem. However, the objection cuts two ways. While it is true that theorems of the two systems cannot contradict each other, it is because they differ in meaning, and to make this observation is to reinforce the point already made that terms shift meanings. And behind this point is the fact that the terms have different meanings because they are manifestations of different conceptual frameworks. Like the surfaces they describe, they belong to different conceptual spaces. If this is the relation between S_1 and S_2, there is no constructive reason for calling the latter an extension of the former.

Now I want to suggest that the case that I have just described—that of replacing one axiom with an inconsistent one—is especially relevant to understanding the relation of S_1 and S_2. For the chief formal difference between the systems consists of the replacement of an axiom of S_1 with an axiom incompatible with it: SA is replaced by H. It is possible to call the two systems incompatible because their principles are incompatible. But if the analogy to the geometrical systems holds, to explore the incompatibility of the two philosophical systems will ultimately be unfruitful because the chief manifestations of that incompatibility will lie in the conceptual shifts between the systems—shifts that produce not incompatibility but a failure of correlation between terms and propositions of the two systems. In order to confirm IH and to grasp the consequences of the hypothesis, one needs to examine those failures of correlation at the outer edges of their networks. To make such a study is to raise questions that have been much discussed in recent philosophy of science under the rubric of *incommensurability*. Since a version of IH which stresses the incongruence of the two systems rather than their logical incompatibility seems most promising as an explanatory hypothesis, I shall henceforth advocate the Incommensurability Hypothesis (ICH), to wit: S_1 and S_2 are incommensurable systems. In order to pursue this hypothesis we must give some content to the notion of incommensurability.

4.3   THE INCOMMENSURABILITY OF S_1 AND S_2

4.3.1   *Paradigms and Incommensurability*

Thomas Kuhn (1970[1962]) has argued that conflicts between different scientific approaches are complicated by the fact that their proponents see things differently. For instance, what to a chemist of one school was a compound appeared to a chemist of another school an element. Differences of theory often result from deeply rooted differences of assumption and perception about the nature of the problem and of the structure of the world. Because of these basically philosophical differences, proponents of one approach cannot directly confront proponents of another approach with their experimental results. Scientists of different persuasions have difficulty communicating because they learn their method by imitating paradigmatic examples of successful research—'paradigms', as Kuhn calls them. Much of the scientist's method is embedded in the concrete examples and is difficult or impossible to isolate from the actual practice of science. Scientists who use different paradigms comprehend the world so differently that they cannot learn from each other. Kuhn calls this situation the incommensurability of scientific traditions (p. 148). It is because of the failure of communication and common bases of dialogue that scientific 'progress' is discontinuous and that new approaches are revolutionary in a significant sense.

In explicating the problem of incommensurability, Kuhn gives three species of disagreement between competing paradigms. First, adherents of different paradigms 'often disagree about the list of problems that any candidate for paradigm must resolve' (p. 148). Thus they do not even agree about what they are supposed to explain. Secondly, although a new paradigm often takes over terminology and experimental apparatus, it employs these in a new way. In their new setting, the old elements express new conceptual relationships. But because of the superficial similarities of terminology and experimental method, differences of approach between new and old paradigms are all the harder to detect and misunderstandings are encouraged. For instance, the term *space* is used equivocally in Newtonian and Einsteinian physics, rendering debate between proponents of the respective paradigms difficult. Finally, Kuhn notes, 'In a sense that I am unable to explicate further, the proponents of competing paradigms practice their trades in different worlds' (p. 150). Scientists bring to their research a world-view, with accompanying dispositions to perceive the world in certain ways and in accordance with a certain outlook. Because of this holistic involvement, adopting a new paradigm for a scientist is something like a conversion experience or the flipping of a psychological *Gestalt* switch.

Now the second characteristic of incommensurable paradigms that Kuhn mentions seems to correlate with the situation we have observed in the case of alternative geometries. Incompatibility in the respective sets of postulates manifests itself in meaning shifts of terms and theorems between systems. Kuhn's analysis enriches the notion of meaning shifts between systems—what we may call formal incommensurability—with notions of motivation and outlook within the pragmatic social and psychological setting in which scientific research takes place. Thus Kuhn's view allows us to see formal incommensurability as a dimension in a living social environment and hence as a dynamic factor in theory change. Because his view puts incommensurability in a wider context, it will help us locate formal incommensurability within the framework of a whole philosophy of the world.

So far I have argued for ICH purely by elimination. If this hypothesis is correct, however, there should be ample evidence of incommensurability of the two systems—in the determination of problems, in conceptual articulation, in fundamental outlook. In this section I propose to identify cases of each kind of incommensurability. The results should confirm the Incommensurability Hypothesis of the relation between S_1 and S_2, and at the same time show that, like Kuhn's paradigm shifts, the conflict between the two is more than a matter of logic.

The simplest and most straightforward case of incommensurability between two systems is that manifested by terms whose similarity of pronunciation or inscription belies semantic differences. I shall begin this study of incommensurability by examing a set of terms having an undeniably central role in the metaphysics of S_2. I shall show that they have different roles in S_1.

4.3.2 Theoretical Terms in S_1 and S_2

Since we have located a gulf between S_1 and S_2 in the absence or presence of hylomorphism, a study of the cluster of terms which represent metaphysical concepts associated with this theory seems in order. The terms for form are εἶδος and μορφή, while the term for matter is ὕλη. The terms for form have a functional opposite in privation, or στέρησις, and actuality or ἐνέργεια is identified with the formed object. By examining these terms we can see at least in a preliminary way how significant is the difference between the two systems.

In S_2 εἶδος is paired with ὕλη in a conceptual opposition which encompasses the two aspects of determination and indeterminate medium. Although the term εἶδος has a wide variety of possible applications, the meaning is circumscribed. εἶδος is form, shape, or the principle of determinacy. By contrast, εἶδος never means form in S_1. Most commonly Aristotle uses the term in the sense of 'species', and, in particular, in contrast to the genus. In this sense I have counted over 100 occurrences of the term in the *Topics* alone; this use appears also in both *Analytics* and in the *Categories*. Aristotle uses εἶδος to designate the Platonic Form several times,[8] and he also uses it twice to mean the 'sense' of a word in the context of a discussion of equivocity.[9] I find only two occurrences

---

[8] *Top.* vi. 8, 147ᵃ6, 7; *A.Po.* i. 11, 77ᵃ5 and 22, 83ᵃ33.
[9] *Top.* vi. 10, 148ᵃ30, 33.

of the term which might plausibly be construed to imply a theory of hylomorphism, and in both the uses are attenuated and indecisive.[10]

The term μορφή is a synonym for εἶδος in S$_2$. It is rare in S$_1$, but it appears in a revealing context. In discussing the various kinds of quality in the *Categories*, Aristotle notes that the fourth class is that of σχῆμα or μορφή, that is, figure or shape (8, 10^{a}11 f.). Here it appears that μορφή is not in the category of substance at all, but in the subordinate category of quality. It seems unlikely that Aristotle could conceive of μορφή as a term for a species of quality and at the same time as designating substantial form, that which determines what the nature of a thing is. μορφή belongs to a different constellation of terms which signify contingent characteristics of an individual but which do not tell what it is.

Perhaps the most important term for comparing S$_1$ and S$_2$ is ὕλη. The term appears frequently in the treatises of S$_2$, in which it means 'matter', that is, the substratum of a composite substance, of which the form is predicated. There are many kinds of matter, but all of them are in some sense a substratum for form. What is striking about this term is that it does not appear in S$_1$ anywhere. There is not a single instance of the term in all the *Organon*. The general term for substratum, ὑποκείμενον, does appear in S$_1$ as in S$_2$, with the same meaning. But Aristotle's failure to use the special term for matter anywhere in S$_1$ calls for an explanation.

In *Physics* i and *Metaphysics* xii form and matter are associated with another term, στέρησις, which there signifies privation or the lack of a form. The matter goes from a state of privation to a state of having the form in a γένεσις. The στέρησις provides a conceptual foil for εἶδος as the absence of the form, the possession of which confers on the matter a higher degree of organization. In general the term στέρησις designates a metaphysical state of being in which matter is incompletely organized.

S$_1$ also uses the term στέρησις, but the meaning is different. The central meaning seems to be 'deprivation', usually connoting the lack of a natural faculty. Aristotle's most common example is that of blindness in relation to sight. His discussion in the *Categories* is significant:

---

[10] *A.Po.* i. 33, 89^{a}20; ibid. 13, 79^{a}6–10, where εἶδος is opposed to ὑποκείμενον, but where it is also asserted that the εἶδος is not predicated of a substratum; evidently the Platonic conception of εἶδος is meant here.

Deprivation and possession [στέρησις and ἕξις] are said of the same subject, as sight and blindness of the eye; and to speak generally, the natural subject of possession is the subject of both possession and deprivation. We say any of the subjects capable of possessing a faculty is deprived just when the faculty is completely absent from the subject to which it naturally belongs at the time when it should naturally belong to it. (10, 12^{a}26–31)[11]

The definition is explicit restricted to contexts in which one can say it is *natural* (πέφυκεν) for x to have possession P. He seems to have in mind mainly biological subjects with natural attributes of some kind, as his following examples of blindness and toothlessness indicate. His definition does not seem to apply, for example, to shapelessness in a quantity of bronze, for it is no more natural for bronze to have the shape of a man than to have a nondescript shape. The shapelessness of bronze is a privation but not a deprivation. Aristotle is adamant on the connotations of naturalness to a subject in his S_1 treatment. He criticizes the definition of coldness as 'the deprivation of what is naturally hot' not for its vacuousness, but because 'naturally' is redundant (*Top.* vi. 3, 141^{a}10–14). Aristotle does use στέρησις in broader contexts, specifically of a deprivation of light in an eclipse. Here the domain of evidence is not merely the biological world; but the term still fits the definition cited above, since it is natural for the moon to be illuminated in the middle of the month.[12] He also uses στέρησις to designate a term that stands to another term in the semantic relation of not-F to F, which is typically marked in Greek by the 'alpha-privative' as in the relation of ἀνισότης 'inequality' to ἰσότης 'equality'.[13] In one passage in S_1 Aristotle states that στέρησις is opposite to εἶδος. Is this a case of privation vs. form? No: εἶδος here is 'species', and Aristotle uses his example of blindness and sight to illustrate the fact that the deprivation and the species are in different genera. Deprivation, Aristotle continues, can be exploited in a constructive argument only by showing that

---

[11] The passage is from the latter part of the *Categories*, the 'Post-Predicaments', which has been suspected of being spurious. But while the last part of the *Cat.* may be originally from another treatise, there are strong arguments that Aristotle is the author and that it is contemporaneous with the *Cat.* proper. See ch. 11 n. 9. For other uses of the blindness example, cf. *Top.* vi. 6, 143^{b}33–5; ii. 8, 114^{a}10 f.; ii. 2, 109^{b}22; vi. 9, 147^{b}34 f.

[12] *A.Po.* ii. 2, 90^{a}16.

[13] *Top.* vi. 9, 147^{b}4–17; cf. the use of στέρησις as a logical term in *DI* 10, 19^{b}24.

98   The Incommensurability of the Systems

as the deprivation is to not-F, so the possession is to F (*Top*. iv. 4, 124^a35-^b6). The passage thus shows no awareness of the relation between privation and form presented in S_2.

Type I	Type II
building vs. able to build	articulated from matter vs. matter
awake vs. sleeping	fashioned vs. unfashioned
seeing vs. having sight with eyes closed	

FIG. 4.1.   Types of Ἐνέργεια

The term ἐνέργεια along with its cognate verb ἐνεργεῖν are closely associated with the hylomorphism of S_2, for the matter in its formed state is said to be fully actual or to have reached its actuality. We have noted already in Chapter 3 that ἐνέργεια contrasts with δύναμις or potentiality, which Aristotle associates with matter in contrast to the completed object. We must now note that there are two senses of δύναμις-ἐνέργεια. In *Met*. ix. 6, Aristotle says that the senses are one by analogy, and he gives examples of the two types (1048^a37-^b4) as in Fig. 4.1. He characterizes Type I as having the relation of κίνησις in relation to δύναμις and Type II as having the relation of substance to matter ($^b8$ f.). The difficult relationship to explain is that of Type I. Shall we say the first item stands to the second as motion to potentiality? The latter translation seems tautologous, since we are trying to explain a species of potentiality. The former gives a false reading. For there is no inherent sense of motion in being awake or seeing. Both being awake and seeing are states.[14] The basis of contrast in Type I is the fact of a state of *activity* on the one hand vs. a state of *capacity* on the other. I shall designate this as the activity sense of ἐνέργεια in contrast to the substance sense (= Type II), abbreviating to ἐνέργεια-A and -S, respectively. I intend to key on ἐνέργεια rather than on δύναμις because the latter term has more senses, many of which are irrelevant to the present discussion.

Only ἐνέργεια-S has explicit connections with hylomorphism (1048^b8 f.). The question of the relation between S_1 and S_2

[14] The morphology of ἐγρηγορώς 'awake' shows this, since the Greek perfect is stative in aspect; ὁρῶν 'seeing' is the participle of an inherently stative verb. See Graham (1980). Note also Plato's careful distinctions between the state and the transition to it in his treatment of being awake in *Phd*. 71 C–D.

becomes with respect to the present term, whether ἐνέργεια-S appears in S_1 or only ἐνέργεια-A. In the *Organon* we find examples of ἐνέργεια or ἐνεργεῖν in contrasting the activity of knowing with the corresponding capacity;[15] and similarly Aristotle singles out the activity of seeing.[16] He recognizes an activity of building,[17] and an activity of courage.[18] He points out that it is a category mistake to call a ἕξις, that is, a state of capacity, an ἐνέργεια. For instance, if one should define perception as change (κίνησις) one would be in error, since perception is a state of capacity, but change is ἐνέργεια (*Top.* iv. 5, 125^{b}15–19). The contrast with ἕξις shows that ἐνέργεια must be used in the activity sense. Aristotle further glosses the contrast between potential and actual perception as the difference between αἴσθησιν ἔχειν 'having perception' (cf. ἕξις, a cognate of ἔχειν) and αἰσθήσει χρῆσθαι 'using perception'.[19] In considering the logic of tenses in argument, he makes a similar equation:

If δύναμις is disposition [διάθεσις] and being able [δύνασθαι] is being disposed [διακεῖσθαι], and if ἐνέργεια is the use of something [τινος ἡ χρῆσις], ἐνεργεῖν is using and ἐνηργηκέναι is having used. (*Top.* iv. 4, 124^{a}31–4, cf. 20 f.)

Again the relationship between δύναμις and ἐνέργεια is one of capacity to activity. One final example of ἐνέργεια is that of enjoying or being pleased (ἥδεσθαι), another case of activity.[20]

There is but one passage in the *Organon* which makes use of ἐνέργεια-S. At *DI* 13, 23^{a}21–6 (cf. ^{a}7 ff.), Aristotle maintains that what is necessary is actual, and he makes a classification of things into a class of items which are actual and do not have potentiality, such as the primary substances, items which have both actuality and potentiality, and items which have potentiality without actuality. I wish to reject this passage as an insertion (by Aristotle no doubt) which does not belong to the original version of the *DI*. I have no philological objections to raise to the passage, but note how the use of 'primary substance' seems to invoke the S_2 conception, and in particular the concept of the Unmoved Mover.

---

[15] *A.Pr.* i. 21, 67^{b}3, 5; *A.Po.* i. 24, 86^{a}29.
[16] *Top.* i. 15, 106^{b}17, 20.
[17] *Top.* iv. 4, 124^{a}20 f.
[18] *Top.* iii. 2, 117^{a}32.
[19] *Top.* v. 2, 129^{b}33 f.
[20] *Top.* vi. 8, 146^{b}13–19. Note the striking equation of γίνεσθαι and ἐνεργεῖν in ^{b}15 f., which, however, Aristotle seems to retract as he further considers the problem in the following lines.

In order to disarm this passage, however, we shall have to examine the contents of the two systems.[21] For now, it will suffice to summarize the meanings of metaphysical terms typical of each system in Fig. 4.2.

The differences of meaning between systems are pronounced. But do they constitute a shift of meaning? Strictly speaking, no, for certain other background conditions must be fulfilled before we can identify a shift of meaning. Most notably there must be a temporal sequence from one system to another, and secondly there must be some kind of replacement of concepts in the one system by those of another. So far we have not even addressed the question of temporal sequence, much less that of further conceptual relations. Yet the meaning differences we have found provide a kind of prima-facie case for meaning shifts. Since I believe the missing pieces of the puzzle can be found, I shall use the present data as tentative grounds for assuming a meaning shift between systems. It may be objected that since the original senses of at least εἶδος and ἐνέργεια persist in S₂, what we have is not a meaning shift but a proliferation of meanings. Yet in both cases the new meaning more or less subsumes the old and the old loses its centrality.[22] Thus a kind of replacement or displacement seems to take place.

Term	S₁	S₂
εἶδος	species	form (also: species)
μορφή	shape (a kind of quality)	form
ὕλη	[does not occur]	matter
στέρησις	deprivation (usu. of a natural capacity)	privation (lack of a positive attribute)
ἐνέργεια	activity e.g. being awake vs. being asleep	actuality e.g. statue vs. bronze (also: activity)

FIG. 4.2.   Differences in the Meaning of Terms of S₁ and S₂

[21] The *DI* offers some unique problems for dating; see ch. 11 n. 10.

[22] This is strikingly in evidence with εἶδος, which surprisingly loses its contrast with γένος in the biological works: Balme (1962). ἐνέργεια-A becomes a subordinate part of a complex scheme (*Met.* ix. 6, 1048ᵃ37 ff.): see ch. 7 below. The clarification in this paragraph is in response to a challenge raised to me by Richard Sorabji.

4.3.3   Shifts in Statement Meaning in S_1 and S_2

A systematic shift in the meaning of terms between one system and another is perhaps the most obvious manifestation of incommensurability. However, the real test of incommensurability must be the degree to which these terms fall into incongruent relationships. In fact, it is only by noting that the similar terms enter into inconsistent statements that we can tell that they have a different meaning. For instance, by observing that in Euclidean geometry the sum of interior angles of a triangle is 180 degrees, but that in Riemannian geometry the sum of interior angles of a triangle is greater than 180 degrees and varies with the size of the triangle, we are justified in inferring that the term 'triangle' has a different meaning in the two geometries. This in turn means not that the two statements of the angle sum are really incompatible, but only what I shall call (following Ernest Nagel 1961: 237) prima-facie incompatible. It is because two systems such as those of Euclidean and Riemannian geometry never give the same theoretical accounts of things—because metaphorically speaking they do not impose the same principle of mensuration—that they are incommensurable.

In so far as they are considered as formal systems, incommensurable systems cannot contradict one another. In fact, they may even, as is generally the case with non-Euclidean geometries vis-à-vis Euclidean geometry, be able to be mapped one to one. For by finding an appropriate model for a non-Euclidean geometry, for example, a spherical surface for Riemannian geometry, one can interpret theorems of Riemannian geometry as theorems of (solid) Euclidean geometry. However, one will have to translate, for example, 'triangle' in Riemannian geometry into a different term and make other such adjustments. Thus it may turn out that one can have one's cake and eat it too: for on a certain interpretation, both geometries are true at the same time. The catch, of course, is the phrase 'on a certain interpretation'. For on other interpretations, including the one which takes 'triangle' to have the same referent, the systems can contradict one another. So when we are dealing with interpretations, there is room for actual contradictions between systems.[23]

With this background in mind, we may intelligently ask the

---

[23] For a discussion of these points, see Nagel (1961: 250–3).

question whether S_1 and S_2 are incommensurable. The question can now be narrowed to the following: can we discover at least one theorem of S_1 that is false in S_2; and can we establish the intended interpretations in such a way that S_1 and S_2 contradict one another? If we can answer these questions in the affirmative, we shall have established that S_1 and S_2 are incommensurable in principle and incompatible in fact.

Consider now a passage from the *Categories*:

Substance does not seem to receive the More and the Less. I do not mean to say that one substance is not more or less substance than another (for I have made this point already), but that each substance is not said to be either more or less what it is. For instance, if the given substance is a man, it is not more or less man, either in the sense that he is more a man than himself or in the sense that he is more a man than another man. For one man is not more a man than another as this white is more or less white than another . . . (5, 3^b33-4^a1)

Aristotle carefully distinguishes his present thesis from an earlier point, namely that a man is not more a substance than a horse nor is the species man more a substance than the species horse (2^b22-8). Here his point is that for individuals a and b of species S, a is not more a substance either than itself (presumably at a different time) or than b. His main argument seems to be, expressed in the formal mode, that we do not use the adverbs 'more' and 'less' with substantial predicates like 'man'. When we say in English 'You're not man enough' or 'He is more of a man than you' we are speaking figuratively and not using the term 'man' in its usual (relatively non-evaluative) sense.

Now although Aristotle presents this point, like most of the characteristics of *Cat.* 5, in an almost inductive way, and although he appeals to ordinary language intuitions to support the point, I suggest that we have here something like a *theorem* of S_1. For according to principle SA, primary substance is simple and unanalysable. Thus it follows that there can be no degrees of being a substance: either x is a substance or it is not. There is no room in the metaphysical picture for Socrates to be more of a substance than Callias, or for Socrates-at-t_2 to be more of a substance than Socrates-at-t_1. So although our linguistic habits confirm that substancehood is an absolute condition, the point really follows from the ontology of the system. I shall call Aristotle's theorem the Absoluteness of Primary Substance (APS).

S_2 offers a thesis that may be compared with APS:

. . . the things that are posterior in generation are prior in form and substance (e.g. man is prior to boy and human to seed, for the one already has the form while the other does not) . . . (*Met.* ix. 8, 1050^a4-7)

Here the man is *prior in substance* to the boy. Surely the boy is a substance according to Aristotle. But he does not have the complete form of the man, and so he is not fully a substance. In fact, although Aristotle does not use the words, the boy is less of a man than the adult.

This thesis, which I shall call the variability of concrete substance (VCS), seems to follow from the principles of S_2. According to H, concrete substance is composed of form and matter. According to the principle of Actualism, the concrete substance exhibits more actuality to the degree its form is more completely realized in its matter. Since actuality is a measure of the perfection of substance, the individual substance can exhibit different degrees of substancehood.

APS and VCS are prima facie incompatible. According to the former, there are no degrees of substancehood; according to the latter there are. Are the two theorems actually incompatible? I suggest that they are. For although 'substance' *means* something different in each theorem—in the former the term stands for primary substance in the S_1 sense, in the latter it stands for concrete substance—the reference of the two terms is the same. For instance if Socrates is a primary substance for S_1, he is also a concrete substance for S_2. According to S_1 he cannot be more complete with respect to his nature at time t_1 than at time t_2; according to S_2 he can—and for at least some time co-ordinates he *is* more truly of his nature at a later than an earlier time.

I conclude that S_1 and S_2 are incommensurable in Kuhn's second sense, the sense in which they make use of different conceptual frameworks, which are organized in different ways with results that sometimes conflict.

4.3.4 Differences of Outlook and of Problems

Beside the area of terminological and conceptual differences, Kuhn finds that incommensurable systems exhibit differences in what they regard as problems to be solved and in general outlook. In this section I shall explore an area of difference between S_1 and

S_2 in which these kinds of differences surface most clearly, namely in the treatment of science.

S_1 conceives of a science as a set of propositions arranged as a formal deductive system. The component propositions are categorical propositions which can be arranged in syllogisms linking the terms in a descending sequence from the most general term, which represents the subject of the science. On this account science manifests two salient characteristics. First, it is constructive rather than analytic: it tends to explain phenomena by projecting a connection between two entities rather than by breaking down a single entity into components. For instance, S_1 is at its best explaining an eclipse of the moon. An eclipse is the blocking out of the sun's rays by the earth. Here we have an attribute (eclipse) of a substance (the moon) explained by the state of a substance (position of the earth). The explanation treats the items involved as separate entities which are capable of determinate relationships among themselves. The 'discovery' consists of locating a previously unknown connection between the items.

Secondly, S_1 science tends to give a *static* account of phenomena. The structure of science is a-temporal: it consists of a set of universal statements linked to a common subject genus. These statements are ideally tenseless generalizations whose significant interrelationship is not temporal but logical. Even an occasional event like an eclipse is explained without reference to time. The modern scientist thinks it one of his primary tasks to predict an eclipse; Aristotle simply defines it. He shows no further interest in questions of mathematical calculation, temporal prediction, or experimental confirmation. The whole schematic conception of science in S_1 presupposes that the practice of science is largely a matter of syllogistic logic. Discoveries are made, but these are merely perceptions of missing steps in deductive chains. They do not require appreciation of dynamic relationships between entities. Furthermore, they do not involve—but rather exclude—questions about the genesis of entities or situations. Aristotle has nothing to say about processes of change as such in his scientific scheme in S_1. A process is a dynamic situation that must be explained in a temporal way. Hence it does not surrender to the kind of logical analysis we have found in S_1. Processes are beyond the pale of science. Even an eclipse is treated only by virtue of the fact that it is conceived as a recurrent event rather than as a process or change.

According to S_2, a scientific analysis consists of an examination of the four causes: the material, formal, efficient, and final. By identifying all causes we make an exhaustive scientific study of a phenomenon. There are only these four causes and Wisdom consists in knowing them. For example, the formal and final cause of an animal is the soul; the efficient cause is the parent of the animal, or perhaps the generative organs; and the material cause is the body or the bodily parts.

S_2 science differs from S_1 science in showing diametrically opposite traits: (1) it is analytic and (2) it is dynamic. S_2 tends to solve problems by breaking down entities into their component parts and then analysing them as to their causal influence. A typical scientific project of S_2 is to isolate the biological causes, as in the example I have just given. This task requires not that we project relationships between different animals but that we separate the animal into its components—its form and matter—and then assign to these their causal roles. Aristotle never states a recipe for scientific research, but if he did the instructions would no doubt consist of two steps: (a) breaking down the subject into its metaphysical components; in cases of earth-bound science, these are typically the form and matter; (b) identifying the four causes. The formal (and sometimes the final) cause is generally identifiable as the form; the material cause is typically the matter; the efficient cause is what generates the subject; the final cause is the goal of the process. A metaphysical analysis is preliminary to a scientific study and presupposed by it.

Secondly, S_2 science is dynamic in outlook. Although the matter–form analysis is not necessarily dynamic in character, it lends itself to a dynamic interpretation. One can treat form and matter merely as contemporaneous aspects of a concrete individual without temporal implications. But one can also ask the question how this form came to be associated with this matter; the question is a dynamic one that seeks for an elucidation in terms of a process of temporal development. Because of their close association with matter and form, the material and formal causes can thus be construed as answers to a question about the development of a situation. Furthermore, the efficient and final cause are naturally construed as answering developmental questions, namely: what caused situation S to come to be (efficient cause)? and: for what end did S come to be? Because of the atpness of the four causes to explain processes, S_2 includes within the purview of scientific explanation natural processes. Thus it is a scientific question how, for example, Bucephalus came to be. Accordingly, the apparatus of the four causes can be brought to bear to explain this particular process, which is no different from the general problem of animal generation except in its individuality.[24] Of course it is more scientific to give a general account of a general process than a particular account of a particular process; but that is a difference of degree rather than of kind.[25]

I would like to suggest that the different characteristics of S_1 and S_2 science are differences of outlook. Each system has a different perspective on what it is to engage in science. For S_1 it is formally to structure the insights into reality antecedently won by induction. To engage in science is essentially to lay out the relationships between universals in an axiomatic system, and to make a scientific discovery is to locate a link in a chain of deductions. According to the view of S_1 there is only one correct scientific system for each field of inquiry, and that is the one that organizes all the truths of science into the appropriate logical order. For the Aristotle of S_1, a scientific system should be consistent, complete, and unique.

For S_2, to engage in science is to analyse a situation into its causal factors, using the four cause scheme as a touchstone. Not any causal analysis will count as scientific, since there are accidental descriptions of causes: one can give causes under an irrelevant description.[26] But if we rule out irrelevant descriptions, there are still many possible causal descriptions of a given situation. The most scientific one will give the universal cause of the event-type in question rather than the particular cause of the event-token. But alternate answers are still scientific. Thus there are no sharp boundaries between scientific and non-scientific analyses. S_2 science is vague and open-textured where S_1 science is precise and rigorous. But S_2 science is also flexible and pluralistic instead of rigid in its approach to problems. And S_2 science arguably has pragmatic advantages over that of S_1, given the state

---

[24] *Ph.* ii. 3, 195ᵃ32–5, ᵇ25–7.   [25] Ibid. ᵇ21 ff.

[26] In Aristotle's terms, this is to give an accidental cause. See *Ph.* ii. 3, 195ᵃ32 ff.

of scientific research in Aristotle's time and the limited potential of the S_1 model.[27]

Not only are the outlooks of the two sciences different, but they address different problems. The S_1 approach to problems comes out clearly in Aristotle's discussion of scientific questions at the beginning of *Posterior Analytics* ii. Although there is some problem in interpreting his examples, the kinds of question he seems to recognize are (1) Is x F?, (2) Why is x F?, (3) Is there an F?, (4) What is an F? Questions (2) and (4) are follow-up questions to (1) and (3), respectively, when these are answered affirmatively. Aristotle goes on in Chapter 2 to equate questions (2) and (4):

In all these cases it is clear that the question 'What is it?' and the question 'Why is it?' are the same. What is an eclipse? Deprivation of light from the moon by the interposition of the earth. Why is there an eclipse, or Why is the moon eclipsed? Because light fails owing to the interposition of the earth. (90^a14-18)

In Chapters 4–10 Aristotle gives a detailed and not always clear discussion of the question whether there is demonstration of essential nature—that is, whether the definition of the nature of a thing can be demonstrated syllogistically. The argument is complex and the conclusions ambiguous, but roughly Aristotle seems to say that scientific demonstration, definition of essence, and statements of cause (answers to the why question) are all somehow related (see 10, 94^a1 ff.). In modern linguistic terms, we might say that demonstration, definition, and causal explanation are all transformationally equivalent.[28] What this means is that all scientific questions can in effect be reduced to requests for definitions. And in fact, Aristotle's paradigm examples of scientific research in S_1 are cases that lend themselves to this approach: What is an eclipse? What is thunder? What is a man?

[27] S_2 science avoids the incoherence which Gaukroger (1978: 124) discovers in Aristotelian science, namely that knowledge of principles comes by induction, which cannot provide the necessary premisses needed for demonstration. This incoherence is generated only within the S_1 conception of science. In any case although S_1 science is an interesting anticipation of the deductive–nomological model of science, that model seems much less promising for qualitative schemes like Aristotle's than for quantitative formulations like those of modern science.

[28] e.g. 'Thunder is quenching of fire, quenching of fire is in cloud, therefore thunder is in cloud' (demonstration); 'thunder is the quenching of fire in cloud' (definition); 'there is thunder because fire is quenched in cloud' (causal account) have a common content, differing only in logical form.

In S_2 the focus is on a different type of problem. Aristotle is aware that in one area where other philosophies are especially weak, his is especially powerful: 'Yet why there will always be generation, and what the cause of generation is, no one says' (*Met.* xii. 10, 1075[b]16 f.). Aristotle uses his ability to explain generation to ideological advantage against Plato, for he charges that the Forms cannot explain change, and thus 'the whole study of nature is undermined.'[29] In general, the four cause theory gives Aristotle the ability to account for generation and process in a way that had not been available to the tradition since Parmenides attacked the notions. Armed with this theory, he can address problems like those of fundamental generation and destruction (in the *GC*), generation of animals (*GA*), principles of generation (*Ph.* i and *Met.* xii), and in general problems of change, heavenly rotations, natural movements, and even (though he does not study the topic in a systematic way) historical development.[30] On the other hand, he seems relatively uninterested in problems of definition and even finds that the complexity of causal relations militates against simple definitions:

. . . we must try to classify animals by their genera as laymen do, recognizing a genus of birds and one of fish. Each of these genera is distinguished by plural differentiae, not by a simple dichotomy. (*PA* i. 3, 643[b]10–13)

More fruitful than the search for simplistic definitions is the quest for causal nexuses in the field of research. The task of S_2 science is to show how natural bodies (including biologically organized bodies) behave in relation to one another, not to define them.

The scientific problems of S_1 and S_2 are different. For S_1 the problem of definition is dominant. The task of science is to answer, either directly or indirectly through demonstration, the question 'What is an F?' for a certain F within the domain of inquiry. For S_2 the dominant problem is the problem of change: 'Why does F come to be, or move or alter or grow?' Definitions take second place, and the capacity to explain much outstrips the capacity to define in S_2. Thus what counts as a scientific problem in one system

---

[29] *Met.* i. 9, 992[b]8 f., cf. 992[a]24 ff., 991[b]3–5, xii. 6, 1071[b]12–19, *GC* ii. 9, 335[b]17–23.
[30] Aristotle did undertake an extended history of thought in the lost *On Philosophy*, a work that probably belongs to S_2 (see ch. 11.3.3).

may either not qualify or not be considered significant in the other. Questions of change are in principle ruled out by S_1—unless they can be expressed in such a way that a definition can be given. In general, this is to say that they must be restated in such a way that they are not questions of change at all. For instance, in S_1 we cannot ask, 'How did the moon *come to be* eclipsed?', but we can ask 'What is an eclipse?' In S_2, on the other hand, Aristotle gives the eclipse example once, but relegates it to the role of a defective case—for not all the causes are relevant![31] It is a striking confirmation of the difference between S_1 and S_2 science that a case that was a paradigm example of scientific explanation—indeed almost a Kuhnian paradigm of successful problem-solving—in the former should be demoted to a place of obscurity in S_2. For science within a hylomorphic framework, eclipses are not very interesting phenomena and their explanation is not a great scientific feat. Science aims at illuminating change, process, development, and only instances of change display in their complexity the full range and power of the four cause scheme.

At this point it is perhaps fitting to go back to Aristotle's criticisms of Platonism in *Met.* i. 9. One of the major points he scores against Plato is that Plato cannot account for change:

In general, although Wisdom seeks the cause of phenomena, we [Platonists] have abandoned our quest, for we say nothing about the cause of movement . . . [992^{a}24–6] Neither do the Forms have anything to do with the cause which we see is the cause of the sciences and the object for which all mind and nature act—the cause which we say is one of the first principles—but philosophy has now degenerated into nothing more than mathematics, even though we claim that mathematics should be studied as a means to other things. [^{a}29–^{b}1] . . . Concerning movement, if [the Great and Small] are movement, clearly the Forms will be moved. If not, where did movement come from? Thus the whole study of nature is undermined. (^{b}7–9)

Curiously, this criticism seems effective not only against Plato, but also against the science of S_1. The paradigm cases of scientific explanation have nothing to say about the cause of movement (^{a}24–6) or the final cause (^{a}29–^{b}1). They are effective only for explaining such phenomena as can be accounted for by a definition—for example, thunder or an eclipse.[32] They cannot

---

[31] *Met.* viii. 4, 1044^{b}6 ff.
[32] Of course thunder and eclipses both involve movement, but Aristotle explains

explain the growth of a plant or the movement of an animal. Thus, in so far as nature is conceived as being essentially a system in motion, S_1 science undermines the study of nature. Of course Aristotle claims that his middle term theory of cause can accommodate the four causes (*A.Po.* ii. 11), but I shall dispute that claim below (in 6.1.1). Only a limited range of phenomena which do not essentially involve motion are subjects for explanation. What S_1 does offer is explanations in the form of essential definitions. That is, it offers essential causes as the only real explanantia. Hence the mode of explanation does not differ from Platonic explanation, which is likewise in terms of essential causes.[33] Moreover, the whole ideal of science in S_1 is the mathematical ideal of a closed deductive system in which a few axioms, definitions, and postulates generate all the timeless truths of the system. S_1 science thus seems to be mathematical in a way that is anathema to the S_2 conception. In general, the criticisms Aristotle levels against Plato from the perspective of S_2's dynamic principles seem to apply equally well to S_1 science. And the substance of his criticism is that Platonic philosophy does not address the real problems of science. By parity of reasoning it must follow that S_1 does not address the problems of real (that is, S_2) science.

In summary, then, we see that S_1 and S_2 exhibit the signs of incommensurability of the three types identified by Kuhn. (1) They address different problems. (2) The respective terms and statements have systematically different meanings. And (3) the two systems manifest different outlooks. I conclude that they are incommensurable systems.

4.3.5   *Metaphysical Roots of Incommensurability*

It is not an accident that S_1 and S_2 are incommensurable. The differences between them are systematic, and they can be traced to differences in metaphysical principles. S_1 begins from an atomistic perception of reality to build a conception of the world that is constructive and static. S_2 begins from a hylomorphic point of view to create a system that is analytic and dynamic. The systems are in a real sense the outgrowths of a central conception. S_1 cannot be

them not *qua* moving: they are explained *qua* properties of a subject. In effect, he explains them as if they did *not* involve movement.

[33] *Met.* i. 6, 988ᵃ8–11; Plato *Phd.* 100 B ff.; cf. Vlastos (1969), Shorey (1924).

analytic beyond a certain point because the atomic substance sets a term for analysis. On the other hand the finite set of secondary substances which stand above each primary substance hold out the promise of a kind of science built on conceptual geography: each substance has a place in a conceptual network that can be mapped and classified. Indeed, one can derive a calculus to plot locations within the scheme. This kind of science is deductively rigorous in principle, but it is also static in its approach to the world. The statements of the system are timeless and the relations studied are unchanging.

S_2, by contrast, is founded on a metaphysic whose central insight is an analysis. The tendency to analyse phenomena is thus built into the system. A hylomorphic ontology does not of itself destroy a constructive approach to science such as is found in S_1. However, the fact that the sensible individual is not metaphysically simple tends to suggest that it is unscientific to focus on this individual as a whole; rather one should seek the determining factor in the individual and explain that. Seen as conceptually unstable, the concrete substance ceases to be a terminus for explanation. There is still a network of entities, but it is interpreted as a network of forms, and the scheme is complicated by the fact that relations of matter must also be taken into account. The matter–form relationship has a temporal interpretation which lends itself to explanations of development and hence in general to a dynamic science. The task of science is explanation of change and the focus is on situations which manifest change, most notably in the realm of biology.

The traits that S_1 exhibits—its constructive and static approach to explanation—are a manifestation of its atomistic foundations. Similarly, the analytic and dynamic character of S_2 results from its hylomorphic foundations. The differences that we saw in the way that S_1 and S_2 treat the same phenomena are reflexes of that fundamental difference of principle. S_1 will tend to interpret phenomena in light of relations between discrete entities; S_2 will tend to dissect entities. S_1 will tend to highlight and explain static, often taxonomic relationships; S_2 will focus on and investigate the dynamic factors that influence change. The collection of all the tendencies of each system is in a way the outlook of the system. And that in turn is largely a product of the principles of the system.

Thus we have two sets of principles generating two different approaches to the world. In other words, we have two distinct philosophies. That one philosopher should produce two incompatible philosophies may seem at first to be an anomaly or a scandal. Yet if we reflect on the history of philosophy we shall realize that it is neither. There are many precedents for philosophers presenting different views—only think of Kant's pre- and post-Critical work or the early and the late Wittgenstein. Some cases can be explained by developmental hypotheses, such as the foregoing, others by non-developmental hypotheses, such as Russell's account of Leibniz's two philosophies. But in any event, it would be a scandal for a philosopher to produce two philosophies only if there were no adequate explanation for his doing so. In the next section I shall sketch an explanation for Aristotle's two systems.

4.4   THE GENETIC RELATION OF S_1 AND S_2

We have considered several hypotheses concerning the relation between S_1 and S_2. I have argued against those which sought to reconcile the two either by counting them as having different domains of evidence or by explaining one as an extension of the other. I have attempted to show that the two systems overlap in their domains of evidence, and that they treat some of the same phenomena in different ways. This difference of treatment is not an accident, but the result of deep-seated differences of their metaphysical foundations. If my argument is correct, there are still some major debts to pay. Most pressing is the question of why Aristotle would produce two inconsistent or incommensurable systems when either one would seem to be potentially satisfactory by itself.

We have not yet introduced the means for a solution of this problem. The reason for this deficiency is that we have hitherto limited the discussion to a systematic analysis. But as I noted in Chapter 1, there is another kind of approach, one that raises questions concerning the temporal order of composition and the change of doctrine embodied in the works of the corpus. This genetic analysis must come second methodologically, for inquiries into the development of an author's thought must await the identification of differences of thought. We have, however, identified important differences, and we have seen that these are not accidents of given occasions, but that they are thoroughgoing and show a high degree of correlation with a certain grouping of works of the corpus. Furthermore, systematic considerations have failed to produce a satisfactory solution to the alleged inconsistencies of the corpus: the fact that one group of works is concerned with logical matters and the other with empirical and ethical matters is not sufficient to explain the discrepancies, since a closer look reveals that the domains of evidence are not so strictly delimited. It seems, then, appropriate to turn to genetic explanations for a solution.

Crudely, genetic explanations of a thinker's development have the following form:

> *Genetic Explanation* (GE): At time t_1 thinker A holds doctrine D_1; at time t_2 A holds D_2 which entails not-D_1; therefore, A's thinking develops.

As we noted in Chapter 1, such a method of explanation has the advantage of saving A from the charge of inconsistency. It does this by relativizing his doctrines to time, since it portrays A as holding D_1-at-t_1 and D_2-at-t_2, but not D_1-and-D_2-at-t_2. Still, the scheme for genetic explanation seems inadequate as it stands, since it can be used to beg the question of inconsistency for any two doctrines that are shown to be stated at different times, whether or not the thinker has repudiated the earlier one. What we should require of an adequate genetic explanation is at least that it show some reason for A's *changing* his views from D_1 to D_2: without this condition we have no assurance that there is an actual development of ideas going on. In other words, the reason A has for embracing D_2 should constitute a reason for abandoning, or at least going beyond, D_1. If we can establish this condition, we have some right to claim that there is a development between positions.

We could remedy the defect of the kind of genetic explanation typically invoked by developmentalists if we could build into it a requirement that the putative doctrinal development be philosophically motivated:

> *Philosophical Genetic Explanation* (PGE): At time t_1 philosopher A holds doctrine D_1; at t_2 he holds D_2 which entails not-D_1; D_2 has philosophical advantage R over D_1; A recognizes R as a reason for preferring D_2 over D_1 and therefore chooses D_2.

PGE, like GE, is like a kind of theory that has been called a transition theory.[34] It aims to explain why a new state S_2 replaces a prior state S_1. PGE in particular adduces intentions as explanantia for the transition. A full philosophical genetic account requires not only that there be some reason for preferring D_2, but that it be a philosophical reason. But there might be several philosophical reasons for preferring D_2. A reconstruction can be made on the basis of any one of those reasons. But it will be a historical fact that A followed R_1 rather than R_2, and ideally the available texts will support one reason over another.

But how, it might be objected, can we be assured that there is a philosophical reason for a development? By making philosophical motivation a desideratum a priori for genetic explanation we seem to be prejudging the situation. I must admit that in a certain sense we are prejudging the case, but I do not think the requirement is unjustified. It is simply a fact that like Saussure's chess game, philosophy is an intentional enterprise. Philosophers philosophize with objects in view; they intend their theories to solve problems; they also reform and modify their views so as to achieve consistency and coherence in the combination of their theories. To be a philosopher is just to engage in such intentional activities. To borrow a notion from Thrasymachus in the *Republic*, in so far as a thinker, fails to conform to this ideal, he is not functioning as a philosopher. It seems to me, accordingly, that it is right to expect a philosopher to have reasons—and indeed philosophical reasons— for changing his philosophical views. I think this expectation should be a defeasible one—that is, one which can be rejected for a given case, but only after due consideration of the evidence. To require any less is to allow the history of philosophy to degenerate into psychoanalysis or sociology or a theory of humours.

We seem thus to have the following requirements for an adequate genetic explanation of philosophical development:

(1) We must distinguish D_1 and D_2 which entails not-D_1.
(2) We must be able to assign a temporal order to D_1 and D_2.
(3) We must be able to assign a philosophical reason R for preferring D_2 to D_1.

[34] Cummins (1983: 1 ff.) provides a helpful anatomy of scientific theories. His classification is meant only for mechanistic theories; nevertheless the formal properties of his transition theories are similar to those of the kind of intentional theories I am exploring here.

(4) We must be able to confirm that A recognized R and actually made R his reason for choosing D_2.

Thus far we have (1) distinguished S_2 from S_1 and established that S_2 entails not-S_1. In fact, this is just to establish the non-historical preliminary to identifying a development. Can we then establish (2) for TSH?

There are many conflicting accounts concerning the dating of Aristotle's works, but fortunately the order of the main works that are of concern to us is not in dispute. For the logical works are generally considered to be among Aristotle's earliest works.[35] Early doubts about the authenticity of the *Categories* have been dispelled, and now it is generally held that the *Categories*, *De Interpretatione*, and *Topics* as well as the *Rhetoric* are earlier than the *Analytics*. Virtually all commentators would put all the above works, with the possible exception of the *Analytics*, before the physical and metaphysical works. As to the *Analytics* there is some disagreement both about the relative dating of the *Prior* and *Posterior Analytics* (on the received view the *A.Po.* is considered the later) and about whether they overlap with the physical and metaphysical treatises. Only the latter question is of importance to us here. Those who would argue for a relatively late date for the *A.Po.* would at most have it overlap with the earliest works of S_2.[36] Thus S_1 is in general earlier than S_2 by all accounts, and at most there is a relatively brief period of overlap between them.

There are many details of the relative dating that are worth considering; however, at this stage of the argument it is desirable to develop TSH without getting bogged down in details. And the *communis opinio* seems sufficiently favourable on the matter of the relative dating of S_1 and S_2 that we may cite the authorities and move on. It will be important to return to the question of relative dating and to confirm the temporal priority of S_1. Indeed, I shall want to argue that the evidence is against any significant overlap between S_1 and S_2. But for now let it be granted that S_1 is in general temporally prior to S_2 in the opinion of the wise. In due time I shall address the relevant problems in dating (11.3).

---

[35] See e.g. Solmsen (1929), Ross (1939a), (1949: 6–23), Düring (1966: 54 ff.).

[36] Ross (1949: 22 ff.). Barnes (1981) would not only date the *A.Pr.* later than the *A.Po.* but put the *A.Pr.* quite late in the period of S_2; his hypothesis is both unusual and unnecessary, however, as I shall show below (ch. 11.5.3).

4.5 THE MOTIVATION FOR DEVELOPMENT

We now have a correlation between doctrines and times. We further have a presumptive direction of change: from S_1 to S_2. Next comes the most challenging and most neglected aspect of developmental explanation. We must give a philosophical reason why Aristotle—or anyone with a view like S_1—would modify it in such a way as to produce S_2. The task is really twofold. For not only must we give a philosophical rationale for the change, we must also show that it was in fact *Aristotle*'s rationale. The first task belongs to philosophy, specifically systematic analysis; the second to history of philosophy. For there may in fact be more than one reason for changing from S_1 to S_2. But we must find which one in fact was Aristotle's. Thus the potential routes a philosopher could take are a matter for philosophical speculation; but the actual route Aristotle took, being a historical accident, is a matter for historical research. I know of two promising hypotheses of change from S_1 to S_2.[37]

According to the first hypothesis, Aristotle perceived that there was something wrong with his account of predication in S_1. Consider the substratum of all attributes, the primary substance of S_1. What is this to be identified with? Is it, for example, Socrates, the substance with all its attributes? This seems to be what Aristotle has in mind as being the sensible thing we are familiar with. This sensible conglomerate has the advantage of being the common-sense object of knowledge. But if this is the case, then when Socrates changes in some respect, he ceases to be Socrates. By getting a sun-tan he would become a different primary substance. But this runs counter to Aristotle's intent. Accordingly,

---

[37] A third one has been proposed by Turnbull (1958: 143). Aristotle is concerned with the problem of how a nature (in contrast to a Platonic Form) can be *in* an individual. There is a danger that we will need to postulate a further nature to account for the connection, so Aristotle analyses substance into form and matter to make the connection between subject and nature immediate. Turnbull does not develop this account, and it seems to me that the Said-of talk in the *Categories* is meant to forestall thinking of the secondary substances as being in the primary. Accordingly, some further motivation for thinking of the universal as in the particular seems to be needed. Bos (1975: 63 ff.) presents a fourth view according to which the concept of matter originally was conceived of as a kind of physical basis for the world of changing things, a determinate version of Plato's Receptacle. His view requires a conjectural reconstruction of the *On Philosophy* and ignores the evidence of treatises that are earlier than that exoteric work.

we must not identify Socrates with all his attributes, but only the essential ones. Essentially, he is a man. But according to S_1 his being a man is derivative of his being Socrates. Yet once we have taken away all the non-essential attributes, what is there left to explain Socrates being Socrates and not Callias? At this point we seem driven to posit some recondite entity that might account for Socrates' being Socrates. In fact, there are two functions we must explain: what is left as a subject of the attributes? And what is the cause of Socrates' being a man? If we now posit an entity to fulfil each function, we can account for both the uniqueness of Socrates, which is a result of his being a unique subject, and his manhood, which makes him like other men. The first entity is matter, the second form. Thus we solve a problem of the subject of predication by positing matter and form. I shall call this account the Subject Hypothesis (SH).[38]

The alternative account stresses a problem of change rather than of predication. According to this hypothesis, Aristotle could not account for a type of change in S_1, namely the coming to be of substances. For substances are simple and hence either are or are not in such a way that there is no explaining their coming into being. In order to make room for substantial change Aristotle posited matter as a substratum for substance, and form as the component that organizes matter into a substance. By making this move he was able to save the phenomena by explaining how substances, for example, Socrates, come to be, as we believe they do. Thus Aristotle introduces hylomorphism to solve a problem of change which it is impossible to solve under the assumptions of S_1. I shall call this account the Change Hypothesis (CH).[39]

Both hypotheses take into account the important differences in the systems we have noted. Both recognize real deficiencies in S_1 and provide a plausible philosophical motivation for a change to S_2. But only one of them fits the evidence of the corpus as to Aristotle's actual motivation. In the following chapter I shall make

[38] For a statement of SH, see Frede (1978: 32). So far as I know no attempt has been made to provide historical evidence that SH embodies Aristotle's real reason for modifying S_1.

[39] This hypothesis has been suggested a number of times; e.g. Fitzgerald (1963: 82), Owens (1962: 108 f.), Owen (1965a: 148 f.), S. Mansion (1971: 79), Dancy (1975: 372 f.), Berti (1977: 297–9), Driscoll (1981: 157 f.). But it has been developed in detail only in Dancy (1978) and Graham (1984).

a detailed study of the work which I maintain effects the transition from S_1 and S_2 to show that CH offers the correct explanation. The turning-point in Aristotle's philosophy is *Physics* i, the earliest work of S_2.

5

The Hylomorphic Turn

Physics i introduces the correlative concepts of matter and form.[1]
Since the other works of S_2 presuppose an understanding of these
concepts, *Physics* i is prior to them in order of exposition.
Furthermore, Jaeger's reconstruction of the early *Metaphysics* has
made it evident that *Physics* i and ii are among the earliest works
of the physical and metaphysical treatises.[2] Thus they provide an
appropriate place to look for clues to the transition from S_1 to S_2.
In this chapter I wish to argue that *Physics* i provides just the clues
we need to reconstruct the transition; for the argument of the work
documents a dialectical development in Aristotle's thought. In
grappling with a certain problem, Aristotle takes a path that leads
him to posit the existence of form and matter. Thus the first book
of the *Physics* embodies a philosophical discovery or, from
another point of view, an invention, which enables Aristotle to
solve certain problems but which also enforces a modification of
his earlier views. *Physics* i exhibits the motivation for the ontology
of S_2 and also chronicles Aristotle's adoption of the new position.
The subject of the book is change, and in particular the number of
principles that are needed to explain change. Before we turn to the

---

[1] For reviews of the literature on matter, see Cencillo (1958: 150–68), Happ
(1971: 2–49).
[2] Jaeger (1923, pt. II, ch. 3 = 1948, ch. 7) demonstrates that *Met*. i, iii, and xiv
constitute the earliest stratum of the *Metaphysics*; they were probably composed at
Assos soon after Aristotle left the Academy. Jaeger's reconstruction of the early
Metaphysics is generally accepted today as a secure landmark of Aristotle's
development. (See Ross 1957: 72.) *Met*. i refers to the four cause theory of *Ph*. ii. 3
and 7 at 3, 983^a24-^b1; 4, 985^a11 f.; 7, 988^a20-2; 10, 993^a11 f.; cf. 1, 981^a18-20 with
Ph. ii. 3, 195^a32 ff.; and of course the whole of *Met*. i is an extended application of
the four cause theory to the history of philosophy. Furthermore, *Met*.i. 5, 986^b27-
31 refers to *Ph*. i. 2–3, and *Met*. xiv. 5, 1092^a33-5 presupposes *Ph*. i. 7. Finally, *Ph*.
ii itself at 3, 194^b23 f. presupposes *Ph*. i. 9, 192^a31 f. and the background argument
of *Ph*. i. 7–8. Thus *Ph*. i antedates *Ph*. ii and both seem to have been written before
Aristotle left the Academy and began the *Met*. (cf. Jaeger 1948: 296, 299; Ross
1936: 7–9).

discussion of change in *Physics* i we need to see what S_1 has to say on the subject.

5.1 CONCEPTS OF CHANGE IN S_1

Overall, Aristotle does not address problems of change in S_1. This is not to say that he has no interest in questions of change, since, as we shall see, he does deal with certain puzzles relating to change, and he does have certain ways of dealing with change. But despite various hints and partial treatments, we find no unified theory of change in S_1, nor any attempt to provide one. What we find in fact is a way of treating change that tends to obscure its problematic nature *vis-à-vis* certain other phenomena.

Aristotle provides an implicit classification of change in the *Categories*. His list of entities in Chapter 4 contains four types which have to do with action. These are the last four types of entity: posture, possession, action, passion. In giving examples of all of these Aristotle uses finite verbs. Thus 'is reclining', 'is sitting' are examples of posture; 'is shod', 'is armed' of possession; the active-voice constructions 'is making an incision', 'is cauterizing' exemplify action, and the corresponding passive-voice constructions passion. Several problems arise concerning this classification. In the first place, just how general are the classes meant to be? The examples seem surprisingly anthropocentric. Should the class that I have translated 'posture' ($\kappa\epsilon\hat{\imath}\sigma\theta\alpha\iota$) be rather rendered more generally 'position' as some translators do? Should 'possession' ($\check{\epsilon}\chi\epsilon\iota\nu$) rather be translated 'state'? The evidence consists mainly of the examples themselves. Note that 'position' cannot here mean 'place', which is a separate category, and it cannot include predicates like 'to the left of', which would be relatives for Aristotle.[3] Similarly, we cannot understand 'state' in too wide a sense because postures are states no less than are possessions. Aristotle seems to have in mind for $\check{\epsilon}\chi\epsilon\iota\nu$ the fact that 'is shod' and 'is armed' can be glossed by 'has shoes on' ($\check{\epsilon}\chi\epsilon\iota\ \upsilon\pi o\delta\acute{\eta}\mu\alpha\tau\alpha$) and 'has arms' ($\check{\epsilon}\chi\epsilon\iota\ \check{o}\pi\lambda\alpha$), respectively.[4] The problems one meets in trying to generalize these categories suggest that Aristotle had not thought them through in a more than superficial way. The fact that

---

[3] *Cat.* 7, 6^{b}11 f.; cf. 9, 11^{b}8–10.

[4] For arguments that the categories are derived from an anthropocentric conception, see Gillespie (1925: 80–3); cf. Owens (1960–1: 78 n. 19).

Aristotle has so little to say about these four categories, which I shall hereafter call the verbal categories, may indicate that Aristotle saw no particular problems with them.[5]

As curious and anthropocentric as they are, the first two verbal categories do not have significant implications for a theory of change precisely because they deal with states, that is, those situations which do not change. On the other hand, the last two verbal categories, action and passion, do have implications for a theory of change. The examples Aristotle gives of action and passion are drawn from medical terminology. He uses transitive verbs in the active and passive voice respectively: '*x* operates on *y*' gives an example of an action; '*y* is operated on by *x*' gives an example of a passion. Now if we look at the categories of action and passion as an attempt to analyse changes, we find that the attempt is not very successful. For any values we can substitute for '*x*' and '*y*', the two sentences above describe the same event. There is no reason to have two separate verbal categories related as active to passive in one's ontology. There simply are not two distinct phenomena which an active and a corresponding passive construction denote. Here is a case in which a difference of surface syntax is misleading. Aristotle himself notes the identity of the underlying event in S_2, aptly noting with Heraclitus that the way up and the way down are one and the same, only described from different points of view (*Ph*. iii 3, 202ᵃ17–21). Here, however, he says nothing.

Although the active–passive distinction is unhelpful as an approach to change, the assumption that underlies it poses an even greater obstacle to understanding change. The assumption is that change can be handled as a predicate, of the same order as other predicates such as those of quality and quantity. Aristotle advertises the categories as classes of simple entities. If change is one of these, it seems to follow that it is ontologically simple and hence unanalysable. By making this assumption Aristotle seems to preclude the possibility of breaking down actions into components,

---

[5] Note the cursory treatment in *Cat*. 9. Aristotle lists different numbers of categories in different places; see Bonitz 378ᵃ45 ff. While in many cases his lists are incomplete, several times he drops only posture and possession (Bonitz, ibid., 50–4); once he drops all the verbal categories and replaces them with κίνησις, *Met*. vii. 4, 1029ᵇ24 f.; once he includes κινεῖσθαι and κινεῖν, *EE* i. 8, 1217ᵇ26–9. This indicates his dissatisfaction with the original classification of action in the *Categories*.

assigning to them identity conditions, and otherwise inquiring into their structure. Specifically, this approach seems to rule out querying the number of principles involved in change. For to try to count principles is to deny the simplicity of change—to cease to treat it as an ultimate predicate.

Against this unpromising background, we find in the *Categories* one important glimmer of an insight into the nature of change. In reciting the characteristics of substances, Aristotle notices a 'special property' unique to substances: they are receptive of contraries while remaining one and the same (5, 4ᵃ10 ff.). For instance, a certain man can be pale or dark without changing identity; but the same colour cannot be pale or dark. Aristotle tacitly assumes that the man in the example is light or dark *at different times* (ὅτε μέν . . . ὅτε δέ . . ., ᵃ19) but he does not call attention to the qualification. In fact, he omits any mention of time in his definition of the special property of substance: substance is 'receptive of opposites while remaining the same and one in number' (ᵃ10 f.), he notes, but he fails to say 'at different times'. By contrast, his statement of the law of non-contradiction in *Metaphysics* iv (3,1005ᵇ19 f.) explicitly includes the important restriction that the same attribute cannot belong to the same thing in the same respect ἄμα 'at the same time'.[6] Aristotle's inattention to the time factor in the *Categories* passage is significant. What this means is that Aristotle is not focusing on change *per se*. For temporal succession is an essential condition of change. Thus the *Categories* passage not only is not an explicit theory of change, it is not even an account of change. Nevertheless, his remarks are suggestive of a theory in a way that his treatment of changes as predicates is not. For in his comments we can glimpse a potential account of the structure of a change.

For example, Socrates, who is pale, becomes tan. According to the *Categories* scheme, we find the following elements: (1) there is a substratum, namely the substance Socrates, which remains self-identical through a change. (2) There is a succession of attributes, specifically the contrary qualities light and dark (Gr. λευκός, μέλας). One quality is present at one time, another at another. (3) There is a time parameter in terms of which the change must be

---

[6] Cf. Plato, *Rep*. iv. 436 B 8 f. who also recognizes the need for temporal qualifications in similar contexts (using ἄμα, B 9).

described; one quality follows another in a temporal sequence.[7] In terms of this scheme we may propose an account of change: *change is an exchange of contrary attributes of a substratum in time.* Since properly speaking only substances are substrata, we may give the equivalent statement that change is an exchange of contrary attributes of a substance in time.

One limitation that is immediately apparent is that the present account deals only with accidental change, that is, change in the accidents of substance. Thus it is at best only a fragment of a general theory of change. Aristotle provides no directions in S_1 for extending the account to cover all cases of change, on the presumption that there are more kinds of change than accidental (an assumption confirmed in *Cat.* 14).[8] Moreover, it is difficult to see how Aristotle might extend the theory, since it is so anchored to the categorial structure of S_1 that there is little room to expand the theory without undermining that structure. But the whole question of adequacy of a theory of change revolves around the problem that had to be solved in the fourth century. We must look more closely at the problem and the possible lines for a solution.

5.2 S_1 AND THE ELEATIC PROBLEM OF CHANGE

It is clear from the overall argument of *Ph.* i that Aristotle takes the traditional problem of change seriously. Although he points out that it is not the natural philosopher's task to defend against objections to the possibility of change, he nevertheless addresses the question in Chapters 2 and 3. It is appropriate that he should, for *Ph.* i is not really a book of natural philosophy, but a methodological prologue to such a study. After examining the methods of the natural philosophers and extracting certain principles, as well as developing his own general schema of

---

[7] Plato, *Phd.* 70 D ff., seems to arrive at the same scheme. However, note that he so de-emphasizes the role of the substratum that it passes unnoticed until 103 A–B. Thus it takes him more than 30 Stephanus pages to get back to what Aristotle would say is the most important element of the scheme.

[8] 15^a13–33. It may be objected that this passage comes from the second half of the *Categories*, which is sometimes called the *Post-Predicaments* and treated as spurious. Against this, see ch. 11 n. 9. The treatment of στέρησις in *Cat.* 10 can be seen to be early by contrast with the S_2 account; see ch. 5.4.4. It is also interesting that Aristotle does not make use of a categorial distinction to account for the different kinds of change in *Cat.* 14. This suggests that his classification there may be pre-theoretic.

change, Aristotle returns to the problem of change in Chapters 8 and 9 to show how his approach solves the problem and does so in a more rigorous way than Plato's theory. Thus Aristotle conceives of his theory of change as the fruits of a dialogue with the traditional opponents of change. His theory is designed to resolve traditional puzzles and to lay to rest some ghosts of the past. At the same time as he engages his philosophical predecessors, he introduces his own logical distinctions and metaphysical apparatus. It is by a sensitive application of his own philosophical advances that he claims to be able to overcome past obstacles to an adequate philosophy of nature.

The problem of change originates with Parmenides, who attacks the assumptions of natural philosophy. He first makes a distinction between a positive method of Is and a negative method of Is Not (B 2, B 6). Only the former route of inquiry is intelligible. By an elaborate tapestry of nested *reductio* arguments, he claims to identify the signposts along the route; these show that being is (1) without beginning or end, (2) homogeneous, (3) unchanging, and (4) determinate (B 8.1–4).[9] Parmenides intends his attack to invalidate philosophical cosmogonies and cosmologies, as shown by the second half of his poem, 'The Way of Opinion', as it became known in the tradition. There he constructs what he claims to be a superior cosmology, only to undercut it by diagnosing a fallacious premiss in its construction (B 8.50 ff.).

Parmenides' arguments did not put an end to natural philosophy, but they did force a radical rethinking of the assumptions which underlay it. Empedocles, who in rhetoric, poetic form, and argument acknowledges his debt to Parmenides, continues to pursue natural philosophy only by adopting a plurality of Eleatic beings, namely the four elements, which individually conform to the four signposts of Parmenides. He preserves natural change only by making it an epiphenomenon of the elements. Roughly, he seems to have construed Parmenides' case against change in the following way:

(1) If something changes, it comes to be.
(2) Nothing comes to be.
(3) Therefore, nothing changes.

---

[9] Mourelatos (1970: 92 ff.); for other views on signposts, see ibid., p. 95 n. 2.

As a (partial) follower of Parmenides, he accepts (2).[10] But as a natural philosopher, he can not accept (3). Accordingly, he denies (1). He sees a way to rehabilitate change by making it a product of the mixture of pre-existing beings possessed of Eleatic properties.[11] Thus he accommodates change, since he interprets it in such a way that it does not entail coming to be, at least in the sense of physical generation. A corollary of his approach is that change is not really real: it is an accident of interrelations between the real things, the elements. In particular, coming to be and perishing do not occur at all, but are only appearances corresponding to qualitative redistributions, which are the only changes possible.

Other post-Parmenidean system-builders use similar strategies to accommodate change within an Eleatic framework which rules out generation. Anaxagoras follows Empedocles in both his ideological rejection of generation and his adoption of mixture as a method of accounting for change. However, he seems to have gone farther than Empedocles in multiplying elemental bodies, and in rejecting the nascent account of chemical combination of Empedocles. For Anaxagoras there is only physical mixture and a dominance of the element that exceeds in quantity. The atomists, on the other hand, make their beings discrete and microscopic and account for change by the physical arrangements of aggregates.

In their desperate attempts to justify change within the framework of Eleatic assumptions, the Presocratics never thought to attack premiss (2) of the Eleatic objection to change. Why is there no coming to be? Parmenides' key argument seems to proceed as follows (B 8.7 ff.):

(1) If what is comes to be, it must come to be from what is not.
(2) It is impossible for it to come to be from what is not.
(3) Therefore, what is does not come to be.[12]

---

[10] B 8, B 12, B 16.   [11] B 8, B 9, B 23.

[12] Aristotle gives a similar argument as follows (*Ph*. i. 8, 191^{a}27–31):

(1a) If what is comes to be, it must come to be either from what is or from what is not.
(2a) If it comes to be from what is, it does not come to be.
(3a) It is impossible for it to come to be from what is not.
(4a) Therefore, what is does not come to be.

It is often assumed that Aristotle is commenting on Parmenides (e.g. A. Mansion 1945: 75). He may infer the first half of the dilemma from B 8.11 or he may regard it as tacit, for he introduces his analysis as something of a diagnosis rather than a report. The dilemma may also have been in Aristotle's text, if Tarán is right to

The key premiss is (2). Parmenides' first supporting reason is that it is not sayable or thinkable ὅπως οὐκ ἔστι (lines 8 f.). Depending on whether we supply a subject or whether we see the last phrase as a sentence-frame, whether we understand the verb as existential, copulative, or something else, there are a large number of possible interpretations. I cannot here explicate the argument further. But it should be apparent that there are many possible ways of interpreting, and hence of attacking, the argument. What is surprising is that none of the Presocratics makes that attempt to attack this argument. It becomes a philosophical orthodoxy that what is cannot come from what is not.

Plato does take on Parmenides' account of not-being in his famous discussion in the *Sophist*. Yet he never makes use of his conceptual tools to attempt a unified theory of change. Aristotle is probably right in seeing the influence of Cratylus in Plato's acceptance of a primordial flux (*Met.* i. 6, 987^{a}32–^{b}1). The belief in a fundamental condition of change absolved him from the need to explain change. What needed explaining was rather the constancy exhibited in phenomena. In any case, when Parmenides' assumptions concerning being and non-being were finally challenged, the objections were not immediately applied to the problem of change. Plato himself had at least two accounts of change. The argument from opposites in the *Phaedo* contains a striking anticipation of the *Categories* account of change as an exchange of contraries. Like many Platonic theories, however, it appears as a somewhat *ad hoc* construction to serve another purposes (the agument for immortality), and Plato never takes up the theory again. Subsequently, the *Sophist* treats change (or, more precisely, motion) as one of the highest kinds, that is, as an irreducible principle in much the same way that the verbal categories of Aristotle are irreducible. But Plato does not elaborate this theory either, so we are left without a general Platonic theory of change.[13]

emend ἐκ μὴ ἐόντος in 8. 12 to ἐκ τοῦ ἐόντος (see Tarán 1965: 96 ff.). However, it seems more likely overall that Aristotle's argument is following a later dilemmatic version of the argument given by Melissus and reported by Simplicius *in Ph.* 103.15–19; cf. Cherniss (1935*b*: 61 n. 254).

[13] Aristotle refers to Plato's account of the Receptable and of the Great and Small as predecessors of his own account, *Ph.* i. 9, 191^{b}35 ff. and *GC* ii. 1, 329^{a}13–24, pointing out defects in the Platonic theory. While Aristotle may have found an anticipation of his own theory and even inspiration in Plato's concepts, it is doubtful that Plato intended his concepts (which are difficult to interpret) to solve

In *Physics* i Aristotle is aware of himself as a scion of a long line of natural philosophers who have been troubled by the objections the Eleatics raised. Unlike the Presocratics, he is not afraid to challenge Eleatic principles of being, and he comes to the conflict armed with technical advances of the Academy, expertise in logic, and a sophisticated metaphysical machinery. But we must ask to what extent the principles of S_1 enable him to reply to the Eleatics. As we have seen, S_1 gives him the concepts of substance as a substratum and contrary predicates as the termini of change and thus suggests a paradigmatic account of change.

We can immediately note some advantages of this account. In the context of Eleatic objections that change involves postulating that what is comes to be from what is not, the above account provides grounds for a reply. If the substance and the attributes pre-exist, there is no reason to worry that what is has come to be from what is not. For there was already something present. On this account, then, change is not radical in the way the Eleatic fears. Furthermore, there is something that remains constant in the change, namely the substance. Thus in a certain sense constancy is prior to change. Finally, there is, metaphorically speaking, a foundation for change, which is the substance. Since this entity is one of the fundamental realities in the first place, its presence provides a metaphysical guarantee that there will be no *ex nihilo* creations and hence no metaphysical discontinuities in the world.

The primacy of substance thus serves to underwrite the possibility of change in Aristotle's system. Perhaps this is no accident, for primary substance has been endowed with the properties of Eleatic being: it is one, self-identical, complete and determinate, and in itself changeless. Unlike Parmenides' ἐόν, οὐσίαι are not unique. There are a plurality of primary substances, each with its own independent integrity. Like Parmenides' ἐόν, primary substance is self-sufficient and perfect. Yet there is a sense in which the scheme of S_1 offers little more than the Presocratic pluralists. They too had posited beings with Eleatic properties, and they could account for certain kinds of change. The one thing they never did accomplish, however, was to restore the concept of generation to a place in the theoretical account of change.[14] Now

problems of change. Rather they seem to be part of an account which aims at grounding the existence of sensible objects.

[14] Cf. *GC* i. 3, 317^{a}32–^{b}35. In *GC* i. 1, Aristotle claims that those who have a

Aristotle's S_1 provides categorial distinctions of an order of sophistication far beyond that of the Presocratics, but does his system provide the means for rehabilitating generation?

In fact, the Eleatic properties of primary substance stand in the way of such an account. The problem of generation, stated in terms of Aristotelian categories, is how do things, that is, substances, come to be?[15] The challenge, which I shall hereafter call the Eleatic challenge, is to give a satisfactory answer to the question, 'How can what is come to be from what is not?'[16] At the level of accidental change, the challenge does not seem problematic: we have a continuum underlying the change and attributes which are participating in the change. But what of substances? They are, *ex hypothesi*, simple. If they come to be, it appears that they must come to be from nothing, for there is nothing which constitutes a substance and hence nothing that can be an ingredient in its production. The metaphysics of atomic substantialism systematically precludes an answer to the problem of generation, which is the outstanding problem of change.

5.3   ARISTOTLE'S OPTIONS

Aristotle does take the Eleatic challenge seriously. He also maintains in S_1 that there are generations and destructions (*Cat.* 14, 15^{a}13). And he holds that primary substances are metaphysically indivisible. These tents seem to involve an inconsistent set of beliefs, which can be articulated as follows:

El: What is does not come from what is not.

G: Primary substances come to be.

SA: Primary substances are metaphysically simple.

The Eleatic principle (El) is easily interpreted as an injunction against *ex nihilo* creation. The principle of generation (G) seems

---

plurality of elements should have recognized generation, though they did not. But of course their elements are the substantial entities of their systems, and these are not generated (with the possible exception of Empedocles' four elements which arise out of the one). Hence the pluralists are justified in denying generation from their own point of view.

[15] *GC* i. 3, 317^{b}20 ff.

[16] *GC* i. 3, 317^{b}23–31; *Ph.* i. 8, 191^{a}24–33 presents the Eleatic challenge as a dilemma concerning whether being or not-being is the source. (See n. 12.) In what follows I shall concern myself only with the more problematic claim that not-being is the source.

to be what Aristotle has in mind when he speaks of genesis or absolute coming to be: coming to be is by definition a change in the category of substance.[17] When these two principles are conjoined with Substantial Atomism (SA), we find that there is nothing which primary substance could be created out of, since it has no components and hence no ingredients. It seems impossible to hold all three principles as they stand; at least one must be given up.

There is something to be said for rejecting each of the principles, and some difficulty in doing so. There is one case in Aristotle in which he is willing to reject EI—in a way. He points out that mathematical points appear without a mediating process of change (*Met.* viii. 5, 1044^{b}21 f.). The same remarks apply to sensations,[18] forms and essences,[19] and to causes and principles.[20] However, Aristotle refuses to call such appearances generations (γενέσεις) or to say that they come to be (γίγνεσθαι).[21] In each case we are dealing with something metaphysically simple, and hence an entity whose appearance cannot be mediated by a process of becoming. But that very fact causes Aristotle to deny that such things come to be, since for him coming to be is a process, not an immediate change. Thus, while Aristotle is willing to take this option, he is not willing to call such changes generations, and consequenty he cannot use this approach to solve his problem of generation.

Because Aristotle is unwilling to compromise on considering immediate changes as generations, it seems that even if he should reject EI, he would also reject G. But since the set of propositions can be rendered consistent simply by rejecting G, let us consider that move by itself. There does seem to be some precedent in Aristotle's tradition for making such a move. Not only do the Presocratics after Parmenides reject generation, but Plato himself, at least in one context, makes such a move. For in the Middle Dialogues he maintains that the soul is eternal. Hence there is at least one type of continuing nucleus for attributes in the world. Of course, if we go to the first principles of Platonism, we find that the Forms are Eleatic beings which are eternal and perfect; however,

[17] *Met.* xii. 2, 1069^{b}9–13; *Ph.* v. 1, 225^{a}12 ff.; cf. *Top.* v. 2, 139^{b}20.
[18] *DS* 6, 446^{b}2–4.
[19] *Met.* vii. 14, 1039^{b}20–6; viii. 3, 1043^{b}14–18; ibid. 5, 1044^{b}21–3.
[20] *Met.* vi. 3, 1027^{a}29 f.
[21] *Met.* vii. 8, 1033^{b}5–8; viii. 5, 1044^{b}21–3.

because of their pristine self-sufficiency, they cannot be the subjects of change. Hence they do not provide the models for a (limited) theory of change that Platonic souls do.

Finally, Aristotle could put an end to the inconsistent set of premises by rejecting SA. By breaking primary substance down into components, he might locate a component which formed a basis for substantial change. Thus he would have the means for bringing generation within the pale of a rational explanation, one which would remove the stigma imposed by Parmenides. Within the scope of S_1 there is no hint of how this analysis of substance might proceed. We might expect, however, that the attempt would continue the general strategy of the pluralists, who identified some continuing element that was the subject of attributes which had the potential to change. The rejection of SA would, nonetheless, be a radical departure from Aristotle's previous philosophy, for it would entail a denial of one of the principles of S_1.

A denial of any of the three propositions above gives a potential solution to the problem. But from Aristotle's point of view, not all of them are live options. As we have seen, he will not countenance a rejection of EI as regards substances. In this respect he is faithful to his philosophical roots. Furthermore, his commitment to a philosophy of common sense makes it impossible for him to reject G. For it is a commonly accepted fact that men, animals, and plants come to be and perish. In his attempt to justify the beliefs of common sense Aristotle carries a heavier burden than the pluralists, who did not blush to call generation a matter of appearance, or to call a perception a matter of convention. Aristotle, for his part, is committed to saving the phenomena, and he regards G as part of the phenomena. In any case, a denial of G is really no solution to the Eleatic challenge, but only a concession to it that the most problematic species of change cannot be defended as part of a rational philosophy of nature. The only live option is to deny SA, and hence to reject one of the props of S_1. At this point a modification of S_1 becomes a reality. The only question is, how serious the modification will be.

But the immediate problem is to determine how one should analyse subtance so as to answer the Eleatic challenge for subtantial change. And here the schema of accidental change we found in S_1 comes into play. According to the schema, there is a substratum, S, which continues throughout the change. There are also two contrary attributes, say F and H, which are in the substance at successive time. S can serve as a foundation for the change: there is always some being present, so the danger of something coming to be from nothing does not arise. Similarly, F is a being, so that when H appears it does not replace nothing but rather another being. Within the context of the schema, no radical deficiencies of being appear. The key to this schema is primary substance. Since, according to the principles of S_1, everything that is is either a primary substance or predicated of a primary substance—that is, dependent on it in some way—the presence of primary substance is enough to ensure a continuity of being throughout the change. We have noted already the Eleatic character of primary substance. In terms of that character, we can say that primary substance is the source of being in S_1 and thus is able to validate any change by underlying it. Thus a change will have the same degree of reality that any non-substance has: it will be a modification of a substance.

The schema succeeds in providing an explanation and validation for a limited range of changes. Can the insights of the schema now be exploited to justify substantial change itself? The schema itself has roots in the pluralists and in Plato's *Phaedo* account, but the former do not recognize the integrity of substance and the latter never clearly articulates the range of application of the principles in question. Can the analysis of a situation of change into a substratum and contrary attributes be applied recursively to a change of a substance itself? Note that the invocation of a substratum, Aristotle's One Under Many principle, is his most fundamental insight into the nature of reality in S_1. In his formal ontology, it is the one under many which is endowed with the full measure of reality. From this standpoint, to extend the concept of substratum is consistent with the perception that the world must be constructed from the foundations up. It is perhaps to be expected that Aristotle should try to posit a substratum for substance. But even given his predisposition to favour a solution appealing to substrata, the quest for a new foundation is not an easy one.

5.4 MODELS AND THE SCHEMA OF CHANGE

5.4.1 *The Principles of Change*

In *Physics* i Aristotle confronts the problem of change. The argument of the book documents a dialectical path to the discovery of matter. I shall not attempt to give a detailed commentary on the book, since the progress of Aristotle's inquiry can be noted by a few landmarks along the way. But I shall provide a loose philosophical commentary designed to bring out the structure of his inquiry. What I wish to stress is that the nature of the problem itself, together with certain philosophical commitments and predilections that Aristotle brings to it, enforces a rethinking of the premises of his philosophy. By observing the dynamics of Aristotle's inquiry we can identify the occasion on which the momentous passage from S_1 to S_2 took place and motivate that development.

First let us note some preliminary steps that Aristotle takes. In addressing the problem of change he formulates the question in terms of the number of principles required to explain change. The inquiry takes on a Platonic ring when he begins laying out the problem systematically at the beginning of Chapter 2. Are the principles one, or more than one; if one, motionless or in motion; if more than one, finite or infinite? The carefully martialled phalanx of double questions recalls Plato's painstaking scrutiny of being in the *Parmenides*. Nevertheless, the queries provide the occasion for a dialectical survey of opinions. Aristotle notes that it is not properly part of a study of natural philosophy to refute denials of motion, but true to form, he engages in the debate. The result of his skirmish with the Eleatics is mainly negative—to reject one alternative. However, he does tacitly create an important framework for the ensuing discussion: he provides a historical and dialectical backdrop for the inquiry concerning change. It is indeed thanks to the Eleatics that natural philosophy has to take the problem so seriously. Yet one would think from his cavalier handling of the Eleatics (3, 186ª10 ff.) that the challenge was a trivial one. The structure of the rest of the book belies this impression, as well it ought.

Aristotle pursues a more constructive path through the *physikoi* in Chapters 4–6. He extracts from them first the point that the contraries must be principles (5, 188ª19 ff.), which point he seconds and supports (ª30 ff.). Change cannot come from any chance attribute, for example, from musical to white, but it must come from an opposite, for example, not-white, and specifically an appropriate contrary, for example, black. Waterlow (1982: 7) has argued that this requirement is not a merely logical one, but one that reflects actual constraints on change.[22] For instance, in order for an object to become white it must previously be coloured, that is, have an attribute in the same range as white. Waterlow is right in saying that Aristotle's point is not merely logical. But his point still seems to be a conceptual rather than an empirical one. For the presupposition of a change is some contrast between the initial state and the final state, where this contrast is based on a difference within the same *conceptual* category. An account of the physical causes and conditions of a change must be posterior to the conceptual recognition of the change.

In Chapter 6 Aristotle extracts the further point that there must be a substratum for the contraries. That substratum is the substance in which contraries inhere. Aristotle's arguments here, for example, are that Love and Strife (of Empedocles) must have a third thing to act on—a point that does not establish Aristotelian substance as a third thing—and that contraries are not the substance of anything, a question-begging piece of Aristotelianism. Satisfied with these dialectical arguments, Aristotle comes to the tentative conclusion that there are three principles of change ($189^{b}16$–18).

Aristotle's survey of the literature shows an Aristotelian bias. It is not by chance that the principles he turns up are precisely those of the *Categories* schema of change. This is not to say Aristotle is being disingenuous; he is simply making his usual assumption that the history of ideas is cumulative and directed toward the true philosophy, which happens to be realized in his own theory. But for our part, we need not be taken in. The historical discussion is a mask behind which Aristotle introduces the schema of change we have already met. Thus far, then, we have nothing new in the way of philosophical insight other than an explicit invocation of the schema as a potential solution to the problem of change.

5.4.2   A Generalization of the Schema

Chapter 7 is the pivotal chapter of the book, and indeed the turning-point of Aristotelian philosophy. In it Aristotle takes recourse to some facts of ordinary language to tease out the

---

[22] On some problems with Aristotle's claims see Bostock (1982: 190).

solution to the Eleatic challenge.[23] He asks us to consider three sentences:

(1) The man becomes musical (or educated, cultured).
(2) The unmusical becomes musical.
(3) The unmusical man becomes a musical man.

He distinguishes between simple elements of this hypothetical situation, namely Man, Unmusical, Musical, and compounds, for example, Musical Man. On the assumption that all these sentences describe the same situation, we make the following observations: the compound does not remain through the change, for Unmusical Man becomes Musical Man. On the other hand, not every element changes, for Man continues through the change.

Seizing on this example, Aristotle generalizes the point to apply to all cases of change (190^a13 ff.). In every case there is a factor that continues throughout the change and a factor that does not continue. What does not continue is the contrary attribute that is replaced by its contrary. Again appealing to the linguistic evidence, Aristotle cites the following sentences:

(4) The man comes to be musical from being unmusical.
(5) The statue comes to be from bronze.

Aristotle uses these sentences to illustrate the point that in general, though not without exception, the contrary is said to be that *from* which something comes to be. We say (4) but we do not say 'He came to be musical from being a man.' On the other hand we do mention the continuant in (5) as the source, whereas we do not say (in Greek) 'The bronze becomes a statue.'[24]

As yet Aristotle has not made an explicit application of his

---

[23] Cf. Wieland (1960: 212–14) and (1962: 112 ff.), Charlton (1970: pp. x–xii), Jones (1974: 477 ff.), Bostock (1982: 183), Waterlow (1982: 12).

[24] Code (1976: 360 f.) interprets 190^a25 f., '[we say] not [the] bronze [comes to be a] statue' as meaning 'we *not only* say . . .'. He argues that if we do not interpret the passage this way it will contradict both 189^b32–190^a13 and the lines that follow 190^a25 f.. I do not agree. 189^b32 ff. deals with accidental change, as does the passage following the quotation. But 190^a25 f. deals with change of a stuff, a change which Aristotle later denies is alteration (*Ph.* vii. 3, 245^b3 ff.), citing linguistic evidence: we use the adjectival 'thaten' expression in such cases. (Cf. Ross's references, 1936: 492 ad loc.) In other words, the matter is not spoken of in nominal form, as a subject (cf. Wieland 1962: 131 f.). But we do refer to the matter by the noun form in cases of accidental predication or alteration (245^b12–6^a1). There is, then, a difference in the logical form of a description of a material changing its shape and the description of an accidental change. Note also that in the disputed passage, Aristotle marks a transition to descriptions of accidental change

principle that there must be some continuing factor to the case of substantial change. At ᵃ33 ff. he argues for such an application:

In other cases [sc. than those of substantial change] it is clear that something must underlie what comes to be . . . But that substances too, and everything else[25] which is said to come to be *simpliciter*, come to be from some substratum, can be seen by investigation. For there is always something which underlies, from which something comes to be; for instance plants and animals come to be from a seed.

As a preliminary, note that Aristotle refers to the coming to be of substances and similar things as coming to be *simpliciter* (or, absolutely, ἁπλῶς). He has in mind the syntax of a statement describing this kind of coming to be: we say of a substance simply that it comes to be (or is born, Gr. γίγνεται), that is, we use no further predicate. But for an accidental change, we add a predicate, for example, 'Socrates came to be *dark*.' The description of substantial change is marked by being simple or absolute, that is, without a predicate, and hence by metonymy Aristotle calls the species of change in question absolute coming to be.[26] By referring to generation in this way Aristotle reinforces the problem that substantial change does not seem to manifest a complex structure in the way that accidental change does. Now we have in the above passage an argument from induction for the principle that, notwithstanding the apparent simplicity of generation, there is a substratum for substantial change:

(1) In all other cases there is a substratum.

(2) In each case of substantial change there is a substratum.

Therefore,

(3) There is a substratum for substantial change.

Unfortunately, however, the inductive evidence given for (2) is in error. For in the paradigm cases, a substratum continues in such a way that it is present in the final product as well as the initial state.

---

with 'however' (μέντοι, 190ᵃ26), signalling a contrast in the logic of the two kinds of expressions. Aristotle's remark seems to be a report of ordinary langauge usage which we should take as a datum. (Bostock 1982: 183 n. 7 thinks Aristotle is guilty of a linguistic confusion here; but there is confusion only relative to English intuitions.)

[25] Ross (1936: 492) excludes ἄλλα (ᵇ2) and reads the καί (ᵇ1) as epexegetical. If he is right, Aristotle may be speaking of substantial change alone.

[26] Cf. the treatment of existence as Being *simpliciter*, A.Po. ii. 2, 90ᵃ9 f., 12.

For instance Man is present in Unmusical Man and also in Musical Man; Bronze is present in Unformed Bronze and Bronze Statue. This requirement is essential for something's being called a substratum, and indeed Aristotle writes the requirement into the definition of matter (9, 192^{a}31 f.). But the seed does not continue in the final product; it has long since disappeared when the organism reaches maturity. Thus the seed is not the substratum of the animal, and there is no evidence to support (2), and hence (3) remains unproved.[27] Aristotle's list of five kinds of unqualified generation (190^{b}5–9) is meant to provide further inductive confirmation that there is always a substratum (^{b}9 f.). Yet three of the kinds are illustrated by examples of artefacts while the remaining two do not obviously confirm the claim in question.[28] Thus Aristotle fails to establish that there is a substratum for substantial change.

After giving an exhaustive list of five different ways in which things come to be, Aristotle states two general principles on which his new-found theory of change is predicated:

All the things that come to be in these ways clearly come to be from substrata. So it is clear from the argument that everything that comes to be is always composite: there is something which comes to be, and there is something which comes to be this in one of two senses—as either the substratum or the opposite. (190^{b}9–13)

[27] For an attempt to save Aristotle's seed example, see Waterlow (1982: 47). She holds (p. 22) that for Aristotle 'the possibility of change and becoming depends upon the metaphysical distinction between things and properties that are not things . . .'. On my interpretation this is false: the possibility of change depends upon the more general distinction between *substrata* (including non-substantial matter) and *features* (including substantial form). Jones (1974: 488–90 *et passim*) argues that e.g. the animal comes from the embryo, which does not remains, and that in general the matter is not a continuant but an individual item from which the resultant comes to be. Cf. Charlton (1970: 131 f.). This view seems to contradict Aristotle's definition of matter at *Ph.* i. 9, 192^{a}31 f. and to make nonsense of his whole notion of substratum. See the criticisms of this position in Code (1976). On the seed example, see Code (1976: 364 f.). Couloubaritsis (1980: 177) stresses that the seed example is pre-theoretical.

[28] Bostock (1982: 185 f.) rightly notes that 190^{a}31–^{b}10 is essentially an empirical inquiry that prepares for a conceptual argument on the need for a substratum for substance. Yet it is important to realize that the empirical inquiry does not offer strong support for a substratum for substance. The two non-artefact examples Aristotle gives are that things come to be by addition, as in the case of things that grow, and those that come to be by alteration (ἀλλοίωσις), as in the case of things whose matter is transformed. But the former is a case of growth, not genesis, and the latter is problematic because it requires us to distinguish a kind of alteration that is not qualitative change but substantial change.

The two principles Aristotle recognizes here are the following:

SC: There is a substratum for every change.

CC: All things that come to be are composite.

Aristotle holds that it is a fact that substances come to be:

GS: Substances come to be.

From these the two principles and the fact, it follows that

CS: Substances are composite.

But CS entails not-SA. And SA is an axiom of S_1. Thus we have as a conclusion of the argument in *Ph.* i. 7 the theorem that overthrows S_1. So far, however, we have no more evidence for SC than for (2) above. Aristotle has plainly moved from the relatively unproblematic case of accidental change to the problematic case of substantial change to establish the result. Yet his only proof for the claim that there is substratum for substantial change is the false analogy that plants and animals come to be from a seed. He has picked up on a sentence whose surface structure misleadingly suggests that it describes a generation from a substratum, whereas it only describes a generation from a previously existing source. Is that sufficient reason to overthrow a first principle of S_1?

5.4.3 *Obstacles to the New Theory*

Thus far what we have observed is a hasty generalization from the schema of change implicit in the S_1 characterization of substance to a general schema of change, in which it is asserted that there is a substratum for every change. Call this principle the Substratum for Change principle, SC above. The chief attraction of SC seems to be the promise that it holds the key to answering the Eleatic challenge. In Chapter 8 Aristotle exploits the schema to that end. Perhaps an examination of his use of the new principle will shed light on his justification for it.

Aristotle makes use of the description of a doctor doing something or changing to expose a fallacy in the Eleatic challenge (8, 191ᵃ36 ff.). For instance, we may say 'The doctor builds a house' or 'The doctor turns grey.' These statements can be true decriptions of events, but they are misleading. For it is not in the doctor's capacity as a doctor that he builds the house, or in his professional role that he turns grey. He builds in his capacity as a builder, and he turns grey in so far as he is dark-haired—or, even more precisely, his hair turns grey in so far as it was not grey. Ordinary descriptions like 'The doctor builds a house' and 'The doctor turns grey' invite sophistical objections to scientific inquiries and thus generate misinformation. The source of the problems is that the events in question are described under an *irrelevant* description (κατὰ συμβεβηκός). The remedy is to give a properly scientific description of the facts—what I shall call a perspicuous description. By constructing perspicuous descriptions we can forestall or dissolve various pseudo-problems, sophistical and otherwise. The philosopher can accept ordinary descriptions for everyday purposes, but if objections arise based on a mistaken dependence on irrelevant details of the description, he should take recourse to the perspicuous description.

Now the Eleatic understands the statement 'The doctor came to be grey from not being grey' as an instance of the scheme '*S* came to be from not being', and he understands this scheme in the sense of 'What is came to be from what is not.' Now even this sentence is ambiguous, but as Aristotle notes, the Eleatic understands 'what is not' as 'what is not *as such*' (191ᵇ9 f.), that is, 'What exists comes from what does not exist.'[29] This, according to the Eleatic, is the deep structure of every description of change; and since the statement is paradoxical, change is impossible.

According to Aristotle, the Eleatic gives a mistaken interpretation. What we assert when we say that the doctor turns grey from not being dark is not that he, or his hair, or greyness comes into being from non-existence. We mean that what is grey comes to be so from not being grey. In Aristotelian terminology, the substratum comes to be in a certain state from its privation. Schematically, *S* comes to be *F* from being not-*F*. Now what we represent schematically by not-*F* is exactly what Aristotle means by 'privation'. Aristotle's reply to the Eleatics is that 'What is comes to be from what is not' need not entail 'Something comes to be out

---

[29]   *GC* i. 3, 317ᵇ25–31 suggests that Aristotle's paradigm case of what-is-not as such is not so much one of simple non-existence, i.e. non-being, as one of complete indeterminacy or nothingness, i.e. not-being *F*, for any *F* whatsoever. This seems to mark a general tendency of the Greek tradition. See Mourelatos (1976) on the early tradition, Owen (1971: 247 *et passim*) on Plato. But whatever Aristotle's specific analysis of what is not, the diagnosis of the contrast between the Eleatic's interpretation of the phrase and the interpretation relevant to the context can be paralleled by the 20th-century contrast between existential and the predicative senses of the verb 'to be'.

of nothing.' Although a description of a change always involves a negative, the negative does not denote non-existence but rather a deprived state. In terms of Aristotle's scheme, the Eleatic takes the negation to attach to Being *simpliciter*, whereas it only applies to a particular mode of being, being *F*. The perspicuous description always describes the change in question in terms of a contrast between not being *F* and being *F*, so that the possibility of absolute Being arising from absolute Non-Being never presents itself. In Aristotle's words:

We ourselves say that nothing comes to be absolutely from what is not, but that in some sense there is coming to be from what is not, in an incidental way—for something comes to be from privation, which is of itself not-being, but which does not persist as an ingredient. Yet this is perplexing, and it seems paradoxical that something should come to be from what is not. (191^{b}13–17)

In a similar way, a positive description of a change, say 'The hair became grey from being black' does not license an inference to 'Being comes to be from Being', for it is always some mode of being that is described as contrasting with another in the pespicuous description: *S* comes to be *G* from being *F* (^{b}17 ff.).

Thus Aristotle has used his distinction to overthrow the Eleatic challenge. This is no small feat, and indeed merits the greatest praise for the author. However, we must return to the question which we asked before looking at the argument of Chapter 8. What justifies Aristotle in generalizing the schema of change to substances? Thus far we have seen no further need or justification for that step. For the fallacious Eleatic inference can be blocked without including substance in the theory of change. All that is needed is a conspicuous counter-example to the Eleatic's move from a negative description of change to the assertion that something comes to be from nothing.

We must note three factors that come into play here. (1) Aristotle evidently is not merely interested in subverting the Eleatic prohibition against change. He wishes to come up with a general theory of change of his own. As we have noted, the schema of change borrowed from *Categories* 5 is the most promising account in S₁. (2) As we have also noted, Aristotle believes that as a matter of fact, substances do come into being and perish. This is a datum of ordinary experience that must be defended philosophically. (3) Substantial change itself is the most vulnerable kind of change. Since substance is the ground of being in the Aristotelian philosophy, there is a real threat the substance may prove to be a being that comes to be from non-being or absolute not-being. Thus it is incumbent to provide the same sorts of protection for substantial change as for accidental change. Given Aristotle's commitments to a general theory of change, to the genesis of substances, and to the avoidance of creation *ex nihilo*, and to the prior One Under Many principle, there is a presumption in favour of extending the schema of change.

Let us return for a moment to the S_1 schema of change. There is a substratum, namely substance, which supports contrary features at different times. We might diagram the schema as shown in Fig. 5.1. If we imagine the vertical axis of the diagram to represent the

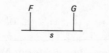

FIG. 5.1. S_1 Schema of Change

scale of being with reference to universality, such that F and G are universals and s is a particular, and if we take the horizontal axis to represent time, we have a picture of one feature succeeding another in time. Now with reference to the schema of change thus represented, we can ask some difficult questions of substantial change. The point that I wish to make is that even granted a strong motivation on Aristotle's part to generalize the schema, and even excusing his mishandling of the evidence for a substratum of substantial change, there remain serious conceptual obstacles to a generalization of the schema. The problems that arise are these: (1) what is the substratum for substantial change? (2) What are the features that enter into the substratum? (3) How are these features contraries? The problems are in part conceptual and in part empirical. The conceptual part consists of trying to make sense of the elements of the schema as applied to substantial change. The empirical part consists in trying to identify the physical counterparts of the theoretical elements so as to interpret and confirm or correct the general conception.

Let us take as an example of substantial change the coming to be of an oak tree. Aristotle is inclined to identify the substratum of the change as the acorn. But as we have seen, this identification cannot be correct. For the acorn does not persist in the change. Furthermore, there is no feature that seems to enter into the acorn *per se* such that the tree can be said to be the product of the modification of the acorn by that feature. And *a fortiori* there is no contrary to such a feature. Thus we are without any empirical basis for applying the schema of change to the case of an oak tree. The oak tree has a *source*, but it does not have a substratum as far as we have seen.

Do the linguistic descriptions of change with which Aristotle started in Chapter 7 reveal any basis for applying the schema? The cases of accidental change of course do not show how to apply the schema, which is modelled on accidental changes, to substantial changes. The descriptions of substantial change to which Aristotle alludes are of the type 'The oak comes to be from the acorn'—which we have seen presents a specious analogy to a description of something arising out of a substratum. But there is one example which precisely describes something arising out of a substratum: 'A statue comes to be from bronze' (190^a25). Here we have a case in which the ἐκ 'from' identifies the substratum; there is a substratum; and there is an object that comes to be in a non-accidental sense.

5.4.4 The Model for Substantial Change

The bronze statue example is introduced without fanfare, and indeed Aristotle produces it only to show that there are exceptions to the rule of thumb that 'from' singles out the contrary. For in the bronze statue description, 'from' introduces the substratum.[30] I would like to suggest, however, that this unpretentious example is in a certain sense the turning-point of Aristotelian philosophy. For although the example appears unobtrusively and as part of an oblique argument, it provides a conceptual bridge that makes the transition from the atomism of S_1 to the hylomorphism of S_2 possible. In brief, it suggests a *model* for substantial change.

We will not be in a position to appreciate the role of the statue example without a preliminary understanding of the place of

[30] See Barnes (1982: 39 f.), Waterlow (1982: 11, 17 f.) on the logic of ἐκ 'from'/ 'out of'. Although Aristotle could have exploited the logic of ἐκ to make his points, he does not do so here. Notice that he sometimes does emphasize the semantic analysis: *GA* i. 18, 724^a20 ff.; *Met.* v. 24; xiv. 5, 1092^a21 ff.

models in general in theory formation. Mary Hesse (1966) has made an especially perceptive study of models and their role in science.[31] According to her, models are not simply tools to be used in the context of discovery and then discarded when a satisfactory formalization is reached. For although formalization is one of the chief victories of science, it is also one of the chief obstacles to further research. In a highly formalized theory it becomes problematic what empirical phenomena correlate with the terms and statements of the theory. It is precisely at this point that the model becomes indispensable. The model provides a concrete analogy to the highly abstract and formal theory in such a way that it suggests correlations. Moreover, the model assists the scientist to exploit the theory in new ways, since it suggests new areas of exploration. In certain cases the points of analogy with the model may break down; for instance both the wave model and the particle model of light fail to account for all the phenomena. However, this does not mean that we can dispense with models in our theorizing. It simply means that sometimes we need a complex model or a plurality of models. Overall, models provide the scientist with a non-arbitrary method for introducing new correlations and testing these, one which is essential if a theory is to grow and submit to new tests.

Much of Hesse's argument in her first essay is directed toward the controversy between those who, like N. R. Campbell, hold that models are an essential part of scientific theorizing, and those who, like Pierre Duhem, hold that they are dispensable adjuncts to the essentially formalist project of science. Into that controversy we need not enter, since we are not dealing with science *per se*, but rather a quasi-scientific philosophy. What is crucial for the present study is to determine the role of models and the extent of their importance for Aristotle. Of course Aristotle himself has a kind of meta-theory in the *Posterior Analytics*, which we may or may not wish to take as indicating a meta-theoretical commitment to formalism.[32] However, we have already noted that Aristotle's commitments in S_1 do not necessarily carry over to S_2. In any case, we shall be dealing chiefly with his *practice* in S_2 and not his meta-theoretical view of what he is doing. Thus it is to illuminate Aristotle's actual practices in theory construction and elaboration

---

[31] Cf. also Black (1962: ch. 13).
[32] On this question, see Łukasiewicz (1957: 15–17).

that we must consider the general function of models in theories.

Before we return to Aristotle, I would like to call attention to one more way in which models may be seen as crucial to theories. This is in the terminology used and even in the conceptualization that results from using certain terms with their conceptual connotations. At a certain inchoate stage of a scientific theory the scientist may borrow terms from another theory because he is trying to analyse a problematic subject-matter in terms of an established science.[33] The terms become imbedded in the very principles of the theory and tend to structure the theory according to their own internal logic. For instance, the early theory of electricity was understood by analogy to hydraulic phenomena. Hence terms like 'current', 'capacity', 'resistance', and 'electron flow' came to be applied to electrical phenomena. As electrical theory developed equations of its own and disanalogies were found with hydraulic phenomena, the theory became less dependent on the model. In this way terms can come to be fossilized within a theory. At one time such terms may have been an organic part of a vibrant theory. On the other hand, a theory may not outgrow the model, or it may not yet have outgrown it at a certain stage of development. When this is the case, that is, when the model itself plays a role in actually structuring a theory, I shall call the model a *constitutive model*.

Accidental Change		Craft Production		Substantial Change
qualities		shape		?
———	: :	———	: :	———
substance		material		?

FIG. 5.2.   Analogy between changes

I would like to suggest that the obstacles we have observed in generalizing the schema of change of S_1 can partially be overcome by using a model, and that Aristotle did tacitly use a model to overcome them. We have seen that in *Physics* i. 7 Aristotle found that ordinary language descriptions of changes supported the schema to the extent of showing a complex relationship of

[33] Kuhn's findings (1970: 132–4, cf. 90) suggest that revolutionary new paradigms of scientific research may result from applying the concepts of one science to those of another under certain circumstances.

exchange of features in a substratum. In the problematic case of substantial change, however, the linguistic evidence gave no similar grounds for analysis. Incidentally, Aristotle noticed that a case like a description of the coming to be of a statue did refer to a substratum. Fig. 5.2 considers an analogy as a proportion.[34]

In the case of accidental change, we have contrary qualities (or quantities or places) which belong to a substance at different times. The overall structure is one of a substratum with incompatible features which cannot inhere in it at the same time, but which can replace each other at different times. In the case of craft production, differences of shape inhere in the material. Those differences are incompatible with one another, and they do exist as modifications of a substratum. The substratum is a stuff which lends itself to different shapes.

How then can we bring the problematic case of substantial change under the schema? By making use of the analogy of craft production as a model for substantial change we can solve two-thirds of the conceptual problem. For if we take craft production as paradigmatic, we can determine analogically what the substratum and what the features are of substantial change. This will leave us only with the problem of determining in what sense there are contrary features in the change. The final feature in the coming to be of a substance will be whatever corresponds to the shape of the craft product. The substratum will be whatever corresponds to the material. What these things actually are may still be problematic, but the problem will be one of a lower order than the conceptual problem. It will be a relatively empirical problem to determine what fills the role of shape and material. If one should make a mistaken identification, this will not overthrow the conceptual scheme, but only call for a more careful interpretation of that scheme.

The strategy which I have just sketched for generalizing the schema of change can be discerned in *Physics* i. 7—not, perhaps, so much in a conscious plan as in the unfolding of the exposition. I have already noted that the statue example is introduced by the way. At 190^b5 ff. Aristotle introduces a list of different kinds of changes to show that all involve a substratum.

The things that come to be in an absolute way come to be either (*a*) by change of shape, as a statue, (*b*) by addition, as things that grow, (*c*) by

---

[34] See Hesse's treatment of proportion in analogies (1966: 64 ff.).

subtraction, as a herm from stone, (d) by composition, as a house, (e) by alteration, as in things whose material [ὕλη] turns.

Note that in these five examples three are drawn from craft productions. The last example is one in which the alteration is not an accidental change but a transformation of a material resulting in a new object.[35] Here again the material–shape analogy is not far removed from the case at hand. I suggest that Aristotle is thinking in terms of the craft analogy as he elaborates these examples. Strictly speaking changes of shape should, on the S_1 analysis, count as accidental changes, since shape is a kind of quality.[36] But here Aristotle is not attending to this restriction, which he abandons in S_2.[37] In his mind the craft production is more closely linked with substantial change than accidental change, and paradigmatic for an understanding of substantial change.

Aristotle pushes the model by treating craft productions as paradigm examples of the feature–substratum analysis:

So it is clear from the argument that everything that comes to be is always composite: there is (1) something which comes to be, and there is (2) something which comes to be this in one of two senses—as either (a) the substratum [ὑποκείμενον] or (b) the opposite [ἀντικείμενον]. I mean by 'opposite' Unmusical and by 'substratum' Man, and furthermore Formlessness and Shapelessness and Disorder are opposites, Bronze and Stone and Gold are substrata. (190ᵇ10–17)

After giving his examples in terms of the unproblematic case of accidental change, he applies the distinctions to craft examples, which evidently are stand-ins for substantial change.

We have left till now the problem of what the contraries could be. The passage just quoted shows what Aristotle's answer is: one feature is described in positive terms and the other as the negation of that feature. Thus the opposite of Musical is Unmusical, of Formed is Unformed. This analysis marks a departure from the schema of S_1, in which the features involved in a change are both described in positive terms, for example, 'black' and 'white'. It was

---

[35] See Ross (1936: 493) for an explication of (e): e.g. wine turns to vinegar. Ross takes ὕλη here as an anticipation or a gloss. On the contrary, it is perfectly in place as a *non-technical* use of the term, as Wieland (1962: 125) and Bostock (1982: 187 n. 12) observe. On the semantic development of the term ὕλη see A. Mansion (1945: 74 and n. 65), Solmsen (1961) and (1963: 492), Wieland (1962: 135 f. and n. 24, 210), Bostock (1982: 187), Graham (1984: 48 f.).

[36] *Cat.* 8, 10ᵃ11.   [37] See *Ph.* vii. 3, 245ᵇ6 ff.

146 The Hylomorphic Turn

required that these features be contraries, but they were not analysed as contradictories. Here Aristotle uses the correct general term for 'opposite', ἀντικείμενον rather than the specific term for 'contrary', ἐναντίον, to designate the positive feature and its negation.[38]

The new analysis seems to grow out of the problematic of *Physics* i. For the underlying problem of the book is to formulate a reply to the Eleatic challenge: 'How can what is come to be from what is not?' It is only by studying changes under a description where there is a process from what is not to what is that Aristotle can face this challenge. Of course it is also true that only by studying such a contrast can even all cases of accidental change be brought under a single description-type. For there is no contrary to Musical as there is to White. Nonetheless, in making this simple move Aristotle has transcended the schema of change he suggested in *Categories* 5 and reiterated in the earlier chapters of *Physics* i. Now he requires that the features in a change be not contraries but contradictories.[39]

This move is essential for allowing Aristotle to bring substantial change into a general theory of change. For it is a characteristic of substance that it has no contraries (*Cat.* 5, 3^b24 f.). Thus there could be no way to generalize the S_1 schema if we kept the requirement that the features be contraries. But for every possible feature it makes sense to talk of a contradictory. For the feature Formed there is the feature Not-Formed. Of course a problem arises as to whether this negative feature is really a feature or the absence of a feature. Aristotle's language in Chapter 7 does nothing to dispel the impression that the negative description of the feature denotes an actual feature.[40] However, he does finally give a technical term to what is denoted: στέρησις (191^a14, also 190^b27). As we have seen, this term signifies a deprivation in S_1. Here, however, it means a privation, something, Aristotle says in Chapter 8, that is 'of itself not-being' (191^b15 f.). This may be a roundabout way of saying what we would like Aristotle to say, that

---

[38] Cf. Wieland (1962: 127 f.), who interprets the move as part of an attempt to identify the subject of change.

[39] On στέρησις as a contradictory, see *Met.* x. 4, 1055^b3 ff. Of course in one sense only propositions can be contradictories.

[40] Note the treatment of the privation in 190^a17–21, where it is spoken of as a positive element.

a privation is not a negative feature, but the absence of a feature.[41]
With the concept of privation established, Aristotle can safely
proceed to generalize the schema of change to the most problematic
case.

To be precise, however, we must note that the new schema of
change is neither a generalization, nor a logical extension, of the
old one: it is a more general schema that grows out of it. For there
are fundamental differences between the S_1 schema and the newly
won S_2 schema. Most notably, the new schema does not treat the
features as contraries. Consequently, change cannot in general be
analysed as an exchange of contraries. The features are opposites,
and in particular contradictories, or at least expressed by contradictory predicates. Since, however, there is reason to believe that
the negatively expressed term does not denote a real predicate,
but rather the absence of a predicate, change is not an exchange of
features at all. Rather *it is the acquisition of a positive feature*,
which paradigmatically is a structural determination, by the
substratum. Change is a process from not-being to being, and
ideally a progression toward a higher level of integration. The
direction of change from privation to possession carries with it an
inference that change is naturally progressive—a suggestion that
will have interesting implications for the development of S_2.[42]

Thus although S_1 does not really have a developed theory of
change, it implies one. And although the S_2 theory of change
grows out of the tacit S_1 account, nevertheless, the S_2 theory of
change is *different* from the S_1 theory in a fundamental way. For
there is a symmetry about the S_1 theory which is not present in the
S_2 theory. According to the S_1 theory change is mere exchange of
features. Since these are ontologically indifferent qualities, there is
in principle no distinction in value between a change from F to G
and a change from G to F—say between Socrates' changing from

---

[41] See also 191ª6 f., where the talk of a privation and form is reduced to talk of
the absence/presence of a feature. This is Aristotle's considered position. See *Met.*
x. 4, 1055ᵇ3–29; vii. 7, 1032ᵇ3–5; iv. 6, 1011ᵇ19 f. and references at Bonitz 700ª3 f.
Against this, see Cherniss (1944: 270 f.), who claims that στέρησις is not mere
negation.

[42] Of course changes to a less organized state are describable in this mode also.
Cf. Wieland (1962: 134 n. 24), who, however, goes too far in saying that no value
judgement is involved in the scheme. Strictly speaking, he is right, but our
preferred way of referring to changes *suggests* a favoured direction of change. The
thesis of *Met.* ix. 8, that actuality is prior to potentiality, is a philosophical
justification of this pre-theoretical suggestion. See ch. 7.3.

pale to tan or tan to pale. But in the S_2 theory, change is from absence to presence of a feature. If that feature is a feature of a higher ontological order—for example, a substantial form—there will be a progression in one direction and a regression in another. On the basis of this asymmetry we might consider change in one direction to be natural and the other unnatural. Here a subtle revision of principles presents us with a radically different perspective on change. This is perhaps the first instance in which the hylomorphic turn produces revolutionary insights into the world.

Yet we are ahead of ourselves. For as yet Aristotle has not recognized matter as a principle, nor has he clearly moved from the logical to the ontological plane. Turning to the question of how many principles there are, Aristotle observes:

The substratum is one in number but two in form—for the man, the gold, and in general the *matter* are countable. For they are more particular, and what comes to be does not come to be from them in an incidental way. But the privation and the contrary are incidental to the process. (190ᵇ23–7)

Here 'matter' still appears in a non-technical sense.[43] It is simply a generic term for material or the material object in such a way that it is conceived of as continuous with a concrete substance like man. Yet we can see from this use how matter might by extension come to apply to substratum for change, again as a generic term.

What we might expect Aristotle to call matter, namely the substratum for substantial change, Aristotle calls in 191ᵃ8 the 'underlying nature' (ὑποκειμένη φύσις):[44]

The underlying nature is knowable by analogy. For as the bronze is to the statue, or the wood to the bed, or the matter and[45] what is formless before it gets form to one of the things having form, so is the underlying nature to the substance and the particular and the being. (191ᵃ7–12)

---

[43] Cf. Wieland (1962: 130 n. 19), Bostock (1982: 187 n. 12). I previously (1984: 49) took this occurrence in a quasi-technical sense to anticipate the definition at 192ᵃ31 f.; that view now seems to me an overinterpretation.

[44] Cf. Bostock (1982: 187).

[45] Diels and Ross exclude the three preceding words (omitted by Simplicius) on the grounds that they spoil the analogy between unformed : formed and matter : substance. But 'unformed' is tacit in all the examples, while the substratum is explicit, so some mention of the substratum is necessary to preserve the points of similarity. See also Bostock (1982: 187 n. 12), who stresses that ὕλη is used non-technically.

Aristotle does not apply the term 'matter' directly to the substratum for substantial change, but only to the model. Nonetheless, the model of craft production determines the conceptualization of the relevant states of affairs. The proportion Aristotle uses to explicate the elements of substantial change is: material : form [in craft products] :: x : substance. The x must be understood as the analogue of material in a product, whatever that may signify for a natural substance. The concept of matter as the substratum for substantial change is clearly present here, as an extension of what Aristotle calls matter in 190^{b}25. It is interesting to note Aristotle's suggestion here that for the understanding of the substratum for substantial change there is no recourse but to the model. The analogy to the model exhausts the cognitive content of this sense of matter.

Thus far we have seen some striking evidences of how the example of craft production, introduced as it is in an incidental way, insinuates itself as a paradigm example of change and then begins to serve as a model for the problematic case of substantial change. But we can step back and look at the influence of the example in a broader context of conceptualization. From this seemingly innocent discussion of change in Chapter 7 we see a new technical terminology emerging: the elements of change are matter and form. The term ὕλη, which Aristotle had never used before, now comes to stand for the substratum of change; the term εἶδος, which he had used only to designate species or Platonic Form, now comes to stand for any feature arrived at by change. Where do these terms come from, or, in the case of εἶδος, what motivates the change of meaning? The obvious answer is that they are dictated by the model. In its technical use, ὕλη is co-opted from the term for material. εἶδος, as Aristotle's use of μορφή in 191^{a}10 f. shows, is used by analogy to the non-technical sense of 'figure, shape'. There are, no doubt, some hidden reminiscences of Platonic conceptions here,[46] but for now the important fact is the connection to the model. What we seem to have here is a case like that of early electrical theory in which terms like 'current' and 'electron flow' are borrowed from another subject-matter in order

---

[46] See Cherniss (1944: 90 f.) Solmsen (1960: 83) on the *Phaedo* as an inspiration for Aristotle's principles of change.

to explicate by analogy a relatively obscure field of inquiry.[47] We do not know what the substratum for matter is, nor what feature comes to be present in it. But we do understand an analogous phenomenon in which something comes to be in absolute sense by the shaping of material. We adopt the conceptual categories appropriate to the analogue, thereby taking it over as a model.

It is as yet an open question how significant the craft model is for S_2. A model can serve a merely heuristic function which, although it is important for a certain stage of theory construction, may be dispensable. On the other hand, a model may prove to be what I have called a constitutive model, one so intimately linked to a theory that it cannot be dissociated from it. I shall argue that the craft model is closely connected both with the initial articulation of S_2 and its continued interpretation. For now we may note that the model is crucial for an adquate account of change—an account which meets the Eleatic challenge for all recognized types of change. On the basis of the model we can now fill out the conceptual development from the S_1 scheme of change to the S_2 scheme, as shown in Fig. 5.3. Fig. 5.4 shows how change can be represented still more schematically, so that we see more clearly the influence of the model on the S_2 scheme. As the unformed material is to the formed material in a craft production, so the privation is to the form in the matter of a substantial change. By replacing the m of S_2 with a substratum in general, we get a perfectly general account of change—one which can comprehend the S_1 scheme of accidental change of a substance as well as genesis. Thus the craft analogy, by becoming a model for a hitherto intractable kind of change, mediates the transition to a new conception of change.

S_1	Craft Model I	S_2
qualities	shapes	privation/form
—— : :	—— : :	——
substance	material	matter

FIG. 5.3   Craft Model I

[47] See Hesse (1965) following Black (1962: 38 ff.) on the value of metaphor in extending the terms of an observation language. Of course I claim that the language being developed is ultimately not the *observation* language but the theoretical language.

S_1	Craft Model II	S_2
$Q_1 \to Q_2$	not-$F \to F$	not-$F \to F$
$\dfrac{}{s}$ ::	$\dfrac{\phantom{\text{not-}F \to F}}{m}$ ::	$\dfrac{\phantom{\text{not-}F \to F}}{m}$

FIG. 5.4   Craft Model II

From this point on Aristotle is committed to explicating the phenomena of change in a way consistent with the model. The model of course imposes strictures on our conceptualizing, but in return it promises to provide answers to the hitherto intractable questions of genesis. In Kuhnian terms, it promises to provide a paradigm which will transform problems into puzzles to be solved by following its procedures. Thus there is a pragmatic justification for this hylomorphic turn. Note, however, that the turn is, in substance if not in intent, revolutionary. At one point in the argument Aristotle sets out his general position:

It is clear then that if there are causes and principles of natural entities, from which they ultimately derive and from which they come to be—not accidentally, but with regard to the substance by which they are identified—everything must come to be both from substratum and form [μορφή]. For the musical man is in a certain way composed of Man and Musical; for it is analysed into the definitions of these. It is clear then that everything would come to be *from these elements*. (190^{b}17–23)

Here Aristotle makes use of an example drawn from accidental change to defend the substratum-form analysis for substantial change. The result is an ontological analysis into form and matter. For the final sentence states what the ontological components of things that change are, not the causal sources, since the form is not a source in any sense. Obviously the analysis applies to substance, and consequently Aristotle hereby abandons the ontological simplicity of substance. He invokes SC, the principle that there is a substratum for every change. As we have seen, the evidence for SC in the problematic case of substantial change is its close analogy to craft production. With a new ontology buttressed by a new model the theory of change will be built on a new foundation. Aristotle gives up his first ontology in order to gain a more powerful theory—one that will give a unified theory of change. To use Kuhnian categories again, we may say that the old paradigm generated an anomaly that proved fatal to its extension: it treated substance as ontologically simple while holding that there was subtantial change and holding that change could only be accounted for by analysis. And it is precisely in accommodating substantial change that the new theory proves its worth.

5.5   CONCLUSION

In this chapter we have seen how the problematic of *Physics* i. together with Aristotle's prior commitments to certain philosophic positions and certain 'facts' generate a conception of form and matter. To recapitulate: Aristotle sets himself the task of giving a general account of change, one which will be proof against the Eleatic challenge, namely: 'How can what is come to be from what is not?' In the face of Eleatic refutations, the tradition has managed to justify change at the expense of generation, that is, absolute coming to be. Aristotle, however, has a commitment to defend the phenomena of everyday experience, one of which is generation. But he accepts the Eleatic refutation of *ex nihilo* creation. Thus the only avenue open to him is to show that generation, like other forms of change, consists of a rearrangement of pre-existing elements. At the same time he must show that this particular kind of rearrangement found in generation differs significantly from other kinds of change. Aristotle appeals to his One Under Many principle, which perhaps embodied the most basic insight on his S_1 ontology. There must be an entity to underlie generation as substance underlies accidents and hence accidental change.

The obstacles to this analysis are considerable because, while the elements of accidental change are easily identified from ordinary-language decriptions of a given change, the elements of generation are not so identified. What is the substratum, what are the features that inhere in it, how are these features contraries? Descriptions of natural generation give no clue, because they describe the event in absolute terms, for example, 'Socrates came to be (was born)'. But by examining the text of Chapter 7, we can find that Aristotle, almost by accident, hits upon a kind of change that in important respects mimics natural generation, for which the elements can be identified. In craft production there is a substratum (the material); a prior, relatively unformed state; and a posterior, relatively formed state. By exploiting the characteristics of this example, that is, using it as a model for natural generation, he can solve the conceptual problems of generalizing the schema of change found in S_1. The problem of finding actual realizations of the elements, the matter, privation, and form, can be left as a puzzle to be resolved later.

Thus we can trace the development of hylomorphism from the S_1 conception of substance. We find in *Ph.* i the opportunity and the problem which can make sense of a revision of his principles. Indeed, not only can we tell a good story around *Ph.* i, but we find in the book traces of a dialectic that leads from a non-technical use of the term ὕλη to a technical use. Aristotle introduces the term here in a way which transparently reveals his motivation in introducing it. As Aristotle observes elsewhere, 'The solution of a problem is a discovery' (*EN* vii. 4, 1146^b7 f.). By this account, his postulation of matter is a discovery, one which he reaches by wrestling with a traditional problem within the context of certain constraints. Furthermore, as we argued at the outset of the chapter, *Ph.* i is the earliest work of the physical and metaphysical treatises. Thus it seems plausible to suppose that *Ph.* i not only introduces matter but indeed provides the locus of Aristotle's discovery. This book is a document of the hylomorphic turn. After this landmark work, no theory could be quite the same, and indeed the other physical and metaphysical works presuppose its concepts. *Ph.* i thus opens the door both to the philosophy of nature and to a new metaphysical conception of the world. Accordingly, in resolving the problem of change Aristotle precipitates the development of a new metaphysical system, S_2. The development we have uncovered is an instance that confirms the Change Hypothesis which was proposed at the end of the last chapter. There is no need for any other developmental hypothesis.

There is, however, one kind of hypothesis which we have not considered. That is that there is no development at all: Aristotle always had a theory of matter and only formally introduced it in *Ph.* i. There are two grounds that are sometimes advanced for this claim. First, Aristotle's early works contain theories that entail the existence of matter. Happ (1971: 270), following a remark by Düring (1955: 156) that the early *Protrepticus* makes use of the δύναμις–ἐνέργεια distinction, which presupposes the matter–form distinction, thus infers the existence of a concept of matter in the early Aristotle. But we have already seen that only ἐνέργεια-S presupposes the matter–form distinction, and this concept does not appear in the *Protrepticus* (or in any other early work).[48]

Secondly, Aristotle's predecessors (that is, Plato, or the Academy, or the Presocratics, or all of them) already had the concept of matter and hence it is arbitrary to suppose Aristotle did not inherit the notion.[49] Of course Aristotle encourages this view by his schematic history of philosophy in *Met.* i and his acknowledgement of Plato's receptacle as a forerunner of his concept of matter.[50] Yet a distinction must be made if we are to settle the question. There is a major philosophical difference between a concept of matter as the stuff of the universe, and a concept of matter as a substratum for change. The first notion is essentially a physical, the second a metaphysical concept. Most of Aristotle's predecessors had the former concept, for which Aristotle did the service of providing a generic term. But none of them had the second concept.[51] In particular, Plato's receptacle will not do as a source because it does not form the basis for a theory of change, being rather a locus for instantiation.[52] Of Aristotle's predecessors only Plato comes close enough to Aristotle's level of abstraction to have conceived of a general substratum of change—but Plato approaches the problem in the *Phaedo*, not the *Timaeus*, and he fails to generalize his results in such a way as to

[48] See ch. 4.3.2. Furthermore it is not clear that the *Protrepticus* provides the earliest occurrences of δύναμις-ἐνέργεια, as is often claimed (e.g. by Jaeger 1928: 632–4); I would date the work around or after the transition to S$_2$: see 11.3. On the δύναμις-ἐνέργεια distinction, see ch. 7.

[49] See e.g. Berti (1977: 297–9), Couloubaritsis (1980: 200 ff.).

[50] *Ph.* i. 9, 191^{b}35 ff.; iv. 2, 209^{b}11–16, ^{b}33–210^{a}2; *GC* ii. 1, 329^{a}13–24. Note, however, that in the same breath that Aristotle attributes hylomorphic notions to Plato, he accuses him of conceptual confusions—thus providing prima-facie evidence against his own interpretation. See de Vogel (1949: 204).

[51] See Happ's survey (1971: 82–270), Cherniss (1944: 172 f.).

[52] Cf. Cherniss (1944: 170–3), Ross (1951: 125, 221 f., 233), Solmsen (1960: 42 f.), (1961: 395), Happ (1971: 121–35). The famous gold analogy (*Tim.* 50 A–C) is introduced as the answer to a problem of reference (cf. E. N. Lee 1971: 231); its value for understanding the nature of the receptacle is unclear. Note also that it cannot be taken for granted (as it almost always is) that the *Timaeus* was written before *Ph.* i: on the traditional dating, the Platonic dialogue is late, whereas the Aristotelian treatise was written while Aristotle was at the Academy. See Düring (1955: 154, 156), who raises this possibility against Claghorn (1954)—though the positive evidence he adduces for the view is faulty (Graham 1984: 37–9). Of course if *Ph.* i were the earlier treatise, at least part of ch. 9, which discusses the *Timaeus*, would have to be a later addition. Owen (1953) has argued that the *Timaeus* should be dated early; against this see Cherniss (1957).

arrive at a theory of matter = substratum-for-change.[53] Further-more, since Aristotle's discovery of matter results from his inquiry into the problem of change rather than a problem of material composition, we can infer that the early concept of matter as the stuff of the universe did not play a formative role in the origin of the concept (though it may have influenced its subsequent articulation, as no doubt the *Timaeus* discussion did).[54] Thus there is no reason to maintain the anti-developmentalist position that Aristotle always had a theory or concept of matter.

We have seen that Aristotle arrives at a satisfactory account of change through what amounts to a dialectical engagement with the Greek philosophical tradition. His newly won position leads, however, to the denial of his old position. For the theory of change entails that substance is ontologically complex, which in turn entails that SA is false, from which it follows that S_1 is false. Aristotle does not approach the problem of change with the intention of subverting his own established position, nor does he focus on the metaphysical consequences of his theory of change. He is merely following out an argument to its conclusion. In this sense, he is not a revolutionary. Indeed, given the problem and the constraints, Aristotle's rejection of SA is philosophically economical and eminently sensible—even conservative. Nevertheless, the consequences of his new theory are revolutionary with respect to S_1. But hylomorphism opens new horizons, and henceforth Aristotle is firmly committed to the principle. And so, without methodological fanfare or ideological polemic, Aristotle quietly and unwittingly passes from one world-view to another.

[53] See above, n. 7.
[54] This consideration counts against the theory of Bos (1975); see ch. 4 n. 37.

6

The Growth of S₂: The Four Causes

In Chapter 4 I argued that the Incommensurability Hypothesis was needed to explain the differences between S_1 and S_2. In Chapter 5 I presented a developmental hypothesis which motivated the shift from S_1 to S_2, locating the occasion for the shift in Aristotle's examination of principles of change found in *Ph.* i. If my developmental hypothesis is correct, it should illuminate not only Aristotle's theory of change but also other theories that make up S_1 and S_2. Ideally, the developmental hypothesis CH should reveal how other differences which we have noted between S_1 and S_2 come about—how, for instance, concepts in the philosophy of science are revised and reinterpreted in the new system. Conversely, we would have strong confirmation of the developmental hypothesis if we should find that theories straddling S_1 and S_2 were modified in S_2 in light of hylomorphic principles. In the following chapters I shall undertake two studies which focus on theories appearing in both systems. First I shall examine the development of the four cause theory (FCT) in Chapter 6,[1] and then the theory of actuality in Chapter 7. In these studies I wish to show that characteristic theories of S_2 are the product of a systematic revision of the concepts found in S_1.

6.1 THE DEVELOPMENT OF THE FOUR CAUSE THEORY

The most obvious problem for a developmental theory of FCT to face is that of accounting for the S_1 version of FCT, which appears only in *A.Po.* ii. 11. There are some major prima-facie disagreements between the S_1 account and the S_2 account. In particular, the S_1 account seems to lack a conception of both a *material* cause and a *formal* cause. Scholars have focused on the former, since the latter is usually conflated with the essential cause by scholars and,

---

[1] I shall not distinguish between FCT and FCT* here because I wish to consider the theory as a single theory developing over time.

arguably, by Aristotle. Ross (1949: 638 f.) argues that the logical ground of a conclusion introduced in *A.Po.* ii. 11 is not the material cause; noting differences between the two, he observes that the term for matter appears nowhere in the *Organon*. He hypothesizes that either (*a*) this is an early exposition, before Aristotle had come to his classical four causes, or (*b*) because the material cause will not work as a middle term, he substituted a cause that would work. Barnes (1975: 215 f.) notes that the logical ground is subsumed under the material cause in the *Physics* and *Metaphysics*,[2] and takes this fact as supporting the identity of the causal schemes in S_1 and S_2. Ross seems to think that the material cause is inadequate as a middle term because in *Ph.* ii. 9 Aristotle argues that the matter does not necessitate the form—hence, presumably, the material cause cannot necessitate the conclusion. Barnes rightly objects that material causes can function as middle terms of a syllogism and thus satisfy the thesis of the *A.Po.* As an example, consider the following:

(1) Iron is hard.
(2) The knife is iron.
(3) Therefore, the knife is hard.

This syllogism seems to provide all that is required to certify that the material cause is a middle term.

Barnes's objection suffices to overthrow hypothesis (*b*). But does it overthrow (*a*)? I think not. Rather, it gives added fuel to the other hypothesis. For if Aristotle had recognized that the above syllogism is possible, he would have had a much easier time demonstrating that the material cause is a middle term. Instead, he takes a much more obscure case and fails to convince us of his thesis. Indeed, on Barnes's account, Aristotle's method is logically flawed. For all that Aristotle manages to prove is that a *special case* of the material cause is a middle term, not the generic notion. Thus, although this method would show that one kind of material causes are middle terms, it would not show that all material causes are.[3]

If, then, we suppose that Aristotle writes the S_1 account of FCT in full awareness of the material cause, we are forced to suppose

---

[2] *Ph.* ii. 3, 195^{a}15–19 = *Met.* v. 2, 1013^{b}16–21; ibid., 1, 1013^{a}14–16.
[3] See also Dancy's arguments against taking the logical ground as matter (1978: 373–7). Against Barnes see ibid., nn. 9–11.

that he bungles his exposition. It seems more promising to hypothesize that he composes the S_1 account in ignorance of the material cause. Now at this point we have already amassed considerable evidence to support the view that S_1 has no concept of matter or material causes and that it precedes the discovery of the concept. Accordingly, there is no need to reargue the case for the present passage. What *A.Po.* ii. 11 can provide is a test case for the developmental hypothesis I have supported. Can that hypothesis accommodate an alleged development in FCT? It might seem obvious that it can. But there is at least one major obstacle: if Aristotle did not have the classical theory of causes in mind when he wrote *A.Po.* ii. 11, why did he produce a scheme of *four* causes? Where did that scheme come from if not from an awareness, for example, of the formal and material, the final and efficient causes as complementary pairs? Indeed, since we have seen that FCT is at best peripheral to the S_1 account of scientific explanation, why should he have even developed such a scheme independently of S_2? I regard these problems as serious challenges to a developmental account of FCT. If they can be met, their explanation will provide a preliminary corroboration for TSH. The ultimate test of TSH in this study will be its ability to account for the total development of FCT.

6.1.1   First Stage: Independent Causes

In the *A.Po.* passage Aristotle asserts that since (1) we have knowledge (ἐπίστασθαι) when we know the cause and (2) there are four causes, (3) all of these are middle terms (94ᵃ20–4). The missing premiss of his argument is the assertion that (4) every cause is a middle term, an identification argued for by induction in *A.Po.* ii. 2. Now that Aristotle has distinguished four causes, he must defend (4) in detail. His argument is revealing.

The Logical Ground. He first addresses the mysterious cause he calls the logical ground. After repeating his logical doctrine that two premisses are necessary for a syllogism, he points out that there must be a middle term common to them, which then is the real cause of the deduction. As an example, he gives the syllogism: right angle (A) belongs to half-of-two-right angles (B), B belongs to the angle inscribed in a semicircle (C), hence A belongs to C. The middle term, B, allegedly represents the ground of the deduction, that is, is a kind of cause of it. Commentators tend to focus on the intriguing interrelations between the Aristotelian proof and that of Euclid. But for our purposes the real problem is in the Aristotelian example. For Aristotle to win his point, he must establish that the ground of a conclusion is a middle term. But there is something distinctly odd about the present case. In all the other cases the cause is *expressed* by the middle term; in the present case it is *identical* with the term. For the logical ground of the conclusion is not half-of-two-right-angles but the formal identity of terms expressing half-of-two-right-angles in the two premisses. In other words, it is the identity of the tokens '*B*' and '*B*'. But what makes the tokens identical is just that they are tokens of type '*B*'. Thus the logical ground of the conclusion is not *B*: half-of-two-right-angles, but '*B*': 'half-of-two-right-angles'. Aristotle makes a kind of use/mention error in assimilating the present case to that of the middle term theory of cause.

Essential Cause. Aristotle finds that the geometric syllogism also exemplifies the essential cause (94^a34 f.) In this case there should be no problem: the essential cause is the cause which paradigmatically fits the middle-term scheme ($^a35$ f.). There is, however, an anomaly in the example. If we are to subsume the geometrical syllogism under the essential cause, each predication should represent an essence (τὸ τί ἦν εἶναι). But both of the predications of the example fail to exemplify that relation. For it is certainly not a truth of definition that (*A*) right angle belongs to (*B*) half-of-two-right-angles. Nor is it by definition that *B* belongs to (*C*) angle inscribed in a semicircle.[4] As Kant would say, the judgements in question are synthetic, not analytic. Aristotle could easily have chosen an example in which the predication was essential—for example, Living Thing-Animal-Man. It is curious that he does not supply such an example here. For the real challenge is not to come up with exotic instances of essential causation, but to show that the other causes conform to the pattern of this cause. But what is striking in the present case is that the logical ground and the essential cause allegedly *coincide*. In S₂ it is an established principle that three of the causes can and often do coincide in the case of natural substances: the final, formal, and efficient causes

---

[4] See Ross (1949: 641 f.) and Barnes (1975: 217) for problems in interpreting the essential predication. I am reading $^a35$ f. as a sequel to $^a34$ f.

can be the same; but the material cause is always opposed to the other three.[5] Here a single example illustrates both essential cause and logical ground. This high degree of correlation would be startling if the logical ground really were the material cause.

Moving Cause. As for the cause of movement, Aristotle gives the example of War (A) belongs to the first aggressors (B), B belongs to the Athenians (C), therefore A belongs to C, that is, the Athenians have war waged upon them. The first cause of conflict is B, which shows why A belongs to C. Here the dummy connective 'belongs to' seems problematic in the first premiss. The only relevant way that A can 'belong to' B in the example is for A to be the result of B, or stated as an inverse relation, for B to be the cause of A. But now the syllogism seems to be question-begging, since we have already assigned a causal role to B. One might reply that the syllogism reveals the relation of A to C, and this is not question-begging. Even if we allow this, however, a problem remains of how to construe 'belongs to' in the second premiss so that it is univocal in both uses. That does not seem possible, since in the first premiss the relation is causal, in the second premiss predicative (or perhaps is the relation of identity).[6] Now we might be tempted here to say that although the present example is not a good one, others can be found. But that will not work. For if Aristotle is right all moving causes should be able to be explicated as middle terms, but the present case seems to resist explication. Hence we have not an example but a counter-example.[7]

Final Cause. As an example of final cause, Aristotle gives Health (A) belongs to non-regurgitation of food (B), B belongs to after-dinner walk (C), hence A belongs to C. Aristotle immediately runs into a problem here because the final cause is A, not the middle term B. He assures us that A and B are interchangeable because B is like a definition of A, and thus we can rewrite the syllogism (94^b19–23). What we are supposed to get is not at all clear. Suppose we convert the first premiss:

---

[5] See e.g. *DA* ii. 4, 415^{b}9 ff.

[6] Ross (1949: 643) makes a similar charge against Aristotle's example of the final cause, but he does not notice the problem in the moving-cause example.

[7] See Barnes (1975: 217 f.) on problems with the present cause.

Original syllogism: $A–B$, $B–C$, hence $A–C$
Converted syllogism: $B–A$, $B–C$, hence $A–C$

This rewriting changes the figure of the syllogism, but it does nothing to change the fact that B is the middle term. If he means, on the other hand, that we should replace every occurrence of 'A' with 'B and vice versa, we can at least make the final cause (A) the middle term:

Syllogism interchanging 'A' and 'B': $B–A$, $A–C$, hence $B–C$.

Now the conclusion is that non-regurgitation belongs to after-dinner walk. But health does not mediate this relationship.[8] For although health is a predicate of after-dinner walk, non-regurgitation is not in fact a predicate of health. It is not an accident that the example does not work. To be sure, the kind of explanation we get with final causes is sequential in a way that can be exhibited by a syllogism. But, as Plato taught—and Aristotle realized in his more lucid moments—the sequence is one of means–ends.[9] If I walk after dinner, I do it in order to keep my food down, and I do this for my health, thus C is for the sake of B, which in turn is for the sake of A. The middle term of this series is an end relative to C but a means relative to A. And this holds true for any sequence of final causes: the mediate end is a middle term relative to the final end. Now Aristotle is interested in the final end, which according to Platonic value theory is the only important one.[10] Thus the final cause *per se* does not satisfy Aristotle's formal characterization of causes.[11]

Commentators on *A.Po.* ii. 11 have noticed many, if not all, of the problems in trying to fit the present four causes to the Procrustean middle term theory of cause. Simply put, *none* of the four causes fits the theory. Only the essential cause in general can be accommodated, and we have seen that even that cause admits of counter-examples. It seems to me that there is an

---

[8] Cf. Barnes (1975: 220).

[9] Plato *Lysis* 219 D–E; cf. Aristotle *EN* i. 1, 1094[a]1–22.

[10] Plato *Lysis* 220 A–B; cf. Aristotle *A.Po.* i. 2, 72[a]29 f. Barnes (1975: 220) thinks one example works: shelters for belongings are roofed; houses are shelters for belongings; therefore, houses are roofed. It seems to me that this example provides an essential cause, but not a final cause. For to give a final cause is just to exhibit an explanation as an end or goal, which the example does not.

[11] On the failure of the final cause to satisfy conditions of the middle term, cf. Ross (1949: 642 f.), Hocutt (1974, sec. 6). On further problems with Aristotle's account, see Ross, pp. 643–5.

obvious moral to the story, one that the commentators have been loath to draw: FCT does not support MTC, and in fact is incommensurable with it. This conclusion, however, seems to drive us back to S_2 as a source for FCT. For if FCT is not an integral part of S_1 but it is an integral part of S_2, how else can we account for its appearance in S_1?

Yet if FCT owes its origin to S_2 and it is inserted back into a work of S_1 (or a later draft of such a work), we should expect it to exhibit traits of the S_2 account. Perhaps the most common assumption from the S_2 version is that the four causes form a *system*.[12] Accordingly, we might ask if the account of FCT in the *A.Po.* forms a system as it should on the present hypothesis. In fact there is no evidence that it does. We have found that the logical ground and the essential cause may coincide. But this coincidence is more of an embarrassment than a piece of evidence, because if one is thinking of the logical ground as a version of the material cause, it will be anomalous to have it coincide with the formal cause. On the other hand, if the logical ground is merely a logical cause, it is quite unexceptionable to view it as potentially identical to the essential cause. But now any systematic relation between the two causes in question is at least a different one from the classical relation according to the S_2 account. As for the moving and final causes, Aristotle observes that 'It is possible for the same thing to be for the sake of something and to be from necessity', that is, to have both a final and a moving cause (94^{b}27 ff.). For example, thunder can be explained as the quenching of fire and (on the Pythagorean account) as having the end of frightening the inhabitants of Tartarus.[13] This shows that the latter two causes can be compatible with one another, but Aristotle never suggests that they are essentially correlative; indeed, the thunder example works only on a mythological interpretation. By contrast, Aristotle's paradigm examples of these two causes in the *Physics* (ii. 7, 198^{a}19 f.) makes them correlative: in the example of an occasion for war (Aristotle is thinking of the Persian War) the moving cause might be an

[12] Hereafter I shall argue that the four causes are conceived as a system only in a later stage of S_2.

[13] Aristotle first gives the example of light particles passing through the pores of a lantern. This example contrasts the *necessity* of transmitting light with the *purpose* of the user. But it does not clearly isolate the *moving cause* in contrast to the *final cause*.

invasion, the final cause so that the defenders might conquer and rule the invaders. The S$_1$ version does not provide any such close association between causes. Rather it demonstrate the compatibility between the logical ground and the essential cause on the one hand, and the moving cause and the final cause on the other.

We seem to have reached an impasse: the S$_1$ version of the FCT cannot be explained within the theoretical framework of S$_1$, and it does not exhibit the characteristics of the S$_2$ account, so that it must not be borrowed from S$_2$. Perhaps Ross (1936: 37) is right when he says, 'We do not know how Aristotle arrived at the doctrine of the four causes; where we find the doctrine in him, we find it not argued for but presented as self-evident.'[14] But I think we are in a better position than Ross to discover what the source of the doctrine is. I have already referred to the analysis of cause as the answer to the question Why?[15] We have found that Aristotle explicitly makes the connection between the four causes and the four kinds of Why questions in *Ph*. ii. This account gives a sufficient reason not only for the *Ph*. ii account, but for the *A.Po.* account as well.

Although Aristotle does not make any meta-theoretical remarks about his four causes in S$_1$, he presupposes a certain linguistic framework. In each case the causes of S$_1$ are answers to the question Why:

(1) Why [διὰ τί] is the angle inscribed in a semicircle a right angle? (94^{a}28)
(2) Why [διὰ τί] did the Athenians get embroiled in the Persian War? (^{a}36 f.)
(3) Why [διὰ τί] does he go for a walk? (^{b}9)
(4) Why [διὰ τί] is this a house? (^{b}9)[16]

Most notably Aristotle makes (2) logically equivalent to 'What is the cause [τίς αἰτία] of the Athenians going to war?' (^{a}37). In the above passages he gives a Why question to correspond to each of the four causes other than the essential cause; and he omits this

---

[14] Ross goes on to suggest that if Aristotle came to the theory by reflection on examples, his reflection was at least informed by the work of his predecessors as chronicled in *Met*. i and elsewhere. But this is weak: Aristotle's critique of the tradition is posterior to and dependent on his prior recognition of the four causes.

[15] See ch. 3.3.2, following Wicksteed and Cornford (1929), Wieland (1962), Vlastos (1969), Hocutt (1974), Moravcsik (1974).

[16] Cf. also ^{b}11, ^{b}20; in all Aristotle's other examples it is an easy exercise to state the request for the cause in the διὰ τί mode.

presumably only because (1) would serve the essential cause as well as the logical ground. Thus we find the Four Becauses are perfectly applicable to the four causes of S_1.

What then is the source of the because theory of causation? It is simply ordinary language analysis (OLA).[17] One notes a correlation beween causal assertions and Why questions; one analyses the contexts in which Why questions appear and one orders the list of causes accordingly. This is a straightforward piece of methodology for the ordinary language analyst, for whom meaning is use. On this account there is no ultimate answer to the question why there should be four and only four causes. For OLA is essentially an open-ended enterprise. It follows the vagaries of linguistic usage and offers no a priori schemes. However, OLA provides just the background we need to understand why Aristotle provides these four causes. He simply finds four different kinds of questions that are asked. Why does he not have a material cause? Because he had not worried about material explanations to date. When he did finally turn his attention to such explanations (urged on, as I maintain, by a new ontology in S_2), he could find reasons for assimilating the new kind of cause to the logical ground. His reasons are in fact not good ones, and he is misled by a propensity to schematize the four caues in a way that linguistic usage does not countenance. But strictly speaking there is nothing surprising about his recognizing the logical ground as a cause while he overlooks the material cause. For he had been intensely engaged in logical theory and had had no occasion to work on physical theory in his earlier work. Thus he was well aware of questions of the form 'Why does conclusion C follow from premisses P?, but unaware of questions of the form 'Why is the knife hard?'[18]

It may seem disappointing to discover the dependency of the FCT on OLA, for the connection suggests that the FCT is only speciously scientific. Indeed, the discovery may confirm our suspicions that Aristotle is being too liberal with his notion of cause, or that his notion is so all-inclusive that it has little to do

[17] Sorabji (1969) stresses the differences between Aristotle's methods and those of the ordinary language analysts. Certainly one has to beware of differences. Aristotle uses his analysis in the service of metaphysics instead of as a replacement or a therapy for it; but he does make extensive use of the method, and there is thus much to be said on the positive side of a comparison.

[18] On Aristotle's failure to perceive the possibility of material analysis in S_1, see Graham (1984: 40).

with ours.[19] Yet this is to concede too much to the current scientific notion of cause, informed as it is by centuries of philosophical consideration. For the present-day scientific/philosophical notion of cause does not by any means exhaust our present-day ordinary language notion of cause. In a careful study of current notions, Hart and Honoré (1959: chs. 1–2) have shown how the philosophic concept of cause fails to address important questions that arise in the philosophy of law. They find that the common-sense conception has a core meaning that by contrast does illuminate these issues. In the course of examining the common-sense concept they observe,

On the one hand it is perfectly common and intelligible in ordinary life to speak of static conditions or negative events as causes: there is no convenient substitute for statements that the lack of rain was the cause of the failure of the corn crop, the icy condition of the road was the cause of the accident, the failure of the signalman to pull the lever was the cause of the train smash. On the other hand the theorist, when he attempts to analyse the notion of a cause, is haunted by the sense that since these ways of speaking diverge from the paradigm cases where causes are events or forces, they must be somehow improper. The corrective is to see that in spite of differences between these cases and the simple [common-sense] paradigms, the very real analogies are enough to justify the extension of causal language to them. (pp. 28 f.)

Here the common-sense conception agrees perfectly with Aristotle: privations and static conditions can be causes. Indeed, so much does the everyday notion of cause parallel Aristotle's that even a motive can count as a cause (p. 40). In the realm of interpersonal transactions there is a special need to deal with reasons for actions, reasons which serve to explain why people act the way they do (pp. 48 ff.). These reasons and motives are Aristotelian final causes, which though shunned by modern philosophic theories of cause, are important features of the common-sense notion. In general, then, while there is a major discrepancy between the Aristotelian concept of cause as expressed in FCT and the modern philosophical concept of cause, the present-day common-sense concept is quite similar to Aristotle's—even in its relevance to certain philosophical concerns.[20]

[19] Vlastos (1969: 292–6) stresses the difference between the Greek concept of αἰτία and the English notion of cause—unnecessarily assimilating the English notion to the current philosophical notion.
[20] Indeed the legal context that Hart and Honoré examine has close ties with the

Thus the FCT of S_1 is explicable as the product of OLA against a background interest in understanding causes in terms of the way they are expressed in language. We have already seen that the *Categories* ontology itself is a piece of OLA, so there is nothing anachronistic about imputing this method to S_1. What makes this account of FCT especially attractive is that it exhibits FCT as independent of the middle term theory and the related missing link theory of cause. If FCT does not fit the mould, it is because it owes its origins to OLA and not to a logical account of causation based on the syllogism. This means that FCT is not likely to be central to S_1—as indeed it is not—because it squares only imperfectly with the a priori desiderata of a causal explanation given the principles of S_1. But it also means that FCT is in a better position to survive the demise of S_1. For it does not share in the demerits of the early system. Overall, then, we are justified in positing for FCT an initial stage in which it is loosely annexed to S_1 but independent of it in origin and content.

6.1.2 Second Stage: Correlative Causes

Of course, FCT becomes a centre-piece of S_2 with the material and formal causes reflecting the hylomorphism of the new ontology. But the transformation of the theory is not immediate. A close look at passages from the earlier period of S_2 will reveal that there is a continuity between the S_1 account and the early S_2 account and that the FCT attains its mature form only gradually.

FCT appears in S_2 first in *Physics* ii. In Chapters 3 and 7 Aristotle itemizes the causes and fits them into a broader context of causal explanation. In Chapter 3 the causes are identified as the following (194^b23 ff.):

(1) The continuant from which something comes to be ($\tau\grave{o}\ \dot{\epsilon}\xi\ o\hat{\upsilon}$ $\gamma\acute{\iota}\gamma\nu\epsilon\tau\alpha\acute{\iota}\ \tau\iota\ \dot{\epsilon}\nu\upsilon\pi\acute{\alpha}\rho\chi o\nu\tau os$).

(2) The form and the archetype ($\tau\grave{o}\ \epsilon\hat{\iota}\delta os\ \kappa\alpha\grave{\iota}\ \tau\grave{o}\ \pi\alpha\rho\acute{\alpha}\delta\epsilon\iota\gamma\mu\alpha$).

(3) The first source of movement and rest ($\acute{o}\theta\epsilon\nu\ \dot{\eta}\ \dot{\alpha}\rho\chi\grave{\eta}\ \tau\hat{\eta}s$ $\mu\epsilon\tau\alpha\beta o\lambda\hat{\eta}s\ \dot{\eta}\ \pi\rho\acute{\omega}\tau\eta\ \ddot{\eta}\ \tau\hat{\eta}s\ \dot{\eta}\rho\epsilon\mu\acute{\eta}\sigma\epsilon\omega s$).

(4) The end ($\dot{\omega}s\ \tau\grave{o}\ \tau\acute{\epsilon}\lambda os$).

Greek notion: for the Greek terms $a\check{\iota}\tau\iota o\nu/a\grave{\iota}\tau\acute{\iota}\alpha$ are adopted from concepts of legal responsibility: Frede (1980: 222 f.). Note also that if van Fraassen (1980*a*: ch.5; 1980*b*) is right in his bold analysis of explanation, the correct philosophic account of cause and explanation is not very different from that of Aristotle.

The last two causes do not differ significantly from those of the
A.Po.: there the moving cause was called ἤ τι πρῶτον ἐκίνησε—
here the notion is slightly expanded to include the cause of rest;
the final cause was called τὸ τίνος ἕνεκα, and here in Chapter 3
Aristotle glosses the fourth cause with τὸ οὖ ἕνεκα (ᵇ33). He even
gives some examples of these causes in Chapter 7 (198ᵃ19 f.) which
are reminiscent of the causes of war examples in the *A.Po.* The
first two causes, however, merit some attention.

It is evident from the similarity of terminology that the first
cause is based on the concept of matter of *Ph.* i.²¹ The initial
examples are likewise illuminating: the cause is found in the
bronze of a statue and the silver of a drinking cup (194ᵇ25).
However, Aristotle does not use the term ὕλη here to designate
the first cause, and when he does give a fuller charactrization of it,
we find that the notion of this cause is broader than we might
suppose:

All the aforementioned causes fall into the four obvious classes. For the
letters of syllables, the material of utensils, fire and such components of
bodies, the parts of the whole, and the conditions of the conclusion
function as causes *from which*. And of these the former members function
as the substratum, for instance the parts, and the latter as the essence,
namely the whole, the compound and the form. (195ᵃ15–21)

Now although Aristotle has already used the term ὕλη to
characterize bronze in its causal relation to a statue (195ᵃ8), here
he demurs: he confines the term ὕλη to its non-technical use as
signifying the material of which artificial objects are created. In
other words, ὕλη appears in the role of a *species* of the first cause.
To preserve the separation from the classical notion of material
cause I shall call this cause the component cause. There are several
species of component cause: discrete elements such as letters,
material stuffs as of craft products, chemical elements, parts, and
premises. In each of these species some different relation obtains
between the component or substratum, and the essence.

Note also that for each species of component cause there is a
species of essential cause (τὸ τί ἦν εἶναι), of which Aristotle
names as species the whole, the compound, and the form (ᵃ20 f.).
Thus the formal cause, like the material cause, is only a single

²¹ Cf. the definition of the material cause at *Ph.* ii. 3, 194ᵇ24 with that of matter
at *Ph.* i. 9, 192ᵃ31 f.

species of a generic kind. And it is the generic kind which is properly one of the four causes.

The passage that we have just examined is careful and correct: material and form are only one species of their respective classes of cause. And yet there is an obvious sense in which they seem to be taking over by metonymy. At 194^{b}26 εἶδος and a term with similar connotations, παράδειγμα are the only names given for the essential cause, although ὁ λόγος ὁ τοῦ τί ἦν εἶναι is given as a gloss (^{b}27). As for the component cause, its general name is given, but only material-artefact examples are provided in the initial statement (^{b}24 f.). Aristotle's whole exposition reveals a tension between a drive to classify correctly the causes taking care to separate generic and specific examples, and a drive to subsume the whole scheme under the concept of craft production.

Aristotle's FCT as here expressed shows a further area of integration when compared with the S₁ account. Here we find that either essentially or typically the component cause and the essential cause are *correlative*. There was no such indication in the S₁ account, and indeed in Aristotle's main example, the two were so far from being correlatives that they coincided. In *Ph.* ii. 3 the 195^{a}15 ff. passage treats all component causes as having a corresponding essential cause. Aristotle emphasizes that the causes can be reciprocally related, referring to work as the cause of health and health of work (^{a}8–11). Here clearly there is a final cause functioning as a correlative of a moving cause. The reciprocity seems to hold also for most or all cases of component and essential causes, but Aristotle does not explicitly notice that fact. What seems to emerge is two pairs of *potentially* reciprocal causes, the moving–final and the component–essential. We have at least a higher level of organization than in the S₁ account.

Yet there is a curious sort of atavism in the Chapter 7 account to consider. There Aristotle seems to restrict the causes to certain contexts such that he does not anticipate their use in systematic correlations. He notes that the essential cause applies to the essence in things without motion, giving mathematics as the chief example (198^{a}16 f.). And he says that the cause in things that come to be is matter (^{a}20 f.). In the following passage (^{a}24 ff.) Aristotle drops these restrictions and treats the four causes as a system. However, this passage has the earmarks of an insertion informed by later biological researches. The former passage seems to indicate that Aristotle had some trouble integrating what came to be the material and formal causes. The restriction of the essential cause to the realm of immovable things seems to be in accord with the *A.Po.* account and to represent no advance over it. In any case, at the stage of development in which we see S₂ in *Ph.* ii, the four causes have incorporated notions of matter and form, but they do not represent a complete system.

In the *Physics* passages Aristotle makes some remarks about the usefulness of the four causes for the natural philosopher, but he makes no claims that they are necessary for the metaphysician. However, in *Metaphysics* i, written not too long after *Physics* ii, he makes some bold claims for the causes outside the realm of natural philosophy:

Since it is clear that we must get knowledge of the original causes (for we say we know each thing when we think we are acquainted with the first cause), and the causes are of four kinds . . . (3, 983ᵃ24–6)

In the previous chapter Aristotle makes it clear that knowledge of causes confers Wisdom, that it is the most exact, universal, knowable, self-sufficient, liberal, and even divine of sciences. Thus a knowledge of the four causes seems to possess the characteristics of the best science. The remainder of the book is devoted to showing that none of Aristotle's predecessors has ever found a cause other than Aristotle's four, and, incidentally, that no one has ever recognized them all simultaneously.

The message is clear: FCT is the nucleus of a methodology that will encompass all the causal explanations of his predecessors, and hence it is at once more powerful and more exact than any previous analytic technique. It is more exact in that it formulates with precision the questions that previous philosophers had posed only rather 'darkly', 'obscurely and unclearly', only 'faintly glimpsing' their objects, like one who lisps because of youth, or like untrained soldiers in battle.[22] By contrast, FCT articulates the questions correctly and thus allows one to discover the correct answers. FCT is more powerful than previous approaches because it is *complete*. It does not leave out any relevant questions concerning the matter at hand:

[22] 5, 987ᵃ10 (reading μορυχώτερον with Ross); 4, 985ᵃ13; 7, 988ᵃ23; 10, 993ᵃ15; 4, 985ᵃ13 f.

That all philosophers have sought the causes discussed in the *Physics*, and that we cannot name any cause except these is clear from our previous argument. (10, 993^{a}11–13)

Aristotle's survey of the history of philosophy in *Met.* i has demonstrated that his list of causes is complete. Since a cause is by definition an answer to the question Why, FCT provides a systematic closure to any inquiry. Once the relevant questions have been posed and answered properly, there is no more to inquire about.

Seen from this perspective FCT gives Aristotle a great ideological advantage over his predecessors. For it allows him to claim a comprehensiveness of treatment that none of them could possibly have attained to. It also allows him to proceed with the confidence that his own analyses are methodologically beyond reproach. For they incorporate every theoretically possible viewpoint that can be applied to a subject-matter. As we have noted, the OLA that generates and justifies FCT is itself an open-ended method. And as thorough as Aristotle's historical survey may be, it has provided him only with inductive evidence for the completeness of the scheme. Aristotle's faith that FCT is complete must issue from some other source. The power of the theory and its balanced symmetry seem to confirm that the scheme is comprehensive. His historical survey in *Met.* i, one-sided though it is, confirms his expectations. Certainly Aristotle's studies are characterized by a confidence of method and a care for system that set them apart from previous philosophical inquiries.

But perhaps Aristotle's most impressive intellectual virtue is his persistence in actually applying the four cause scheme to his scientific inquiries. Aristotle's discussion of soul is not complete until he has enumerated the three senses in which soul is a cause (*DA* ii. 4, 415^{b}7 ff.). And indeed from his account of the generation of the elemental bodies (*GC* ii, esp. Ch. 9) to the Unmoved Mover at the pinnacle of actuality (*Met.* xii. 7, 1072^{b}1 ff.) Aristotle's universe is plotted on a grid of the four causes. Unlike the otiose missing link theory of cause advocated in *A.Po.* ii, FCT is a working hypothesis that Aristotle constantly invokes to clarify explanatory relationships in the phenomena under investigation. Overall, FCT forms the basis of scientific analysis in S$_2$.

6.1.3   Third Stage: A System of Causes

Previously we have seen how the FCT of S_1 was not an integral part of the method of S_1, whereas the FCT of S_2 takes a central role in the methodology of science and philosophical inquiry in general. One of the reasons for adopting FCT, as Aristotle argued for it in *Met.* i, was its claim to completeness: it embraces all possible scientific questions and thus leaves out no relevant considerations. This suggests another important feature of the FCT of S_2: it provides a *system* of causes. We have seen that this feature was not clearly depicted in *Ph.* ii. Although the material–formal and the efficient–final cause pairs appear to be reciprocal causes, the exposition falls short of tying all four causes together in a system, and indeed the opening remarks of Chapter 7 seem to obscure even the material–formal cause connection.

Yet it becomes Aristotle's practice to invoke all four causes in many situations. For instance, in *DA* ii. 4 he finds that the soul is the formal, final, and efficient cause of the body, which is the material cause of the soul. Here it is evident that all four causes apply to a situation *simultaneously* in such a way that it is illuminating, and even imperative, to pose all four causal questions at the same time. In the opening passage of the *GA* Aristotle makes it clear that he conceives of his biological treatises as forming a coherent whole because they are structured around the four causes: after dealing with the formal and final causes (in the *DA*?) and the material causes of animal, which are their parts (in the *PA*), he will investigate their efficient causes, that is, their generative systems, in the *GA*. Here at a macroscopic level, Aristotle applies the four cause scheme to a whole series of treatises to give them a relational unity. There seems, then, to be a presumption that the philosopher should seek all four causes of any phenomenon unless he becomes aware that some cause does not apply. This attitude is the diametrical opposite of that suggested by the *Ph.* ii. 7 account, which tended to delimit causes to certain domains of application beyond which it was a priori impossible to apply them.

The culmination of Aristotle's tendency to apply the causes systematically can be seen in the late *Met.* viii account we have already called attention to. There Aristotle gives a recipe for applying the causes:

Whenever one seeks the cause, since 'cause' is said in many ways, one should *give all possible causes*. For instance, [1] what is the material cause of man? Perhaps the menstrual fluid? [2] What is the moving cause? The seed? [3] What is the formal cause? The essence. [4] What is the final cause? The end. (Perhaps these last two are the same.) And one should give the proximate causes. (4, 1044^a32-^b2)

Here Aristotle counsels the philosopher–scientist to seek all possible causes, and he gives an example in which all four causes apply to the situation at once. He is not of course claiming that all the causes are immediately clear. Nor is he supposing that each cause will necessarily be distinct from every other; on the contrary, he suggests that in case at hand two of the causes coincide. In fact he does not really give *any* definitive answers to the causal questions. His answers to the first two are rhetorical questions. The last two responses come close to being tautologies. But the point here is not so much to find the answers as to learn how to look for them. Aristotle goes on to examine how the questions apply to an eclipse of the moon. He finds that the material cause applies only in a qualified sense, and that there probably is no final cause.[23] This example thus demonstrates that all causes do not apply to all situations. Finally he asks for the causes of sleep. Here he is even more tentative than before, showing that at least for present purposes the question is more important than the answer.

6.2   EXPLANATION OF THE DEVELOPMENT OF FCT

We have now seen a development of FCT which can be roughly divided into three stages: (1) a stage in S_1 in which the four causes do not constitute a system, and in which each cause may possibly be limited to a certain domain of application, and in which there is no material cause: (2) a stage in which two pairs of causes are recognized, the material–formal and the efficient–final, with claims that the causes are a complete set and hints that they form a system; (3) a stage in which the four causes clearly form a system. In the process of this development FCT goes from being an appendix to the philosophy of science to being its centre-piece. I have already offered a preliminary explanation of the origin of FCT in order to make plausible the claim that FCT might have

[23] For a discussion of this example in relation to S_1 see ch. 4.3.4: what for S_1 is a paradigm example of causal explanation is for S_2 a defective case.

appeared in S_1 without the contaminating influence of S_2. The task now before us is to show how the dialectic of S_2's development itself might account for the growth of FCT beyond its original content in S_1.

We have a lead to follow in the difference of the list of causes between stages (1) and (2). We find no material cause in (1) but we find it in (2) and (3). Furthermore, I have already suggested that the crucial difference between S_1 and S_2 is the presence of the doctrine of hylomorphism in the latter, and I have shown how the problem of change leads Aristotle to make the hylomorphic turn. It seems plausible to infer from this background that behind the difference between stages (1) and (2) is likewise the respective absence and presence of hylomorphism. What then precipitates a new relationship between the causes is the background assumption that substances are composed of matter and form. Once Aristotle has come to this metaphysical insight, he is able to reconceive the four causes in such a way that the previously unrelated causes are seen to have a correlation.

In stating how Aristotle revises FCT, one is inclined to say simply that he now makes the matter and form of *Ph*. i into causes, which then absorb the previously unrelated causes of the logical ground and the essence. However, such an interpretation is too hasty; it misstates the relationship between the hylomorphism of *Ph*. i and the FCT of *Ph*. ii. The first theory is an *ontological* theory, the second a theory of *explanation*. Matter and form are components of reality; they are not *per se* causes. A cause, as we have seen, is the answer to a Why question. As such it is an explanatory statement, or perhaps more precisely for Aristotle, a factor on the basis of which something is to be explained—the ground of an explanatory statement. Now a component of a substance could, under favourable circumstances, count as a cause, that is, a factor which explains something. On the other hand it is not necessarily a cause. To identify something as a cause is to locate it in the context of an explanation in which that item appears as the referent of the explanans. For instance, to note that a statue is composed of a certain form and matter, say the form of Pericles and bronze, is not to give form and matter as causes. For them to be causes, one must presuppose a situation in which some question arises requiring explanation. For instance, one might ask, 'Why is that statue green?' The informed guide would reply that the statue is made of bronze, and bronze turns green when it is oxidized. In this case the matter has been invoked as a cause, an explanatory factor. But matter is not by definition a cause.

It should be clear, then, that matter and form are not causes *per se*. On the other hand, to embrace the doctrine of hylomorphism is to accept a fundamental restructuring of the world, one which invites a re-evaluation of the four causes. Indeed, once matter and form become the fundamental components of reality, they *assume an explanatory value*. To provide an analysis of a concrete substance is at the same time to tell *why* it is the way it is. In a sense, the ultimate entities are the ultimate explanantia, and it becomes inevitable that they should be accommodated within the scheme of the causes, however many there might be. It does not follow that they should become paradigmatic for two of the causes, since they are initially only species of more general types. But once they become paradigmatic types of causes, there is an easy and almost inevitable transition to conceiving them as reciprocal causes, for matter and form are correlative concepts. Thus to explain something in terms of matter is to presuppose a form, and conversely. Hence it is plausible that once Aristotle adopted H, he should restructure his set of causes, and restructure them in such a way that a material and a formal cause would be correlative causes.

We noted another pairing of causes in stage (2): the efficient and final causes seemed to be reciprocal causes at least for some events. I believe that this relationship can be explained independently of the foundations of S_2. One prominent example of the moving cause in *A.Po.* ii. 11 is the cause of the Persian War: the Athenian participation in the raid on Sardis. This event is recalled again in *Ph.* ii. 7, and with it goes a final cause, in order to rule. Aristotle provides a number of craft and biological examples in *Ph.* ii 3—the adviser and sculptor and parent as moving causes, health as a medically directed final cause—but the historical example of Chapter 7 stands out and harks back to the *A.Po.* account. The problem of explaining the Persian War reminds one of a famous historical problem in Thucydides. In the first book of his history of the Peloponnesian War, he discusses the cause of the latter conflict. He notes various conflicts as *grounds* for initiating the war, but maintains that the real *cause* is the fear the Peloponnesians had of the growing Athenian power.[24] Here, significantly, we have a historian thematizing for us the problem of explaining the outbreak of a war. The early problem of historiography calls for an analytical awareness of the concept of a cause in the context of human activity. We further find at least a preliminary analysis of causality: Thucydides distinguishes two different senses of cause. And finally, and perhaps most revealing of all, we find something like an inchoate distinction between a moving cause—the events, occasions, and conflicts that preceded the war—and a final cause—a deeper purpose that underlies the particular events.[25]

Here the homely means–ends distinction suggested by craft analogies seems to have profound implications. As, for example, exercise is the moving cause of health and health the final cause of exercise (195^{a}8–11), so historical events have motivations and motives inspire incidents. The means–ends correlation thus has application to the conspicuous domain of politics, where it effects a striking synthesis between superficially disparate phenomena. A tentative link between the moving and the final causes accordingly finds a pragmatic justification in its ability to illuminate complex and obscure political-historical relationships.

I do not wish to claim that the efficient–final cause distinction came to Aristotle already worked out by historians. But I do wish to suggest that a serious groundwork had been laid already by historians and perhaps other intellectuals who looked beneath the surface of the fast-moving stream of history to find a deeper source

---

[24] Thucydides 1.23.5–6 distinguishes between the various αἰτίαι and διαφοραί on the one hand the ἀληθεστάτη πρόφασις on the other. The significance of the word choice has been much debated, but Rawlings (1975) gives a convincing argument that there are two homonymous πρόφασις lexemes, an earlier one deriving from φημί and a later one originating in Hippocratic medicine deriving from φαίνω. The former term has the subjective meaning 'pretext' or 'alleged cause', the latter signifies an objectively determinable antecedent condition or characteristic symptom. Rawlings's study renders obsolete the claims that there is no recognizable difference in Thucydides' terms for 'cause' (e.g. Cornford 1907: 59, Gomme 1945: 153, Ste. Croix 1972: 53 f.), and hence the inference that he is confused (Cornford, ibid.). Cf. Lloyd (1979: 54 n. 231).

[25] In the many modern interpretations of Thucydides' terminology the distinction between moving and final causes does not seem to have been articulated clearly. Kirkwood (1952: 51) does stress that the πρόφασις is a 'motive'. Of course I do not maintain that Thucydides' *terminology* points to a distinction between moving and final causes, but that the specific factors he isolates exemplify the respective types and that his very distinction between the grounds given and the truest cause shows an appreciation for their different roles.

of unity. At least in this case the raw material of Aristotle's causal scheme had been prepared for his working, and a test case had been provided for vindicating that scheme. Whereas in the *A.Po.* account Aristotle had used the outbreak of the Persian War to illustrate only the efficient cause, in *Ph.* ii he perceptively exploits the example to illustrate the efficient and final causes as complementary explanatory factors of the same situation. Aristotle's synoptic grasp of the causes relevant to this problematic situation represents a perceptive abstraction: the philosopher renders in general terms a distinction the historian has adumbrated in a particular setting. Where Thucydides sees a concrete problem in historical explanation, Aristotle finds a paradigmatic case illustrating the structure of historical explanation. What Aristotle appreciates in the S_2 account that he had ignored in the S_1 account is the complexity of the historical example.

Both the final and the efficient causes have antecedents in Plato as well. In the *Phaedo* (97 c ff.) Plato criticizes the Presocratics for failing to recognize or (in the case of Anaxagoras) to exploit a kind of explanation that Aristotle would call final cause explanation. Utimately Plato settles for a kind of formal cause explanation instead (99 c ff.). In the *Timaeus* Plato pursues final-cause type explanations in detail, without, however, producing any meta-theoretical account of what he is doing there.[26] The *Philebus* produces a scheme of explanatory factors which includes something like the efficient cause (26 E ff.). Yet this cause is not contrasted to the final cause but rather to the limit, the unlimited, and the product of the limited and unlimited (27 B). Accordingly, while the efficient and final causes can be attributed to Plato in some form, the juxtaposition of the two causes cannot be traced to his influence.

Thus the efficient–final-cause pair seems to emerge from political–historical discussions as a vital correlation. The material-formal-cause pair, on the other hand, seems to result from an

---

[26] Although the Demiurge is a kind of transcendent efficient cause that works with a purpose, Plato does not thematize this relationship; when he comes to analyse the factors necessary for becoming he gives more of an ontological than an aetiological schema: *Tim.* 51 E–52 c. On the other hand, the Reason–Necessity opposition manifests a marked aetiological contrast between purpose and material constraints: Cornford (1937: 162–77). Overall, both in the *Phaedo* and the *Timaeus* Plato tends to read the main contrast in explanation as between the final and the material causes rather than between the final and efficient causes.

adaptation of the hylomorphism of S_2. The correlative pairs of stage (2) show an increasing level of integration in the causal scheme compared with stage (1)—a development which is wholly natural given the Change Hypothesis and contemporary interest in historical explanation. We have yet to explain the systematic character of FCT as exhibited most clearly in stage (3). How is it that the two pairs of causes come to be seen as themselves part of a larger system in which all four causes apply simultaneously and in a complementary manner? One could have had a scheme in which the two pairs occupy a different logical space, such that one or other of the two pairs applies to any given context, but not both. For instance, it would be plausible to suppose that the efficient–final pair applies to human activities but not necessarily to mathematics—for in this realm there are no changes and hence no moving causes or purposes. We noticed that Aristotle did rule out one of the causes in the realm of astronomy—but still his presumption was that the four causes *generally* apply. There are even more complex problems for some individual causes, in particular the final cause. Does this cause apply within the realm of nature? Aristotle's answer in *Ph.* ii. 8 is yes; but in his confidence he seems to go beyond the original application of the concept. For surely we ask 'For the sake of what . . .?' properly only of human endeavours. Aristotle has taken this notion out of the language game to which it belongs and applied it to an alien situation. Similar problems arise with respect to the material and formal causes. Granted that they apply to analyses of things, initially craft products, what assures us that they also apply, first to natural objects, and secondly to non-objects such as events, for example, wars? How can Aristotle maintain that in general one should seek all four causes in a given situation?

For one who looks to biology or to common sense or to biographical details to provide the background to Aristotle's philosophy, the question is baffling. But given the presuppositions we have uncovered in articulating TST, the answer is not far to seek. In a sense it is before our eyes constantly in Aristotle's terminology, his analogies, his choice of examples. We noted in the last chapter that what made the transition to a theory of matter possible was an analogy between coming to be in nature and craft production in the realm of human endeavour. We see the traces of similar analogies in all of Aristotle's S_2 treatments of FCT. But what I would like to suggest is that in this case a craft analogy provides another model for a theory. It provides a model by which Aristotle could fit each of the four causes into the logical space of a coherent description of the world, and do it in such a way that the simultaneous applicability of the four causes was assured.

In order to see how this could come about, consider a case in which a craftsman produces an artefact in his workshop. A thorough observer might note (1) there was a workman skilled in the trade required for the production. (2) The workman had a plan, a conception, whether written down, drawn, or internally digested. (3) The workman made use of some material, whether clay, wood, metal, flour and water, or whatever, which he moulded, carved, cast, or kneaded to produce his result. And (4) in the process of the activity he engaged in, the workman transformed his material by imposing on it a shape or characteristic it had not possessed prior to his activity. All of these elements are present in any craft production; to leave one out would be to give an incomplete description. But the four factors seem to exhaust the relevant features of the situation. Any further determination can be classified under one of the headings already given. For instance, we could call attention to the need for tools. But tools can be subsumed under the agency of the craftsman, since they are an extension of his own movements and efforts.[27] Thus the analogy provides a situation in which a finite number of causal factors can explain an infinite range of outcomes.

Now the account I have given may seem commonplace and even hackneyed. But note that accounts like the above are usually provided in textbooks to *illustrate* how to apply the four causes. If my story is homely, the application I am putting it to is novel: I am claiming that the story *structures* the four cause theory itself. *Of course* it is helpful to apply the four cause theory to a situation like the one above—because that is precisely the sort of situation that gives to the FCT its systematic character. Then to turn about and locate the four causes in the picture is strikingly easy and encouraging precisely because the causes are already embedded in the example. Without that example, there would be no assurance that the four causes either all applied at once or that they applied in a complementary way. Indeed, in no other situation do all four

---

[27] As Aristotle recognizes, even one's hands are tools for extending one's power as a mover: *PA* iv. 10, 687ª10, 19–23, ᵇ2–4; *DA* iii. 8, 432ª1 f.

causes apply unequivocally. As soon as we turn to the realm of nature, for instance, it becomes highly problematic whether there is matter, or an efficient cause, or particularly a final cause. To be sure Aristotle has likely candidates for all of these roles, but at best such factors are one with the paradigmatic four causes only by a strained analogy. What makes Aristotle's explanations work is the power of the model, as we may often glimpse even in the biological works:

It is clear that the natural philosophers have the wrong method [of explaining animals]; rather one must state that the animal is such, and both concerning it and its parts, one must explain what are the essence and the characteristics, just as if one were describing the form of a couch. (*PA* i. 1, 641ᵃ14–17)

Because we can control the answers to questions about a couch, it serves as model for understanding the answers to questions about animals. On any other account than the present one, such analogies are inept, embarrassing, wrong-headed, or at least superfluous and dispensable. But if the crafts are a model, the analogies are crucial.

What I am arguing then is that the example of craft production is not merely (or not accidentally) a good illustration of the four causes: it is a *model* which exhibits the four causes as part of an integrated system of explanation (See Figs. 6.1 and 6.2). In the paradigmatic situation, all four causes apply, and each accounts for one relevant aspect of the total situation. In so far as this situation serves as a model, this systematic conception of the causes is projected on to the world. Aristotle assumes that the four causes apply to normal situations; if they do not, the situation must be in some way defective.

It is *because* of the craft model that Aristotle can advance form

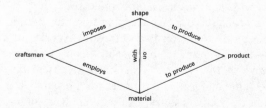

FIG. 6.1. The Craftsman Situation. The craftsman imposes a shape on a material in accordance with his craft to produce a product.

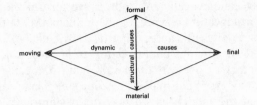

FIG. 6.2. The Four Causes. By using the craft situation as a model, Aristotle can organize the two pairs of correlative causes into a system which represents all possible relations between causal factors.

and matter to the status of paradigmatic causes over such other candidates as essence, whole, synthesis; and substratum, parts, logical ground. In terms of the model, form and matter are the ideal exemplifications of two kinds of cause. There are, to be sure, other examples; but they do not belong to the model. If we understand the relationship of, for example, matter to the other three causes, we understand one sort of cause. On the other hand, if we understand the parts in relation to the whole we do not necessarily understand the relation of one sort of cause to all the others.

When we appreciate the role of the craft model in FCT of S$_2$, we are also in a position to see how it is that Aristotle can make the extravagant claim that to know the four causes is to possess Wisdom. Given the model, the four causes are all the causes that are 'logically' possible—that is, according to the logic of the model, or relative to its logical space. Of course Aristotle uses a survey of the history of philosophy to prove this point in *Met.* i. But this serves to glorify the theory more than to ground it, since the scheme itself is prior to the survey and organizes it. The survey is really a beauty contest for FCT in which it reveals its charms in comparison with theories less amply endowed.

I raised a problem above concerning how the specific material and formal causes could displace the other species of causes in their class—the component and essential causes—to become the representative of the whole class. Obviously, from an inductive point of view, the material and formal causes are only one of many kinds in their respective classes. If, then, one were simply to claim that they were the only kind of cause in their class, one would be in error. Once the craft model becomes operative in relation to FCT, however, the role of the material and efficient causes changes. For the model becomes the standard by which FCT is interpreted and applied to the world. In fact, it becomes integrated with FCT, and without it FCT cannot be properly applied. The partial integration of the theory with the model is the outcome of Aristotle's rethinking of FCT in stage (2). In stage (3) the integration has been completed. There is a canonical list of causes which potentially apply to every situation. The causes form a closed system with respect to explanation. Once we interpret FCT in accordance with the craft model, we are licensed to promote the material and formal causes to the role of prototypes within their classes. For they are now theoretically inseparable from the class. The model has become part of the theory—a constitutive model—and so all four causes are to be understood by analogy to the paradigmatic situation of craft production. In other words, the new role of the material and formal causes is not the product of a hasty generalization; it is the result of a theoretical leap by which they have become central features of the theory itself.

6.3 CONCLUSION

We have examined the development of FCT from its appearance in S_1 to its maturity in the late works of S_2. The direction of development is from a collection of unrelated factors to a system of complementary explanatory functions. We have found that the theory originates from Aristotle's attention to an ordinary language analysis of explanatory statements. Aristotle's new theory of hylomorphism leads him in *Ph.* ii to associate two causes with matter and form and to conceive them as reciprocal causes, as he conceives of efficient and final causes in the light of historical analysis. Even at this point the systematization is only beginning, for Aristotle now tacitly makes use of an analogy of craft production to find a simultaneous interpretation for all four causes, in which all account for simultaneous aspects of a single situation. By making this analogy into a model, and moreover a constitutive model, Aristotle is able to underwrite the general applicability of FCT to all situations and to make the formal and material causes paradigmatic for their classes.

At this point we have accounted for the observed development of FCT by appealing to our account of the hylomorphic turn in

Aristotle. This turn was crucial for the re-evaluation of FCT, which seems to have followed soon after the discovery of matter. The full development of FCT seems to have resulted from the S_2 conception in a more roundabout way. Rather than resulting directly from hylomorphism, the full elaboration of FCT came about as a result of the craft model. This model, however, is in essence the same model that allowed Aristotle to include matter in his S_2 ontology. Hence not only did the new principle of hylomorphism play its part, but the model that interpreted the new ontology decisively influenced Aristotle's theory of cause. Here we are getting close to a view of a new way of looking at things—a new paradigm or a root metaphor that makes us see the world in a different way. I have said that the influence of the S_2 conception on FCT was indirect in this case; but, in reality, perhaps it is a kind of deep influence that is more direct conceptually even if less direct logically. If theories are judged more by their potential than by their immediate explanatory power,[28] the new system seems far to outstrip the old in its appeal. For the craft model brings with it a wealth of suggestive parallels to the natural world. As a model that helps to constitute both Aristotle's ontology and his theory of explanation, it seems fair to say that it is indeed a constitutive model for the whole system. Because of its suggestive implications, it provides a powerful impulse for Aristotle to rethink his whole philosophy.

[28] As Kuhn (1970: 157 f.) and Lakatos (1970) suggest.

7

The Growth of S$_2$:
Potentiality and Actuality

We have looked briefly at Aristotle's concept of actuality and
potentiality in chapters 3 and 4. We have found at least two
concepts under the rubric of ἐνέργεια. One of these, ἐνέργεια-A
(hereafter EA), was associated with activity, for instance seeing as
opposed to merely having sight or being awake as opposed to
being asleep. The second sense, ἐνέργεια-S (hereafter ES), was
associated with substance or form. In this sense ἐνέργεια is as a
statue compared with the matter it is made of, or a house as
opposed to the bricks.[1] As we have seen,[2] Aristotle seems to think
that ἐνέργεια can only be defined inductively or by analogy. We
have found that only EA appears in S$_1$, and that ES appears only
in S$_2$. Moreover, actuality appears as a metaphysical principle only
S$_2$. Since S$_1$ is earlier than S$_2$ and S$_2$ results from a development of
S$_1$, it would seem plausible to expect that ES is in some sense a
development of EA. To show how and why ES grew out of EA
would corroborate our developmental hypothesis and also bring
more order to our understanding of Aristotle's theory of actuality.
Let us turn then to the problem.

First it will be useful to look at Aristotle's comments on the
relation between EA and ES. For he makes some observations
which have developmental implications—and this is one of the few
cases in which he shows some faint awareness of a development of
his own theory. Of course Aristotle devotes a whole book to the
concept of actuality, *Met.* ix, which book reflects in its structure
the presence of two chief senses of actuality and and potentiality.
At the outset he notes:

. . . we shall explicate potentiality [δύναμις] and realization [ἐντελέχεια],
and first the chief sense of δύναμις, which is not, however, the most useful
for our present purposes. For δύναμις and ἐνέργεια have a wider sense

---

[1] See chs. 4.3.2 and 3.1.2.   [2] Ch. 4.3.2; *Met.* ix. 6, 1048^{a}35–7.

than merely the activity sense [τῶν . . . λεγομένων κατὰ κίνησιν]. But when we have discussed this sense we shall also talk about the others in explicating the concept of actuality. (1, 1045ᵇ34–6ᵃ4)

Here Aristotle mentions the 'chief' sense of potentiality (and presumably actuality) as the sense of κίνησις—the same sense that he identifies with certain examples of activity in Chapter 6 (1048ᵇ8, with ᵃ37–ᵇ2). He seems to think this sense is less philosophical, or at least less relevant to understanding Being in the sense of actuality, which is the subject of the book (1045ᵇ27 ff.). In general, it is a less metaphysical sense, as we have noted already, than ES.[3]

Aristotle also makes an etymological–historical comment:

The term actuality, which tends to mean realization [ἐντελέχεια], has come to apply to other objects from originally applying to activities [κινήσεις], for activity especially seems to be actuality . . . (3, 1047ᵃ30–2)

Here Aristotle explicitly notes that EA is temporally earlier than ES (or any other sense), and hence provides a comfirmation of our relative dating of the two concepts. It is curious, however, how he treats the concepts. It is probable that he himself invented the term ἐνέργεια. Yet instead of discussing the term and the concepts it represents as something that he had developed and manipulated, he speaks as if they have a life of their own. Perhaps this attitude is not surprising in light of certain views he holds concerning the history of philosophy—that philosophers have been led on by the truth itself to new discoveries.[4] This suggests that the terms and concepts of philosophy are not private property or the products of personal viewpoints, but part of a living organism with its own τέλος. In any case, the original sense of the term is clear from his remark. There is the further suggestion of a direction of development in Aristotle's mention of the synonym ἐντελέχεια. This word seems to represent the new meaning. With its connotations of completeness (cf. ἐντελής 'complete') and even the possession of a goal (τέλος),[5] it seems to represent ES, which

---

[3] See ch. 3.1.2.   [4] Met. i. 3, 984ᵇ10 f., 984ᵃ18 f.

[5] Aristotle himself endorses the etymology for ἐντελέχεια deriving from ἐν [ἑαυτῷ] τέλος ἔχειν, Met. ix. 8, 1050ᵃ21 ff. Notwithstanding the fact that Aristotle must have coined the word himself, his etymology is false: the term must derive from the phrase ἐντελῶς ἔχειν. On another false etymology (that of Hirzel 1884) see Diels (1916). Although the term ἐντελέχεια has different connotations from ἐνέργεια, it is used interchangeably with it; see Chen (1958), Blair (1967), Reale

applies to the completed substance. Aristotle makes an etymological connection between ἐντελέχεια and ἐνέργεια later in the book (8, 1050^{a}21–3):

Action [ἔργον] is an end [τέλος] and the actuality is an end, therefore even the name 'actuality' [ἐνέργεια] is derived from 'action' and tends to mean realization [ἐντελέχεια].

Here a free-wheeling association of terms allows Aristotle to make semantic connections between his synonyms. The observation has little value for formal etymology, but it does show the close connection ἐνέργεια came to have with the notion of completeness, a notion proper to ES. Taken with the previously quoted passage, this passage indicates the close ties the concept of actuality developed with the concept of completeness. But clearly the original concept is mainly associated with activity. Thus Aristotle confirms our hypothesis that EA is earlier than ES and genetically related to it.

7.1 'Ενέργεια-A

One approach to understanding the original concept of actuality is to examine its etymology. Since Aristotle presumably coined the word, the roots of the word may cast light on its meaning. As we have seen, Aristotle gives a derivation of the term which cites ἔργον as its source. Formally speaking, this is incorrect. It may seem curious that Aristotle could coin a word and then make an error about its derivation. However, the situation is not difficult to explain. In the first place, the ability to create new words in one's native tongue is something of a competence that is acquired along with the ability to speak the language. Etymology, on the other hand, is a theoretical attempt to explain what happens when words are (or were) coined. The dismal state of etymological science in classical Greece is parodied by Plato in the *Cratylus*. R. Eucken (1869) has studied Aristotle's attempts at etymology, and finds them of little linguistic value; typically, however, they are not the product of free associations such as we find in the *Cratylus* but are advanced as confirmations of some theory Aristotle holds on other grounds. Aristotle's etymologies fall under the linguist's classification

(1962: 175–7, 196–205), Bonitz (1849: 387 f.). Aristotle may have intended to use ἐντελέχεια to signify ES alone, but if so, he failed to maintain his distinction. On the etymology of the term, see Frisk (1960: 524), Ross (1924, i. 245 f.).

of folk etymologies. Such etymologies are common from early Greek literature down to classical times, but as Hermann Diels (1916: 201) has pointed out, they have little or no influence on the actual practice of word-formation. The mature native speaker of a language is competent to create new words that conform to the canons of his native tongue. The ability to do this, however, does not entail the ability to comment intelligently on the process of word-formation. It is only with the rise of modern linguistics that secure principles of etymology have been established.

Taking this preamble into account, then, let us examine the etymology of the neologism ἐνέργεια. The term is a descendant of the adjective ἐνεργός, which in turn presumes a prepositional phrase ἐν ἔργῳ 'at work'. The adjective is attested first in Herodotus (8. 26), who speaks of a group of Arcadians ἐνεργοὶ βουλόμενοι εἶναι 'desiring to be employed'. The basic sense of the adjective is 'employed, busy, occupied', which is extended in military contexts to those 'on duty' and to units and equipment 'fit for service' (LSJ, s.v.). The abstract noun ἐνέργεια cannot itself be constructed directly from ἐνεργός, since the adjective form corresponding to nouns ending in -εια is the -εσ-stem adjective.[6] Now the adjective ἐνεργής is not attested in the fourth century. Aristotle does use a form presupposing ἐνεγρής, namely the comparative ἐνεργέστερον, in *Top.* i. 12, 105ᵃ19, but he also uses a superlative derived from ἐνεργός in the same work: vii. 4, 154ᵃ16).[7] Much more frequent and philosophically important in Aristotle is the verb ἐνεργεῖν. This verb is a 'denominative' which must derive from ἐνεργός as, for example φιλεῖν 'love' derives from φίλος 'friendly' and the former must mean ἐνεργὸς εἶναι 'be employed, active' as φιλεῖν means φίλος εἶναι 'be friendly', for the -εω verb typically denotes a state or activity corresponding to the noun or adjective (Smyth 1956: 245). In the absence of an adjective ἐνεργής attested in Aristotle's time, it is attractive to take the verb ἐνεργεῖν as the source of ἐνέργεια, and thus recognize the noun as a 'deverbative'.[8] Moreover, ἐντελέχεια, another noun in -εια with

---

[6] On the relation of the noun and adjective, see Buck and Petersen (1945: 121), Schwyzer (1959: 469); on the origin of -εια nouns, see Felix Solmsen (1909: 248–53), Chantraine (1933: 86–8). A complete list of -εια nouns is contained in Buck and Petersen (1945: 128–35).

[7] ἐνεργέστερον may have been suggested by analogy with forms of ἐναργής, whose noun form ἐνάργεια appears to have been coined by Plato.

[8] This is the derivation favoured by Bonitz (1849: 387).

Aristotle coined and associated with ἐνέργεια, lacks an attested adjective from which it can be derived, but can be constructed from a verb phrase. Models of the type βοηθεῖν : βοήθεια were available to Aristotle,[9] and he seems to have been prolific in coining nouns ending in -εια.[10]

If the etymology I have proposed is correct, we may expect that ἐνέργεια is capable of expressing a contrast with a condition of not being employed. And so we find in an example from the *DA*: ὁ δὲ τέκτων μεταβάλλει μόνον εἰς ἐνέργειαν ἐξ ἀργίας (The builder merely changes from idleness to activity) (ii. 4, 416ᵇ2 f.). It is plausible to think that such a paradigm situation of changing from idleness (ἀργία, i.e. ἀ-εργία) to employment inspired the philosophical notion of ἐνέργεια. For the contrast between the potential and the actual use of a faculty is analogous to that between the inactivity and activity of an agent. It is not difficult to cast this relationship into an analogy of proportion: ability : x :: inactivity : activity (or in Greek, δύναμις : x :: ἀργία : ἐνέργεια). The term for 'employment, activity' can be co-opted to supply the missing term, and the result is the opposition δύναμις : ἐνέργεια. The situation of the builder, by the way, shows how the connotation of work (ἔργον) might cling to the notion of activity, and thus provides a kind of justifiable *semantic* and synchronic interpretation for Aristotle's etymological and diachronic remarks connecting the terms ἔργον and ἐνέργεια.[11]

One way of capturing the difference between inactivity and activity would be to designate the activity as a κίνησις. Certainly this term for motion is directly applicable to the paradigm situation. It could easily be extended as a quasi-technical term to cover more abstract notions, and specifically to the property which characterizes an ἐνέργεια by contrast with a faculty. In this way ἐνέργεια and κίνησις might come to be practically synonymous, and the latter term would be a more vivid one to stress the

[9] βοήθεια is actually derived from *βοήθοια (Schwyzer 1959: 469).

[10] Twenty-three -ειᾰ nouns are first attested in Aristotle, 18 in Plato (Buck and Petersen 1945: 128 ff.). In the great majority of cases an -εσ-stem adjective is also attested for these nouns, sometimes for the first time in the author that first uses the noun.) N.B. I am counting only -ειᾰ nouns, not including -είᾰ formations, though the latter have some affinities with the former—see references in n. 6—and sometimes the evidence is ambiguous between forms.)

[11] This derivation of ἐνέργεια from a model of human activity is favoured by Aquinas *Super libros sententiarum* i. 42, 1, 1, c; Meyer (1909: 69 ff.); Jaeger (1923: 410 f.); Smeets (1952: 132 f.), Stallmach (1959: 45).

condition of activity. It would not necessarily be the case, however, that ἐνέργεια would involve motion, since κίνησις would now be a technical term whose meaning was determined by its place in a theory. Thus seeing as opposed to merely having sight would exemplify κίνησις, even though seeing is not essentially a motion or a change. In this way we can justify Aristotle's explications of actuality as a κίνησις without discounting his examples.[12]

Thus far we have been discussing the etymology of ἐνέργεια with a view to explaining the meaning of the term in its original context. We have found that it must mean activity or employment. Of course the term is put to use in Aristotle's philosophy, and the real test is how he actually applies the term. As we have noted earlier,[13] the δύναμις–ἐνέργεια distinction is used in the *Topics* to distinguish between different senses of the same term. For instance, one can be said to perceive something in both a potential and an actual sense. In the first sense, one would have the power of perception without using it; in the latter, one would be employing that power (v. 2, 129ᵇ33 f.). Aristotle makes a similar distinction for knowledge and virtue.[14] In these contexts the contrast is one between a power or faculty and a corresponding activity or exercise. The main object of the distinction seems to be Aristotle's effort to avoid logical mistakes which result from conflating the senses. For instance, Aristotle exposes a fallacy in defining perception as a motion through the body (κίνησις διὰ σώματος): perception is a state (ἕξις), but motion is an activity (ἐνέργεια), so the proposed definition rests on a category mistake (Top. iv. 5, 125ᵇ15–19).

The early appearance of EA in the service of logical clarifications may suggest that the concept owes its origin to logical concerns. However, another early source provides evidence for another origin. The term ἐνέργεια appears in two fragments of the lost dialogue *Protrepticus*. In both fragments 6 and 14 (Ross) the term is contrasted with δύναμις and in both EA rather than ES is intended. Aristotle's argument in fr. 14 is particularly instructive. He begins by making the δύναμις–ἐνέργεια distinction:

---

[12] See discussion of examples in ch. 4.3.2.
[13] See ch. 4.3.2.
[14] *A. Pr.* ii. 21, 67ᵇ3, 5; *A. Po.* i. 24, 86ᵃ29; Top. iii. 2, 117ᵃ32.

'Living' seems to have two senses, one the potential, the other the actual sense. For we say those animals see which have sight and are naturally able to see, even if they happen to have their eyes closed, and also those which are employing this power and making use of their sight. Similarly for 'understanding' and 'knowing', in one sense we mean using knowledge and contemplating, in one sense possessing the power and having understanding. If now we distinguish between living and non-living things by the presence of perception, and 'perception' has two meanings—in the primary sense it signifies using the senses, but also having the power . . . it is clear that 'living' will consequently have two senses. For he who is awake should be said to be alive in the true and primary sense, but he who is asleep because he is able to change into this activity [μεταβάλλειν εἰς ταύτην τὴν κίνησιν] in virtue of which we say he is awake and having some perceptions . . . (Iamblichus *Protrepticus* 56. 15–57. 6 Pistelli)

The distinction is in keeping with that of the *Organon* distinction between faculty and activity. Aristotle even uses the term κίνησις as a rubric for the condition in which the faculty is active. The examples of understanding, knowing, and perceiving are all paralleled in the logical works. But the *Protrepticus* goes beyond the *Organon* in actually putting the distinction between potentiality and actuality to work in the context of a specific philosophical problem. The problem is an ethical–valuational one: what is the good life? By making the distinction between potentiality and actuality, Aristotle can make finer discriminations between various candidates for the good life.

Aristotle's strategy is to identify living in the fullest sense with activity rather than a potentiality to be active. He further associates the good life with the exercise of the best of several faculties, and indeed the correct exercise of it. But man's best faculties are those of thinking and calculating, so 'he lives best who thinks right, and most especially he who thinks truly, and this is he who thinks and contemplates in accordance with the most exact science' (fr. 14, 58. 6–9 Pistelli). Furthermore, the most complete activity brings enjoyment (τὸ χαίρειν), and hence contemplative activity brings the greatest enjoyment. Overall, the argument has much in common with Aristotle's definition of happiness in *EN* i. 7. What is important for the present study is that here the potentiality–actuality distinction is not a mere text-book convention, but a crucial feature of a major argument.

It is perhaps significant that all the examples that appear in S₁

have some relevance to the ethical argument. It is possible that
Aristotle developed the distinction to forestall sophistic refutations
which traded on an ambiguity in verbs (especially of knowing and
perception?) and their nominal counterparts. But it seems unlikely
that the distinction would merit serious attention and even a name
of its own unless its author perceived some positive application for
it. I suggest that the intended application is just the realm of value
theory which the *Protrepticus* fragment exemplifies. One might
even wish to invoke the *Protrepticus* testimony as the earliest
extant source on the potentiality–actuality distinction, as Jaeger
(1928: 632 f.) does. However, I do not believe that the work
antedates the *Topics*, and indeed, if Düring's earlier dating of
Aristotle's works is correct the *Protrepticus* may even come near
the end of the composition of the *Organon*.[15] But as in historical
linguistics the earliest attested uses of words are not always the
most primitive, so in this case temporal priority may not be as
important as philosophical relevance. Moreover, the relatively
early *Eudemian Ethics* employs the concept of ἐνέργεια to argue
for a conception of happiness in a passage reminiscent of the
Protrepticus and anticipating the ἔργον argument of *EN* i. 7;[16] and
in that argument Aristotle invokes a distinction between ἐνέργεια
and ἕξις which appears in the *Topics*.[17] All our evidence points to
the fact that the logical contexts in which ἐνέργεια first appears
find immediate applications in ethical arguments.

As Jaeger (1928: 634) has pointed out, the origin of the
potentiality–actuality distinction can be traced to a Socratic–Platonic
argument in the *Euthydemus* (280 c ff.). There Socrates contrasts
possessing things (κεκτῆσθαι) with using them (χρῆσθαι).[18] The
goods we have will benefit us only if we use them, and use them
correctly. If we should use our goods without wisdom, we would
be less likely to do ill if we had less opportunity. Interestingly, one
of the examples of having less opportunity is being ἀργός rather

[15] Düring (1966: 59) suggests that Aristotle finished the *Organon* by 355; the
Protrepticus is usually dated no earlier than 355. On questions of dating, see ch.
11.3.

[16] This has been the generally accepted view since Jaeger (1923). Kenny (1978)
has disputed this ordering, but his evidence is not conclusive. See the criticisms in
Cooper (1981).

[17] *EE* ii. 1, 1219ᵃ29 ff.; *Top.* iv. 5, 125ᵇ15–19.

[18] As usual—and in contrast to Aristotle—Plato avoids developing a technical
terminology; he uses the verb-forms by preference to the nouns κτῆσις and χρῆσις,
which he uses only in passing.

than ἐργάτης—unemployed rather than employed (281 c 7 f.).
The purpose of the discussion is to reveal the conditions for
attaining happiness (εὐδαιμονία). As is typical in the earlier
dialogues, the distinction between possession and use is *ad hoc* and
is not further developed for its own sake. Nevertheless, the basic
materials for the distinction between potentiality and actuality in
the activity sense are all there. And perhaps it is not a coincidence
that the purpose for introducing the distinction is to determine the
nature of happiness, as is the case for the potentiality–actuality
distinction in the *Protrepticus*. At least the circumstantial evidence
suggests that the original motivation for Aristotle's distinction, as
for its Platonic prototype, is ethical.

The main feature of EA appears to be its contrast to the
underlying faculty. In fact, what we have in all the examples is a
contrast between, roughly, an inert state and an active state of
some subject. The result is analogous to a concept which is a
descendent of EA, that of potential and kinetic energy. A body
has a certain potential energy because of its physical properties
and its location. For instance, a brick on a table has potential
energy proportionate to its height above ground. If it falls off, the
potential energy is converted into kinetic energy. But perhaps even
more apt would be a comparison between potentiality–actuality
and different energy *levels*. For instance, an electron in an atom
may have one of several different energy levels, and it may go from
a higher to a lower level or vice versa. Aristotle plainly conceives
of a person who is exercising knowledge as occupying a higher
level than one who merely possesses the knowledge. In just what
the higher level consists is unclear; however, at least actuality involves
a higher *value*. Since the value in question is identified with
activity, I shall call it kinetic value. That value is expressed in part
by saying that, for some verb V, actually V-ing is the primary sense
of V-ing. Although it might seem appropriate to look for multiple
levels of value, in fact the examples never presuppose more than
three: one level of potentiality and two levels of actuality.[19] It is
important to note that there is no continuity in these energy levels:
rather they are discontinuous states and the transformation from

---

[19] e.g. the ability to learn to read, the acquired state of being able to read, the
activity of reading. Cf. *DA* ii. 1, 412ª9–11; cf. 5, 417ª22–ᵇ2, where the first two
cases are considered species of potentiality and the last a single case of actuality
(ª30).

one to another is a leap rather than an evolution. One is either asleep or awake, not seeing or seeing, possessing knowledge or exercising it. Aristotle treats the changes as immediate, that is, as what Vendler characterizes as achievements.[20]

Aristotle does not comment on the ontological status of actualities and potentialities, but the examples significantly all conform to a single type: all are states of a substance. Being awake, perceiving, knowing, are states of substances, and in particular of animals. The obvious inference is that potentiality–actuality is a concomitant of attributes of substance. Certain attributes may inhere in substances without actively manifesting themselves. Potentiality and actuality are ways of being for such attributes. They are almost adverbial notions. As some epistemologists have sought to analyse statements like 'Mary sees green' by the locution 'Mary sees greenly', Aristotle seems at times to disambiguate a statement like 'Mary sees' into 'Mary sees potentially' and 'Mary sees actually.' For he frequently uses the dative noun in an adverbial way—δυνάμει, ἐνεργείᾳ: 'potentially, actually'—to capture the distinction. The adverbial modification does not apply to the subject, but to the predicate—a predicate adjective or a verb—to qualify its sense. Actuality and potentiality are thus without direct connection to the substance. They signify ways of being F for some attribute F of a substance.

7.2 'Ενέργεια-s

ES is the concept which Aristotle explicitly identifies with substance: as matter is to what is articulated from matter, and the unworked is to the worked, or in general matter is to substance, so is potentiality to actuality (*Met.* ix. 6, 1048[b]3 f., [b]9). Here actuality is not to be identified with a state of a substance, but with the substance itself, by contrast to the material from which it is formed. As Aristotle puts it: 'Thus it is clear that the substance and the form are actuality' (8, 1050[b]2 f.). In the substantial sense, ἐνέργεια and δύναμις are correlates of form or substance and matter, respectively. Thus they distinguish a complete and an incomplete level of organization. The state of actuality is a state of completeness, or ἐντελέχεια in its pregnant sense. ES carries with

---

[20] See the typology of actions in Vendler (1967: ch. 4).

it a notion of value, but it is *ontological* value rather than the kinetic value of EA. An actual statue or an actual horse is more complete and hence more *real* than a potential statue or horse.

Because of the close connection between potentiality and matter on the one hand, and actuality and form on the other, the two schemes become almost interchangeable and the terms synonymous. As Aristotle puts it in the application of these schemes to soul: 'matter is potentiality and form is realization [ἐντελέχεια] . . .' (*DA* ii. 1, 412^{a}9 f.). In general both the matter–form scheme and the potentiality–actuality scheme can do the same work (*Ph.* i. 8, 191^{b}27–9). The schemes are largely coextensive. They differ mainly in intension, for the matter–form scheme analyses substances in the terms of their components while the potentiality–actuality scheme analyses them in terms of their relative completeness or ontological value. Yet the latter scheme is in a sense dependent upon the former in that one must appeal to the degree of organization or integration of components in order to judge the level of completeness. Indeed, before even judging that some matter is potentially some substance, we must verify that the matter in question is appropriate as a substratum for that substance (*Met.* ix. 7, 1048^{b}37 ff.).

ES differs from EA in that it presupposes a continuum of value. Aristotle makes this clear in his discussion of the building of a temple in *EN* x. 4, 1174^{a}19 ff. The many tasks that go to the creation of a temple are incomplete by themselves, but they each contribute to the completeness of the temple. Similarly, in the case of walking (^{a}29 ff.) the several stages of progression are distinct from the whole walk, of which they constitute parts.[21] Indeed, movement itself is an incomplete actualization which ceases when its goal, the complete actualization, for example, the temple, exists (*Ph.* iii. 1). In general it is possible to chronicle the development of some matter into actuality. As an acorn (which is not itself matter, but contains matter) develops it goes through stages which bring it closer to being a complete oak tree.[22] Thus in contrast to EA, which presupposes a discontinuity between potentiality and actuality, ES presupposes a continuous development. The two concepts clearly differ in significant respects

[21] For discussions of the logical form of κίνησις-descriptions see Penner (1970), Graham (1980).
[22] See ch. 5.4.2.

although they share a common name, and, according to Aristotle, are genetically related.

7.3   THE DEVELOPMENT OF THE CONCEPT OF ACTUALITY

We have seen that EA applies to states of substances, to which it ascribes kinetic value. ES applies to substances, differentiating form from matter, and ascribes ontological value. The former concept presupposes discontinuous energy levels, the latter a continuum of development. Aristotle himself recognizes EA as earlier than ES and the source for the later concept. Can we explain the growth of the new concept on the basis of our developmental hypothesis? I believe we can. I have already suggested a possible origin for EA: the need to distinguish between different states of action in the context of a determination of the good life. Now the actual distinction may be due simply to a desire to make some clarifications in light of sophistical objections; but the philosophical motivation for promoting the distinction to a place of prominence is likely to have been ethical. In any case, once it was established it was adequate for performing the task required of it in ethics. The real problem is to explain the motivation of ES: why did Aristotle need to develop a new concept of ἐνέργεια?

7.3.1   The Need for a New Concept

The need for ES can be glimpsed in the conditions which attend substantial change in S₂. As we have noted, Aristotle precipitated the move to a hylomorphic metaphysics when he forged his new theory of generation. According to the theory, a substance comes to be when some appropriate matter, which lacks a certain form, receives that form. Thus the analysis of generation yields three items: the matter, the privation, and the substantial form. Of these, the matter and the form are clearly entities; the privation is best taken as the absence of an entity. From an ontological point of view, accordingly, generation consists of the informing of a material by an organizing form. But there is one grave problem with this account: *the form is ontologically simple.*[23] If we were to

---

[23] Aristotle recognizes this characteristic by noting that forms, like other simple entities, cannot undergo genesis: *Met.* viii. 5, 1044^{b}21–3; vii. 8, 1033^{a}28–^{b}7.

explain generation as merely the coming to be present in matter of a form, it would follow that generation should be immediate and absolute. At time t_0 there would be no form present; at time t_1 the form would suddenly appear, without a process or development.

Now in fact, substances such as Aristotle interprets them to be do not come to be in this fashion. They develop gradually from small beginnings into a mature organism. The theory of generation is intended to account for our experience of nature—to save the phenomena. An account which treats generation as immediate fails to explain the phenomena.

What Aristotle needs is a *metaphysical basis* for explaining generation as a gradual process. The scheme of three principles Aristotle develops in *Ph.* i obviously does not provide the means for solving the problem. However, it does provide some direction for a solution. For according to the scheme, as we have noted, change is no longer exchange of features in a substratum as it was in the *Categories* but development from a negative to a positive condition. That is, it is built into the scheme that a typical change is from not-*F* to *F*. If this is so, change is inherently progressive and constructive.[24] The paradigmatic change is in the direction of greater integration, organization, and order. But if this is so, change is inherently goal-directed, since whenever a process tends toward an end, it exists for the sake of that end (*Ph.* ii. 8, 199ª8 f.). It is furthermore the case that the goal of the process has a higher metaphysical value than the starting-point. Thus change typically increases value. From a cosmic perspective, this account introduces a sort of inverse of the law of entropy in Aristotle's system.

Of course there are objections to such a cosmic leap. The description of a change is relative to our interests, and we can describe changes so as to emphasize the negative or privative outcomes, as Aristotle is well aware.[25] Nonetheless, Aristotle believes that some points of view are more equal than others. The very fact that in nature organisms grow to full maturity if nothing impedes them and processes follow regular courses is remarkable and important.[26] That nature is creative is a datum that must be

[24] See ch. 5.4.4.
[25] See ch. 5 n. 42. Cf. *Ph.* v. 5 229ª25–7; *Met.* ix. 9, 1051ª5–11 asserts the potential for each of two opposites, but the following lines use the fact to argue for the superiority of actuality over potentiality, on which cf. ibid., ch. 8.
[26] See Cooper (1982) for a discussion of the naturalistic basis of Aristotle's teleology.

acknowledged in natural philosophy. Hence the intimation of the schema of change that change is inherently progressive is confirmed by the facts.

7.3.2   *From Energy Levels to the Curve of Becoming*

There is an analogy between potentiality–actuality in the activity sense and generation. For potentiality and actuality apply to two successive states of a substance, of which the latter possesses higher kinetic value. Thus we have a substratum which exhibits two states which are differentiated by their level of value. For instance, a human being at different times is asleep and awake. In the case of generation there is a substratum, the matter, and also two successive states, one without form and one with. The latter has a higher level of ontological value. The anology is close enough that potentiality–actuality can serve as a model for generation, and the deprived state can be identified with potentiality while the informed state of matter can be identified with actuality (see Fig. 7.1). Nevertheless, the scheme of EA presupposes only *discontinuous* energy levels whereas Aristotle needs a *continuum*. The difficulty is not insurmountable: the discontinuity is an incidental feature of the EA scheme and not part of its definition. More important is the fact that the very discontinuity presupposes a scale of value. The scale itself is continuous, and it can be invoked to account for the continuity of generation.

knowing	reading	level 3	scale of
awake	literate	level 2	activity
asleep	illiterate	level 1	($\grave{\epsilon}\nu\acute{\epsilon}\rho\gamma\epsilon\iota\alpha$)
subject 1	subject 2	substance	

FIG. 7.1.   Energy Levels (EA)

I suggest that Aristotle did invoke the potentiality–actuality scheme to solve the continuity problem for generation. What it provides is another dimension, as it were, for the representation of generation. For as time unfolds along a horizontal axis, completeness can be measured along a vertical axis—against a continuous scale of reality. Thus we can plot a *curve of becoming* which shows a continuum of growth and development (see Fig. 7.2). Of course Aristotle did not conceive of the process in a graphic way, but the

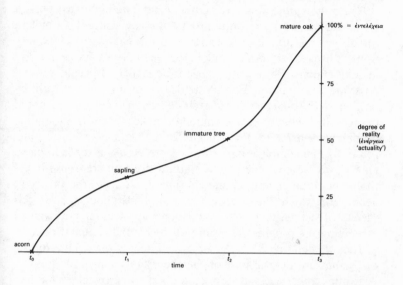

FIG. 7.2.   Curve of Becoming (ES)

exercise gives an interpretation to the phenomenon he was attempting to account for: the continuity of change. For instance, at t_0 we have an acorn, at t_1 a sapling, at t_2 a small tree, and at t_3 a mature oak. Note that the same scheme can be applied also to gradual accidental changes, such as the change in colour of a ripening apple. Such changes are not as problematic as generation, but they also deserve to be accounted for.

By comparing EA in Fig. 7.1 and ES in Fig. 7.2 we can also observe an important ontological distinction between them. As the diagrams show, EA is always a state of a *substance*. ES, by contrast, is properly a state of *matter*. EA is the only kind of actuality available for a theory such as S_1 which construes substances as atomic subjects; the ES scheme could have no place in S_1 because it presupposes—indeed defines—varying degrees of substantiality. For S_2, on the other hand, EA becomes merely a limiting case in which the substratum is a substance and the form in question is an attribute of substance, while ES is central. The ontological correlations between the two systems and the two types of actuality thus confirm and clarify the historical correlations.

By extending the notion of actuality and potentiality to apply to substantial changes, Aristotle produced a new concept. Complete actuality is the full exemplification of form; complete potentiality is the absence of form. And in between lies a space for the incremental growth of form. Since form is metaphysically simple, Aristotle accounts for the varying degree of presence of form by *positing a concomitant scale of exemplification*. The new concept of potentiality–actuality thus embodies a strategy for grounding continuous generation. For actuality is the metaphysical measuring-rod of formal completeness. In this sense ἐνέργεια tends to mean ἐντελέχεια 'completeness' and justifies the common-sense belief that generation is gradual and continuous. Indeed, the theory of generation would be incomplete and inadequate without this theory of actuality, for it would leave us without any way of explaining the progressive nature of substantial coming to be.

Thus we find that ES is not a mere adjunct to the hylomorphism of S₂, but an integral part of the theory of change. Without it, Aristotle could account for generation only by claiming that generation was a sudden and immediate change. But this is not how generation in fact occurs. Thus he must supplement his account of the principles of change with that of a metaphysical continuum of reality. And this is actuality in the substantial sense.

7.3.3   Degrees of Reality

We have already seen in chapter 4.3.3 that the principle of actuality of S₂ is prima facie incompatible with S₁. For, according to S₁, no individual substance is more of a substance than any other individual substance, or than itself at another time. But according to A, an individual substance can develop so as to be more of a substance than it was, and one substance can be more of a substance than another. We noted the conflict of the two systems on this point, but we have not explained the reasons for it. Now we are in a position to do so. They key to explaining the conflict is Aristotle's attempt in S₂ to accommodate generation. In effect, Aristotle is forced to deny the simplicity of substance in order to explain generation; accordingly, he divides substance into form and matter. But in order to explain the *continuity* of generation, he must also deny the absoluteness of substance: if substancehood is an either-or affair, then there can be no continuous process of coming to be for substances. In that case, either a candidate is or is not a substance; there can be no middle ground and hence no process. But if we can determine a scale of substancehood, then it will not be impossible for a substance to develop gradually out of its matter.

Actuality is a scale of reality or being—of the degree of presence of form in matter. Since concrete substance is the union of form and matter, actuality is a scale of substancehood. Aristotle has limited the Eleatic perfection of the primary substance of S_1 in order to make room for generation. The pristine conception of substance that underlies the S_1 world-view gives way to a complex analysis. No more impassible, sensible substance is now a compound of matter and form; and these components are not united in a simple nexus, but in a variable bond that permits quantitative differentiation. Instead of being either a substance or not, an individual may be more or less of a substance. This raises the question whether concrete substance can be really real inasmuch as it admits of varying degrees of reality. From one point of view, to pose this question is to answer it—in the negative. But this leaves the problem of what is the true reality or substance. To this question we shall turn in the next chapter.

7.4. POTENTIALITY IN *MET.* IX

I began the discussion of actuality by referring to Aristotle's own remarks in *Met.* ix, which distinguished between an earlier and a later sense of potentiality and actuality. I identified EA and ES with the earlier and later senses of ἐνέργεια. For convenience I shall designate the corresponding senses of δύναμις as DA and DS, respectively. Now, does the distinction I have drawn agree with the one Aristotle suggests in Book ix? The answer is a complex one.

After warning us that there are two senses of potentiality and actuality in the opening chapter, Aristotle goes on to identify the sense of potentiality which is connected with κίνησις with what I shall call the concept of power:

We have elsewhere shown that δύναμις and δύνασθαι have many senses. Let us dismiss the senses that are equivocal . . . those that are defined with relation to the same form all designate sources and are defined in relation to a primary sense, which is 'a source of change in another in so far as it is other'. (1046ᵃ4–11)

Alluding to his discussion of δύναμις in *Met.* v. 12, Aristotle makes use of his definition of power. The definition involves a transitive or 'transeunt' sense of potency in which an agent is conceived of as acting on a patient. For instance, if billiard ball *A* strikes billiard ball *B* so as to dislodge it, *A* has manifested a power of moving *B*, and *B* has manifested a passive power of being moved by *A*. The main term that contrasts with power is nature or φύσις, which Aristotle defines as 'a certain source and cause of motion and rest in that to which it belongs primarily and in a proper, not an incidental, sense' (*Ph.* ii. 1, 192^{b}21–3).[27] A substance has a nature in so far as it has a tendency to stay at rest or to move—that is, not to move *something else* but to move itself. Thus whereas the concept of power presupposes a transitive action verb: *A* V*s* *B*, the concept of nature presupposes an intransitive or reflexive sense : *A* V*s* or *A* V*s* *A*.[28]

Now what does power have to do with DA? Consider Ross's analysis:

> The relation [between ἐνέργεια and δύναμις] is of two main kinds: (1) that of movement to *power*, (2) that of substance to matter. We recognize in the first of these a reference to the transeunt δύναμις, ἡ κατὰ κίνησιν λεγομένη δύναμις, with which the first half of [*Met.* ix] was occupied. A power in *A* to produce change in *B* is at the same time an immanent δύναμις in *A*. In producing change in *B*, *A* is itself passing from potentiality to actuality. (1924, i. p. cxxvii, italics added)

According to Ross, DA is identical to δύναμις in the sense of *power* (hereafter: DP). For DA is a source of change in another. But consider Aristotle's examples at *Met.* ix. 6, 1048^{a}37–^{b}4, as shown in Fig. 7.3. The builder's potentiality may consist in the source of changing bricks into a building. But sleeping does not consist in a source of change in another. Nor does having sight.[29] Indeed, the builder can be an active builder even without actually moving anything if he is planning the construction.[30] Furthermore, a little reflection on the scheme will show that potentiality could not possibly be identical with power, since it makes sense to speak of a power as either *potentially* or *actually* operating.

---

[27] The final qualifications are designed to rule out cases like the doctor doctoring himself, a feat carried out by τέχνη, a species of power.

[28] Cf. Mourelatos (1967: 99 f.).

[29] Seeing often involves an object, but the object is not affected by the seer, as Aristotle was well aware. Cf. *SE* 22, 178^{a}15–19.   [30] Cf. *Met.* vii. 7, 1032^{b}15 ff.

DA/EA	DS/ES
(1) able to build/building	(1) matter/articulated from matter
(2) sleeping/awake	(2) unfashioned/fashioned
(3) having sight/seeing	

Fig. 7.3.   Types of Potentiality–Actuality.

This last observation suggests the radical difference between DP and DA. DP is *essentially* transitive or transeunt in nature, as Aristotle's definition in *Met.* v. 12 shows. But DA is not essentially transitive. In fact, the examples suggest that it is essentially non-transitive, and that objects of action such as buildings for builders are only incidental to the actualization of DA. What is necessary for the builder is to do whatever it is he needs to do to use his capacity. For the builder that will ultimately involve moving something or someone, but in the case of the seer it will not involve moving anything.[31] Thus the transitivity present in DA is due only to the nature of the specific capacity in question, not to the nature of potentiality. Furthermore, DP differs from DA simply in that the former can be defined, whereas the latter can be known only inductively, through examples (1048^a35-7).[32] There is an underlying reason for this superficial distinction: DA is essentially a *correlative* notion, whereas DP is not. It is impossible to understand what a given instance of DA is without understanding what the corresponding EA is.[33] For instance, we cannot understand what it is to be a builder without understanding building. But it is possible to understand power apart from its homonymous actuality-term. For instance, instead of saying heat is what heats, we can say that heat is the tendency to associate things of like nature.[34] Because power is the source of change in another, it can be defined

---

[31] Note that Aristotle argues that the most practical activity is thought itself: 'But it is not necessary that the practical life should be a life in which one interacts with others, as some think, nor that only those thoughts should be practical which are performed for the sake of their results, but much rather those which are complete in themselves and those contemplations and reasonings which exist for their own sake. For good activity is an end in itself, so that it is a kind of action. Indeed we say even of those engaged in productive activities that they who direct the work with their minds [τοὺς ταῖς διανοίαις ἀρχιτέκτονας] are active in the strictest sense' (*Pol.* vii. 3, 1325^b16-23).

[32] Thus Aquinas *in Met*, sec. 1826 (Cathalá), Smeets (1952: 96–9), Reale (1962: 162 f.).

[33] Cf. Reale (1962: 163), Arnold (1965: 150).   [34] *GC* ii. 2, 329^b26 f.

in terms of its effects on that other without merely repeating the same term.

Thus DP and DA are very different concepts. The majority of scholars seem to take them as identical as does Ross.[35] I think Aristotle means us to make the identification, reading κίνησις at $1048^{b}8$ as the fulfilment of his promise to link a kinetic sense of δύναμις–ἐνέργεια to the sense which tends to mean ἐντελέχεια. But Aristotle has confounded DP and DA to make the identification.[36] What this means in effect is that he does not really explain how DS/ES came to be. This throws us back on our own devices. I have already presented my views on the development of the concept-pair as consistent with TST. But there are a number of competing theories of the potentiality–actuality development. I do not wish to examine these in detail, since I think most of them are implausible. But it will be useful to compare them with my account. There are two main lines of thought on the development of the theory of actuality.

A number of scholars who have expressed themselves on the subject assume that Aristotle did not have a theory of δύναμις–ἐνέργεια in the earliest period. Following the lead of Gohlke (1924) they stress the absence of the term and concept of ἐνέργεια in the definitions of Met. v. 12 and the early books of the Physics.[37] But Jaeger (1928) argues against Gohlke that he has ignored the evidence for the potentiality–actuality contrast in the fragments of the Protrepticus.[38] Berti (1958), accepting Jaeger's views, has stressed the development from DA/EA to DS/ES and from immediate experience of activity to a reflective understanding of its basis in actuality.[39]

---

[35] Wundt (1953) sees Met. ix. 1–5 as dealing with DP only. This makes it difficult to see the connection between the two halves of the book. But the connections are obscure in any case.

[36] Bonitz (1849: 379 f.) stresses Aristotle's failure to keep his terms separate: '. . . Ac posse quidem duo δυνάμεως genera distingui nemo infitiabitur; sed et admodum subtile et minutum esse haec discrimen apparet, neque ipsum Aristotelem satis caute versatum in tenenda ea distinctione, ut alios libros ne adeamus quidem, ex hoc ipso libro, in quo eam distinctionem proposuit, facile potest cognosci.' Bonitz focuses on the confusion of potency and possibility in ix. 3.

[37] Thus Wundt (1953: 79–102), Stallmach (1959; ch. 4), Gohlke (1954). Cf. also Jaeger (1923: 222).

[38] Berti (1958: 481) cites also Eudemus fr. 2, but the passage does not reveal the distinction in the Eudemus.

[39] This general line of interpretation is anticipated by Meyer (1909: 69 ff.), who speculated that the potentiality–actuality distinction was arrived at independently

Those in the first group who have bothered to reply to Jaeger have argued that the words of Iamblichus' paraphrase from which the *Protrepticus* fragments are drawn are not reliable.[40] But the δύναμις-ἐνέργεια distinction is an integral part of the *Protrepticus* argument, not an incidental feature, and it is therefore not likely that Iamblichus can be blamed for introducing the references.[41] Furthermore, the *Topics*, which is likely to be earlier than the *Protrepticus*, contains a number of unimpeachable instances of DA/EA.[42] This seems to me to provide conclusive evidence against the first approach, whatever merits the reconstructions may have in their details.[43] This leaves Berti's account, which is

from the matter–form distinction, the former based on a model of human activity, the latter on a model of natural process; and the schemes were later combined. (Jaeger 1923: 410 f. followed by Smeets 1952: 131–4 rightly notes that *both* schemes are modelled on human activity.)

[40] Wundt (1953: 18 f.), Gohlke (1954: 7 f.). Jaeger (1928: 633) takes a dim view of this approach: 'Die Naivität dieser "Philologie" entspricht der Kindlichkeit des philosophischen Missverständnisses der Methode des Aristoteles . . .'

[41] Note also that recent scholarship has tended to confirm Iamblichus' value as a source. As Düring (1954: 144) puts it, 'We can be fairly sure that Iamblichus followed the Aristotelian original rather slavishly. When he departs from it, he immediately shows his incompetence.' Guthrie (1981: 76) calls Iamblichus 'a word-for-word plagiarist as his borrowings from Plato prove'. Actually, what he was doing is perhaps better seen as thematic anthologizing. On Iamblichus' method, see Düring (1961: 24–7).

[42] Virtually everyone who has written on the development of the concept of actuality has overlooked this evidence. Wundt (1953: 98), after observing that Waitz's index to the *Organon* fails to record any occurrences of ἐνέργεια, attempts to remedy the defect; but he himself fails to note any occurrences in the *Topics*! See ch. 4.3.2. for a discussion of the *Topics* passages.

[43] Stallmach (1959: ch. 4) provides an interesting account. He recognizes three main stages: (1) beginning with δύναμις as a principle of change in another, Aristotle elaborates an account of the process of change in such a way that it comes to incorporate the relations able-to-build (active power) and able-to-be-built (passive power). But these two (horizontal) correlations of ground-of-change : change cause the (vertical) relation of the agent to the patient to be transcended. An element of immanent fulfilment is introduced. (2) The passive δύναμις, connected with ὕλη in relation to form and divested of power, comes to be conceived as mere potentiality. (3) The new conception of δύναμις lacks a correlative term. Aristotle uses the δύναμις : ἔργον and ἕξις : ἐνέργεια terminologies (cf. *EE*) to build a δύναμις : ἐνέργεια pair. This pair of terms, which first corresponds to the active power, is extended by the influence of the passive sense of δύναμις and the relation of δύναμις to matter in the matter : form opposition to produce a new potentiality : actuality opposition.

I think the scheme is overworked. But it is possible that some such cross-fertilization of notions took place, and I do not regard my own account of DA/EA to DS/ES development as necessarily capturing all the complex interaction of the several concepts.

correct in its overall conception.[44] The alternative reconstructions simply fail to account for the relevant data.[45]

There is one problem or set of problems that an account of the first type brings to the fore. Why does Aristotle fail to mention ἐνέργεια in his philosophical dictionary, *Met.* v, and further in his critiques of his predecessors in *Met.* i, and in the early books of the *Physics*, notably Book i?[46] Some scholars want to use the absence of the concept to make the potentiality–actuality distinction a relatively late development.[47] TST, however, can explain the absence of the concept in the early books of the *Physics*: the DS/ES distinction that is relevant to metaphysics post-dates the hylomorphic turn, and hence the notions of actuality and potentiality should enter metaphysical discussion only gradually. And the early books of the *Metaphysics*, including Book v, are on the standard account also written soon after *Ph.* i, which I claim heralds the discovery of matter.

But one might object that *Met.* v, though relatively early, was written after the *Topics* and probably the *Protrepticus*. Thus it was

---

[44] I disagree with Berti in that he supposes Aristotle begins from a Platonic stage which I do not believe was present (see ch. 11.3). I also think his stress on the role of immediate experience in suggesting the DA/EA distinction invites a naïve view of this theory-construction. Berti gives an interesting account of the metaphysical value of the DS/ES distinction (1958: 490, 504); but he implies that it is Parmenides' Non-Being–Being dichotomy that forces the development of the concept, whereas I claim it is the further problem that Aristotle's own candidate for Being, namely form, is indivisible.

[45] A further possibility is that no developmental account is needed; this is the conclusion Reale (1962: 193 f.) arrives at. But such a view fails to account for the consistent difference of meaning we have found between S₁ and S₂.

[46] Aristotle's reference to potentiality and actuality in Book i, 8, 191ᵇ27–9, reads like a later insertion.

[47] Gohlke (1954, cf. 1924) thinks that *Ph.* i, v, and vi–viii in an older recension than we now have (of which the β-version of vii is a relic) are earlier than ii–iv. Runner (1951: 66 f.) gives some hasty arguments for taking vii as early. Düring (1966: 291 f., 306 f.) thinks Book vii is a collection of notes or sketches that is earlier than much of the *Physics*. Ross (1936: 1–19) considers i–vii fairly early, possibly all written in the Academy, iii–vii having been composed in roughly their present numerical order (though vii is not an integral part of the series). Düring's view of Book vii as a collection of notes seems attractive, but observe that in any case ch. 3 presupposes the matter–form distinction, and hence Book i. See also Bos (1973) for a different reconstruction of the early physical works. Whatever the precise details, virtually everyone regards i as early.

Gohlke also argues that early books of the *Met.* did not mention the potentiality–actuality distinction. But there are numerous references e.g. in Books iii, v, xiii, and xiv. Gohlke tries to excise many of these by a circular argument (e.g. pp. 94 f.). For criticism, see Reale (1962: 184–9; index of terms, 196–204).

written well after the concepts DA/EA were known. Should it not then contain an entry for ἐνέργεια? And although the book perhaps focuses on metaphysical concepts and the like, the terms discussed often include only marginally relevant homonyms of the main entries, as is the case in Chapter 12. Why then, when Aristotle is not loath to discuss even arguably non-philosophical terms, does he fail to mention DA as a respectable sense of δύναμις, in his entry for that term? I have no conclusive answers. But it seems to me that Aristotle's tendency in *Met.* ix to conflate DP and DA may cause him to think that in giving DP he has given DA. And there is no reason to suppose that Aristotle should feel obliged to create a separate entry for ἐνέργεια, since even form and matter come in only as an afterthought in *Met.* v. 8. His list of terms is a haphazard one that seems to reflect a state of research characteristic of early S₂, but which often fails to reproduce state-of-the-art discriminations.[48] I do not think much can be proved from *Met.* v other than the relative unimportance of the potentiality–actuality distinction in the early works of S₂.

Aristotle's remarks in *Met.* ix show that he is aware of some kind of development in his concepts of potentiality–actuality. But an examination of his account shows that he is not clear about the nature of that development. Even if he were explicit about the relation between DP, DA/EA, and DS/ES—which he is not—he should still tell us *why* the concepts developed the way they did. And this he never attempts. Nonetheless, we can reconstruct the order of development from his texts. From his earliest extant writings we find the DA/EA distinction; the DS/ES distinction appears only in S₂. The matter–form distinction ushers in S₂ and makes possible an identification between potentiality and matter, actuality and form. Furthermore, as we have seen, the matter–form analysis as it develops in the context of the problem of change requires some parameters. For since form is indivisible it must be instantiated immediately unless some continuous scale of exemplification is additionally posited. And that scale is precisely what DS/ES provides. TST *accommodates* the data (as most other

---

[48] Thus ch. 2 is a boiler-plate from *Ph.* ii. 3 representing up-to-date S₂ casual theory, but ch. 22 on στέρησις recognizes only the S₁ conception of deprivation, not the new S₂ conception of privation. Note also that ἐνέργεια, ἐνεργεῖν, and ἐντελέχεια occur 19 times in *Met.* v; see Reale's table, 197 f. Thus the potentiality–actuality distinction is not unknown in *Met.* v.

developmental theories do not) and also *explains* them. The structure of *Met.* ix does not strongly support the TST account, but then Aristotle's mistaken identification of DP and DA would cause problems for any account. On the positive side, the *Met.* ix account does confirm that the sense of δύναμις and ἐνέργεια that has to do with κίνησις is the early one; and if we interpret κίνησις as 'activity' rather than 'movement' Aristotle's remarks turn out to be accurate and illuminating. Thus TST accounts for the development which Aristotle adumbrates in *Met.* ix.

7.5   CONCLUSION

In this chapter and the previous one we have observed the growth of two Aristotelian theories. In one case Aristotle gives no notice of the development; in the other he recognizes it but makes some misleading observations. Despite the difficulties in tracing a development, there are clear indications of the direction of development for both theories. In both cases, theories that were peripheral to S$_1$ were transformed under the pressure of new principles to become key components of the new system. In tracing the growth of the theories we have seen how they were able to conform to new requirements and to resolve problems that came with the new system. The fact that we have been able to correlate important stages in the development of these theories with the changeover to S$_2$ provides confirmation for our developmental hypothesis. By recognizing the hylomorphic turn in Aristotle's early physical speculation we can understand variations in Aristotelian theories in a systematic way. The absence of a material and a formal cause in the *A.Po.* account of the four causes is not an accident; the absence of DS/ES in early accounts of actuality makes sense. Overall, we see how Aristotle's progress from S$_1$ to S$_2$ allowed him to achieve a greater integration of his theories while expanding the range and explanatory power of his philosophy. A larger question remains to be answered. To what extent did S$_2$ solve the problems it was designed to solve? Despite the greater integrity and power of the new system, there are some serious obstacles to the fulfilment of Aristotle's programme. In the next chapter we shall examine these obstacles.

8

The Paradoxes of Substance: Matter

Thus far we have examined the contents of the two systems, S_1 and S_2; we have found that they were not identical but rather incommensurable; we have seen that S_1 is earlier than S_2 and that S_2 results from a development of S_1 motivated by Aristotle's desire to explain substantial change; and finally we have seen that important components of S_2 develop from unimportant components of S_1 under the impetus of the new system. One serious gap remains in the account of the relation of S_1 and S_2: how did Aristotle see their relation? The question becomes a pressing one when we realize that if he retained S_1 as part of his mature philosophy, he must have held incompatible principles. This would entail that his philosophy was inconsistent, and it would cause us to expect contradictory statements in his mature writings—statements that would be deducible from the incompatible principles he espoused. In this chapter and the next I shall examine these questions and argue that Aristotle in fact did not abandon S_1. And I shall claim that a record of the consequences is to be found in that compendium of Aristotelian paradoxes, *Metaphysics* vii. Accordingly, in the course of this chapter and the next I shall produce a reading of *Met.* vii which, unlike the majority of present and past interpretations, purports not to find *the* real solution to the problem of substance but to show that there is *no* unique solution to the problem.

8.1 ARISTOTLE'S CONTINUED ACCEPTANCE OF S_1

There is no evidence that Aristotle ever abandoned S_1. Throughout the corpus, he makes backward references to the works of S_1, citing them as providing illumination for theories under discussion. This of course implies that he still accepts the expositions in question without reservations. One might wonder whether he accepts other sections of the *Organon* treatises which he does not refer to. There are at least no grounds for believing that he rejects them. He never explicitly repudiates the works as a whole nor the principles found in them. There are specific theories within them that scholars have thought were rejected in later writings. For instance, the *A.Po.* view of division may be under attack in Aristotle's criticism of the method of division in the *PA*. Even in this relatively limited case, however, it is not clear whether the target of criticism is Aristotle's own theory or someone else's version of division.[1]

On the other hand, there are some obvious cases in which propositions from S_1 are out of step with those of S_2. We have already examined such cases as the conflict of the indivisibility vs. the divisibility of substance and the disagreement over whether there are degrees of substancehood. In these cases that seem to beg for a clarification, Aristotle surprisingly has nothing to say. This silence on his part has encouraged the unitarian interpretation of Aristotle. I have already argued for the inadequacy of this view. But Aristotle's silence does seem to provide evidence that his own view of his work was unitarian in character. Either he saw no problem or he thought the problem was so easily resolved that it did not call for comment.

Furthermore, Aristotle actually asserts some key principles of S_1 in works of S_2. In particular, he invokes certain of these obsolete principles in *Met.* vii. Since we shall examine the relevant passages in some detail in what follows, I shall not discuss the cases now. But the fact is that, far from repudiating S_1, Aristotle continues to make use of its principles, even in the context of metaphysical expositions in S_2

I have noted already Aristotle's general insensitivity to developmental questions regarding his own philosophy.[2] However, we have seen that he recognized, albeit obscurely and somewhat inaccurately, a development in the theory of actuality. This small area of awareness indicates that Aristotle did not totally ignore or discount matters of his own philosophical development. If, then, he had some awareness of his developing view of substance, and if further he regarded some explanation as necessary, and if he held

---

[1] Some scholars have argued that Aristotle's target in *PA* i. 2–4 was his own early view on the subject (see Düring 1943: 109 f. followed by Lloyd 1961: 59 f.). However, Balme (1972: 104 f.) rejects this interpretation.

[2] See chs. 7.0, 7.4.

a unitarian view of his own philosophy, he must have held either the *Organon* Hypothesis or the Extension Hypothesis. For only these two hypotheses would justify a unitarian view of his theories.

Which of these views he held it is not possible to say in the absence of direct evidence. There may be some indirect evidence in the fact that he does not seem to restrict the validity of his early theories to logical contexts when he cites them. This may suggest that he did not view the *Organon* as narrowly logical in its applications, and hence that he did not hold OH, but EH. As Düring (1966: 53) notes, the view that logic does not belong to philosophy is probably imported by later commentators reacting to Stoic theories. Thus there may be a slight presumption in favour of Aristotle's holding EH. Furthermore, given Aristotle's teleological view of the history of ideas,[3] it is likely that he would tend to see any development of his own views as a natural extension of his earlier position, and hence, even if he held OH, to confound this view with EH. In any case, his historical views would tend to encourage the optimistic view that his earlier and later theories could be reconciled in principle, on the ground that philosophical development is cumulative.

Like most philosophers, Aristotle probably evaluated his principles on the basis of the problems they helped to solve. He seems to have largely closed the book on the *Organon* problems when he turned to natural philosophy. He thus had no need critically to re-examine the principles of S_1 and may have never had occasion to compare them with those of S_2. The S_1 principles worked in their context; the S_2 principles worked in theirs. Thus, whether or not he espoused OH, he may have in practice assigned the principles to non-overlapping domains and thus have failed to note any conflict. Aristotle's own model of the understanding seems to explain his oversight:

In having knowledge but not using it we see a different state [from having it and using it], so that in a sense one has knowledge and in a sense one does not, as in the case of the sleeper, the madman, and the drunk. (*EN* vii. 3, 1147^{a}11–14).

Aristotle's oversight need not result from somnolence, strong drink, or excess of passion—preoccupation with other matters seems sufficient excuse. His failure to note the inconsistency of

[3] Cf. *Met.* i. 3, 984^{a}18 f., ^{b}9–11; xii. 8, 1074^{a}38–^{b}14.

parts of his theory marks a failure to exercise his knowledge of different propositions at the same time. Since Aristotle was conditioned by his own philosophy to minimize the effects of development and to compartmentalize his studies, it is plausible to think that he did not find occasion to compare, contrast, and criticize the principles of his earlier and later systems, or even to view the systems as two.

Whatever Aristotle's views on the unity and consistency of his philosophy, it is certain that if he did retain the two sets of incompatible principles, there would be tensions in his thought. Whether these tensions were made explicit in contradictions would depend on whether or not he drew out enough consequences from his principles to exhibit the incompatibility. But clearly it would be possible in principle to produce contradictions from such a system. I have already noted some tensions in the theory of substance that produce contradictions on the asumption that 'substance' has a common reference: Socrates is both a simple substance and not a simple substance, and in his childhood he is both a complete substance and not a complete substance. Unfortunately, these examples do not result from a confrontation of systems and are not even noticed by Aristotle. Accordingly, we cannot say that he is confronted with the conflict. *A fortiori*, neither can we say that he would maintain S_1 principles in the face of such a conflict. However, I shall argue that there is a work in which Aristotle presents principles from both his systems and precipitates a conflict of major proportions. This work can serve as a test case both for viewing the effect of mixing the principles in question and for observing Aristotle's reaction to the conflict. The work is *Metaphysics* vii.

8.2 THE PROBLEM OF *METAPHYSICS* VII

Metaphysics vii is regarded by many commentators as the pinnacle of Aristotelian metaphysical speculation. In it Aristotle undertakes to solve the problem of substance, namely what is substance, once and for all. However, his exposition is notoriously difficult. In addition to the difficulty of understanding Aristotle's solution to the problem, there is a second-order problem of why Aristotle finds it so difficult to come to a solution. In section 8.3 I shall examine his attempts at finding a solution. But for now I wish to

concentrate on examining the problem Aristotle sets for himself
and the conditions for an adequate solution that he recognizes.
For by understanding the problem we shall be in a better position
to understand the sources of conflict.

8.2.1 The Problem of Substance

Aristotle devotes *Met.* vii to a central question of metaphysics that
he notes has challenged generations of philosophers:

> ... the question that is and always has been asked and always has puzzled
> philosophers is: What is being? [τί τὸ ὄν]; and this question is just: What
> is substance? For some say that this is one while some say it is more than
> one; and some say it is of a limited number while others of an unlimited
> number. Therefore we too must consider especially and first and only, so
> to speak, what is the nature of this kind of being. (1, 1028ᵇ2–7)

Aristotle sees himself as part of a philosophical tradition with a
shared problem. The problem is the nature of being. He claims
that his predecessors and contemporaries all are or have been
seeking to discover what being is. But this question is just the
question of substance. Here Aristotle must be taking 'substance' in
a broad sense such that it does not refer merely to Aristotle's
technical definitions, or the identification would be patently false.
'Substance' means roughly 'the ultimate entity', that is, the real
being that is the ground of all existence. Yet Aristotle's invocation
of substance here is not altogether innocent of Aristotelian theory.
For he prefaces the above remark with an exposition of the
categories of being in order to show that substance is the central
sense of the term. He seems to believe that the commitment to a
substantival concept of being is shared by the tradition. In other
words, it has been a common assumption that the answer to the
question of being is to be a *thing* or some *thinglike* entity. There
seem to be some grounds for acknowledging this much agreement
in the tradition, with perhaps the exception of Heraclitus, whom
Aristotle does not understand very well.[4]

Book vii thus appears to address a general philosophical
problem. By the end of Chapter 3, however, it becomes evident
that Aristotle not only has a traditional question to ask, but that he
is wrestling with the implications of his own philosophy. For he

---

[4] On the substantiality of being and Heraclitus' opposition to it, see Mourelatos
(1973). On οὐσία as an antecedently understood term, cf. Loux (1984: 241).

suddenly becomes embroiled in a difficult question internal to his system: is the composite, or form, or matter the substance? Of course in one sense the answer is that they all are. But this does not satisfy the inquiry, and so we are forced to recognize that what Aristotle is after is not just a vindication of his view of substance *vis-à-vis* the tradition, but a determination of the ultimate ground of reality *in his own system*. Indeed, as Aristotle's argument progresses in Book vii it becomes evident that the real focus of the book is a tension in his own philosophy, and only by the way does he undertake to refute some erroneous conceptions of substance. I would like to suggest that the real motivation for Book vii is not Aristotle's perception of inadequacies in the tradition, but his concerns about the status of his own concept of substance.

In fact, it is precisely the transition from S_1 to S_2 that makes the question 'What is substance?' an urgent one.[5] For the whole concept of substance becomes problematic within the context of S_2. In S_1, we recall, substance is whatever fills the requirement of not being in anything or said of anything. We have noted that these requirements determine an entity that is always a *subject* and never a predicate. This subject is τόδε τι signifying at least that it is indivisible and one in number (*Cat.* 5, 3ᵇ10 ff.). Thus, according to S_1, substance in the primary sense consists of a particular subject. Aristotle interprets these formal requirements as applying to at least particular living organisms. Hence Socrates is a primary substance. In general S_1 has a clear and unambiguous account of primary substance, and moreover one which satisfies Aristotle's predilection for common-sense philosophy by identifying the really real with what is most familiar and accessible to us.

The hylomorphism of S_2, however, shatters this comfortable picture of harmony. For it identifies Socrates with the composite of two ontological components, form and matter. To be sure, Socrates is still a substance, but the new arrangement raises nagging doubts about the status of Socrates as a substance. How can we say that he is an example of the *ultimate* reality? Are not the components themselves the ultimate simples in the equation? What implications does this have for the concept of substance in general? Moreover, if we decide that one of the components of Socrates is the real substance, how are we to understand what the

[5] Cf. Dancy (1978: 382 f.).

component consists of? For we know (or seem to know) what Socrates is; but what do we know of his metaphysical components? How are we to interpret them?

We see, then, that at the root of *Met.* vii is the need to articulate a new concept of substance that conforms to the ontology of S_2 and puts the several elements of substance in a proper perspective. In general, Aristotle is concerned with a matter of priority of elements, so much so that he believes that he can solve the problem of substance only by determining which element is prior. Aristotle identifies ultimate reality with ontological priority, so that it cannot be an insignificant matter to determine the prior element. This element, whichever it is, will win the title of primary substance which has been unclaimed since the sensible substance of S_1 relinquished it.

According to the above characterization, *Met.* vii is an attempt to complete the work of articulating S_2. It is as if Aristotle, having worked out the ramifications of his hylomorphism with a theory of causation, a theory of actuality, and so on, and after having successfully applied many of this theories to scientific problems in diverse fields, returns in this relatively late work to some unfinished business concerning the foundations of his system. For he wishes now to clarify the nature of the primary elements of reality and in doing so to put the whole system on a secure footing. Yet we recall that Aristotle has never cut his ties with S_1. And at the same time that the overall thrust of his inquiry is to articulate the foundations of S_2, we shall find that he is importing conceptions proper only to S_1. If this observation is correct, there is an underlying problem in Book vii, and that is the problem of reconciling the principles of S_1 and S_2. Instead of merely articulating the metaphysical foundations of S_2, then, Aristotle is also trying to achieve a synthesis of his two systems—a task that we know is logically impossible to achieve. And I suggest that the impasse that he reaches is not due to the inherent incoherence of S_2, but to the interference of S_1 in the inquiry.

8.2.2 The Problem of Substance as a Puzzle

It is time now to examine terms under which Aristotle will accept a solution to the problem of substance. First we must draw some preliminary distinctions. Kuhn (1970: 35 ff.) has argued that it is characteristic of scientific inquiries that they attempt to reduce problems to the status of puzzles. Puzzles are marked by having determinate solutions which can be reached by using accepted procedures. To solve a puzzle requires skill in applying the rules of a practice, but it does not necessarily involve novelty. In fact, novelty is ruled out by the restrictions the practice places on the methods of solution. Now, while it might seem that reducing a scientific problem to the status of a puzzle would limit one's creative freedom, from the standpoint of the scientific community the loss is more than compensated by the promise that the puzzle has a solution and an established procedure for attaining that solution. It is just by turning problems into puzzles that steady scientific progress can be made within the framework of a scientific paradigm.

Kuhn's characterization of normal science as puzzle-solving has some obvious applications to philosophy. Many philosophers have aimed at establishing a method that will transform the problem of philosophy into puzzles amenable to the method in question. Richard Rorty (1979) has studied the efforts of philosophers to replace speculation by method, and has pointed out both how pervasive the desire to make the replacement is, and how paradoxical. For to replace speculation with method is to turn philosophical inquiry into 'a boring academic specialty' (p. 385). In a sense, it is to do away with philosophy altogether. But as curious as the concept of a philosophy to end all philosophies is, it seems to exercise a powerful influence on the Western tradition. I suspect that the effort to find a final solution, far from being a bane to philosophical inquiry, may be a necessary condition for philosophy as we know it, just as the concept of winning is necessary to competitive games, even though the game will be played over next year on the same ground. But whether the scientific tendency is good or bad in philosophy, it is a common tendency, and Aristotle certainly subscribes to the position that philosophical problems should be cut down to size and solved once and for all. And in fact, the early chapters of *Metaphysics* vii make perfect sense as an attempt to lay down the ground rules for an exercise in puzzle-solving. The puzzle to be solved is no less than the question, 'What is being?'

After introducing the categories of being and arguing that the question of being is the question of what is substance, Aristotle gives several examples of items that are recognized as substances

(Chapter 2). In the first place there are (1) bodies such as (*a*) animals, plants, and their parts, or (*b*) the 'natural' bodies (φυσικὰ σώματα), for example, fire, water, and earth, or portions of these or physical structures composed of these, for example, the universe or the heavenly bodies. Furthermore, some consider (2) the limits of body such as planes and lines to be substances. Finally, some think that (3) there are eternal substances such as the Forms or mathematical entities. Clearly Aristotle is trying to capture here the range of possible examples of substance without committing himself to accepting the examples. The only examples that Aristotle would accept are those under (1*a*) and possibly the heavenly bodies under (1*b*). But he does not wish to rule out any of the examples a priori. Rather he wants to survey the field of possible examples and later give reasons for accepting or rejecting some of them, as he does in Chapter 16.

What Aristotle has done is to survey the claims of earlier and contemporary philosophers as these concern the question of being, and to distil the different positions. Roughly his three classes of alleged substances are those recognized by the φυσικοί, the Pythagoreans, and the philosophers of the Academy. The list of examples seems to be something of an Aristotelian commonplace.[6] His method will be to examine the φαινόμενα which Owen (1961: 85 ff.) has shown to include the λεγόμενα 'matters of linguistic usage' and the commonly held opinions, as well as the observed facts. Even in supposedly scientific inquiries, as Owen points out, Aristotle has recourse to common conceptions on the subject at hand, which he considers to be part of the data of the problem.[7] The method is actually in keeping with the modern practice of beginning with one's own pre-philosophical intuitions on a topic as a starting-point for an adequate philosophical theory and a touchstone for its success. In *Met.* vii the problem is one concerning the nature of substance, and Aristotle begins, as is his wont, with a survey of the opinions of experts. The survey in Chapter 2, then, is an integral part of the argument—one that Aristotle is compelled to recapitulate with the summary of the argument in *Met.* viii (1, 1042ᵃ6 ff.). For it provides a point of departure for the discussion and a point of reference for

[6] Cf. Aristotle's surveys in *Met.* v. 8 and viii. 1, 1042ᵃ6 ff.
[7] For a reconsideration and vindication of Aristotle's methodology, see Nussbaum (1982).

determining the adequacy of the solution reached. The inquiry will reach its closure when Aristotle discovers a solution that will resolve the problems of substance and at the same time show what is right and what is wrong with traditional answers. In other words the solution must exhibit the erroneous conceptions as mistakes, revealing why their proponents were misled. Thus a complete solution not only solves the residual problems but exposes the attempted solutions of others as mistakes.

Having established in concrete terms what some of the leading contenders for substancehood are, we still want to know what the abstract qualifications, the criteria or principles, are. For instance, what is it about natural bodies that makes them likely candidates? The determination of concrete examples is only preliminary to this more fundamental question, and to this Aristotle turns in Chapter 3. Without justifying his classifications, he identifies four senses in which something can be substance: essence, universal, genus, and substratum. Presumably one could establish this classification by examining the examples of substance Aristotle has already identified, and by determining the rationale for choosing the various kinds of examples. In each case the rationale would reduce to one of the four senses of substance. For instance, if one claimed that all things were composed of air, one would be implying that the fundamental reality was material in nature, that is, was something underlying the derivative entities we experience; hence he would be committed to the claim that substance is substratum. Thus in *Met.* v. 8 Aristotle finds four concrete candidates for substance: natural bodies, souls, limiting parts, and essence. He claims that it follows from these examples that the ultimate substratum and the form are substance—that is, the abstract kinds of substance (1017^b23–6). It is not clear that the supposed conclusion follows; certainly it does not without some auxiliary premisses. But evidently Aristotle thinks that the inference is unproblematic. He may think that in a similar way all four principles of substancehood in vii. 3 can be inferred from the ἔνδοξα.[8]

---

[8] A comment in the latter passage (1042^a12 f.) suggests that the arguments that establish substratum and essence are independent of the data. In Book vii the case for substratum and essence are presented as a separate stage of the argument. It is interesting to note that 1042^a8–11, which is ostensibly a recapitulation of the claim that natural bodies are substance, provides a more orderly taxonomy than does

Unlike the two principles of substancehood from *Met.* v, however, the list of *Met.* vii includes some candidates that Aristotle is not sympathetic with, and will ultimately reject. The list is thus not to be taken as generated from within Aristotle's system, but as derived from the commonly accepted philosophical views on being. Aristotle is attempting to set up the discussion in such a way that he does not rule out a priori any of the alleged answers to the question. He is, then, setting up the problem so as to avoid begging the question. His aim is to show that in a fair contest between the contenders, the Aristotelian candidate for substance will win.

However, as we have noted, Aristotle is not quite certain what his own answer to the question should be. Thus the inquiry will be more open than one might expect. To be sure, Aristotle has a favourite, namely essence. But he is not without sympathy for substratum, which after all he has championed in previous discussions. Thus we may hope for a more balanced treatment of substance than we usually get from Aristotle.

As a final preliminary to the investigation proper, Aristotle presents us with some *criteria* for determining the correct answer to the question 'What is substance?' He does not present these *as* a preliminary standard, but his first argument makes use of them and hence indicates that they will be operative in the inquiry. Having first introduced substratum in the sense of matter as a candidate, he considers a criterion it satisfies—(1) that it is the ultimate subject—and then rejects it because it does not conform to two other criteria. These are (2) substance must be separable (χωριστόν); and (3) substance must be τόδε τι. Although Aristotle presents the three criteria as straightforward and unproblematic, some difficult questions immediately arise. What does each of these criteria consist of? Are these criteria internal to Aristotle's system, or are they meant to be theory neutral? Are these the only criteria that will be operative in the inquiry?

The questions are not totally independent, because if we answer the first in a certain way, we may be forced to interpret the criteria as internal to Aristotle's system, in answer to the second question. And if the criteria are internal to Aristotle's system, it will become

---

1028^{b}8–13, in so far as it presents the bodies in an ascending order of complexity. On the other hand, the Book viii passage drops (2) as a separate class of examples. For a discussion of *Met.* v. 8, see Polansky (1983).

imperative to seek some theory-neutral criterion or criteria to complement the internal argument, lest Aristotle be shown to beg the question. Here we can only give a provisional answer to the questions.

1. The criterion of being the ultimate subject immediately recalls *Cat.* 2. However, we should not jump to the conclusion that it has no relevance to the philosophical tradition. On Aristotle's reading of the history of philosophy, the first candidate for substance was matter, which he understands as the substratum of change.[9] Thus Aristotle would claim that the early Presocratics tacitly accept his criterion of substance: the real is a substratum in that it is a subject of ephemeral affections. Consequently, his use of the criterion does not beg the question against the tradition in general; rather, it is very much in keeping with one important philosophical movement within the tradition.

2. The criterion of separability is one that can be identified with the notion of independence in the *Categories*. The In tie was explained as involving ontological dependence upon a subject, which is ontologically independent of the accident that is in it. However, the notion of separability is not one that is confined to Aristotle. Indeed, Aristotle uses the term to reproach Plato for his metaphysical principles.[10] For Aristotle claims that Plato is wrong to separate the Forms from their instances. It thus seems likely that the general conception derives from Plato, and that Aristotle thinks that he is not begging the question against Plato by calling substance separable; on the contrary, he is preserving a Platonic criterion.[11] Similarly, those who claim that certain natural bodies are substances would hold that these are separable: for Empedocles the four elements have separate existence, but the compounds of them only come to be after a manner of speaking. For the atomists the atoms are separate realities and the bodies that come together from these are only chance congeries. Those who hold that planes,

---

[9] *Met.* i. 3, 983^{b}6 ff.; note the reference to the substratum at ^{b}16.

[10] A survey of Ast (1836, s.v. χωρίζω), shows that Plato does not apply the term in this way in the dialogues. Cf. Ryan (1973: 213 and n. 10). However, Plato does clearly hold that the Forms are separate. There are also some very loose anticipations of the terminology of χωρισμός in Plato's use of the cognate adverb/preposition χωρίς in the *Parmenides*, e.g. 130 B, 159 B 6 f.—where, however, the term does not seem to connote ontological priority but only distinctness. See Ast ibid., s.v. χωρίς, for passages.

[11] Cf. Polansky (1983: 62 f.).

lines, and points are substances would hold that these are entities separate from the bodies they bound. Thus this criterion is theory-neutral: it does not pick out a priori any one candidate for substance.

3. Aristotle's third criterion for substance is that it should be τόδε τι. We have met the concept of τόδε τι already in the *Categories*. However, we have no assurance that the same term here refers to the same concept. In fact, there is a presumption against the term having the same meaning, since in the *Cat.* it picked out the particular, whereas here it picks out the form. What indeed does τόδε τι mean? I shall leave this question for the next chapter, in which a more detailed study of Aristotle's position is appropriate. For now, suffice it to say that Aristotle seems to have in mind a notion of definiteness such that a demonstrative (τόδε 'this') could pick out a given object. If we take the criterion in this way, it is possible to find that the examples of substance put forth by the tradition in general satisfy the criterion. Indeed, Parmenides seems to have advanced a forerunner of this requirement in asserting that what is must be τετελεσμένον 'complete, perfect'—an attribute he connected with having limits. These limits in turn he represents (at least metaphorically; perhaps literally) as spatial boundaries.[12] Thus Aristotle's criterion of 'thisness' is at least compatible with an Eleatic principle of being which influenced the philosophical tradition.

All Aristotle's criteria can be understood as theory-neutral conditions that the tradition has placed on substance, or the really real entity. The candidates for substance, both concrete and abstract, both examples and principles, have tacitly had to conform to these conditions to be seriously considered. Thus atoms are both separate realities and they are definite objects. Plato's Forms are separate from their instances and they are definite. It seems fair, then, to recognize the criteria Aristotle refers to as constraints on the inquiry into being for the whole tradition. The criteria are ἔνδοξα no less than some of the examples of substance.

Like ἔνδοξα, however, the criteria are subject to evaluation from the point of view of the new inquiry. They may be interpreted to

---

[12] Parmenides, B 8.4 (with emendations—see Tarán 1965: 93–5, Mourelatos, 1970: 96), 8.32 f., 8.42–9.

bring them into line with a correct view of reality. And in fact, as we shall see, Aristotle's criteria do lend themselves to a strict Aristotelian interpretation. The criteria, like the examples of substance and the definitions of substancehood, will become grist for Aristotle's mill, and will be transformed into a uniquely Aristotelian product. But all the while it will be important for Aristotle to conform to the tradition in his main assumptions so that he can offer a solution that is arguably a solution to the problems his predecessors faced. Aristotle is conscious of this responsibility and opportunity.

The picture that emerges from this study of Aristotle's preliminary chapters is one of a carefully prepared inquiry. Aristotle shows that the problem of being reduces to a problem of substance; he identifies the contenders for substancehood both as to concrete examples and as to abstract principles; and he makes use of some relatively theory-neutral criteria to decide the issue. In the opening statement Aristotle thus treats the problem at hand as a scientific (in a broad, Aristotelian sense of that term) inquiry which has a definite question to answer, a clearly defined set of hypotheses for answering the question, and an objective method for reaching a solution. In short, Aristotle presents the inquiry as having the form of a puzzle which admits of a solution within the framework of Aristotelian Normal Science, that is, here his philosophical method.

This is not to say that Aristotle is going to be, or going to pretend to be, a perfectly disinterested arbiter of the dispute over substance. He has a stake in the investigation and he is only too aware of his role as a partisan. But at the same time, the very terms in which he presents the problem show that he is confident that he can initially offer a neutral characterization of the question and its alleged answers, invoke a neutral method, and still have his investigation vindicate his position. The point is that, led on by the truth itself, as it were, we shall be compelled to agree with Aristotle's assessment of substance as against rival theories. An inquiry which clearly lays out the problem and uses a rational scientific procedure will perforce arrive at the right answer, which incidentally is the Aristotelian answer.

The irony of *Met.* vii is that Aristotle's best-laid plans go agley. He finds no answer. Or, perhaps more accurately, he finds too many answers to the question 'What is substance?' Instead of a puzzle with a unique and definite solution, Aristotle finds a confusing plurality of solutions, all of which have some plausibility with respect to the method, but each of which is defective in some important respect. In the terms of Kuhn's analysis of science, Aristotle comes up with an anomaly. Something has gone wrong: the paradigm is no longer adequate. It is time to turn to the argument of *Met.* vii.

8.3 THE CONFLICT OF S_1 AND S_2 IN *MET.* VII

The anomalous character of Aristotle's inquiry into substance manifests itself in contradiction. From Chapter 4 on Aristotle studies form and essence with an eye to revealing how they are true substance. In the process of his discussion it becomes clear that form is to be identified with essence, which is correlated with definition and expresses the universal character of the individual. But in Chapter 13 Aristotle unexpectedly asserts that substance is what is unique to its subject and no universal is a substance. Suddenly substance is what is not universal. Thus we find that in *Met.* vii substance is and is not universal.

The logical difficulty of Aristotle's position has long been recognized. As Eduard Zeller (1897, i. 339) expresses it, 'It only remains, then, to recognise in this point, not merely a lacuna, but a deep contradiction in the philosophy of Aristotle.' Since Zeller, there have been many attempts to rescue Aristotle.[13] None of these has met with general approval, and indeed, it seems accurate to say that the interpretation of *Met.* vii and viii is one of the most vexed issues of contemporary Aristotelian scholarship. The solutions that have been offered include some radically different alternatives: primary substance is particular; primary substance is universal; it is both; it is neither. While there is always the hope that some ultimate solution will be found, perhaps the failed efforts of a century of scholarship should provide some inductive evidence that a solution is beyond reach. The alternatives may not be genuine options but rather antinomies whose rival claims can never be adjudicated given the presuppositions. If such is their status, the alternatives may require diagnosis rather than partisan

---

[13] Yet there have been surprisingly few attempts to attribute contradictions to Aristotle. Two limited essays in this direction are Chen (1964) and Lacey (1965*b*).

support. In the spirit of such a critique, I turn to the argument of *Metaphysics* vii.

8.3.1 *The Hylomorphic Conception of Substance*

Aristotle begins his study by considering the candidacy of the concept of substratum. He defines substratum as 'that of which other things are said, but which is not itself said of another' (3, 1028^b36 f.). The definition is that of the *Categories* concept of primary substance. Yet it quickly becomes clear that he will apply this concept to the ontology of S_2. For in the following lines he distinguishes the matter, the form, and the compound as possible instances of substratum:

> The primary substratum especially seems to be substance. In one sense matter is said to be substratum, in another sense form, and in a third sense the compound of these (I mean by the matter for instance the bronze, by form the outline of the shape, by the compound the whole statue) . . . (1029^a1-5)

Aristotle's example shows that he has the S_2 conception of substance in mind, in all its analogically robust reality. It is curious that he should naïvely invoke a concept of substance so intimately connected with the atomic entities of S_1 in trying to explicate the ontology of S_2. It is also curious how, after carefully setting up the problem as a general question pertinent to the whole philosophical tradition, he should so quickly narrow in on questions internal to his own system. The fact is that Aristotle is preoccupied with his own housekeeping, and the source of his worries is the agreement of S_2 with the principles of S_1. He is right to assign pride of place to the claims of substratum, since substratum is historically the starting-place of his own quest for substance. But as to the congruence of this conception with the S_2 ontology, there are grave problems.

The Compound as Substance. In Chapter 3 Aristotle considers briefly the claims of all three senses of substance to be considered substratum. The compound he considers only to reject out of hand: 'The substance composed of both elements, namely matter and form, may be dismissed; for it is posterior and obvious' (a 30–2). The reason that the compound is posterior is evidently that it is derivative: it is by its very definition composed of elements. And as Aristotle will later say (in the context of a definition of the form) at least some of the parts of a formula are prior to the formula (10, 1035^b4–6). In general he seems to hold that if there is a formula for a thing, the thing is complex as opposed to its elements, which are either simple or at least more simple than the compound; and hence they have a greater claim to ultimacy than does the complex.[14] Aristotle's dismissal of the compound thus seems to stem from an unexamined assumption that what is simple is prior to what is complex. There is a presumption in favour of reductionism that colours his thinking here, a presumption that is one aspect of his earlier position of substantial atomism. I shall not undertake to analyse Aristotle's assumptions here, other than to point out their close connection with the world-view of S_1.

Matter as Substance. Matter has a strong prima-facie claim to being substance in the sense of substratum. For it is the substratum for form. Aristotle gives more attention to matter in Chapter 3 than to any other contender. But after he presents the case for matter, he quickly rejects the candidacy of matter—not because of any implausibility in the argument for matter but because it does not satisfy the criteria of separability and thisness. Although he does not examine the position in detail, it is not difficult to see why he cannot accept matter as substance.

To be sure, matter fits the conception of substratum. But we must distinguish between different levels of matter. There is the final matter that is the substratum of, for instance, a fully formed substance. In this sense the body is the matter of a human being. But that body may in turn be broken down into its underlying parts and their substrata and the tissues that underlie the non-homogeneous parts may in turn be analysed until we reach the elements, which in turn must have matter because they are transformed into one another. By this route we would finally reach a level of matter that is not in turn a compound composed of some further matter and its form. The matter for elements is traditionally known as prime matter (following Aristotle's apparent reference to πρώτη ὕλη).[15] I shall call this method of

---

[14] This is the implication of 1029^a5–7 (if we read τοῦ ἐξ ἀμφοῖν in line 6 as the logic of the passage demands—see Ross ad loc.): if form is prior to matter it is *a fortiori* prior to the compound.

[15] *GC* ii. 1, 329^a29 f., where the πρώτην is really a predicate. Cf. *Met.* ix. 7, 1049^a25 f.

analysis *metaphysical analysis*, and the resulting matter PM. Now if we view PM as substance we will admirably fulfil the requirement that PM be that of which all other things are predicated but will not be predicated of anything itself. But there will be a serious problem for this conception of substance in that it will turn out to be completely indeterminate in that of itself it has no characteristics. In Aristotle's words, 'If this is substance, it eludes us what else substance is' ([a]10 f.). In a sense, by invoking the criterion of thisness, Aristotle seems to be reacting precisely to this deficiency in PM.

8.3.2 The Paradoxes of Matter

But the notion of prime matter is not as simple as my sketch suggests. Although there is evidence for the metaphysical analysis of substance in the physical and biological treatises, as well as evidence (which is much disputed) about PM,[16] Aristotle does not perform a metaphysical analysis here, nor does he precisely arrive at PM. Rather than undertaking to decompose a substance into its physical parts or metaphysical components, Aristotle looks at the substance from a logical point of view. In a thought experiment he imagines stripping away the other attributes of substance until only the three dimensions of length, width, and depth are left.[17] Then he imagines stripping those away and finds that we are left only with what is determined by its attributes. If this is what matter is, it is neither substance nor quantity nor anything else by which being is determined ([a]20 f.). Thus it is different from all the categories of being, since it is their subject, either directly, as the subject of 'substance,' that is, form, or indirectly, as in the case of accidents which inhere in 'substance' and hence derivatively inhere in matter ([a]21–4). The process of analysis Aristotle envisages is thus not a metaphysical one of going from higher-level biological components to lower-lever biological and physical ones, but a

---

[16] King (1956) and Charlton (1970, appendix) and Jones (1974) have denied that Aristotle had a notion of PM; their views have been controverted by Solmsen (1958), Robinson (1974), Dancy (1978), and Williams (1982: 211–19); see also Lacey (1965a). Charlton (1983) has recently replied to his critics, and his view has found support from Cohen (1984). I find the arguments against PM inadequate, and the following characterization will provide some systematic support for the notion. See also Dye (1978: 80 n. 52) and Graham (1987).

[17] Aristotle's reference to the dimensions tends to suggest a physical or geometrical analysis; but his further remarks do not bear out this impression.

logical analysis of stripping away the categorial attributes of a substance until one arrives at what we may call the logical subject. We are assured by the very process of arriving at the logical subject that it is totally indeterminate.

I shall call the kind of matter that results from the categorial analysis of substance logical prime matter (LPM). What is the relationship between PM and LPM? And what is their status as substance? The two conceptions are the product of two different sorts of analysis. Discussions of the passage often conflate the two notions of matter. But we must not beg the question by assuming their identity. Aristotle is examining the candidacy for substancehood of some kind of basic matter. But it is not immediately clear what kind of matter he is examining or what the context is. Is Aristotle looking for a straw man? Or is he seeking to curb some natural tendency from within his own position to overestimate matter? Ultimately, what are the implications of his argument for the status of matter in his own system? I am not certain that all the questions this passage raises can be answered definitively. However, we can make some progress by getting clear on the role of prime matter in Aristotle's system.

PM is posited to explain how one of the four elements (earth, air, fire, water) can be transformed into another, as Aristotle holds they can.[18] For instance, water can be transformed to air. The process of evaporation is just an instance of this physical–chemical change, which takes place when one of two determinant powers of an element changes. Every element consists of an ordered set of two powers, the first one either hot or cold, the second either wet or dry, exemplified in matter. Thus using the first letters of the powers to designate them, we can create a matrix to define the four elements (see Fig. 8.1). On this analysis Air = HW, Water = CW, Fire = HD, Earth = CD. Aristotle explains the evaporation of water as a transformation of water to air, or schematically, $CW \rightarrow HW$. This change is not an accidental change but a substantial one, for water and air are distinct substances. According to the theory of change of *Ph.* i, there must be some matter for any substantial change. The matter for elemental change is PM. By hypothesis PM has no characteristics of its own: it is the material bedrock of all physical composition

[18] The main evidence for the reconstruction is in *GC* i. 3; ii. 1–5, 7; cf. *DC* iii. 8, 306^b16–22; iv 5, 312^a30–3.

H	HW	HD
C	CW	CD
	W	D

FIG. 8.1. Combinations of Powers

and so must be without an essence of its own. If it did have an essence of its own, it might arguably be a substance in its own right; then there would not really be four elements, or, as Aristotle calls them, simple bodies, but only the one stuff.[19]

Aristotle attempts to shore up the theory of PM by assuring us that PM is never found by itself: it always has some powers inhering in it.[20] But his whole account is radically flawed. To see how it is, we must recognize that, given Aristotle's theory of change and his belief that elemental change is an empirical fact, the doctrine of PM is entailed. Aristotle espouses the following principles:

SC: There is a substratum for every change.
EC: The elements change from one to another.
ES: The elements are the most simple bodies.

From these theses we can deduce the following:

EM: There is a matter for elemental change.

But by definition:

PM: The matter for elemental change is prime matter.

Thus the doctrine of prime matter is, given Aristotle's belief in EC, a theorem of the system. Furthermore, there is ample textual evidence that Aristotle embraced this consequence.[21]

There are still serious problems for PM, however. Recall the rationale for the theory of matter in *Ph.* i: matter is the enduring entity which underlies change, and it is especially crucial for an account of substantial change, in which there is no apparent substratum. It is posited precisely to provide a structural answer to the Eleatic challenge, which asks how what-is can come to be from

[19] Cf. *GC* i. 1, 314^{a}8–11, ^{b}1–4.
[20] *GC* ii. 1, 329^{a}24–6; cf. i. 3, 319^{b}2–4.
[21] The textual evidence is controversial, but it seems to me that overall the opponents of PM have to force their readings of key passages. The texts are much discussed in the works cited in n. 16.

what-is-not. Aristotle's answer provides a *something* as the foundation for change, and particularly substantial change. To the Eleatic Aristotle can reply that change presupposes some entity underlying the change. The entity may be relatively less developed than the resulting product of the change—for instance the bronze is less organized than the statue—but it is *something*. Thus something always comes to be from something. For every change, there is some substratum S that comes to be F from being not-F.

But now consider PM. According to ES, the four elements are the simplest bodies. That is, they are independent entities with their own characteristics, but nothing of a lower order is independent in this way. Hence,

NC: PM has no characteristics of its own.

It follows that PM can have no essence of its own. If it did, it would become the ultimate simple body, displacing the four elements. But if PM has no actual features of its own, that is, if for all features F PM is not-F, is not PM something like pure indeterminacy? And pure indeterminacy more than non-existence is for Aristotle and his tradition (the Eleatic tradition) probably the paradigm case of nothingness.[22] He sees the threat of indeterminacy clearly in setting up the case against PM:

If [unqualified not-being means an absolute denial of being], not-being will be a complete negation of all attributes in general, so that what comes to be will necessarily come to be from *nothing*. (*GC* i. 3, 317^{b}11–13)

To be completely characterless is to be nothing. Aristotle sees the difficulty, but when it comes to a solution he settles for an inadequate one: he claims that there is no problem for PM because it is always found exemplifying some power or other (at least one power stays identical, even during a change) (*GC* ii. 1, 329^{a}24 ff.). Aristotle's explanation fails because whether PM exemplifies some power or not is irrelevant. It is like defending bronze as the substratum for the creation of a statue by saying that it keeps its colour throughout the change. Yes, it does, but its colour is an accidental feature of bronze.[23] What accounts for the bronze being a substratum is that it has a certain melting-point, physical properties suitable to casting, etc. In other words, it has some

---

[22] See ch. 5 n. 29.

[23] Note Aristotle's definition of matter as something ἐνυπάρχον μὴ κατὰ συμβεβηκός, *Ph* i. 9, 192^{a}31 f.

essential characteristics in virtue of which it is able to function as a substratum in a certain context of change. Likewise, if PM is to function as a bona fide substratum it must have some features in virtue of which we can explain the change. It must *be* something. If PM has no characteristics besides the powers—which are not essential to it, since it need not have any given pair of them—it is essentially indeterminate. And it seems that it cannot have any other attributes besides the four powers, since they are the most primitive tactile characters (*GC* ii. 2). Hence PM can have no determining characteristics. For the Eleatic then, PM is a nothing, a mere *flatus vocis* invented ad hoc to save appearances. It is a something-I-know-not-what conjured up to beg a question. Even Aristotle's appeal to potentiality is misplaced, since there must be a ground for potentiality.[24]

The concept of PM can be attacked from another angle also. By Aristotle's definition in *Ph* i. 9, matter is the ingredient of a change that endures in an essential way as a substratum. If this is true, one would expect that we should be able to identify the alleged substratum S at time t_0 at the beginning of a change and at time t_1 at the end. However, there is no feature by which we could identify PM either at the beginning or at the end of a change: all we can identify is the set of powers in it. And these may change completely in the process of change, for example, from *CW* to *HD*. Interestingly, Aristotle faces the fact that there is no continuing mark of PM, but he makes it almost a criterion for substantial change (*GC* i. 4, 319^{b}14 ff.). There he concentrates on the conditions of perception of change. Yet the real problem is not epistemological but metaphysical: what does it even *mean* to say that S at t_0 is identical to S at t_1 if S has no features of its own — if, for all F, S is not-F? How could there then be identity conditions? How could any principles such as Leibniz's Law apply?[25]

---

[24] Note Aristotle's appeal to potentiality in *GC* i. 3, 317^{b}16–18; on the need for a basis of potentiality, *Met.* ix. 7, 1048^{b}37 ff., *DC* iii. 2, 302^{a}6–9; cf. Dye (1978: 79 n. 51). For a similar point in the contemporary theory of dispositional properties, see Cummins (1983: 18 f.).

[25] This line of argument was suggested to me by Panayot Butchvarov. Cf. Butchvarov (1979: 165–9), also Lacey (1965a: 466). For a defence of Aristotle on this point see Dye (1978: 70). To defend Aristotle, Dye must construe PM as extension, as Sokolowski (1970) and Cohen (1984) interpret it. I reject the identification (Graham 1987).

Aristotle does have a concept of PM. The concept is, however, highly problematic, even paradoxical. Those who have tried to exorcise the notion from Aristotle are right at least in trying to save Aristotle from it. What does emerge from this critique is that the notion of matter is central and defensible in Aristotle's system. The notion of prime matter is derivative and problematic. The medieval tradition has turned Aristotle upside-down in making the notion of PM central. In fact it is a limiting case of the concept of matter, one that is attenuated and even defective. In order to serve its dialectical function of providing an ontological ground for change, matter must be determinate in some respects. By progressively emptying each lower level of matter of its features until he finds one that has none, Aristotle has created a philosophical anomaly.

Let us return now to the question of LPM. In presenting the case for LPM being substance Aristotle has not used his own physical theory. Does he himself subscribe to the existence of LPM? The tone of his own presentation suggests that he may not: he may regard LPM as merely a straw man to reveal the inadequacy of matter as substance.[26] On the other hand, the analysis and its presuppositions are so Aristotelian that the suggestion of LPM seems to be one that could only arise internally to Aristotle's system. Does he himself find LPM an attractive candidate? I have no novel answer to the question as stated. However, the previous discussion will help us deal with the problem. Whatever may be Aristotle's attitude to LPM, the same problems that arise for PM can be raised for LPM, *mutatis mutandis*. Conversely, the problems Aristotle sees for LPM can be raised for PM. There is indeterminacy of substratum for PM and indeterminacy of subject for LPM. There is a failure of identity conditions through time for PM, and a failure of identity conditions at the same time for LPM. In the latter case one cannot tell whether the LPM of Socrates is identical to the LPM of Callias. In either case, the ultimate matter comes as close to being nothing as any entity could in Aristotle's system.

[26] Another possibility, argued by Schofield (1972), is that LPM is a straw man designed to show that only matter in a more familiar Aristotelian sense (i.e. not PM but a higher-level kind of matter) is substance on the proposed criterion. Stahl (1981) claims that the answer to the riddle of what is left is that the original substance is still the subject even when the attributes are stripped away.

S_2 divides the sensible substance into a subject-component and a feature-component. The formal condition for substancehood in S_1 clearly identified the metaphysical subject of S_1 as the really real entity. As applied to S_2, the condition has curious results. It makes us bypass the high-level, relatively complex matter that provides the focus of Aristotle's account of substance in favour of the most primitive kind of matter. This is plausible enough from an ontological point of view, since higher-level matter is itself a compound built up from another, lower-level matter; and thus the higher-level matter is not an ultimate subject, but only a relative subject. The notion of a subject itself is ambiguous: a subject may be either a diachronic substratum for change or a synchronic subject of properties. In either case, we can hypothesize an ultimate subject, PM or LPM, respectively. And in either case, the subject is deficient. But it is not merely deficient in that it lacks separability or determinateness, which are the grounds for Aristotle's rejection at least of LPM. The fact is that the concept of these entities borders on incoherence. The ultimate subject, either of change or of predication, turns out to be almost paradigmatically nothing. The ultimate subject is ultimately indeterminate, insubstantial; it is a kind of not-being seemingly at the foundation of the system. Aristotle may uncover the problem only for dialectical purposes — to advance the candidacy of form. But his probing reveals a deep structural flaw in the edifice of his philosophy.

According to the formal criterion of S_1, the ultimate subject is the basic substance. But as we descend through the layers of physical stuffs or the hierarchy of predications in S_2, we seem to wander farther and farther from basic substance. At the end of the journey is a substratum that is paradigmatically a subject in that it is never a predicate in any context; but that subject is at the same time paradigmatically not-being, for it has no characteristics of its own. The conflict between the criteria of the ultimate subject and of the fully determinate individual suggests a possible source of the conflict: the application to S_2 of a criterion appropriate only to S_1. For while the subjecthood criterion and the determinacy criterion both pick out substantial individuals like Socrates in S_1, they pick out different entities in S_2. The ultimate subject is the most primitive substratum, but the most determinate individual is

Socrates or his manhood. Perhaps the paradox of prime matter results from applying to S_2 an obsolete or irrelevant criterion of substancehood. The positing of matter in S_2 entailed recognizing a subject which though prior as a subject to the substantial individual was posterior as a substance. Accordingly, to reinvoke the criterion of subjecthood in S_2 is to court disaster.

Earlier I raised the question of what Aristotle thought of LPM. I have not answered that question but have rather pointed to some problems raised for Aristotle's system by the concepts of PM and LPM. It would be interesting to speculate about Aristotle's own views on LPM. Unfortunately, I do not find any decisive evidence to help resolve the question. What can be said is that LPM is the limiting case of logical analysis as PM is of metaphysical analysis. LPM might plausibly be seen as a synchronic version of PM as matter-as-a-synchronic-component is related to matter-as-a-diachronic-substratum-for-change. In other words, LPM is to PM as logical subject is to metaphysical substratum. But we cannot be sure on the basis of the limited evidence that Aristotle made such an analogy.

There is one interesting ontological lesson to be learned from the discussion of LPM in *Met.* vii. 3. If Aristotle had endorsed LPM as the real substance, he would have overthrown his whole metaphysical foundation. For LPM could not possibly be substance in the Aristotelian sense. One thing that distinguishes substance in every genuinely Aristotelian theory is essence. Without essence we have not substance but something less. In the case of LPM we get a subject devoid of any proprietary characteristic whatsoever. This concept brings us close to the modern notion of a bare particular. To found one's ontology on bare particulars is to abandon substance metaphysics in favour of something like logical atomism. The resulting system is congenial to an empiricist, but anathema to a rationalist. For in making a categorial separation between the subject and all its characters it promotes the chance and contingent over the determinate and intelligible. That much Aristotle appreciated, and in preferring the criterion of determinacy to that of subjecthood he clearly cast his lot in favour of the intelligible.

Nevertheless he leaves us with the tension between criteria and the paradox of an entity that is both paradigmatically real and paradigmatically unreal. Instead of facing this paradox Aristotle turns his attention to a more promising candidate which satisfies other criteria (1029^{a}27 ff., cf. ^{a}9). We shall find, however, that the candidacy of form is no less pradoxical than that of matter. And that at the root of both paradoxes is a common problem.

9

The Paradoxes of Substance: Form

In the last chapter we saw how Aristotle's discussion of matter as substance in *Met.* vii. 3 suggested a deep incoherence in the status of matter. Prime matter turns out to be both ultimately real and ultimately unreal. Nevertheless, the analysis of matter is only a dialectical foil to the analysis of form and essence, which provides the focus of Aristotle's argument in Book vii. In this chapter we shall examine the status of form and the closely related notion of essence. I shall argue that the concepts of form and essence show an incoherence similar to that of matter, and I shall offer a preliminary diagnosis of the problem. We take up the problem of substance where we left off, in vii. 3.

9.1 FORM AS SUBSTANCE

The criterion of subjecthood is a legacy from the S_1 conception of substance. To invoke this criterion is to invite the conclusion that matter is substance. Yet Aristotle clearly is a partisan of form, which seems most removed from a concept of substratum. It is instructive to see how he handles the claims of form as substance against the background of substance as substratum.

One obvious strategy for accommodating form would be simply to dismiss substratum as a consideration. Barring that, one could grant that substratum has something to do with substance, but maintain that it determines substance in a subordinate or ancillary sense. Thus one could concede to PM a place in the pantheon of substance without awarding it primacy. However, Aristotle adopts neither of these strategies. Rather, he aims at *extending* the notion of substratum so as to include form. The one clue as to how form could qualify at all as substratum is his remark that other predicates attach to 'substance' and substance to matter (1029^a23 f.). Now here 'substance' cannot be matter, and it cannot be the compound, since the compound already includes matter; by elimination, 'substance' must be a *lapsus calami* for 'form'. But in what sense is form the subject of predication of accidents? It seems rather that the compound is the relevant subject. In any case, form will not be the ultimate subject. At this point Aristotle extricates himself by appealing to the criteria of separability and thisness. He thus diverts attention from the problem at hand and never really resolves the rival claims of form and matter with respect to the criterion of subjecthood.

Aristotle's appeal to the criteria of separability and thisness in the context of his argument seems to indicate that these are at least concomitant criteria of substratum. But this inference is in doubt, for at *Met.* v. 8, 1017^b23-6 Aristotle identifies two disjoint senses of substance: the ultimate substratum on the one hand,[1] and what is τόδε τι and separable on the other. We can bring at least the latter sense into line with the concept of substratum.[2] For as I have mentioned, the criterion of separability can be linked to the feature of the substratum that it is not In another, that is, it is ontologically independent. The primary substance of S_1 was also rated as τόδε τι. Although in S_1 all these criteria pointed to the same entity as primary substance, in S_2 Aristotle will invoke the latter two to forestall the consequence of the first. But he is able to do so only at a price: he must reconceive the latter two criteria so that they will single out—indeed, even apply to—form.

Now if the criterion of separability applies to the primary substance of S_1 at all, it must be in the sense that substance is ontologically basic, and thus forms the nucleus of all existence. The evidence for such a claim would presumably be that the existence of particulars is a stubborn fact, one more stubborn than that of features of particulars. Aristotle does not explicitly call the substances separable in the *Categories*. He does in general use the terms for separability as a mark of disapprobrium for Plato's Forms: one of their chief defects is that they are separate from their instances.[3] Yet in the criticism is the key to Aristotle's

---

[1] Ross (1924) ad loc., says that Aristotle here means the individual compound, based on the examples in 1017^b10-14. But the concluding lines of the chapter do not build on the examples in a very clear way (indeed although they read as a conclusion, the inference from the examples seems forced at best), and in any case the examples may be merely dialectical ones.

[2] Aristotle does treat all three criteria as criteria of substratum at *Met.* viii. 1, 1042^a26-9.

[3] *Met.* vii. 16, 1040^b27 ff.

understanding of the concept. For his precise complaint is that Plato turns the Forms into particulars: 'They make the Ideas universal and at the same time *separate* and individual [τῶν καθ' ἕκαστον]' (*Met.* xiii. 9, 1086^{a}32–4, cf. ^{b}3 f.). To be separate is to be self-existent in a way that is only appropriate to particulars. Indeed, Aristotle even links the property of being separable with that of being a particular subject of predicates:

Some things are separable and some are not; the former are substances. *Because of this property* [διὰ τοῦτο] substances are the cause of all things, since without them there are no modifications [πάθη] or activities [κινήσεις]. (*Met.* xii. 5, 1070^{b}36–1^{a}2)

Here separability seems to amount to ontological priority: S is separable if for all A which coexist with S, S can exist without A but A cannot exist without S. Thus far separability is very much in harmony with the characteristics of substance Aristotle stresses in S_1. We find, however, that Aristotle revises this notion of separability so that it can apply to form. Aristotelian form cannot be actually separate in the way that Platonic Form is. Thus Aristotle introduces the notion of something that is separable in definition.[4] By making this move, he can apply the criterion to form and thus provide another grounds for its being a substratum and hence a substance. But what this new criterion really means is obscure. Many things are separable in definition. Why does this characteristic confer any advantage on them? Is it that the definiens is prior to the definiendum? Such a priority would seem to be epistemological rather than ontological. Aristotle does argue later for the priority of the parts of essence over the essence, but such an argument would be a consideration in favour of form being essence, not substratum. Thus although Aristotle succeeds in applying the criterion of separability to form, to do so he must reinterpret the criterion and ultimately render the criterion problematic as a standard for substratum.

We have briefly discussed the use of τόδε τι to characterize primary substance in the *Categories* (2.1.2). The term is treated as equivalent to 'indivisible and unitary' (5, 3^{b}12), and evidently signifies what is particular. Since primary substance is particular as well as being the ultimate subject in S_1, no conflicts result from

---

[4] I am following Ross (1924, i. 311) on this point; cf. *Ph.* ii. 1, 193^{b}3–5; *Met.* viii. 1, 1042^{a}26–9. However, see Ch. 10 below on a form separable in actuality.

using this concept as an auxiliary criterion of substancehood. The S_1 concept, however, will clearly not do for form. Aristotle must reinterpret this notion also if he is to extend it as a criterion to admit form as substratum.

It is time to take a closer look at the concept of τόδε τι, and this in turn requires that we take a closer look at the meaning of the Greek words. The classic study of the term is a brief note by J. A. Smith (1921). He distinguishes between three ways of taking the words: (1) the first word is a demonstrative, the second a pronoun. The meaning is 'this somewhat'. Smith objects that this reading presupposes a class of somewhats, which seems otiose. (2) Alternatively, the first word is a pronoun, the second an indefinite article, and the meaning is 'a this'. Smith objects to this reading that the notion of a universal class character of thisness is un-Aristotelian and the suggested meaning does not agree with Aristotle's actual use. (3) Finally, both words function as co-ordinate nouns. The meaning is 'anything which is both this and a somewhat'. Smith advocates this position. But his argument fails for a number of reasons.

In the first place, he ignores the evidence of the *Categories* passage cited above, the earliest document of Aristotle's meaning. That passage assigns no role whatever to universality; rather it identifies being τόδε τι with being indivisible and unitary. This rules out (1) and (3). Secondly, Smith claims that τόδε τι does not have meaning (2) in Aristotle's works; yet Aristotle uses the phrase τόδε τι with the required sense, and notably even in a non-technical utterance. In *DC* i. 8 he argues that if there is natural movement, particular bodies of the same kind must move toward a place that is numerically one, for example, toward τόδε τι μέσον or τόδε τι ἔσχατον (276ᵇ29–32). Here τι cannot be a pronoun because μέσον and ἔσχατον function as nouns; it cannot function as an adjective modifying the nouns ('a certain . . .') because it would cancel the effect of the τόδε. It must function as an indefinite article, which would then render τόδε a stand-in for a particularizing reference; thus the phrase means 'a particular centre or a particular extremity' (Oxford trans.). What we are talking about in each use of τόδε τι is a so-far unspecified place that is numerically one.

Finally, Smith takes a naïve view of the function of the terms in the phrase. In each case he assigns the word a literal meaning in conformity with its use. But if (1) were the correct way to relate the words, his translation would still not be revealing. For Aristotle might be using the term τι not literally, as a class name, but as a stand-in for an indefinite noun, that is, a variable: 'this F'. This latter observation can help us to reply to his objection to (2). In (2) the term τόδε does not function in a literal way; it is not *used* but *mentioned*. Being a stand-in for an expression denoting a particular, it must serve not precisely as a pronoun F but a pro-proper-name N. To co-opt the demonstrative in this way is appropriate since the indexical 'this' is normally used, together with a context of utterance which includes a deictic gesture, to denote a particular. Thus 'a "this"' functions like 'an N' where N is a variable ranging over proper names, and means something like 'a thing-such-as-is-designated-by-a-proper-name'.[5]

The use–mention distinction helps to reply to a potential philological objection to (2). It might seem that the τι is redundant and unnecessary. But on the present reading the term is not redundant precisely because Aristotle needs to signal that the term τόδε is not being used but mentioned. Greek orthography did not possess inverted commas (or other punctuation) in Aristotle's time. An article must be used, as commonly the neuter definite article is, for mentioned words and phrases; but here an indefinite article is called for, which must be supplied from the indefinite pronoun since there is no indefinite article as such in Greek. Without the article, the τόδε will be taken demonstratively and not, contrary to normal usage, as a predicate or a stand-in for a predicate.

Note that when Aristotle does want to say something such as alternatives (1) and (3) suggest, he uses a different terminology. In *Met.* vii. 8 (1033[b]19 ff.) he points out that the craftsman makes a 'such' (τοιόνδε) out of this (τόδε), producing a 'this-such' (τόδε τοιόνδε). This seems to be Aristotle's expression for a particular F, where τόδε expresses the particularity and τοιόνδε the universal or kind. In contrast, Aristotle uses Callias and Socrates as examples of what he calls 'the whole this' (τὸ δ' ἅπαν τόδε, [b]24 following Ross's translation).

---

[5] Cf. Preiswerk (1939: 85 n. 3), who approves of Smith's general conclusions but rejects the philological analysis. Preiswerk's own version takes 'a "this"' as 'an F', where 'F' is to be filled in by an essence. Since Preiswerk takes *Met.* vii as his point of departure, he too ignores the evidence of the *Cat.*

I take it, then, that the term τόδε τι means 'a This', that is, 'an N', where 'N' is to be filled in by a word denoting a particular. On this reading it is not difficult to see how a primary substance of S₁ is τόδε τι. And indeed the conclusion that τόδε τι signifies the particular agrees with our conclusions in Chapter 2.1.2 based on the indexicality of the demonstrative pronoun and the textual evidence of the *Categories*. But we encounter a serious problem in applying the notion of τόδε τι to the forms of S₂. There is a controversy as to whether substantial form is to be taken as universal or particular in *Met*. vii; but in Chapter 3 we cannot suppose that this issue has been decided. Since Aristotle ascribes thisness to form without argument, he must have in mind a relatively obvious sense in which form is τόδε τι. If, accordingly, we broaden the meaning of the term to encompass whatever is determinate, we can see how Aristotle would say that form but not matter is τόδε τι. Of course even here we must be careful, because in a sense form, considered as separable, is not so much determinate, as if it were on a par with the compound, as it is the *source* of determination.[6] But Aristotle does not seem to focus on this nicety, and he is content to leave form as what is determinate in contrast to matter.

Thus we see how form can satisfy the criterion of thisness. But lest we should now assume that form is simply the particular of S₂, we must note again that τόδε τι has shifted its meaning. Form satisfies some sort of requirement of thisness, but it is no longer the same requirement that we found in S₁. Correspondingly, if we say that form is substratum because it is τόδε τι, it is no longer clear that we mean by 'substratum' what we meant in S₁. And indeed, it seems as if all the landmark terms of S₁, by which we might get our bearings in that system, have shifted meaning on us. In *Met*. vii substratum is still substance; and it is still what is the ultimate subject and is endowed with separability and thisness. But none of the criteria is really the same, nor, consequently, does 'substratum' mean what it used to. If 'substratum' has changed meaning, we have no guarantee that even 'substance' means what is used to. Of course, I have already argued that it does not: the incommensurability of S₁ and S₂ involves a shift of meaning in the theoretical terms of S₁. But in the shift of meanings of the criteria

[6] Cf. *Met*. vii. 8, 1033ᵇ19 ff.

for substancehood we now see a confirmation of our earlier conclusion.

In Chapters 1–3 of *Metaphysics* vii Aristotle has succeeded in employing some shibboleths of S_1, but he has failed to apply them in such a way that they prove the substancehood of form. For given the shifts of meaning in the terms that appear toward the end of Chapter 3, the criteria for substratum have changed, and consequently the very concept of subtratum invoked in *Met.* vii is a new one. We are left in uncertainty concerning the meaning of substratum and hence concerning what it means to say that substratum is substance. What does emerge from Chapter 3 is Aristotle's predilection for form. But much remains unclear about form: precisely how is it substance, and indeed, what is form in the last analysis? Aristotle next examines the candidacy of essence, and in the process makes some important connections between essence and form. Perhaps by understanding the claims of essence we shall come to understand the claims of form to the title of substance.

9.2 ESSENCE AS SUBSTANCE

Aristotle concludes his study of substance in Chapter 3 with a programmatic remark that form must be examined further. The following Chapters 4–6 and 10–11 are devoted to a study of essence. But in his discussions he identifies form with essence, so he must be carrying out the programme he has promised by studying essence. Aristotle seems hopeful that by examining the claims of essence, he can show how form alone of the three senses of Aristotelian substance qualifies as the really real.

He begins his study with a preliminary specification of essence. Essence is what a thing is in its own nature ($\kappa\alpha\theta$' $\alpha\mathring{v}\tau\acute{o}$) (4, $1029^{b}14$). It is expressed in a formula which describes the nature of the thing in question while omitting the name of the thing ($^{b}19$ f.). In other words, an essence is the real correlate of a definition. The definition cannot include the definiendum in the definiens or it would be circular. Aristotle's doctrine of Essentialism ensures that every concrete substance has an essence. His present hypothesis is that that essence is the substance of a given thing.

We have seen in Chapters 2 and 3 that Essentialism (E) is a part of S_1 and the corresponding principle of Essentialism* (E*) is part of S_2. The following set of doctrines comprises E:

Secondary Substantialism (SS): Every primary substance falls under a secondary substance.

Definibility (D): Every species is either identical to a primitive genus or is identical to the differentia of a genus.

Naturalism (N): Species and genera are natural kinds.

E* consists of the D and N, with FS replacing SS:

Formal Substantialism (FS): Every concrete substance falls under a species, which is identical with its form.

It seems plausible and conformable to common sense that Aristotle should espouse Naturalism and that he should identify the sensible particulars of his system with specimens of a natural kind. But E and E* say more than this: they say that each concrete substance has a nature that can be described by means of a unique definition. In fact, as Aristotle's study progresses we see that the definition will be *per genus et differentiam* (Chapter 12). The thesis D which embodies Aristotle's view of definition is neither self-evident nor easily justifiable. In Aristotle's discussion of essence in *Met.* vii, D plays a prominent but ambivalent role. It is on this component of Aristotle's essentialism that we must focus first.

In Chapter 12 we can glimpse the operation of a procedure derived from Plato's method of division. This suggests that behind D there is a logical, or perhaps biological, method of classification. Plato's method no doubt plays some genetic role in accounting for Aristotle's theory of essence. But as Aristotle clearly points out in the *Analytics* (*A.Pr.* i. 31, *A.Po.* ii. 5), the method of division begs the questions it examines and hence fails to demonstrate essence. Aristotle clearly wants more from essence than the method of division can give him. I suggest that a linguistic model lies behind the doctrine of essence. We have noted already the assumption of isomorphism that Aristotle makes in the *Categories*. The realm of language and the realm of things are alike composed of simples arranged into complexes. Moreover, the structure of language is the structure of the world and conversely. Thus by studying grammatical properties of language we can study the logical structure of the world.

Now it seems reasonable to suppose that each descriptive term of our language has a definition, and furthermore that each common noun has a definition that can be expressed in a string composed of an adjective and a more general noun, the adjective specifying the general noun more completely. For each meaning there will be a unique definition of such a noun. There may be some nouns that are so general that they do not in turn have definitions, but these may be assigned a different role in the semantic system. If this semantic structure is taken as typical of the structure of the world, we have a guarantee of a unique definition of each thing's nature. For the linguistic definition becomes a model for the natural object: as the definiens is to the definiendum, so the nature is to its object. Its nature is a complex entity consisting of a specific characteristic and a generic universal—in Aristotelian terminology a differentia and a genus. Thus, I suggest, it is a linguistic model that underwrites Aristotelian Essentialism.

I have already discussed the model lying behind Aristotle's hylomorphism. The craft model governs the interpretation of the substratum as matter and the feature as form. The model becomes so much a part of S_2 that it helps to constitute a privileged interpretation of the theory. We see a manifestation of that constitutive role in *Met.* vii. 3 when Aristotle explicates matter, form, and compound as bronze, shape, and statue, respectively (1029^a3-5).

Thus we see that *essence* and *form* are supported by *different models*. The point is not merely a genetic one. Each conception belongs to a different matrix of theoretical assumptions, to a different language game. Now Aristotle is committed to arguing that essence is substance, and he expects this argument to verify that form is substance. But the whole argument presupposes a prior one, namely that form *is* essence. Yet the fact that form and essence belong to different language games raises a serious question about their ability to be identified. We may find that we are left with little better than a mixed metaphor. On the other hand, identifications of the sort that cross categorial boundaries are often the most philosophically important ones, and the possibility of such definitions cannot be ruled out a priori.[7] What is

[7] This point has been made in recent literature in connection with the identity theory of mind. See Place (1956), Smart (1959), Cornman (1962: 492).

at stake is a synthetic view of substance which will combine certain features of the S_1 theory with certain of the S_2.

We do not find an explicit Aristotelian argument for the identity of form and essence. However, it is possible to glimpse some connections that make the identification plausible or even inevitable. The connections concern the interpretations of the relatively abstract notions of form and essence. In the first place, note how essence is understood in S_1. Each primary substance falls under a secondary substance. According to the interpretation of S_1, a secondary substance is a species (εἶδος), which in turn falls under a genus. The species is understood as a natural entity, either as a class or a universal. For instance, Socrates falls under the species Man. But Man in turn falls under the genus Animal, and can be uniquely specified by the aid of some differentia such as Rational (or Two-footed—unfortunately, Aristotle is never very confident as to what the right differentia is). Thus the notion of a species is interrelated with the notion of an essential definition. Species is properly what gets defined in stating an essence—it is what is identical with a certain specification of a genus.

On the side of form there is a similar identification: form is often interpreted to be species. Thus the form of Socrates can be stated as Man. When Socrates comes to be, some sort of animate protoplasm comes to exemplify the form Man. This is not to say that form is always or in every context interpreted as species. In the *De Anima* account, form is soul. On the other hand, it is not clear how far Aristotle wants to separate soul from species. Perhaps Socrates' soul just is the manifestation of his humanity, and human soul in general just is the species *Homo sapiens*. In any case, at least some of the time and in some explanatory contexts, the form of biological substances is their species. It is for this reason that when Aristotle says that the efficient cause of an animal is identical with the formal cause his statement is not false: both are manifestations of a single species.[8] There is a further reason that the identification may seem obvious: both concepts are expressed by the same term, εἶδος. To be sure, Aristotle is capable of subtle differentiations of sense, but at the same time he often slides between meanings. Given his propensity to take species as the proper interpretation of form in the context of

[8] e.g. *Ph.* ii. 7, 198ª25–7.

biological substances, it is not surprising if he does not trouble himself to make an explicit identification of the two concepts.

Thus Aristotle makes two separate identifications:

(1) Species is essence.
(2) Form is species.

As an easy consequence, he can infer

(3) Form is essence.

The definition given by a statement of essence is a definition of species, which in turn is form. In vii. 4 Aristotle explicitly argues only for (1):

> Therefore there is an essence only of those things whose formula is a definition. But we have a definition not where we have a word and a formula identical in meaning . . . but where there is a formula of something primary; and primary things are those which do not imply the predication of one element in them of another element. Nothing, then, which is not a species of a genus will have an *essence*—only species will have it, for these are thought to imply not merely that the subject participates in the attribute and has it as an affection, or has it by accident . . . (1030^a6–14, trans. Ross)

Aristotle seems to believe that he has also proved (3), for he speaks interchangeably of essence as form and as primary substance. Indeed, he almost takes form and essence as synonymous: 'I understand "form" to mean the essence of each thing and its primary substance' (7, 1032^b1 f.).[9] It appears that for Aristotle (2) is almost analytic and hence (3) results from a straightforward substitution of (2) in (1). In any case, he clearly accepts (3), and consequently holds that form is an object of definition.

Thus Aristotle combines the notions of form and essence into a single concept. It may appear to Aristotle that the relationship of the two notions is analytic, but in reality it is synthetic. The notion of form is a notion of a principle of structure and determinacy relative to some medium. The notion of essence is the notion of definability and analysis into kind and characteristic. Each notion comes trailing clouds of theoretical associations, and Aristotle seems to receive these without reservation. The concept of form–essence seems attractive to him in so far as it synthesizes the several aspects of his systems. It is as if he had been playing music

---

[9] Cf. also 1032^b14; 10, 1035^b32; 11, 1037^a5 f., $^a29$ f.

in two different modes on two different sets of piano keys. In order to be able to extend the possibilities of performance, he tunes the keys so that one black key, for example, can serve as either a sharp for the white key below or a flat for the white key above it, even though the sharp and the flat are not precisely the same note. This is roughly the practice used by Bach and his contemporaries in tuning 'the well-tempered clavier'. In fact it is a strategy for dealing with a phenomenon of incommensurability in music, for certain tonal progressions are incommensurable with each other. One compromises by tuning the keys such that no progression will be quite correct in order that no other progression will be terribly wrong.

I suggest that something like this is what Aristotle is attempting in *Met.* vii. The objective of his identification of form and essence is the well-tempered substance. A synthetic concept will serve to solve a wider range of problems than either of its component concepts, and will bring into unity the so far disjoint sets of principles that have governed his philosophy. Now when I say that he is attempting to synthesize the two concepts, I am speaking structurally or dialectically: I do not claim that that is what Aristotle *thinks* he is trying to do. For be probably thinks that the identity of form and essence is analytic.[10] But the best interpretation we can put on his identification of form and essence in light of the dialectical background of the two systems is the one I am recommending.

9.3 PROBLEMS OF THE WELL-TEMPERED SUBSTANCE

It is perhaps the effort to effect a synthesis of concepts from both systems that gives to *Met.* vii its desperate grandeur. From the point of view of the Two Systems Theory it is impossible to effect a thoroughgoing synthesis of the systems—logically impossible. For their respective principles are incompatible. It is only as long as the two systems can be contained within their own non-overlapping domains that they can be saved from doing violence to each other. The question concerning *Met.* vii is whether Aristotle can bring in concepts from the different systems without bringing

---

[10] Of course even the analytic–synthetic distinction is anachronistic; but if he understood our terminology he would assert that the connection was an analytic one—one true by definition.

along their presuppositions. In this section I shall examine the notion of essence—a notion proper to S_1—as it appears in S_2 in order to suggest that it will be problematic in any context in S_2. I would like to call attention to three problems in particular.

9.3.1 The Empirical Problem

At least one important dimension of Aristotelian theory is its applicability to scientific problems. The biological realm is especially significant as a potential testing-ground for theory because of the central place of biological individuals as exemplary natural substances. We might expect that Aristotle would find that essence was an invaluable concept for investigating biological phenomena, particularly in light of the connection between species and essence. But what Aristotle finds in his biological researches is the inadequacy of essence.

In *PA* i. 2–4 Aristotle argues against a method of classifying animals by dichotomous division. He finds that the method is artificial and introduces a number of strictures that prevent us from arriving at a natural characterization. His positive recommendation is that we abandon such a priori methods of analysis in favour of a more flexible approach:

. . . we must try to classify animals by their genera as laymen do, recognizing a genus of birds and one of fish. Each of these genera is distinguished by plural differentiae, not by a simple dichotomy. (3, 643[b]10–13)

The problem with dichotomy is that it fails to take into account the multiplicity of characteristics that go into a distinction between two species. We must key on elements of the οὐσία ([a]27 f.), but there is no guarantee that the differences will reduce to a single feature—indeed the facts are otherwise. 'It is impossible', Aristotle maintains, 'for a single differentia to characterize a species . . .' ([b]28 f.).

Aristotle does not explicitly reject essential definitions here. His target is an artificial method of arriving at definitions of animals. However, his argument against dichotomy raises some troublesome questions for a theory of essence. If it is not in general possible uniquely to characterize an animal species by citing a single differentia from a single path of divisions, what reason is there for thinking that an animal can be uniquely characterized by any single differentia? And if we decide that it cannot, as Aristotle's last-quoted remark suggests, what is left of the theory of essence? Will we not have to abandon the insight that to every common noun there corresponds a unique definition? In short, will we not be compelled to admit that even if there is a fixed nature shared by members of a species, there is no simple description of that nature?

At this point we would do well to make a distinction in our use of the word 'essence'. We might use it to mean simply the fixed nature of a particular that is shared by all members of a species. Or we might use it to mean such a nature as it is given in a definition. The former sense of essence is the weaker one. The latter sense is proper to S_1, but it becomes problematic for S_2. The immediate cause of the problem is that Aristotle seems to take a more empirical and less schematic view of biological research. The more he investigates biological phenomena the farther recedes the dream of finding a simple feature on the basis of which all other features can be explained. It is in the realm of language and perhaps of mathematics that the simple definition can be discovered and applied. In the complex and elusive realm of empirical biology the naïve rationalism of grammar and geometry must perish.

9.3.2 The Analytic Problem

One would expect that Aristotle's biological researches and his methodological reflections on them would spur him to abandon the Essentialism* of S_2 in favour of a view which does not require that the nature of a natural kind have a definition.[11] In other words, we might posit a modified essentialism which omits thesis D. D has its roots in the linguistic model of S_1, but it has no rationale in S_2, so by excluding D we are doing no harm to S_2. Perhaps it is a testimony to the strong hold that the S_1 picture has on Aristotle that he does not waver in his allegiance to D in *Met.* vii. Much of his discussion of essence is devoted to working out problems of definition associated with essence. Clearly Aristotle has not learned his lesson from his forays into biology. But in

---

[11] I am assuming, with the prevailing view, that *Met.* vii is a late work written after Aristotle had done much of his biological research and probably after he had written the *PA*.

dealing with problems of definition he comes up against a problem that is more serious to the degree that it is more theoretical.

The problem is one that seems to lie behind many of Aristotle's worries in Chapters 4–6 and 10–12, although he sometimes talks around the problem instead of confronting it directly. The problem is simple to state: if a species is defined by a statement of its essence, and the essence is a complex of elements, are not the elements (or some subset of them) prior to the species?[12] In Chapter 10 Aristotle accepts a similar suggestion on the grounds that this will make form superior to matter. The focus there, however, is on a definition of a concrete substance in which the definiens in question consists of a term denoting the matter and another term denoting the form. Yet the real problem case is not the definition of a concrete substance but the definition of the species, that is, of the formal element of the concrete individual. Suppose that species is identical with essence, as Aristotle argues in Chapter 6, that essence is complex, as he maintains in Chapter 10, and that the elements of essence are differentia and genus, as Aristotle implies in Chapter 12. Now can Aristotle still maintain that form is substance? (1) Genus cannot be substance, because then he will have to forfeit to Platonism. (2) Then it seems that the differentia must be substance. But the differentia is not even substantive. It is a characteristic like Two-Footed or Rational, expressed by an adjective designating not a thing but a modification of a thing.

Aristotle realizes part of the problem, but he does not seem to appreciate that it is a dilemma. In Chapter 12, in order to save himself from a capitulation to Platonism, he accepts (2). Indeed, he even construes differentia in a way that presupposes the method of division (though not necesarily dichotomous division).[13] If we follow the method of division we will have a single differentia that comprises the whole difference and which constitutes the substance of the species.[14] The solution follows logically from the assumptions, but to take such a position would be no less fatal to substantialism than would (1). For we would find that what is at least arguably substantial, namely form, is in fact a non-substantial characteristic—not a natural kind, however

[12] Cf. 10, 1035^{b}4–6.
[13] However, 1038^{a}12–15 suggests that he has dichotomous division in mind.
[14] Cf. ^{a}19 f., 25 f., 28–30.

general, but a way of being a kind. Aristotle extricates himself by a disclaimer at the end of the chapter—suggesting that perhaps it was all an exercise in dialectic after all. He notes that there is no priority in substance and thus the preceding argument is otiose. The remark is almost cryptic, and it leaves us wondering just how much of the previous discussion is cancelled.

Aristotle's investigation of essence reads like a series of flirtations with the sirens of Platonism. In the light of TST it is possible to see the attraction a Platonic position might have for him. In S_1 Aristotle had an account of essence as revealing the structure of the species. But the species was not an independent entity: it was anchored to primary substance. Hence whatever analysis might be made of species, the result was not a reduction of species to genus and/or differentia, for there was a built-in downward link to the particular. As Aristotle repeatedly asserted, species was more substantial than genus. And clearly it must be, for it was closer to the ontological basis of the system. But in S_2, Aristotle cuts loose from the basic particular, and now there is nothing to keep substance from being identified with the most universal and generic of elements. In other words, reductionism can operate on the equation of species and essence to break up species into one or more of the universals that make up essence.

The temptation to reduction brings its own problems. If the elements of essence turn out to be the real substance, then we must ask (1) what the relation between the elements is and, as a connected question, (2) which of the elements is the real substance. These questions concern Aristotle in Chapter 12 and, in an oblique way, Chapters 13, 14, and 16. Aristotle seems to envisage two possible relationships of the elements of essence, which we can represent schematically as follows (S = species, D = differentia, G = genus):

(a) $S = D + G$
(b) $S = D (G)$

If we take scheme (a) above as representative of the relation between differentia and genus, we seem to have two equivalent elements. It is difficult to see how they can be unified into a single account. If they cannot, we are left with *two* substances. When Aristotle notices this consequence, he rejects interpretation (a).[15]

---

[15]   13, 1039^a3–5; 16, 1041^a3–5.

The alternative seems to be to subordinate one element to another. (*b*) suggests this by making *S* a function of *G*. The function then becomes the real substance, and this function is *D*, the differentia. The genus appears merely as an argument in the function, or, in metaphysical terms, an indeterminate entity. I take it that this interpretation lies behind Aristotle's strategy in Chapter 12:

> If then the genus does not exist in its own right apart from the species of the genus, or if it exists, but as matter (for [e.g.] voice is the genus and matter and the differentiae form the species, which are letters, from this), evidently the definition is the formula of the differentiae. (1038ᵃ5–9).

Because genus plays the role of an indeterminate element and a potentiality in this interpretation, it can be equated with matter by analogy. Some interpreters would like to make this move the foundation of Aristotle's solution to the problem of substance.[16] But the view that genus is matter is at best an attenuated conception of matter, and one that seems based more on logical exigencies of the moment than deeply rooted biological insights. In any case, Aristotle fails to develop the interpretation, and his remarks at the end of the chapter look like a disclaimer for the preceding approach. Aristotle officially rejects the present interpretation because he finds the notion of priority (of elements in a definition?) incoherent. As I have noted, he is well advised to abandon the view, since to reduce substance to differentia would be a fatal blow to substantialism.[17]

9.3.3 The Conceptual Problem

This brings us to the final problem for taking essence as substance. The analytic problem consisted in the fact that once species is cut loose from the basic particular, there is no way to block reductionism, which threatens to reduce substance either to what is generic or what is non-substantial altogether. But the danger of reductionism calls attention to a feature of essence that seems to disqualify it from being substance at all: it is irrevocably universal, and its elements are universals. To identify substance with essence

[16] Rorty (1973); see criticisms in Grene (1974) and reply in Rorty (1974). See also criticism in White (1975).

[17] He seems to return to this position in a guarded way in Book viii (2, 1043ᵃ4 ff.). However, his approach in Book viii ultimately leads him in a different direction; cf. ch. 9.5.

thus seems to amount to a capitulation to a relatively Platonic way of seeing the world.

The problem is not really unique to essence. Form also must be universal. For according to the craft model, a form is imposed on a material to arrive at a product. Notice that the form is not unique to the material on which it is imposed: a smith can turn out a dozen statues embodying the same form, which, according to Aristotle, is in the mind of the craftsman—or, more abstractly, in the smith's art—before it is realized in the metal.[18] Thus the form is not in any significant sense particular. To call it τόδε τι does not make it particular because, as we have seen, the phrase changes meaning in S_2. On the other hand, it is easier to lose sight of the fact that form is universal than it is in the case of essence. For form can be manifested as shape, and shape can be felt to be peculiar to an individual, particularly someone as uniquely shaped as snub-nosed Socrates. In each case what makes form individual is really a certain instantiation, but there is a temptation to think of shape as individual because of the way it manifests itself. Thus it is relatively easy to ignore the ontological status of form as a universal.

But it is crucial to the interpretation of Aristotle's doctrine of substance just how we construe the ontological status of form. In general there are four possibilities: (1) form is universal; (2) form is particular; (3) form is neither universal nor particular; (4) form is both universal and particular. Although (1) is the obvious, and I think correct, interpretation, it is not popular because of Aristotle's conflicting claims in vii 13. Woods (1967) defends this interpretation by drawing a distinction between being predicated universally and being universal. However, the distinction has little textual support.[19]

There is textual evidence to support proponents of (2), but the evidence is limited and ambiguous.[20] Moreover, advocates of particular form have a difficult task in giving an account of what philosophical sense we can make of particular form. Hartman (1976: 552 f.) makes a serious attempt to explain how one individual's form can be different from another's; what he finds is

---

[18] Cf. *Met.* vii. 7, 1032[b]11–14; 8, 1033[a]28 ff.; 9, 1034[a]21–4; xii. 3, 1070[a]13–19.
[19] See Lesher (1971: 170–4).
[20] For statements of the position see Sellars (1957), Harter (1975), Hartman (1976); for problems see Albritton (1957).

that the difference must depend upon matter. If that is so, the individuating factor is matter, not form, and form is particular only in so far as it is instantiated in matter. But this is compatible with—and even implies—that form is universal, not particular.[21]

Interpretation (3) entails that form be distinguished from such universal entities as essence and species and from concrete particulars. Thus form will have to turn out to be *sui generis*.[22] Advocates of this position often stress the difference between the matter–form tie and predication; since according to *DI* 7, 17[a]39 f. the universal is what is predicated of many things, if form is not predicated of matter it is not universal. The problem with this view is that it entails distinctions between universals and forms which are ill-supported by the texts. If this is Aristotle's view, it is curious that he fails to make or maintain vital distinctions.[23] Thus (3) tends to collapse into (1), which brings back the threat of contradiction in vii. 13.

Finally, according to (4) form can be construed as both particular and universal.[24] The challenge with this view is to avoid creating a philosophical monster. Aristotle himself diagnoses the Third Man Argument as resulting from a confusion of particular and universal and he explicitly rejects the identification (vii. 13, 1039[a]1–3). He thinks of the two ontological properties as of incompatible types. It would be surprising, then, if he should view (4) as a viable answer to the problem.[25] The conceptual problem of form remains intractable to ordinary and even extraordinary analysis.

In general, Aristotle's statements in Book vii seem to entail that form is universal at the same time that they make it impossible to embrace the conclusion. Both form and essence are problematic as candidates for substance because they are universals. Explicitly to recognize a universal as substance would be a major reversal of

[21] Cf. Lesher (1971: 175) against Albritton, whom he takes to be an advocate of (2).

[22] For versions of this approach see Owens (1951: chs. 11 and 13), Haring (1956–7), Loux (1979), Code (1982).

[23] For criticisms, see Lacey (1965*b*: 61–3) on Haring.

[24] This interpretation is suggested by Owen (1978) and defended by Modrak (1979).

[25] Modrak makes a distinction between substance-types and other universals, so that in effect she sees an ambiguity in Aristotle's rejection of universals in vii. 13. Her overall strategy is similar to that of Woods (1967) and her view tends to collapse into a version of (1).

position for Aristotle. The candidacy of essence especially calls attention to the anomaly because there is no effective way of denying the universality of essence. But the conflict is more easy to detect than to eliminate. For there seems to be no viable alternative to taking form and essence as universals. Ironically, the concept of essence was appropriated from S_1 precisely to clarify the function of form in S_2. Instead it precipitates a major crisis by focusing attention on its differences from the classical conception of substance. In Chapter 13 Aristotle raises the question of the universality of essence and comes face to face with the consequences of mixing substantial atomism and hylomorphism.

9.4   THE INCOMPATIBILITY OF THE SYSTEMS

The progress of Aristotle's argument has taken him through the candidacy of substratum, essence, and genus. He now addresses the claims of the universal in Chapter 13. He is conscious that the present question has implications for the debate with Platonism, for he applies the conclusions of Chapter 13 to a Platonic position in Chapter 14. He does not seem to anticipate the consequences his argument will have for his own position; at least he does not prepare the reader for the difficulties ahead. At the close of the chapter, however, he calls attention to a serious anomaly that arises from the critique of the universal. I shall argue that the present chapter has disastrous consequences for his own philosophy, and that the problem arises from his adoption of obsolete principles.

Aristotle begins his brief against the universal by citing two principles of substance: (a) substance is what is unique to an individual (1038^b10); (b) substance is what is not predicated of a substratum ($^b15$). By using these principles, he hopes to be able to show that the universal is not substance. Now (a) is evidently a principle that expresses the thesis of substantial atomism: the indivisible particular is substance in the primary sense. The principle is stated oddly, because according to SA we would not even speak of *a* substance that is peculiar to an individual, because the individual just *is* the substance. However, the statement of (a) seems to be an effort to capture SA in a manner of speaking that is more appropriate to S_2. (b) is a straightforward restatement of the criterion of subjecthood of S_1: substance is that which is always a subject and never a predicate, that is, substance is the ultimate subject.

Aristotle uses these principles as criteria of substance. Not surprisingly, he finds that they rule out the universal. (*a*) immediately rules out the universal because the universal is by definition common to many (*b*11 f.). It is almost superfluous for Aristotle to provide a brief *reductio ad absurdum* argument to make his point (*b*12–15). The statement of (*b*) gives an immediate refutation of the thesis that the universal is substance, since it is a corollary of the definition that the universal is said of a subject (*b*15 f.). Some more complex arguments follow to show that the universal is not substance. (1) To the suggestion that some element of the essence is a universal, Aristotle argues that the case reduces to making substance a common predicate, which is ruled out by (*a*) (*b*16–23). (2) Furthermore, if we say the elements of essence are substance, there will be a substance made up of non-substances, since general terms do not stand for substances but for features (*b*23–1039*a*2). (3) If we do not observe this distinction between substances and features, we will generate the Third Man Argument (*a*2 f.). (4) If we derive substance from the elements of essence we make a single actual substance to be two actual substances, which is impossible: two actual entities are never actually one (*a*3–11). (5) Similarly number is not a compound of units actually present in it.[26]

All these arguments seem to aim at blocking the ascent from the particular to the universal. If we take the universal to be substance, many absurdities follow. (*a*) and (*b*) seem to provide the basic presumptions that militate against the universal in all Aristotle's arguments. If substance is what is unique to the individual, and if substance is not said of a subject, then universals must be ruled out, either directly by confronting the criteria or indirectly by producing results which are paradoxical given the criteria.

Through all this Aristotle seems to think he can attack the universal without discrediting essence. He begins (1) by giving the advocate of universals a rejoinder: 'But even if [the universal] cannot be [substance] in the same way as essence, nevertheless it is in this . . .' (*b*16–18). The implication seems to be that the

---

[26] I am generally following Ross's analysis of the argument.

argument is not directed against essence, but only against the universal, and that it is agreed by both parties that essence is substance. But as I have indicated already, essence *is* universal, and hence the argument attacks essence *ipso facto*. Aristotle himself recognizes that definitions have universal application, which should lead him to see that essence, as the correlate of a definition, is universal. And indeed, he does seem to say this.[27] In any case Aristotle holds that essence is a complex analysis of species, and if the elements are universal, essence is undermined indirectly. Aristotle seems to hint that the universals are not actually present in the essence (cf. Chapter 12), but he does not say what function they have. At best essence enjoys a very precarious immunity to the onslaught of Aristotle's dialectic.

But at the end of the chapter (1039[a]14 ff.) the latent paradox of his position seems to catch up to Aristotle:

The resulting theory seems to produce an anomaly (ἀπορία). For if no substance can come from universals because these stand for a Such but not a This, and no substance can be a compound of actual substances, every substance would be uncompounded, so that there would not be a definition of any substance. But it is generally held and was asserted some time ago that substance only or especially has a definition. Yet now it turns out that even it has no definition. Thus there will be no definition of anything. Or in one way there will and in another there will not be. This will become clearer from the following remarks. ([a]14–23)

Aristotle never makes good on his final promise. But he does now see the difficulty of his position, at least from one point of view. Substance is what is by nature definable, and yet it is not definable. The first conjunct is proved in Chapter 4, the second in Chapter 13. The statement is a contradiction generated by Aristotle's assumptions. It is not difficult to see why the contradiction arises at the end of Chapter 13. For in the argument of this chapter Aristotle has brought back the principles of S_1 that are inconsistent with the hylomorphism of S_2. According to SA substance is the indivisible particular. But according to H there is no indivisible particular, and hence there is nothing to satisfy criteria (*a*) and (*b*). Rather the form is substance in S_2. But form is identified with

---

[27] On definitions, see *Met.* xii. 8, 1074[a]34 f.; cf. *Cat.* 1, 1[a]6 f., 5, 2[a]19–21; on the connection between definition and essence, *Met.* vii. 4, 1030[a]6 f.; on the essence as universal, cf. *Met.* vii. 10, 1035[b]27 ff., and especially [b]34 f.: '. . . the definition is of the universal.'

essence, so essence is also substance; and essence is the correlate of definition, so substance is definable. But if, as Aristotle sees, substance is not universal, it has no definition.

Let us consider the argument that emerges from this chain of reasoning:

(1) Form is substance. (vii. 3)

(2) Form is essence. (vii 4, 6)

∴ (3) Essence is substance. (1), (2)

(4) Something is definable if and only if it has an essence. (vii. 4)

∴ (5) Form is definable. (2), (4)

∴ (6) Substance is definable. (3), (4)

(7) Definition is of the universal. (vii. 10)

(8) Substance is not universal. (vii. 13)

∴ (9) Substance is not definable. (7), (8)

Of course (6) and (9) are contradictory propositions. The ἀπορία Aristotle hits on is, to be precise, a paradox. The deduction above is a classical *reductio ad absurdum*, and it seems to require that we jettison one of our independent premisses. According to the principles of S_2 as they are developed in *Met.* vii we should reject (8). Furthermore, from the point of view of TST this principle appears to be an intrusion from S_1. However, Aristotle suggests that we should rather give up the claim that substance is universal. But that claim is not even a line of the proof. To introduce the claim, we should need an auxiliary premiss such as

(6a) Essence is universal.

Combined with (3), (6a) gives us

(6b) Substance is universal.

The conclusion (6b) is certainly an Aristotelian tenet. But since it is now a consequence of other premisses, the inconsistency must be traced back to at least one of those: either (3) or (6a) must be rejected. Now it is not clear how Aristotle could deny (6a)—how could essence *qua* essence not be universal? So perhaps we should consider rejecting (3). But since (3) is a consequence of (1) and (2), one of these must be at the root of the problem. But clearly Aristotle can not reject (1) without undermining his whole project in *Met.* vii. And as we have already noted, he shows no disposition to question the identity in (2).

In general, then, the paradox of definition seems to issue from a
contradiction deep within Aristotle's set of privileged assumptions.
For the contradictions that are generated by the argument of vii.
13 can be traced back to the principles which direct the whole
inquiry into substance. The ἀπορία Aristotle finds in vii. 13 is thus
not a minor stumbling-block. It suggests a deep incoherence in
Aristotle's position. According to TST the paradox of definition is
just the manifestation of a latent contradiction in Aristotle's
position, for he has not renounced the principles of S_1 which are
inconsistent with the principles of S_2. The opening lines of vii. 13
are just a reiteration of S_1 principles, which are not now vital
elements of his current system, but adventitious dogmas inherited
from an earlier stage of thought. They provide gratuitous
assumptions which do not further but rather obfuscate the
argument of Book vii.

One of the major inadequacies of most interpretations of Met.
vii is that they have failed adequately to explain the aporetic
character of Aristotle's Sisyphean argument. One recent approach
to the puzzles about substance tries to correct this deficiency by
incorporating the aporetic structure into the interpretation.[28] The
approach is initially attractive because it would allow one to
discount a good many of Aristotle's remarks as preliminary and
dialectical. Yet except for the Topics Aristotle never raises puzzles
just for the exercise of it, as his interpreters are well aware. Sooner
or later he must solve the riddle, and the interpreter must tell us
how he does so. However dialectical his argument is, Aristotle
must bring the argument home and resolve the puzzles; he must
find a solution, then exhibit it as a resolution to the real puzzles
and/or a dissolution of the various pseudo-problems the dialectic
generates.[29] And when it comes to identifying the solution to the
puzzles the aporetic interpretation runs into the same obstacles as
the standard interpretations. It is difficult to discern a solution and
more difficult still to find an instance of Aristotle exploiting the
solution to solve the problems of substance.

If Aristotle has a simple solution, he should clarify and apply it
soon after Chapter 13. We expect him to warn us that form is not
the same as essence, and only form is substance. Curiously,
though, he never confronts the implications for essence of the

[28] See Owen (1978), Code (1982), Loux (1984).
[29] EN vii. 3, 1146^{b}6–8.

paradox of definition. He gladly uses his conclusions against Platonism in Chapter 14 before he returns to the problem in Chapter 15. Then he invokes a distinction between the concrete individual and the λόγος (a new version of the distinction between compound and form) to save his position. The concrete individual is not definable or demonstrable because it has matter which can either be or not be; it is thus known only by opinion. But the λόγος is neither created nor destroyed. Thus we can know the individual through its λόγος. Aristotle's whole argument here is an *ignoratio elenchi*. The problem that arises in vii. 13 is not that concrete substance is not universal and definable; we could easily accept that. It is that *form* is not universal and definable: that is shocking and revolutionary. Aristotle responds to a vexing problem about the nature of primary substance with a truism about concrete substance. He merely uses his distinction between the concrete substance and the λόγος to restate a naïve version of his position, not to defend it against a challenge posed by the paradox of definition—one which would sever the link between concrete substance and λόγος altogether.

Thus Aristotle shows no signs of having learned a lesson from the paradox of definition—either the lesson of the incommensurability of his systems or that of the anomalous character of form. But on the other hand he does not seem satisfied with his immediate solution. For if he were satisfied, he should cease pursuing the question and move on to another. But so far from giving up the search, he generates two more distinct solutions to the problem, as we shall see.

9.5 ARISTOTLE'S OTHER SOLUTIONS

In Chapter 16 Aristotle applies his findings to show that most of the concrete candidates for substancehood fail. The details need not concern us. The main significance of the chapter is that it seems to provide a closure for Aristotle's study. As I have noted, Aristotle sets up the problem of being as a puzzle having a determinate solution to be reached by the proper method. The ἔνδοξα or preliminary facts (and intuitions) to be explained include the concrete candidates for substancehood. When Aristotle brings the discussion back to the ἔνδοξα he signals that the problems have been met and the results are sufficient to exhibit the truths that were obscurely grasped as preliminary facts. Thus one would expect that the inquiry is officially over. Aristotle even provides a final sentence to sum up the results of the inquiry: 'It is plain that neither are any of the things said universally substance nor is any substance composed of other substances' (1041^a3–5). But, as if Aristotle realizes that this answer is unsatisfactory, he does not end his inquiry here. He provides another solution to the problem of being in Chapter 17, and then goes on to add a whole appendix on to Book vii, namely Book viii. In the appendix he gives yet another solution, which he and many commentators seem to think is equivalent or supplementary to the Chapter 17 solution.[30]

In Chapter 17 Aristotle examines the question of substance from the standpoint of cause. He begins with an account of cause reminiscent of *A.Po.* ii. 1–2. However, he makes use of the form–matter distinction to identify the essential cause with the form which unifies the matter (1041^b7–9). Then using an analogy of a syllable composed of letters, he argues that the syllable is not simply identical to the letters; nor is it identical to the letters plus another element, which is the form. For then we would have to explain how the first set of elements plus the new element are a unity. Thus Aristotle uses something like Bradley's regress argument to point out that the formal cause is not an element, but a principle of another logical order. It is a principle of combination according to which the many parts are constituted into a unity.

Here Aristotle is attempting to identify substance with essence through a new route. He identifies the essence with the formal cause and the formal cause with the form. The argument is interesting because it is perhaps the closest Aristotle gets to combining an account from S_1 and an account from S_2. The argument for the essence being a cause is straight out of the *A.Po.* while the connection between that cause and the form is unique to S_2 accounts of causality. The solution has the advantage that a particular can be the formal cause of a particular thing, as, for instance, Socrates' soul can be the cause of Socrates. Unfortunately, however, if Aristotle wants to maintain the identity of essence and formal cause, which is an integral part of the present argument, he must admit that from the point of view in which the formal cause is identical to the essence, it is universal. At this point all the problems seem to return.

[30] Most recently, Loux (1984).

In *Met.* viii Aristotle recapitulates his argument, digresses, and finally works out another solution to the problem of substance. In Chapter 6 he raises again the question of unity of essence: what makes parts of the definition a unity (1045^a12-17)? The question is made especially interesting by the fact that Book viii is a continuation of vii, and Aristotle seems to put forth the query as a continuation of vii. 17. There he gave no sign that he thought the problem of unity applied to parts of the *essence*, since his examples used objects with a plurality of material parts. But perhaps he had in mind the identity of essence. If so, his answer in vii. 17 is curious because the formal cause is the cause of unity of the essence—that is, there is a form of form which is the real substance—a most curious result. In viii. 6, however, Aristotle identifies the elements in a unity as matter and form, which are related as potentiality and actuality ($^a23-5$). The argument is cryptic, especially since we are not sure what elements Aristotle is identifying with matter and form. Are we still talking about elements of a definition, that is, the genus and differentia? Both of these are elements of form, but perhaps the genus is potential–material relative to the differentia, which is actual–formal, since the differentia determines the genus (cf. vii. 12, 1038^a5-9). Aristotle's initial discussion in viii. 6 about the unity of definition ($^a7$ ff., $^a14$ ff.) suggests this reading. Perhaps, on the other hand, the elements in question are simply the matter and form of a compound. The example Aristotle exploits is that of a bronze sphere, which suggests that he has in mind the latter paradigm ($^a25$ ff.).[31] Furthermore, after drawing out the consequences of the example, he resumes the discussion by considering the unity of the *proximate* matter and the form—a definite reference to an instance of concrete unity ($^b17-19$).

Thus it is not at all clear even what the domain of inquiry is. Nevertheless, we do see Aristotle making some very interesting moves in his inquiry. Using the bronze sphere analogy he argues that the question, 'What makes the elements a unity?', is misplaced:

What then is the cause of this, the potential being actual, except the maker, in the case of things that come to be? For there is no other cause of the potential sphere becoming actual but that this was their essence. ($^a30-3$)

[31] Note, however, how he slides into this example from a counterfactual definition.

The philosophical strategy seems remarkably modern: show that the question is meaningless because it makes presuppositions that fail. Why should one even ask the question? Only if one confused the question 'What is the cause of unity?' with the genetic question 'How did this unity came into being?', would one press the inquiry. In the last analysis 'the ultimate matter and the shape are one and the same, the one potentially, the other actually . . .' (^{b}17–19).

Now this final solution to the problem of substance is, surprisingly, a new one. According to it the *elements* are as form and matter. In vii. 17, by contrast, the elements were identified with the matter; the form is not an *element* but a unifying principle of a higher order. In vii. 17 it made sense to ask what the cause of unity was, and the answer was the formal cause. In viii. 6, the question is exposed as misguided, and in so far as it has an answer, the answer is only the efficient cause. Here form and matter are not really different; they are merely two aspects of the same reality, so intimately connected that it makes no sense to ask what makes them one. In the vii. 17 solution the causal question is the only relevant one, and the formal cause is the appropriate answer; in the viii. 6 solution the causal question is misplaced and can only be answered by giving the incidental efficient cause. Somehow essence gets lost in the last solution. Either Aristotle has dropped the identification of form and essence and answered the question with respect to form and matter alone; or the elements of the unity *are* the elements of the essence. In this case we again get a kind of second-order solution to the problem. For on the latter interpretation the principles of matter–form and potentiality–actuality are taken out of their original domain of application and reapplied to elements of essence, which elements were originally identified exclusively with form and actuality. Now we seem to have a form and a matter of essence, that is, a form and matter of form.

What we find after vii. 16 is that Aristotle adds two new solutions to the problem of substance. Both seem hasty and both suggest that Aristotle may be forcing the inquiry into higher-order analyses to solve the problem. The two solutions are different, contrary to what Aristotle leads us to believe. Overall they leave the impression that Aristotle was not satisfied that he had solved the problem, and that he was starting to go in circles by reapplying principles in different contexts. In any case, he fails to address the real problem that lies behind the paradox of definition and the deeper inconsistency in his position that generates the paradox. That is to say, he fails to tell us how substance can be both universal and not universal. If the Two Systems Theory is correct, the fatal flaw lies in Aristotle's tenacious reliance on concepts and principles drawn from S_1. Indeed, one of the objectives of *Met.* vii seems to be a synoptic view of substance which takes into account principles of both systems. His appeals to principles of S_1—or at least specious imitations of them—in Chapters 3, 12, 13, and 17 show that the S_1 viewpoint is an integral part of his inquiry. But a stubborn insistence in Chapter 13 on the unmitigated S_1 criteria of substance in contrast to the mitigated criteria of Chapter 3 brings his investigation into inner conflict, and his continued dependence on S_1 principles in Chapter 17 shows that he has not learned his lesson. Yet his ongoing inquiry into substance after Chapter 16 at least shows that Aristotle is not content; and it provides strong prima-facie evidence that Aristotle has not found a solution to his problem, or that if he has he does not know it.

9.6 CONCLUSION

In this chapter and the previous one we have discovered confirmation of TST in the paradoxes of substance of *Met.* vii. Matter, in particular prime matter, proves to be paradigmatically substantial and paradigmatically non-substantial; form proves to be particular and non-particular, universal and non-universal, and by extension substantial and non-substantial. Where we find the paradoxes we find that Aristotle has appealed to S_1 principles. TST predicts that contradictions will be generated if Aristotle invokes principles of both systems at the same time. In the paradoxes of substance we find confirmation of the prediction. Thus our interpretive theory supplies a diagnosis— indeed a *single* diagnosis—for two sets of well-known anomalies in Aristotle's metaphysics: the paradoxes of matter and the paradoxes of form. Furthermore, we can verify that Aristotle fails to address the premises that generate the paradoxes, and instead of a definitive solution to the paradoxes he gives us a series of different solutions. None of the solutions is adequate, and Aristotle does not even seem to be clear as to whether the solutions are the same or different. This tends to show that while Aristotle recognized he had a serious problem in harmonizing elements of his system, he did not correctly diagnose the cause of the problem or recognize that he was working with two systems.

I have argued that the paradoxes of substance result from Aristotle's accepting an inconsistent set of principles. If my diagnosis is correct, we should be able to eliminate the paradoxes by eliminating the offending principles. But will that save Aristotle's theory of substance? We still have not solved the problem of *Met.* vii: what is the real substance? The principles of S_2 alone seem to generate this problem, since hylomorphism by splitting the atomic substance of S_1 raises questions of priority for the substantialism of S_2. So even if we can save matter and form from being incoherent elements of S_2, we must still face the problem of *Met.* vii. Can TST resolve this problem and, as it were, show Aristotle what he could and should have said?

10

S₂ without S₁:
What Aristotle Should Have Said

We have seen that the paradoxes of *Met.* vii result from combining the principles of S_1 with those of S_2. In a sense Aristotle has failed to give S_2 a fair chance. Instead of determining what answer to the question 'What is substance?' is appropriate to S_2, he seeks an answer that is compatible with the demands of S_1. But it is logically impossible to produce such an answer. What Aristotle should have done is to determine an answer to the question which captures the basic notion of substance within the hylomorphic system. In this chapter I shall attempt to discover what the real substance is for S_2, and thus to construct the basis for a consistent hylomorphic substantialism.

10.1 THE CLAIMS OF FORM

In *Met.* vii. 3 Aristotle introduced three criteria of substantiality, as we have noted: (*a*) being a subject, (*b*) being separable, and (*c*) being a This. If we were to look at these criteria without a bias toward any of the three candidates, namely form, matter, and the composite, which would the criteria favour? Criterion (*a*) seems most obviously to favour matter, which is the subject for form and hence the ultimate subject of predication. The separability referred to in (*b*) seems to be paradigmatically self-existence. For to be separable in thought or definition is a trivial property of almost anything that can be named. The most obvious candidate for an independently existent object is the compound of matter and form, since it is not clear in what sense either matter or form exists apart from the composite. As for (*c*) being a This, again the composite seems the most obvious choice. The entity that is singled out by ostension is the composite, not its form or its matter.

Of course Aristotle slants the interpretation of the criteria so that they pick out form as the real substance. He is evidently not a disinterested observer in the debate over the real substance. There is something about form that Aristotle finds promising. It is not the presence of tacit assumptions from S$_1$ which dictates his choice of form, since considerations of S$_1$ tend to favour matter over form. Rather, certain systematic considerations proper to S$_2$ seem to motivate Aristotle's choice. By seeing what these considerations are, we can determine whether the claims of form can be vindicated. I shall provide a cursory survey of some well-known theories in Aristotle's philosophy to show how the primacy of form provides certain benefits for those theories.

10.1.1 Form and Psychology

One important application of the matter–form analysis is to the living organism. As applied to living things, whether plants or animals, Aristotle finds that the matter is to the form as the body is to the soul (*DA* ii. 1). Because of the correlation between body–soul and matter–form the question of priority between matter and form has immediate implications for the body–soul contrast: if matter is prior to form, then body is prior to soul. If, on the other hand, form is prior to matter, soul is superior to body. Since Aristotle inherits the Platonic bias in favour of soul over body this one case creates a strong presumption in favour of form over matter.

But of course the other choice is possible. The atomists for instance view the soul as merely a collection of fine atoms. Thus it is basically a physical construct which can survive only as long as the body is properly organized and operating.[1] A slightly more complex materialistic view is the quasi-Pythagorean view that the soul is a harmony of the body. According to this view soul is an emergent property, but it is a function or dependency of the physical state of the organism. This view is not far removed from Aristotle's own in some respects. For Aristotle too sees the soul as dependent on a harmonious organization of parts—indeed it almost is the functional disposition of the body. Thus it is difficult to see how Aristotle's mature theory of soul differs from the harmony view of soul Plato criticizes in the *Phaedo*, except that

---

[1] *DA* i. 3, 406^{b}15–22 = DK 68 A 104.

Aristotle has a complex hylomorphic model instead of a crude musical metaphor to interpret the theory.[2]

Yet although Aristotle's view could easily be recast in materialistic mould, Aristotle himself stoutly resists such a move.[3] He does not mean for his concept of soul to be reduced to bodily function. He consistently treats the soul as superior to the body and as ruling it—contrary to Plato's critique of the soul as function of the body. For Aristotle the soul is a function not merely in the sense of an epiphenomenon, but in the sense of an emergent property. Thus after giving his famous definition of soul as first actuality of the body, Aristotle compares the body to an axe; he argues that the soul is to the body as the essence of an axe is to an axe: if the essence disappears, the axe ceases to be an axe except in name.[4] To fill out his example: the essence of an axe is the capacity to cut; without this an object shaped like an axe is not really an axe. By analogy, a body is organized to function in a certain biological way; without this capacity, which is realized in the soul, it is not really a body. Accordingly, far from the soul being a mere epiphenomenon, it is the condition for a body's being a body: it is *essential* to the organism.

Perhaps in part to secure further the primacy of soul, Aristotle also retains the active νοῦς or agent intellect as a transcendent element of soul which does not perish at death and which is superior to and impervious to the affections of the soul.[5] It is as though Aristotle leaves this one element as a fossil of Platonism to assure that soul should not be reducible to body. Certainly without this transcendent active νοῦς, the soul would be completely dependent on the body for its existence and would perish utterly when the body perished.

What seems to emerge is that Aristotle's philosophy of mind could be revised in a materialistic way without doing violence to his ontology. But the result is inconsistent with his ideological orientation. When given a choice between an idealism which exalts

---

[2] *Phd.* 91 E–94 E.

[3] For a materialistic interpretation of Aristotles philosophy of mind, see Hartman (1977).

[4] *DA* ii. 1, 412^{b}11–17.

[5] *DA* iii. 5. For a review of the interpretations by the Greek commentators of this difficult passage, see Ross (1961: 41–4). Hicks (1907: 505–10) followed by Hamlyn (1968: 141 f.) tries to explain away the apparent reference to a transcendent νοῦς, but the interpretation seems forced.

soul and a materialism that debases it, Aristotle chooses the idealism—even to the point of positing a kind of residual dualism of *νοῦς* and body. He chooses form over matter in part to anticipate his psychology. It is not precisely that his psychology demands the ontological priority of form, but that his idealistic bias as expressed in psychology promotes it.

10.1.2 Form and Theology

Another important application that Aristotle often anticipates in his discussions of substance is that of theology. For instance, in *Met.* vi. 1 and Book xii Aristotle finds that a study of being naturally leads to a study of the divine. Of course, if studies are to be individuated by their object and if the object of the first science is immovable substance and if this immovable substance is God, then the first science is theology. At this point metaphysics and theology coincide and the principles of philosophy must be adequate to generate a satisfactory theological account.

There are constraints on what counts as an adequate theology in the Greek tradition. The characteristics of deity were formulated by Xenophanes and became so entrenched in the philosophical tradition that they became *ἔνδοξα* for his successors. He found that the divine should be (1) a single entity rather than a plurality; (2) complete and apparently homogeneous; (3) sentient and omniscient; (4) unchanging and yet (5) able to control the world; (6) happy, or at least untroubled.[6] Aristotle saw the opportunity to incorporate all these attributes into a single being if that being were form. The form would be a separately existing mind (*νοῦς*) with cosmic influence. It would be (1) single by hypothesis,[7] (2) complete and homogeneous by being an *ἐντελέχεια* without parts that could be heterogeneous,[8] (3) sentient as a mind, and possibly omniscient as well as a fully actual mind.[9] (4) It would not change,[10] but (5) it would be the source of movement in the cosmos by being an object of desire;[11] and (6) it would be perfectly happy because of the contemplative and indeed self-contemplative life it led.[12]

[6] Xenophanes B 23–6.
[7] *Met.* xii. 8, 1074ª36 f.   [8] Ibid. ª35 f.; 7, 1073ª5–7.
[9] Ibid. Ch. 9; 7, 1072ᵇ14 ff.; on the objects of the Unmoved Mover's thought see Norman (1969).
[10] *Met.* xii. 7, 1071ª25; 9, 1074ᵇ25–7.   [11] Ibid. 7, 1072ᵇ3 ff.
[12] Ibid. 7, 1072ᵇ14–30; ch. 9; cf. *EN* x. 8, 1178ᵇ7 ff.

Thus the recognition of form as substance seems to facilitate the construction of a theology which satisfies Xenophanes' requirements. The identification of form and substance allows one to attach the positive values that are associated with form—activity, intelligibility, goodness, completeness, etc.—to the highest entity in the cosmos. It makes it possible for Aristotle to reconcile the tensions of the impassivity of God implied in (4) and the activity implied in (5), the perception implied in (3) with the bliss implied in (6). God becomes a kind of self-contained activity that by its perfection commands the reverence and emulation of all beings in the cosmos. Aristotle supposes that any admixture of matter could only introduce potentiality and imperfection into the notion of deity. Hence the choice of form as substance is the only option which anticipates Aristotle's theology.

10.1.3 Form and Value Theory

Implicit in both Aristotle's psychology and his theology is the assumption that form is the bearer of value. The properties of form: intelligibility, order, determinacy, discreteness, organization—these are the ultimate values. By contrast the characteristics of matter *qua* matter are unintelligibility, disorder, indeterminacy, continuity, and lack of organization. Thus form has a positive value in the scale of intrinsic goods while matter has a negative value. The composite owes any intrinsic good it enjoys to the presence in it of form, not matter. Thus form enjoys a clear-cut axiological priority over matter and the composite.

The good that is achievable by human agency is the realization of value in the context of a human life. The good life sketched in *EN* i. 7 and expanded in x. 6–8 is the life consisting of realizing one's potentialities as a human being. In other words, it is a state of complete instantiation of the human form, which at its highest levels entails the performance of characteristically human activities. The good for man is a certain kind of life in accordance with human virtue. Since the highest and most characteristic human capacity is reason, the good for man is a life lived in accordance with the intellectual virtues. The good for a horse is a certain kind of life in accordance with the virtues of horses. And in general the good for anything is a life or a functioning in accordance with the capacities of that entity—the realization of its form.

Thus although value is species relative, it is relative in such a way that the value in question is a constant function of the form of the species. The ideal form that might be realized is the standard of value which is the measure of all specimens of a species. Thus not only is the (actual) form the bearer of the (actual) value of an individual, but the ideal form of a species is the standard of value. Form and value are intimately connected in Aristotelian value theory.

From the standpoint of value theory we come to the same conclusions about the soul and about God as we do by hylomorphic analysis. If we take as data the fact that the soul is better than body, and form as opposed to matter is the bearer of value, then soul must be form. If God is the best thing in the universe and there is nothing better than form, then God must be form. To recognize the ontological priority of form makes possible a consistent value theory that also confirms the results of psychological and theological investigation.

We must conclude, then, that Aristotle has some strong systematic reasons for preferring form. His choice provides for a harmonious account of psychology, theology, and value theory. The primacy of form over matter anticipates and justifies the primacy of soul over body, of the divine over the profane, and of the pursuit of excellence over the pursuit of sensual indulgence. Yet on the other hand the ontology itself does not determine the idealistic interpretation of principles. There is a kind of supervenient ideology which orders the principles of S_2. When Aristotle is given a choice between idealism and materialism, he chooses idealism; when he is given a choice between rationalism and empiricism, he chooses rationalism—for the ultimate formal entities, soul and God are not known through the senses. In fact there is a kind of Platonism present in Aristotle's interpretation of S_2 principles that is not predictable from his own formal ontology or from his standard craft model. But is Aristotle's Platonism consistent with his Aristotelianism?

10.2 PROBLEMS WITH ARISTOTLE'S PLATONISM

The net result of Aristotle's attempts to promote form to an exalted status in his ontology and his axiology is to create a notion of form that is increasingly independent of matter. With the differentiation of substance into form and matter in *Ph.* i it appeared that matter and form were correlative notions—that it made no sense to conceive of matter without form and form without matter. To posit matter was just to envisage a possible scenario in which the matter came to have form. By extension, to think of matter or form in a synchronic rather than diachronic perspective was just to conceive of the contrast of two correlative components of a concrete whole. It is surprising then to meet with forms like the agent intellect and the Unmoved Mover which require no material substrate and can exist independent of any other entity. Several problems arise for such a notion of form.

10.2.1 Three Problems

Metaphysical Problems. What does it mean to say that a totally disembodied form exists? Is that not a contradiction in terms? Is not the whole notion of a form inextricably connected with the notion of matter?[13] Certainly in the way that the notions of form and matter are introduced it is difficult to see how they can exist independently. But suppose they can. Will the supposition produce a coherent account of substance or a *reductio ad absurdum*? If forms can exist independently, Aristotle seems to have a kind of form that transcends the world. It seems proper to ask where and how forms exist apart from matter. In the case of the agent intellect (AI) the problem is notoriously difficult. Aristotle's cryptic remarks about the AI in *DA* iii. 5 have given rise to conflicting traditions of interpretation concerning the nature of the AI. Are there monadic AIs or only a single AI of which all intellectual creatures have some share? There are no generally accepted answers to the questions that Aristotle raises. In a way, the status of the AI is even more obscure than that of the Unmoved Mover (UM), since the former is not only capable of existing separately but capable of existing in a soul. In any case, Aristotle's own remarks on the AI are brief and programmatic and therefore insufficient to decide the issue.

With the UM Aristotle gives us more information. And since

[13] It is a common and, I think, correct criticism of Aristotle's mature theory that he unjustifiably posits the existence of a pure form such as is exemplified by the active intellect and the Unmoved Mover. Ryan (1973) argues against those who raise this criticism (e.g. Cherniss 1944: ch. 3, Lacey 1965*b*) that Aristotle does not posit pure form. Yet Ryan recognizes that the Unmoved Mover is pure actuality, and in view of Aristotle's identification of form and actuality, it is difficult to see how he can maintain his rejection of pure form.

the UM may possibly be a special instance of the AI, to understand the UM may be to understand the AI as well. Thus it is important to consider the problems that arise for the UM. Aristotle tells us how the UM exists: as pure activity. Yet we well may ask where it exists. For we typically understand activity to be activity of something in some respect. Aristotle tells us that the UM enjoys pure noetic activity, and we are given to understand that the UM is a single discrete entity that is mental in character. But does it exist in some place? He states that it exists at the circumference of the cosmos.[14] But he also claims that the UM has no dimensions.[15] Now according to Aristotelian theory, what has no dimensions exists either as a unit if it has no position, or as a point if it has position (θέσις).[16] Since the UM has a position it must be a point. But in Aristotle's physical system the geometrical point is something of a mathematical fiction.[17] To have a position is not to have a *place*, and in the physical world to exist is to have a place. Only extended objects occupy a place, by the very definition of place. Non-extended objects can have place derivatively; for example, soul occupies place by virtue of its association with a body.[18] In general a point could have a place by virtue of its connection with an extended entity from which it is abstracted. But what is that entity with which the UM is connected? It is not dependent upon any body and hence has no such connection. It appears then that the UM has no place in the physical cosmos.

Furthermore, in one passage Aristotle states that there is no place or time outside the heaven; from this point he draws the conclusion that whatever exists there enjoys the best kind of life.[19] Presumably he is alluding to the UM and saying, among other things, that it exists outside time and space. Does it then belong to

---

[14] *Ph.* viii. 10, 267ᵇ6–9.   [15] Ibid. ᵇ17–26; *Met.* xii. 7, 1073ᵃ5–11.

[16] Cf. *Met.* xiv. 3, 1090ᵇ5–13; ibid. v. 6, 1016ᵇ24–6 and ᵇ29–31.

[17] See *Met.* xiii. 2, 1077ᵇ12–17.

[18] See *DC* iii. 6, 305ᵃ25 f.; *Ph.* iv. 4–5, esp. 212ᵃ20 f., ᵇ7–12 and ᵇ24 ff.

[19] *DC* i. 9, 279ᵃ17–22: 'It is clear then that there is neither place nor void nor time outside [the heaven]. Accordingly the things there [τἀκεῖ (!)] cannot be in place, nor does time age them, nor is there any change in the things ranged beyond the outermost orbit; but unaltered and impassible they continue through their whole existence living the best and most self-sufficient of lives.' This lyrical passage is reminiscent of *Met.* xii. 7, 1072ᵇ13 ff. in its encomium of the divine life. Ross (1924, i. p. cxxxiv) thinks that the UM is truly not in space. Yet it is curious how anything can be 'there' where there is neither place nor void—in a space that is no space.

a different realm of being—a second world? Yet according to Aristotelian theory only universals (or mere potentialities) fail to have a specific location in the world, and there is no other world; hence the UM, which is a particular—a This—must have a place. Thus the UM is and is not located. There is something metaphysically paradoxical about the notion of the UM.

The problem of location allows us to focus on a deeper metaphysical problem of which it is a manifestation. Location is characteristic of particulars; lack of location (or plurality of location) of universals. Is the UM a particular or a universal? Aristotle claims that it is one in number;[20] this suggests that it is particular, as does his description of it as enjoying a life of pure thought.[21] But he also claims that the UM is one by definition.[22] This characteristic suggests that the UM is a fully determinate universal. Furthermore, he calls the UM an essence (τί ἦν εἶναι) and states that it has no matter.[23] Thus it is pure form, and we may well wonder how it can possibly be anything but a universal. To say that the UM is both one in number and in definition suggests that it is both particular and universal. But if so, it seems to fall victim to the criticisms that Aristotle makes of Plato's Forms. According to Aristotle, the fact that the Forms are both universal (one over many) and particular (the entities we refer to) generates the Third Man Argument.[24] The UM is protected from the Third Man Argument by the technicality that it is not said of anything, and hence is not a universal in the technical Aristotelian sense. But it seems likely that the combination of properties of particularity and universality that we find in the UM is responsible for problems like that of location.

Furthermore, there are yet other problems that seem to have deep roots in the concept of the UM. We learn in *Met.* xii. 9 that the UM is both the thinker and the object of its thought. This paradoxical relation seems to result from conceiving of the UM as both a composite substance—with a formal and a material component corresponding to soul and body, actuality and potentiality, agent and patient, active intellect and passive intellect—and a simple substance. The UM has both an active and a passive aspect, yet it is in no way passive or potential; it is both

---

[20] *Met.* xii. 8, 1074ᵃ36 f.   [21] Ibid. 7, 1072ᵇ13–30; 9, 1074ᵇ15–35.
[22] Ibid. 8, 1074ᵃ35–7.   [23] Ibid. ᵃ35 f.
[24] *Met.* vii. 13, 1038ᵇ34–9ᵃ3; i. 9, 990ᵇ15–17.

thinker and thought, agent and patient, without being a patient.
First we think of the UM on the model of a composite thinking
substance, then we think away the material–potential component
and we have the thought of thought. Yet the very conception
of a composite that is not composite seems incoherent. This
incoherency seems to account for the paradoxical character of
νόησις νοήσεως. Yet curiously Aristotle makes a virtue of this
paradoxical description of the UM's activity. Wherever we turn,
the UM appears to be an ontological anomaly: it is there where
there is no space, it is a particular universal, a composite simple.

Epistemological Problems. Given that the AI and the UM
transcend the world of sense, how can we know them? Aristotle
gives philosophical arguments for them which support the claim
that they exist. But at least in the case of the UM he makes the
stronger claim that it is the cause of the motion—specifically of the
eternal motion—of the cosmos. It moves all things by being loved
(*Met*. xii. 7). Now to say that *x* moves *y* by being loved by *y* does
solve the paradox of saying that something can move another
without itself moving. But we still must wonder how *y* can love *x*.
In the everyday cases *y* loves *x* only if *y* finds *x* beautiful or
attractive or desirable in some way. Now *y* can find *x* desirable
only if *y* perceives *x* (or conceives it in some fairly concrete way).
But if the UM utterly transcends sensation, we must ask in what
other way it can be perceived. Since no one before Aristotle
recognized a UM, it is not obvious how we can maintain that
anyone perceives it at all. At best we seem to come to know it
through abstract philosophical speculation. But such speculation
does not confer genuine perception on the speculator. How then
does the UM keep the cosmos in motion? Perhaps it is enough that
the intelligences associated with the planetary spheres perceive the
UM. By their own motion the spheres and their heavenly bodies
control the seasons and years. Thus they are efficient causes of the
other motions.[25] Yet this account also suggests that the world of

[25] This is not the line that Aristotle actually takes; he claims that all movement is
for the sake of the stars (1074ᵃ27 f.), i.e. the motion of the stars is the final cause of
other motions. Now Aristotle does explicate natural final causes such that they are
the terminus of a series without necessarily being conscious goals (*Ph*. ii. 8,
199ᵃ8 f.); yet the UM is not in any sense an event which is the terminus of a natural
series. Mover, Aristotle tends to suggest that the UM is an object of emulation, not
a mere terminus: *Met*. xii. 7, 1072ᵇ2 f., ᵇ24–6; 10, 1075ᵃ14 f. For further criticisms
of the concept of the UM, see Ross (1924, i. p. cxlix).

the UM is radically disconnected from the world of experience and that we have no real access to it.

Causal Problems. The preceding remarks reveal some causal problems. For although the UM is allegedly the final cause of the cosmos, it is unclear how it can function as a final cause except for the intelligences of the spheres.[26] The spheres themselves seem to control the seasons and cycles of life as efficient causes. But if this is so it seems that the world of nature does not have a single teleological focus in the way that Aristotle sometimes suggests it does.[27] As for the AI, Aristotle treats it as a formal and perhaps efficient cause of understanding. But it is not clear how it can be either. If it is so radically different from the soul itself, which is an actuality of an organic body, how can it interact with the soul and the body? What precisely does it contribute, and how? Aristotle gives us only metaphors—art in relation to its material, light in relation to colours. Similarly in the case of the UM, we are told that the final cause moves by being loved. But by neglecting the details Aristotle fails to show clearly how the metaphors apply.

What seems to emerge is that Aristotle's forms create problems for a consistent theory of substance. The kinds of problems that arise are analogous to problems Aristotle recognizes for Platonic Forms. He complains that they belong to a hypothetical other world;[28] that they are unknowable;[29] that they are causally inefficacious;[30] and furthermore that key relations in his system are explicated merely by empty metaphors.[31] In each case a comparable objection can be levelled against Aristotle's disembodied forms: they do not exist in our world; they are unknowable; their causal operation is problematic; and they are explicated by metaphors. What we seem to observe is that Aristotle's revised hylomorphism is in danger of collapsing into

---

[26] Aristotle's scheme of causal interaction is actually complicated and obscure. Besides the UM there are 55 spheres, their intelligences and their souls; possibly the intelligences and the souls are to be identified. See Ross (1924, i. pp. cxxxvi f.). For problems in Aristotle's calculations of the number of spheres, see Dicks (1970: 200 ff.).

[27] *Met.* xii. 10; *Ph.* ii. 8; for rational creatures, cf. *EN* i. 1, 1094ᵃ1–3; 2, 1094ᵃ18–22.

[28] e.g. *Met.* i. 9, 992ᵃ24–7.

[29] *Met.* vii. 16, 1040ᵇ30–4.

[30] *Met.* i. 9, 991ᵃ8 ff.   [31] Ibid. 992ᵃ26–9; 991ᵃ20–2; 6, 987ᵇ10–14.

Platonism. Aristotle's theory of substance could easily fall prey to the same kinds of problems that he attributes to Plato's theory of Forms.

10.2.2 Platonism and the One Under Many

When we observe that Aristotle becomes a target for a *tu quoque* type of criticism we see that there is something radically wrong with the choice of form as substance. By preferring form and attributing to form the characteristics of primary substance such as independent existence and determinacy Aristotle has come dangerously close to espousing Platonism. With forms as primary substances Aristotelian forms will be scarcely distinguishable from Platonic Forms. In attempting to secure the foundations of Aristotelianism, Aristotle seems to be selling out to Platonism.

Yet we can ask whether Aristotle's Platonism is so bad after all. Perhaps Aristotle's main difference with Plato is merely ideological: Aristotle prefers the worldly to Plato's other-worldly. Perhaps a Platonism with a this-worldly emphasis will be reasonable and acceptable. On this account Aristotle's disagreement with Plato is one over values, not over ontology.

This sort of perspective provides a sense of ecumenical accommodation which has often been sought by syncretistic interpreters. But it belies a more basic philosophical difference. I have argued already that the basic insight of Aristotelian philosophy is the One Under Many (2.1.1). When the atomic substantialism of S$_1$ failed to deal with the fact of substantial change Aristotle did not abandon OUM but rather extended the insight: he posited another substratum below the level of substance (see Chapter 5). The new substratum became matter and of course brought with it problems of interpretation in a situation of theory change. But it was true to Aristotle's basic pre-theoretical orientation. However, when Aristotle conceives of forms as primary substances, he in effect pries them loose from the ontological foundation of the system. He betrays OUM for the One Over Many.

It seems to me that this betrayal is something much more damaging than a lapse of ideology. In the case of OUM we have a principle which is arguably the fundamental insight of Aristotle's whole philosophy. S$_1$ and S$_2$ can be viewed as successive articulations of this insight. And OUM can be regarded as providing the philosophical thrust of which Aristotle's animadversions on Platonism are merely a superficial manifestation. For Aristotle the sources of ontology must be found in our world and their epistemological correlates must be objects of our acquaintance. To abandon this orientation is to abandon anything that can be called genuinely Aristotelian. When Aristotle flirts with Platonic identifications of form and primary substance, he is being untrue to his own pre-theoretical insights and hence betraying his philosophical roots.

Aristotle's Platonism is a mistake of major proportions. It is a mistake independent of his conflation of S_1 and S_2. In fact it is only the latter mistake that seems to save Aristotle from the former. For it is only when Aristotle reminds himself in *Met.* vii. 13 of his ontological commitments in S_1 that he draws back from a wholesale endorsement of a Platonic ontology. But this leaves us with the task of saving Aristotle from Plato within the constraints of S_2. We must identify what the real substance is and diagnose Aristotle's error in accepting form as primary substance.

10.3 THE COMPOSITE AS PRIMARY SUBSTANCE

10.3.1 *Matter as Substance*

If form is not primary substance, is matter? We have seen that if we combine S_1 with S_2 principles we can demonstrate that prime matter is substantial and non-substantial. If we drop the S_1 principles will matter still be disqualified? In S_2 taken by itself we can still find serious anomalies in matter, even if we do not generate formal paradoxes. The low-level, relatively indeterminate matter which underlies higher-level matters and substances becomes the primary reality. What is least organized becomes the standard of reality; what is least intelligible becomes the primary object of knowledge; what is least orderly comes to be the primary source of value. Not surprisingly Aristotle does not give extended consideration to this option. Indeed, if he had chosen matter as primary substance, his theory would have run the risk of collapsing into a materialism reminiscent of some of the Presocratics he criticizes. The source of reality in the world would be the material substrate, the prominent form of explanation the material cause. Yet the choice of matter as substance would seem more in keeping with OUM than the choice of form. Thus given a choice between the two, matter has at least as good a claim to be primary substance as form.

10.3.2 The Middle Way

Between the Scylla of form and the Charybdis of matter, between Platonic idealism and Presocratic materialism, we must find some middle way. It seems to me that the right course is to choose the one candidate Aristotle never seriously considers—the composite. As I have noted already, criteria (b) and (c), separability and thisness, seem most obviously to pick out the composite. The composite is clearly an entity that exists independently; and it is clearly a particular and determinate object—a genuine This. Furthermore the composite is (a) a paradigm logical subject.To be sure it is not the subject of substantial form. But it is more obviously a subject than form itself and certainly the foundation of everything except substantial forms. Thus there seems to be a good prima-facie case for the composite.

The case can be made out more strongly by turning to ontology. Consider what it is that makes an Aristotelian substance an Aristotelian substance, whether in S_1 or in S_2. The substance seems to have two characteristics in general: it is particular and it is intelligible. In the paradigm S_1 case Socrates is a substance. Socrates is unique and concretely existent—a clear-cut particular. But he is also a man. His manhood in S_1 is called a secondary substance. But it is assumed that no particular fails to instantiate some secondary substance. In *Met.* vii Aristotle's prestidigitation with form seems designed to preserve the fact that primary substance is both particular and intelligible. There is a unique form which is a specific form with an essence.

By contrast Plato's Forms are intelligible without being particular in a strong sense.[32] They are basically universals which have been reified; they exist separately, but not in our world of time and place. On the other hand the atomists produce atoms which are particular without having essence to them. In fact, in order to keep any hint of uniformity from the atoms, Democritus claims that

---

[32] Although Aristotle views them as Thises, Plato rejects the claim that they must exist in our world of time and space (*Tim.* 49 E–52 C). By ruling out the spatio-temporal parameters he in effect denies particularity to the Forms.

they are infinitely various in shape and size.[33] Finally one can imagine a pair of correlative kinds of entity such that one kind has all the attributes of particularity and the other all the attributes of intelligibility. This will be something like twentieth-century Logical Atomism with its thises and thats on the one hand and its whites and reds on the other.

Aristotle's substances differ in that they are both things in our environment here and now and things of which we can say what they are. They are men and trees and horses and, by extension, sticks and stones, chairs and tables. If Aristotle succeeds where Plato, the atomists, and the Logical Atomists have failed it will be because his entities are richer in content and more familiar than other entities. Of course Aristotle may be asking too much of his substances. But at least we can say that if entities fail to be particular and intelligible, they will fail to be what Aristotle thinks of as substances and collapse into something else. Aristotle's ontological experiments show how easily his substances can turn into something else. When he interprets substance as form he nearly accepts Platonism; when he considers matter he raises the possibility of a materialistic interpretation; and when he pushes LPM to the limit in *Met.* vii. 3 he comes up with something resembling the Logical Atomist's bare particular. There is little room for him to manœuvre. Yet although the alternative positions narrowly circumscribe Aristotle's theory, they also show that within its perimeter it has its own unique perspective that is not reducible to any other philosophical view.

Given the Aristotelian desiderata for the primary entities, only the composite substance possesses the conceptual richness required. It is both particular and intelligible. Socrates is both uniquely identifiable and generally classifiable. Is this asking too much? I think not. For if Socrates were not one he could not really be the other. That is, if he were not really *this* thing, he could not be a man; but if he were not a man, there would be no thing that was a This. Epistemologically speaking, the act of perceiving an individual and the act of conceiving a kind seem to be correlative.[34] Linguistically speaking, referring to an individual (as

---

[33] Theophrastus *ap.* Simplicius *in Phys.* 28.9 ff.; Aristotle *DC* iii. 4, 303ᵃ5 ff.; Simplicius *in DC* 295.1 ff. = Democritus A 37; Dionysius *ap.* Eusebius *Praeparatio Evangelica* 14.23.3.

[34] Cf. *A.Po.* ii. 1, 89ᵇ32–5; 8, 93ᵃ24–6, where Aristotle seems to argue that existence and essence are known together.

a This) and sorting it (as a Such) are correlative acts. In general, it seems plausible to think that there can be no identification without classification and no classification without identification. And since the things we humans seem to be most adept at identifying and classifying are middle-sized particulars, it seems plausible to hypothesize that these are the primary substances.

Aristotle clearly adopts middle-sized particulars as primary substances in S$_1$: he makes Socrates and Callias and such things the primary substances. What is puzzling is why he abandons them in S$_2$. To understand this is to provide a diagnosis of how Aristotle goes wrong in S$_2$.

10.3.3 Analysis and Reductionism

According to hylomorphism the concrete substance is divisible into form and matter. This is a fundamental fact of analysis of S$_2$: the sensible substance is a composite, not a simple individual. The analysis seems to invite a question about the composite itself: which component makes the substantial compound substantial? Is it form or matter? Since the sensible substance is analysed into two components, one of them must be responsible for the substantiality of the whole.

Yet this simple inference from hylomorphic analysis to a claim that one component is the source of substantiality is the root of the problems we have encountered. Because Aristotle analyses the sensible substance into form and matter, he assumes that it must be *reduced* to form and matter. In seeking for the true substance in *Met.* vii. 3 Aristotle notes, 'The substance composed of both elements, namely matter and form, may be dismissed; for it is posterior and obvious' (1029^{a}30–2). Sensible substance is posterior and obvious because it is derivative. Aristotle assumes that since it is a compound its important properties must derive from its components. Yet it is a fallacious step to suppose that because an object has a property its components must necessarily have that property also. From the fact that the compound of form and matter are substance we cannot deduce that form or matter individually is substance. Moreover, Aristotle unjustifiably assumes that since the components are also substance, the composite must *derive* its substantiality from them.

Why should Aristotle make these assumptions? What we in fact observe in going through the hierarchy of composition of natural substances is that nothing is as substantial as the individual organism. The organs and bodily parts are less substantial than the organism; the tissues and homoeomerous parts are less substantial than the organs; the elements are less substantial than the tissues. As we descend from higher-level composition to lower-level, we observe less organization and less substantiality. Similarly, as we ascend up through the hierarchy of forms from species to higher-level genera we get farther and farther removed from substance. It is the individual organism that is the focal point of substantiality. To divide this into its ontological components and to identify one component as the source of a composite's substantiality is to falsify the true relation: substantiality applies only and properly to the compound itself. From this standpoint any analysis is a destructive analysis that cannot capture the source of substantiality.

How then should we view form and matter? It seems to me that we should take them not as components in the normal sense. If they are components—metaphysical components—they may exist separately and be bearers of substantiality. We should rather conceive of them as *aspects* of the sensible substance. In this capacity they can be separated in thought from the sensible substance, but there is no implication that the substance is put together from them or dependent upon them in any way. They are clearly posterior to sensible substance. Indeed the sensible substance is not truly a compound or a composite on this account. Now of course the bronze exists before the statue; but the bronze exists as a quasi-substance. The bronze is matter only relative to a scenario in which it is cast as a statue. As such the notion of a matter separate from the statue is the notion of an intentional description of a quasi-substance; the lump of bronze is described in terms of what it may be used to make. But then to describe it as matter is tacitly to describe it as matter *for* some substance—in this case the statue. In general to be matter (or form) is to be matter (form) for some substance. Hence the notions of matter and form are dependent on or derivative from the notion of a concrete substance.

This interpretation corresponds to some things that Aristotle says in *Met.* viii. 6. There he speaks as if the form and the matter taken together just are the substance; there is no cause of their being substance other than perhaps the efficient cause which brought the substance into being. The unity of form and matter is just a fact which has no real explanation. We may interpret the chapter as implying that form and matter are not really components but aspects of the substance whose presence in it defies analysis. Thus the aspect account of hylomorphism has some basis in Aristotle's own theory. However, I do not wish to assert that this is Aristotle's considered position. It conflicts with much of what Aristotle actually says about form and matter, and the mere fact that he seems to think the aspect account is compatible with other things he says shows that he is not very clear about his own position. Had he seen the full implications of the aspect account, he would have been obliged to do some serious revising in his metaphysics. Yet he at least glimpses the value of such an account.

10.3.4 Reconciling S_2 and S_1

Adopting the aspect account of form and matter has interesting implications for the relation between S_1 and S_2. The component account, which is at least Aristotle's dominant conception of form and matter in S_2, enforces a major break between S_1 and S_2 on the topic of substance. For in S_1 the real substances were biological individuals like Socrates, Callias, and Bucephalus. But in S_2 the real substances are substantial forms such as, perhaps, Socrates' soul. This is a major difference since different objects qualify as the real substances for S_1 and S_2. On the aspect account, however, the same objects in our environment turn out to be the real substances in both systems. The identification of Socrates with the real substance in S_2 preserves a greater degree of continuity between the systems. It also maintains Aristotle's biological orientation, which his abandonment of the sensible substance as the primary substance tends to undermine.

There will still be a good deal that is discordant between S_1 and S_2. S_2 will allow for things to be more or less substances, which S_1 prohibits; S_2 will see the relation between certain lower-level substances and certain higher-level substances such as brass and statues to stand in a relation of matter and substance—a relationship that would be meaningless in S_1. Thus the aspect interpretation would not effect a full reconciliation between S_1 and S_2. But it would provide a greater measure of agreement on the basic notions, most notably concerning which items in the world are the real substances. The real substance of S_2 would be analogous to the real substance of S_1. In Aristotle's own preferred account the real substances of S_2, the substantial forms, are analogous not to the primary substances of S_1 but to the secondary substances. The promotion of substantial forms is a mistake, and by rejecting the mistake we can provide a smoother transition from S_1 to S_2 and a greater continuity between the systems.

10.4 RESOLVING THE ANTINOMIES OF SUBSTANCE

If we now step back from S_2 we can see some interesting relationships. Initially Aristotle divides substance into form and matter; then he asks which component is the real substance; he finds some compelling arguments in favour of matter; he rejects these because of prior commitments; finally he advances compelling arguments for form. Yet we have seen that neither matter nor form is really substance in the full sense. The pattern of inquiry we find in *Met.* vii. 1–12 reminds one of a pattern Kant found in the history of philosophy. We identify a concept C that seems to be comprehensive in scope. One party argues that a certain property F belongs to C, advancing compelling reasons; another party argues that not-F belongs to C, for compelling reasons. Both arguments seem equally valid. Such a debate is the result of a dialectical illusion; the deadlock between opinions can be settled only by realizing that both sides are in error because neither F nor not-F applies to C at all. This kind of debate is called an antinomy.[35] One Kantian example of the Antinomy of Pure Reason is the contradictory set of theses that the world has a beginning in time and that it has no beginning in time. The conflict can only be stopped by showing that the concept of the world is a transcendental one that does not admit of application to experience; hence it is meaningless to say either that the world has a beginning or that it has not as if the world (that is, the universe) were just another event in the world.[36]

Now consider the case of substance in S_2. The evidence for asserting that some entity is primary substance is that it is (*a*) an ultimate subject, (*b*) separable—that is, independently existent—

[35] *Critique of Pure Reason*, A 405 ff., B 432 ff. I am omitting a good deal of Kantian background theory.
[36] Ibid. A 426 ff., B 454 ff.

and (c) a This—that is, particular. We have noted that one can generate paradoxes by interpreting the three criteria first in the sense of S$_1$ then in a different sense which Aristotle employs in S$_2$. But suppose we forget about the S$_1$ sense at least in so far as it is derived from S$_1$. Can we generate another set of paradoxes just within S$_2$? I believe so.

For instance, logical prime matter is an ultimate subject, for it is the subject of the form. On the other hand, it is not the ultimate subject, for it is not the subject of all the properties of the thing. Moreover, the form is the ultimate subject, for all the properties of the object belong to the object in virtue of the form. But it is not the ultimate subject because it belongs to a prior subject, the logical prime matter.

As regards criterion (c), LPM is particular in virtue of providing a ground for this thing being here at all. But it fails to be particular in that it fails to be determinate in any way. The form, on the other hand, is particular in so far as it confers the determinacy on this thing. But it is not particular in that it does not make this thing unique.

Aristotle does not argue for all the above positions. Clearly he has a predilection for form and he tends to overlook or explain away the claims of matter. Yet he does seem to present both positions in some cases, notably the conflicting arguments concerning the ultimate subject. Moreover, the antitheses can be made out in cases where Aristotle pleads for only one side. It is unfortunate that Aristotle does not set up the opposition more completely, for it might have exposed the ambivalence of his position. In the case of particularity the reason for the ambivalence of interpretation begins to emerge. There are really two interpretations of 'particular' that are operating: the particular can be understood as a *unique* individual or as a fully *determinate* individual. On one interpretation matter has the advantage, on the other form.

This discovery might lead us to conclude that in reality there is no serious problem here: we simply need to get straight as to which is the right interpretaton in order to avoid equivocating. But a closer look indicates that equivocation is inevitable in the present situation. Kant's insight into problems of this nature is that the terms are simply not applicable in the problematic cases. He argues that concepts like the world (that is, the universe) are of a logically or epistemologically different order from concepts like those of everyday objects (for example, substances). When we try to talk about the world having a beginning in time we *ipso facto* apply to a concept which transcends any possible experience a predicate that applies only within experience. A modern linguistic version of the Kantian strategy of dealing with antinomies is Gilbert Ryle's notion of a category mistake: we sometimes create philosophical pseudo-problems by applying to concepts predicates that are irrelevant to them.[37] Now a Rylean or Kantian analysis seems to offer a resolution of the antinomies of substance. For the precise problem with saying that either matter or form is particular is that the notion of a particular or τόδε τι simply is not defined for matter or form. What does it mean to say that form is τόδε τι? Obviously it is not a This in the way that Socrates is a This—a thing that we can refer to by a proper name, single out by ostension, identify, classify, and re-identify. Accordingly we must slide into some other notion of particularity which will make sense for a substantial form (and presumably rule out its rivals). But at this point equivocation is part of the game, not an incidental mistake to be avoided.

We see a similar situation in regard to the other criteria. We know what it means to say that Socrates is a man or Socrates is pale. But we do not know what to say when we have stripped away from Socrates all his properties. Is there some bare particular that is the subject for Socrates' manhood? Given that Socrates is a compound of matter and form, is his form or his matter the subject of his accidents? One might develop the theory of predication so as to answer these questions. But one cannot appeal to ordinary language intuitions to resolve the problem. For according to our intuitions, Socrates is the ultimate subject; there is no further ground of his properties.[38] When we go beyond our intuitions we must avail ourselves of some theoretical perspective. LPM is an ultimate subject in virtue of being the limit of a series of substractions. Form is an ultimate subject by virtue of supplying

[37] More precisely: similarities in the surface form of expressions cause us to overlook differences in logical form. In an early statement Ryle observes, 'Paradoxes and antinomies are the evidence that an expression is systematically misleading' (1931: 168). Ryle (1949: ch. 1) is a famous exemplar of the method.

[38] Stahl (1981) argues for this interpretation of the stripping away of properties in *Met.* vii. 3. This is probably what Aristotle should have said, but I do not believe it is what he meant to say in the chapter.

the condition for being an empirical subject. But the concept of an ultimate subject is equivocal.

In the case of separability we find that our experience and our ordinary language intuitions support the claim that the sensible substance is separable. We recognize it as an entity in our environment which behaves independently of other entities. We refer to it by name or pick it out by its attributes, we make assertions of it and apply attributes to it. But what of matter and form? The material which is potentially a composite substance can exist as a pile of bricks or a lump of bronze. But it is difficult to identify it except by reference to external measures such as piles and lumps. And we think of its existence as somehow subservient to that of the substances formed out of it. Forms are more easily identifiable; but when we refer to them it seems that we are typically referring not to the forms themselves but to the things which exhibit the forms. Nor do they obviously exist independent of the things which exhibit them. We seem to know forms only derivatively, through particular things having the forms. And we do not know what it would mean to say that they exist, apart from the obvious claim that there are things with those forms in our environment. In any case, neither matter nor form seems to exist separately in any obvious sense. If we claim that they do, we seem to be applying language outside its standard domain.

Well is it harmful to apply language in such a way? After all, every theoretical discourse is a specification of language in a way that departs from the ordinary. It seems perfectly justifiable for Aristotle to extend the concepts of ordinary language. The objection is correct so far as it goes. But I am not criticizing Aristotle's use of language for not being ordinary; I am criticizing it for being inconsistent or ambiguous.[39] In extending language we must be careful to apply terms in a consistent and meaningful way. The problem with Aristotle's criteria of substancehood is that they are interpreted differently in different contexts. If he were out to extend the domain of his terms, he should specify how those terms are being applied, why the terms need to be altered, and how the criteria newly defined are appropriate criteria. He seems to expect us to assent to the criteria because we are familiar with them from

---

[39] Thus I am making only minimal use of the transcendental critique found in Kant and (in a different form) in Ryle; I am not assuming that where concepts are not applicable their use inevitably produces incoherency.

S_1, and to assent to his application of the criteria because their applications are intuitively obvious. But in so far as the criteria are reminiscent of S_1, the applications are not obvious; and in so far as the applications are obvious, the criteria are not reminiscent of S_1.

The result of this looseness with the criteria of substancehood is that we can generate antinomies of substance that rival the paradoxes of substance found in and suggested by vii. 13. We found that the problems of vii. 13 resulted from Aristotle's introduction into S_2 of the strict S_1 interpretations of the criteria for substance. Yet even if we refuse to introduce these S_1 interpretations, they can sneak in the back door through terminological ambiguities. Thus the ambivalence of interpretation in S_2 can generate antinomies. And the antinomies of substance recapitulate the paradoxes of substance which the clash of S_1 and S_2 generates. To protect S_2 from S_1 we must block the antinomies. The way to block them is to do what Kant requires: to rule out the unwarranted applications of terms to domains in which they do not apply. Now we can be more accommodating than Kant by allowing for extensions of terminology. But any extension of terms should be made explicitly and defended. In absence of such an extension, the technical terms should mean what they standardly mean.

If we observe these principles, we shall find that neither matter nor form has any claim at all on primary substancehood. What they supply are conditions for the generation and destruction of substances in a diachronic analysis and the conditions of determinacy in synchronic analysis. They allow us to extend the theory of substance to contexts unknown to S_1. They do not compete for primacy with the concrete substance nor do they exist apart from that substance in a fully substantial way. Matter and form can be called substances only by courtesy and in so far as they are components (in some weak sense) or aspects of primary substance. For they are correlative notions which are not defined apart from each other or apart from their potential incorporation in some primary substance. As Kant speaks of his pure concepts of understanding having reference to some possible experience, so we must speak of matter and form as having reference to some possible concrete substance. Apart from such a (perhaps hypothetical) context, it is meaningless to call something matter or form. But then matter and form are notionally dependent on the concrete substance. Hence *they*, not concrete substance, are the derivative entities.

Why then does Aristotle make the concrete substance derivative? There is what Kant would call a natural dialectic at work here. In seeking for the ultimate reality we desire to identify the simple elements of the world. We are tempted to say that these are the realities, since all things are compounds of them. Analysis is the most intuitive form of explanation; and mereological analysis of a whole into its parts and physical analysis of a collection into its members are its most primitive forms. Reductionism is just a methodological application of these natural modes of analysis. It may be dogmatic or naïve; in the case of the ancients it seems typically to be naïve.[40] Reductionistic systems have a certain intuitive, almost aesthetic, appeal because their form provides a natural closure to explanation.[41] Thus it is part of the intuitive attraction of atomic substantialism (as it is of Democritean Atomism) that the substances are the basic components of the world.

One of the most revolutionary implications of hylomorphic substantialism is that simplicity is no longer a characteristic of substancehood. Aristotle recognizes this point tacitly in his claim that the concrete substance is more real than its component matter. In this context he abandons the identification of substance with what is simple. But curiously he is unwilling to extend this insight to the realm of form. He wants primary substance to be something indivisible, even at the cost of losing the identification between primary substance and what is familiar to us.

We have already seen that Aristotle makes a reductionistic assumption that forces him to go beyond the concrete substance to

---

[40] The Presocratics from the Milesians on dominantly practised some form of reductive explanation. Parmenides stipulated that What Is must be ἕν (B 8.6). This seems to be a homogeneity principle (cf. Mourelatos 1970: 111–14) which demands a qualitative simplicity. The Eleatic concept of qualitative simplicity influenced Plato's conception of the Forms. Among the Socratics the school of Antisthenes taught an extreme form of reductionism for which Aristotle thought them naïve (ἀπαίδευτοι): *Met.* viii. 3, 1043ᵇ23–32; cf. v. 29, 1024ᵇ32–4; however they are not *methodologically* naïve but dogmatic, since they self-consciously pursue a reductive programme.

[41] Of course the simple elements must be known by some non-analytic mode of knowledge. Thus a reductionistic account of the world presupposes at least a twofold epistemological account: one dealing with the complexes, one dealing with the simples. Cf. Aristotle *A.Po.* i. 3, 72ᵇ18–25; *EN* vi. 6.

its components in search of primary substance. The reductionistic tendency is a persistent one. Not until Wittgenstein do we find a strong rejection of the tendency to identify the ultimate reality with some allegedly simple component of the world.[42] Nevertheless Aristotle's own position entails that the concrete substance is more real than some of its components (namely matter), and it was not impossible for him to draw the inference that substance in S$_2$ is not what is most simple but what is most concrete.

The last point accords with ontological observations we made earlier (10.3.2). Ontologically speaking, substance theory differs from other theories in that it posits an entity that is both a particular and a member of an intelligible class of things. Socrates is a primary substance, but he is also a man, and there is no primary substance without (in S$_1$ terms) a secondary substance. Thus there is a conceptual complexity to substance: it is both particular and universal, a This and a Such. The primary substance exists at a given time and place, but it is also a member of a kind in the intelligible order of things. Thus substance is already a kind of concrete object in a way that a Democritean atom or a Platonic form is not. There is a temptation to ask what is the real notion of substance. But this is a gambit which the Aristotelian must refuse. For any answer to the question will leave us with something that is less than a substance. The critic may object that the notion of substance is incomprehensible because it combines particular and universal features. The defender of substance must hold the line nevertheless. He may reply that substance is no more incomprehensible than the things in our environment; we perceive them as having both particularizing location and universal intelligibility. There could be no identification without classification and no classification without identification. We can intellectually separate the particular and universal aspects of the thing. But there could be no thing without both aspects. We can analyse primary substance into matter and form, particular and universal, this and such, but we cannot reduce it to any of these aspects, for fear of destroying the concept of substance.

[42] In the *Tractatus* he implicitly resists reductionism by identifying the world with a set of states of affairs which are prior to the simple objects that compose them (secs. 1.1–2.02). Later in the *Philosophical Investigations* he attacks reductionism explicitly (secs. 46–8).

10.5 CONCLUSION

In this chapter we have examined S_2 without S_1. I have argued that when Aristotle identifies form with substance in S_2 he makes an unnecessary and damaging concession to Platonism. He seems to be drawn into Platonism by the reductionistic assumption that one of the components of concrete substance must be the real substance, together with the evaluative assumption that idealism is better than materialism. But the first assumption is as unwarranted as the second is unnecessary. For there is no reason internal to S_2 why substance should be simple; on the contrary, the logic of Aristotle's position dictates that the concrete substance must be more real than any component or aspect of it, much less any ideal component. The most striking evidence against reductionism is the fact that when Aristotle adopts reductionistic assumptions his position generates antinomies. By promoting concrete substance Aristotle can stay true to his Aristotelianism: he can maintain that reality is the One Under Many, and that the locus of real being is in our world. He can also avoid the antinomies that result from extending concepts definitive of substance beyond their intended domain. This interpretation of S_2 has the effect of bringing S_2 closer to S_1 in spirit; it does not remove the logical differences, but it does preserve the emphasis and point of view of S_1 in S_2. Thus the present interpretation provides for a more consistent Aristotelianism in the sense that it resolves the antinomies inherent in S_2 and in the sense that it helps to reconcile S_2 with S_1.

I began this book with some relatively modest claims about the need to unify developmental with unitarian accounts of Aristotle. The inquiry has led us to posit two systems in Aristotle which stand in a genetic relation to one another. The interpretive viewpoint that emerges from this study has enabled us to disentangle some threads from S_1 and S_2 that become tangled in the *Metaphysics*, and now to criticize Aristotle's mature conception of substance. Evidently the Two Systems Theory generates a complete interpretation of Aristotle, one which provides a basis both for understanding Aristotle's dialectical development and for critically evaluating his theories—that is, it provides a complete developmental and systematic account of Aristotle. Thus TST must compete with well-developed interpretations of Aristotle in the market-place of ideas. In the following chapter I shall discuss the status of TST in relation to established interpretations of Aristotle, detailing its affinities and differences, disadvantages and advantages.

The Two Systems Theory as an Interpretation of Aristotle

I have argued that the Two Systems Theory (TST) provides a coherent interpretation of Aristotle's philosophy that integrates both systematic and developmental points of view. My study has been directed toward working out the details of TST and showing how it illuminates various aspects of Aristotle's philosophy. In the course of developing the present interpretation I have argued that its various components present better accounts than competing hypotheses for certain explananda. I have not, however, undertaken an overall evaluation of TST in relation to competing theories. In this final chapter I wish to raise the question of the comparative merit of TST. Although I shall, of course, be presenting the case as a partisan of TST, I shall try to present my view as a contender in a field of possible interpretations of Aristotle—that is, in as objective a way as possible. Thus I shall not in general argue from inside TST that the theory accomplishes its goals, but from the outside that TST competes well relative to independent criteria of theory choice. I hope to show that from this relatively detached perspective TST has more to recommend it than major alternative interpretations. I shall first recapitulate the main lines of my argument, then examine potential problems of my theory, and finally explore several actual advantages it enjoys relative to the competition.

11.1 RECAPITULATION

In the first chapter I noted different interpretative approaches to Aristotle. The unitarians view Aristotle as having a unified system which it is the interpreter's task to reconstruct, harmonizing apparent conflicts. The developmentalists attempt to trace the growth of Aristotle's thought and see conflicts as evidence of different temporal strata from which the stages of development can be reconstructed. We noted problems for both views: the developmentalists tend to fragment Aristotle's thought, while the unitarians try to reconcile too much. I suggested a synthetic view in which we should distinguish two stages of thought, each of which contains a system of its own.

To show that there are two systems in Aristotle I made a stipulation that the *Organon*, together with the *Rhetoric*, should be regarded as embodying a system designated S_1, and the remainder of the corpus should be regarded as embodying system S_2. I then explored the characteristics of S_1 (Chapter 2) and S_2 (Chapter 3) independently, and without prejudging what the relation between the two systems was. In the course of the examination it became apparent that while S_1 and S_2 did indeed appear to form coherent systems on their own, they used different concepts and differed from each other in content. It thus became evident that the relation between S_1 and S_2 was not one of simple identity.

In Chapter 4 I examined leading hypotheses concerning the relation between the two systems. The previous examination of systems provided enough evidence to reject the view that S_1 was merely a collection of analytic tools rather than a philosophic position. Moreover, logical considerations led to rejecting the view that S_2 was a logical extension of S_1. We were left with the hypothesis that S_2 was incompatible with S_1. Further considerations suggested that it would be fruitful to consider S_1 and S_2 as incommensurable rather than as incompatible systems.

By establishing that the two systems were incommensurable we raised the question of why there should be two such systems in Aristotle. At this point the developmental claim that S_2 was later than S_1 was advanced. A preliminary consideration of dating seemed to agree with the proposed temporal ordering. In Chapter 5 we explored a possible philosophical motivation for the shift from S_1 to S_2 and found the trail of just such a development in *Physics* i. Thus we had evidence for a specific path of development from S_1 to S_2.

On the general hypothesis that S_2 developed from S_1, we were able to find evidence for two concomitant theories that straddled both systems and developed in response to a shift in metaphysical principles. The four cause theory (Chapter 6) and the theory of actuality (Chapter 7) were both found to be transformed by the exigencies of the new system and in fact to become more integral in their new configurations. Thus the general developmental hypothesis, which keyed on a revision of metaphysical principles, was found to be corroborated by specific developments in subsidiary theories.

In Chapters 8 and 9 we scrutinized the problems of *Met.* vii. I argued that although Aristotle set up his inquiry as a puzzle with a discoverable solution, he in fact raised troubling questions about his own principles and exposed some deep-seated paradoxes. His attempts to identify what was primary substance revealed fundamental incoherences in his concepts of both matter (Chapter 8) and form (Chapter 9). I traced the paradox of definition to a conflict concerning the universality of substance. The source of the conflict proved to be Aristotle's retention of S_1 principles which were contradicted by the new system. I claimed that Aristotle's assertion of inconsistent principles made a solution to the problems of *Met.* vii impossible.

Aristotle's failure to resolve the problem of what primary substance is raises the question of what the solution is according to TST. In Chapter 10 I argued that the correct solution is that the composite is primary substance. Aristotle overlooks this answer because he is committed to some reductionistic assumptions that are extrinsic to his own metaphysics and actually inconsistent with it. He also has systematic reasons for preferring form to matter. Nevertheless, his preference for form leads him in the direction of a Platonism that is inconsistent with his basic insights. Adopting the composite as primary substance allows us to save him from an ill-advised Platonism and also to forestall certain antinomies of substance that arise from applying concepts definitive of substance to form and matter.

It should be clear from this overview that while TST starts from an analysis of one body of writings in relation to the others, it issues in a comprehensive interpretation of Aristotle, one with implications for a general critique of his position. It seems appropriate, then, to evaluate TST according to standards applied to interpretative theories and to examine its strength relative to other general interpretations of Aristotle. The most obvious problem for TST is the fact that it creates a bifurcation in Aristotle, and moreover justifies the bifurcation on developmental lines without saving Aristotle from inconsistency. Let us turn to the question of a coherent and consistent Aristotle.

11.2 TOWARDS A CONSISTENT ARISTOTLE

Let us begin with a simple but important methodological objection to TST. This theory divides Aristotle into two logically incompatible systems—it gives him two philosophies, if you will. On methodological grounds it is preferable to make an interpretation which attributes only one self-consistent philosophy to Aristotle. The objection is of course a general one which supports any unitarian view against any developmental view. But from the unitarian perspective, even the traditional type of developmental views do not go so far as TST. They find inconsistencies, it is true, but theirs are localized conflicts resulting from alleged piecemeal revisions of Aristotelian principles. Thus one can be a developmentalist of the traditional sort without making the radical claim that Aristotle has two separate, distinct, and incommensurable philosophies. Surely it is implausible to think that so great a mind as Aristotle would produce two ultimately inconsistent philosophies without even noticing what he had done.

The objection is a serious one. And the methodological premiss on which it is based is quite unexceptionable. Nevertheless, like any methodological objection, it is based on a comparison of two theories which are evaluated as equivalent in all other respects. My reply is simply that other interpretations do not deliver what they promise, a coherent and consistent Aristotle. As I have already indicated, *Met.* vii offers a proving ground for unitarian interpretations, and to date if any scholar has succeeded in solving its problems, he has failed to convince his peers. To be sure, there are many promissory notes outstanding, but these cannot be redeemed in advance to argue against my position. At this time enough interpretations have failed, to justify the Kantian move of searching for a diagnosis of what I claim to be antinomies in Aristotle's position. This will not stop scholars from seeking for unitarian solutions—nor is it intended to—but it does define an alternative that has been too long absent in the repertoire of end-game manœuvres.

As to the complaint that Aristotle would not make the kind of mistake TST attributes to him, we must distinguish two versions. The first is the psychological claim that Aristotle is too good a philosopher to let a shift of such major proportions get by him. I am not impressed by this claim. I find ample evidence that Aristotle is capable of such an oversight. Besides his frequent vacillations on specific points—which perhaps are not too telling, since they occur over more limited questions—Aristotle shows some tendencies which would make his ignorance of the systematic differences in his positions difficult for him to detect.[1] In the first place, he is not critical of his own views in the way he is of others— a common failing among Greek philosophers and scientists.[2] Evidence of this tendency is found simply in his failure to address such problems as how his S_1 ontology is meant to relate to his S_2 ontology—or, in his terms, how we should read the *Categories* relative to the *Metaphysics*. His few hints on the matter show that he has not seen the real conflict. Secondly, as we have noted, he has a teleological view of the history of philosophy and the history of ideas which tends to obscure developments, especially revolutionary ones.[3] Because he sees his mature view as the *natural* one, to which all his previous thoughts—as well as the theories of all previous philosophers—tend, he has a licence to ignore changes of detail. This might include, on occasion, shifts in the meaning of terms, shifts in the interpretation and scope of theories, and differences of doctrine on specific points. In other words, he might be induced to ignore all the specific items of evidence that we have used to demonstrate a change of theory. Finally, Aristotle understands the developments he does note as showing an accumulation of knowledge. He is thus inclined, when he interprets his own philosophy, to downplay the respects in which his early views are not commensurable with the later. He has a tendency to 'rewrite the textbooks', as Kuhn would put it. And of course he is in a unique position to do so in a way that will decisively obscure his own development. As I shall argue later, I do not think his rewriting is so extensive that we are not able to trace any development. But his introductory and transitional remarks often suffice to gloss over problems in continuity so as to

---

[1] An example is *DA* ii. 12, 424^{b}3–18, in which Aristotle does an about-face on what objects affect the perceiver. Of course Aristotle can drag out his vacillations over entire books, as *Met.* vii shows.

[2] See Lloyd (1979: 168, 200, 224), Barnes (1982: 51 f.).   [3] See ch. 7.0.

obscure from him as well as from us the underlying changes in view. For all these reasons I do not think Aristotle is immune from mistaking his own development.

There is a second way of taking the objection that Aristotle would not make such a mistake. This is a purely methodological one: that it is a violation of the so-called principle of charity to attribute a weak view to a philosopher when one can attribute a strong one. One should put the most favourable construal possible on a position. The objector can point out that TST is less favourable to Aristotle than some unitarian interpretation. Moreover, he can take advantage of another aspect of TST: its claim that Aristotle never abandoned the principles of S_1. Thus TST attributes to Aristotle an inconsistent position. Now it may be psychologically possible that Aristotle holds such a position, or even plausible that he does not perceive the inconsistency, but it is not charitable to attribute an inconsistent position to him. Indeed, of all the errors we could attribute to Aristotle, that of logical inconsistency is the worst.

The objection does bring out a serious demerit of TST. But again the principle of charity can decide the matter only if we establish that TST is no better than competing hypotheses on other grounds. And I shall argue that it is in fact superior on other grounds, so that, whether it reflects credit on Aristotle or no, TST is the best interpretation of Aristotle.

There is, however, one important question that can be raised about the extent to which TST is unfavourable to Aristotle. Is the inconsistency an unavoidable part of Aristotle's thought, or can his philosophy be saved from logical ruin? If we answer the former question affirmatively, we have an irremediable deficiency; but if the latter way is correct, the inconsistency is accidental and the conflict in his thought is correctable. It should be fairly evident that I hold that latter view. The conflict which we find expressed in *Met.* vii is the result of the retention of obsolete principles of S_1. If Aristotle would renounce those principles, he would save himself from inconsistency.

I introduced further complications to this position in Chapter 10: Aristotle's choice of form as primary substance in S_2 is inconsistent with the fundamental insight of Aristotelian metaphysics even apart from S_1. Furthermore, on the reductionistic assumptions Aristotle uses in S_2 he can and does generate antinomies which recapitulate the paradoxes of substance. Nevertheless, I showed how by rejecting reductionism and promoting the composite as primary substance we can derive a consistent hylomorphic theory. Thus the inconsistencies of Aristotle's mature theory are explicable as the results of some ill-advised moves on Aristotle's part; they are generated by his adoption of concomitant assumptions that are inconsistent with hylomorphic substantialism. But the axioms of hylomorphic substantialism are self-consistent. What I have done is to reject certain unwarranted assumptions of Aristotle in order to save S_2 from inconsistency.

Of course the Aristotelianism I am willing to defend as consistent is a revised Aristotelianism. For that, however, I do not apologize. It seems to me that an adequate interpretation of Aristotle—indeed any adequate essay in history of philosophy— ought to treat its subject as any philosopher should be treated: with respect but not deference. History of philosophy lives in the interval between a cataloguing of doctrines, which when it is isolated is doxography, and a retailing of their modifications, which gives rise to a history of ideas. It is a kind of golden mean between the relative vice to which an a priori unitarianism tends, and that to which an a priori developmentalism tends.[4] Its object is to discern what, in philosophical terms, the philosopher is trying to do, and to what extent he succeeds. If we can understand his philosophical projects, we have a control on his philosophy such that it is possible to criticize him from his own perspective as well as from ours. Accordingly, the history of philosophy is properly not simply descriptive in its aims, but normative, not simply historical but philosophical.[5] I suggest that the revisionary Aristotelianism I have offered is one that is based on Aristotle's own philosophical perspective and is both fair and potentially acceptable to him. Thus I maintain that while Aristotle is not consistent in his presentation of his philosophy, the incoherence is not a congenital defect. The condition can be remedied by simple, if extensive, surgery.

---

[4] Of course there is value in both doxography and history of ideas; but they should not usurp the role of history of philosophy.

[5] I have developed my ideas on the history of philosophy in Graham (1988).

11.3 PROBLEMS OF DATING

One set of serious problems remains: can TST be shown to be consistent with what we know about the dates of Aristotle's works? Our knowledge of dating, both absolute and relative, is far from complete, but there are sufficient points of agreement to make it imperative that any developmental theory should be reconciled with the known data. At the end of Chapter 4 I suggested that in general the works of S_1 were thought to be written before the works of S_2, but I did not wish to break the train of argument with a detailed study of the alternatives. And indeed, the problems of dating are relevant to more than just the question of the historical possibility of a development from S_1 to S_2; they also can help to choose between alternative developmental theories. Thus the question is best dealt with in the present chapter in which we are evaluating the relative strength of TST.

We may distinguish three preliminary questions which will shed light on the general problem of dating S_2 relative to S_1. (1) What are the dates of the works of S_1 relative to each other? (2) What are the dates of the works of S_1 relative to the early works of S_2? And (3) what are the dates of Aristotle's dialogues relative to the works of S_1 and S_2? The first question is important because it is chiefly the later works of S_1 which are sometimes thought to overlap with S_2, and we must identify which these are. The second question is obviously the main object of the present study. But it can perhaps best be illuminated by providing a synchrony with the dialogues in answer to (3). The dialogues provide important evidence because they tend to be occasion pieces which can be given absolute (if approximate) dates on the basis of their relation to external events. A great deal of attention has been directed to answering these questions, especially since Jaeger (1923), and much progress has been made; nevertheless there is much that is still controversial. Accordingly, we shall have to be content with probabilities rather than certainties in this inquiry. But if TST is defensible, it should accord with the probabilities.

11.3.1 Relative Dates of the Works of S_1

The two methods of assigning relative dates to the works of S_1 are style and content on the one hand and cross-references on the other. One can use the internal evidence of differences in doctrine, sophistication of technique, or correlations of style to argue the priority of one work relative to another. Or one can study the passages in which Aristotle mentions another work, assuming in general that a reference is from a later work to an earlier, especially if the reference plays an integral role in an argument and is not simply an aside.[6] Stocks (1933: 115 f.) studies references in the *Topics* and two *Analytics*, finding that *Top.* i–vi refer to no other works of the corpus. The last three books of the *Topics* make references to the *Analytics*, while the *A.Pr.* refers to the *Topics*, suggesting that these works overlap.[7] The *A.Po.* does not refer to the *Topics* but does refer to the *A.Pr.*[8] Düring (1966: 54 ff.) further considers references in all the works of the *Organon*. The *Cat.* seems to be very early, containing no references to other works.[9] The *DI* has references to the *A.Pr.*, *SE*, and the *DA*, the last of which is probably a later insertion.[10] It also contains a

---

[6] Bonitz 95^{b}49 ff. provides an analytic index of cross-references in Aristotle. Thielscher (1948) examines references having a determinate temporal reference. His study provides a useful provisional ordering of works, but because he fails to consider the possibility of later insertions and revisions of works, his results must be viewed with caution.

[7] The *SE* is another name for *Top.* ix.

[8] The *A.Po.* (ii. 12, 95^{b}10–12) also refers to *Ph.* vi; Stocks is concerned only with the relative chronology of the *Analytics* and the *Topics* and does not mention this reference.

[9] Düring (1966: 54 f.). Chs. 10–15 (the 'Post-Predicaments') of the *Cat.* address a different topic from the first 9, and may have originally constituted a separate treatise; however they seem to be a genuine early Aristotelian work (Düring ibid., Husik 1904, Frede 1981: 3). On the relative dating of the *Cat.*, see n. 17 below; on the genuineness of the work, see n. 43.

[10] 10, 19^{b}31 referring to *A.Pr.* i. 46, 51^{b}36 ff.; 20^{b}26 referring to *SE* 5, 167^{b}38 and 6, 169^{a}6; 16^{a}8 referring to *DA*. (Cf. Düring 1966: 55.) Düring does not mention the first reference. Ross treats it as a later insertion since he regards the *DI* as prior to the *A.Pr.*: see his argument *contra* Maier in Ross (1949: 421 f.). Ross ibid., and Düring (1966: 55) agree that the *DI* was written after Plato's *Sophist* but before Aristotle's *A.Pr.* and stands between them in terms of the development of the doctrine of judgement.

Maier (1900b) provides an extended argument for the *DI* being genuine but late. Cf. also Zeller (1897, ii. 66 n. 1, 157 f.). However, D. Frede (1970: 81–3) gives convincing reasons for taking at least chs. 1–6 as very early—evidently written after the *Top.* but before the *Analytics*. She finds that chs. 7–11 including ch. 9 (see p. 107 n. 19) and esp. chs. 12 and 13 are later insertions. Her results agree well with TST: chs. 1–6 are crucial to the reconstruction of S_1, while ch. 13 shows clear connections with S_2 conceptions (see following note).

Maier may be right to assert that the *DI* was not a part of Aristotle's regular lectures on logic. He also offers a brilliant analysis of the 16^{a}8 reference to the *DA*, revealing it to be a marginal note later inserted into the *wrong place* in the text (pp. 36 f.); this account effectively disqualifies the reference in question from

passage that seems to allude to the Unmoved Mover, which seems to be a later doctrine.[11] Thus a study of references does not give any unequivocal answer concerning the relative dates of the works of S_1.

The generally accepted order of works of the *Organon* is that originally put forth by Maier.[12] *Top.* ii–vii. 2 are the earliest major works, followed by *Top.* i, viii, and ix. Roughly *A.Pr.* i precedes *A.Po.* i, after which come *A.Pr.* ii and *A.Po.* ii. Solmsen (1929) used Jaegerian methods to argue for a more complex development in which *A.Po.* i follows *Top.* i–vii and the *Rhetoric*, *Top.* viii and ix follow *A.Po.*i, and then come *A.Po.* ii and the *A.Pr.* in that order.[13] Solmsen dates the first part of the *Top.* and the *Rh.* to the Academic period but considers Aristotle's analytic as seen in the latest works to belong to Aristotle's final period as head of the Lyceum. Ross (1939a) examines Solmsen's view and finds strong, and I think convincing, reasons for returning to Maier's general position.[14] Most impressive is his marshalling of passages of the *A.Po.* which presuppose the syllogistic theory of the *A.Pr.* One obvious problem for Solmsen is the peroration of *Top.* ix (183^b17 ff.) which treats Aristotle's efforts as a major advance in logical theory, and a paradigm to be followed in further studies of τὸ συλλογίζεσθαι (184^b1)—a position that could hardly be held after the development of the axiomatic theory of *A.Po.* i. There have been some recent attempts to revive a view like that of Solmsen's, but they have a lot to prove.[15]

The *Organon* does not contain much that is of help for the purposes of absolute dating. A possible reference in *A.Pr.* ii. 24,

indicating a late date for the *DI*, and shows that Andronicus' rejection of the work (because no passage in the *DA* satisfies the reference as it is now located in the text) is unnecessary.

[11] *DI* 13, 23^a21–6 at least makes use of substantial actuality, which it attributes to primary substances. D. Frede (1970: 81 n. 16) recognizes it as a late insertion (cf. preceding note).

[12] Maier (1900a: 56 ff. and esp. 78 n. 3).

[13] Solmsen's argument is conveniently summarized in Stocks (1933).

[14] Solmsen (1941) replied to Ross (1939a) but Ross did not change his position (see Ross 1949: 6–23). Cf. also Shorey (1924).

[15] See Barnes (1981), who has an ulterior motive for bringing back the Solmsen view, namely to explain the failure of the corpus to exemplify the scientific method of the *A.Po.* On this problem, see Ch. 11.5.3. Cf. also Smith (1982), who argues for a conclusion similar to Barnes's. In private conversation Smith has convinced me that parts of the *A.Pr.* were written after parts of the *A.Po.*; however, I am not willing to follow Barnes in his more radical conclusions about dating.

69^a2 to the Third Sacred War with a date of 353 is too vague to be relied on.[16] A more promising line is to pursue some striking stylistic and terminological correlations that lead Huby (1962) to a date of around 360 for the earliest books of the *Topics* (p. 75).[17] She also points out that the theory of Forms described in the *Top.* does not contain the Pythagorizing elements found in the *Metaphysics* accounts.[18] On the lower end of the time-scale, Ross (1949: 22 f.) argues that the *A.Po.*, which he takes as the latest work of the *Organon*, should be assigned to the period 350–44. He points out that since the *A.Pr.* is referred to in the *EE* and *Rh.* and the *A.Po.* is referred to in the *Met.*, the *EE*, and *NE*, they cannot be too late. His main reason for putting the *A.Po.* as late as he does is the argument that it must have taken Aristotle some time to develop from a Platonic position, and to produce so elaborate a theory as we find in the *Analytics*.[19]

11.3.2 *The Dating of S_1 in Relation to S_2*

This brings us to the problem of overlap in the two systems. It is generally agreed that the most secure point in Jaeger's reconstruction is his claim that the original version of the *Met.* was written in Assos soon after Aristotle left the Academy.[20] Now since the early books i and xiv refer to *Ph.* i and ii, not in passing, but as providing the groundwork for the *Met.*, we must assign at least part of the *Physics* to the Academic period. As we have seen, *Ph.* i and ii provide the starting-point for S_2. But if Ross's dating of the *A.Po.* is correct, part of S_1 is probably later than part of S_2.

---

[16] See Düring (1966: 54) *contra* Ross (1949: 22).

[17] The interesting verbal and doctrinal correlations Husik (1904) finds between the *Cat.* and the *Top.* indicate a similar date for the *Cat.*

[18] Evans (1977) explores theories of the *Top.* to show that it is not naïve or inconsistent with Aristotle's mature works. See also Weil (1951) for a similar approach. Although we may grant there are many sophisticated features in the *Top.*, we need not depart from the general consensus that makes the work a very early one.

[19] Nuyens (1948: 106–18) gives his dating of works of the *Organon*. He finds that the *Cat.* and *Top.* are early, the *DI* and *Analytics* belong to Aristotle's middle period. What is unique in his dating method is his use of a criterion based on the notion that Aristotle's theory of soul developed from a dualism in the *Eudemus* to a hylomorphic theory in the *DA*. He thus presupposes a kind of continuum of development which may seem natural to a historian of ideas, but which seems highly unnatural from a philosophical point of view. Nevertheless his arguments and certain synchronisms he finds with metaphysical and biological works are interesting.

[20] Ross (1957: 72).

This is awkward for TST, though perhaps not an insuperable obstacle; for it might take Aristotle some time to appreciate the profound changes of viewpoint that S₂ entails. Yet it seems especially difficult for these particular works to overlap. We have seen how the four cause theory of *A.Po.*ii. 11 lacks a concept of matter and form; here of all places a conflict between systems would be expected to appear. If Aristotle had already developed the hylomorphism of S_2, he should have incorporated it in the *A.Po.*

Let us consider, then, the grounds for putting the *A.Po.* late in the Academic period (or even in the Assos period). As Ross sees it, there are two problems with putting the work early: (1) the theories of the *Organon* must have taken considerable time to elaborate; and (2) Aristotle needed some time to develop from a Platonic position. There is no question that Aristotle needed some time to work out the theories he gives. They are complex and sophisticated, a major advance over anything previously seen— even the *Topics* theory, as Aristotle notes. On the other hand, Aristotle spent 20 years in the Academy, from 367 to 348 or 347. We might also note by way of comparative judgements, that mathematicians and logicians often do their best work at a remarkably young age; youth seems to be no barrier to logical studies.[21] Thus we cannot rule out a priori the possibility that Aristotle was young when he did his logical work. When he left the Academy he was about the same age as Russell when he finished the manuscript of the *Principia Mathematica* and about the same age as Einstein when he published the general theory of relativity. Of course in discussing the achievements of genius, we can at most cite exemplary cases and statistics. Such data as we have, however,

---

[21] e.g. Pascal wrote his essay on conic sections at 17 and developed a calculating machine at 19; Leibniz wrote *De Arte Combinatoria* at 20 and developed the foundations of calculus at about 29; Newton independently developed the calculus around 26–8 years of age; Gauss produced his *Disquisitiones Arithmeticae* at 24; Frege published the *Begriffschrift* at 31 and *Die Grundlagen der Arithmetik* at 36; Russell finished his *Principles of Mathematics* at 30, Wittgenstein his *Tractatus* MS at 29; Einstein published his special theory of relativity at 26; Quine's *System of Logistic* and *Mathematical Logic* were produced at 26 and 32, respectively; Kripke had produced his important papers on modal logic by 27. Aristotle himself recognizes that a παῖς can be μαθηματικός (*EN* vi. 8, 1142ᵃ12–18). In philosophy rather than logic Hume had finished his MS of the *Treatise of Human Nature* by 26. Certainly Aristotle was the intellectual equal of any of these geniuses, the Master of Those Who Know.

indicate that it is not at all unusual for young thinkers to make remarkable contributions. In one interesting study on age and achievement, Lehman (1953) finds that the average age for major works is 35–9 for both philosophy and logic, 30–4 for mathematics, but 40–4 for works specifically in metaphysics. Moreover, there are notable cases in all fields of creative endeavour of young prodigies making major contributions before the age of 21.[22]

The one point that might keep scholars from putting Aristotle's work too early would be the belief that he did not finish his preliminary studies until about 357, in accordance with the educational programme of Plato's *Republic*.[23] But the programme of the *Republic* is designed for an ideal state. We have no knowledge that this programme was actually followed in the Academy. Even if it was in general, exceptions might be made. And with a genius of Aristotle's type, we canot assume that he was held back to preliminary studies for the prescribed period—if there was a prescribed period.[24] I therefore see no reason to rule out an early date simply on the grounds of the time needed to develop the theory.

11.3.3 The Relation of the Dialogues to S_1

This leaves us with the second reason for putting the *A.Po.* late: that Aristotle needed time to develop from a Platonic position. The assumption here is that we must first have a period of Platonism, and then a period of logical researches. The evidence for the Platonism consists of fragments from lost dialogues. Thus we must evaluate the relation of the dialogues to the works of S_1. If we have both a Platonic and an anti-Platonic period between 367 and 347, we shall indeed have difficulty fitting all the logical works into the Academic period. An alternate possibility is that Aristotle developed the logical doctrines somewhat independently and only later saw that they were inconsistent with Platonism, as Jaeger supposed. Finally, Aristotle may have been an opponent of Plato

[22] See Lehman (1953: 38 ff.) for philosophy; summary of all fields, pp. 324 ff. For examples of signal achievements before age 21, see pp. 200 ff.

[23] *Rep.* vii. 537 D; cf. Cherniss (1945: 68–70), who takes this programme seriously for reasons extraneous to developmentalist accounts of Aristotle.

[24] That Aristotle was regarded as an exceptional student even in his first years would be confirmed if we could verify that the Aristotle of Plato's *Parmenides* was a representation of our Aristotle. Wundt (1953: 18) finds the identification appealing.

from the earliest period of his writing. This is the position that Düring has taken in his interpretations of Aristotle.

There are several dialogues that are of special importance in reconstructing Aristotle's early thought. The *Gryllus*, which can be dated around 360, was apparently an attack on rhetorical education aimed at Isocrates.[25] The reconstruction must be largely conjectural because of the paucity of evidence, but the dialogue seems to have propelled Aristotle into the public eye. For it is likely that on the basis of this work Plato appointed him to give afternoon lectures in rhetoric in the Academy,[26] and he became a target for attacks by Isocrates and his followers. In the *Eudemus* Aristotle gives an argument for the immortality of the soul in a style like that of the *Phaedo*, giving a number of arguments that are similar to Plato's. Because the dialogue is written on the occasion of the death of a friend and colleague, we can date it to around 352. The *Protrepticus* is probably a reply to Isocrates' *Antidosis*, which is in turn a reply to the *Gryllus*; it was written around 352–350. These are the main dialogues that might throw light on an alleged Platonic period. The *On Philosophy* was written between 350 and 348; in it Aristotle used the form–privation distinction developed in *Ph.* i, and hence had developed the conceptions of S_2 by the time of its writing.[27] Thus, since the *Gryllus* is so obscurely known (and perhaps did not deal with main-line philosophical topics anyway), it is the *Eudemus* and *Protrepticus* that might provide evidence of a Platonic phase of Aristotle's thought.

Now the *Eudemus* is remarkable for the other-worldly spirit it breathes. The author recalls, for instance, a story in which Silenus tells Midas that it is best not to be born, but the second best thing

[25] I shall follow Chroust in his general reconstruction: he is careful and thorough in his research and has no philosophical axe to grind. See 1973, ii. 1–14 for suggested dating of all works, and chapters devoted to individual works. Note that I am using the term 'dialogue' loosely here: not all of Aristotle's works were in dialogue form, and we do not always have sufficient evidence on the genre of specific works. On the *Gryllus* see Chroust (1973, i. 105 ff.).

[26] These may form the basis of the *Rhetoric*, which shows signs of early composition; cf. n. 35 below.

[27] Plutarch, *Mor.* 370 C = fr. 6. In the dialogues *On the Good* and *On the Ideas* Aristotle criticized Platonic theories of ethics and metaphysics and developed his own; Chroust dates these works to 357–355. Unfortunately we cannot be very precise about the dates. If they should be correct, however, it would follow that both the *Eudemus* and the *Protrepticus* postdate Aristotle's explicit break with the theory of Forms, and hence cannot be Platonic in a strong sense.

is to die as quickly as possible (fr. 6 Ross). Aristotle gives several proofs of the immortality of the soul, some of which are restatements of arguments from the *Phaedo*. This provides some prima-facie grounds for attributing to Aristotle a Platonic point of view. However, there are serious problems in taking the Platonism at face value. The first problem is that the Platonism of the *Eudemus* is an *obsolete* Platonism. For Plato had passed far beyond the vale-of-tears attitude in subsequent works, and his simple treatment of the soul had yielded to a complex analysis. Why should Aristotle go back to an outdated approach?[28] It seems likely that the melancholy ambience of the dialogue reflects conventions of the literary genre, dictated by the occasion of its composition. As for the doctrine of the soul, we must beware not to assimilate it to Plato's too hastily.

Philoponus gives the following as an original argument from the *Eudemus*:

'Harmony has an opposite, disharmony; the soul does not have an opposite; therefore, the soul is not a harmony' (*in DA* 144.24 f. = fr. 7).

The syllogistic character of this argument has often been noticed. The form suggests at least that Aristotle was aware of the basics of syllogistic reasoning when he wrote the *Eudemus*. But further-more, the line of argument suggests that Aristotle has in mind the doctrine of the *Cat.* that substances do not have contraries—and indeed, in his version, Olympiodorus adds to the second premiss the explanation 'for it is a substance'.[29] If these words are a quotation, we must suppose that Aristotle had expounded his doctrine of substance in the *Cat.* prior to writing the *Eudemus*. In any case there is a strong possibility that Aristotle had already developed the fundamentals of his doctrine of substance before the *Eudemus*. The doctrine of substance is incompatible with the theory of Forms, to which it provides an alternative. Thus it is implausible to think that the dialogue would advocate the existence of Platonic Forms. Now Simplicius reports that Aristotle called the soul εἶδός τι.[30] Commentators have often tried to

[28] For considerations of this problem, see Wundt (1953: 17 f.), Rees (1960: 191–3), Berti (1962: 416 f.), Owen (1965a: 126 f.).
[29] Olympiodorus *in Phd.* 173.20 = fr. 7.
[30] Simplic. *in DA* 221.20 ff. = fr. 8. Note that the words following the quoted phrase do not refer to the *Eudemus* but to the *DA*: Guthrie (1981: 70 n. 3).

connect this remark with Plato's theory of Forms,[31] but of course to call the soul a Form is in Plato's system a category mistake. On the other hand, if we are dealing with a remark from S_2, the assertion makes perfect sense.[32] Yet then it is difficult to see how Aristotle could support the immortality of soul. Overall, the remark is too brief and problematic to support either side of the debate. But there seems to be no strong argument forthcoming that the *Eudemus* presupposes the theory of Forms. It seems therefore that we can accept the mood as a stylized touch of *Il Penseroso* without accepting the doctrines as Platonic.

The ample fragments of the *Protrepticus* are largely devoted to ethical arguments, many of which prefigure arguments of the *Ethics* and present no particularly Platonic bent. The concept of ἐνέργεια appears in two fragments (6, 14), but only in the activity sense, so that they do not demonstrate a connection with S_2. The one fragment that sounds Platonic is 13:[33] there Aristotle claims that the philosopher differs from other craftsmen by looking to the original and not copies. However, he explains this claim by saying that 'he alone lives by fixing his gaze on *nature* and the divine . . .'. Thus it seems likely that his original is not a Form or set of Forms, but Nature, and the other-worldly tone of the fragment does not imply an other-worldly metaphysics. In fact, what is striking about the *Protrepticus* as a whole is the robust sense of reality in its outlook—the emphasis on living as richly and fully as possible, the goal of the good life, the contrast between active and inert states. The sudden turnabout of attitudes is difficult to explain, given the

---

[31] Cf. Chroust (1973: ii. 68).

[32] Philoponus *in DA*, 144.25–30, thinks Aristotle should add that body and soul are as privation and form, and in this sense opposite. He evidently puts a hylomorphic construction on the passage. As he recognizes, privation–form comprises a different species of opposition from contrariety. However, the fact that Aristotle does not use the privation–form schema here may be evidence that he has not yet developed the *Ph*. i analysis. See Ross (1957: 66), who contrasts the tentative assertion of a hylomorphic analysis of soul in *Met*. xiii. 2, 1077ª32–4 with the confident assertion in *DA* ii. 1, 412ª19–21 and elsewhere. Since *Met*. xiii belongs to the middle period or later, this comparison might suggest a later date for Aristotle's applying a hylomorphic analysis to soul.

[33] Chroust (1973, ii. ch. 8) argues that lines 55.7–56.2 (Pistelli) of fr. 13 are an intrusion perhaps from a passage of Aristotle's *Politicus*, inferring a discontinuity from an inconsistency in the notion of φύσις in the fragment. It seems to me that the apparent conflict can be resolved by noticing a tacit distinction between the *principles* of nature (πρῶτα, 55.9) and its *manifestations*, which are known by experience (ἐμπειρία, 55.11). Thus the argument is a conventionally Aristotelian one, and 'nature' is not to be understood in a Platonic way in 55.26.

only two or so years between the *Eudemus* and *Protrepticus*, unless we take the melancholy of the former to be more of a posture than a conviction. Aristotle's use of imitation and craft similes also has Platonic overtones, but he deploys them for Aristotelian ends.

So far we have seen a Platonism of style rather than substance. But can we definitely exclude a Platonic period? I believe there is a good case for doing so. Recall that stylistic and doctrinal grounds suggested a date of 360 for the early books of the *Topics*. The *Gryllus* was written about that time and soon after Aristotle was lecturing on rhetoric. Although we have no positive evidence on the point, there seems to be no reason in principle why Aristotle could not have been teaching dialectic as well, that is, the material of the *Topics*. One of the criticisms levelled in a general way against Aristotle and Plato was that their methods were pettifogging and useless,[34] and this could well be explained by a second-hand acquaintance with Aristotle's compendium of dialectical strategies. There are signs that both the *Topics* and the *Rhetoric* were written when Aristotle accepted some of Plato's theories uncritically—for instance his theory of pleasure.[35] On the other hand, we see evidence of Aristotle's independence, originality, and power of organization throughout. I conceive of the *Topics* as Aristotle's doctoral dissertation—a major piece of original research done within the framework of a loosely Platonic normal science. But even in the *Topics* Aristotle has a nascent theory of substance that is subversive of Platonic metaphysics. And indeed the most important piece of evidence for dating S_1 relative to the exoteric works is the indication discussed above that one argument for immortality of the *Eudemus* presupposes the S_1 theory of substance. This datum reveals an anti-Platonic metaphysic lurking behind the Platonic façade of Aristotle's most other-worldly essay.

The weight of evidence points to the conclusion that at least some of the works of the corpus, or some parts of them, are as early as the earliest dialogues. If this is so, we have a control on the alleged Platonic phase of Aristotle's development. To be sure,

[34] Isocrates *Antidosis*, 258 f., 266; Ps.-Isoc. *Ad Demonicum*, 3.

[35] *Rh.* i. 11, 1369^{b}33–5; cf. *Philebus* 31 D ff., *Tim.* 64 C–D, 65 A. The *Topics* seems to accept Plato's tripartite soul and thus to antedate the *Protrepticus*: Verbeke (1960).

these early works do not address all problems we might wish to know about. Nevertheless, they do allow us to see what some of Aristotle's technical accomplishments were in his earliest period. He must have attained the distinction of predicates into accidents, genera, properties, and definitions in his earliest period, since *Top.* ii–vii are constructed as an inquiry into the dialectical strategies associated with each type. This distinction in turn suggests a recognition of the distinction of subjects and predicates. Might this be a merely logical distinction? It does not seem likely in view of the four classes of predicates, which represent not so much logical classes as classes of real characteristics.[36] Although Aristotle does not develop a positive metaphysical theory in *Top.* ii–vii, as is appropriate given the nature of the work, he does discuss the theory of Forms in a critical way,[37] and he once suggests a definition of soul as a *substance* (οὐσία) receptive of knowledge (vi. 14, 151^{b}1), suggesting that he holds a theory of substance already.[38]

Thus Aristotle does not appear to be an orthodox Platonist even in the books that we have reason to believe are as early as the earliest dialogues. And in fact we can assert that we have a more or less continuous record of Aristotle's thought before us in the works of the *Organon*. This does not mean that it is easy to see the temporal order of his development from the works of S$_1$, but it does mean that we do not have to rely too heavily on conjectural reconstructions of early dialogues to furnish the foundations of Aristotle's thought. For the *Organon* itself is a record of early Aristotelian positions, sometimes overlaid with transitional and programmatic connections. The dialogues can still provide helpful insights into Aristotle's early ethical and psychological thought— that is, on areas not well covered in S$_1$ treatises. But we need not continue to suppose that there is a mysterious stage of Aristotle's thought represented only by the fragments of dialogues and revealing a very different Aristotle from the one we know.

[36] *Top.* i. 5; although Book i is perhaps later in composition than ii to vii, the schema of the four classes of predicates is obviously early since it defines the structure that the succeeding books follow.

[37] *Top.* vi. 6, 143^{b}23 ff.; 10, 148^{a}14–22.

[38] Frede (1981) argues that the *Topics* is a better source for our understanding of the term κατηγορία than the *Cat.* If he is right about the origin of the term, the passage in *Top.* i. 9 shows how the term οὐσία might have first signified a way of predication and only later an ontological particular. Thus the notion of οὐσία in *Top.* i is conceptually earlier than that of the *Cat.*

Aristotle may not have begun his philosophical career as a confirmed antagonist of Plato, but the thrust of his logical analyses carried him toward a hypostasis of the logical subject and thus a head-on collision with Plato's Forms. There is within S_1 a development in the direction of atomic substantialism, but that development is natural and continuous. There was no major shift from Platonism to S_1 that we can trace, but only the formulation of an increasingly coherent position.[39]

Thus it seems reasonable to suppose that Aristotle produced the works of S_1 relatively early, soon realizing that his theories were incompatible with those of his master. Aristotle's argument that the soul is immortal and has no contrary suggests to me that he did not have a hylomorphic conception of soul when he wrote the *Eudemus*. His interest in nature and actuality in the *Protrepticus* suggests a possible correlation between that work and *Ph.* ii. Perhaps sometime around or soon after 352—after 15 years in the Academy—Aristotle came to analyse substance into matter and form, initially to save the appearances concerning the coming to be of substances. By the time he had left the Academy in 348/7, he realized the implications that a matter–form ontology had for his philosophy, and in *Met.* i set about to rethink the history of philosophy in light of the four cause theory.

There are perhaps grounds for one more objection to TST based on historical sequence. This is the presence in early Aristotelian texts—both in the corpus and the fragments—of a theory of homoeomereity.[40] Homoeomerous things have parts that are like the whole, as part of a quantity of water is water. Now it would seem that if Aristotle has an early theory of homoeomereity, he has an early theory of matter, and thus TST is false. I think that the inference is fallacious: a theory of homoeomereity does not

[39] Cf. Bos (1973: 101): 'Aristotle's development was not: gradual attainment of an independent conception, but rather: evolution from a rough conception of his own, with markedly Platonic characteristics, to another detailed system in his period as scholarch' (italics omitted). Of course I hold that there is a radical change of position before Aristotle becomes scholarch—but it is not to be explained directly by his relation to Plato. Cf. Owen (1965a: 131 f.) on failure of evidence for a Platonic period. Owen (pp. 127–9) attacks the notion that Aristotle's logic and philosophy developed independently (*contra* Jaeger 1948:46). He is surely right, although the full implications of his logical analyses may not have occurred to Aristotle immediately.

[40] *Top.* v. 5, 135^{a}20–^{b}6; Philoponus *in DA* 144.21 ff. = *Eudemus* fr. 7; on the first passage see Evans (1978). Evans personally suggested the problem to me.

entail a theory of matter—in the relevant sense of matter. For a homoeomerous stuff is one which has *physical parts* of a certain kind, and homoeomereity presupposes a physical analysis. But hylomorphism is a *metaphysical* doctrine presupposing a metaphysical analysis. It is quite true that Aristotle from the start has a conception of stuffs; and we can even say that stuffs are matter. But they are not matter in the sense of a metaphysical component of substance—the substratum of change or the subject of predication. In the sense of matter = stuff all the Presocratics and Plato may have had a concept of matter. But in the sense of matter = logical–metaphysical substratum only Aristotle has the concept. From the physical conception we cannot infer the metaphysical. Hence the passages in question cannot overthrow TST.[41]

One residual problem with my argument is that I have argued that Aristotle did some rewriting of the textbooks, revising them so as to minimize the changes of viewpoint. If this is so, how can we in principle expect to have any evidence of a historical development? The answer is simply that Aristotle's rewriting or revising is neither extensive nor thorough. In general he seems to have confined himself to providing programmatic introductions to assign works a place in his developed theory, occasionally (but rarely) adding cross-references, and making a few transitions. Thus the *Topics* has a long methodological introduction, the first book, which assigns the work a subordinate place in a logical theory that had overtaken it. Yet Aristotle fails to eliminate the long closing passage of Book ix which exhibits the *Topics* as his greatest achievement. Aristotle does not seem to tinker with the contents of individual books, although he sometimes does connect books from different periods into a longer work. In fact, we cannot imagine that Aristotle had much time to rewrite extensively in the less than 40 years of his philosophical publishing activity. For the mass of his output is so great that he must have been constantly more occupied with new compositions than old. His presently extant works are comparable to an encyclopaedia, even without the many books of lost dialogues and treatises. Thus both on a

---

[41] There are those who hold that Aristotle inherited his conception of matter from the tradition, and who would therefore reject TST, e.g. Berti (1977). However, for the reasons given, their view seems to me untenable. See arguments against a Platonic concept of matter in Ross (1951: 125, 221 f., 233), Solmsen (1961: 395), Happ (1971: 121–35); cf. Aristotle's ambivalent account, *GC* ii. 1, 329^{a}13–24 and *Ph*. iv. 2, 209^{b}11–13.

priori grounds and in fact, there is a good deal of coherence in Aristotle's works from the standpoint of time of composition. What Aristotle's rewriting accomplished was to create a veneer of unity in a stratified compilation of works.

11.4 CONTEXTUAL ADVANTAGES OF TST

I have thus far detailed some potential disadvantages of TST in comparison with other hypotheses. I now wish to examine what I take to be actual advantages. In this section we shall consider some advantages TST has in the context of the larger setting of biography, history, and philosophy. I take it that such contextual advantages are not decisive in themselves, but they may offer a presumption in favour of one of a set of competing theories.

11.4.1 Biographical Advantages

There are three important hypotheses concerning the course of Aristotle's philosophical development. On Jaeger's view, Aristotle begins his career as a confirmed Platonist and gradually establishes his independence, moving to more empirical and practical interests. On Owen's view, Aristotle begins as a critic of Platonism and gradually through the dialectic of his own philosophy, he comes to appreciate and embrace certain principles of Platonism, always with the needs of his system in mind.[42] Ingemar Düring's view makes Aristotle a philosopher who is critical of Plato from his earliest period, and one who makes no significant concessions to Platonism but only works out the implications of his own philosophy.

Of these hypotheses, TST follows the general lines of Owen's view (although it adduces different evidence for it). His and Düring's views seem to be the most plausible hypotheses given the general *status quaestionis*. The Jaeger view is on weak ground because the consensus on dating key works counts against it. For instance the *Categories* is agreed to be among Aristotle's earliest treatises, but in it we see an ontology that is diametrically opposed

---

[42] There is a view that combines features of Owen's and Jaeger's views: first there is a Platonic period represented by the dialogues, then an anti-Platonic period, then a revised-Platonic period. This view is recommended by de Vogel (1960). I have already argued against the first period; what is left of her reconstruction is similar to Owen's view.

to Plato's as the One Under Many is opposed to the One Over Many. On the other hand, the central books of the *Metaphysics* are agreed to be among Aristotle's latest works. And they, and in particular *Met.* vii, are among the most Platonic in outlook. Jaeger argued, on unconvincing grounds, that the *Cat.* was a later work by a pupil, but his arguments have not been accepted.[43] Furthermore, there is evidence that Aristotle began his biological researches in his middle period, and hence that his more empirical work is not confined exclusively to his latest period.[44] Moreover, as Ross (1957: 72 ff.) has argued, it is implausible to suppose that effective scientific research can go on in the absence of theories to validate their method. Thus we should not suppose that an increased effort in the direction of empirical studies ruled out theoretical interests. Finally, as we have already argued, the evidence of an early Platonism is more ambiguous than Jaeger supposed.

The Düring hypothesis is more defensible, and is indeed the view I think Aristotle would have taken of his own work. My recommendations for dating of the early works follow Düring's and I find much that is valuable in his position. It is largely on the grounds of the content of S_2 that I must depart from his view. For Aristotle's anti-Platonic ideology notwithstanding, his work increasingly reveals a Platonic strain that is implicit in the S_2 ontology, and he does not attempt to palliate that Platonism until he comes face to face with serious paradoxes in *Met.* vii.

Overall the Owen thesis is attractive despite its initial implausibility. For although the development may seem to be backwards, it makes a kind of psychological sense. Aristotle, the brilliant young philosopher, establishes himself in the Academy as a perceptive critic of his master. He elaborates his own position by contrasting it to that of Plato, and wins the admiration of Plato and his other students by sharpening their understanding of the issues.

---

[43] Jaeger (1948: 46 n. 3). On the authenticity of the *Cat.* see Husik (1904), (1939), Ross (1939*b*), de Rijk (1951).

[44] Thompson (1910: p. vii); cf. Jaeger (1948: 329 ff.). H. D. P. Lee (1948) has been influential in suggesting that Aristotle conducted much of his biological research in his middle period. Solmsen (1978) disputes some of his data but does not significantly revise the timetable. See now Lee (1985). See also Preus (1975: 45–7) on dating the biological works. Gaiser (1985) has recently suggested that Aristotle may have gone to Lesbos specifically to conduct biological research with Theophrastus.

After Plato's death—indeed even before—Aristotle finds a need to incorporate a more Platonic view into his metaphysics in order to accommodate certain otherwise recalcitrant problems. Led on by the truth itself, as it were, he makes concessions to a position that is more like his own philosophy than he realizes. Thus the Owen hypothesis seems plausible after all, and it fits well with the data of Aristotle's writings and their dates.[45]

11.4.2 Historical Advantages

The historical plausibility of TST is a function of its ability to reveal Aristotle as the heir of a tradition. Because this study is limited to an exposition of Aristotle's thought I cannot here do more than sketch a programme for a defence of TST. In Chapter 5 I argued that Aristotle's attempt to explain the coming-to-be of substances led him to posit form and matter; and further that the need to provide a conceptual interpretation for the notions led him to invoke the craft analogy, which then became integral to the theory of form and matter. Now the craft analogy is a prominent legacy of Socrates' ethical thought.[46] Although Plato's use of the analogy is sometimes misunderstood, it is clear that Plato modified and developed the analogy in his own mature thought, and that it became an important feature of his later scientific views. When Aristotle takes up the craft analogy in S_2, he is harking back to his philosophical tradition; he takes an instrument of Socrates' and Plato's philosophical analyses and applies it more systematically and rigorously to central philosophical problems. If these observations are correct TST not only puts Aristotle in a plausible historical context, but generates a new dimension of continuity from Socrates to Aristotle. By contrast, both the Jaeger and the Düring hypotheses stress the discontinuity of the Athenian philosophical tradition—on Jaeger's view because Aristotle tends to resign from philosophical speculation, on Düring's because Aristotle is an implacable opponent of Plato's thought. I claim,

[45] Although I approve of Owen's account of the general direction in which Aristotle's thought developed, it should be clear from the last chapter that I think Aristotle conceded too much to Plato. Aristotle's hylomorphism is an acceptable concession, but not his adoption of an independently existent form. In general, my endorsement of Owen's Platonism of Aristotle thesis is an endorsement of a descriptive developmental thesis. It should not be understood as an endorsement of a normative synchronic thesis that Aristotle was right to adopt a strongly Platonic position.

[46] See Kube (1969), Irwin (1977a: 71 ff.).

then, that from a historical point of view TST has a prima-facie advantage.

11.4.3 Philosophical Advantages

By far the most important context for judging the competing developmental hypotheses is the philosophical: the course of development should make sense in philosophical terms, that is, as the sort of path a philosopher would be likely to take for philosophical reasons. From this point of view the Düring thesis is adequate only in so far as it seems that there is no significant development to explain between S_1 and S_2. The evidence indicates that there is a problem, and since Düring puts the works of S_1 clearly before those of S_2, it must be in part a developmental problem. But here the difference between Düring and TST comes down to a difference of evidence, which must be dealt with in the next section.

Jaeger's view shows a significant weakness on the question of philosophical motivation. In general Jaeger finds no philosophical reasons for Aristotle's progress. There are, of course, disagreements with Plato, but these are vague and general, for instance:

. . . the things he is most concerned to bring out are the collapse of the invisible world of Ideas erected by Plato as the paradigm or pattern of the visible cosmos, his own dislike of mere speculation without the support of experience, and his sceptical attitude towards several of the bursts of unverifiable cosmological fancy into which many Academi[c]s had been led by their taste for Pythagorean philosophy . . . (1948: 308)

The points of contention come off more as differences of humours than of philosophic theses. At some level differences between philosophers do reduce to differences in point of view that may seem like questions of taste. And insights into the varying points of view can be valuable, as are some of Jaeger's extended remarks on Aristotle's Place in History (1948: ch. 15). But since he sees Aristotle not as an opponent of Plato from the cradle, he owes us more of an account than Düring, for example. For he makes Aristotle's point of departure Plato's philosophy as a whole, which he allegedly accepts in his early career; to develop from that position requires some motivation, and we should expect a specifically philosophical motivation. But Jaeger only makes vague remarks about Aristotle's growing independence. Furthermore,

Jaeger sees development after his initial break with Platonic philosophy, for which he also owes us philosophic reasons. Instead he makes faintly Hegelian observations like the following:

> His metaphysics arises out of that inner tension between intellectual conscience and longing for a religious view of the world which constitutes what is new and problematic in his philosophical personality. (p. 377)

What we find is a gradual personality development rather than a philosophical progression from an inadequate or untenable position to a defensible one.[47] In short, we are unable to descry any philosophical reasons either for Aristotle's alleged break from Platonism or for his further progress towards a scientific attitude. And indeed, Jaeger's schematic view of Aristotle's progress seems to preclude a philosophical motivation in the long run, for Jaeger sees him as becoming less philosophical as he becomes more empirically minded. We should note, moreover, that the failure to adduce philosophical reasons for changes in philosophy seems to be endemic to those who follow in Jaeger's footsteps: they are typically more interested in sequences and trends than in philosophical justifications.

It is one of the signal strengths of TST that it gives a philosophical motivation for the progress from S_1 to S_2. The account I have given of the changeover from the earlier to the later system is not the only possible one. Owen (1965a) gives an alternate account in arguing for the development towards a modified Platonism. I shall comment on this account below (11.6.4), but for now suffice it to say that a recognition of two systems at least makes possible a *philosophical* explanation of Aristotle's development.

11.5 EVIDENTIAL ADVANTAGES OF TST

Contextual advantages provide a presumption in favour of TST, but they do not of themselves decide the issue. The most important dimension of a theory is its ability to interact with the data of a problem and to connect them into a network of evidential

---

[47] Nuyens (1948: 43) makes this approach into a virtue, noticing what is unHegelian in it: 'Nôtre interêt se concentre précisément sur ce qui apparaît trop peu dans l'interprétation systématique (surtout hegelienne): ce qu'il y a de personnel, de caractéristique chez un grand penseur tel qu'Aristote.'

relations which makes sense of the data. In this section I shall discuss the advantages of TST in its handling of the data in general, then its potential for confirmation and its treatment of certain so far intractable problems.

11.5.1 Data and Evidence

In the first place we expect the best of several competing theories to be able to make better use of the data than its rivals. That better theories make better use of the data is a truism, but it conceals a number of important relationships between theories and evidence that we must be aware of in evaluating the theories. First one should make a distinction between pre-theoretical and post-theoretical information. I shall call the former 'data' and the latter 'evidence'. The former consist of truisms, 'facts', observed regularities, etc.—Aristotle's ἔνδοξα. It is sometimes held that there are no facts apart from theories, but even if this is true—which it may not be—one can still distinguish between facts which are associated with relatively incoherent or incomplete conceptions of the world and those which have a place in a highly criticized and organized theory.[48] The data can be rejected outright or explained away as well as transformed into evidence in a theory. But we expect the theory to do justice to the data in general, which are the manifestation of our pre-theoretical insights into the problem. Secondly, let us make a distinction between a primary and a secondary domain. The primary domain consists of the explananda of the immediate problem; the secondary domain is a field of data of wider scope that the theory has implications for explaining. It is a generally accepted principle that the best theories not only explain the immediate explananda but have implications for the understanding of a wider range of phenomena. For instance, the theory of relativity not only explains the constancy of the speed of light, but has implications concerning the convertibility of mass and energy. If a theory has no further implications, it is under suspicion of being *ad hoc*.

Given these distinctions, I suggest the following criteria for evaluating theories: (1) the best theory should explain the data in its primary domain best; (2) it should transform more data into evidence; (3) it should be more fruitful, that is, have more

---

[48] Cf. Pepper (1942: 39 ff.), Gaukroger (1978: 46 ff.).

implications for further testing, or have a more extensive secondary domain. Of course the ultimate test is whether the theory agrees with the evidence it adduces, but since often all theories agree with their evidence (or are adjusted to do so) these criteria are important for measuring the theories' performance.

The primary domain of TST is the difference between the language and doctrines of the *Organon* and the rest of the corpus. In this domain the nucleus of the theory, the Incommensurability Hypothesis (ICH), is in competition with the *Organon* Hypothesis (OH) and the Extension Hypothesis (EH). I have argued in Chapter 4 that OH is untenable and that logical considerations rule out EH. On the other hand, ICH seems to fit the data and to make sense of them. Thus TST has major evidential advantages over its competitors in the limited domain on which it initially focuses. Ultimately the main target of TST is the dominant unitarian interpretation. Since this interpretation requires OH or EH to account for discrepancies between sections of the corpus, it is seriously compromised by the failure of those subsidiary hypotheses in part of its domain.

I claim also that TST transforms more data into evidence, and thus satisfies (2). One clear mark of success in a theory is its ability to turn mere observed correlations, that is, data of a certain sort, into evidence. For instance, ancient astronomers had long been aware of a correlation between planets' cycles of anomaly (the period between successive episodes of retrograde motion), their revolutions of longitude (return to the same position in the heavens), and solar years. For the Ptolemaic theory this was merely a coincidence; for the Copernican it was evidence.[49] The difference in the evidential relations the two theories bore towards the data was a mark of difference in explanatory power, one that favoured the new theory. In just the same way, I suggest, the correlations between the meanings of terms and their location in S_1 or S_2 is merely a coincidence for OH and EH—in fact the extent of the meaning difference is largely ignored by them. On the other hand, ICH (supplemented by a developmental hypothesis) both suggests the examination of the data, and transforms them into evidence for the theory. Similarly, the difference in the four cause theory of S_1 and that of S_2 is merely a coincidence for the unitarian

---

[49] See Glymour (1980: 183 ff.).

(since the proferred explanations do not work), but it is evidence for TST. And the difference in the theory of actuality, which has hitherto been ignored or misunderstood, is evidence for TST.

Finally, ICH obviously does have implications for a wider domain than its primary domain, and with the addition of a suitable developmental hypothesis, it suggests a general re-interpretation of Aristotle. On the other hand, so far from having further implications, OH actually prizes off S_1 from S_2 as not a part of Aristotle's philosophy. EH allows for some developmental insights, but does not in general have important implications for understanding Aristotle's philosophy, for which unitarian hypotheses are employed. I suggest then that on the basis of criteria (1) to (3), TST and in particular ICH, have advantages over their competitors.

11.5.2 Bootstrapping and Confirmation for TST

Perhaps the most important recent contribution to the theory of confirmation is that of Clark Glymour (1980). He holds that scientific theories can be confirmed, but in a way different from what most previous realist theories have held. According to him, we use evidence together with theoretical claims to deduce instances of other theoretical claims. Thus, 'Confirmation or support is a relation among a body of evidence, a hypothesis, and a theory . . . the evidence confirms or disconfirms the hypothesis with respect to the theory' (p. 110). What we test are not whole theories or networks of beliefs, as Quine would have it, but single hypotheses composing a theory. Thus it is important that a theory be articulated into component hypotheses and be testable individually against evidence in conjunction with other hypotheses. For instance, we might use a set of values for pressure, volume, and temperature to calculate the constant k in the theoretical equation $PV = kT$. Then we might use a second set of values for the variables to confirm or disconfirm the equation (p. 111). Thus we use values given in experience together with a hypothesis to compute an instance of the hypothesis, and then use another set of values with the newly discovered constant to instantiate the equation and see if the predicted relationship holds. In this way components of theories and ultimately whole theories can be tested against the evidence by objective procedures in a hierarchy of confirmations Glymour calls 'bootstrapping'.

I claim that TST, which is a theory of interpretation, can be, and has been, so tested. For it is composed of a set of hypotheses each of which addresses a different domain or subdomain of evidence, such that one can be used to test another. Consider the following hypotheses:

(1) ICH, the Incommensurability Hypothesis: S_1 and S_2 are incommensurable.

(2) PS_1, the Priority of S_1: S_1 is prior in time of composition to S_2.

(3) DM, the Discovery of Matter: Aristotle postulates form and matter as a solution to the problem of change; this postulation is the beginning of S_2.

(4) DA, the Development of Actuality: Aristotle develops a conception of substantial actuality in S_2.

(5) DF, the Development of the Four Cause Theory: Aristotle develops a new version of FCT in S_2.

(6) AU, Aristotle's Unitarianism: Aristotle holds a unitarian view of his own work.

(7) IZ, the Incoherence of *Met.* vii: *Met.* vii is logically incoherent.

(8) ED, the Date of the Early Dialogues: the date of Aristotle's allegedly Platonizing dialogues is posterior to certain works of S_1.

(9) OT, the Owen Thesis: Aristotle develops toward a more Platonic position.

This is not an exhaustive list of hypotheses in TST, but it does present some of the more important components, and it does give a sample of both systematic and developmental hypotheses. Let us look at some relations between them.

In the first place I argued for ICH, a systematic hypothesis. Having done so, I noted that another set of evidence supported PS_1. Since the major difference between S_1 and S_2 had been shown to be the presence of hylomorphism, we expected that some philosophical justification might lead Aristotle to posit the existence of matter and form early in S_2. Thus, roughly (using the arrow for entailment):

(a) ICH, $PS_1 \rightarrow$ DM

We found, in fact, evidence to substantiate this prediction in the form of an argument leading to the positing of matter in *Ph.* i, arguably the earliest work of S_2. Subsequently we noted that differences in the configuration of the theory of actuality and the four cause theory in S_1 and S_2 suggested that they might be explained in terms of the discovery of matter. Thus:

(b) ICH, DM → DA, DF

Thus instances of both hypotheses on the left predicted instances of hypotheses on the right, and we were able to find evidence confirming our expectations. We further noted that Aristotle had not actually renounced S_1, but rather retained its principles, at least nominally. Furthermore, he restated those principles in *Met.* vii. This suggests that the logical incompatibility of principles of S_1 and S_2 would be manifest in *Met.* vii:

(c) ICH, AU → IZ

Subsequently we found evidence that the problems of that book were best understood as logical paradoxes generated by incompatible assumptions characteristic of S_1 and S_2. In the present chapter we noted that the dating of S_1, of the early dialogues of Aristotle, and of the discovery of matter as instantiated in *Ph.* i led to a rejection of the Jaeger thesis and an acceptance of the Owen thesis:

(d) PS_1, ED, DM → OT

As we subsequently noted, OT is the most plausible overall developmental thesis.

On the basis of these and other connections between hypotheses, I hold that TST is highly tested on the basis of a large body of data, and that it is furthermore highly confirmed. Although it is in principle possible to disconfirm the hypotheses at many points, including a number of places where it goes out on a limb—such as with IZ—it finds confirming evidence. Thus TST is powerful and effective in explaining a wide variety of evidence, as is shown by its conformity to the requirements of an important theory of confirmation.

11.5.3 The Dissolution of a Problem

One bonus of TST is that it dissolves one serious and so far intractable problem in harmonizing Aristotle. The problem is that while Aristotle prescribes a formal structure for science, he fails to exemplify that structure in any extant scientific treatise. Indeed, although he makes syllogism the foundation of scientific proof, there is virtually no straightforward syllogism in all the scientific treatises. Barnes (1969) has effectively criticized many attempts to solve the problem, and has come up with a solution of his own which has been widely accepted. According to him, 'the theory of demonstrative science was never meant to guide or formalise scientific research: it is concerned exclusively with the teaching of facts already won . . . it offers a formal model of how teachers should *present and impart* knowledge' (p. 138).

Barnes's solution might work if one could maintain a distinction between mere pedagogy on the one hand and epistemological justification on the other. But while *A.Po.* i. 1 stresses the first aspect of demonstration, Chapter 2 insists on the second as well: demonstration confers scientific knowledge—indeed it *comprises* such knowledge (71^b17–19). What is at stake with demonstration is not mere education, but a foundationalist epistemology in which our aquaintance with first principles makes possible an inferential knowledge of facts (72^a25 ff.). Barnes's interpretation trivializes demonstration by ruling out its justificatory role in warranting our knowledge. Barnes entertains the objection that on his own view Aristotle's scientific works should still be demonstrative, since they are designed as lessons. In reply, Barnes notes the signs of revision in the writings and infers that '. . . Aristotle did not intend his treatises to be pieces of formal intruction: they are progress-reports, not text-books . . .' (p. 145). But surely this is not at all what Aristotle thinks of his treatises.[50] Consider for instance the long methodological preface to the *Parts of Animals* (i. 1), which is conceived as a prologue to a pedagogical exposition, not a progress report. In any case, if Aristotle himself was not

[50] Dirlmeier (1962: 40–3) rightly criticizes Jaeger (1923: 399, 401) for claiming that Aristotle's system is open and provisional; see also his criticisms of Düring (1954: 164), (1961: 229–31). Aristotle holds that the limits of human knowledge can quickly be reached: Cicero, *Tusc.* 3.28.69 = *Protrepticus* fr. 8: 'Aristoteles . . . ait . . . se videre quod paucis annis magna accessio facta esset, brevi tempore philosophiam plane absolutam fore.' Since the world is everlasting and along with it the human race, and since periodic world disasters have destroyed human civilization, the arts and sciences have often been fully developed and then lost. Cf. Iamblichus *Comm. Math.* 26 = *Protr.* fr. 8; *DC* i. 3, 270^b19 f.; *Mtr.* i. 3, 339^b27–30; *Met.* xii. 8, 1074^b10–13. For discussions of Aristotle's views on progress, see Edelstein (1967: 69 f., 87–92, 118–28), Dodds (1973: 14). Aristotle's view that all knowledge can be attained in a finite time seems to have been shared by the early modern progressive Francis Bacon: Bury (1932: 57 f.).

in a position, after starting from the first principles of natural philosophy, to provide more than a 'progress report', how could he expect anyone to execute such a monumental task as deducing the details of a science from their axioms?[51]

Barnes now advocates a developmental theory which seems in part to render his previous account unnecessary. For in a recent article (1981) he undertakes to show that the theory of syllogism is later than the theory of demonstration in the 'order of discovery', although in present form the two *Analytics* are interrelated. Barnes suggests that the *A.Pr.* was composed no earlier than the 340s.[52] Thus Aristotle's failure to make use of syllogistic in his science may be explainable by its late date (pp. 58 f.). Barnes's dating seems to have little evidence in its favour. Against it there is the failure of the *A.Pr.* to make any connections with Aristotle's later thought.[53] This point might be dismissed as an argument from silence. But there is at least one surprising theoretical lapse in the *A.Pr.*: Aristotle never makes use of what seems to us a natural extension of the matter–form conception—the distinction of arguments into a formal and a material component. Yet the Greek commentators freely use this distinction.[54] Certainly Aristotle has the general notion of an argument *form*, and it is one of his signal contributions to the history of logic.[55] But the intuitive extension of hylomorphic language to the realm of logic—the terminology of formal arguments and argument forms, of the matter and form of an argument—never appears in Aristotle. Aristotle has intelligible form and separable form, but not logical form. I suggest that the lack of a hylomorphic terminology in Aristotle's syllogistic creates a strong presumption against its being a late development.

[51] For other criticisms of Barnes, see Burnyeat (1981: 116–20).

[52] His main evidence for an absolute date is a passage in *A.Pr.* ii. 24 which Düring (1966: 54) finds inconclusive. See ch. 11.3.1.

[53] Cf. Burnyeat's objection in Barnes (1981: 57 n. 66).

[54] e.g. Alexander *in A.Pr.* 52.19–25, 53.28–31, 55.21 ff. clearly recognizes the difference between logical form and different material exemplifications of it, and uses form–matter terminology to explicate the difference. Philoponus uses form–matter terminology to explicate Aristotle's definition of the syllogism into a formal and a material factor; he finds in the distinction the basis for the order of exposition in the *Analytics*: see *in A.Pr.* 32.31–33.21, 270.17, 387.9–11, *in A.Po.* 57.19–23. Furthermore, the commentators regularly use expressions such as ἐπὶ ὕλης to designate exposition 'by concrete examples' as opposed to e.g. exposition ἐπὶ στοιχείων (using letters, i.e. variables): Alexander *in A.Pr.* 53.28–31, 55.23, 222.8, 414.9; Philoponus *in A.Pr.* 48.4 f., 47.5, 75.12.

[55] Łukasiewicz (1957: 7 f.), Ross (1949: 29).

One suggestion for reconciling the lack of syllogisms in Aristotelian science that I find more attractive than the preceding ones is one that makes a distinction between the surface structure and the deep structure of science.[56] Perhaps what Aristotle wishes to maintain is not that every scientific argument should be reduced to syllogistic form in actuality, but that it should be reducible in principle. Below the less formal surface of scientific explanation is a formal structure that can be asserted, though for convenience it is not. The line would not be too different from that of a proponent of the hypothetico-deductive model of science: for he would claim not that all scientific exposition is in fact deductive, but that it can be rendered so in principle. Although this line seems promising, Aristotle himself does not seem to have made the requisite distinction between surface structure and deep structure in his own theory of demonstration, and his own foundationalist remarks seem to require a strict application of formal deduction in demonstration. Accordingly, I do not think this interpretation works either.

Thus the attempts to save Aristotle's science from his own formal requirements, which he does not fulfil, have so far failed. The advantage that TST has in this case is that it dissolves the problem: the theory of demonstration belongs to S_1, the scientific treatises to S_2. And the scientific method of S_2 goes back to the principles of *Ph.* i and ii rather than those of the *Analytics*. It is only to be expected then that the scientific treatises will reflect not the formal deductive methods of S_1, but the pluralistic and analytic aetiological approach of S_2. Indeed, far from being an embarrassment, the lack of syllogistic in Aristotelian science is another piece of evidence in favour of TST. From the point of view of TST, the problem of demonstration is just another anomaly created by the unitarian interpretation of Aristotle; it is not a problem for Aristotle but for an interpretative theory. Of course we must again concede to the unitarian that according to TST Aristotle does not renounce the principles of S_1 in his mature thought; but this does not mean TST has to accommodate S_1 principles in its interpretation of S_2. We are justified in following Aristotle's practice—since in practice he is more consistent than in

---

[56] Alexander Mourelatos first suggested this idea to me; William Wians has defended an interpretation like this in a paper read at the American Philosophical Association Western Division Meetings, 1986.

theory—of ignoring S_1 principles in S_2 science. I claim, then, that TST provides at least one less paradox for the interpretation of Aristotle. From the point of view of TST, the problem of scientific argument is one that is created by the refusal to recognize two systems.

Thus TST seems to have advantages over competing theories in explaining the data. It makes certain predictions, including some unconventional and risky ones, which disagree with those of standard theories. These predictions are confirmed, and furthermore certain anomalies are eliminated—that is, TST does not make certain predictions that are not confirmed. Accordingly TST stands up well under evidential tests.

11.6 TST AND OTHER INTERPRETATIONS

Thus far I have argued that TST can meet objections, and that it has contextual and evidential advantages over certain rival theories. These arguments create a presumption in favour of TST. But they cannot decide the issue in themselves. What is at stake is the adequacy of TST as a general theory of interpretation. Tactical victories in limited theatres of operation do not necessarily win the war. The ultimate test for TST, as for any theory that attempts to provide an overall interpretation of Aristotle, is how satisfactorily it integrates the diverse components of his philosophy. In metaphorical terms, does this interpretation present the kind of perspective that allows for a synoptic view of Aristotle? Any answer to the question is bound to be subjective to a certain degree: does this viewpoint accord with what we know or think we know about Aristotle? Does it suggest new lines of inquiry? Does it correct misconceptions about Aristotle? We cannot answer such questions except from some perspective or other. Nevertheless, we can evaluate differences of perspective in a critical way. For we can judge the assumptions that the viewpoint presupposes to see if they are justified. Moreover, if one perspective is able to expose the inadequacies of another it is to that degree more powerful.

In this discussion I shall criticize some standard views of Aristotle on the basis of what has been established so far in the argument for TST. The views include both scholarly and popular (pedagogical) expositions. The reason for making no distinction between scholarly and popular types is that what is at stake is the validity of the perspectives, nor the rigour or detail with which they are worked out. One test of the power of TST is its ability not only to provide a satisfactory account of Aristotle but to furnish a diagnosis of what is wrong with other perspectives. I shall try to show that TST does provide a synoptic view of Aristotle which exposes the weaknesses of current influential perspectives.

11.6.1 Aristotle as a Philosopher of Common Sense

It is often said that Aristotle's philosophy is a philosophy of common sense.[57] In a way this is obviously true: a continuing desideratum of Aristotelian philosophy is that it accommodate our pre-theoretical intuitions, the ἔνδοξα. And clearly Aristotle's early ontology is designed to put biological individuals of the sort we are familiar with in ordinary experience at the foundation of his world-view. However, we have reason seriously to doubt the overall claim that Aristotle is a philosopher of common sense. In the first place, while the *interpretation* of his S_1 ontology connects it with the middle-sized objects of common sense, the *formal* ontology itself is not a datum of common sense. Rather it is a highly abstract construct modelled on grammatical forms. Furthermore, when Aristotle must modify his ontology to save the phenomena of substantial change—itself a concession to common-sense beliefs—he transforms his principles into an even more complicated scheme. By introducing a substratum for substance, he is forced to find an interpretation which assigns to that substratum a referent in the world of nature. By modelling this new ontology on the crafts, he is able to connect the mysterious substratum with material and hence derive a notion of matter, which can be connected with the homoeomerous stuffs of the world. But the concept remains problematic at the level of the biological individual, since it is unclear what the appropriate matter of an animal or plant is. The new ontology drives a wedge between the biological individual and the really real, such that Aristotle ultimately assigns ontological priority to something far removed from common-sense conceptions. Thus we must conclude that while Aristotle holds common sense in high esteem, his theory itself is an abstract and sophisticated construct that is not itself a product of common sense. And the direction of his own

---

[57] The most extended development of this approach is in Veatch (1974).

elaboration is rather away from common sense than toward it.

Perhaps another dimension of the common-sense interpretation is the belief that Aristotle's categories and principles are so natural that he must have obtained them by observation. This belief seems to me to incorporate an egregious methodological error. To say that Aristotle derived his potentiality–actuality distinction from an episode of watching a plant grow, or that he arrived at his matter–form distinction by observing the nature of living things is naïve. It is comparable with the myth that Newton discovered gravity by watching an apple fall off a tree. It is true that such an event might possibly be the *occasion* of a conceptual discovery; but human beings—and brilliant ones too—had been watching apples fall off trees for millennia without producing theories of gravitation. Similarly, humans had been observing plants for millennia before Aristotle without producing a theory of actuality or matter. One gets out of a conceptual discovery roughly what one puts in to it. Platonic accounts of power and exercise, form and participants, and Aristotelian concepts of substratum and predication all went into Aristotle's discoveries. No doubt there is a kind of inspiration that reveals the relevance of conceptions and unifies the ingredients into a new whole, perhaps in a flash of insight as one contemplates a natural event. But as Kant recognized long ago, nature has no secrets to divulge to those who do not know how to ask. From the point of view of the historian of philosophy it is the preconceptions that are important because it is they that can be controlled and shown to be unique; the observations are common to all and hence can explain nothing. Thus on the grounds of observation Aristotle cannot be avowed to be more commensensical than any other thinker.[58]

11.6.2 Biological Approaches to Aristotle

We have already noted the prominence of the biological individual in Aristotle's interpretation of his metaphysics. This suggests another line of interpretation, one which in fact has been very influential. Armed with some biographical facts about

[58] Cf. Tonelli (1962: 293): 'Parfois ce qui paraît avoir été créé *ex nihilo* derive non pas de la tradition, mais de l'observation directe ds choses, c'est-à-dire, plus exactement, non pas tout court de la tradition mentale, verbalisée ou non, mais d'une réaction nouvelle provoquée entre cette tradition ou une conséquence qu'on en tire, et ce qu'on appelle "réalité"; ce qui, à son tour, est dit "observation".'

Aristotle and the evidence of his biological writings, some scholars have thought that the key to understanding him is his biological orientation. Born the son of a physician, he was educated in anatomy and dissection and applied his biological acumen to problems of philosophy. His skill and interest in biology is evident in his scientific writings; but his philosophy as a whole bears the stamp of a biologist in its systematic organization and its metaphysical categories.[59] Biology provides a model or explanatory scheme for Aristotle's philosophy.

Although this view is initially plausible and attractive as an integration of biography and philosophical doctrine, there are fatal objections. In the first place, the theory commits a serious anachronism: there was no real biology before Aristotle developed his own; and we can trace his biological researches to his stay on Lesbos at the earliest, that is, after 344; but by this time Aristotle had developed all his metaphysical principles and had probably written his fundamental physical treatises and all the *Organon*.[60] Furthermore, proponents who connect primary substance with biological categories fail to analyse the relation of ontology and nature carefully. The formal ontology cannot be accounted for biologically, but rather on a linguistic model; only the interpretation connects the abstract scheme with biology. Yet when we speak of the substance as a biological individual, we are not using 'biological' in a scientific sense, but only to indicate that it is the living thing that is important. In any case, Aristotle's S_2 ontology moves farther away from biology, as we have noted, a move that cannot be explained on the biological theory of interpretation.[61]

I maintain that the craft model (and the linguistic model in S_1) explain more rigorously and effectively what the bioloical model is purported to explain, the concepts and schemes of Aristotle's thought. Indeed, there is a remarkable instance of the priority of

---

[59] See Grene (1963) for the fullest development of such a position.

[60] Grene (1963: 32) attempts to get around this problem by attributing the present corpus to a course of study Aristotle composed after he had organized his biological research. Even if there were evidence for a general restructuring of Aristotle's writings, which there is not, there are still sufficient traces in the corpus to show the relative temporal priority of metaphysics to biology, and hence to demonstrate the conceptual independence of the former.

[61] See Graham (1986) for an extended critique of biological interpretations in their several versions; see also Jacobs (1978) for a limited critique.

the craft model to the biological one in Aristotle's *Generation of Animals* (i. 22): when Aristotle comes down to the final explication of the mystery of conception, he invokes the crafts of carpentry, pottery, and architecture in an extended analogy that is his *only* explanation. In general Aristotle makes frequent use of craft analogies in his scientific treatises, using them often in preference to the biological analogies we might expect.[62] And although Aristotle officially regards the crafts and nature as complementary phenomena, he makes craft analogies do much more work in his system.[63]

There is, however, one sense in which biology does play a creative role in Aristotle's philosophy. That is in providing a pre-theoretical insight into the nature of things. For Aristotle the world is not radically defective as it is for Plato; it is a self-determining and organic whole which exists and can continue to exist without outside interference or an external standard of comparison. It is significant that while Aristotle continues to depend on craft analogies like those Plato uses in the *Timaeus*, he makes *Nature* the craftsman. He has no use for a Demiurge or a transcendent creator of any kind. Thus there is a kind of reflexivity to his concept of the world, as is seen in his image of the doctor doctoring himself.[64] Yet in noting this important role for biology, we must nevertheless observe that *scientific* biology adds nothing to this picture; rather it is biological science which is dependent on the four cause theory and other concepts connected with the craft model for its foundation.

11.6.3 The Craft Analogy as a Root Metaphor

One view that has some important similarities to TST is that of Wilfred Sellars (1967). He states that 'the "root metaphor" of the Aristotelian system is the making of artifacts by skilled craftsmen who understand the purpose their products are to serve' (p. 77). I think he is on the right track in pointing to the importance of the craft analogy. However, there are two major problems with his interpretation. In the first place, he takes a unitarian position and

[62] See examples in Jacobs (1978).
[63] *Ph.* ii. 8; see Jacobs (1978: 25 f.), who argues that the crafts and nature should be taken as complementary. He fails to note that the relevant conflict does not concern Aristotle's theory but a meta-theoretical analysis of Aristotle's motivation.
[64] *Ph.* ii. 8, 199^{b}30–2; cf. Solmsen (1963: 490 f.), Preus (1975: 221 ff.).

tries to read the craft analogy into S_1 as well as S_2. I find no evidence that the analogy is operating as an important element of S_1, although Sellars's reconstruction is an interesting attempt to tie in the craft analogy.

Secondly, and more fundamentally, the root metaphor theory is inadequate in general, and inadequate specifically in explaining Aristotle. The root metaphor theory to which Sellars alludes is a meta-philosophical theory of Stephen Pepper (1942).[65] In a sophisticated argument, he claims that philosophical positions tend to gravitate toward a finite number of 'world hypotheses' or integrated world-views, and that each of these world hypotheses is in fact generated by a root metaphor, a kind of foundational analogy in terms of which the details of the philosophy are worked out. This is not the place for a general critique of Pepper's interesting theory; but I can show what is wrong with it in resepct of Aristotle, and the problems can be generalized as problems for the root metaphor theory as a whole.

In describing the positions of Plato and Aristotle, Pepper attributes to both of them the root metaphor of Formism, which is the somewhat vague metaphor of resemblance and difference. He suggests that for Plato this is understood by analogy to the crafts, while Aristotle stresses the biological side (pp. 162 f.). From what we have seen, however, Aristotle is just as dependent if not more so than Plato on the craft analogy. Thus it would follow that both Plato and Aristotle use the same version of the same root metaphor. But if this same metaphor can generate such conflicting world-views as those of Plato and Aristotle, those world-views must be radically underdetermined by their root metaphors.

In fact, if my analyses of Aristotle are correct, we find that there are principles which Aristotle holds to prior to his use of analogies, principles such as the One Under Many. One could try to extract a root metaphor from some of these principles, but since we find some significantly different interpretations of the same principles from S_1 to S_2, it appears that the attempt would be doomed to failure. For the principles are so abstract that they can admit of many interpretations. And the point at which analogies come in is not at the level of first principles, but at the level of interpreting those principles. Thus the analogies can serve as models, and if

[65] See ch. 2.1.1.

they become absorbed into the actual theory, as constitutive models. This, I claim, is the role of the craft analogy in Aristotle: it is a constitutive model of the second stage of his philosophy. Thus it is an essential feature of that philosophy, but it is not the sole factor that generates the philosophy, nor is it the ultimate touchstone of its coherence.

11.6.4 Owen and the Platonism of Aristotle

Previously I have defended the general developmental thesis of Owen according to which Aristotle developed from an anti-Platonic position toward a revisionary Platonism. Owen, however, argues for a different path of development from the one I have presented. While his view is not obviously incompatible with my own, it is not obviously compatible either. Accordingly, it will be helpful to compare his own theory of development with TST.[66]

Owen portrays Aristotle as taking an early stand against Plato in his rejection of the unity of science. Plato views dialectic as a master science which holds the principles of all the sciences. Aristotle, by contrast, argues in his earlier works that there is no single sense of being; there are as many senses of being as there are categories, and hence there can be no science of being. Later, however, Aristotle develops the notion of πρὸς ἕν equivocity, or focal meaning, as Owen calls it, by which he is able to overcome his early scruples against a general science of being. For according to the theory of focal meaning, homonymous terms may have a central meaning such that all secondary senses of the term refer to the primary sense, and thus their difference in meaning does not preclude a single account of them. *Met.* iv exploits the theory of focal meaning to introduce the science of being *qua* being. Thus Aristotle's early rejection of a general metaphysics gives way to a pursuit of metaphysics, and Aristotle progresses from an anti-Platonic to a Platonic position.

Owen finds the main evidence for Aristotle's early rejection of a science of being in the *EE*.[67] He argues that the notion of a science of being *qua* being is absent from the *Organon*, and in fact is missing even in the earlier works of the *Met.* In general the difference between the earlier stage without a science of being and the later stage with one cannot be synchronized with my division

[66] Owen's view is presented in Owen (1960), (1965a), cf. (1965c).
[67] (1960: 165 ff.), relying esp. on i. 8, 1217^{b}25–35.

between S_1 and S_2. However, there seems to be no obvious incompatibility between Owen's developmental scheme and TST. Owen's account, nevertheless, seems to have some problems of its own making. For in the first place Owen is compelled to acknowledge that Aristotle had the concept of focal meaning even in the *EE*.[68] This is an awkward datum to have to explain away. Secondly, it is possible to interpret the main piece of evidence for Aristotle's rejection of a science of being as more correctly a rejection of a *single* science of being (i. 8, 1217^b34 f.). It would not follow then that the early Aristotle was anti-metaphysical in a strong sense. Furthermore, one could ask: what is the *Cat.* if not a science of being? It may be that the *Cat.* does not qualify because it does not conform to the principles of the *A.Po.*, but that restriction seems a bit contentious since Aristotle never produced a work that did conform to those principles. Many questions remain unanswered.

Perhaps more serious than these queries is the problem of motivation. Although Owen goes beyond Jaeger in seeing the conflict between Aristotle and Plato as having philosophical rather than psychological causes, he still fails to work out some important details of the story. He presents Aristotle's theory of homonymy as the vehicle for an attack on Plato's concept of a science of being, and to this extent as having a dialectical motivation. But we are left to wonder why he so modified it as to take away its sting, and further to wonder why he so persistently applied it as to undermine his original objection. Perhaps he was led on simply by some new logical insights which he had the intellectual integrity to pursue wherever they led. On the other hand, if he still had serious doubts on other grounds about a unified science of being, the theory of focal meaning would not have been sufficient to silence them. Concerns such as these lead some scholars to question the theory of focal meaning as an explanation of the change to the *Met.* iv position.[69]

In general it is not clear how opposed Aristotle was to a science of being in his early thought and how significant the concept of focal meaning was to a change of viewpoint. And in any case focal

[68] (1960: 169): Aristotle uses the concept at vii. 2, 1236^a17–33. Curiously, Owen (1965a: 127, 130) takes Jaeger to task for supposing that Aristotle's logic and metaphysics could develop quite independently, when his own account makes a similar demand on our credulity.

[69] See problems raised by Dybikowski (1972), Irwin (1977b: 220 n. 14), and Kung (1981).

meaning did not make possible the inquiry into metaphysical questions *per se*, since the early books of the *Metaphysics* antedate the discovery of the science announced in Book iv. Thus I take it that the alleged development to a science of being *qua* being has limited implications for an understanding of Aristotle's development as a whole. On the other hand, if TST is correct, there is a profound development from one system to another such that hardly any feature of the first system remains untouched by the transformation. Thus TST contains a more powerful developmental theory than that of Owen. Moreover, the sense in which TST reveals a return to Platonic principles is more strict than that of Owen's theory to the extent that it is based on an *ontological* comparison rather than a *methodological* one. For TST atrributes the Platonism of Aristotle to Aristotle's postulation of forms, which become the ground of reality for him as Plato's Forms do for Plato. Thus while it is possible that Aristotle develops in the way Owen hypothesizes, the change in viewpoint is not so far-reaching or so clear-cut as that between S_1 and S_2. Aristotle's discovery of matter and his construction of a hylomorphic philosophy deserve to take precedence over the development of a concept of being *qua* being and, as far as I can see, over every other development that has been postulated to date.

11.7 CONCLUSION

I conclude that TST is the best interpretive theory of Aristotle. It faces no insurmountable objections; it has advantages over competing theories in the contexts of biography, history of philosophy, and philosophical motivation; it is more powerful in organizing and exploiting the data as evidence; and it avoids and exposes the difficulties of leading interpretations.

TST has important implications both for systematic and for genetic studies of Aristotle. It entails that studies of Aristotle's system be relativized so as to consider either S_1 or S_2 without reading in distinctions from one system to another. Thus it would rule out discussing the primary substance of the *Categories* as concrete substance, and seeking for a syllogistic demonstration of theorems in the biological works. In the realm of genetic studies it would suggest rethinking the development of Aristotelian theories in terms of their interrelations with Aristotle's two successive metaphysical foundations. If the results were generally positive, it might make it possible to determine further synchronisms in Aristotle's work.

As I have mentioned, I think that much of the better Aristotelian scholarship takes into account the interplay of his system and his development. I hope that the present study will provide a secure foundation for such practices as well as a point of reference for further and more penetrating researches into Aristotle's philosophy. There are no doubt other developments in Aristotle's thought than the hylomorphic turn, and other subsystems worth identifying and exploring. However, I do not think that any development is more significant than the one I have traced, and I do not think that this one can be overlooked without doing violence to Aristotle's philosophy.

What emerges is an Aristotle that is bifurcated into a young philosopher with brilliant logical insights and the energy and organization to work out their implications while astutely applying them to design a priori a programme of scientific research; and a mature philosopher with a powerful and flexible theory which better adapts itself to the more practicable scientific projects which he engages in carrying out. Aristotle's early system was elaborated on a linguistic model that rendered it particularly suitable for generating a logical system of discrete terms in which strict connections could be established. Dependent from the start on the craft model, the later system was less rigorous in its articulation but more flexible in application, pluralistic in its outlook but more powerful in scope, less perspicuous in dealing with phenomena but more penetrating in analysis. The reason for the change of systems was not an altered relation to Plato but a confrontation with a philosophical problem. In solving the problem of substantial change Aristotle revised his metaphysical foundations so thoroughly that he precipitated a changeover to a new philosophy. Although his polemics against Plato increased, his new system was more Platonic in ontology and more Socratic–Platonic in its central model than the old. The late Aristotle wished to integrate his early principles with his later ones, his Aristotelianism with his Platonism. He never succeeded, and he could not have, for the gulf between the systems was a logical one. But in the process of developing his theories he gave us two of the greatest philosophies the world has known.

REFERENCES

Note: Entries marked 'BSS' are reprinted (foreign language articles in English translation) in J. Barnes, M. Schofield, and R. Sorabji, eds., *Articles on Aristotle*, 4 vols., London: Duckworth, 1975–9.

Ackrill, J. L. 1963. *Aristotle's* Categories *and* De Interpretatione. Oxford: Clarendon Press.

Albritton, R. 1957. 'Forms of Particular Substances in Aristotle's *Metaphysics*', *Journal of Philosophy* 54. 699–708.

Allen, R. E. 1969. 'Individual Properties in Aristotle's *Categories*', *Phronesis* 14. 31–9.

Annas, J. 1982. 'Aristotle on Inefficient Causes', *Philosophical Quarterly* 32. 311–26.

Anton, J. and Kustas, G. L., eds. 1971. *Essays in Ancient Greek Philosophy*. Albany: State University of New York Press.

Arnold, U. 1965. *Die Entelechie: Systematik bei Platon und Aristoteles*. Vienna: Verlag R. Oldenbourg.

Ast [Astius], S. F. 1836. *Lexicon Platonicum*. 2 vols. Repr. Bonn: R. Habelt, 1956.

Balme, D. M. 1962. 'Γένος and Εἶδος in Aristotle's Biology', *Classical Quarterly* N.S. 12. 81–98.

—— 1972. *Aristotle's* De Partibus Animalium *I and* De Generatione Animalium *I*. Oxford: Clarendon Press.

Bambrough, R., ed. 1965. *New Essays on Plato and Aristotle*. London: Routledge & Kegan Paul.

Barnes, J. 1969. 'Aristotle's Theory of Demonstration', *Phronesis* 14. 123–52. BSS.

—— 1975. *Aristotle's* Posterior Analytics. Oxford: Clarendon Press.

—— 1981. 'Proof and the Syllogism' in Berti (1981), 17–59.

—— 1982. *The Presocratic Philosophers*. Revised edn. London: Routledge & Kegan Paul.

Berti, E. 1958. 'Genesi e sviluppo della dottrina della potenza e dell'atto in Aristotele', *Studia Patavina* 5. 477–505.

—— 1962. *La filosofia del primo Aristotele*. Padua: CEDAM.

—— 1977. *Dalla dialettica alla filosofia prima*. Padua: CEDAM.

—— ed. 1981. *Aristotle on Science: The* Posterior Analytics. Padua: Editrice Antenore.

Black, M. 1962. *Models and Metaphors*. Ithaca, NY: Cornell University Press.

Blair, G. A. 1967. 'The Meaning of "Energeia" and "Entelecheia" in Aristotle', *International Philosophical Quarterly* 7. 101–17.

Bonitz, H. 1849. *Aristotelis* Metaphysica. Vol. 2. Repr. Hildesheim: Olms, 1960.

Bos, A. P. 1973. *On the Elements of Aristotle's Early Cosmology*. Assen: Van Gorcum.

—— 1975. '*Hylè* in de wijsbegeerte van Aristoteles', *Philosophia Reformata* 40. 47–71.

Bostock, D. 1982. 'Aristotle on the Principles of Change in *Physics* I' in Schofield and Nussbaum (1982), 179–96.

Bradley, F. H. 1897. *Appearance and Reality*. 2nd edn. London: George Allen & Unwin.

Bromberger, S. 1966. 'Why-Questions' in *Mind and Cosmos: Essays in Contemporary Science and Philosophy*, Pittsburgh: University of Pittsburgh Press (University of Pittsburgh Series in Philosophy of Science, vol. 3).

Buck, C. D. and Petersen, W. 1945. *A Reverse Index of Greek Nouns and Adjectives*. Chicago: University of Chicago Press. Repr. Hildesheim: G. Olms, 1970.

Burnyeat, M. F. 1981. 'Aristotle on Understanding Knowledge' in Berti (1981), 97–139.

Bury, J. B. 1932. *The Idea of Progress: An Inquiry into its Origin and Growth*. New York: Macmillan.

Butchvarov, P. 1979. *Being Qua Being: A Study of Identity, Existence and Predication*. Bloomington, Ind.: Indiana University Press.

Cencillo, L. 1958. *HYLE: Origen, conceptos, y funciones de la materia en el Corpus Aristotelicum*. Madrid: Instituto Luís Vives.

Chantraine, P. 1933. *La formation des noms en grec ancien*. Paris: Librairie C. Klincksieck.

Charlton, W. 1970. *Aristotle's* Physics: *Books I and II*. Oxford: Clarendon Press.

—— 1983. 'Prime Matter: A Rejoinder', *Phronesis* 28. 197–211.

Chen, Chung-Hwan. 1958. 'The Relation Between the Terms Ἐνέργεια and Ἐντελέχεια in the Philosophy of Aristotle', *Classical Quarterly* 52. 12–17.

—— 1964. 'Universal Concrete: A Typical Aristotelian Duplication of Reality', *Phronesis* 9. 48–57.

Cherniss, H. 1935a. Review of Werner Jaeger, *Aristotle*, *American Journal of Philology* 56. 261–71.

—— 1935b. *Aristotle's Criticism of Presocratic Philosophy*. Baltimore: Johns Hopkins Press.

—— 1944. *Aristotle's Criticism of Plato and the Academy*. Vol. 1. Baltimore: Johns Hopkins Press.

—— 1945. *The Riddle of the Early Academy*. Berkeley: University of California Press.

—— 1957. 'The Relation of the *Timaeus* to Plato's Later Dialogues', *American Journal of Philology* 78. 225–66.

Chroust, A.-H. 1973. *Aristotle: New Light on his Life and Some of his Lost Works*. 2 vols. London: Routledge & Kegan Paul.

Claghorn, G. S. 1954. *Aristotle's Criticism of Plato's* Timaeus. The Hague: Nijhoff.

Code, A. 1976. 'The Persistence of Aristotelian Matter', *Philosophical Studies* 29. 357–67.

—— 1982. 'The Aporematic Approach to Primary Being in *Metaphysics* Z' (abstract), *Journal of Philosophy* 79. 716–18.

Cohen, S. 1984. 'Aristotle's Doctrine of the Material Substrate', *Philosophical Review* 93. 171–94.

Cooper, J. M. 1981 Review of A. Kenny, *The Aristotelian Ethics*, *Nous* 15. 381–92.

—— 1982. 'Aristotle on Natural Teleology' in Schofield and Nussbaum (1982), 197–222.

Corcoran, J., ed. 1974*a*. *Ancient Logic and its Modern Interpretations*. Dordrecht: Reidel.

—— 1974*b*. 'Aristotle's Natural Deduction System' in Corcoran (1974*a*), 85–131.

—— 1974*c*. 'Aristotelian Syllogisms: Valid Arguments or True Generalized Conditionals?', *Mind* 83. 278–81.

Cornford, F. M. 1907. *Thucydides Mythistoricus*. London: E. Arnold.

—— 1937. *Plato's Cosmology*. London: Kegan Paul, Trench, Trubner & Co.

Cornman, J. W. 1962. 'The Identity of Mind and Body', *Journal of Philosophy* 59. 486–92.

Couloubaritsis, L. 1980. *L'Avènement de la science physique: Essai sur la Physique d'Aristote*. Brussels: Éditions OUSIA.

Cummins, R. 1983. *The Nature of Psychological Explanation*. Cambridge, Mass.: MIT Press.

Dancy, R. M. 1975. 'On Some of Aristotle's First Thoughts About Substances', *Philosophical Review* 84. 338–73.

—— 1978. 'On Some of Aristotle's Second Thoughts About Substances: Matter', *Philosophical Review* 87. 372–413.

Dewey, J. 1933. 'Logic' in *Encyclopedia of the Social Sciences*, New York: Macmillan, 9. 598–603.

Dicks, D. R. 1970. *Early Greek Astronomy to Aristotle*. Ithaca, NY: Cornell University Press.

Diels, H. 1916. 'Etymologica: 3. ʼΕντελέχεια', *Zeitschrift für vergleichende Sprachforschung* 47. 200–3.

Dirlmeier, F. 1962. 'Merkwürdige Zitate in der *Eudemischen Ethik* des Aristoteles', *Sitzungsberichte der Heidelberger Akademie der Wissenschaften*, philosophische-historische Klasse, Nr. 2. Heidelberg: C. Winter.

Dodds, E. R. 1973. *The Ancient Concept of Progress and Other Essays on Greek Literature and Belief*. Oxford: Clarendon Press.

Driscoll, J. A. 1981. '*Εἴδη* in Aristotle's Earlier and Later Theories of Substance' in O'Meara (1981), 129–59.

Düring, I. 1943. *Aristotle*: De Partibus Animalium. Göteborg: Elanders.

—— 1954. 'Problems in Aristotle's *Protrepticus*', *Eranos* 52. 139–71.

—— 1955. Review of Claghorn (1954), *Gnomon* 27. 154–7.

—— 1957. *Aristotle in the Ancient Biographical Tradition*. Göteborg (Studia Graeca et Latina Gothoburgensia 5).

—— 1961. *Aristotle's* Protrepticus: *An Attempt at Reconstruction*. Göteborg (Studia Graeca et Latina Gothoburgensia 12).

—— 1966. *Aristoteles: Darstellung und Interpretation seines Denkens*. Heidelberg: C. Winter.

—— and Owen, G. E. L., eds. 1960. *Aristotle and Plato in the Mid-Fourth Century*. Göteborg (Studia Graeca et Latina Gothoburgensia 11).

Dybikowski, J. C. 1972. 'Professor Owen, Aristotle, and the Third Man Argument', *Mind* NS 81: 445–7.

Dye, J. W. 1978. 'Aristotle's Matter as a Sensible Principle', *International Studies in Philosophy* 10. 59–84.

Edelstein, L. 1967. *The Idea of Progress in Classical Antiquity*. Baltimore: Johns Hopkins Press.

Euken, R. 1869. 'Beiträge zum Verständnis des Aristoteles: Die Etymologien bei Aristoteles', *Neue Jahrbücher für Philologie und Pädagogik* 99. 243–8.

Evans, J. D. G. 1977. *Aristotle's Concept of Dialectic*. Cambridge: Cambridge University Press.

—— 1978. 'Aristotle *Topics* E 5, 135^{a}20–^{b}6: The Ontology of '*Ὁμοιομερῆ*', *Archiv für Geschichte der Philosophie* 60. 284–92.

Fitzgerald, J. J. 1963. ' "Matter" in Nature and the Knowledge of Nature: Aristotle and the Aristotelian Tradition' in McMullin (1963), 79–98.

Frede, D. 1970. *Aristoteles und die 'Seeschlacht'*. Göttingen: Vandenhoek & Ruprecht (*Hypomnemata* 27).

Frede, M. 1978. 'Individuen bei Aristoteles', *Antike und Abendland* 24. 16–39.

—— 1980. 'The Original Notion of Cause' in Schofield, Burnyeat, and Barnes (1980), 217–49.

—— 1981. 'Categories in Aristotle' in O'Meara (1981), 1–24.

Frisk, H. 1973. *Griechisches etymologisches Wörterbuch*. 3 vols. 2nd edn. Heidelberg: C. Winter.

Fritz, K. von. 1931. 'Der Ursprung der aristotelischen Kategorienlehre', *Archiv für Geschichte der Philosophie* 40. 449–96.

—— 1961. 'Der Beginn universalwissenschaftlicher Bestrebung und der Primat der Griechen', *Studium Generale* 14. 546–83, 601–36.

Furth, M. 1978. 'Transtemporal Stability in Aristotelean Substances', *Journal of Philosophy* 75. 624–46.

Gaiser, K. 1985. *Theophrast in Assos*. Heidelberg: C. Winter.

Gaukroger, S. 1978. *Explanatory Structures: A Study of Concepts of Explanation in Early Physics and Philosophy*. Atlantic Highlands, NJ: Humanities Press.

Gillespie, C. M. 1925. 'The Aristotelian Categories', *Classical Quarterly* 19. 75–84. BSS.

Glymour, C. N. 1980. *Theory and Evidence*. Princeton: Princeton University Press.

Gohlke, P. 1924. 'Die Entstehungsgeschichte der naturwissenschaftlichen Schriften des Aristoteles', *Hermes* 59. 274–306.

—— 1954. *Die Entstehung der aristotelischen Prinzipienlehre*. Tübingen: Mohr.

Gomme, A. W. 1945. *A Historical Commentary on Thucydides*. Vol. 1. Oxford: Clarendon Press.

Graham, D. W. 1980. 'States and Performances: Aristotle's Test', *Philosophical Quarterly* 30. 117–30.

—— 1984. 'Aristotle's Discovery of Matter', *Archiv für Geschichte der Philosophie* 66. 37–51.

—— 1986. 'Some Myths About Aristotle's Biological Motivation', *Journal of the History of Ideas* 47. 529–45.

—— 1987. 'The Paradox of Prime Matter', *Journal of the History of Philosophy* 25. 475–90.

—— 1988. 'The Structure of Explanation in the History of Philosophy', *Metaphilosophy* 19. 158–70.

Grene, M. 1963. *A Portrait of Aristotle*. Chicago: University of Chicago Press.

—— 1974. 'Is Genus to Species as Matter to Form?', *Synthese* 28. 51–69.

Guthrie, W. K. C. 1981. *A History of Greek Philosophy*, vol. 6, Cambridge: Cambridge University Press.

Haldane, E. S. and Ross, G. R. T. 1970. *The Philosophical Works of Descartes*, 2 vols. Cambridge: Cambridge University Press.

Hamlyn, D. W. 1968. *Aristotle's De Anima Books II and III*. Oxford: Clarendon Press.

Happ, H. 1971. *HYLE: Studien zum aristotelischen Materiebegriff*. Berlin: W. De Gruyter.

Haring, E. S. 1956–7. 'Substantial Form in Aristotle's *Metaphysics*', *Review of Metaphysics* 10. 308–32, 482–501, 698–713.

Hart, H. L. A. and Honoré, A. M. 1959. *Causation in the Law*. Oxford: Clarendon Press.

Harter, E. D. 1975. 'Aristotle on Primary *Ousia*', *Archiv für Geschichte der Philosophie* 57. 1–20.

Hartman, E. 1976. 'On the Identity of Substance and Essence', *Philosophical Review* 85. 545–61.

—— 1977. *Substance, Body, and Soul*. Princeton: Princeton University Press.

Heath, T. 1921. *A History of Greek Mathematics*. Vol. I. Oxford: Clarendon Press.

Heinaman, R. 1981. 'Non-Substantial Individuals in the *Categories*', *Phronesis* 26. 295–307.

Hesse, M. B. 1965. 'The Explanatory Function of Metaphor' in Y. Bar-Hillel, ed., *Logic, Methodology and Philosophy of Science*, Amsterdam, 249–59. Repr. in Hesse, *Revolutions and Reconstructions in the Philosophy of Science*, Bloomington, Ind.: Indiana University Press, 111–24.

—— 1966. *Models and Analogies in Science*. Notre Dame: Notre Dame University Press.

Hicks, R. D. 1907. *Aristotle*: De Anima. Cambridge: Cambridge University Press.

Hintikka, J. 1967. 'Time, Truth and Knowledge in Ancient Greek Philosophy', *American Philosophical Quarterly* 4. 1–14

—— 1972. 'On the Ingredients of an Aristotelian Science', *Nous* 6. 55–69.

Hirzel, R. 1884. 'Über Entelechie und Endelechie', *Rheinisches Museum* 39. 169–208.

Hocutt, M. 1974. 'Aristotle's Four Becauses', *Philosophy* 49. 385–99.

Huby, P. M. 1962. 'The Date of Aristotle's *Topics*', *Classical Quarterly* 1962. 72–80.

Husik, I. 1904. 'On the *Categories* of Aristotle', *Philosophical Review* 13. 514–28.

—— 1939. 'The Authenticity of Aristotle's *Categories*', *Journal of Philosophy* 36. 427–31.

Irwin, T. 1977a. *Plato's Moral Theory: The Early and Middle Dialogues*. Oxford: Clarendon Press.

—— 1977b. 'Aristotle's Discovery of Metaphysics', *Review of Metaphysics* 31. 210–29.

—— 1982. 'Aristotle's Concept of Signification' in Schofield and Nussbaum (1982), 241–66.

Jacobs, W. 1978. 'Art and Biology in Aristotle', *Paideia*, Special Issue, 16–29.

Jaeger, W. 1923. *Aristoteles: Grundlegung einer Geschichte seiner Entwicklung*. Berlin: Weidmann.

—— 1928. Review of P. Gohlke, *varia*, *Gnomon* 4. 625–37.

—— 1948. *Aristotle: Fundamentals of the History of his Development*. (Trans. of Jaeger 1923 by R. Robinson.) 2nd edn. Oxford: Clarendon Press.

Johnson, W. E. 1921. *Logic: Part I*. Cambridge: Cambridge University Press.

Jones, B. 1972. 'Individuals in Aristotle's *Categories*', *Phronesis* 17. 107–23.

—— 1974. 'Aristotle's Introduction of Matter', *Philosophical Review* 83. 474–500.

Kapp, E. 1931. 'Syllogistik', *Paulys Real-Encyklopädie der classischen Altertumswissenschaft*. Rev. by G. Wissowa. 2nd ser. Stuttgart: A. Druckenmüller, vol. IVA, pt. 1, cols. 1046–67. BSS.

Kenny, A. 1978. *The Aristotelian Ethics: A Study of the Relationship Between the* Eudemian *and the* Nicomachean Ethics *of Aristotle*. Oxford: Clarendon Press.

King, H. R. 1956. 'Aristotle without *Prima Materia*', *Journal of the History of Ideas* 17. 370–89.

Kirkwood, G. 1952. 'Thucydides' Word for "Cause"', *American Journal of Philology* 73. 37–61.

Kneale, W. and M. 1962. *The Development of Logic*. Oxford: Clarendon Press.

Kube, J. 1969. *Τέχνη und 'Αρετή: Sophistiches und platonisches Tudend-wissen*. Berlin: De Gruyter.

Kuhn, T. S. 1970. *The Structure of Scientific Revolutions*. 2nd edn. Chicago: University of Chicago Press.

Kullman, W. 1981. 'Die Funktion der mathematischen Beispiele in Aristoteles' *Analytica Posteriora*' in Berti (1981), 245–70.

Kung, J. 1981. 'Aristotle on Thises, Suches and The Third Man Argument', *Phronesis* 26. 207–47.

Lacey, A. R. 1965a. 'The Eleatics and Aristotle on Some Problems of Change', *Journal of the History of Ideas* 26. 451–68.

—— 1965b. '*Οὐσία* and Form in Aristotle', *Phronesis* 10. 54–69.

Lakatos, I. 1970. 'Falsification and the Methodology of Scientific Research Programmes' in I. Lakatos and A. E. Musgrave, eds., *Criticism and the Growth of Knowledge*, Cambridge: Cambridge University Press, 91–196.

Lear, J. 1980. *Aristotle and Logical Theory.* Cambridge: Cambridge University Press.

Lee, E. N. 1971. 'On the "Gold-Example" in Plato's *Timaeus*' in Anton and Kustas (1971), 219–35.

—— Mourelatos, A. P. D., and Rorty, R., eds. 1973. *Exegesis and Argument: Studies in Greek Philosophy Presented to Gregory Vlastos.* Assen: Van Gorcum (*Phronesis* suppl. vol. 1).

Lee, H. D. P. 1948. 'Place-Names and the Dates of Aristotle's Biological Works', *Classical Quarterly*, 62–7.

—— 1985. 'The Fishes of Lesbos Again' in A. Gotthelf, ed., *Aristotle on Nature and Living Things*, Bristol: Bristol Classical Press, 3–8.

Lehman, H. C. 1953. *Age and Achievement.* Princeton: Princeton University Press, for the American Philosophical Society.

Lesher, J. 1971. 'Aristotle on Form, Substances, and Universals: A Dilemma', *Phronesis* 16. 169–78.

Lloyd, G. E. R. 1961. 'The Development of Aristotle's Theory of the Classification of Animals', *Phronesis* 6. 59–81.

—— 1968. *Aristotle: The Growth and Structure of his Thought.* Cambridge: Cambridge University Press.

—— 1979. *Magic, Reason and Experience: Studies in the Origin and Development of Greek Science.* Cambridge: Cambridge University Press.

Loux, M. J. 1979. 'Fǫrm, Species and Predication in *Metaphysics Z, H,* and *Θ*', *Mind* 88. 1–23.

—— 1984. '*Ousia*: Prolegomena to *Metaphysics Z* and *H*', *History of Philosophy Quarterly* 1. 241–65.

Łukasiewicz, J. 1957. *Aristotle's Syllogistic from the Standpoint of Modern Formal Logic.* 2nd edn. Oxford: Clarendon Press.

Maier, H. 1900*a*. *Die Syllogistik des Aristoteles.* Vol. 2 (2nd half). Tübingen: Verlag der H. Laup'schen Buchhandlung.

—— 1900*b*. 'Die Echtheit der aristotelischen *Hermeneutik*', *Archiv für Geschichte der Philosophie* 13. 23–72.

Mansion, A. 1945. *Introduction à la physique aristotelicienne.* 2nd edn. Paris: J. Vrin.

Mansion, S. 1971. 'Sur la composition ontologique des substances sensibles chez Aristote' in R. B. Palmer and R. Hamerton-Kelly, eds., *Philomathes: Studies and Essays in Humanities in Memory of Philip Merlan*, The Hague: M. Nijhoff. BSS.

Matthews, G. B. and Cohen, S. M. 1968. 'The One and the Many', *Review of Metaphysics* 21. 630–55.

McMullin, E., ed. 1963. *The Concept of Matter in Greek and Medieval Philosophy.* Notre Dame: Notre Dame University Press.

Meyer, H. 1909. *Der Entwicklungsgedanke bei Aristoteles*. Bonn: P. Hansteins Verlagsbuchhandlung.

Modrak, D. 1979. 'Forms, Types, and Tokens in Aristotle's *Metaphysics*', *Journal of the History of Philosophy* 17. 371–81.

Moraux, P. 1973. *Der Aristotelismus bei den Griechen: Von Andronikos bis Alexander von Aphrodisias*. Vol. 1. Berlin: De Gruyter.

Moravcsik, J. M. E. 1967*a*. *Aristotle: A Collection of Critical Essays*. Garden City, NY: Anchor.

—— 1967*b*. 'Aristotle's Theory of Categories' in Moravcsik (1967*a*), 125–45.

—— 1967*c*. 'Aristotle on Predication', *Philosophical Review* 76. 80–96.

—— 1974. 'Aristotle on Adequate Explanations', *Synthese* 28. 3–17.

Mourelatos, A. P. D. 1967. 'Aristotle's "Powers" and Modern Empiricism', *Ratio* 9. 97–104.

—— 1970. *The Route of Parmenides*. New Haven: Yale University Press.

—— 1973. 'Heraclitus, Parmenides, and the Naïve Metaphysics of Things' in Lee, Mourelatos, and Rorty (1973), 16–48.

—— 1976. 'Determinacy and Indeterminacy, Being and Non-Being in the Fragments of Parmenides, *Canadian Journal of Philosophy* suppl. vol. 2. 45–59.

Mueller, I. 1974. 'Greek Mathematics and Greek Logic' in Corcoran (1974*a*), 35–70.

Mure, G. R. G. 1949. 'Aristotle's Doctrine of Secondary Substances', *Mind* 58. 82–3.

—— 1975. 'Cause and Because in Aristotle', *Philosophy* 50. 356–7.

Nagel, E. 1961. *The Structure of Science*. New York: Harcourt, Brace & World.

Norman, R. 1969. 'Aristotle's Philosopher-God', *Phronesis* 14. 63–74. BSS.

Nussbaum, M. C. 1982. 'Saving Aristotle's Appearances' in Schofield and Nussbaum (1982), 267–93.

Nuyens, F. 1948. *L'Évolution de la psychologie d'Aristote*. (Trans. of *Ontwikkelingsmomenten in de zielkunde van Aristoteles*, 1939.) Paris: J. Vrin.

O'Meara, D., ed. 1981. *Studies in Aristotle*. Washington: The Catholic University of America Press.

Owen, G. E. L. 1953. 'The Place of the *Timaeus* in Plato's Dialogues', *Classical Quarterly* N.S. 3. 79–95.

—— 1960. 'Logic and Metaphysics in Some Earlier Works of Aristotle' in Düring and Owen (1960), 163–90. BSS.

—— 1961. '*Τιθέναι τὰ φαινόμενα*' in *Aristote et les problèmes de la méthode*, Louvain: Publications universitaires, 83–103. BSS.

—— 1965*a*. 'The Platonism of Aristotle', *Proceedings of the British Academy* 50. 125–50. BSS.

—— 1965*b*. 'Inherence', *Phronesis* 10. 97–105.

—— 1965*c*. 'Aristotle on the Snares of Ontology' in Bambrough (1965), 69–95.

—— 1971. 'Plato on Not-Being' in Vlastos (1971), 223–67.

—— 1978. 'Particular and General', *Proceedings of the Aristotelian Society* 79. 1–21.

Owens, J. 1951. *The Doctrine of Being in the Aristotelian* Metaphysics. Toronto: Pontifical Institute of Medieval Studies.

—— 1960–1. 'Aristotle on Categories', *Review of Metaphysics* 14. 73–90.

—— 1963. 'Matter and Predication in Aristotle' in McMullin (1963), 99–115.

Patzig, G. 1968. *Aristotle's Theory of the Syllogism*. Trans. by J. Barnes. Dordrecht: D. Reidel.

—— 1981. 'Erkenntnisgründe, Realgründe und Erklärung (zu *Anal. Post.* A 13)', in Berti (1981), 141–56.

Penner, T. 1970. 'Verbs and the Identity of Actions—A Philosophical Exercise in the Interpretation of Aristotle' in O. P. Wood and G. Pitcher, eds., *Ryle: A Collection of Critical Essays*, Garden City, NY: Doubleday, 393–460.

Pepper, S. C. 1942. *World Hypotheses: A Study in Evidence*. Berkeley: University of California Press.

Place, U. T. 1956. 'Is Consciousness a Brain Process?', *British Journal of Psychology* 47. 44–50.

Polansky, R. 1983. 'Aristotle's Treatment of *Ousia* in *Metaphysics* V, 8', *Southern Journal of Philosophy* 21. 57–66.

Preiswerk, A. 1939. *Das Einzelne bei Platon und Aristoteles*. Leipzig: Dieterich'sche Verlagsbuchhandlung (*Philologus* suppl. vol. 32).

Preus, A. 1975. *Science and Philosophy in Aristotle's Biological Works*. New York: Olms.

Quine, W. V. 1960 *Word and Object*. Cambridge, Mass.: Harvard University Press.

Randall, J. H. Jr. 1960. *Aristotle*. New York: Columbia University Press.

Rawlings, H. R. III. 1975. *A Semantic Study of Πρόφασις to 400 BC*. Wiesbaden: Franz Steiner Verlag. (*Hermes* Einzelschriften 33.)

Reale, G. 1962. 'La dottrina aristotelica della potenza, dell'atto, e dell'entelechia nella "Metafisica"' in *Scritti di filosofia e di storia della filosofia in onore di Francesco Olgiati*, Milan: Vita e Pensiero, 145–207.

Rees, D. A. 1960. 'Theories of Soul in the Early Aristotle' in Düring and Owen (1960), 191–200.

Rijk, L. M. de. 1951. 'The Authenticity of Aristotle's *Categories*', *Mnemosyne* 4th ser. 4. 129–59.

Robin, L. 1944. *Aristote*. Paris: Presses universitaires de France.

Robinson, H. M. 1974. 'Prime Matter in Aristotle', *Phronesis* 19. 168–88.

Rorty, R. 1973. 'Genus as Matter: A Reading of *Metaphysics Z–H*' in Lee, Mourelatos, and Rorty (1973), 393–420.

—— 1974. 'Matter as Goo: Comments on Grene's Paper', *Synthese* 28. 71–7.

—— 1979. *Philosophy and the Mirror of Nature*. Princeton: Princeton University Press.

Ross, W. D. 1923. *Aristotle*. London: Methuen.

—— 1924. *Aristotle's* Metaphysics. 2 vols. Oxford: Clarendon Press.

—— 1936. *Aristotle's* Physics. Oxford: Clarendon Press.

—— 1939a. 'The Discovery of the Syllogism', *Philosophical Review* 48. 251–72.

—— 1939b. 'The Authenticity of Aristotle's *Categories*', *Journal of Philosophy* 36. 431–3.

—— 1949. *Aristotle's* Prior *and* Posterior Analytics. Oxford: Clarendon Press.

—— 1951. *Plato's Theory of Ideas*. Oxford: Clarendon Press.

—— 1957. 'The Development of Aristotle's Thought', *Proceedings of the British Academy* 43. 63–78. BSS.

—— 1961. *Aristotle:* De Anima. Oxford: Clarendon Press.

Runner, H. E. 1951. 'The Development of Aristotle Illustrated from the Earliest Books of the *Physics*', Diss., Free University of Amsterdam.

Ryan, E. E. 1973. 'Pure Form in Aristotle', *Phronesis* 18. 209–24.

Ryle, G. 1931. 'Systematically Misleading Expressions', *Proceedings of the Aristotelian Society*, N.S. 32. 139–70.

—— 1949. *The Concept of Mind*. London: Hutchinson.

—— 1953. 'Categories' in A. Flew, ed., *Logic and Language* (Second Series), Oxford: Basil Blackwell, 65–81.

Sachs, D. 1948. 'Does Aristotle Have a Doctrine of Secondary Substances?', *Mind* 57. 221–5.

Ste. Croix, G. E. M. de. 1972: *The Origins of the Peloponnesian War*. London: Duckworth.

Saussure, F. de. 1915/1966. *Course in General Linguistics*. C. Bally and A. Sechehaye, eds., trans. by W. Baskin. New York: McGraw-Hill.

Schofield, M. 1972. '*Metaphysics Z* 3: Some Suggestions', *Phronesis* 17. 97–101.

—— Burnyeat, M., and Barnes, J., eds. 1980. *Doubt and Dogmatism: Studies in Hellenistic Epistemology*. Oxford: Clarendon Press.

—— and Nussbaum, M. C., eds. 1982. *Language and Logos: Studies in Ancient Greek Philosophy Presented to G. E. L. Owen*. Cambridge: Cambridge University Press.

Schwyzer, E. 1959. *Griechische Grammatik*. Vol. 1. 3rd edn. Munich: C. H. Beck. In W. Otto, ed., *Handbuch der Altertumswissenschaft*, div. 2, pt. 1, vol. 1.

Sellars, W. 1957. 'Substance and Form in Aristotle', *Journal of Philosophy* 54. 688–99

—— 1967. 'Aristotle's *Metaphysics*: An Interpretation' in *Philosophical Perspectives*, Springfield, Ill.: Thomas.

Shorey, P. 1924. 'The Origin of the Syllogism', *Classical Philology* 19. 1–19.

—— 1933. 'The Origin of the Syllogism Again', *Classical Philology* 28. 199–204.

Smart, J. J. C . 1959. 'Sensations and Brain Processes', *Philosophical Review* 68. 141–56.

Smeets, A. 1952. *Act en potentie in de Metaphysica van Aristoteles*. Louvain: Leuvense universitaire uitgaven (Université de Louvain Recueil des travaux d'histoire et de philosophie, 3ᵉ série, 49ᵉ fascicule).

Smiley, T. J. 1973. 'What is a Syllogism?', *Journal of Philosophical Logic* 2. 136–54.

Smith, J. A. 1921. '*Τόδε τι* in Aristotle', *Classical Review* 35. 19.

Smith, R. 1982. 'The Syllogism in *Posterior Analytics* I', *Archiv für Geschichte der Philosophie* 64. 114–35.

Smyth, H. W. 1956. *Greek Grammar*. Rev. by G. Messing. Cambridge, Mass.: Harvard University Press.

Sokolowski, R. 1970. 'Matter, Elements and Substance in Aristotle', *Journal of the History of Philosophy* 8. 263–88.

Solmsen, Felix. 1909. *Beiträge zur griechischen Wortforschung*. Vol. 1. Strasburg: K. Trübner.

Solmsen, Friedrich. 1929. *Die Entwicklung der aristotelischen Logik und Rhetorik*. Berlin: Weidmann.

—— 1941. 'The Discovery of the Syllogism', *Philosophical Review* 50. 410–21.

—— 1958. 'Aristotle and Prime Matter', *Journal of the History of Ideas* 19. 243–52.

—— 1960. *Aristotle's System of the Physical World*. Ithaca, NY: Cornell University Press.

—— 1961. 'Aristotle's Word for "Matter"' in S. Prete, ed., *Didascaliae: Studies in Honor of Anselm M. Albareda*, New York: B. M. Rosenthal, 395–408.

—— 1963. 'Nature as Craftsman in Greek Thought', *Journal of the History of Ideas* 24. 473–96.

—— 1978. 'The Fishes of Lesbos and Their Alleged Significance for the Development of Aristotle', *Hermes* 106: 467–84.

Sorabji, R. 1969. 'Aristotle and Oxford Philosophy', *American Philosophical Quarterly* 6. 127–35.

—— 1980. *Necessity, Cause and Blame: Perspectives on Aristotle's Theory*. Ithaca, NY: Cornell University Press.

Stahl, D. E. 1981. 'Stripped Away: Some Contemporary Obscurities Surrounding *Metaphysics Z* 3 (1029^{a}10–26)', *Phronesis* 26. 177–80.

Stallmach, J. 1959. Dynamis *und* Energeia. Meisenheim: A. Hein.

Stocks, J. L. 1933. 'The Composition of Aristotle's Logical Works', *Classical Quarterly* 27. 115–24.

Strawson, P. F. 1959. *Individuals*. London: Methuen.

Tarán, L. 1965. *Parmenides*. Princeton: Princeton University Press.

Thielscher, P. 1948. 'Die relative Chronologie der erhaltenen Schriften des Aristoteles nach den bestimmten Selbstzitaten', *Philologus* 97. 229–65.

Thom, P. 1981. *The Syllogism*. Munich: Philosophia Verlag.

Thompson, D'A. W. 1910. *Aristotle:* Historia Animalium. Oxford: Clarendon Press.

Tonelli, G. 1962. 'Qu'est-ce que la histoire de la philosophie?', *Revue philosophique de la France et de l'étranger* 152. 289–306.

Trendelenburg, A. 1846. *Geschichte der Kategorienlehre*. Berlin (repr. Hildesheim: G. Olms, 1963).

Turgendhat, E. 1958. Τὶ κατὰ τινός: *Eine Untersuchung zu Struktur und Ursprung aristotelischer Grundbegriffe*.Freiburg i.B. and Munich: Karl Alber.

Turnbull, R. G. 1958. 'Aristotle's Debt to the "Natural Philosophy" of the *Phaedo*', *Philosophical Quarterly* 8. 131–43.

van Fraassen, B. C. 1980a. *The Scientific Image*. Oxford: Clarendon Press.

—— 1980b. 'A Re-Examination of Aristotle's Philosophy of Science', *Dialogue* 19. 20–45.

Veatch, H. B. 1974. *Aristotle: A Contemporary Appreciation*. Bloomington, Ind.: Indiana University Press.

Vendler, Z. 1967. *Linguistics in Philosophy*. Ithaca, NY: Cornell University Press.

Verbeke, G. 1960. 'Plutarch and the Development of Aristotle' in Düring and Owen (1960), 236–47.

346   References

Vlastos, G. 1969. 'Reasons and Causes in the *Phaedo*', *Philosophical Review* 78. 291–325.

——, ed. 1971. *Plato I: Metaphysics and Epistemology: A Collection of Critical Essays*. Garden City, NY: Doubleday.

—— 1973. *Platonic Studies*. Princeton: Princeton University Press.

Vogel, C. J. de. 1949. 'Problems concerning Later Platonism I', *Mnemosyne* 4th ser. 2. 197–216.

—— 1960. 'The Legend of the Platonizing Aristotle' in Düring and Owen (1960), 248–56.

Waterlow, S. 1982. *Nature, Change, and Agency in Aristotle's* Physics: *A Philosophical Study*. Oxford: Clarendon Press.

Weil, E. 1951. 'La Place de la logique dans la pensée aristotelicienne', *Revue de métaphysique et de morale* 56. 283–315. BSS.

White, M. J. 1975. 'Genus as Matter in Aristotle?', *International Studies in Philosophy* 7. 41–56.

Wicksteed, P. H. and Cornford, F. M., trans. 1929. *Aristotle:* The Physics, vol. 1. London: Heinemann.

Wieland, W. 1960. 'Das Problem der Prinzipienforschung und die aristotelische Physik', *Kant-Studien* 52. 206–19. BSS.

—— 1962. *Die aristotelische Physik*. Göttingen: Vandenhoek & Ruprecht.

Williams, C. J. F. 1982. *Aristotle:* De Generatione et Corruptione. Oxford: Clarendon Press.

Woods, M. J. 1967. 'Problems in *Metaphysics Z*, Chapter 13' in Moravcsik (1967a), 215–38.

Wundt, M. 1953. *Untersuchungen zur Metaphysik des Aristoteles*. Stuttgart: W. Kohlhammer Verlag.

Zeller, E. 1897. *Aristotle and the Earlier Peripatetics*. 2 vols. Trans. by B. F. C. Costelloe and J. H. Muirhead. London: Longmans, Green & Co.

INDEX LOCORUM

Alexander of Aphrodisias
in A. Pr.
1.3–4.29: 88 n. 3
3.2–4: 88
52.19–25: 42 n. 39, 321 n. 54
53.28–31: 42 n. 39, 321 n. 54
54.21 ff.: 41 n. 37, 321 n. 54
55.21 ff.: 42 n. 39
55.23: 321 n. 54
222.8: 321 n. 54
414.9: 321 n. 54

in Top.
74.29–31: 87

Aristotle
A. Po.
i. 71b9–12: 46
71b17–19: 320
71b20–3: 46
72a8 f.: 39 n. 32
72a16 f.: 47
72a25 ff.: 320
72a29 f.: 161 n. 10
72b18–25: 47, 286 n. 41
73a21–4: 47
73a34–b4: 49
73b4 f.: 49
74b5 f.: 47
75b37–40: 47
76a37 f.: 47
77a5: 95 n. 8
77a5–7: 24 n. 8
77a9: 24 n. 8
77a22: 95 n. 8
79a6–10: 96 n. 10
83a2 ff.: 69 n. 17
83a33: 95 n. 8
83a33–5: 24 n. 8
84a11 f.: 49
84a17–28: 49
86a29: 99 n. 15, 188 n. 14
89b7–9: 88 n. 2
89a20: 96 n. 10
ii. 89b32–5: 277 n. 34
90a9, 12: 135 n. 26
90a14–18: 107

90a16: 97 n. 12
93a24–6: 277 n. 34
93a29 ff.: 50
94a1 ff.: 107
94a20–4: 51, 158
94a28: 163
94a34 ff.: 159
94a36 f.: 163
94b9: 163
94b11: 163 n. 16
94b19–23: 160
94b20: 163 n. 16
94b27 ff.: 162
95b10–12: 298 n. 8
100a7: 24 n. 8
100a12 f.: 82 n. 35

A. Pr.
i. 24a16 f.: 39 n. 32
24b18–20: 41
24b22–4: 42
24b26–30: 32 n. 21
25b32–6a2: 44 n. 44
26a17–28: 44 n. 44
43b3–5: 23
51b36 ff.: 298 n. 10
ii. 67b3, 5: 99 n. 15, 188 n. 14
69a2: 299–300

Cat.
1a14 f.: 40 n. 34
1a6 f.: 254 n. 27
1a27 f.: 28
1b3–9: 28–9
1b4 f.: 25
1b6–9: 25 and n. 9
1b10–15: 33
1b25 ff.: 38, 39 n. 31
2a4–10: 39
2a11–19: 22
2a19–21: 254 n. 27
2a13 f.: 25
2a14–17: 31, 32
2a14–19: 25
2a34–b6: 36
2b15–17: 23
2b22–8: 102

2b37–3a1: 23
3a21–b9: 33 n. 23
3b2–7: 33
3b10–13: 25, 212
3b10–23: 39
3b12: 25 n. 9, 235
3b13–21: 31
3b13–22: 25
3b17: 25
3b24 f.: 146
3b33–4a1: 102
4a10 ff.: 122
4a19: 122
4a23 ff.: 40
6b11 f.: 120 n. 3
6b11–14: 39 n. 31
10a11: 145 n. 36
10a27–32: 40 n. 34
11a20–38: 30 n. 20
11b8–10: 120 n. 3
12a26–31: 97
15a13: 128
15a13–33: 123 n. 8

DA
i. 406b15–22: 264 n. 1
ii. 412a9 f.: 193
412a9–11: 191 n. 19
412a19–21: 60 n. 1, 305 n. 32
412b11–17: 265 n. 4
415b7 ff.: 170
415b7–28: 77
415b9 ff.: 160 n. 5
416b2 f.: 187
417a22–b2: 191 n. 19
417a28 f.: 27
424b3–18: 294 n. 1
iii. 432a1 f.: 178 n. 27

DC
i. 270b19 f.: 320 n. 50
276b29–32: 236
279a17–22: 270 n. 19
iii. 302a6–9: 228 n. 24
303a5 ff.: 277 n. 33
305a25 f.: 270 n. 18
306b16–22: 225 n. 18
312a30–3: 225 n. 18

DI
16a3 ff.: 39 n. 30
16a5–8: 46
16a8: 298 n. 10
16a13 ff.: 39
16a33–b1: 40 n. 34

16b16–18: 40 n. 34
16b26–8: 39
17a2–5: 39
17a5–7: 40
17a8 ff.: 39 n. 32
17a9–11: 39
17a15–22: 40
17a39 f.: 251
17a39–b1: 31
19b24: 97 n. 13
19b31: 298 n. 10
20b26: 298 n. 10
23a7 ff.: 99
23a21–6: 99, 299 n. 11

DS
439b19 ff.: 28 n. 18
446b2–4: 129 n. 18

EE
i. 1217b25–35: 329 n. 67
1217b26–9: 121 n. 5
1217b34 f.: 330
ii. 1219a29 ff.: 190 n. 17
vii. 1236a17–33: 330 n. 68

EN
i. 1094a1–3: 273 n. 27
1094a1–22: 161 n. 9
1094a18–22: 273 n. 27
vi. 1142a12–18: 301 n. 21
vii. 1146b6–8: 256 n. 29
1146b7 f.: 153
1147a11–14: 209
x. 1174a19 ff.: 193
1174a29 ff.: 193
1178b7 ff.: 266 n. 12

Eud.
fr. 6 (Ross): 304
fr. 7: 304 and n. 29, 308 n. 40
fr. 8: 304 n. 30

GA
i. 715a4–18: 77
724a20 ff.: 141 n. 30
730a32–b24: 60 n. 4

GC
i. 314a8–11: 226 n. 19
314b1–4: 226 n. 19
317a32–b35: 127 n. 14
317b8–11: 66 n. 11
317b11–13: 227
317b16–18: 228 n. 24
317b20 ff.: 128 n. 15

317b23–31: 128 n. 16
317b25–31: 138 n. 29
319b2–4: 226 n. 20
319b14 ff.: 228
ii. 329a13–24: 126 n. 13, 309 n. 41
329a24 ff.: 227
329a24–6: 226 n. 20
329a29 f.: 223 n. 15
329b26 f.: 201 n. 34
335b17–23: 108 n. 29

Met.
i. 981a18–20: 119 n. 2
983a24–6: 169
983a24–b1: 77, 119 n. 2
983b6 ff.: 218 n. 9
984a18 f.: 184 n. 4, 209 n. 3
984b9–11: 209 n. 3
984b10 f.: 184 n. 4
985a11 f.: 119 n. 2
985a13 f.: 169 n. 22
986b27–31: 119 n. 2
987a10: 169 n. 22
987a32–b1: 126
987b1–4: 52 n. 56
987b10–14: 273 n. 31
988a8–11: 110 n. 33
988a20–2: 119 n. 2
988a23: 169 n. 22
990b7 f.: 24 n. 8
990b15–17: 271 n. 24
991a8 ff.: 273 n. 30
991a20–2: 273 n. 31
991b3–5: 108 n. 29
992a24 ff.: 108 n. 29
992a24–6: 109
992a24–7: 273 n. 28
992a26–9: 273 n. 31
992a29–b1: 109
992b7–9: 109
992b8 f.: 108 n. 29
993a11 f.: 119 n. 2
993a11–13: 170
993a15: 169 n. 22
iv. 1003b20 f.: 27 n. 14
1005b19 f.: 122
1011b19 f.: 147 n. 41
v. 1013a14–16: 157 n. 2
1013b16–21: 157 n. 2
1016b24–6: 270 n. 16
1016b29–31: 270 n. 16
1017b10–14: 234 n. 1
1017b23–6: 216, 234
1024b32–4: 286 n. 40

vi. 1027a29 f.: 129 n. 20
vii. 1028b2–4: 57
1028b2–7: 211
1028b8–13: 217 n. 8
1028b36 f.: 222
1029a1–5: 222
1029a2 f.: 58
1029a3–5: 241
1029a4: 68
1029a5–7: 223 n. 14
1029a10 f.: 224
1029a20 f.: 63
1029a20–4: 224
1029a20–6: 58
1029a23 f.: 63, 64, 233
1029a26 f.: 68
1029a27–9: 58, 232
1029a30–2: 58, 222, 278
1029a30–b2: 58
1029a32 f.: 60
1029b14: 239
1029b19 f.: 239
1029b24 f.: 121 n. 5
1030a6 f.: 254 n. 27
1030a6–11: 60
1030a6–14: 243
1030a10 f.: 58
1030a11–14: 60
1032a18 f.: 59
1032b1 f.: 243
1032b3–5: 147 n. 41
1032b14: 243 n. 9
1032b15 ff.: 200 n. 30
1033a5 ff.: 70 n. 20
1033a28–b7: 194 n. 23
1033b5–8: 129 n. 21
1033b19 ff.: 237, 238 n. 6
1033b24: 237
1034a5–7: 60 n. 2
1035b4–6: 223, 247 n. 12
1035b27 ff.: 254 n. 27
1035b32: 243 n. 9
1035b34 f.: 254 n. 27
1037a5 f.: 243 n. 9
1037a5–10: 69 n. 15
1037a29 f.: 243 n. 9
1037b2 f.: 60 n. 5
1037b3 f.: 58
1038a5–9: 249, 259
1038a12–15: 247 n. 13
1038a19 f.: 247 n. 14
1038a25 f.: 247 n. 14
1038a28–30: 247 n. 14
1038b10: 252

1038b11–9a11: 253
1038b15: 252
1038b34–9a3: 271 n. 24
1039a1–3: 251
1039a3–5: 248 n. 15
1039a14–23: 254
1039b20–6: 129 n. 19
1040b27 ff.: 234 n. 3
1040b30–4: 273 n. 29
1041a3–5: 248 n. 15, 258
1041b7–9: 258
1041b11–34: 21 n. 3
viii. 1042a6 ff.: 215
1042a8–11: 216 n. 8
1042a12 f.: 216 n. 8
1042a26–9: 234 n. 2, 235 n. 4
1043a4 ff.: 249 n. 17
1043b14–18: 129 n. 19
1043b23–32: 286 n. 40
1044a32–b2: 172
1044a34 f.: 60 n. 4
1044b6 ff.: 109 n. 31
1044b21 f.: 129
1044b21–3: 129 n. 19, 129 n. 21,
    194 n. 23
1045a7 ff.: 259
1045a12–17: 259
1045a14 ff.: 259
1045a23–5: 259
1045a25 ff.: 259
1045a30–3: 259
1045b17–19: 259, 260
ix. 1045b27 ff.: 184
1045b32–6a4: 61 n. 6
1045b34–6a4: 184
1046a4–11: 199
1047a30 f.: 61 n. 7
1047a30–2: 184
1048a30 ff.: 61 n. 6
1048a35–7: 181 n. 2, 201
1048a37–b2: 184
1048a37–b4: 98, 200
1048b3 f.: 192
1048b8: 184, 202
1048b8 f.: 98
1048b9: 192
1048b37 ff.: 193, 228 n. 24
1049a18 ff.: 70 n. 20
1049a25 f.: 223 n. 15
1049a30–b2: 70 n. 21
1050a21 ff.: 184 n. 5
1050a21–3: 185
1050b2 f.: 192

1050a5–11: 195 n. 25
x. 1055 b3 ff.: 146 n. 39
1055b3–29: 147 n. 41
xii. 1069b9–13: 129 n. 17
1070b36–1a2: 235
1071a25: 266 n. 10
1071b12–19: 108 n. 29
1072b1 ff.: 170
1072b2 f.: 272 n. 25
1072b3 ff.: 266 n. 11
1072b13 ff.: 270 n. 19
1072b13–30: 271 n. 21
1072b14 ff.: 266 n. 9
1072b14–30: 266 n. 12
1072b24–26: 272 n. 25
1073a5–7: 266 n. 8
1073a5–11: 270 n. 15
1074a27 f.: 272 n. 25
1074a34 f.: 254 n. 27
1074a35 f.: 266 n. 8, 271 n. 23
1074a35–7: 271 n. 22
1074a36 f.: 266 n. 7, 271 n. 20
1074a38–b14: 209 n. 3
1074b10–13: 320 n. 50
1074b15–35: 271 n. 21
1074b25–7: 266 n. 10
1075a14 f. 272 n. 25
1075b16 f.: 108
xiii. 1077a32–4: 305 n. 32
1077b12–17: 270 n. 17
1079a9: 24 n. 8
1086a32–4: 235
1086b3 f.: 235
1087a16–21: 27 n. 14
xiv. 1090b5–13: 270 n. 16
1092a21 ff.: 141 n. 30
1092a33–5: 119 n. 2

Mtr.
i. 339b27–30: 320 n. 50

PA
i. 641a14–17: 179
643b10–13: 108, 245
643b27 ff.: 245
ii. 646a12 ff.: 59
iv. 687a10, 19–23, b2–4: 178 n. 27

Ph.
i. 186a10 ff.: 132
188a19 ff.: 132
188a30 ff.: 132
189b16–18: 133
189b32–190a13: 134 n. 24

190a13 ff.: 134
190a17–21: 146 n. 40
190a25: 141
190a25 f.: 134 n. 24
190a31–b10: 136 n. 28
190a33 ff.: 135
190b3–5: 60 n. 3
190b5 ff.: 144–5
190b5–9: 136
190b9 f.: 136
190b9–13: 136
190b10–17: 145
190b17–23: 151
190b23–7: 148
190b25: 149
190b27: 145
191a6 f.: 147 n. 41
191a7–12: 148
191a10 f.: 149
191a14: 146
191a24–33: 128 n. 16
191a27–31: 125 n. 12
191a36 ff.: 137
191b9 f.: 138
191b13–17: 139
191b15 f.: 146
191b17 ff.: 139
191b27–9: 193, 204 n. 46
191b35 ff.: 126 n. 13
192a31 f.: 70 n. 19, 72 n. 23, 119 n. 2,
   136 and n. 27, 227 n. 23
ii. 192b21–3: 200
193b3–5: 235 n. 4
194b9: 59
194b23 ff.: 119 n. 2, 166
194b23–33: 73, 76
194b24 f.: 168
194b25: 167
194b26–7: 168
194b33: 167
195a8: 167
195a8–11: 168
195a15 ff.: 75–6, 168
195a15–19: 157 n. 2
195a15–21: 167
195a19–21: 76
195a20 f.: 167
195a32 ff.: 106 n. 26, 119 n. 2
195a32–5: 106 n. 24
195b21 ff.: 106 n. 25
195b25–7: 106 n. 24
198a8–11: 175
198a14–16: 73

198a16 f.: 168
198a19 ff.: 162, 167
198a20 f.: 72, 168
198a24 ff.: 168
198a25–7: 242 n. 8
199a8 f.: 195, 272
iii. 202a17–21: 121
iv. 209b11–13: 309 n. 41
212a20 f.: 270 n. 18
212b7–12: 270 n. 18
212b24 ff.: 270 n. 18
v. 225a12 ff.: 129 n. 17
227b7–11: 28 n. 18
229a25–7: 195 n. 25
vii. 245a12–14: 70 n. 22
245b3 ff.: 134 n. 24
245b6 ff.: 145 n. 37
245b9–12: 70 n. 20
245b12–6a1: 134 n. 24
viii. 267b6–9: 270 n. 14
267b17–26: 270 n. 15

Poet.
1456b20 ff.: 39 n. 29

Pol.
vii. 1325b16–23: 201 n. 31

Protr.
fr. 6 (Ross): 188, 303 n. 27, 305
fr. 8: 320 n. 50
fr. 13: 305 and n. 33
fr. 14: 188, 305

Rh.
i. 1369b33–5: 306 n. 35

SE
167b38: 298 n. 10
169a6: 298 n. 10
178a15–19: 200 n. 29
183b17 ff.: 299
184b1: 299

Top.
i. 101b39: 33
102a18 f.: 34
102b4–9: 27
104b1–3: 88 n. 2
105a19: 186
105b19–25: 88 n. 2
105b25–9: 88 n. 2
106b17, 20: 99 n. 16
ii. 109b22: 97 n. 11
114a10 f.: 97 n. 11
iii. 117a32: 99 n. 18, 188 n. 14

iv. 122b16 f.: 33 n. 23
124a20 f.: 99 n. 17
124a31–4: 99
125b15–19: 99, 188, 190 n. 17
127a20–5: 28 n. 18
128a26 f.: 33 n. 23
v. 129b33 f.: 99 n. 19, 188
135a20–b6: 308 n. 40
vi. 139b20: 129 n. 17
141a10–14: 97
142b30 ff.: 27 n. 14
143b23 ff.: 307 n. 37
143b33–5: 97 n. 11
144a18 ff.: 33 n. 23
146b13–19: 99 n. 20
147b4–17: 97 n. 13
147a6,7: 95 n. 8
147b34 f.: 97 n. 11
148a14–22: 307 n. 37
148a30, 33: 95 n. 9
151b1: 307
vii. 154a16: 186

Cicero
Tusc.
3.28.69: 320 n. 50

Democritus
DK 68 A 37: 277 n. 33
A 104: 264 n. 1

Empedocles
DK 31 B 8: 124–5
B 9: 125
B 12: 124–5
B 16: 124–5
B 23: 125

Eusebius Caesariensis
PE
14.23.3: 277 n. 33

Herodotus
8.26: 186

Iamblichus
Comm. Math.
26: 320 n. 50

Protr.
55.7–56.2: 305 n. 33
56.15–57: 189
58.6–9: 189

Isocrates
Antidosis
258 f., 266: 306 n. 34

Olympiodorus
in Phd.
173.20: 304

Parmenides
DK28 B 2: 124
B 6: 124
B 8.1–4: 124
B 8.4: 219 n. 12
B 8.6: 286 n. 40
B 8.7 ff.: 125 f.
B 8.11: 125 n. 12
B 8.12: 125 f. n. 12
B 8.32 f.: 219 n. 12
B 8.42–9: 219 n. 12
·B 8.50 ff.: 124

Philoponus, J.
in A. Po.
57.19–23: 321 n. 54

in A. Pr.
8.26 ff.: 87
32.31–33.21: 321 n. 54
46.25 ff.: 42 n. 39
47.5: 321 n. 54
48.4 f.: 321 n. 54
75.12: 321 n. 54
270.17: 321 n. 54
387.9–11: 321 n. 54

in DA
144.21 ff.: 308 n. 40
144.24 f.: 304
144.25–30: 305 n. 32

Plato
Crat.
385C: 38 n. 27

Lysis
219D–E: 161 n. 9
220A–B: 161 n. 10

Euth.
280C ff.: 190
281C7 f.: 191

Parm.
130B: 218 n. 10
159B6 f.: 218 n. 10

Phd.
70D ff.: 123 n. 7
71C–D: 98 n. 14
91E–94E: 265 n. 2
97C ff.: 176
99C ff.: 176
100B ff.: 110 n. 33
102B: 40 n. 34
103A–B: 123 n. 7

Phil.
17B6–9: 27 n. 14
26E ff.: 176
27B: 176
31D ff.: 306 n. 35

Rep.
436B8 f.: 122 n. 6
537D: 302 n. 23

Sph.
261E–2A: 38 n. 27

Tim.
49E–52C: 276 n. 32
51E–52C: 176 n. 26
52B: 26 n. 13
64C, D, 65A: 306 n. 35

Plutarch
Mor.
370C: 303 n. 27

Ps.-Isocrates
Ad Demonicum
3: 306 n. 34

Simplicius
in Cat.
20.11 f.: 87

in DA
221.20 ff.: 304

in DC
295.1 ff.: 277 n. 33

in Ph.
28.9 ff.: 277 n. 33
103.15–19: 126 n. 12

Thucydides
I.23.5–6: 175 n. 24

Xenophanes
DK 21 B 23–6: 266 n. 6

SUBJECT INDEX

Absoluteness of Primary Substance (APS), 102 f., 198
Abstractionism (Ab), 83 fig. 3.2
Accidental Predication (AP, AP*), 40 f., 45, 66
accidents, 27 ff., 35, 65 ff., 123
Ackrill, J. L., 28 n. 15, 32 n. 22, 38 n. 27, 45 n. 47, 333
activity, 98 f., 100 fig. 4.2, 201 fig. 7.3, 183 f., 185–92, 194, 196 f.; *see also* ἐνέργεια (EA); κίνησις
Actualism (A), 62, 80 fig. 3.1, 103, 198
actuality, 61, 98 f. and fig. 4.1, 100 fig. 4.2, 183 ff., 201 fig. 7.3; *see also* ἐνέργεια (ES); ἐντελέχεια
αἰτία, 73 f., 163, 165 n. 19, 175 n. 24; *see also* Four Cause Theory
Albritton, R., 250 n. 20, 251 n. 21, 333
Alexander of Aphrodisias, 41 n. 37, 42 n. 39, 87, 88 and n. 3, 321 n. 54
Allen, R. E., 28 n. 15, 333
Anaxagoras, 125, 176
Andronicus of Rhodes, 88
Annas, J., 73 n. 24, 333
Antinomies, 281 ff., 295 f.
Antisthenes, 286 n. 40
Aquinas, T., 187 n. 11, 201 n. 32
Arnold, U., 201 n. 33, 333
Ast, S. F., 218 n. 10
Atomic Substantialism (AS), 36, 54, 81, 84, 274, 308
atomism, 111, 218, 264, 276 f., 287; *see also* Atomic Substantialism; Substantial Atomism
atomism, logical, 21, 277
ἄτομον, 25

Bacon, F., 34, 320 n. 50
Balme, D. M., 100 n. 22, 208 n. 1, 333
Barnes, J., 47 n. 49, 51 n. 54, 73 n. 24, 78 n. 31, 79 n. 32, 115 n. 36, 141 n. 30, 157, 159 n. 4, 160 n. 7, 161 nn. 8 and 10, 294 n. 2, 299 n. 15, 320 f., 333
Because Theory of Causes (BTC), 73–5, 81 fig. 3.1, 164
Berti, E., 117 n. 39, 154 n. 49, 202,

203 f., 204 n. 44, 309 n. 41, 333
biology, 77, 105, 108, 246, 325–7
Black, M., 142 n. 31, 150 n. 47, 333
Blair, G. A., 184 n. 5, 334
Boethius, 44 n. 46
Bonitz, H., 121 n. 5, 147 n. 41, 185 n. 5, 186 n. 8, 202 n. 36, 289 n. 6, 334
Bos, A. P., 116 n. 37, 155 n. 54, 204 n. 47, 308 n. 39, 334
Bostock, D., 133 n. 22, 134 nn. 23 and 24, 136 n. 28, 145 n. 35, 148 nn. 43, 44, and 45, 334
Bradley, F. H., 21, 258, 334
Bromberger, S., 73 n. 24, 334
Buck, C. D., 186 n. 6, 187 n. 10, 334
Burnyeat, M. F., 321 nn. 51 and 53, 334
Bury, J. B., 320 n. 50, 334
Butchvarov, P., 228 n. 25, 334

Campbell, N. R., 142, 334
categories, 21–36, 120 f.
Cencillo, L., 119 n. 1, 334
Change Hypothesis (CH), 117, 153, 156, 177
change, substantial, 96–8, 123 n. 8; *see also* generation
change, theories of, 117, 119–55
Chantraine, P., 186 n. 6, 334
Charlton, W., 73 n. 24, 134 n. 23, 136 n. 27, 224 n. 16
Chen, C.-H., 184 n. 5, 221 n. 13, 334
Cherniss, H., 7 f., 126 n. 12, 147 n. 41, 149 n. 46, 154 nn. 51 and 52, 269 n. 13, 302 n. 23, 334–5
Chroust, A.-H., 303 n. 25, 305 nn. 31 and 33, 335
Cicero, 320 n. 50
Claghorn, G. S., 154 n. 52, 335
Code, A., vii f., 134 n. 24, 136 n. 27, 251 n. 22, 256 n. 28, 335
Cohen, S., 63 n. 8, 224 n. 16, 228 n. 25, 335
Cohen, S. M., 28 n. 15
Cooper, J. M., 190 n. 16, 195 n. 26, 335
Corcoran, J., 42 n. 40, 43 n. 42, 335

Cornford, F. M., 73 n. 24, 163 n. 15, 175 n. 24, 176 n. 26, 335, 346
Cornman, J. W., 241 n. 7, 335
Couloubaritsis, L., 136 n. 27, 154 n. 49, 335
craft analogy; *see* model, craft
Cummins, R., 114 n. 34, 228 n. 24, 335

Dancy, R. M., vii, 117 n. 39, 157 n. 3, 212 n. 5, 224 n. 16, 335
Definability (D), 33, 35, 61, 62, 80 fig. 3.1, 240, 246
Democritus, 264 and n. 1, 276 f. and n. 33, 286
Demonstrative Knowledge (DK), 47 f., 80 fig. 3.1
deprivation, 96–8; *see also* privation; στέρησις
Descartes, R., 34
developmentalism, 3 ff., 113–18, 310–14, 329–31
Dewey, J., 89 n. 6, 335
Dicks, D. R., 273 n. 26, 335
Diels, H., 148 n. 45, 184 n. 5, 186, 335
Dionysius, 277 n. 33
Dirlmeier, F., 320 n. 50, 336
Dodds, E. R., 320 n. 50, 336
Driscoll, J. A., 32 n. 21, 117 n. 39, 336
Düring, I., 87, 88 nn. 2 and 4, 115 n. 35, 153 f., 154 n. 52, 190 n. 15, 203 n. 41, 204 n. 47, 208 n. 1, 209, 298, 298 nn. 9 and 10, 303, 310 f., 312 f., 320 n. 50, 321 n. 52, 336
Duhem, P., 142
Dybikowski, J. C., 330 n. 69, 336
Dye, J. W., 224 n. 16, 228 nn. 24 and 25, 336
δύναμις (DA, DS), 61, 98, 153 f., 183 ff., 199–206; *see also* ἐνέργεια; ἐντελέχεια

Edelstein. L., 320 n. 50, 336
εἶδος, 58, 72, 95, 96 and n. 10, 97, 100 and fig. 4.2, 149, 168, 242; *see also* form; μορφή
Einstein, A., 301
Eleatics, 128 ff., 229 f.
Eleatic principle (E), 128–31
Empedocles, 124 f., 133, 218
ἔνδοξα, 45 n. 47, 216, 219, 257 f., 266, 315, 324
ἐνέργεια (EA, ES), 61, 95, 98–100, 100 fig. 4.2, 153 f., 183 ff., 199–206, 305

ἐνεργεῖν, 98 f., 186, 205 n. 48
energy levels, 191 f., 196 f., 196 fig. 7.1
ἐντελέχεια, 61, 183–5, 192 f., 197 f., 202, 205 n. 48, 266
epistemology, 82 f., 89, 272 f., 286 n. 41
essence (τὸ τί ἦν εἶναι), 33, 49, 51, 60, 72, 76, 159, 167, 221, 231, 233, 239–50, 252–5, 258–60, 271
essential cause, 159 ff., 167 f.
Essential Predication (EP, EP*), 40 f., 45, 66
essentialism (E), 35, 239–41, 246
Euclid, 52
Euken, R., 185, 336
Eusebius Caesariensis, 277 n. 33
Evans, J. D. G., 22 n. 1, 300 n. 18, 308 n. 40, 336
Extension Hypothesis (EH), 85 f., 90–2, 209, 316 f.

first principles, 47, 51 f.
Fitzgerald, J. J., 117 n. 39, 336
form, 58–66, 72, 74–6, 81, 95–8, 108 f., 119, 129 f., 149–51, 173 f., 183, 194 f., 196–8, 233–62, 263–75, 278–87, 303 ff.; *see also* εἶδος; μορφή
Formal Substantialism (FS), 62, 80 fig. 3.1, 240
Formism (F), 61, 80 fig. 3.1
Four Cause Theory (FCT, FCT*), 51, 72–8, 81 fig. 3.1, 105 ff., 108, 110, 156 ff.
Frede, D., 298 n. 10, 299 n. 11, 307 n. 38, 336
Frede, M., 1 f., 25, 28, 30, 74, 117 n., 38, 166 n. 20, 298 n. 9, 336
Frege, G., 301 n. 21
Frisk, H. 185 n. 5, 337
Fritz, K. von, 52 n. 55, 337
Furth, M., 1 f., 85, 337

Gaiser, K., 311 n. 44, 337
Gaukroger, S., 21 n. 1, 36 f., 38 n. 26, 107 n. 27, 315 n. 48, 337
Gauss, K. F., 301 n. 21
generation, 125–31, 133 ff., 141 ff., 194–9
Generation, principle of (G), 128–31
Genetic Explanation (GE), 113
Gillespie, C. M., 45 n. 47, 120 n. 4, 337
Glymour, C. N., 316 n. 49, 317, 337

Gohlke, P., 202 and n. 37, 203 n. 40, 204 n. 47, 337
Gomme, A. W., 175 n. 24, 337
Graham, D. W., 70 n. 18, 98 n. 14, 117 n. 39, 145 n. 35, 148 n. 43, 154 n. 52, 164 n. 18, 193 n. 21, 224 n. 16, 228 n. 25, 296 n. 5, 326 n. 61, 337
Grene, M., 249 n. 16, 326 nn. 59 and 60, 337
Guthrie, W. K. C., 87 n. 1, 203 n. 41, 337

Hamlyn, D. W., 265 n. 5, 337
Happ, H., 119 n. 1, 153 f., 154 nn. 51 and 52, 309 n. 41, 337
Haring, E. S., 251 n. 22, 338
Hart, H. L. A., 165, 338
Harter, E. D., 250 n. 20, 338
Hartman, E., 250 and n. 20, 265 n. 3, 338
Heath, T., 52 n. 55, 338
Heinaman, R., 28 nn. 16 and 18, 338
Heraclitus, 121, 211 and n. 4
Herodotus, 186
Hesse, M. B., 24 n. 6, 142, 144 n. 34, 150 n. 47, 338
ἕξις, 97, 99, 188, 203 n. 43
Hicks, R. D., 265 n. 5, 338
Hintikka, J., 40 n. 33, 48 n. 53, 53 n. 59, 338
Hirzel, R., 184 n. 5, 338
Hocutt, M., 73 n. 24, 74 nn. 25 and 26, 161 n. 11, 163 n. 15, 338
homoeomereity, 308 f.
Honoré, A. M., 165, 338
Huby, P. M., 300, 338
Hume, D., 301 n. 21
Husik, I., 298 n. 9, 300 n. 17, 311 n. 43, 338
ὕλη, 58, 95, 100 fig. 4.2, 145 and n. 35, 148 n. 45, 149, 153, 167, 203 n. 43, 223; see also matter
Hylomorphic Substantialism (HS), 81 f., 84
Hylomorphism (H), 61 f., 75 f., 80 fig. 3.1, 82 f., 91 f., 98, 110 f., 119 ff., 173 f., 176 f., 198, 212 f., 278–80
ὑποκείμενον, 23, 45 f., 96 and n. 10, 145

Iamblichus, 189, 202 f., 320 n. 50
incommensurability, 93–5, 101–3, 110–12, 244
Incommensurability Hypothesis (ICH), 93, 316–17, 318–19
Incompatability Hypothesis (IH), 86 f., 93
Irwin, T., 39 n. 30, 67 n. 12, 312 n. 46, 330 n. 69, 338
Isocrates, 303, 306 n. 34

Jacobs, W., 326 n. 61, 327 nn. 62 and 63, 339
Jaeger, W., 4 ff., 119, 154 n. 48, 187 n. 11, 190, 202, 203 nn. 39 and 40, 300, 302, 308 n. 39, 310 f., 311 n. 44, 312–14, 320 n. 50, 330, 339
Johnson, W. E., 21, 339
Jones, B., 28 n. 15, 134 n. 23, 136 n. 27, 224 n. 16, 339

Kant, I., 64 n. 9, 112, 159, 281, 283, 284 n. 39, 285 f., 325
Kapp, E., 39 n. 32, 52 n. 56, 339
Kenny, A., 190 n. 16, 339
κίνησις, 121 n. 5, 184, 187 ff., 202, 206
King, H. R., 224 n. 16, 339
Kirkwood, G., 175 n. 25, 339
Kneale, W. and M., 44 n. 44, 339
Kripke, S., 301 n. 21
Kube, J., 312 n. 46, 339
Kuhn, T. S., 93 f., 103, 110, 143 n. 33, 182 n. 28, 213 f., 339
Kullman, W., 52 n. 57, 339
Küng, J., 330 n. 69, 339

Lacey, A. R., 221 n. 13, 224 n. 26, 228 n. 25, 251 n. 23, 269 n. 13, 339
Lakatos, I., 182 n. 28, 339
Lear, J., 42 n. 40, 340
Lee, E. N., 154 n. 52, 340
Lee, H. D. P., 311 n. 44, 340
Lehman, H. C., 302, 340
Leibniz, G., 112, 228, 301 n. 21
Lesher, J., 250 n. 19, 251, n. 21, 340
Lloyd, G. E. R., 87 n. 1, 175 n. 24, 208 n. 1, 294 n. 2, 340
Logical Prime Matter (LPM), 225–32, 277, 282, 283
λόγος, 39, 46, 257
Loux, M. J., 211 n. 4, 251 n. 22, 256 n. 28, 258 n. 30, 340
Łukasiewicz, J., 41 nn. 37 and 38, 42 nn. 39 and 40, 89 n. 6, 142 n. 32, 321 n. 55, 340

Maier, H., 39 n. 29, 298 n. 10, 299, 340
Mansion, A., 125 n. 12, 340
Mansion, S., 117 n. 39, 340
Mass Terms (MT), 69–72, 80 fig. 3.1
mathematics, and syllogistic, 52; and
 EH, 92; and shift in terms, 101
matter, 58–66, 68, 72, 75 f., 81, 95–8,
 105, 119, 123 n. 8, 132 ff., 148–50,
 153 f., 173 f., 196 f., 207 ff., 268 f.,
 275–80, 285, 287, 309 n. 41; see also
 ὕλη
Matthews, G. B., 28 n. 15, 340
Melissus, 126 n. 12
Meyer, H., 187 n. 11, 202 n. 39, 340
Middle Term Theory of Cause (MTC),
 49–51, 78, 81 fig. 3.1, 110, 158 f.,
 161 f., 166
Missing Link Theory of Cause (MLC),
 50 f., 78, 81 fig. 3.1, 55, 166, 170
model, craft, 131 ff., 178–81, 327–9
Modrak, D., 251 nn. 24 and 25, 341
Moraux, P., 88 nn. 2 and 4, 341
Moravcsik, J. M. E., 28 n. 15, 38 n. 27,
 45 n. 47, 73 n. 24, 74 n. 27, 163 n. 15,
 341
μορφή, 58, 95 f., 100 fig. 4.2, 149; see
 also form; εἶδος
Mourelatos, A. P. D., x, 26 n. 12, 46 n.
 48, 124 n. 9, 138 n. 29, 200 n. 28, 211
 n. 4, 219 n. 12, 286 n. 40, 322 n. 56,
 341
Mueller, I., 52 and n. 55, 341
Mure, G. R. G., 74 n. 26, 89 n. 6, 341

Nagel, E., 101 and n. 23, 341
Naturalism (N), 26 f., 35, 60 f., 62, 80
 fig. 3.1, 240
Newton, I., 301 n. 21, 325
Norman, R., 266 n. 9, 341
νοῦς, 265 f.
Nussbaum, M. C., 215 n. 7, 341
Nuyens, F., 5, 300 n. 19, 314 n. 47. 341

Ockham, Wm of, 39 n. 29
Olympiodorus, 304
One Under Many (OUM), 24, 68, 131,
 140, 152, 274 f.
Ordinary Language Analysis (OLA),
 164–6, 170
ὄργανον, 85, 87 f.
Organon Hypothesis (OH), 85, 87–90,
 209, 316 f.
οὐσία, 22–4, 211 n. 4, 245, 307

Owen, G. E. L., viii, 10 f., 28 n. 15, 45
 n. 47, 73 n. 24, 79 n. 33, 117 n. 39,
 138 n. 29, 154 n. 52, 215, 251 n. 24,
 256 n. 28, 308 n. 39, 310–12, 314,
 329–31, 341
Owens, J., 117 n. 39, 120 n. 4, 251 n.
 22, 342

Parmenides, 108, 124 ff., 204 n. 44, 219
 and n. 12, 286 n. 40
Pascal, B., 301 n. 21
Patzig, G., 41, 42 n. 40, 43 n. 41, 44 nn.
 44, 45, and 46, 48 n. 52, 342
Penner, T., 193 n. 21, 342
Pepper, S. C., 24, 315 n. 48, 328, 342
Petersen, W., 186 n. 6, 187 n. 10, 334
Philoponus, J., 42 n. 39, 87, 304, 305 n.
 32, 308 n. 40, 321 n. 54
Philosophical Genetic Explanation
 (PGE), 113 f.
Place, U. T., 241 n. 7, 342
Plato, 23 f., 26 n. 13, 27 n. 14, 38 n. 27,
 40 n. 34, 98 n. 14, 108–10, 110 n. 33,
 116 n. 37, 122 n. 6, 123 f. and n. 7,
 126, 132, 154, 161 nn. 9 and 10, 176
 and n. 26, 185, 190 f., 218 and n. 10,
 219, 264 f., 265 n. 2, 274 f., 276 n. 32,
 286 n. 40, 302 n. 23, 303 ff., 306 n.
 35, 310–13, 327
Plutarch, 303 n. 27
Polansky, R., 217 n. 8, 218 n. 11, 342
potentiality, 61, 98 f., 183 ff., esp. 199–
 206 and fig. 7.3; see also activity;
 actuality; δύναμις
power, 200–6; see also δύναμις;
 potentiality
Predication (P, P*), 30, 41, 62–7, 80 fig.
 3.1
Preiswerk, A., 237 n. 5, 342
Preus, A., 311 n. 44, 327 n. 64, 342
Prime Matter (PM), 223–32
privation, 95 f., 100, 123 n. 8, 138 f.,
 146 f., 147 n. 41, 150, 194, 303; see
 also στέρησις
Ps.-Isocrates, 306 n. 34

Quine, W. V., 25, 64 n. 10, 69 n. 16,
 301 n. 21, 342

Randall, J. H., 89 n. 6, 342
Rawlings, H. T. III, 175 n. 24, 342
Reale, G., 184 n. 5, 201 nn. 32 and 33,
 204 nn. 45 and 47, 205 n. 48, 342

Rees, D. A., 304 n. 28
reference, 39, 67–9
Riemannian geometry, 92, 101
Rijk, L. M. de, 311 n. 43, 343
Robin, L., 88 n. 5, 343
Robinson, H. M., 224 n. 16, 343
Rorty, R., 214, 249 n. 16, 343
Ross, W. D., 25 n. 11, 42 n. 39, 47 n.
    49, 52 n. 56, 88 n. 5, 115 nn. 35 and
    36, 119 n. 2, 134 n. 24, 135 n. 25, 145
    n. 35, 148 n. 45, 154 n. 52, 157, 159 n.
    4, 160 n. 6, 161 n. 11, 163, 185 n. 5,
    200, 202, 204 n. 47, 223 n. 14, 234 n.
    1, 235 n. 4, 253 n. 26, 265 n. 5, 270 n.
    19, 272 n. 25, 273 n. 26, 298 n. 10,
    299, 300 and nn. 16 and 20, 301, 305
    n. 32, 309 n. 41, 311 n. 43, 321 n. 55,
    343
Runner, H. E., 204 n. 47. 343
Russell, B., 112, 301
Ryan, E. E., 218 n. 10, 269 n. 13, 343
Ryle, G., 283, 284 n. 39, 343

Sachs, D., 89, 343
Ste. Croix, G. E. M. de, 175 n. 24, 343
Saussure, F. de, 11–14, 114, 343
Schofield, M., 68 n. 13, 229 n. 26, 343
Schwyzer, E., 186 n. 6, 187 n. 9, 344
Scientific Explanation (SE, SE*), 48,
    79, 81 fig. 3.1
Scientific Knowledge (SK), 46 f., 80 fig.
    3.1
Secondary Substantialism (SS), 35, 80
    fig. 3.1, 240
Sellars, W., 250 n. 20, 327 f., 344
Shorey, P., 52 n. 56, 110 n. 33, 299 n.
    14, 344
Simplicius, 87, 126 n. 12, 148 n. 45, 277
    n. 33, 304
Smart, J. J. C., 241 n. 7, 344
Smeets, A., 187 n. 11, 201 n. 32, 203 n.
    39, 344
Smiley, T. J., 42 n. 40, 43 n. 42, 344
Smith, J. A., 25 n. 11, 236, 344
Smith, R., 299 n. 15, 344
Smyth, H. W., 186, 344
Sokolowski, R., 25 n. 11, 63 n. 8, 228 n.
    25, 344
Solmsen, Felix, 186 n. 6, 344
Solmsen, Friedrich, 52 n. 56, 115 n. 35,
    149 n. 46, 154 n. 52, 224 n. 16, 299,
    309 n. 41, 311 n. 44, 327 n. 64, 344

Sorabji, R., 73 n. 24, 100 n. 22, 164 n.
    17, 345
Stahl, D. E., 64 n. 10, 229 n. 26, 283 n.
    38, 345
Stallmach, J., 187 n. 11, 202 n. 37, 203
    n. 43, 345
στέρησις, 95, 96–8, 100 fig. 4.2, 123 n.
    8, 146 f.; see also deprivation;
    privation
Stocks, J. L., 298, 299 n. 13, 345
Stoics, 87 f., 209
Strawson, P. F., 21 n. 4, 25 n. 11, 345
Subject Hypothesis (SH), 117
substance, 22, 25–7, 31, 35 f., 54, 57–
    67, 68 f., 81, 90 f., 99 f., 102 f.,
    110 f., 127–31, 151 f., 196 fig. 7.1,
    197 ff., 206, 210–32, 233–62, 276–89
substance, primary, 24–7, 34, 35 fig.
    2.3, 39, 58, 199, 263 f., 275–81, 285–
    8
Substantial Atomism (SA), 35, 80 fig.
    3.1, 91 f., 128–30, 155, 252–4
Substantialism (S, S*), 35, 61, 80 fig.
    3.1, 247, 249
Substantival Reference (SR, SR*), 39,
    67–9, 80 fig. 3.1
syllogism, 41–56, 107, 158–61, 320–2
Syllogistic Theory of Arguments
    (STA), 42 ff., 80 fig. 3.1

Tarán, L., 125–6 n. 12, 219 n. 12, 345
teleology, 147 f., 184 f., 195 f., 273
Theophrastus, 277 n. 33, 311 n. 44
Thielscher, P., 298 n. 6, 345
Thom, P., 43 n. 42, 345
Thompson, D'A. W., 311 n. 44. 345
Thucydides, 175 and nn. 24 and 25, 176
tie, Said-of, In, 21–3, 40, 41 n. 36, 218;
    form–matter, accident–composite,
    66 f.
τόδε τι, 25, 58, 212, 217, 219, 235–8,
    250, 283
Tonelli, G., 325 n. 58, 345
Trendelenburg, A., 40 n. 34, 45 n. 47,
    345
Tugendhat, E., 23, 25 n. 11, 345
Turnbull, R. G., 116 n. 37, 345
Two Systems Hypothesis (TSH), 15 ff.,
    158
Two Systems Theory (TST), 16

unitarianism, 3 ff., 208 f.; see also
    Extension Hypothesis; Organon
    Hypothesis

Universalism (U), 83 fig. 3.2
Unmoved Mover (UM), 170, 268–74

Van Fraassen, B. C., 73 n. 24, 166 n. 20, 345
Variability of Concrete Substance (VCS), 103, 197–9
Veatch, H. B., 324 n. 57, 345
Vendler, Z., 192 n. 20, 345
Verbeke, G., 306 n. 35, 345
Vlastos, G., x, 32, 73 n. 24, 110 n. 33, 163 n. 15, 165 n. 19, 346
Vogel, G. J. de, 154 n. 50, 310 n. 42, 346

Waterlow, S., 132 f., 134 n. 23, 136 n. 27, 141 n. 30, 346
Weil, E., 300 n. 18, 346
White, M. J., 249 n. 16, 346

Wians, W., 322 n. 56
Wicksteed, P. H., 73 n. 24, 163 n. 15, 346
Wieland, W., 73 n. 24, 134 nn. 23 and 24, 145 n. 35, 146 n. 38, 147 n. 42, 148 n. 43, 163 n. 15, 346
Williams, C. J. F., 224 n. 16, 346
Wisdom (W), 77 f., 80 fig. 3.1, 105, 109, 169, 180
Wittgenstein, L., 30, 44–5, 64 n. 10, 112, 287
Woodruff, P., x
Woods, M. J., 250, 251 n. 25, 346
Wundt, M., 202 nn. 35 and 37, 203 nn. 40 and 42, 302 n. 24, 346

Xenophanes, 266 f. and n. 6

Zeller, E., 298 n. 10, 346

The Promise of

Cognitive Psychology

A Series of Books in Psychology

Editors: Richard C. Atkinson
Gardner Lindzey
Jonathan Freedman
Richard C. Thompson

The Promise of
Cognitive Psychology

Richard E. Mayer
UNIVERSITY OF CALIFORNIA, SANTA BARBARA

W. H. FREEMAN AND COMPANY
San Francisco

Project Editor: Judith Wilson

Copy Editor: Sean Cotter

Designer: Sharon H. Smith

Production Coordinator: William Murdock

Illustration Coordinator: Cheryl Nufer

Artist: Ron Newcomer

Compositor: Composition, etc.

Printer and Binder: The Maple-Vail Book Manufacturing Group

Library of Congress Cataloging in Publication Data

Mayer, Richard E   1947-
    The promise of cognitive psychology.

    (Series of books in psychology)
    Includes bibliographical references and index.
    1. Cognition.   I. Title.
BF311.M427   153.4   80-39997
ISBN 0-7167-1275-X
ISBN 0-7167-1276-8 (pbk.)

Dedicated to Beverly, Kenny, and Davey

Contents

Preface   ix

Note to the Reader   xiii

1   Introduction to Cognitive Psychology   1
   Definition of Cognitive Psychology   1
   Three Psychologies   2
   History of Cognitive Psychology   5
   The Tools of Cognitive Psychology   10
   Suggested Readings   14

2   The Information Processing System   15
   The Ability Problem   15
   The Traditional Approach   17
   The Cognitive Approach   23
   Examples of the Cognitive Approach   27
   Applying What You've Learned   35
   Further Applications of the Information Processing Model   36
   Suggested Readings   38

3   Cognitive Process Models   40
   The Procedural Skill Problem   40
   The Traditional Approach   41
   The Cognitive Approach   43
   Examples of the Cognitive Approach   47
   Applying What You've Learned   55
   Further Applications of Cognitive Models   58
   Suggested Readings   59

4   **Cognitive Structure Models   60**
The Verbal Knowledge Problem   60
The Traditional Approach   60
The Cognitive Approach   62
Examples of the Cognitive Approach   68
Applying What You've Learned   75
Further Applications of Structure Models   78
Suggested Readings   80

5   **Cognitive Strategy Models   82**
The Strategy Problem   82
The Traditional Approach   83
The Cognitive Approach   85
Examples of the Cognitive Approach   93
Applying What You've Learned   101
Further Applications of Strategy Models   103
Suggested Readings   106

References   108

Index   117

Preface

This book is intended to serve as a brief introduction to the major themes in cognitive psychology. It describes each of the major analytic tools that have been developed during the last few decades and shows how they can be applied to practical problems that are familiar to the reader. Instead of trying to survey and condense the research currently going on in cognitive psychology, I have provided representative examples of experimental and theoretical work in several key areas.

Readers need not have any previous background in experimental psychology. This book is intended as an adjunct text for courses in introductory psychology; for example, it can be used as a counterbalance for short books on behaviorism such as Skinner's *About Behaviorism* (1974), often used in such courses. It can also be used as an adjunct text for courses in topics such as human learning and memory, cognitive psychology, educational psychology, or problem solving. The general reader who is interested in learning more about the cognitive revolution in psychology will also find it useful.

There is encouraging evidence that the cognitive revolution, born in the late 1950s and early 1960s, has matured greatly during the 1970s. Early works such as *A Study of Thinking* (Bruner, Goodnow, and Austin, 1956), *Plans and the Structure of Behavior* (Miller, Galanter, and Pribram, 1960), and *Cognitive Psychology* (Neisser, 1967) set a tone and a direction that have recently produced some exciting advances. During the past decade there has been a virtual explosion both in the amount of new information and in the sophistication of our explanations of the mechanisms of human learning, memory, and cognition. One of the most significant departures from earlier work in cognitive psychology is that psychologists have become interested in explaining human learning, memory, and cognition within real-world domains. This book, therefore, briefly describes the newly developed cognitive analysis techniques and shows how they can be applied to several real-world problems.

The book is organized into five chapters. The first chapter provides a general overview and history of the cognitive approach to psychology. Each of the subsequent four chapters describes one of the major analytic tools of cognitive psychology, and is organized in the following way:

Problem. First, some familiar problem is presented, such as the question of what is involved in verbal ability tests (Chapter 2), solving arithmetic problems (Chapter 3), reading a story (Chapter 4), or solving algebra equations (Chapter 5).

Traditional Approach. Second, the traditional psychological approach to the problem is presented for the purpose of comparison with the cognitive approach.

Cognitive Approach. Third, the appropriate cognitive tool is described in some detail, including the information processing model (Chapter 2), the process model (Chapter 3), the structure model (Chapter 4), and the means–ends strategy analysis (Chapter 5).

Examples of the Cognitive Approach. The fourth section of each chapter demonstrates how the cognitive tool can be applied to a particular problem. Special care was taken to use examples that are familiar and at the same time demonstrate the advances that can be made using the cognitive approach. These include applying the information processing model to the study of ability (Chapter 2), using process models to describe arithmetic performance (Chapter 3), using structure models to describe reading comprehension performance (Chapter 4), and using means–ends analysis models to describe algebraic problem solving (Chapter 5).

Applying What You've Learned. The fifth section in each chapter gives you a chance to try your model-building expertise so that you can make sure you understand the main ideas presented.

Further Applications. Finally, each chapter closes with some comments concerning future trends and possible extensions of ideas presented in the chapter.

• • •

This book took shape during my sabbatical leave at the Learning Research and Development Center (LRDC), University of Pittsburgh. I am grateful for the hospitality and stimulating atmosphere provided at LRDC by Jim Greeno, Bob Glaser, Lauren Resnick, Jim Voss, Michi Chi, Paul Feltovich, Joan Heller, Mary Riley, Sherm Tyler, and many others. I also appreciated the many useful conversations with Jill Larkin and her colleagues at Carnegie-Mellon University. While these people cannot be held responsible for any shortcomings in this book, it does seem appropriate that this book evolved in Pittsburgh, which has produced much of the pioneering work in cognitive psychology. Finally, I would like to thank my parents, James and Bernis Mayer, and my brothers, Robert and Bernie Mayer, for their much appreciated encouragement; and Beverly, Kenny, and Davey for putting up with me while I worked on this project.

October 1980   Richard E. Mayer

Note to the Reader

In my role as psychology teacher, or as conversationalist at a cocktail party, or even at family gatherings, I am often in the position of having to answer the question, "Exactly what is cognitive psychology?" I find that many people believe psychology consists mainly of putting little white laboratory rats into mazes and putting neurotic people on the therapist's couch. For example, at the beginning of each term I like to ask my introductory psychology class to indicate who they already know in psychology. Almost everyone recognizes the names "Freud" and "Skinner"; however, these are usually the only universally recognized names in psychology.

The purpose of this little book, then, is to introduce a third approach to psychology—cognitive psychology. Even if you already know something about the behaviorist and Freudian theories, you will probably be interested in learning about the cognitive approach as well. Cognitive psychology deserves your attention for several reasons, which I will outline briefly.

Widespread. First, the cognitive approach has become so widespread that it is now a dominant theme in modern psychology. It has had an impact on a wide range of topics in psychology, including how we store and process information, how we form friendships and prejudices, how we think and reason, and how we respond to reinforcement. You cannot have a complete and accurate view of modern psychology without some basic knowledge of cognitive psychology.

Current. Second, cognitive psychology is relatively new, having taken hold only within the last 10 or 20 years. Since it is much newer than either the behaviorist or psychoanalytic approaches, the cognitive approach represents a fresh viewpoint in modern psychology.

Promising. Third, because it offers a new perspective, a way of looking at human behavior from the inside, cognitive psychology offers some promise of furthering psychology both as a science and as a means of promoting human welfare. It has already changed the way we look at questions like: What is intelligence? How do we learn when we read? How do children learn arithmetic? Why are some people good problem solvers? This book focuses primarily on the promising tools and techniques in cognitive psychology that can be applied to these kinds of practical problems.

The Promise of
Cognitive Psychology

1 Introduction to Cognitive Psychology

DEFINITION OF COGNITIVE PSYCHOLOGY

What is cognitive psychology? If you asked several different psychologists this question, you probably would not always get the same answer. Some might try to describe how cognitive psychology is different from other approaches such as the behaviorist or psychoanalytic approaches. Some might emphasize the topics that cognitive psychologists generally study, such as human memory, perception, problem solving, learning, and so forth. Some might emphasize the general theoretical framework that underlies cognitive psychology. This framework—called the information processing model—views all humans as active processors of information; it will be discussed in detail in Chapter 2.

In spite of these conflicting answers to the simple question "What is cognitive psychology?" I think most psychologists would agree on the following very general definition: *Cognitive psychology is the scientific analysis of human mental processes and memory structures in order to understand human behavior.* Let's examine each component of this definition in turn.

Scientific analysis. The first part of the definition refers to the "how" of cognitive psychology. Only the methods of science may be used. This means, for example, that the data we use must be public—any reasonable person should be able to find the same data by following the same procedure. Thus, your own intuitions and feelings about how your mind works are not acceptable bases for cognitive psychology unless you can formulate a prediction that is directly observable by others. This makes the task of cognitive psychology quite indirect—we cannot observe private mental events but can only infer them from someone's behavior. Thus, cognitive psychologists must devise scientific methods to observe mental life indirectly. The principal tools of cognitive psychology involve precise analytic techniques for breaking mental activities down into measurable parts. These tools will be outlined at the end of this chapter.

Mental processes and structures. This part of the definition concerns the "what" of cognitive psychology. The object of study is human mental life. Cognitive psychology studies what is going on inside a person's head when he or she is performing some task —that is, mental processes—and the way a person stores knowledge and uses it in performing some task—that is, mental structures.

Understanding human behavior. The final part of the definition concerns the "why" of cognitive psychology. The goal of cognitive psychology is to produce a clear and accurate description of internal cognitive events and knowledge so that we can better predict and understand human behavior. For example, we study the processes underlying arithmetic problem solving so that eventually we can better predict and understand why some children succeed and some fail in learning simple arithmetic.

THREE PSYCHOLOGIES

It will help you put cognitive psychology into perspective if you assume that there are really many different approaches to psychology. Although this section will focus on three major approaches, you may acquaint yourself with other schools in psychology by referring to the Suggested Readings at the end of this chapter. This section will examine behaviorism (as represented by Skinner), psychoanalytic theory (as represented by Freud), and cognitivism (the subject of this book). In order to understand cognitive psychology you should have some idea how it differs from the alternative approaches.

In the previous section it was noted that cognitive psychology has the following characteristics: Its subject matter is human mental or rational activity; its methods involve the scientific analysis of mental structures and processes; and its goal is the understanding of human behavior.

Let's see how behaviorism stands on each of these three points. First, like cognitive psychology, behaviorism has as its goal the understanding of human behavior. However, unlike cognitive psychology, there is no attempt to understand the internal processes that underly behavior. Second, like cognitive psychology, behaviorism is committed to the rigorous methods of science. However, it must be noted that the particular techniques used in cognitive psychology differ from those used in behaviorist approaches. Third, the major difference between behaviorism and cognitivism concerns the question of what should be the subject matter of psychology. Behaviorists (Skinner, 1953) argue that since internal mental events cannot be directly observed they can never be the legitimate objects of scientific study. Thus the subject matter of psychology must be restricted to what can be directly observed—behavior. Theories about unseen and unseeable mechanisms supposedly underlying behavior have no place because these mental processes and structures cannot be directly observed. According to behaviorists, in order for psychology to be a rigorous, useful. science it must use scientific methods to develop laws of behavior.

The cognitive approach differs from behaviorism mainly on the issue of whether or not it is useful to study mental processes and structures that cannot be directly seen. The cognitive response to the behaviorist position is not that it is wrong, but rather that it is too limiting and restricting. In order to fully understand human behavior it is necessary to understand the mechanisms that underlie behavior. Cognitive theories must be subjected to rigorous testing and changed when the predictions of a theory don't match the actual behavior. However, cognitive theories do have a place in psychology as long as they are stated in a way that allows for some direct, observable test. For example, if the behaviorist approach were applied to other sciences, like chemistry and physics, there could be no theory of atomic structure. Some of the entities making up an atom cannot be seen, yet a theory of atoms can make useful predictions. The same can be said for a germ theory of disease, since germs had not yet been observed at the time of the invention of the germ theory.

Now, let's see how the psychoanalytic approach compares with the others. First, the goal is the same as in cognitive psychology and behaviorism: to understand human behavior. Second, like the behaviorists and cognitivists, the psychoanalytic approach often purports to use scientific methods. However, many criticisms have centered on the claim that the psychoanalytic approach has not yet developed methods of sufficient rigor and power, and that consequently it must often resort to nonscientific methods (like intuition, clinical judgment, or untestable dogma). Third, the major difference between the psychoanalytic approach and the other approaches concerns what should be the subject matter of psychology. Like the cognitive approach, this approach emphasizes the study of internal mechanisms that underlie behavior; however, while cognitive psychologists tend to study the rational or intellectual side of mental life, the psychoanalytic approach emphasizes internal feelings, emotions, and desires. These are very much more difficult to study than the rational side of human mental life, and the necessary analytic techniques have yet to be developed.

Box 1.1 summarizes the similarities and differences among the three psychologies described in this section. They all purport, with varying degrees of success, to use scientific methods and to have as a goal the understanding of human behavior. They differ with respect to the particular tools they use and the subject matter they use the tools on. The behaviorists focus on well-controlled studies of human behavior, the cognitivists study the processes and structures that make up the rational, intellectual side of mental life, and the psychoanalysts focus on the irrational, emotional side of mental life. Certainly, a complete psychology of humans requires that all three components—behavior, cognition, and affect—be clearly understood and related to one another. Hopefully, as psychology progresses, the best features of each approach will be blended into a unified science.

	Uses scientific methods	Goal is to understand human behavior	Research focus on
Behaviorism	Yes (well established)	Yes	Behavior
Cognitivism	Yes (newly established)	Yes	Cognition
Psychoanalytic approach	Sometimes (not yet well established)	Yes	Affect

Box 1.1   Comparison of Three Psychologies

HISTORY OF COGNITIVE PSYCHOLOGY

A complete history of cognitive psychology is beyond the scope of this book. The Suggested Readings at the end of this chapter will help provide you with more detail. However, a summary of the ideas that have led up to the cognitive revolution in psychology will help you understand some of the apparently peculiar arguments and theories you might read about in psychology texts, and will help you appreciate why psychologists are doing the work they are doing today.

Wilhelm Wundt is generally cited as the founder of scientific psychology, and he certainly had a strong influence on the field for a generation or more. When Wundt established a psychology lab at the University of Leipzig in 1879, he also established an approach to psychology called structuralism. It was called structuralism because its goal was to study and analyze all the various parts of human consciousness. Wundt argued strongly that the new science of psychology must use the methods of science. However, the technique that he and his students relied on turned out to be a rather poor one. They used the method of introspection—trained introspectionists would carefully describe what went on inside their heads as they performed some task.

The method of introspection was open to so much abuse that it provoked a very strong reaction, especially in America. By the early 1900s a new movement was taking hold as a reaction against Wundt's structuralism. This movement, called behaviorism under the leadership of John Watson in America, became the dominant force in psychology by 1920, and like structuralism it held on for 30 years. Behaviorists claimed that the methods and subject matter of psychology had to be changed if it was to become a strong and respected science. The method of introspection was out; more rigorous and carefully controlled laboratory studies were in. The subject matter of consciousness was out because it was too nebulous; only behavior was considered the appropriate subject matter of psychology, since only behavior was directly observable. In retrospect, it appears that the behaviorists were certainly correct in emphasizing rigorous methods but perhaps were overzealous in ruling out the study of mental events.

A second reaction against Wundt's structuralism developed mainly in Europe at about the same time that behaviorism came to dominate American psychology. This reaction was called gestalt psychology. Unlike behaviorism, gestalt psychology kept mental processes and structures as the subject matter of psychology; however, like behaviorism it attempted to use rigorous scientific methods more powerful than introspection. Unfortunately, the rigorous tools of scientific analysis were just not available to gestalt psychologists, and eventually their failure to develop precise theories and methods, coupled with the freezing effects of Nazism in Europe, put an end to gestalt psychology. Many psychologists see gestalt psychology as a forerunner of cognitive psychology. The gestalt psychologists asked many of the same questions that cognitive psychologists ask today; however, today we like to think that we have the tools to answer at least some of them successfully.

Finally, a third major approach to psychology began to develop in Europe, mainly as a branch of medical science. In the early 1900s the problem of mental illness was finally being subjected to scientific analysis, and Freud's work in the early 1900s came to dominate the field. Freud's view was truly revolutionary, for he argued that human behavior—and he was especially interested in abnormal behavior—was caused by something that had happened to the patient. This is called the medical model because a mental illness was thought to have a locatable cause, just as physical illness does. Freud's work led to the development of psychoanalytic theory, which attempts to describe the mechanisms underlying human feelings and emotion. While many alternative theories and therapeutic techniques have come and gone since Freud's time, psychology is still seeking to understand the affective side of human beings.

By 1950 or so, the time was right for a change. The hold of behaviorism on American psychology was finally weakening after a 30-year reign. Gestalt psychology and psychoanalytic theory had been torn apart by the upheaval in Europe. The new electronic age was coming, bringing with it a device that would profoundly influence psychology—the computer.

By the late 1950s psychology was being influenced by ideas from at least three sources. First, the impact of the computer was beginning to be felt. Computers could do many of the things that humans did—learn, store, manipulate, and remember information as well as use language, solve problems, and reason. Papers like "Elements of a Theory of Human Problem Solving" (Newell, Shaw, and Simon, 1958) paved the way for recasting old psychological problems in terms of modern computer analogies. Interest in internal processes and structures was again legitimate, since they could be specified precisely in terms of a computer program. Second, in the field of linguistics there was a growing shift away from behaviorist theories of language and toward an analysis of the structures underlying comprehension and production of utterances. This shift was spearheaded by *Syntactic Structures* (Chomsky, 1957), a book that provided for a cognitive analysis of language behavior. A third force involved the growing impact of the work of Piaget (1954). Piaget focused on the growth of internal structures and processes that underlie developmental changes in human behavior. Thus in the computer (or artificial intelligence) approach of Simon, the psycholinguistic approach of Chomsky, and the biological approach of Piaget there was converging interest and success in describing internal cognitive processes and structures.

Even in traditional areas of psychology, the late 1950s were sprinkled with new and powerful ideas. In 1956 Bruner, Goodnow, and Austin provided a cognitive interpretation of the strategies involved in concept learning in a volume entitled *A Study of Thinking*. In the same year, Miller published a landmark paper, "The Magic Number Seven, Plus or Minus Two," which encouraged the development of the information processing model presented in Chapter 2.

In 1960 a book appeared called *Plans and the Structure of Behavior*, by Miller, Galanter, and Pribram. It offered a cognitive alternative to stimulus–response (S–R) behaviorism, and the cognitive revolution was called into action. The main idea in the book was that there were two ways of looking at behavior: (1) The S–R behaviorist approach was to say the unit of behavior is the stimulus–response association. In other words, each situation is associated with a response (or many responses). (2) The alternative approach was to say that the unit of behavior is a plan— a system for generating behavior similar to the feedback loops used in computers. In other words, behavior is generated by a set of mental processes and tests on the environment rather than specifically tied to an environmental stimulus. The human thus is transformed from a passive responder to stimuli into an active processor of information.

By 1967 there was enough research literature for Neisser to produce a well-integrated textbook called *Cognitive Psychology*. Thus, the first successful textbook on cognitive psychology not only built on the theoretical framework of Miller, Galanter, and Pribram (1960) but also provided an integrated summary of actual research. The theoretical contribution of Neisser's book was to posit a general information processing model consisting of a series of distinct memory stores and processes (see Chapter 2 for a further discussion of this model). The research contribution of Neisser's book was to show that it was possible to study internal mental processes using the precise tools of cognitive psychology. While Neisser dealt mainly with research on perception—the main interest of the structuralists and gestaltists, by the way—he also provided a framework for cognitive research in all areas of psychology.

By 1970 there was enough research going on in cognitive psychology that a journal with this name could be established and supported. But work in this area was not confined to one small journal or one small research area. During the 1970s the cognitive revolution came to influence all branches of psychology. What is new and interesting in many areas of psychology today is the application of the new techniques of cognitive psychology to old problems.

For example, in human experimental psychology the cognitive approach has come to dominate the way we understand how humans perceive, learn, remember, and reason. In developmental psychology the cognitive development of humans has become a major theme. Following the pioneering work of Jean Piaget, developmental psychologists have increasingly studied the changes in cognitive processes and cognitive representation of knowledge that occur with growth. In social and personality research, the concept of attribution has been a strong influence on recent research. Attribution refers to the cognitive process of trying to justify one's social behavior or that of someone else. Even in the traditional stronghold of behaviorism—animal learning —new work is progressing in the study of cognitive and memory processes in laboratory animals.

The history of cognitive psychology is summarized in Box 1.2. We can now return to the beginning of this brief history. As you may recall Wundt, in founding psychology, sought for his new science a better understanding of internal cognitive processes such as consciousness and attempted to analyze mental life into its parts. In these respects, cognitive psychology has returned to the origins of psychology. The gestaltists attempted to develop further the study of mental processes and structures; they asked fascinating questions about the nature of mental life but were never able to give fully satisfactory answers. Cognitive psychology has returned to many of these questions, with the hope that now—armed with better tools and years of experience— psychology may at last be able to come to grips with the issues that brought it into being. We still do not know whether this latest attempt to study the mechanisms underlying human behavior will succeed. There are promising signs that it has achieved much progress, and examples are given in the following chapters. As

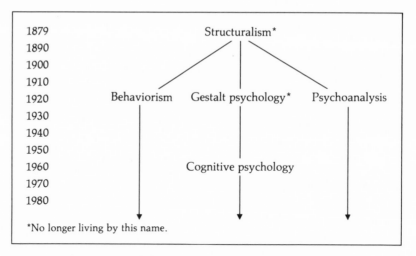

Box 1.2   Summary of the History of Cognitive Psychology

you read these chapters you may think of psychology as returning to the questions posed by the structuralists and the gestaltists, but with one difference—we come equipped with analytic tools that have taken a century to develop. These tools will be described in the next section.

THE TOOLS OF COGNITIVE PSYCHOLOGY

As the previous section suggests, there is an interesting sense in which ideas circulate in psychology until we have the tools to deal with them. Certainly, modern cognitive psychology owes a debt to Wundt for his interest in human mental life. Yet he and his students, while they asked interesting questions, simply lacked the tools to test their ideas adequately. Similarly, cognitive psychology owes a debt to the gestaltists, who formulated many of the most interesting theories and questions in psychology concerning human mental life. Yet, like the structuralists, the gestaltists offered only vague theories and lacked the precise analytic tools to progress. Cognitive psychology even owes a debt to its two rivals—the behaviorist and psychoanalytic approaches—

because they provide constant reminders of what yet needs to be done. Certainly, cognitive psychology must eventually be able to go beyond theories of rational cognitive processes and incorporate the irrational, affective side of human life; and it cannot lose sight of the demand of the behaviorists for a true science based on scientific observation and testable theories.

What are the tools of cognitive psychology that allowed a successful rebirth of interest in cognitive processes? In this book, I will emphasize four major new tools. Each will be briefly described below.

Analysis of the information processing system. The first main tool is what can be called the "information processing model." This model is based on the idea that humans are processors of information: information comes in through our sense receptors, we apply a mental operation to it and thus change it, we apply another operation and change it again, and so on, until we have an output ready to be stored in memory or used to generate some behavior. The information processing model concerns the series of cognitive operations (or processes) that a person uses in a given situation, or to put it another way, the various organizations of information as it progresses through the system. As you may see, this model is based partly on a computer analogy. Humans are like computers in the sense that both can take information, operate on it, and generate some appropriate response. Thus, since computers can do many of the things that humans can do, we can describe the processes that go on inside the human mind in the same terms we use to describe the processes that go on inside the computer. There are certainly some problems with this analogy; for example, it ignores the fact that humans are alive, trying to survive, and full of emotions and feelings as well as intellect. However, put aside your reservations for a moment and first try to understand the information processing framework as described in Chapter 2. You will see what this tool is and how it can be applied to a recurrent issue in psychology—the nature of human intellectual abilities. After reading the next chapter you will be in a better position to judge for yourself whether the cognitive approach helps explain human mental life and behavior.

Analysis of cognitive processes. In addition to the general information processing model, there are more specific techniques for representing what is going on in a person's head while he or she is performing a given task. For example, what is the procedure children have in their heads when they finally learn long division? They have acquired some procedural knowledge that they did not have before. Cognitive psychology provides techniques for analyzing precisely what that new knowledge might be. In general, the analytic technique involves choosing an intellectual task like solving a long division problem, carefully observing and questioning how a person solves it, analyzing the process into small parts consisting of processes (things are manipulated) and decisions (a test is made), then testing the process model that is produced against the actual behavior of a human. The process model that is generated for a given task (like solving long division problems) may be written as a computer program or as a flow chart or in some other way. The techniques for producing a process model to represent someone's cognitive processes for a task and for testing the process model are laid out in Chapter 3. In particular, Chapter 3 shows how to analyze the cognitive processes involved in arithmetic and how to describe the knowledge that a person has in terms of a precise process model.

Analysis of cognitive structures. The previous paragraph introduced the idea of developing a process model to represent a person's procedural knowledge—knowledge about how to do something such as an arithmetic procedure. Another type of knowledge that can be represented using the analytic techniques of cognitive psychology is verbal knowledge—knowledge about some topic, such as a story. Techniques exist for representing the knowledge that a person has when he or she knows a story or some other piece of information. In general, these analytic techniques involve choosing some piece of information, presenting it to the subject as a passage to be read or listened to, then asking questions about the information such as asking the subject to recall it. The information is analyzed into its major parts and the relations between parts. This structure model can then be compared to the actual performance of the subject. The structure model that is created for a given passage may be represented as a tree diagram or as a network or in some other way. The techniques for specifying what people know when they know some verbal information are spelled out in Chapter 4. In particular, Chapter 4 shows how to analyze the cognitive structure acquired when a person learns a story and how to describe this knowledge as a precise structure model.

Analysis of strategies. So far we have mentioned techniques for analyzing the working of the general information processing system, for analyzing procedural knowledge into process models, and for analyzing verbal knowledge into structure models. The fourth major tool of cognitive psychology involves the investigation of techniques people use to control the various pieces of knowledge they have; such techniques are known as cognitive strategies. For example, consider the solution of an algebra problem, like "John drove 20 miles and used 2 gallons of gas. What was his gas mileage?" To answer this you need some verbal knowledge—namely, that mileage equals miles driven divided by the amount of gas used—some procedural knowledge—namely, how to divide—and an information processing system for holding the knowledge. However, in addition, you need a plan of attack, a strategy to help you achieve your goal. In general, cognitive psychologists have attempted to discover the strategies people use by giving them complex problems, asking them to describe their thinking process aloud, trying to develop a precise statement of the strategy (or heuristic) being used, and then testing the strategy model against actual human performance. One common strategy model is called means–ends analysis—a procedure that involves setting subgoals and then trying to find the means to achieve them. Means–ends analysis is more carefully described in Chapter 5, where it is applied to the task of solving algebra problems.

● ● ●

The remainder of this book describes each of the major tools of cognitive psychology in detail and provides examples of how these tools have been applied to real-world situations like reading and arithmetic. It is not intended to provide a broad survey of all the research results and theories in cognitive psychology, but rather to outline the major ideas in this new and exciting area. As you read the following chapters, your goal should simply be to get some idea of what the four cognitive tools are and to see whether or not you think they can be successfully applied to real situations.

SUGGESTED READINGS

Hilgard, E. R., and G. H. Bower. *Theories of learning.* Englewood Cliffs, N.J.: Prentice-Hall, 1980. An introduction to over a dozen major approaches to the study of human learning and behavior.

Humphrey, G. *Thinking: An introduction to its experimental psychology.* New York: Wiley, 1963. An excellent summary of the historical ideas and findings underlying modern cognitive psychology.

Mandler, J. M., and G. Mandler. *Thinking: From associationism to Gestalt.* New York: Wiley, 1964. A set of condensed readings from early studies in the psychology of cognition.

2 The Information Processing System

THE ABILITY PROBLEM

You have probably taken your share of standardized tests during the course of your school career. For example, you have probably taken one like the Scholastic Aptitude Test (SAT), which measures verbal and quantitative abilities and gives a score for each. To refresh your memory, read the passage given in Box 2.1 and then try to answer the questions. This type of test is typical of the items you would find on a standardized test of verbal ability.

Many of us are quick to accept these scores as evidence that we are "smart" or "dumb" in some ability. However, the question posed in this chapter is simply, what are the psychological mechanisms that allow one person to score high on tests of ability (such as that shown in Box 2.1) and another person to score low? These questions form the core of what can be called the *ability problem* —the problem of determining the differences in the cognitive system between people who differ in certain abilities.

People often make assessments of ability. For example, suppose someone told you that "Sue is a mathematical whiz" or "Tom knows everything about English." These sorts of assessments make sense because they tell us what performance to expect from Sue when she works on mathematical tasks or from Tom when he works on verbal tasks. You might translate these comments to mean that Sue has high mathematical ability or Tom has high verbal ability. However, the problem facing psychologists is to determine exactly what Tom has in his head that allows him to perform well on verbal tasks or what Sue has in her head that

Record your starting time: Hour _____ Minute _____ Second _____

The essential trick of the Renaissance pastoral poem, which was felt to imply a beautiful relation between rich and poor, was to make simple people express strong feelings in learned and fashionable language. From seeing elements of the two sorts of people combined like this the reader thought better of both; the best parts of each were used. The effect was in some degree to combine in the reader or the author the merits of the two sorts; he was made to mirror in himself more completely the effective elements of the society in which he lived. This was not a process that had to be explained in the course of writing pastoral poems; it was already shown in the clash between style and subject, and to make the clash work in the right way the writer had to keep up a firm pretense that he was unconscious of it.

The usual process for putting further meanings into the pastoral situation was to insist that the shepherds were rulers of sheep and so compare them to politicians or bishops or what not; this piled the heroic convention onto the pastoral one since the hero was another symbol of his whole society. Such a pretense, no doubt, made the characters unreal, but not the feelings expressed or even the situation (as opposed to the setting) described. The same pretense is often valuable in modern writing.

Which of the following is LEAST likely to be found in a Renaissance pastoral?

(a) Serious intent   (d) Elegance of expression
(b) The heroic convention   (e) Accurate depiction of social structures
(c) Symbolism

In lines 14–16 the author finds it necessary to oppose the situation to the setting because

(a) in pastoral poetry a possibly real situation is conveyed by unreal characters in unreal scenes
(b) setting and situation are natural opposites
(c) the addition of the heroic convention makes the pastoral setting an absurd situation
(d) situation and setting are the same in modern writing
(e) in pastoral poetry the pretense makes the setting even more real than the situation

The author would say that of the following the LEAST artificial element in pastoral poetry is the

(a) heroic convention   (d) underlying emotion
(b) characterization   (e) pastoral convention
(c) level of language

Record your stopping time: Hour _____ Minute _____ Second _____

Source: Adapted from *Principles of Educational and Psychological Testing,* second edition, by Frederick G. Brown. Copyright © 1970 by the Dryden Press Inc. Copyright © by Holt, Rinehart and Winston. Reprinted by permission of Holt, Rinehart and Winston.

Answers: (E), (A), and (D).

Box 2.1   A Reading Comprehension Test

allows her to perform well on mathematical tasks. Again, these problems are at the core of the ability problem.

Finally, suppose you were a school teacher interested in individualizing instruction for your students. In order to be a more effective teacher it would be useful if you knew something about the abilities each student is bringing to your class. How do you find out what a student's abilities or experiences are? In general, this problem has been solved by administering standardized tests to children and then translating their performance into scores for each measured ability. But as a skeptical teacher you might not be satisfied with a list of test scores for various nebulous ability categories. Such information is not very specific and does not really pinpoint what a child's capabilities are. They are, instead, very gross measures. You might therefore ask, what are the particular features of my student's cognitive system that permit a good performance in tests of one ability but a poor performance in tests of another? Again, this is the ability problem, and this chapter will show how cognitive psychologists have attempted to deal with it.

THE TRADITIONAL APPROACH

Very early in the development of psychology, an important observation was made: People differ from one another. They differ in the way they react to certain situations, in the way they interact with other people, in the things they like and dislike, and so on. This observation led to the factor (or trait) theory of human behavior—the idea that certain definable factors or traits underlie human behavior and that each person can be described as scoring at some level on each trait. This was not a particularly novel idea, since philosophers had dealt with the problem of traits for centuries. However, psychologists developed a field called psychometrics to answer the questions of (1) what are the major traits and (2) how can they best be measured? Thus, what had once been a philosophical question turned out to be a problem of how to develop testing techniques.

The first breakthrough came near the turn of this century when Alfred Binet was asked to design a test that would predict success in French schools (see Wolf, 1973). Binet's method of measuring intellectual ability was quite straightforward. First, he selected test items that involved common tasks that children of a given age group could perform, such as reciting the days of the week or making change (see Box 2.2). He then determined which tasks could be performed by the average child in each age group. Next, in order to measure the intellectual ability of a child, Binet noted whether or not the child was able to succeed on tasks that other children of that age group could succeed on; if the child could not, then the score would be below average; but if the child could go on and perform tasks that older children knew then the score would be above average. Finally, the test scores were compared to actual academic performance (such as grades). Test items that were not predictive of school success were dropped from the tests. Binet's test was so successful in predicting school performance that by the 1920s it became the basis for intelligence tests used in America and around the world. Thus, it is clear that from the beginning the measurement of intellectual ability has been validated by comparing test scores to success in schools.

Binet's work showed that it was possible to produce instruments for measuring important abilities. The psychometric (or testing) field of psychology now needed to face the issue of determining the major human traits. In order to solve this problem, new statistical tools were developed that freed psychology from the rhetoric of philosophy and allowed a means of determining the key factors underlying intellectual performance. One of the major statistical inventions was called factor analysis. The general procedure was to give a large number of different types of tests to a large group of people. Then factor analysis techniques were used to determine which tests seemed to be related to one another. For example, if people who scored high on test A also scored high on test B (and people who scored low on test A also scored low on test B, and so on), it could be concluded that test A and test B were really measuring the same single factor.

Spearman (1904; 1927) used factor analysis techniques to show that all tests of intellectual ability were related to one another, although not perfectly. In other words, if you scored high on one you would be likely to score high on others. Thus Spearman pro-

Age two

1. Three-hole Form Board. Placing three geometric objects in form board.
2. Delayed Response. Identifying placement of hidden object after 10-second delay.
3. Identifying Parts of the Body. Pointing out features on paper doll.
4. Block Building Tower. Building four-block tower by imitating examiner's procedure.
5. Picture Vocabulary. Naming common objects from pictures.
6. Word Combinations. Spontaneous combination of two words.

Age six

1. Vocabulary. Correctly defining 6 words on 45-word list.
2. Differences. Telling difference between two objects.
3. Mutilated Pictures. Pointing out missing part of pictured object.
4. Number Concepts. Counting number of blocks in a pile.
5. Opposite Analogies II. Items of form "Summer is hot; winter is _____."
6. Maze Tracing. Finding shortest path in simple maze.

Age ten

1. Vocabulary. Correctly defining 11 words on same list.
2. Block Counting. Counting number of cubes in three-dimensional picture, some cubes hidden.
3. Abstract Words I. Definition of abstract adverbs.
4. Finding Reasons I. Giving reasons for laws or preferences.
5. Word Naming. Naming as many words as possible in one minute.
6. Repeating Six Digits. Repeating six digits in order.

Average adult

1. Vocabulary. Correctly defining 20 words.
2. Ingenuity I. Algebraic word problems involving mental manipulation of volumes.
3. Differences between Abstract Words. Differentiating between two related abstract words.
4. Arithmetical Reasoning. Word problems involving simple computations.
5. Proverbs I. Giving meaning of proverbs.
6. Orientation: Direction II. Finding orientation after a verbal series of changes in directions.
7. Essential Differences. Giving principal difference between two related concepts.
8. Abstract Words III. Meanings of abstract adverbs.

Source: Adapted from *Principles of Educational and Psychological Testing*, second edition, by Frederick G. Brown. Copyright © 1970 by the Dryden Press Inc. Copyright © by Holt, Rinehart and Winston. Reprinted by permission of Holt, Rinehart and Winston.

Box 2.2 Typical Test Items on the Stanford–Binet Test

claimed the "two-factor theory" of intellectual ability—the idea that there is one factor for general intelligence (which he called *g*) and many smaller factors that are specific to individual tests (which he called *s*). Thus, your performance on a test was jointly determined by your general ability plus your specific abilities for the particular type of test.

Later, Thurstone (1938) modified the factor analysis technique and found that all tests of intellectual ability could be grouped into seven primary mental abilities: verbal comprehension, number, memory, perceptual speed, space, verbal fluency, and inductive reasoning. Thus, where Spearman found one primary ability (*g*), Thurstone found seven abilities worthy of measurement.

Finally, Guilford (1959; 1967) developed a system for specifying 120 separate mental abilities. His theory, called structure of the intellect, was not based on factor analysis but rather on a logical analysis of the factors involved in mental functioning. As shown in Box 2.3, he categorized all mental abilities within a framework consisting of three dimensions: the operations that are required in the task, the products of the mental operations, and the specific content of the problem. Since there are 5 operations, 6 products, and 4 contents, there are $5 \times 6 \times 4$ or 120 possible categories of mental abilities. Tests have been found that measure most of Guilford's 120 factors, but there are still no tests for several of them. Box 2.3 shows some examples of the tests corresponding to several factors in this system.

The theories of Spearman, Thurstone, and Guilford demonstrate the problems in locating the major human factors. However, if the psychometricians had trouble in defining factors, they certainly had less trouble in measuring a factor once it was defined. While there are many ways to define a good test, most psychometricians would include the following criteria:

Reliable. The test should result in the same score each time one person takes a version of it.

Valid. The test should measure what it says it is measuring. For example, a test of general intelligence should be able to predict school success.

Objective. The test should be easy to score and should result in the same score regardless of who scores it.

Structure of the Intellect

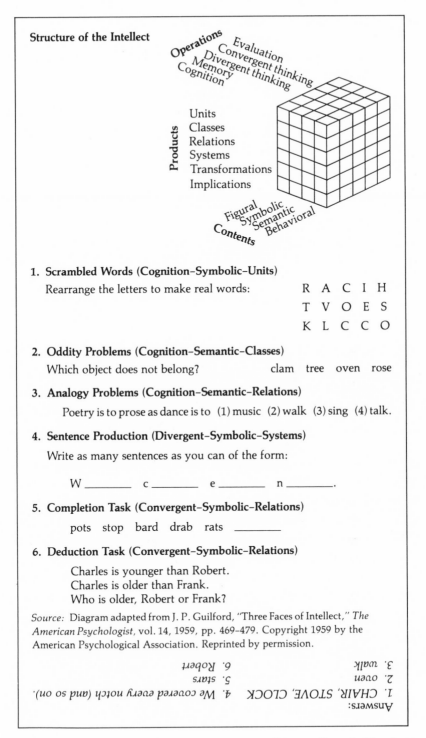

1. **Scrambled Words (Cognition–Symbolic–Units)**

   Rearrange the letters to make real words: R A C I H

   T V O E S

   K L C C O

2. **Oddity Problems (Cognition–Semantic–Classes)**

   Which object does not belong? clam tree oven rose

3. **Analogy Problems (Cognition–Semantic–Relations)**

   Poetry is to prose as dance is to (1) music (2) walk (3) sing (4) talk.

4. **Sentence Production (Divergent–Symbolic–Systems)**

   Write as many sentences as you can of the form:

   W _____ c _____ e _____ n _____.

5. **Completion Task (Convergent–Symbolic–Relations)**

   pots stop bard drab rats _____

6. **Deduction Task (Convergent–Symbolic–Relations)**

   Charles is younger than Robert.
   Charles is older than Frank.
   Who is older, Robert or Frank?

Source: Diagram adapted from J. P. Guilford, "Three Faces of Intellect," *The American Psychologist*, vol. 14, 1959, pp. 469–479. Copyright 1959 by the American Psychological Association. Reprinted by permission.

Answers:

1. CHAIR, STOVE, CLOCK   4. *We covered every notch (and so on).*

2. *oven*   5. *stars*

3. *walk*   6. *Robert*

Box 2.3   Guilford's 120 Mental Factors and Some Sample Test Items

1. Select test items.
2. Determine measurement standards.
3. Administer test to a large sample.
4. Compare test scores to real-world performance of sample. If test is highly predictive, stop. If some of the test items are not predictive, eliminate them and go back to step 1.

Box 2.4   Procedure for Developing a Test

Standard. The test should be given to a large population so that it is possible to tell where a given score stands compared to all others from that population.

Tests that are to varying degrees reliable, valid, objective, and standardized have been developed for many factors (see Buros, 1972, for a listing of existing tests).

The psychometric approach is a scientific approach to the ability problem outlined at the beginning of this chapter. In a sense, it is a self-correcting procedure. If you want a test that will distinguish between students who will do well in learning to read and those who will not, you develop a test, administer it to people, observe whether it predicts performance, change items in the test that don't predict, and so on. This procedure is summarized in Box 2.4. (Further information can be obtained from the Suggested Readings at the end of this chapter.)

By this point, it should be clear that the technology of testing is well established. However, there is something left unfulfilled by the accomplishments of the psychometric approach. The psychometricians were much better at measuring factors than at defining them. For example, Box 2.5 shows that a person's response to a stimulus situation is supposed to be determined by scores for one or more relevant factors; for verbal ability, the relevant factors underlying performance are the ability to use proper grammar, the ability to spell, the ability to retain information from a short passage, and the ability to recognize definitions of words. As you can see, there was not much theoretical work aimed at describing *why* someone who scored high on a certain test would probably

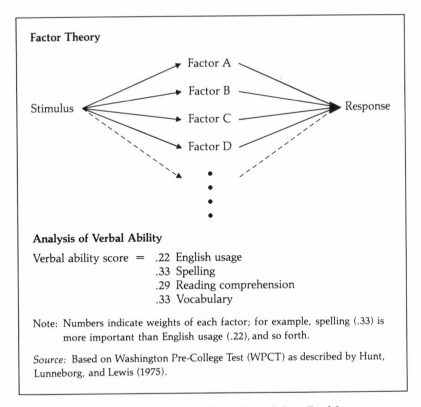

Factor Theory

Stimulus → Factor A, Factor B, Factor C, Factor D → Response

Analysis of Verbal Ability

Verbal ability score = .22 English usage
.33 Spelling
.29 Reading comprehension
.33 Vocabulary

Note: Numbers indicate weights of each factor; for example, spelling (.33) is more important than English usage (.22), and so forth.

Source: Based on Washington Pre-College Test (WPCT) as described by Hunt, Lunneborg, and Lewis (1975).

Box 2.5   Psychometric Approach to the Ability Problem

do well in some future task. The statistical tools allowed the development of measurement instruments, but it was not until the last ten years or so that the tools of cognitive psychology have been applied to the issue of what ability tests measure.

THE COGNITIVE APPROACH

The psychometric approach succeeded in its goals of locating and measuring traits, but it did not really tell us as much as we would like to know about the mechanisms underlying them. The psychometric approach never really developed a strong theoretical basis; it was, apparently, easier to measure abilities than to define or understand them. This is where cognitive psychology can help.

The cognitive tool that is most useful for solving the ability problem is the general information processing model. The main idea is that all humans come equipped with the same basic information processing system (IPS), as shown in Box 2.6. The main components of the information processing system are:

Short-term sensory store (STSS). Information coming in from the outside world impinges on our sense receptors. It is first held in an STSS (also called a sensory buffer by some theorists). This store holds information in its raw physical form exactly as presented. It can hold everything that was presented (unlimited capacity), but information fades very rapidly (rapid time decay). There may be a different STSS for each sense. For example, the STSS for visual information can be thought of as a snapshot that is exact, complete, and fades within a half second.

Short-term memory (STM). If attention is paid to the information in STSS before it fades away, some of it may be transferred to STM. This store may convert the raw sensory information into another modality, such as changing visually presented letters into sounds. The holding capacity of STM is limited to about seven items (limited capacity), although clever chunking techniques can increase the power of STM. Items are lost from STM when they are bumped out by new incoming items or when they are not actively rehearsed. STM can be thought of as conscious memory— it holds all that a person can be aware of at one time.

Working memory (WM). Many theorists add an appendage to short-term memory called working memory or intermediate term memory. Like STM, this memory has limited capacity, stores information in a form other than raw sensation, and forgets due to overloading or failure to rehearse. You can think of working memory as a scratch pad on which you perform conscious mental operations such as mental arithmetic.

Long-term memory (LTM). If information is held in short-term memory, there are encoding processes that allow it to be transferred to long-term memory. Long-term memory, like STSS, is unlimited in capacity, so it can hold vast amounts of information. But unlike STSS, LTM does not fade with time; however, items are lost because new information blocks the routes for retrieval of information from LTM. You can think of LTM as an organized storehouse of information, in which each item must be found by following a search path.

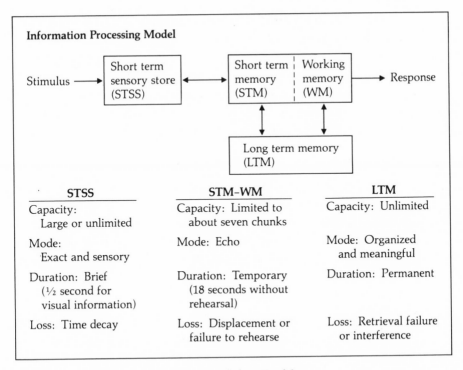

Box 2.6   Cognitive Approach to Ability Problem

Some of the main control processes in the information processing system are

Attention. Transferring information from STSS to STM.

Rehearsal. Keeping information active in consciousness in STM or WM.

Chunking. Techniques for clustering information in STM.

Operations in WM. Manipulating information in working memory.

Encoding. Transferring information from STM to LTM.

Searching LTM. Finding a target item in LTM.

The components and processes discussed above and illustrated in Box 2.6 represent a typical description of the information processing system, although different theorists may use slightly different arrangements. It is beyond the scope of this book to

document the case for the existence of each component and process listed above, but this chapter will attempt to show how this
model can be applied to problems in psychology. (See Lindsay
and Norman, 1977, for a discussion of the IPS.)

Let's assume that all humans possess the same general IPS
system consisting of STSS, STM, LTM, attention processes for
getting information from STSS to STM, rehearsal and chunking
processes for holding information in STM, encoding processes for
getting information from STM to LTM, and search processes for
finding a target in LTM. However, let's suppose that humans
differ with respect to the character and size of each memory store
and control process. For example, some people may be faster in
searching LTM than other people; some people may be able to
hold more information in STM at a time than other people; some
people may have better attentional strategies for getting information into STM before it fades away; and so on.

As an example, let's consider some of the differences that might
be important for reading and verbal processing. For example, the
speed with which one can find a target in long-term memory is
important, since the decoding of letters and words requires such a
search. Hunt, Lunneborg, and Lewis (1975) point out there are
500,000 morphemes (the building blocks of meaning) in a typical
pocket novel. Thus a major part of reading is looking up each
important word or letter group in memory to find its decoded
meaning. Even if people are very fast in recognizing morphemes,
a slight difference in search time would result in considerable differences in reading speed when it is multiplied by half a million.

Another important component of the IPS that may be involved
in reading involves the holding capacity of short-term memory.
How much can be held in STM at one time? If a person can hold
many words at once, without mixing up the order, then the task of
reading should be a bit easier. Even a small difference in capacity
would be magnified greatly when you consider how many times
STM must be filled at the rate of a few words per cycle. Differences in the holding capacity of STM would be especially important when long, complicated sentences are used.

Finally, another important component of the IPS that may be

involved in reading is the speed with which operations can be performed on verbal information in STM. For example, in reading one must keep the words in order and decide which one is the subject, object, predicate, and so on. If mental operations in STM require even slightly more time for some people as compared to others, this difference could show up as a large difference in overall comprehension and reading ability. These components are summarized in Box 2.7.

There are, of course, many other features of the information system that may differ from person to person; examples include the tendency to use verbal versus visual rehearsal mechanisms, the organization strategy of LTM, the speed with which STSS fades, and so on. The main idea here is that differences on tests of ability—such as verbal ability—can be analyzed into differences in the characteristics of people's information processing systems. The next section provides examples of this technique.

EXAMPLES OF THE COGNITIVE APPROACH

Earl Hunt and his colleagues (Hunt, 1976; Hunt, 1978; Hunt, Frost, and Lunneborg, 1973; Hunt and Lansman, 1975; Hunt, Lunneborg, and Lewis, 1975) have successfully applied the cognitive tool described in the previous section to the problem of individual differences. The cognitive tool is the analysis of ability in terms of the components in the information processing system (IPS); that is, in terms of the memory stores and processes that are involved in performing a given task. In particular, Hunt took a group of college freshmen who scored high in verbal ability and a group who scored low in verbal ability as measured by a standardized college entrance exam (like the SAT). He then set out to answer the question, what are the differences between these two groups in terms of their information processing systems?

Decoding Processes in Long-Term Memory

One important component of the IPS that may be relevant to verbal ability is the speed with which a person can search through

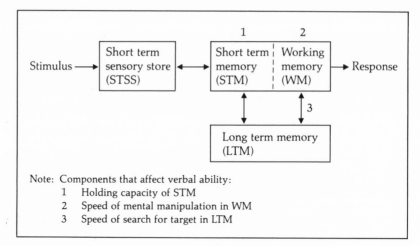

Box 2.7   Cognitive Analysis of Verbal Ability

long-term memory for a particular well-learned piece of information. For example, one very simple decoding process is to recognize a single letter. In reading and verbal comprehension, part of the task is simply to decode the printed letters into an internal representation. A person must be able to look at a printed letter and find its meaning in long-term memory.

How can you measure this simple cognitive process of letter recognition? Fortunately for Hunt, a test of decoding processes in long-term memory had already been developed by Posner, Boies, Eichelman, and Taylor (1969). The general procedure is to present the subject with two letters on a screen—such as Aa—and ask the subject to press a *yes* (same) or *no* (different) button. As shown in Box 2.8, there are two separate tasks. In the physical match task the subject presses the *yes* button if both letters are identical, but *no* if they are not (AA is *yes*, Aa is *no*); in the name match task the subject presses the *yes* button if both letters have the same name and the *no* button if not (Aa or AA are *yes*; AB is *no*).

What cognitive processes are involved in each task? For the physical match task the subject must get the stimuli into STM, make a decision, and then execute a response; for the name match task the subject must get the stimuli into STM, look up the name for each letter in LTM, make a decision, and then execute a

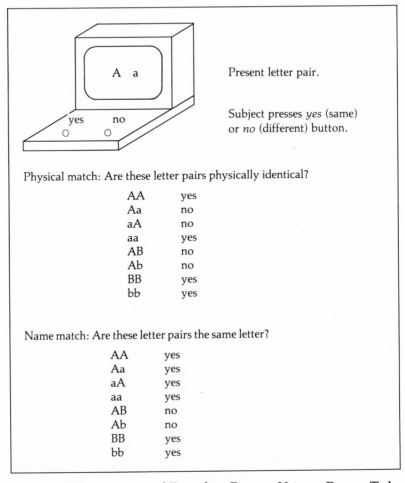

Present letter pair.

Subject presses *yes* (same) or *no* (different) button.

Physical match: Are these letter pairs physically identical?

AA	yes
Aa	no
aA	no
aa	yes
AB	no
Ab	no
BB	yes
bb	yes

Name match: Are these letter pairs the same letter?

AA	yes
Aa	yes
aA	yes
aa	yes
AB	no
Ab	no
BB	yes
bb	yes

Box 2.8   Measurement of Decoding Process Using a Posner Task

response. Thus, the two tasks involve the same processes except that the name match task contains one additional step—searching long-term memory for the names of the two letters. This step is not necessary for the physical match task since it is not necessary to figure out the names of the letters. Thus by using a subtraction technique we can say that the time to look up the name for the letters in LTM equals the time for a name match minus the time for a physical match. Since reading involves many instances of looking up letter names (and morpheme names) in long-term memory, Hunt predicted that he could find a difference on this skill between high and low verbal students.

To test this prediction, Hunt gave a modified version of the physical match test and the name match test to a group of high verbal and a group of low verbal subjects. Their average time to make a physical match was about the same, indicating that the groups did not differ much in how fast they could get letters into STM, make decisions, or execute responses. However, the low verbal group required much more time than the high verbal subjects when performing on the name match test. In one experiment, the difference between the time for a name match and time for a physical match was 33 milliseconds for the high verbal group and 86 milliseconds for the low verbal group. In another experiment, the differences were 64 milliseconds for the high verbal and 89 milliseconds for the low verbal. These results show that the decoding process of finding a name for a letter in long-term memory takes more time for low verbal than for high verbal subjects. Admittedly, the low verbals are just a fraction of a second slower (25 to 50 milliseconds); however, this decoding process must be repeated over and over thousands of times in the course of reading a single passage.

What can be concluded from this IPS analysis of verbal ability? One important implication is that gross differences in verbal ability may be describable in more detail. Note that low verbal students are not slower in getting information into STM and in executing a response (as required in the physical match task). However, low verbal students are consistently slower in searching LTM for a well-known target (as required in the name match task).

Holding Capacity of Short-Term Memory

As verbal information comes into short-term memory, it must be held there momentarily while decoding processes and other comprehension processes are carried out. In reading you must be able to hold the last few letters in memory so that you can later put them together to make a word, or you must be able to hold the last few words in memory so that you can later put them together into a clause. If the holding capacity of short-term memory is small then the process of comprehension will require more work and be subject to more error.

How can you measure the holding capacity of short-term memory? Again, Hunt and his colleagues were fortunate because cognitive psychologists had already developed techniques for measuring the capacity of short-term memory. They used a modified version of a task developed by Peterson and Peterson (1959). In Hunt's version of the task, subjects were presented with four letters on a screen one at a time; then there was a distractor task of reading numbers from the screen for a few seconds; and then subjects were asked to recall the four letters in order (see Box 2.9). This task requires that the person hold information in short-term memory while concentrating on something else. Similarly, reading involves taking in stimuli and holding them in memory for a few seconds while taking in some more.

Hunt gave this recall task to high and low verbal subjects. The results were that the low verbal subjects made more errors on the task than high verbal students; for example, when the retention interval was short, the low verbal students made three times as many errors in recall. Thus the high ability subjects were able to retain the letters in order much better than the low ability subjects. This suggests that the high verbal students have a larger holding capacity for verbal stimuli in short-term memory.

Again, we have been able to describe the difference between high and low verbal students in terms of the differences in their information processing systems.

Manipulation of Information in Short-Term Memory

So far, we have looked at the speed of decoding letter names in long-term memory and the size of short-term memory. Another important IPS process that is crucial for verbal comprehension is the ability to perform rapid operations on the information held in short-term memory. In order to read, a person needs to be able to put letters together into words, words together into clauses, and so on.

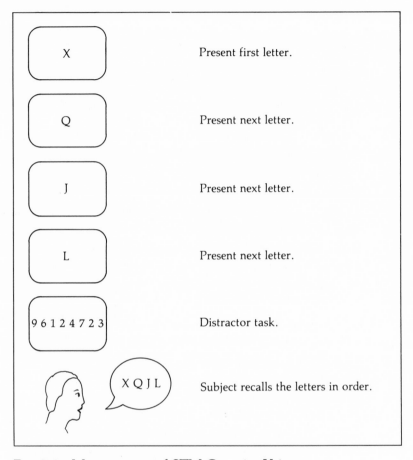

X	Present first letter.
Q	Present next letter.
J	Present next letter.
L	Present next letter.
9 6 1 2 4 7 2 3	Distractor task.
X Q J L	Subject recalls the letters in order.

Box 2.9   Measurement of STM Capacity Using a
Modified Peterson Task

Again, when Hunt sought to measure the speed with which
people can operate on information in short-term memory he
found that cognitive psychologists had already developed some
tests to help him. For example, he modified a task developed by
Sternberg (1969) to produce the following test: The subject is presented with from one to five target letters, one at a time, for about
1 second each; then a probe letter is shown and the subject must
press a *yes* button if the probe is the same as any of the target
letters and a *no* if it is not (see Box 2.10).

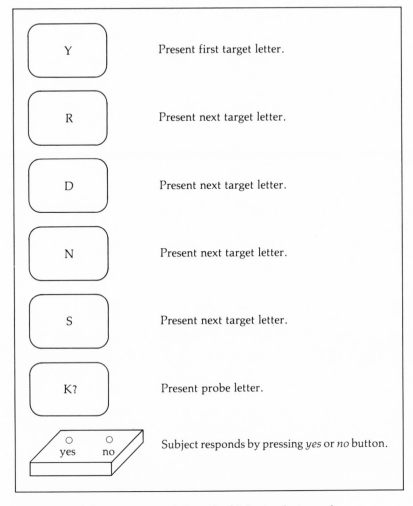

Y	Present first target letter.
R	Present next target letter.
D	Present next target letter.
N	Present next target letter.
S	Present next target letter.
K?	Present probe letter.
○ yes ○ no	Subject responds by pressing *yes* or *no* button.

Box 2.10 Measurement of Speed of Manipulation of Information in Working Memory Using a Modified Sternberg Task

What is involved in this task when there is one target letter and one probe? The subject must get the target into short-term memory, hold it there, get the probe letter into short-term memory, make one mental comparison, and execute the response. When there are two targets everything is the same except that two mental comparisons are made instead of one; the probe is compared to the first letter and to the second letter. When there are three targets there is one more mental comparison, and so on. Thus we can look at the time added by adding one more target to the task by using the following formula: The time to make a mental comparison equals the time to respond when there are n target letters minus the time to respond when there are $n-1$ target letters. Thus the Sternberg task provides a way of measuring the time it takes to make one simple mental operation in working memory.

The results again produced an interesting difference between low and high ability subjects. The reaction time for the one-target problems was at about the same level for both groups, but for each added letter in the target (two-target, three-target, and so on) there were about 80 milliseconds added to the time for low verbal students and only 60 milliseconds added for high verbal students. This difference in the slope of the response time curve means that the time to make a mental operation in short-term memory was considerably less for the high verbal students. In other experiments, more complex mental operations were required and the same results were obtained; the time required for each additional operation was more for the low verbal than for the high verbal students. These results again show that it is possible to describe differences in verbal ability in terms of differences in people's information processing systems.

It is important to note that high verbal people do not perform better on all tasks; rather, they excel on certain measures of relevant processing speeds and memory storage capacities. For example, low verbal people were not slower overall on tasks requiring mainly reading a stimulus and executing a response. However, when we increase the processing required in the task—such as increasing the number of mental operations involved—then differences between high and low verbal people emerge.

● ● ●

The work of Hunt and his colleagues demonstrates how the IPS model can make sense out of the long-standing problem of individual differences in mental ability. Hunt's work provides some reason to believe that gross measures like tests of verbal ability, mathematical ability, or general intelligence may ultimately be understood in terms of differences in very simple cognitive stores and processes. For example, the difference between high and low verbal students seems to include differences in the search speed through LTM, the holding capacity of STM, and the speed of mental operations in STM. These are processes that seem to be fundamental building blocks in reading, processes that would be used over many times in the course of reading a passage. However, Hunt's work also demonstrates that many measures are not important in distinguishing between high and low verbal students; for example, general speed on executing a response is not related to the differences.

APPLYING WHAT YOU'VE LEARNED

So far, we have shown that the IPS model can be used as a way of solving the ability problem when the ability factor is verbal. Now, try to apply this knowledge to a different type of ability. For example, what are the components of the IPS that would be useful for becoming a good piano player? Take a moment and try to generate a list of two or three basic cognitive processes that might be useful in distinguishing a group of excellent piano players from those who are not able to learn piano very well. To start with, you might try to think of some ways of modifying the tasks that were discussed above. Which of the following tasks do you think would be important in characterizing good piano players?

Decoding of tones in long-term memory. First, subjects learn the names for eight different tones. Then, we can use a modified version of the physical and name match tasks. For the physical match we could present two tones and ask the subject to press a *yes* button if they were the same and a *no* button if they were different. For a name match we could present a tone and a name and again ask for a button-pressing response. In the name match task, however, the subject must locate the name of the tone by searching long-term memory. Thus we would measure the decoding time for recognizing a tone as follows: The time to find the name for a tone in LTM equals the time for a name match minus the time for a physical match. Would you predict that the speed of decoding tones would be faster for good piano players?

Holding capacity of short-term memory for tones. First, subjects learn to make eight different tones by pressing one of eight different keys. Then, we can use a modified version of the Peterson and Peterson task. Subjects listen to four tones presented in order, then there is a brief distracting task, then the subject tries to recreate the four tones by pressing four keys in order. Would you expect fewer errors in recall for the good piano players?

Manipulation of tones information in short-term memory. Finally, we can modify the Sternberg task so that the stimuli are tones. A subject listens to a series of from one to five target tones, then a probe tone is given. The subject presses a *yes* button if the probe is the same as any of the targets and a *no* if it is not. The additional time required for each additional tone gives a measure of the time to make a mental operation on tones in short-term memory. Do you predict differences in measure for good and poor piano players?

Can you now think of any other components in the IPS that might be relevant? If you wanted to test your predictions, how would you do it? One method would be to take a group of students who are all beginning piano lessons for the first time; test them with your cognitive tests; and then wait a year and see who are the successful students and who are the dropouts. Finally, compare the scores of the groups to see whether the dropouts have different IPS characteristics than the good piano learners.

FURTHER APPLICATIONS OF
THE INFORMATION PROCESSING MODEL

In a recent symposium on "Intelligence Tests in the Year 2000" several participants were optimistic that tests of the future would be more closely tied to a cognitive analysis of the IPS. For example, Horn (1979) identified the following trends for future testing:

We will measure several basic cognitive processes, de-emphasize the concept of a single attribute of general intelligence, focus on adult tasks, and make more use of computers for testing and scoring. Resnick (1979) predicted that the new cognitive tests would fill important roles in schools, including a means of individualizing instruction. Based on the papers presented at the symposium, Detterman (1979, p. 295) concluded that "intelligence tests will have a very different appearance than they do today."

More recently, Pellegrino and Glaser (1979) have made a distinction between two related cognitive approaches to the ability problem. The "cognitive correlates" approach, such as the work of Hunt discussed earlier, specifies the information processing components that are different in high and low ability groups. The "cognitive components" approach analyzes a task into its parts and seeks to determine which parts of the task are the source of the difference between high and low performers. Recent work using the latter approach has been directed at analyzing the processes involved in common items on IQ tests. For example, a common item on an IQ test is an analogy problem such as:

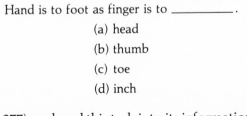

Hand is to foot as finger is to _____ .

    (a) head

    (b) thumb

    (c) toe

    (d) inch

Sternberg (1977) analyzed this task into its information processing components and measured the time required to accomplish each of the subprocesses. Based on his testing of large numbers of subjects, he was able to locate the basic information processes that are most important in distinguishing high from low scorers on an IQ test. Thus, performance on an IQ test can be understood in terms of the speed with which a person performs certain basic cognitive processes.

Another typical IQ test item is a series completion such as

axbxcxd __ __ __

Simon and Kotovsky (1963) have provided an analysis of this task into its information processing components. Further, Holtzman, Glaser, and Pellegrino (1976) have successfully instructed schoolchildren on some of the components of such a test item. Many of the other items on typical tests of intellectual ability are currently being analyzed into the basic cognitive processes that are required.

This chapter has given you a very brief example of how the cognitive revolution is affecting one of the oldest areas in psychology—the measurement and description of individual differences in mental ability. It has provided an example of how one of the tools of cognitive psychology—the IPS model—can be used to take a traditional problem in psychology and make sense out of it. In the not-too-distant future we might no longer say things like, "Tom is high in verbal ability." Instead, it might make more sense to say that "Tom scores high on alphanumeric search speed," or "Tom scores high on the holding capacity of his verbal short-term memory." Perhaps the whole mystique of ability in general and intelligence in particular will finally be laid to rest, and we will at last be able to solve the ability problem raised at the beginning of this chapter.

SUGGESTED READINGS

Hunt, E., C. Lunneborg, and J. Lewis. What does it mean to be high verbal? *Cognitive Psychology*, 1975, 7, 194–227. Describes research project on analysis of verbal ability that is discussed in this chapter.

Intelligence, 1979, *3*, No. 3. This issue of the journal *Intelligence* gives an excellent summary of the current status of the cognitive analysis of ability.

Lindsay, P. H., and D. A. Norman. *Human information processing*. New York: Academic Press, 1977. A general introduction to psychology from the information processing point of view.

Resnick, L. B. *The nature of intelligence.* Hillsdale, N.J.: Erlbaum, 1976. Contains many important papers describing how cognitive psychologists are studying differences in intellectual abilities.

Sternberg, R. J. *Intelligence, information processing, and analogical reasoning: The Componential Analysis of Human Reasoning.* Hillsdale, N.J.: Erlbaum, 1977. Describes a research project aimed at analyzing the information processing components involved in solving verbal analogy problems.

3 Cognitive Process Models

THE PROCEDURAL SKILL PROBLEM

A major component of the early schooling of a child generally involves the learning of basic arithmetic skills such as the ability to add, subtract, multiply, and divide. Many students acquire these skills, although there is some appalling evidence that some do not. The main question raised in this chapter is, what knowledge does a person have when he or she is able to engage in some procedural skill? This question can be called the procedural skill problem. One aspect of the procedural skill problem concerns the acquisition of basic arithmetic skills. For example, consider the following subtraction problems:

$$
\begin{array}{cccc}
763 & 792 & 806 & 890 \\
-541 & -668 & -577 & -722 \\
\end{array}
$$

Can you describe what someone who can solve these problems knows?

Another aspect of this question concerns the knowledge of a person who makes errors on a certain procedure. For example, look at Sheila's performance:

$$
\begin{array}{cccc}
763 & 792 & 806 & 890 \\
-541 & -668 & -577 & -722 \\
\hline
222 & 136 & 371 & 172 \\
\end{array}
$$

Can you describe the procedure that Sheila is using?

Cognitive psychologists seek to answer these kind of questions by providing a detailed description of the procedure a person has acquired for a given task like subtraction. As this chapter will show, the tool that has been most successful in solving the procedural skill problem has been a technique for analyzing a cognitive process into its parts.

THE TRADITIONAL APPROACH

The traditional approach to the procedural skill problem was based on S–R association as put forth by E. L. Thorndike (1913, 1931) in the first third of this century. His description of learning arithmetic skills was quite straightforward: The child simply learns to make many stimulus–response associations. For example, the stimulus is the problem (for example, $5 + 5 = $ _____) and the response is the correct answer (10). The process of learning involves the formation of an association between an individual stimulus and its response.

Suppose that a child learns an arithmetic fact such as $8 - 5 = 3$. Box 3.1 shows how the traditional S–R approach might describe the learning process. At the start of learning, the stimulus $(8-5)$ may be associated with many possible answers in the child's memory; thus, a child may have a mild tendency to respond with 3, 2, 4, 13, or other numbers. Thorndike proposed several laws of learning to account for the acquisition of procedural skills. One such law, the law of exercise, included the idea that the association becomes stronger and stronger as the child practices more and more. Thus as the child recites "$8-5=3$" the association between the stimulus $(8-5)$ and the correct response (3) becomes stronger. Another important law, the law of effect, included the idea that feedback helps strengthen the association with the correct response and weaken associations with other responses. If incorrect responses such as 2 or 13 are punished by the teacher saying "try again," these responses become less strongly associated with the stimulus $(8-5)$. If the correct response is rewarded by the teacher saying "right," it becomes more strongly associated with the stimulus. According to this theory, the learning of basic arithmetic skills involves memorizing many separate S–R associations.

This approach to the learning of procedural skills made some

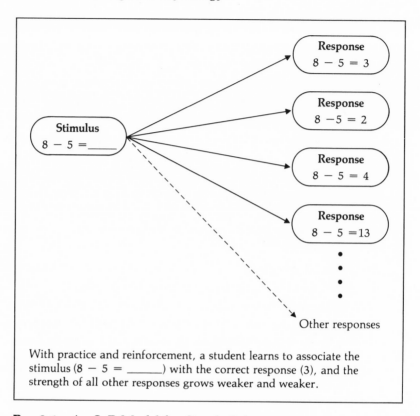

With practice and reinforcement, a student learns to associate the stimulus (8 − 5 = _____) with the correct response (3), and the strength of all other responses grows weaker and weaker.

Box 3.1 An S–R Model for Simple Subtraction

sense to the psychologists and educators of Thorndike's time because it fit the existing theories and tools of psychology. However, consider how many rote pieces of information a student would have to learn according to this theory. For simple addition of one-digit numbers such as 2 + 2 and 5 + 8 there are 90 different problems; if we include two-digit numbers there are over 8000 different addition facts. Furthermore, the same figures apply in turn to subtraction, multiplication, and division. A person would need to memorize literally thousands of arithmetic facts, many of which are never or only rarely used.

According to Thorndike's S–R theory of procedural skill, the best way to learn arithmetic is to perform many problems repeatedly with feedback on each problem, which translates into rote drill and many tests. This approach led to some strong reactions, such as Brownell's (1935) assertion that learning arithmetic should be based on the child's understanding of underlying principles rather than on memorization of isolated facts. It should be noted that Thorndike's approach did have an impact on education, and certainly provided a reform over earlier practices. However, it has not been until fairly recently that psychologists could offer a theoretically useful alternative to Thorndike's S–R approach. Let us now turn to this alternative—the approach of modern cognitive psychology.

THE COGNITIVE APPROACH

The S–R approach emphasized the idea that a person acquires the correct behavior for each given stimulus situation. According to the cognitive approach, a person does not acquire behavior directly but rather acquires a higher-order procedure or rule system that can be used to generate behavior in many situations.

In order to attack the procedural skill problem, cognitive psychologists have had to develop rigorous tools for analyzing a cognitive process into its parts. They have successfully applied several techniques for formally analyzing and specifying the procedural knowledge that a person applies to a given problem. Two useful ways of representing procedural knowledge are to draw flowcharts or to write a program. A program is just a list of things to do that you start at the top and follow one step at a time. A flowchart is a set of boxes and arrows that describes the processes and decisions involved for some procedure. Let's explore each of these cognitive tools.

For example, let's suppose that you know an inventive five-year-old, Kenny, who is able to give correct answers for single-digit subtraction problems. As a good cognitive psychologist you might be interested in figuring out what cognitive procedure he uses to solve the problems. In order to get a better idea of Kenny's procedural knowledge about subtraction, you could interview him about his procedure, try to generate a flowchart or program that corresponds to his procedure, and test it by comparing its performance to that of the five-year-old.

Program for Counting Up Procedure

1. *Set counters.* (Set fingers to smaller number; set voice to zero.)
2. *Do fingers equal larger number?* If *yes*, stop and recite; if *no*, go on to step 3.
3. *Increment counters by 1.*
4. *Go back to step 2.*

Box 3.2   A Process Model for Simple Subtraction
(Program Format)

The first thing to do, then, is to observe and interview our little friend carefully. When we watch him we see that he seems to be using his fingers and his voice to count. For example, if we give the problem "What is 8 take away 5?" he puts out 5 fingers, then 6 fingers and says "1," then 7 fingers and says "2," then 8 fingers and says "3," and finally he says, "The answer is 3." With a little more interviewing and questioning, we find that he has learned to subtract by using what he already knows about counting.

The next step is to look over the protocol of Kenny's subtraction behavior and try to describe it more precisely. Can you describe his procedure as a program? The procedure may be as follows:

1. *Set counters.* Your fingers serve as one counter and your voice serves as another. Put out the number of fingers corresponding to the lower number, and your voice will start out at zero.
2. *Do fingers equal larger number?* Does the number of fingers you have out equal the larger number? If so, stop and recite how many times you have incremented your finger counter. If not, go on to step 3.
3. *Increment counters by 1.* Put out one more finger and also recite by voice how many times you have come to step 3.
4. *Go back to step 2.*

This procedure is summarized in Box 3.2.

You can also represent this procedure as a flowchart as shown in Box 3.3. The diamond represents a decision (whether or not to

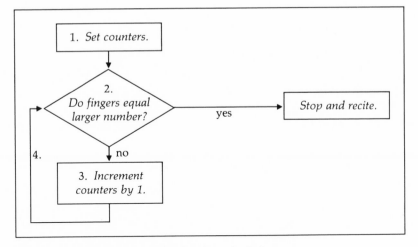

Box 3.3   A Process Model for Simple Subtraction
(Flowchart Format)

stop) and the rectangles represent processes (things to do). Can
you see that the flowchart and the program convey the same
information about the procedure for subtracting by counting?
These analyses of cognitive processes can be called process
models because they are models of what a person knows.

The next step is to test your representation of Kenny's subtraction procedure. You could compare Kenny's performance against
the performance of your representation of his procedure. The
model does not make any errors for single-digit subtraction, and
when we test Kenny we find that he makes no errors either. However, the model does suggest that some problems will be more difficult than others. For example, the more times that step 3 (count
aloud) has to be repeated, the more time the problem will take.

When we apply the model we have built to the 8 − 5 problem
we find the following: The finger counter is set to 5 (step 1), we
have not yet reached 8 so we go on (step 2), we add one finger and
say "1" (step 3), we return to step 2 and see that we still have not
reached 8, we add another finger giving us 7 and say "2" (step 3),
we return to step 2 and still do not have 8 fingers, we add another
finger now giving us 8 and say "3" (step 3), we go back to step 2,
and now we have 8 fingers so we stop and say "3." This solution

1. Put out 5 fingers.
2. Number of fingers is not 8 so go on.
3. Put out one more finger (6) and say "1."
4. Go on to step 2.
2. Number of fingers (6) is not 8 so go on.
3. Put out one more finger (7) and say "2."
4. Go on to step 2.
2. Number of fingers (7) is not 8 so go on.
3. Put out one more finger (8) and say "3."
4. Go on to step 2.
2. Number of fingers is 8 so stop and say "3."

Box 3.4   Performance of Process Model for $8 - 5 = $ _____

procedure is summarized in Box 3.4. The $8 - 5$ problem requires that we go through step 3 a total of three times; $8 - 6$ requires only two cycles through, and $8 - 7$ and $9 - 8$ require only one. If we compare predictions like these to Kenny's speed of solution we can test the accuracy of our model. If Kenny's solution times are longer for the problems that require many cycles (like $8 - 5$) but shorter for problems that require few cycles (like $8 - 7$), then we can say our model fits Kenny's performance. Box 3.5 graphs the model's performance against that of a human.

Resnick and her colleagues (Resnick, 1976b; Woods, Resnick, and Groen, 1975) have developed five simple models like the one described above and found that the performances of school children can be fit to one of them. Younger children tend to use procedures that are not totally efficient (like the model described above), but older children use highly efficient ones. Since these techniques are rarely taught explicitly, it seems that children are able to invent procedures and to revise them with experience. An important implication of Resnick's work is that different children may be giving the same answers for problems and yet be using entirely different procedures for generating them. Thus, instead of focusing on whether or not the child gives the correct answer for each problem (as suggested by S–R associationism), it is useful to focus on which procedure the child is using.

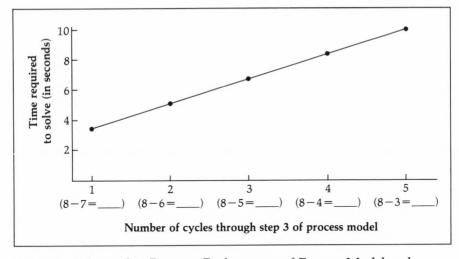

Box 3.5   Relationship Between Performance of Process Model and Performance of Human

    The use of cognitive tools for solving the procedural knowledge problem is an important advance over the traditional approach to arithmetic learning. If we were using an S–R behaviorist approach we would say that when we give Kenny a problem like 8 − 5, he pauses, mumbles, moves his fingers, and says "3." We would not really have a good understanding of what was generating this behavior. However, instead of saying that a child has acquired the correct behavior or has not acquired the correct behavior, it is now possible using the cognitive approach to give a more precise description of the cognitive mechanism that a child uses to generate his or her behavior. Let's now see how this technique can be applied to the learning of other arithmetic skills.

EXAMPLES OF THE COGNITIVE APPROACH

Brown and Burton (1978) have shown how the cognitive process analysis techniques described in the previous section can be applied to the study of the real performance of children on arithmetic problems. In particular, they analyzed the procedure that one must know in order to solve subtraction problems correctly.

Also, they developed a list of bugs that children may incorporate into their own particular procedures, creating procedures that are similar to the correct one but have one or more components that are different.

First, let's try to analyze the procedure involved in subtraction of three-digit numbers such as the following:

763	792	806	890
−541	−668	−577	−722
222	124	229	168

What are the processes and decisions involved in solving these kinds of problems? A step-by-step program for the correct procedure is given below.

1. *Set up problem.* First, you need to recognize the elements in the problem. You need to determine which digit belongs to the units space on top, the tens space on top, the hundreds space on top, the units space on bottom, the tens space on bottom, and the hundreds space on bottom. You can assume there is an erasable scoreboard with 9 spaces that looks something like this:

$$\begin{array}{llll}
& T(\text{hundreds}) = \underline{\quad} & T(\text{tens}) = \underline{\quad} & T(\text{units}) = \underline{\quad} \\
- & B(\text{hundreds}) = \underline{\quad} & B(\text{tens}) = \underline{\quad} & B(\text{units}) = \underline{\quad} \\
\hline
& A(\text{hundreds}) = \underline{\quad} & A(\text{tens}) = \underline{\quad} & A(\text{units}) = \underline{\quad}
\end{array}$$

Each space has a name and a number is stored in that space. Once you have set up the problem you need to recognize that it is a subtraction problem and that you will start at the right, in the units column.

2. *Initiate subtraction procedure.* Now, you may begin the subtraction process, which consists of the following.

   2a. *Find* $T - B$. You must find the number at the top and the number at the bottom for the column you are working on. This involves simply looking in the spaces for the two numbers you need and setting them up as a subtraction problem.

   2b. *Is* $T < B$? Next you need to see whether or not you need to borrow. If the top number is less than the bottom number, you need to jump to the borrow procedure in step 3. If not, you can go on in this procedure to step 2c.

2c. *Subtract and write.* Since the top number is greater than or equal to the bottom number, just generate the answer to this problem and write it in the appropriate space for the column you are working on.

2d. *Continue?* If there are more columns to the left, go on and repeat the subtraction procedure starting at step 2a; otherwise, stop.

3. *Borrowing procedure.* You use this procedure only if you have determined (in step 2b) that you need to borrow.

   3a. *Find next T.* First, you check the top number in the column to the left of the one you are working to see if you can borrow.

   3b. *Is next T = 0?* If the number in the borrow column is equal to zero, you cannot borrow from it so you need to go to the *Borrowing from zero procedure* in step 4; if it is greater than zero, then you can use this borrow procedure and go on to step 3c.

   3c. *Add 10.* Add 10 to the top number in the column you are working on, and write that number in the *T* space.

   3d. *Subtract 1.* Subtract 1 from the top number in the column next to the one you are working on, and write that number in the *T* space in the borrow column.

   3e. *Go to step 2.* You are now ready to carry out the subtraction procedure, so jump back to step 2 and continue from there.

4. *Borrowing from zero procedure.* Use this procedure only if you have determined (in step 3b) that you need to subtract from zero.

   4a. *Find next T.* First, you need to check the top number that is two columns to the left of where you are working.

   4b. *Is next T = 0?* If it is also zero, you need to jump to another procedure (not specified); otherwise, you can continue to step 4c.

   4c. *Subtract 1.* Subtract 1 from the top number that is two columns to the left and write that number in its space.

   4d. *Add 9.* Add 9 to the top number that is in the first column to the left, which contained a zero. That space will now have a 9 in it, so write 9 there.

---

1. *Set up problem*

2. *Initiate subtraction procedure.*

   2a. Find $T - B$.
   2b. Is $T < B$? If so go to step 3, otherwise go on.
   2c. Subtract and write and move to next column.
   2d. Continue? If there are more columns, repeat step 2a; otherwise, stop.

3. *Borrowing procedure.*

   3a. Find next T (from next column).
   3b. Is next $T = 0$? If so go to step 4, otherwise go on.
   3c. Add 10 to top number in current column.
   3d. Subtract 1 from top number in next left column.
   3e. Go to step 2.

4. *Borrowing from zero procedure.*

   4a. Find next T (from next column).
   4b. Is next $T = 0$? If so go to some new procedure, otherwise go on.
   4c. Subtract 1 from top number in second left column.
   4d. Add 9 to top number in left column.
   4e. Add 10 to top number in current column.
   4f. Go to step 2.

Box 3.6 A Process Model for Three-Digit Subtraction
          (Program Format)

    4e. *Add 10.* Now, you can finally borrow the 10 you need for the column you are working on. Add 10 to the top number and write the new number in the space.

    4f. *Go to step 2.* Now you are ready to proceed with the subtraction procedure, so go back to step 2.

As you can see we have written this subtraction procedure as a simple program; that is, as a list of things to do. You start at step 1 and work down; if you jump to a new line, you begin working down from there, ignoring any steps in between (see Box 3.6). We could also write it as a flowchart such as shown in Box 3.7. Note that decisions such as steps 2b, 3b, and 4b are indicated by diamonds, processes are indicated by rectangles, and the order of

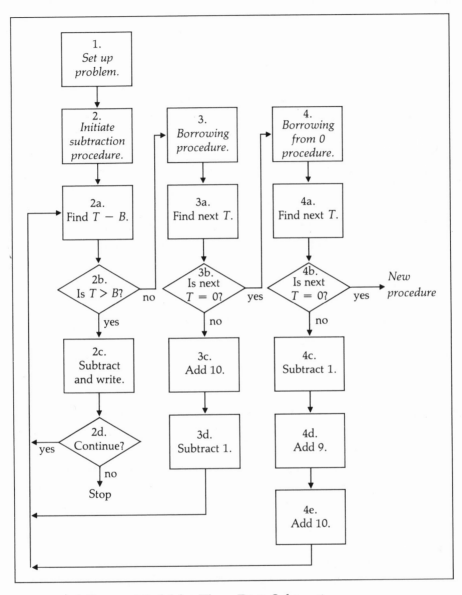

Box 3.7 A Process Model for Three-Digit Subtraction
(Flowchart Format)

work is indicated by arrows. The flowchart in Box 3.7 and the
program in Box 3.6 are really saying the same thing. It is possible
to analyze a person's procedural knowledge using either method.

In order to make sure you understand this analysis of the cognitive processes for subtraction, let's try a problem:

$$846$$
$$-555$$

In step 1 we set up the problem as: T(hundreds) = 8, T(tens) = 4, T(units) = 6, B(hundreds) = 5, B(tens) = 5, B(units) = 5. We start in the right column and go to step 2a, where we find 6 − 5 = _____ as the first part of the problem. In step 2b we determine that no borrowing is needed, so we go on to step 2c, where we find the answer [A(units) = 1] and write it. Since there is another column (as determined in step 2d) we go to the tens column and start over. In step 2a we find 4 − 5 = _____. In step 2b we determine that borrowing is needed so we jump to step 3. The top number in the hundreds column is 8 (step 3a) so we determine that we can continue (step 3b). In step 3c we add 10 to the 4 in top tens column to get 14, and in step 3d we subtract 1 from the 8 in the hundreds column to get 7 there. We can now jump back to step 2a, and in step 2c we write the answer as 9 in the tens column. In step 2d we go to the hundreds column and start over. The last part of the problem is 7 − 5 = _____ (step 2a), which does not require borrowing (step 2b), so the answer is written as 2 in the hundreds column (step 2c) and we stop (step 2d). This process is summarized in Box 3.8.

So far we have looked at how to describe the procedural knowledge required in order to solve certain subtraction problems. However, let's suppose that a child has almost but not quite acquired this procedure; let's suppose that the child has one little bug in his or her procedure for subtraction. For example, what would happen if there were at bug a step 2b; instead of setting up each problem as taking the bottom number away from the top, the child sets up each problem as taking the smaller number away from the larger. In other respects, though, the child's procedure is correct. What answers would this child give for the following problems? (222, 136, 371, 172)

763	792	806	890
−541	−668	−577	−722

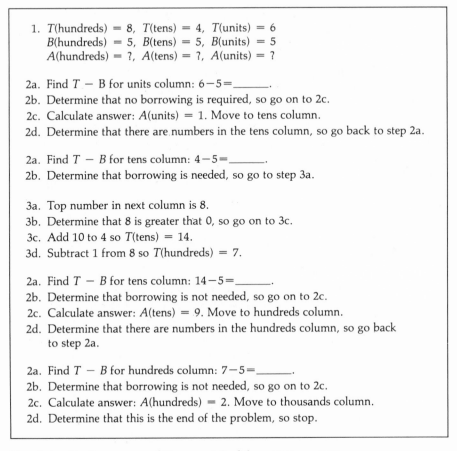

1. $T(\text{hundreds}) = 8$, $T(\text{tens}) = 4$, $T(\text{units}) = 6$
   $B(\text{hundreds}) = 5$, $B(\text{tens}) = 5$, $B(\text{units}) = 5$
   $A(\text{hundreds}) = ?$, $A(\text{tens}) = ?$, $A(\text{units}) = ?$

2a. Find $T - B$ for units column: $6 - 5 = $_____.
2b. Determine that no borrowing is required, so go on to 2c.
2c. Calculate answer: $A(\text{units}) = 1$. Move to tens column.
2d. Determine that there are numbers in the tens column, so go back to step 2a.

2a. Find $T - B$ for tens column: $4 - 5 = $_____.
2b. Determine that borrowing is needed, so go to step 3a.

3a. Top number in next column is 8.
3b. Determine that 8 is greater that 0, so go on to 3c.
3c. Add 10 to 4 so $T(\text{tens}) = 14$.
3d. Subtract 1 from 8 so $T(\text{hundreds}) = 7$.

2a. Find $T - B$ for tens column: $14 - 5 = $_____.
2b. Determine that borrowing is not needed, so go on to 2c.
2c. Calculate answer: $A(\text{tens}) = 9$. Move to hundreds column.
2d. Determine that there are numbers in the hundreds column, so go back to step 2a.

2a. Find $T - B$ for hundreds column: $7 - 5 = $_____.
2b. Determine that borrowing is not needed, so go on to 2c.
2c. Calculate answer: $A(\text{hundreds}) = 2$. Move to thousands column.
2d. Determine that this is the end of the problem, so stop.

Box 3.8 Performance of Process Model on $846 - 555 = $ _____

Or suppose that the child had a bug at step 3d in the borrowing procedure. Instead of subtracting 1 from the borrow column the child simply ignores this step. What answers would this child give to the problems listed above? (222, 134, 329, 178)

Or suppose that the child had a bug at step 4c in the borrowing from zero procedure. Instead of subtracting 1 from the hundreds column, this step is ignored. However, the child retains steps 4d and 4e and all the others. What answers would the child give for the above problems? (222, 124, 329, 168)

As you can see there are many bugs that may be present in the subtraction procedure a child uses. In other words, there are many procedures a child might use that lead to correct answers on some problems but errors on others. A good teacher may be able to look at the test performance of a student and notice which bugs seem to be present in his or her subtraction program. However, it has not been until the last few years that cognitive psychologists could really offer much help.

Brown and Burton (1978) have developed a computer program that uses the cognitive tool of analyzing tasks into process components. They tried to determine all the major bugs that children sometimes have in their programs for subtraction. For example, a group of 1325 students was given a large number of subtraction problems. The mistakes made by each student were carefully studied, and some of the most common bugs found in children's knowledge of subtraction were the following:

1. *Borrowing from zero.* When borrowing from a column that has a zero on top, the student changes it to a 9 but does not subtract 1 from the number to the left. For example, 205 − 126 = 179.

2. *Subtracting smaller number from larger.* When it is necessary to subtract the bottom number in a column from the top number, the student instead subtracts the smaller number from the larger. For example, 205 − 126 = 121.

3. *Moving over zero.* When subtracting the bottom number from the top number and the top number is zero, the student writes the bottom number as the answer. When the student borrows from a column that has a zero on top, the student skips that column and borrows from the next one. For example, 205 − 126 = 29.

Brown and Burton's computer program, called BUGGY, can be used to diagnose students' errors in subtraction. The student sits down in front of a computer terminal and is presented with subtraction problems. The computer has in its memory all the possible wrong procedures (as well as the correct one) that a student could use and tries to find the one that best fits the answers the child gives. For example, if a student behaves like Sheila (see the beginning of this chapter), the computer will find that the number 2 bug (subtracting smaller number from larger) is the one in her procedure. Sometimes more than one bug might be involved and sometimes children are not consistent, so the task of the computer is really a difficult one. BUGGY was moderately successful in characterizing the procedural knowledge of the 1325 children who were tested: 12 percent made no or only one or two errors, 21 percent made errors that could be completely explained by one or two bugs, 53 percent made errors that could partly be explained by one or two bugs, and 16 percent made errors that could not be explained at all by the known bugs. Based on the pattern of errors, the computer prints out the most likely bug or bugs that account for the student's answer. Thus, instead of giving each child a score of how many answers were correct, the BUGGY program is able to tell the teacher (and student) exactly where the procedural bug is located.

The work of Brown and Burton (1978) in developing the BUGGY program gives an excellent example of how the analytic techniques of cognitive psychology can be successfully used. Notice that the main tool of cognitive psychology in this case is the analysis of a cognitive process (the subtraction procedure) into its parts.

APPLYING WHAT YOU'VE LEARNED

We have just seen how the analysis of cognitive processes can be applied to subtraction. Now let's try the same technique with simple addition of two-digit numbers. For example, consider the following kinds of problems:

$$
\begin{array}{r} 22 \\ +23 \end{array} \qquad
\begin{array}{r} 74 \\ +25 \end{array} \qquad
\begin{array}{r} 56 \\ +57 \end{array} \qquad
\begin{array}{r} 24 \\ +82 \end{array} \qquad
\begin{array}{r} 29 \\ +12 \end{array}
$$

First, solve these problems yourself, giving a running description of what you are doing. In generating your protocol try to describe each process and decision you go through. Next, based on your running description, try to determine what processes and decisions are involved in your addition procedure. Take a few minutes to make a list of the steps that you think are involved. Did your program contain the following steps? Can you fill in the details?

1. $T(\text{tens}) = 2,\ T(\text{units}) = 9$
   $B(\text{tens}) = 1,\ B(\text{units}) = 2$

2a. Find $T + B$ for units column: $9 + 2 =$ _____.
2b. Determine that answer is greater than 10, so go to step 3a.

3a. Write answer for units: $A(\text{units}) = 1$.
3b. Determine that there are numbers in the tens column,
    so go on to 3c.
3c. Add 1 to top number in tens column so $T(\text{tens}) = 3$.

2a. Find $T + B$ for tens column: $3 + 1 =$ _____.
2b. Determine that answer is not greater than or equal to 10,
    so go on to 2c.
2c. Write answer for tens column: $A(\text{tens}) = 4$.
2d. Determine that it is time to stop. (Answer: 41.)

Box 3.9   Performance of Complete Process Model
on $29 + 12 =$ _____

1. *Set up problem.*

2. *Add procedure.*

   2a. Find $T + B$ for the column you are on.

   2b. Is $T + B \geq 10$? If so, go to *Carry procedure* (step 3);
   otherwise, go on to step 2c.

   2c. Calculate and write answer for $T + B$.

   2d. Continue? If there is more to do, go back to step 2a;
   otherwise, stop.

3. *Carry procedure.*

   3a. Write right digit as answer for this column.

   3b. Numbers in next column? If there are no numbers in the
   next column, go to step 4; otherwise go on to step 3c.

   3c. Add 1 to top number in next column.

   3d. Go back to step 2.

4. *Carry to zero procedure.*

   4a. Write 1 in next column for answer.

   4b. Stop.

1. $T(\text{tens}) = 2$, $T(\text{units}) = 9$
   $B(\text{tens}) = 1$, $B(\text{units}) = 2$

2a. Find $T + B$ for units column: $9 + 2 =$ _____.
2c. Write answer in units column: $A(\text{units}) = 11$.
2a. Find $T + B$ for tens column: $2 + 1 =$ _____.
2c. Write answer for tens column: $A(\text{tens}) = 3$.
2d. No more columns, so stop. (Answer: 311.)

Box 3.10   Performance of Incomplete Process Model
on $29 + 12 =$ _____

According to this procedure, which of the problems given above will be the most difficult and which will be the easiest? You could count the number of steps each problem takes to determine which takes the longest. Time yourself on each problem. Did your solution times correspond with the predictions of your model? In other words, did the problems that the model says have more steps take longer to solve?

If you were going to generate a BUGGY-like diagnostic system, what are some of the major bugs you would look for? For example, if a child gives answers like the following,

22	74	56	24	29
+23	+25	+57	+82	+12
45	99	1013	106	311

which of the steps in the child's procedure are defective? The problem seems to be that the subject skips step 2b and never uses step 3 or 4. Thus, when the sum of two numbers is a two-digit number both numbers are written in the column for the answer. This procedure consists only of steps 1, 2, 2a, 2c, and 2d. It sometimes gives the correct answer (such as for the first, second, and fourth problems above) but often fails. See Boxes 3.9 and 3.10.

In summary, a cognitive analysis of performance using a process model gives more information about what a child knows than just a raw score of percent correct. The basic steps for constructing a process model are as follows: First, human subjects are interviewed and asked to describe how they solve certain problems; second, a process model is constructed, such as one using flowcharts or a program; third, the performance predictions of the model are compared to the performance of real human subjects to see if they match.

FURTHER APPLICATIONS OF PROCESS MODELS

This chapter has given one example of how the performance of children on arithmetic problems can be analyzed in terms of underlying procedural knowledge. Although this line of research is a relatively new one, it has already displayed some progress. For example, Groen and Parkman (1972) were able to analyze the adding behavior of first graders, and Resnick and her colleagues (Resnick, 1976b; Woods, Resnick, and Groen, 1975) were able to analyze the subtraction behavior of second and fourth graders. In both cases there was evidence that the type of procedure becomes more sophisticated as the child grows. Thus, learning can be viewed as the acquisition of more and more powerful procedures. One promising aspect of this work is that the progress of a child may someday be measured in terms of which algorithms have been acquired rather than how many number facts he or she knows.

A logical extension of this line of work is to try to teach explicitly the higher order procedures that are useful in a subject like arithmetic. If we view skill learning as the acquisition of a useful procedure, why not explicitly teach the procedure? Instead of relying on the student to discover the procedure through drill and practice on problems, why not tell the student exactly what you are trying to teach? This idea has been argued by Landa (1974) and to some extent by Scandura (1977). Ehrenpreis and Scandura (1974) found that it was possible to teach the higher level rules and algorithms as part of a mathematics course, and that students who received this training performed better on later tests than those who were taught in the traditional way. Thus, the cognitive approach holds some promise for changing the way that instruction is carried out.

Finally, the diagnosis and remediation of errors is a crucial problem in education. The BUGGY approach (Brown and Burton, 1978) encourages the hope that someday teachers will be able to give tests that indicate which bugs exist in a student's procedural knowledge rather than how many errors were made. It will then be easier to tailor remediation work to fit the needs of each child.

In recent years, cognitive psychologists have been able to generate process models for many different tasks in addition to basic computational arithmetic. The list of tasks for which process models have been described ranges from solving linear syllogisms (Potts, 1972) to judging whether a simple sentence matches a picture (Carpenter and Just, 1975). Process models thus offer a level of precision and depth that promises even greater progress in the future.

SUGGESTED READINGS

Brown, J. S., and R. R. Burton. Diagnostic models for procedural bugs in basic mathematical skills. *Cognitive Science*, 1978, *2*, 155–192. Descibes the BUGGY research projects discussed in this chapter.

Groen, G. J., and J. M. Parkman. A chronometric analysis of simple addition. *Psychological Review*, 1972, *79*, 329–343. Describes research on process models for simple one-digit addition.

Landa, L. N. *Algorithmization of learning and instruction.* Englewood Cliffs, N.J.: Educational Technology Publications, 1974. A summary of Russian research on teaching algorithms.

Miller, G. A., E. Galanter, and K. H. Pribram. *Plans and the structure of behavior.* New York: Holt, Rinehart & Winston, 1960. Classic book that argues for the use of process models as an alternative to S–R theories.

Resnick, L. B. Task analysis in instructional design: Some cases from mathematics. In D. Klahr (Ed.), *Cognition and instruction.* Hillsdale, N.J.: Erlbaum, 1976. Describes research on process models in simple one-digit subtraction.

4 Cognitive Structure Models

THE VERBAL KNOWLEDGE PROBLEM

Much of what we know about the world comes to us in the form of verbal information. For example, we are told that there was a major earthquake in San Francisco in 1906 or we read a story in the newspaper about a family that won the state lottery. When we listen to or read some verbal information we tend to remember some of it, forget some of it, and add to or change some of it. What is the process by which we acquire new verbal information and how do we store that knowledge in memory? These questions can be called the verbal knowledge problem.

For example, look at the passage given in Box 4.1. Read it over as you would normally read; then, put the passage aside and try to write a summary of the story. Now compare your summary to the actual text. Did you remember the main ideas? Did you forget some ideas? Did you add to or change some of the information?

This chapter will investigate new cognitive techniques for analyzing the structure of a person's verbal knowledge.

THE TRADITIONAL APPROACH

As Cofer (1976) has pointed out, there are two distinct traditional approaches to the verbal knowledge problem: the Ebbinghaus tradition and the Bartlett tradition. The Ebbinghaus tradition is based on the work of Ebbinghaus (1885), who was the first psychologist to study verbal learning and memory seriously. First, he made up lists of nonsense syllables with each syllable consisting of three letters. He then experimented on himself by memo-

There was once an old farmer who owned a very stubborn donkey. One evening the farmer was trying to put his donkey into its shed. First, the farmer pulled the donkey, but the donkey wouldn't move. Then the farmer pushed the donkey, but still the donkey wouldn't move. Finally, the farmer asked his dog to bark loudly at the donkey and thereby frighten him into the shed. But the dog refused. So then, the farmer asked his cat to scratch the dog so the dog would bark loudly and thereby frighten the donkey into the shed. But the cat replied, "I would gladly scratch the dog if only you would get me some milk." So the farmer went to his cow and asked for some milk to give to the cat. But the cow replied, "I would gladly give you some milk if only you would give me some hay." Thus, the farmer went to the haystack and got some hay. As soon as he gave the hay to the cow, the cow gave the farmer some milk. Then the farmer went to the cat and gave the milk to the cat. As soon as the cat got the milk, it began to scratch the dog. As soon as the cat scratched the dog, the dog began to bark loudly. The barking so frightened the donkey that it jumped immediately into its shed.

Source: Perry W. Thorndyke, "Cognitive Structures in Comprehension and Memory of Narrative Discourse," *Cognitive Psychology,* vol. 9, 1977, pp. 77–110.

Box 4.1   The Old Farmer and the Donkey

rizing and then recalling the lists under a number of different conditions. He found, for example, that he remembered more syllables if he practiced the list more and he remembered fewer syllables if he waited a long time for a test. While these may not seem like startling findings, they did form the basis for much subsequent work. As you may have guessed, Ebbinghaus' theoretical approach was a version of S–R associationism; the stimuli went into memory, the response came out, and the main thing to be measured was how much was remembered.

The Bartlett (1932) tradition stands in sharp contrast to the Ebbinghaus tradition. Bartlett was interested in the cognitive question of how verbal knowledge is organized in a person's head rather than the behavioral question of how much is remembered. Instead of using lists of nonsense syllables as his stimuli, Bartlett used an actual story. For example, he asked his subjects to read a folk story from an unfamiliar culture, repeat the story for the next person, let that person reproduce the story for the next person, and so on. By the time the story reached the last person in line, it had been completely changed. Many details and names were missing. References to spirits and ghosts were eliminated. New events were added so that the story would "make sense." In short, Bartlett concluded that humans do not passively record verbal information and randomly forget some of it. Rather humans make "an effort after meaning"—an active attempt to make sense out of the story or information, an attempt to fit the new story to what they already know and are familiar with.

Unfortunately, Bartlett was never able to be very precise about his concept of "effort after meaning," and his work remained largely ignored for decades. On the other hand, Ebbinghaus attracted many followers who worked in his tradition of using word lists. However, while his work was precise and experimentally well controlled, it did not really deal with the complex problems of memory for prose. The dilemma, then, was that the Bartlett tradition raised interesting ideas but lacked the needed tools for analysis, while the Ebbinghaus tradition provided the needed rigor and precision but failed to address the issue of complex verbal learning. However, with the rebirth of interest in cognitive psychology, the questions raised by Bartlett and the tradition of rigorous analysis established by Ebbinghaus have finally come together.

THE COGNITIVE APPROACH

The cognitive approach to the verbal knowledge problem involves an attempt to analyze verbal knowledge into parts and to indicate the structure into which these parts fit. Thus, a structure model of a person's verbal knowledge generally consists of elements and relations among them. Two of the most useful techniques for representing verbal knowledge are networks and trees. A network is a diagram that indicates each of the major elements by a box or oval, with lines among them that specify relations. A tree consists of a diagram that begins at the top and branches to a second level, and then branches from that level to a third, and so on. Let's examine how these work by focusing on how to represent the knowledge in a sentence, and then in a simple narrative.

You are already familiar with sentence grammar—the rules for breaking a sentence into its parts and relations. For example, consider the sentence, *In the afternoon, I get very tired of working*. It can be broken down into a qualifying phrase (*In the afternoon*) and a major clause (*I get very tired of working*). These parts can be broken down further. The major clause consists of a subject (*I*) and a predicate (*get very tired of working*); the predicate consists of a verb phrase (*get very tired*) and an object (*of working*); the verb phrase can be broken into a verb (*get tired*) and an adverb (*very*); while the object decomposes into a preposition (*of*) and a noun (*working*).

Box 4.2 shows how this sentence can be represented as a tree. The top of the tree is the entire sentence. Then, at the first level from the top there is a break, based on the rule,

Sentence = Qualifying phrase + Major clause

At the next lower level, the two clauses are broken down using the rules,

Qualifying phrase = Preposition + Noun phrase

Major clause = Subject + Predicate

At the next level we can apply the following rules for breaking down the test:

Noun phrase = Noun + article

Predicate = Verb phrase + Object phrase

Finally, the last rules applied at the bottom of the tree are

Verb phrase = Verb + Adverb

Object phrase = Preposition + Noun

Thus, under the tree we can now see how each part of the sentence fits into the overall structure.

The rules for breaking a sentence down into its parts such as those listed above are called parsing rules. You may not have been

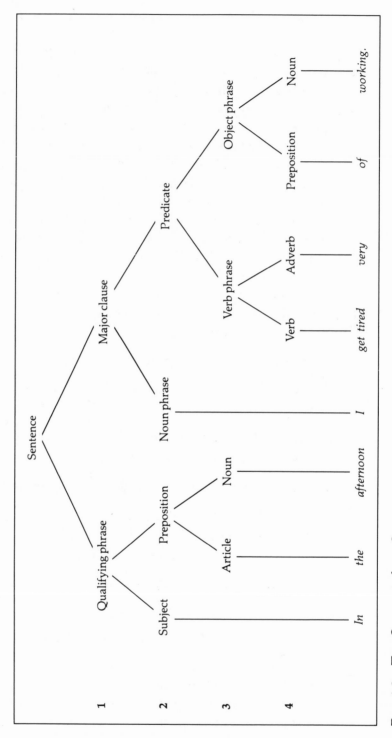

Box 4.2 Tree Structure for a Sentence

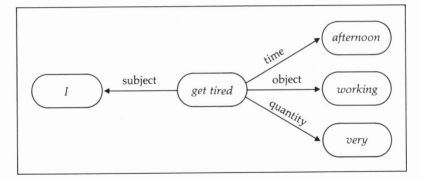

Box 4.3 Network Structure for a Sentence

taught exactly these rules or this type of terminology in your English courses. However, there is some evidence (Anderson and Bower, 1975; Kintsch, 1974) that people do use rules like these for comprehending sentences.

Box 4.3 shows another way of representing the sentence, a network graph. We take the main predicate, *get tired*, as the central node of the network. Then we find the arguments for this predicate, each of which holds a certain relationship to it. For example, we know that a predicate generally has a subject; that is, the person who *gets tired*. In this case the subject is *I*. Also, a predicate needs an object; *I get tired* of what? In this case, the object is *working*. The predicate may also need a setting such as time and place; that is, *get tired* when? In this case, the time argument is *in the afternoon*. The predicate may even have some arguments that modify it, such as *get tired* how much? In this case the argument *very* has a relation to the predicate. Thus, for any predicate in a sentence we have expectations concerning which types of arguments should go with it. In this case, we can summarize the arguments as follows:

> *Get tired*—subject: *I*, object: *working*,
>
> time: *afternoon*, quantity: *very*

This set of rules for finding the relationships between a predicate and its argument is called case grammar (Fillmore, 1968) because each type of relation is specified. The network shown in Box 4.3 specifies the predicate, the arguments, and each of the case relations.

The parsing rules or case grammar for sentences make it easier to represent the elements and overall structure of a sentence— that is, they provide a structure model for the information in a sentence. However, suppose we want to analyze a larger chunk of information, such as a simple narrative, into its parts and relations. Think of stories that you know, like a children's fairy tale or the story in Box 4.1. What are the major parts of such stories and how do they fit together? In essence, you need to determine what cognitive psychologists have called the story grammar. Since we are already familiar with sentence grammar (such as shown in Boxes 4.2 and 4.3), can we apply the same type of analysis to entire stories? For example, we have suggested that people have certain expectations of a sentence: a predicate will have a subject and object, and so forth. Can we specify the same sort of expectations—like parsing rules or case grammar—for stories?

The basic units that make up a sentence are words. What are the larger units that make up a story? In general, let's say that the units are simple sentences or clauses that express one event or one state. Thus, the first thing we can do in analyzing a story is to break it down into a list of simple sentences with each sentence either expressing one event or describing one state.

Now that we have specified the building blocks for our story grammar—states and events—we need to describe the structure into which they can be fit. What are the rules that specify the relations among simple sentences? Thorndyke (1977), building on the work of Rumelhart (1975), has suggested some parsing rules. First, a story can generally be broken down into four parts: We expect a setting, a theme, a plot, and finally we expect that the plot will be resolved. This basic grammar can be summarized as follows:

Rule 1: Story = Setting + Theme + Plot + Resolution

Each of the simple sentences (that is, events and states) should fit into one of these four categories.

Now we can go on and analyze each of these components of a story. A setting generally consists of some characters, a location, and a time. We can summarize this as:

Rule 2: Setting = Characters + Location + Time

We will not break these down any further. In a story we will thus expect to find some event(s) and/or state(s) that refer to characters, some that refer to location, and some that refer to time.

Next comes the theme. A theme of a story generally consists of some goal; sometimes there is an event or series of events that lead up to the need for this goal. This can be summarized as:

Rule 3: Theme = Event(s) + Goal

A goal is just a state. An event, of course, is expressed in a simple sentence as an event.

Now comes the plot. The plot consists of a series of episodes, and can be summarized as:

Rule 4: Plot = Episode(s)

What is an episode? An episode consists of a subgoal, one or more attempts to reach the subgoal, and the outcome of the attempt(s). This can be summarized as:

Rule 4a: Episode = Subgoal + Attempt(s) + Outcome

A new episode can also have its own attempts, and so on.

This brings us at last to the resolution. The resolution consists of an event or a state.

Rule 5: Resolution = Event or State

These few basic rules form the basis of a story grammar that is involved in many types of narratives. They have been modified from a similar set of rules described by Rumelhart (1975) and by Thorndyke (1977), for a variety of stories.

This type of story grammar offers an advance over earlier work, because it allows us to state more precisely what might be meant by "effort after meaning." If adults carry around these story grammar rules and try to use them when they read a story, this means that they try to fit the incoming story into these pre-existing structures for a story. They expect a setting, theme, plot and resolution, and so on. Comprehension and storage of story information may depend on how well the presented information can fit into our story grammar structures.

EXAMPLES OF THE COGNITIVE APPROACH

Thorndyke (1977) has provided a good example of how the analysis of verbal knowledge can be carried out and tested. He asked college students to listen to or read a story such as "The Old Farmer and the Donkey" (given in Box 4.1). Some subjects were given the complete story in its normal order (story group), some were given the story in random order (random group).

One of the major problems in this study was to develop a way to represent the structure of the story—that is, a structure model for the verbal information. First, Thorndyke broke the passage down into propositions, with each proposition presenting either one simple event or one simple state. There turn out to be 35 simple events and states. These are listed in Box 4.4.

Next, it is necessary to arrange these propositions into a structure, as shown in Box 4.5. Using the parsing rules for stories described in the previous section, we can break a story into four parts: setting, theme, plot, and resolution.

Let's look first at the setting of "The Old Farmer and the Donkey." The setting can be broken down into characters, location, and time. The characters are the old farmer (stated in proposition 1) and the donkey (stated in proposition 2). Thus, propositions 1 and 2 fit into the "Characters" part of the tree diagram shown in Box 4.5. We might also suppose that the location is a farm, but since there is no proposition that states this, we will ignore it for now.

Since there are no other propositions that refer to setting, let's move on to the second major section, the theme. Remember that the theme consists of a major goal; this goal may have some event that leads up to it or, as in the present case, may not. What is the

1. There was once an old farmer
2. who owned a very stubborn donkey.
3. One evening the farmer was trying to put his donkey into its shed.
4. First, the farmer pulled the donkey,
5. but the donkey wouldn't move.
6. Then the farmer pushed the donkey,
7. but still the donkey wouldn't move.
8. Finally, the farmer asked his dog
9. to bark loudly at the donkey
10. and thereby frighten him into the shed.
11. But the dog refused.
12. So then, the farmer asked his cat
13. to scratch the dog
14. so the dog would bark loudly
15. and thereby frighten the donkey into the shed.
16. But the cat replied, "I would gladly scratch the dog
17. if only you would get me some milk."
18. So the farmer went to his cow
19. and asked for some milk
20. to give to the cat.
21. But the cow replied,
22. "I would gladly give you some milk
23. if only you would give me some hay."
24. Thus, the farmer went to the haystack
25. and got some hay.
26. As soon as he gave the hay to the cow,
27. the cow gave the farmer some milk.
28. Then the farmer went to the cat
29. and gave the milk to the cat.
30. As soon as the cat got the milk,
31. it began to scratch the dog.
32. As soon as the cat scratched the dog,
33. the dog began to bark loudly.
34. The barking so frightened the donkey
35. that it jumped immediately into its shed.

Source: Perry W. Thorndyke, "Cognitive Structures in Comprehension and Memory of Narrative Discourse," *Cognitive Psychology*, vol. 9, 1977, pp. 77–110.

Box 4.4 List of Events and States for
"The Old Farmer and the Donkey"

main goal discussed in this story? The farmer wants to get the donkey into its shed. Thus, the theme of the story is presented in proposition 3, which states the goal.

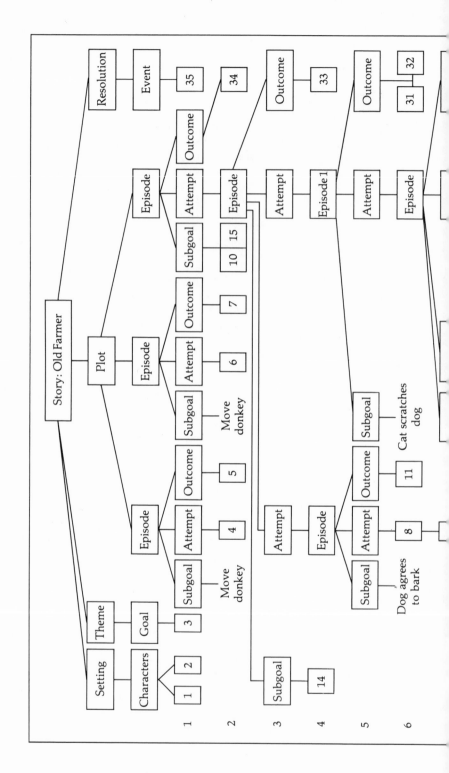

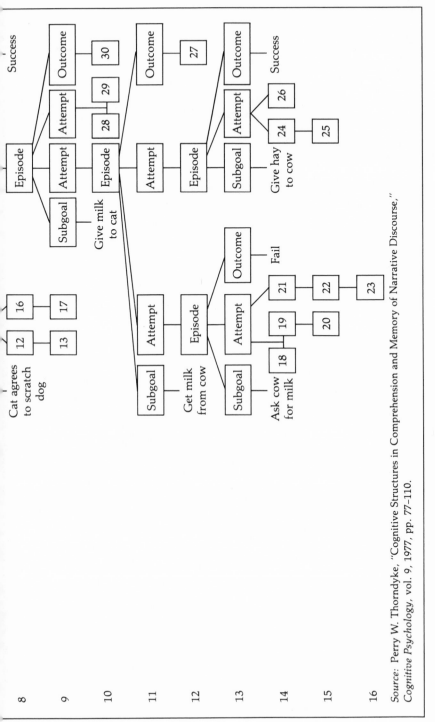

Source: Perry W. Thorndyke, "Cognitive Structures in Comprehension and Memory of Narrative Discourse," Cognitive Psychology, vol. 9, 1977, pp. 77–110.

Box 4.5 Tree Structure for "The Old Farmer and the Donkey"

Since there are no other propositions that deal with this goal or the events leading up to it, let's move on to the third section of the story, the plot. Remember that the plot is made up of many episodes, and that episodes consist of subgoals, attempts, and outcomes. In the first episode, the new subgoal is to pull the donkey; this is attempted (proposition 4) but fails (proposition 5). In the second episode, the subgoal of pushing the donkey is attempted (proposition 6) but also fails (proposition 7). In the next episode, there is a new subgoal—to frighten the donkey, as stated in propositions 10 and 15—and the eventual outcome is success, as stated in proposition 34. However, in the attempt to satisfy this subgoal, there are many new episodes with new subgoals like "have cat scratch dog," "make dog bark," "get milk from cow," and so on. These are listed under the plot in Box 4.5. Finally, the last element of a story that a person expects is a resolution. In "The Old Farmer and the Donkey" the story's main goal—getting the donkey in the shed—is achieved, so proposition 35 states the resolution. Thus, the "Old Farmer and the Donkey" story can be fit into the general structure laid out earlier: there is a clear setting (consisting of two characters), a theme (consisting of the goal of getting the donkey into the shed), a long, complicated plot that begins with the subgoals of pushing, pulling, and finally scaring the donkey and ends with the outcome of scaring the donkey, and a resolution (consisting of getting the donkey into the shed).

Rumelhart (1975) and Thorndyke (1977) have been able to create tree structures like these for a variety of stories. However, Thorndyke was also interested in testing to see whether the structure model he created was a useful or valid one. In order to test his story grammar he asked subjects to recall the story. He predicted that people would recall the propositions that fit high in the tree, since these are most central to the structure of the story. The highest propositions in the tree are 1, 2, 3, and 35—these give the characters, the theme, and the resolution. The next highest are 4, 5, 6, 7, 10, 15, and 34, which give the first simple subgoals and attempts and outcomes. The rest of the propositions are lower because they involve episodes of the subgoal of scaring the donkey.

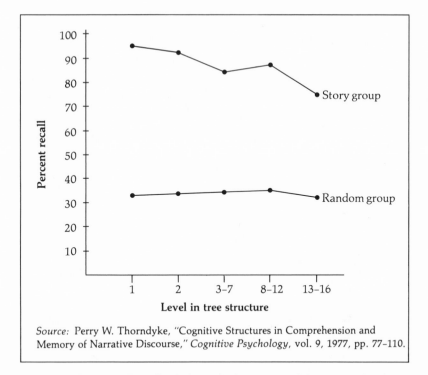

Source: Perry W. Thorndyke, "Cognitive Structures in Comprehension and Memory of Narrative Discourse," *Cognitive Psychology*, vol. 9, 1977, pp. 77–110.

Box 4.6 Percent Recall of "The Old Farmer and the Donkey" Story by Level in the Tree Structure

Box 4.6 shows the percentage of propositions recalled, by level in the hierarchy, for the two groups. The story group recalled almost all of the level 1 information, but less and less of the information in successively lower levels of the tree. The random group, however, shows an entirely different pattern. Since they apparently did not treat the information as forming an organized story, they recalled equivalent amounts from each level of the hierarchy. Thus, the story group behaved as if each reader had tried to build a tree like the one given in the figure and worked from the top down; the random group, however, was not able to build such a structure and remembered the information in a much less organized way.

As another test, Thorndyke produced some versions of the story that did not contain the theme or did not state it until the end. If readers cannot determine the theme, it will be very difficult for them to build a useful internal tree for a story. Thus, he predicted that recall of the remaining propositions would be poorer for these subjects than for subjects who had the theme stated early in the story (that is, the normal story). As predicted, removing or postponing the theme had a strong negative effect on recall, although it was not as harmful as placing the propositions in random order.

Finally, Thorndyke conducted another test of his analysis of cognitive structure for the stories he used. Suppose that people comprehend stories by trying to fit the propositions into a story grammar structure. If two stories are read in order, and if the second has the same structure as the first, but different content, then it should be easier to understand since the reader has just built that particular structure. Understanding the second story means simply fitting the new characters and events into a familiar structure. However, if a new structure is used in the second story, it should be harder to understand because the reader must break out of his previous way of structuring the story and build a new tree. When Thorndyke tested this idea he again found supporting evidence for his predictions. Repeating the same structure across two different stories helped recall, but repeating the same content (characters and events) in a new structure caused interference in recall.

In summary, Thorndyke was successful in analyzing a passage into its parts, determining the structure into which the parts might fit, and testing to see whether humans actually tend to build this structure when they comprehend stories. As you can see, a system like Thorndyke's deals with learning and memory for real-world, meaningful verbal information; thus this line of research is an advance over Ebbinghaus' work on lists of nonsense syllables. The cognitive structures required to represent meaningful verbal information are quite different from those involved in rote learning situations such as Ebbinghaus used. This line of research is also an advance over Bartlett's work on memory for stories. Thorndyke's analysis is far more detailed and precise than Bartlett's and allows for more specific predictions.

APPLYING WHAT YOU'VE LEARNED

In the previous section, we showed how the story grammar approach can be used to specify the structure that a person is likely to acquire from a narrative when he is making "an effort after meaning." The story grammar described in the previous section was developed for use in a wide variety of stories. It is a general purpose story grammar. However, suppose you wanted to develop a more specific set of rules for a more restricted set of stories.

For example, suppose that I said I wanted to tell you about what happened to me when I went and ate at Joe's restaurant last night. You probably have a certain set of expectations when you read or listen to an episode about someone going into a restaurant. Based on your general experience with restaurants, you have some idea of the script for a restaurant episode; as you read or listen to the story you try to fill in the general script with the specific events and situations in the particular story.

Take a minute to write down the main scenes you would expect in a restaurant script; for each scene write down the general events you would expect.

If you are having trouble, first try to list the cast of characters, such as customer, host/hostess, waiter/waitress, chef, cashier, and others. Now, what are the major scenes? The first scene, for example, might be entering and getting seated. What are all of the events you would expect to take place in this scene?

Box 4.7 gives a summary of the restaurant script suggested by Schank and Abelson (1977) in their book, *Scripts, Plans, Goals, and Understanding*. These authors argue that, in addition to general story grammars, adults also have specialized scripts for recurring episodes in their experience. Their version of the res-

Schema: Restaurant.

Characters: Customer, hostess, waiter, chef, cashier.

Scene 1: Entering.
   Customer goes into restaurant.
   Customer finds a place to sit.
    He may find it himself
    He may be seated by a hostess.
     He asks the hostess for a table.
     She gives him permission to go to the table.
   Customer goes and sits at the table.

Scene 2: Ordering.
   Customer receives a menu.
   Customer reads it.
   Customer decides what to order.
   Waiter takes the order.
    Waiter sees the customer.
    Waiter goes to the customer.
    Customer orders what he wants.
   Chef cooks the meal.

Scene 3: Eating.
   After some time the waiter brings the meal from the chef.
   Customer eats the meal.

Scene 4: Exiting.
   Customer asks the waiter for the check.
   Waiter gives the check to the customer.
   Customer leaves a tip.
    The size of the tip depends on the goodness of the service.
   Customer pays the cashier.
   Customer leaves the restaurant.

Source: D. E. Rumelhart, *Introduction to Human Information Processing.* New York: Wiley, 1977.

Box 4.7 Schank and Abelson's Restaurant Script

taurant script consists of four scenes: entering, ordering, eating, and exiting. How does yours compare?

Schank and Abelson also argue that people use scripts for comprehending verbal information. For example, when someone tells you something in a conversation, you try to find the appropriate script in your memory; you ask yourself, "Is this information from a restaurant script, or a taking-the-plane script, or a going-to-in-laws script?" and so on. Once you figure out which script is appropriate, it is much easier to comprehend what is being said.

Suppose you are at a party, and a friend tells you the following story.

> Sally and John and Beth and I decided to go out for dinner last night. Well, we found a table right away and sat down. I got up and ordered the specialty of the house for everybody. It didn't take long for the meals to be ready. I paid for the food, and brought it back to the table. Everyone ate and said the meal was delicious. Then we cleaned up and left.

When you hear this episode, you might be tempted to use your standard restaurant script (as shown in Box 4.7) to understand it. However, as you try to fit the events in the episode into the script, you might have some problems. Suppose you use the Schank and Abelson script. Which events would fit into the script and which events would not? Also, where would they fit into the script?

The episode can be broken down into the following events:

1. Sally and John and Beth and I decided to go out for dinner last night.
2. We found a table right away and sat down.
3. I got up,
4. and ordered the specialty of the house for everyone.
5. It didn't take long for the meals to be ready.
6. I paid for the food,
7. and brought it back to the table.
8. Everyone ate
9. and said the meal was delicious.
10. Then we cleaned up
11. and left.

As you try to fit these events into the restaurant script you would probably find the following:

1. A signal to you to use the restaurant script.
2. Fits into the entering scene.

3. Seems to belong in the ordering scene but does not fit the script since one does not normally get up to order. This might cause you to change your script or to just try to fit event 3 in any way. One way to fit it in is to ignore it. Another is to assume that it is a formal restaurant and it is polite to stand up when ordering.

4. Seems to fit the ordering scene.

5. Fits the eating scene.

6. Does not fit. It is out of order. Again, you could change your script at this point or try to fit in this event in some other way.

7. Also does not fit. The waiter or waitress is supposed to bring the food, according to the script. You should become very skeptical at this point concerning your script. It just does not seem to be able to hold the events in the story.

8, 9. Fit the eating scene.

10. Seems related to the exiting scene but does not fit any of the expected events in the script. By now you should see clearly that a different script is needed.

11. Fits the exiting scene.

As you can see, most of the events fit the script, but there are many that don't. As you listen to the story you might decide that you need to use a modified script—the McDonald's restaurant script, for example. If you use this script, the events in the story fit the expected structure much better: one gets up to order and carry back the food, cleans up before leaving, pays before eating, and so on.

As you can see, one important source of misunderstanding or failure to communicate may be that the sender and receiver are using different scripts. It is useful to tell the listener early in the conversation which script he or she should be using for organizing the statements that will follow. The concept of a script is similar to other concepts such as Minsky's (1975) "frame" or Bransford's (1979) "schema."

FURTHER APPLICATIONS OF STRUCTURE MODELS

The work on story grammars (broadly defined) is a very new area in cognitive psychology, and yet it has already demonstrated much success. Apparently, it is possible to describe the cognitive structures that people acquire from stories and the rules they use for understanding and building them. Results similar to those described in this chapter have also been reported by Kintsch and his colleagues (Kintsch, 1974, 1976; Kintsch and van Dijk, 1978) and by Meyer (1975).

If people have a set of grammar rules about narratives, it is likely that they also have other grammar systems for use in understanding other types of verbal information. For example, Kintsch (1974) has suggested a macrostructure for scientific reports, and Spilich, Vesonder, Chiesi, and Voss (1979) have developed a macrostructure for understanding the radio broadcast of a baseball game. Although the particular rules are different, it is possible to represent a scientific report or a baseball game transcript as a tree diagram and to predict that the upper levels of the tree will be better remembered. As work progresses, there will likely be an explosion of grammars for many particular types of verbal information in addition to stories.

If cognitive psychologists are able to specify the grammars for particular types of information, it seems likely that we can do a better job of presenting information. For example, Stein and Nezworski (1978) found that when stories are presented in the optimal order as prescribed by a story grammar, people remember much more of the story than when the story is slightly or greatly at variance with the expected order. Also, Thorndyke (1977) found that practice with a particular story structure aided comprehension of a story with the same structure. The work on story grammars may eventually lead to prescriptions for writers on how to make sure their prose meshes with people's expected grammars.

An understanding of the structure of verbal knowledge holds other promises as well. If someone is having trouble reading and comprehending a textbook in a certain area, such as American history, perhaps the appropriate remediation would be to make the grammar of the history book more explicit. By giving the student a grammar system for organizing the prose, one could be more confident that the important topics would be remembered and organized well. Thus, it seems likely that we may someday teach people about the grammars of subject areas (like stories) in the same sort of way we now teach students about the grammar of sentences. Recently, Kintsch and van Dijk (1978) have suggested a precise model of how humans read, based on the idea that we try to build hierarchical structures for the information. As we test and refine such theories, we may be in a much better position to teach people how to read in specific disciplines.

Finally, the story grammar approach provides a new way of measuring what a given person knows about a given topic. Instead of saying that "Sharon got 85 percent correct on a test covering the chapter on electricity," we can specify how Sharon has organized the information. We can pinpoint areas that are missing; perhaps part of the grammar is not being used, such as remembering the causal link between two events. New techniques for measuring and representing cognitive structure could lead to better evaluation, diagnosis, and remediation.

In summary, cognitive psychologists have developed systems for describing the verbal knowledge that one acquires from prose. Even the stories that Bartlett used 50 years ago have finally been subjected to story grammar analysis (Mandler and Johnson, 1977). Yet much remains to be done; this frontier, which did not exist a decade ago, is far from being well mapped.

SUGGESTED READINGS

Kintsch, W. Memory for prose. In C. N. Cofer (Ed.),
The structure of memory. San Francisco: W. H. Freeman and
Company, 1976. Describes a research project concerned with
the representation of verbal knowledge in memory.

Meyer, B. J. F. *The organization of prose and its effects on
memory.* Amsterdam: North-Holland, 1975. Describes a
system for analyzing passages using a case grammar
approach.

Rumelhart, D. E. Notes on a schema for stories. In D. G.
Bobrow and A. M. Collins (Eds.), *Representation and
understanding: Studies in cognitive science.* New York:

Academic Press, 1975. Describes a system for analyzing stories into tree structures such as those described in this chapter.

Schank, R. C., and R. P. Abelson. *Scripts, plans, goals, and understanding.* Hillsdale, N.J.: Erlbaum, 1977. Describes a system for representing knowledge about a story; makes heavy use of computer terminology.

Thorndyke, P. W. Cognitive structures in comprehension and memory of narrative discourse. *Cognitive Psychology,* 1977, *9,* 77–110. Describes experiments on story grammars that are discussed in this chapter.

5 Cognitive Strategy Models

THE STRATEGY PROBLEM

When a person is confronted with a problem, there are many things he or she can bring to bear on it. So far we have examined three major features of the human cognitive system: the architecture of the information processing system (Chapter 2), the procedural knowledge brought to a task (Chapter 3), and the verbal knowledge brought to a task (Chapter 4). In this chapter, we will explore a fourth feature of the cognitive system—the general strategy for making the most efficient use of the memory stores, procedures, and knowledge structures that are available.

For example, suppose you had just learned the equations shown below:

$$work = weight \times distance \qquad (1)$$

$$potential\ energy = weight \times height \qquad (2)$$

$$power = \frac{work}{volume} \qquad (3)$$

Now, if you had values for *weight*, *distance*, and *power*, could you determine the value for *volume*? As you attempt to solve this problem, talk aloud so that you are aware of the plan you follow.

In solving this problem, you must make use of your working memory as discussed in Chapter 2, so individual differences in the efficiency of operation of that memory store should affect problem-solving performance. You must also make use of the cognitive procedures discussed in Chapter 3, such as knowing how to multiply, divide, and use algebraic operations. In addition, you must form a knowledge structure as discussed in Chapter 4, in order to represent the three equations. However, as well as all of these factors, you must decide on some plan of attack, some general strategy for solving the problem.

One general strategy you could use is called working forward: Start with the givens (*weight, distance,* and *power*) and work towards the goal (*volume*). You notice that with *weight* and *distance* you can find *work* (using the first equation). With *work* and *power* you can find *volume* (third equation), which is the value you were asked about.

Another strategy is called working backwards, which involves starting with the goal (*volume*) and working towards the givens (*weight, distance,* and *power*). For example, to find *volume* you notice that you must know the values of *power* and *work* (in equation 3). You check your givens and see that you already know *power,* so all you need to find is *work.* To find *work,* you need to know the values of *weight* and *distance* (in equation 1). As you check your givens you notice that you have *weight* and *distance,* so you have solved the problem. (See Mayer and Greeno, 1975, for a more detailed description of strategies for solving this problem.)

These examples show that a person generally has several alternative strategies available in complex problem-solving tasks. The task of the cognitive psychologist is to specify clearly what these strategies (also called heuristics) are and how they are used. This can be called the strategy problem. The remainder of this chapter demonstrates how cognitive psychologists have attacked it.

THE TRADITIONAL APPROACH

Most of the early work on the strategy problem was based on informal observation of people—sometimes famous thinkers—in the act of solving some problem. One of the most common observations was that people tended to go through a series of stages in order to reach a solution. Although there was never much agreement on what the stages were, a typical set of stages was proclaimed by Wallas (1926) in his classic book, *The Art of Thought.*

The four stages in Wallas' system were: preparation (gathering information), incubation (putting the problem aside), illumination (a flash of insight), and verification (working through the solution). Polya (1957, 1968) also suggested a similar set of stages involved in mathematical problem solving.

Other early researchers, mainly gestalt psychologists, noticed that people set up subgoals in solving problems. For example, Duncker (1945) gave a subject the following problem: "Given a human being with an inoperable stomach tumor, and rays which destroy organic tissue at sufficient intensity, by what procedure can one free him of the tumor by these rays and at the same time avoid destroying the healthy tissue which surrounds it?" Duncker found that his subject hit upon a general solution to the problem —a general goal that drives the problem-solving process—before trying specific solutions. For example, a general goal would be "desensitize the healthy tissue" and a specific solution after that would be "immunize by adaptation to weak rays"; another general goal, "lower the intensity of the rays in the healthy tissue," suggests the specific solution "use a lens" (the correct solution). The entire set of goals and specific attempts is given in Box 5.1. Duncker's main point was that people tend to break a problem down into subgoals and then try to solve the subgoals.

Polya (1957, 1968) observed how students solve mathematics problems in high school courses. Like Duncker, he noticed that when a problem seems too difficult to solve, a good strategy is to break it down into smaller problems that can be solved. For example, if your job is to find the volume of a frustum (lower portion) of a pyramid, you may make up an easier subgoal—finding the volume of the entire pyramid. Thus, the idea of stages in problem solving and in particular the idea of subgoals were early contributions to the strategy problem. The general strategy people used seemed to involve breaking a problem down into its parts.

Unfortunately, these ideas never really got off the ground. They were stated so imprecisely that they seemed right but could not really be tested. No predictions could be made about human performance, and people's strategies could not be clearly described.

General Subgoal	Specific Subgoal	Specific Solution
	1a. Use free path to stomach.	1a. Esophagus
1. Avoid contact between rays and healthy tissue.	1b. Remove healthy tissue.	1b. Insert cannula.
	1c. Insert protecting wall.	1c. Feed substance which protects wall.
	1d. Displace tumor toward surface.	1d. By pressure.
2. Desensitize healthy tissue.	2a. Inject desensitizing chemical.	
	2b. Immunize by adaptation to weak rays.	
3. Lower intensity of rays through healthy tissue.	3a. Turn up intensity as ray hits tissue.	
	3b. Concentrate ray at place of tumor.	3b. Use lens.

Source: Adapted from K. Duncker, "On Problem Solving," *Psychological Monographs,* vol. 58, no. 270, 1945.

Box 5.1 Some Subgoals and Attempts in Solving Duncker's Tumor Problem

The required analytic tools were not yet available, and the concept of using subgoals remained a vague idea until the cognitive revolution. Many attempts—such as Polya's (1957) *How to Solve It*—were made to teach problem strategies, and with some success. Thus Polya and others raised interesting issues and challenged modern cognitive psychologists to get to work.

THE COGNITIVE APPROACH

It all began with computers. Electronic computers that could solve a variety of problems were developed during the late 1940s and early 1950s. As computer technology increased in sophistication, it became possible to program them to solve more and more complex problems. However, when computers were programmed to solve problems they needed several things: a set of memory stores and transformation processes (analogous to but quite different in structure from the human IPS discussed in Chapter 2), a set of procedures for accomplishing goals (as discussed in Chapter 3), a set of verbal knowledge (as discussed in Chapter 4), and a set of general strategies or heuristics for controlling the problem-solving process (as discussed in this chapter). Thus it became apparent that problem solving, at least in computers, required precise descriptions of problem-solving heuristics (or strategies). The same tools used for spelling out the strategies used in computers could be used, it seemed, to describe the strategies used by humans.

One of the earliest and best known computer programs related to this problem was called General Problem Solver (GPS). GPS was endowed by its creators (Ernst and Newell, 1969) with a powerful, general strategy that was supposed to enable it to solve a wide variety of problems. Ernst and Newell and, later, Newell and Simon (1972) asked humans to solve problems and to talk aloud as they worked, then abstracted from their subjects' reports the general strategy that they seemed to be using. Finally, the researchers tried to specify this strategy in precise detail so that they could program the problem-solving approach into GPS.

Ernst and Newell's book *GPS: A Case Study in Generality and Problem Solving* (1969) was a significant breakthrough. Until the invention of GPS, individual computer programs had been designed to specialize in just one type of problem; however, GPS was intended to possess a general problem-solving strategy that could be used in many different tasks. In all, Ernst and Newell tried GPS on 11 very different problems. These are listed in Box 5.2. Although GPS was able to solve these 11 problems, it did not always produce a goal structure that was similar to the way humans performed.

In 1972 Newell and Simon produced their monumental treatise, *Human Problem Solving*, which further developed the ideas presented in the earlier book. In addition, this book provided in-depth analysis of the strategies used by people solving cryptarith-

Missionaries and Cannibals

Three missionaries and three cannibals are on one side of a river and want to get to the other side. The only means of conveyance is a small boat with a capacity of two people. If at any time there are more cannibals than missionaries on either side of the river, those missionaries will be eaten by the cannibals. How can you get all six people across the river without any casualties?

Integration

Solve integration problems such as

$$\int [\sin^2(ct)\cos(ct) + t^{-1}]dt$$

Tower of Hanoi

There are three pegs and three (or more) disks. The disks vary in size and are placed on the first peg with the smallest on top and the largest on bottom. The problem is to move the disks to the third peg. The pegs must be moved one at a time, and a larger disk may never be placed on top of a smaller disk.

Proving Theorems

A famous theorem from predicate calculus is given.

Father and Sons

A father and his sons want to cross a river. They use a boat that has a maximum capacity of 200 pounds. Each son weighs 100 pounds and the father weighs 200 pounds. Assuming that the father and either son can operate the boat how can they get across the river?

Monkey Task

A monkey is in a room with a box and some bananas above him out of reach. How can the monkey get the bananas?

Three Coins

Three coins are on a table. The first and third show tails, while the second shows heads. A move consists of turning any two coins over. How can you use exactly three moves to get the coins to show all heads or all tails?

Parsing Sentences

Identify parts of speech in a sentence such as the following:

Free variables cause confusion.

Water Jug

Given a 5-gallon jug and 8-gallon jug, how can you get exactly 2 gallons of water?

Box 5.2 Eleven Problems for GPS (continued on next page)

Letter Series Completion

What is the next letter in the series:

B C B D B E ____

Bridges of Konigsberg

Given a city with seven bridges, can you start at one point and return to it after going over each bridge only one time?

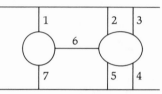

Source: Adapted from G. W. Ernst and A. Newell, *GPS: A Case Study in Generality and Problem Solving.* New York: Academic, 1969.

Bridges: Impossible.
Letter Series: B.
remainder is 2).
Water Jug: 5 + 5 − 8 = 2 (Fill 5 and pour into 8, fill 5 and pour into 8,
confusion—object.
Parsing Sentences: Free—adjective; variables—noun; cause—verb;
Answers:

Box 5.2   Eleven Problems for GPS

metic problems, logic problems, and chess problems. The techniques for representing and testing models of human problem solving were clearly presented and are the basis for the discussion in this chapter.

How do you go about representing someone's problem-solving strategy? In order to understand how GPS does this, let's look at two separate ideas. First, a problem must be represented as a problem space. A problem space consists of the given state of the problem, the goal state of the problem, all possible operations that may be applied to any state to change it into another state, and all intermediate states of the problem. Box 5.3 shows an

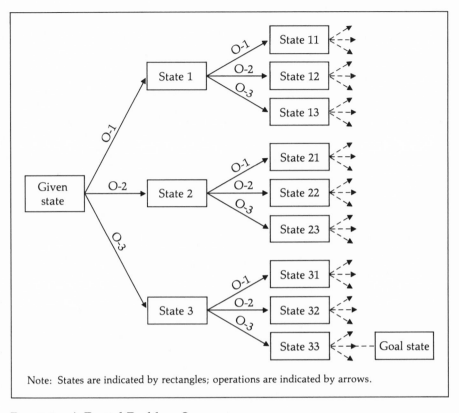

Note: States are indicated by rectangles; operations are indicated by arrows.

Box 5.3 A Partial Problem Space

example of a problem space with three possible operations. As you can see, there may be many useless paths (blind alleys) through the problem space.

Second, the solution to a problem involves a goal-directed searching through the problem space. In this case, problem solving involves finding the correct path from the given state, through some of the intermediate states, to the goal state. The important point here is that the search process is goal-directed. In general, people do not wander blindly or randomly around in the problem space. They have plans and subgoals. The particular planning strategy can be precisely represented in the GPS system.

The basic strategy for searching through the problem space in GPS is called means–ends analysis. Means–ends analysis is just one possible strategy that a person (or computer program) can use, but it is a general and powerful one. Means–ends analysis begins with a clearly specified problem space—all the allowable problem states and operators are specified. Then, the problem solver generates goals and attempts to find operators that can satisfy each goal; if a particular goal cannot be satisfied, a subgoal is created; only one subgoal is worked on at a time.

In GPS there are three general subgoals that can be used in means–ends analysis. They may be used repeatedly in a problem, but at any given point in problem solving only one can be used at a time. The three subgoals are

1. *Transform state A into state B.* This means that the problem is currently in one state (*A*) but you want it to be in some other state (*B*). In order to carry out this subgoal, you must compare state *A* to state *B*. If they are the same, you have succeeded and may go on. If they are different you must clearly specify what that difference (*D*) is. Once you have specified a difference *D* between states *A* and *B* you are ready to use a second subgoal (see below).

2. *Reduce difference D between state A and state B.* This means that you have located the difference *D* between *A* and *B*, and you would like to make the difference less. In order to carry out this subgoal, you must find some operator *Q* that is appropriate for the particular difference you have, and you must make sure that the operator *Q* can feasibly be applied to state *A*. Once you have found a relevant and feasible operator *Q*, you are ready to use a third subgoal (see below).

3. *Apply operator Q to state A.* This means that the problem is currently in state *A*, and that you would like to apply operator *Q* to state *A*. In order to carry out this subgoal, you compare the operator *Q* to the state *A*. If they match, you can apply the operator and produce a new state *A'.* If not, then you find the difference between the operator *Q* and the state *A'* and use subgoal 2 above to reduce it.

The three subgoals are summarized in Box 5.4. As you can see, each subgoal may also involve some of the other subgoals. One

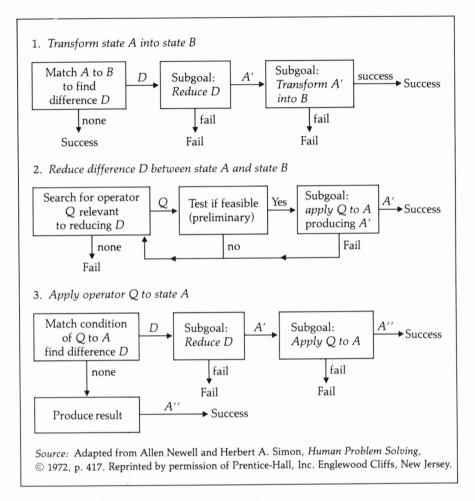

Source: Adapted from Allen Newell and Herbert A. Simon, *Human Problem Solving*,
© 1972, p. 417. Reprinted by permission of Prentice-Hall, Inc. Englewood Cliffs, New Jersey.

Box 5.4   Three Subgoals in Means–Ends Analysis

way of thinking about the subgoals is that each has an input and
an output. The *Transform A into B* subgoal starts with states *A*
and *B* and outputs the difference *D* between them. The *Reduce D*
subgoal starts with the difference *D* and outputs an operator *Q*
that may be applicable to reducing the difference. The *Apply Q*
subgoal takes state *A* and operator *Q* as the starting point and
ends with a new state *A'* that is the result of applying *Q* to *A*.

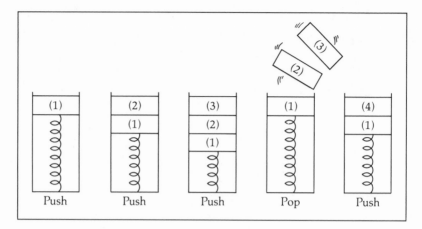

Box 5.5   Push-Down Pop-Up Goal Stack

In problem solving, a person begins with the goal of transforming the given state into the goal state. As you can see, this is a
Transform A into B subgoal. Let's make this the top goal in a
push-down pop-up stack as shown in Box 5.5. We put in the top
goal (1) and find that there is a difference *D*. Thus, the following
subgoal might be *Reduce the difference D*. We have not yet solved
the top goal so it stays in the stack, but we put subgoal (2) on top
of it. In order to accomplish subgoal (2) we must find an operator
and apply it. Let's say we find an operator *Q* and proceed to the
next subgoal (3): *Apply operator Q to state A*. Thus, we now put
subgoal (3) on top of our stack. We try to accomplish this subgoal
and are able to apply *Q* directly to state *A*. Thus subgoal (3) is
complete and can be popped off. This also satisfies subgoal (2), so
it pops off, and now we return to goal (1). We can say that goal (1)
is reinstated, and we must check to see if state *A* is different from
state *B*. If so, we push on a new subgoal (4) of reducing the difference, and so on. As you can see, the push-down pop-up stack
allows you to work on only one subgoal at a time and makes you
set up a new subgoal if you cannot solve the current one. Thus,
the three general subgoals and the stack provide a precise
mechanism for representing the strategy of the problem solver.

So far, we have examined two major representational tools that can be used in solving the strategy problem. These tools are a technique for specifying the problem space and a technique for specifying the goal structure of a problem. In the next section of this chapter we will show how these techiques can be applied to a real-world problem-solving situation—solving algebra problems.

EXAMPLES OF THE COGNITIVE APPROACH

Consider the problem of solving for x in the following equation:

$$2(3x - 11) = 3x + 8.$$

Assuming that the problem solver uses means–ends analysis, how can we represent the problem-solving process?

First, we need to construct a problem space. The initial state is

$$2(3x - 11) = 3x + 8$$

and the goal state is

$$x = \text{some number}$$

The allowable operators involve addition, subtraction, multiplication, and division of numbers and variables as specified by the rules of algebra. For purposes of this discussion let's define five operators:

Move number. Performing the same arithmetic operation on a number on both sides of the equation, such as subtracting 8 from both sides.

Move variable. Performing the same arithmetic operation on a variable on both sides of the equation, such as subtracting $3x$ from both sides.

Combine numbers. Performing an indicated arithmetic operation on two numbers on one side of the equation, such as changing $22 + 8$ into 30.

Combine variables. Performing an indicated arithmetic operation on two variables on the same side of the equation, such as changing $6x - 3x$ into $3x$.

Compute parens. Performing an indicated arithmetic operation between parentheses involving numbers and variables, such as changing $2(3x - 11)$ into $6x - 22$.

Name	Condition	Action
Move variable (MV)	x variable is on right side of equation.	Perform corresponding arithmetic operations to both sides, so as to move the x variable from right to left.
Move number (MN)	Number is on left side of equation.	Perform corresponding arithmetic operations to both sides, so as to move the number from left to right.
Combine variables (CV)	Two x variables on one side of equation.	Perform indicated operation so as to combine them into one x variable.
Combine numbers (CN)	Two numbers on one side of equation.	Perform indicated operation so as to combine them into one number.
Compute parentheses (CP)	Operation is to be distributed across parentheses.	Perform indicated operations so as to eliminate the parentheses.

Box 5.6   Condition–Action Chart

The conditions and actions implied by these five operators are summarized in Box 5.6.

To generate the intermediate states for the problem space, let's start with the given state and see what operators can be applied. We can apply *Move number* to the given state in order to get

$$2(3x - 11) - 8 = 3x$$

We can apply *Move variable* to the given state in order to get

$$2(3x - 11) - 3x = 8$$

We cannot apply *Combine numbers* or *Combine variables* to the given state because there are not two numbers or two variables on one side. We can apply *Compute parens* to the given state on the left side to get

$$6x - 22 = 3x + 8$$

Thus from the initial state there are three states in the first level of the problem space.

Where can we go from each of these states? If we are in the state

$$2(3x - 11) - 8 = 3x$$

we can move back to the start by *Move number,* or we can use *Move variable* to get

$$2(3x - 11) - 8 - 3x = 0$$

or we can apply *Compute parens* to get

$$6x - 22 - 8 = 3x$$

If we are in the state

$$2(3x - 11) - 3x = 8$$

we can get back to the given state by applying *Move variable* or we can apply *Move number* to get

$$2(3x - 11) - 8 - 3x = 0$$

or we can apply *Compute parens* to get

$$6x - 22 - 3x = 8$$

If we are in the state

$$6x - 22 = 3x + 8$$

we can use *Move variable* to get

$$6x - 22 - 3x = 8$$

or we can use *Move number* to get

$$6x = 3x + 8 + 22$$

These equations form the second level in the problem space. Part of the problem space is indicated in Box 5.7. Notice that one of the

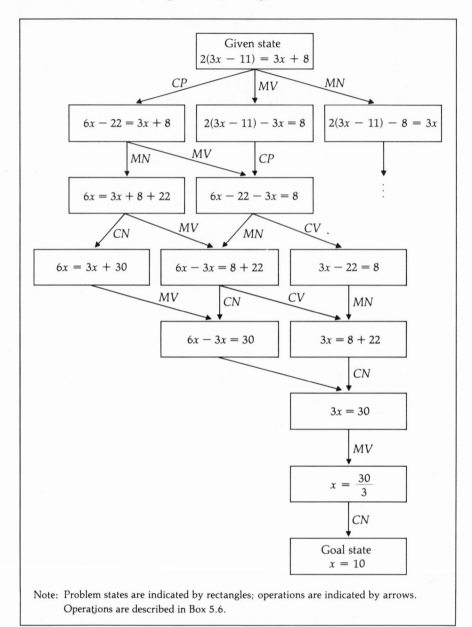

Box 5.7   Part of the Problem Space for $2(3x - 11) = 3x + 8$

five operators is applied in moving from each state to the next.

The next task is to represent the search process that someone goes through in moving across the problem space. We need to bring out our three subgoals as described in the previous section —*Transform A into B, Reduce D,* and *Apply Q*—and we need to bring out our push-down pop-up stack. These are general tools for representing the search process, but we also need to make some specific prescriptions concerning which operator (*Q*) should be applied under which conditions. There are five operators in the problem, and the goal state has *x* on the left side and a number on the right side of the equation. When there is an individual number on the left side of the equation, then we can apply the *Move number* operator. When there is an individual variable on the right side of the equation, then we can apply the *Move variable* operator. When there are two numbers on one side of the equation with an indicated arithmetic operation, we can apply the *Combine numbers* operator. When there are two variables on one side of the equation with an indicated arithmetic operation, we can apply the *Combine variables* operator. When there is an arithmetic operation indicated by parentheses, we can apply the *Compute parens* operator. (See Box 5.6.)

Now we are ready to start the show. You can use Box 5.8 to follow the problem-solving process. Our goal is to transform the given state into the goal state, so that is the top goal in the push-down pop-up stack. When we check for differences we find that there is a single variable on the right, a single number on the left, and a parentheses operation on the left. Since goal (1) cannot be achieved immediately, we create subgoal (2) and put it on top of the stack. This subgoal is to reduce the difference (that is, eliminate the problem that there is a variable on the right). Looking at the condition–action chart in Box 5.6, we see that the appropriate operation is *Move variable*. Thus, we create subgoal (3) to apply this operator; it works, and we create a new problem state. Subgoals (2) and (3) have been popped off, and we return to the original goal. However, there is still a difference between the present state of the problem and the goal state: There is a number on the left side, two separate variables are apart on the left side,

Subgoals in Stack*	Type of Subgoal	Statement of Subgoal	Success
(1)	*Transform*	Find value for x.	No: x on right, number on left, parens.
(2)(1)	*Reduce*	Get x to left.	Yes: Use *MV*.
(3)(2)(1)	*Apply*	Apply *MV*.	Yes: $2(3x-11)-3x=8$.
(1)	*Transform*	Find value for x.	No: Number on left, 2 x's apart, parens.
(4)(1)	*Reduce*	Get x's together.	Yes: Use *CV*.
(5)(4)(1)	*Apply*	Apply *CV*.	No: Parens.
(6)(5)(4)(1)	*Reduce*	Eliminate parentheses.	Yes: Use *CP*.
(7)(6)(5)(4)(1)	*Apply*	Apply *CP*.	Yes: $6x-22-3x=8$.
(5)(4)(1)	*Apply*	Apply *CV*.	Yes: $3x-22=8$.
(1)	*Transform*	Find value for x.	No: Number on left.
(8)(1)	*Reduce*	Get number to right.	Yes: Use *MN*.
(9)(8)(1)	*Apply*	Apply *MN*.	Yes: $3x=8+22$.
(1)	*Transform*	Find value for x.	No: 2 numbers apart, number on left.
(10)(1)	*Reduce*	Get numbers together.	Yes: Use *CN*.
(11)(10)(1)	*Apply*	Apply *CN*.	Yes: $3x=30$.
(1)	*Transform*	Find value for x.	No: Number on left.
(12)(1)	*Reduce*	Get number to right.	Yes: Use *MN*.
(13)(12)(1)	*Apply*	Apply *MN*.	Yes: $x=\frac{30}{3}$
(1)	*Transform*	Find value for x.	No: 2 numbers apart.
(14)(1)	*Reduce*	Get numbers together.	Yes: Use *CN*.
(15)(14)(1)	*Apply*	Apply *CN*.	Yes: $x=10$.
(1)	*Transform*	Find value for x.	Yes: $x=10$.

*Note: The push-down pop-up stack includes the overall goal [goal (1)] as well as subgoals.

Box 5.8   Goal Structure for $2(3x - 11) = 3x + 8$

and there is a parentheses operation specified on the left. We set up subgoal (4) to reduce the difference concerning the two x variables on the left side of the equation. The appropriate operation for this subgoal is *Combine variables*. Thus we set up subgoal (5) to apply this operator, but when we try we fail because we have not yet cleared up the parentheses. There is thus a difference (unfinished parentheses) that is noticed, so subgoal (6) is needed to reduce this difference. We find the operator *Compute parens* to be the relevant one, and set subgoal (7) to apply it. We succeed in applying this operator and create a new problem state. Thus sub-goals (7) and (6) are popped off, and we return to subgoal (5). We can now apply the *Combine variables* operator and create another new problem state. Subgoals (5) and (4) pop off, and we return to the top goal. Again, we find a difference between the current state and the goal state, namely the fact that there is a number on the left. We create subgoal (8) to reduce this differ-ence, and by consulting the condition–action chart we see that the appropriate operator is *Move number*. We set up a subgoal (9) to apply this operator. This succeeds, creates a new state, pops off subgoals (8) and (9), and returns us to the top goal. Now the solu-tion path is fairly clear. Subgoal (10) is established to reduce the difference concerning two numbers on the right; subgoal (11) applies the *Combine numbers* operation to reduce that difference and create a new state ($3x = 30$). In trying the top goal again we find that there is a number on the left, so we seek to get rid of it [subgoal (12)] and apply the *Move number* operator [subgoal (13)] to produce a new state ($x = \frac{30}{3}$). Now we find that there are two numbers and a specified operation on the right, so we seek to eliminate that difference [subgoal (14)] and apply the *Combine numbers* operation [subgoal (15)]. When we return to the top goal we find that we have succeeded. This goal is popped off, and the problem is solved.

You might feel that this representation of the problem-solving process is a bit too tedious and detailed. However, the amount of detail is what makes this representational tool so useful and at-tractive. It is now possible to specify precisely and simply how someone goes about solving a problem. The means–ends analysis tool allows a much more precise description than simply saying that people tend to use goals in problem solving. It allows us to specify exactly how someone goes about using goals.

An important feature of the means–ends model described above is that it is testable. We can compare how the model per-forms with how a real person performs. If the model and the person produce quite different performances, then we must

1. Ugh. I hate algebra problems.
2. OK, let's see. Solve for x.
3. I can get rid of the $3x$ on this side (points to the right),
4. so I have to subtract $3x$ from both sides.
5. (Writes: $2(3x - 11) - 3x = 8$)
6. While I'm at it, I need to get the x's together,
7. but the parentheses are in my way.
8. I'll multiply first, $6x$ minus 22 (points to left side of equation).
9. (Writes: $6x - 22 - 3x = 8$)
10. Now I can get the x's together,
11. which makes $3x$,
12. and I have to get 22 out of there (points to left).
13. Three times x equals 22 plus 8.
14. Three times x equals 30,
15. so x equals 10.
16. That's it.

Box 5.9 Protocol for $2(3x - 11) = 3x + 8$

modify the model. If the person and the model produce quite similar performances, then we have some reason to think that we are on the right track.

In order to test our model, let's give our problem to a subject. Further, let's ask the subject to solve the problem aloud, telling us what he or she is thinking at each step in the problem. A protocol that consists of a written copy of the subject's statements is given in Box 5.9. Numbers are assigned to different statements for convenience.

How well does the subject's protocol fit the performance of the means–ends analysis model? In statements 1 and 2, the subject recognizes that this is an algebra solution problem. Thus, the subject is acting as if he is setting the goal of finding a value for x. In statement 3, the subject points out a difference that must be reduced and finds an operator [as in subgoal (2)]. In statement 4 the *Move variable* operator is applied [as in subgoal (3)] and in statement 5 a new state is created, as in the model. In statement 6, another difference is found [as in subgoal (4)], and in statement 7, there is a recognition of another problem [as in subgoal (5)]. In statement 8, a new operation is found [subgoal (6)] and in statement 9 it is successfully applied [subgoal (7)]. The rest of the protocol also follows the general order of the model. Statements 10 and 11 correspond to subgoals (12) and (13). Statements 14 and 15 correspond to subgoals (14) and (15). Statement 16 corresponds to the accomplishment of the original goal. Thus, it appears that the subject's protocol and the performance of the means–ends model are fairly similar.

The condition–action diagram in the above example was modified from the work of Bundy (1975). Bundy suggested that we should "read between the lines" in analyzing how people solve algebraic equations by examining the major subgoals they have. In the present example, we have created five different condition-action pairs that correspond roughly to those outlined by Bundy. Further, Bundy suggests that the GPS system of means–ends analysis could be applied to the process of equation solving, and provides some examples similar to those used above. Bundy also notes that GPS may have to be modified in order to describe the strategies used by humans; however, he offers no empirical test of his model.

In a recent series of experiments, Mayer, Larkin, and Kadane (1980) found evidence that college students did tend to use a means–ends analysis strategy in solving algebra equations like the example in this section. However, some of the problems were stated in words such as, "Find a number such that if 11 less than 3 times the number was doubled that would be the same as 8 more than 3 times the number." When problems were stated in words, subjects showed no signs of using a means–ends analysis strategy. Apparently, when information gets too complicated humans are not able to make use of planning techniques.

APPLYING WHAT YOU'VE LEARNED

Suppose that you ask a subject to solve the following algebra problem with paper and pencil:

$$5(2x) = 2 + 8x$$

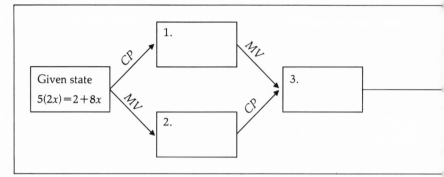

Box 5.10   Problem Space for $5(2x) = 2 + 8x$

The subject writes the following:

$$5(2x) = 2 + 8x$$
$$5(2x) - 8x = 2$$
$$10x - 8x = 2$$
$$2x = 2$$
$$x = 1$$

The subject also comments, "Always try to get the x's on the left and the numbers on the right first." Can you describe a means-ends analysis procedure that would have produced these states and that would be consistent with the subject's remark?

First, let's try to build a problem space so that we can see the paths that are available. Begin with the given state,

$$5(2x) = 2 + 8x$$

and see whether you can apply any of the five operators. Take a few minutes and try to build a problem space. If you have trouble, Box 5.10 provides a problem space for each of the states and gives the operation that leads to it. Can you fill in the states?

The correct states for Box 5.10 are as follows:

1. $10x = 2 + 8x$ 4. $2x = 2$
2. $5(2x) - 8x = 2$ 5. $x = \frac{2}{2}$
3. $10x - 8x = 2$ 6. $x = 1$

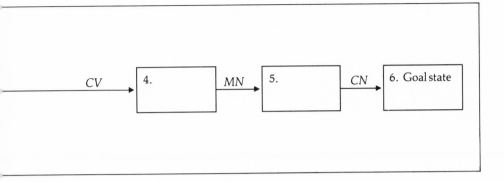

Now that you have built a problem space for the algebra equation problem, let's move on to the means–ends analysis. The same condition–action chart can be used as in Box 5.7. When selecting a difference to be reduced always try first to get the x's together on the left before making any computations with numbers. Box 5.11 provides a framework for this analysis. The top goal is to get a numerical value for x. Specify whether each subgoal is a *Transform*, a *Reduce*, or an *Apply*. If it is a *Transform*, tell what the major difference encountered is. If it is a *Reduce*, tell what the selected operator is. If it is an *Apply*, tell what the newly created state is. Can you fill in Box 5.11? Once you have filled it in, look at the analysis in Box 5.11a. Does your analysis look the same?

FURTHER APPLICATIONS OF STRATEGY MODELS

As you can see, there have been some exciting developments in the psychology of problem solving during the last decade. The beginning of this chapter described early research that suggested that humans use subgoals in problem solving (Duncker, 1945; Polya, 1957). This chapter has demonstrated two new tools for the analysis of problem solving—the problem space and the means–ends analysis of goal structure. These tools allow for a clear statement of the mechanism underlying the use of subgoals, and thus provide a real step forward over older, vaguer theories.

Subgoals in stack	Type of subgoal	Statement of subgoal	Success
(1)	*Transform*	Find value for x.	*No:* x on right, parens.

Box 5.11   Goal Structure for $5(2x) = 2 + 8x$

The pioneering work of Ernst and Newell (1969) and Newell and Simon (1972) demonstrated how a GPS-like system could be applied to a total of 14 different tasks. More recently, cognitive psychologists have been able to make improvements on the means–ends analysis system so that the model more closely fits the performance of human subjects. For example, Atwood and Polson (1976) successfully modified a GPS-like system for solving water jug problems so that they could more accurately predict the relative difficulty of problems. One change was to make some limitations on the system's memory. Egan (1973; Egan and Greeno, 1974) found that GPS was able to predict which steps in the tower of Hanoi problem would be most difficult; however, an even more accurate description could be derived by adding some memory limitations and allowing for more than one systematic planning strategy. Finally, work on a version of the missionaries and cannibals problem by several researchers (Thomas, 1974; Greeno, 1974; Simon and Reed, 1976) indicates that GPS-like systems fit the performance of subjects best when the task is fairly difficult, when the subject has some practice, and when hints are given. In other cases, subjects tend to use more variable strategies.

There have also been improvements in the techniques for generating a problem space. For example, Hayes and Simon's (1974) UNDERSTAND program takes a word problem and converts it into a problem space. The program has been applied to a wide variety of texts such as "instructions" and "directions." Earlier work by Bobrow (1968) produced a program that translated algebra story problems into a usable problem representation.

One useful direction for future research involves the analysis of problem-solving strategies in real-world domains. For example, Bundy (1975) analyzed the process by which people solve algebra equations. Greeno (1978) has analyzed the problem-solving strategies involved in geometry. Larkin (1979) has analyzed the strategies of experts and novices in solving physics problems. As techniques for representing strategies become more refined, we can expect fo find entire domains in mathematics and science mapped out.

As we learn more about the use of strategies in solving complex problems, we will be able to do a better job of teaching people how to solve problems. For example, Wickelgren's book *How to Solve Problems* (1974) provides instructions based on modern cognitive theory. As we are better able to describe the powerful, general heuristics that experts use, we may be able to devise ways of directly teaching these methods to novices.

Another future development may be that computer programs —designed by humans—may someday be able to beat humans in problem-solving exercises such as playing chess. A favorite topic of conversation among builders of problem-solving models concerns the date by which the best chess player in the world will be a computer program. Already, computer programs exist that can defeat very good chess players, but the grand masters are still humans as of this writing. In a recent issue of *Omni* researchers

Subgoals in stack	Type of subgoal	Statement of subgoal	Success
(1)	*Transform*	Find value for x.	No: x on right side, parens.
(2) (1)	*Reduce*	Get x on left.	Yes: Use *MV*.
(3) (2) (1)	*Apply*	Apply *MV*.	Yes: $5(2x) - 8x = 2$
(1)	*Transform*	Find value for x.	No: Two x's on left.
(4) (1)	*Reduce*	Get one x on left.	Yes: Use *CV*.
(5) (4) (1)	*Apply*	Apply *CV*.	No: Parens on left.
(6) (5) (4) (1)	*Reduce*	Eliminate parens.	Yes: Use *CP*.
(7) (6) (5) (4) (1)	*Apply*	Apply *CP*.	Yes: $10x - 8x = 2$
(5) (4) (1)	*Apply*	Apply *CV*.	Yes: $2x = 2$
(1)	*Transform*	Find value for x.	No: Number on left.
(8) (1)	*Reduce*	Get number on right.	Yes: Use *MV*.
(9) (8) (1)	*Apply*	Apply *MN*.	Yes: $x = \frac{2}{2}$
(1)	*Transform*	Find value for x.	No: Two numbers on right.
(10) (1)	*Reduce*	Get one number.	Yes: Use *CN*.
(11)(10) (1)	*Apply*	Apply *CN*.	Yes: $x = 1$
(1)	*Transform*	Find value for x.	Yes: $x = 1$. Stop.

Box 5.11a   Goal Structure for $5(2x) = 2 + 8x$. (One likely sequence of goals and subgoals.)

speculated that a machine will be the world champion within a few years. What this means is not that humans will have lost their place as thinkers in the world; quite the contrary, many cognitive psychologists will take pride in this event as evidence that the tools of science can successfully be applied to the study of the last frontier—the human mind.

SUGGESTED READINGS

Mayer, R. E., J. Larkin, and J. Kadane. *Analysis of the skill of solving algebra equations.* Santa Barbara, Calif.: University of California, Department of Psychology, Technical Report No. 80–2, 1980. Describes a system for representing the strategy a person uses in solving algebra equations.

Newell, A., and H. A. Simon. *Human problem solving.* Englewood Cliffs, N.J.: Prentice-Hall, 1972. A highly influential book that describes how means–ends analysis can be used to represent human problem-solving performance.

Wickelgren, W. A. *How to solve problems: Elements of a theory of problems and problem solving.* San Francisco: W. H. Freeman and Company, 1974. Discusses the concepts of problem space and means–ends analysis; provides descriptions of the major problem-solving strategies.

References

Anderson, J. R., and G. H. Bower. *Human associative memory.* Washington, D.C.: Hemisphere Press, 1973.

Atwood, M. E., and P. G. Polson. A process model for water jug problems. *Cognitive Psychology,* 1976, *8,* 191–216.

Bartlett, F. C. *Remembering.* Cambridge: Cambridge University Press, 1932.

Bobrow, D. G. Natural language input for a computer problem-solving system. In M. Minsky (Ed.), *Semantic information processing.* Cambridge, Mass.: MIT Press, 1968.

Bransford, J. D. *Human cognition.* Belmont, Calif.: Wadsworth, 1979.

Brown. F. C. *Principles of educational and psychological testing.* New York: Holt, Rinehart & Winston, 1976.

Brown, J. S., and R. R. Burton. Diagnostic models for procedural bugs in basic mathematical skills. *Cognitive Science,* 1978, *2,* 155–192.

Brownell, W. A. Psychological considerations in learning and teaching arithmetic. In *The teaching of arithmetic: Tenth yearbook of the National Council of Teachers of Mathematics.* New York: Columbia University Press, 1935.

Bruner, J. S., J. J. Goodnow, and G. A. Austin. *A study of thinking.* New York: Wiley, 1956.

Bundy, A. *Analysing mathematical proofs.* Edinburgh: University of Edinburgh, Department of Artificial Intelligence, Research Report No. 2, 1975.

Buros, O. K. (Ed.). *Mental measurements yearbook.* (7 vols.) Highland Park, N.J.: Gryphon Press, 1938–1972.

Carpenter, P. A., and M. A. Just. Sentence comprehension: A psycholinguistic processing model of verification. *Psychological Review,* 1975, *82,* 45–73.

Chomsky, A. N. *Syntactic structures.* The Hague: Mouton, 1957.

Cofer, C. N. An historical perspective. In C. N. Cofer (Ed.), *The structure of memory.* San Francisco: W. H. Freeman and Company, 1976.

Detterman, D. K. A job half done: The road to intelligence testing in the year 2000. *Intelligence,* 1979, *3,* 295–306.

Duncker, K. On problem solving. *Psychological Monographs,* 1945, *58* (No. 270).

Ebbinghaus, H. *Memory.* New York: Dover, 1964. (Originally published in 1885.)

Egan, D. E. The structure of experience acquired while learning to solve a class of problems. Ann Arbor, Michigan: Department of Psychology, Doctoral Dissertation, 1973.

Egan, D. E., and J. G. Greeno. Theory of rule induction: Knowledge acquired in concept learning, serial pattern learning, and problem solving. In L. Gregg (Ed.), *Knowledge and cognition.* Hillsdale, N.J.: Erlbaum, 1974.

Ehrenpreis, W., and J. M. Scandura. Algorithmic approach to curriculum construction: A field test in mathematics. *Journal of Educational Psychology,* 1974, *66,* 491–498.

Ernst, G. W., and A. Newell. *GPS: A case study in generality and problem solving.* New York: Academic Press, 1969.

Fillmore, C. J. The case for case. In E. Bach and R. T. Harms (Eds.), *Universals in linguistic theory.* New York: Holt, Rinehart & Winston, 1968.

Greeno, J. G. Hobbits and orcs: Acquisition of a sequential concept. *Cognitive Psychology,* 1974, *6,* 270–292.

Greeno, J. G. A study of problem solving. In R. Glaser (Ed.), *Advances in Instructional Psychology.* New York: Wiley, 1978.

Groen, G. J., and J. M. Parkman. A chronometric analysis of simple addition. *Psychological Review,* 1972, *79,* 329–343.

Guilford, J. P. The three faces of intellect. *American Psychologist,* 1959, *14,* 469–479.

Guilford, J. P. *The nature of human intelligence.* New York: McGraw-Hill, 1967.

Hayes, J. R., and H. Simon. Understanding written instructions. In L. W. Gregg (Ed.), *Knowledge and cognition.* Hillsdale, N.J.: Erlbaum, 1974.

Hilgard, E. R., and G. H. Bower. *Theories of learning.* Englewood Cliffs, N.J.: Prentice-Hall, 1980.

Holtzman, T. G., R. Glaser, and J. W. Pellegrino. Process training derived from a computer simulation theory. *Memory and Cognition,* 1976, *4,* 349–356.

Horn, J. L. Trends in the measurement of intelligence. *Intelligence,* 1979, *3,* 229–240.

Humphrey, G. *Thinking: An introduction to its experimental psychology.* New York: Wiley, 1963.

Hunt, E. Varieties of cognitive power. In L. B. Resnick (Ed.), *The nature of intelligence.* Hillsdale, N.J.: Erlbaum, 1976.

Hunt, E. Mechanics of verbal ability. *Psychological Review,* 1978, *85,* 109–130.

Hunt, E., N. Frost, and C. Lunneborg. Individual differences in cognition: A new approach to intelligence. In G. Bower (Ed.), *The psychology of learning and motivation* (Vol. 7). New York: Academic Press, 1973.

Hunt, E., and M. Lansman. Cognitive theory applied to individual differences. In W. K. Estes (Ed.), *Handbook of cognitive processes: Introduction to concepts and issues* (Vol. 1). Hillsdale, N.J.: Erlbaum, 1975.

Hunt, E., C. Lunneborg, and J. Lewis. What does it mean to be high verbal? *Cognitive Psychology*, 1975, 7, 194–227.

Intelligence, 1979, 3, 215–306.

Kintsch, W. *The representation of meaning in memory.* Hillsdale, N.J.: Erlbaum, 1974.

Kintsch, W. Memory for prose. In C. N. Cofer (Ed.), *The structure of memory.* San Francisco: W. H. Freeman and Company, 1976.

Kintsch, W., and T. A. van Dijk. Toward a model of text comprehension and production. *Psychological Review*, 1978, 85, 363–394.

Landa, L. N. *Algorithmization of learning and instruction.* Englewood Cliffs, N.J.: Educational Technology Publications, 1974.

Larkin, J. H. Models of strategy for solving physics problems. Paper presented at annual meeting of the American Educational Research Association, 1979.

Lindsay, P. H., and D. A. Norman. *Human information processing: An introduction to psychology.* New York: Academic Press, 1977.

Mandler, J. M., and N. S. Johnson. Remembrance of things parsed: Story structure and recall. *Cognitive Psychology*, 1977, 9, 111–151.

Mandler, J. M., and G. Mandler. *Thinking: From association to gestalt.* New York: Wiley, 1964.

Mayer, R. E., and J. G. Greeno. Effects of meaningfulness and organization on problem solving and computability judgments. *Memory and Cognition,* 1975, *3,* 356–362.

Mayer, R. E., J. Larkin, and J. Kadane. *Analysis of the skill of solving equations.* Santa Barbara, Calif.: University of California, Department of Psychology, Technical Report No. 80–2, 1980.

Meyer, B. J. F. *The organization of prose and its effects on memory.* Amsterdam: North-Holland, 1975.

Miller, G. A. The magic number seven, plus or minus two. *Psychological Review,* 1956, *63,* 81–97.

Miller, G. A., E. Galanter, and K. H. Pribram. *Plans and the structure of behavior.* New York: Holt, Rinehart & Winston, 1960.

Minsky, M. A framework for representing knowledge. In P. H. Winston (Ed.), *The psychology of computer vision.* New York: McGraw-Hill, 1975.

Neisser, U. *Cognitive psychology.* New York: Appleton-Century-Crofts, 1967.

Newell, A., J. C. Shaw, and H. A. Simon. Elements of a theory of human problem solving. *Psychological Review,* 1958, *65,* 151–166.

Newell, A., and H. A. Simon. *Human problem-solving.* Englewood Cliffs, N.J.: Prentice-Hall, 1972.

Pellegrino, J. W., and R. Glaser. Cognitive correlates and components in the analysis of individual differences. *Intelligence,* 1979, *3,* 187–214.

Peterson, L. R., and M. J. Peterson. Short-term retention of individual verbal items. *Journal of Experimental Psychology,* 1959, *58,* 193–198.

Piaget, J. *The construction of reality in the child.* New York: Basic Books, 1954.

Polya, G. *How to solve it.* Garden City, N.Y.: Doubleday, 1957.

Polya, G. *Mathematical discovery.* New York: Wiley, 1968.

Posner, J., S. Boies, W. Eichelman, and R. Taylor. Retention of visual and name codes of single letters. *Journal of Experimental Psychology Monographs,* 1969, *79* (1, Pt. 2).

Potts, G. R. Information processing strategies used in the encoding of linear orderings. *Journal of Verbal Learning and Verbal Behavior,* 1972, *11,* 727–40.

Resnick, L. B. *The nature of intelligence.* Hillsdale, N.J.: Erlbaum, 1976a.

Resnick, L. B. Task analysis in instructional design: Some cases from mathematics. In D. Klahr (Ed.), *Cognition and instruction.* Hillsdale, N.J.: Erlbaum, 1976b.

Resnick, L. B. The future of I.Q. testing in education. *Intelligence,* 1979, *3,* 241–254.

Rumelhart, D. E. Notes on a schema for stories. In D. G. Bobrow and A. M. Collins (Eds.), *Representation and understanding: Studies in cognitive science.* New York: Academic Press, 1975.

Rumelhart, D. E. *Introduction to human information processing.* New York: Wiley, 1977.

Scandura, J. M. *Problem solving.* New York: Academic Press, 1977.

Schank, R. C., and R. P. Abelson. *Scripts, plans, goals, and understanding: An inquiry into human knowledge structures.* Hillsdale, N.J.: Erlbaum, 1977.

Simon, H. A., and K. Kotovsky. Human acquisition of concepts for sequential patterns. *Psychological Review,* 1963, *70,* 534–546.

Simon, H. A., and S. K. Reed. Modeling strategy shifts in a problem-solving task. *Cognitive Psychology,* 1976, *8,* 86–97.

Skinner, B. F. *Science and human behavior.* New York: Free Press, 1953.

Skinner, B. F. *About behaviorism.* New York: Knopf, 1974.

Spearman, C. General intelligence objectively determined and measured. *American Journal of Psychology,* 1904, *15,* 201–293.

Spearman, C. *The abilities of man.* New York: Macmillan, 1927.

Spilich, G. J., G. T. Vesonder, H. L. Chiesi, and J. F. Voss. Text processing of domain related information for individuals with high and low domain knowledge. *Journal of Verbal Learning and Verbal Behavior,* 1979, *18,* 275–290.

Stein, N. L., and T. Nezworski. The effects of organization and instructional set on story memory. *Discourse Processes,* 1978, *1,* 177–193.

Sternberg, R. J. *Intelligence, information processing, and analogical reasoning: The componential analysis of human abilities.* Hillsdale, N.J.: Erlbaum, 1977.

Sternberg, S. Memory-scanning: Mental processes revealed by reaction time experiments. *American Scientist,* 1969, *57,* 421–457.

Thomas, J. C., Jr. An analysis of behavior in the hobbits-orcs problem. *Cognitive Psychology,* 1974, *6,* 257–269.

Thorndike, E. L. *The psychology of learning.* New York: Columbia University Press, 1913.

Thorndike, E. L. *Human learning.* New York: Century, 1931.

Thorndyke, P. W. Cognitive structures in comprehension and memory of narrative discourse. *Cognitive Psychology,* 1977, *9,* 77–110.

Thurstone, L. L. *Primary mental abilities.* Chicago: University of Chicago Press, 1938.

Wallas, G. *The art of thought*. New York: Harcourt, 1926.

Wickelgren, W. A. *How to solve problems*. San Francisco: W. H. Freeman and Company, 1974.

Wolf, T. H. *Alfred Binet*. Chicago: University of Chicago Press, 1973.

Woods, S. S., L. B. Resnick, and G. J. Groen. An experimental test of five process models for subtraction. *Journal of Educational Psychology*, 1975, *67*, 17–21.

Index

Abelson, R.P., 75–76, 81, 113
Ability
  cognitive theories of, 23–39
  examples of tests of, 15–17
  traditional theories of, 17–23
Addition, cognitive theories of, 55–58
Algebra problem solving, 82–107
Analogy problems, 21–37
Anderson, J.R., 65, 108
Arithmetic
  cognitive theories of, 43–59
  examples of, 40–41
  traditional theories of, 41–43
Attention, 25–26
Attribution, 9
Atwood, M.E., 104, 108
Austin, G.A., ix, 7, 108

Bartlett, F.C., 61, 108
Baseball, comprehension of, 79
Behaviorism. See also S–R associationism
  compared to cognitivism, ix, 3–5
  history of, 6
Binet's test of intelligence, 17–19
Bobrow, D.G., 80, 105, 108, 113
Boies, S., 28, 113
Borrowing procedure, in subtraction, 49–51
Bower, G.H., 14, 65, 108, 110
Bransford, J.D., 78, 108
Bridges of Konigsberg problem, 88
Brown, F.C., 16, 19, 108
Brown, J.S., 47, 54–55, 59, 108
Brownell, W.A., 43, 108
Bruner, J.S., ix, 7, 108
BUGGY, 54–55, 57, 59
Bugs, in arithmetic procedures, 47–58
Bundy, A., 101, 105, 109
Buros, O.K., 22, 109
Burton, R.P., 47, 54, 55, 59, 108

Carpenter, P.A., 59, 109
Case grammar, 65–66

Chess, 105–106
Chiesi, H.L., 79, 114
Chomsky, N., 7, 109
Chunking, 25–26
Cofer, C.N., 60, 80, 109, 111
Cognition. See Cognitive psychology
Cognitive development, 4, 7, 9
Cognitive processes, 12, 25–26, 40–59
Cognitive psychology
  analytic techniques, 10–14
  compared to behaviorism, 2–5
  definition of, 1–2
  history of, 5–10
  information processing system, 15–39
  process models, 40–59
  strategy models, 82–107
  structure models, 60–81
Cognitive strategies, 82–107
Cognitive structures, 12–13, 60–81
Cognitivism. See also Cognitive psychology
  compared to behaviorism, 3–5
Collins, A., 80, 113
Comprehension, of prose, 60–81
Computers
  analogy for human information processing, 11–12
  in BUGGY, 54–59
  in GPS, 86–93
  impact on cognitive psychology, 7–8
  in intelligence testing, 37
Condition–action chart, 94, 101
Consciousness, 5
Control processes, 25–26

Decoding process, 27–30
Deduction problems, 21
Detterman, D.K., 37, 109
Developmental psychology, 4, 7, 9
Duncker, K., 84–85, 103, 109

Ebbinghaus, H., 60–61, 109
Effort after meaning, 62

Egan, D.E., 104, 109
Ehrenpries, W., 58, 109
Eichelman, W., 28, 113
Emotion, relation to cognition, 4
Encoding, 25–26
Ernst, G.W., 86–88, 104, 109
Errors, in arithmetic procedures, 47–58

Factor analysis, 18
Factor theory, 17–23
Fillmore, C.J., 65, 110
Flowchart
   definition of, 43
   examples of, 43–45, 51
Frames, 78
Freudian psychology. *See* Psychoanalytic
      psychology
Frost, N., 27, 111

Galanter, E., ix, 8, 59, 112
General intelligence, 20
General Problem Solver (GPS), 86–93
General solution, 84–85
Gestalt psychology, 6–7, 10
g-factor, 20
Given state, in problem space, 88–89
Glaser, R., 37–38, 110, 112
Goals
   in problem solving, 84–85, 90–106
   in story grammars, 67–75
Goal stack
   definition of, 92
   example of, 98, 104
Goal state, in problem space, 88–89
Goal structure, 90–93, 98, 104
Goodnow, J.J., ix, 7, 108
GPS (General Problem Solver), 86–93
Grammar
   for sentences, 62–66
   for stories, 66–80
Greeno, J.G., 83, 104, 105, 109, 110, 112
Groen, G.J., 46, 58–59, 110, 115
Guilford, J.P., 20–21, 110

Hayes, J.R., 105, 110
Heuristics, 13, 82–107
Hilgard, E.R., 14, 110
Holtzman, T.G., 38, 110
Horn, J.L., 36, 110
Human information processing, 11–12,
      23–39
Humphrey, G., 14, 110
Hunt, E., 23, 26, 27–35, 38, 110, 111

Individual differences
   in information processing, 23–39
   measurement of, 15–23

Information processing system, 11–12,
      23–39
Instruction
   for arithmetic, 58
   for intelligence tests, 38
   for problem-solving strategies, 105
   for text processing, 79–80
Intelligence
   cognitive analysis of, 23–39
   psychometric measurement of, 17–23
   tests of, 15–17
Introspection, in structuralism, 5–6

Johnson, N.S., 80, 111
Just, M.A., 59, 109

Kadane, J., 101, 106, 112
Kintsch, W., 65, 79, 80, 111
Klahr, D., 59, 113
Knowledge
   procedural, 12, 40–59
   strategic, 13, 82–107
   verbal, 12–13, 60–81
Kotovsky, K., 38, 113

Landa, L.N., 58–59, 111
Landsman, M., 27, 111
Larkin, J.H., 101, 105, 106, 111, 112
Learning, from prose, 60–81
Lewis, J., 23, 26, 27–35, 38, 111
Lindsay, P.H., 26, 38, 111
Linguistics
   impact on cognitive psychology, 7
   sentence structure, 62–66
Long-term memory
   definition of, 24–25
   search for target in, 27–30, 35–36
Lunneborg, C., 23, 26, 27–35, 38, 111

Mandler, G., 14, 112
Mandler, J.M., 14, 80, 111, 112
Mathematics
   addition, 55–58
   algebra, 82–106
   subtraction, 41–55
Mayer, R.E., 83, 101, 106, 112
Means–ends analysis
   definition of, 90–93
   examples of, 93–106
Memory
   definition of structures and processes,
      24–26
   individual differences in, 26–39
   for prose, 60–81
Memory processes
   definition of, 25–26
   individual differences in, 26–39

Memory stores
  individual differences in, 26–39
  long-term memory, 24–25
  short-term memory, 24–25
  short-term sensory store, 24–25
  working memory, 24–25
Mental comparisons, 32–34
Mental factors, 20–21
Meyer, B.J.F., 79–80, 112
Miller, G.A., ix, 8, 59, 112
Minsky, M.A., 78, 108, 112
Missionaries and cannibals problem, 87
Morphemes, 26
Music ability, cognitive analysis of, 35–36

Narrative discourse, 60–81
Neisser, U., ix, 8, 112
Network structure, 62, 66
Newell, A., 7, 86–88, 91, 104, 107, 109, 112
Nezworski, T., 79, 114
Nonsense syllable, 60–61
Norman, D.A., 26, 38, 111

Objectivity, of tests, 20
Oddity problems, 21
Organization of memory, 60–81

Parkman, J.M., 58, 110
Parsing rules
  for sentences, 63
  for stories, 66–67
Pellegrino, J.W., 37–38, 110, 112
Peterson, L.R., 31–32, 112
Peterson, M.J., 31–32, 112
Piaget, J., 7, 113
Plan, as an alternative to S–R
  psychology, 8
Polson, P.G., 104, 108
Polya, G., 84–85, 103, 113
Posner, M., 28–29, 113
Potts, G.R., 59, 113
Pribram, K.H., ix, 8, 59, 112
Primary mental abilities, 20
Problem solving
  in algebra, 85–107
  in arithmetic, 40–59
  in GPS, 86–93
  in intelligence tests, 15–23
Problem space
  definition of, 88–89
  examples of, 94–97, 102–103
Problem states, 88–90, 94–97, 102–103
Procedural knowledge
  cognitive theory of, 43–59
  definition of, 40–41
  traditional theory of, 41–43
Process models, 12, 43–59

Program
  definition of, 43
  examples of, 43–44, 48–50, 56
  in GPS, 86–93
Propositions, 68–75
Prose processing, 60–81
Protocol
  in algebra problem solving, 100
  in mental arithmetic, 44
Psychoanalytic psychology
  compared to cognitivism, 3–5
  history of, 6–7, 10
Psycholinguistics
  impact on cognitive psychology, 7
  in sentence structure, 62–66
  in story structure, 66–80
Psychometrics, 17–23
Push-down pop-up stack
  definition of, 92
  example of, 98, 104

Reaction time
  in mental arithmetic, 46–47
  in Posner task, 27–30·
  in Sternberg task, 32–34
Reading
  cognitive analysis of, 26–39
  learning from, 60–61
  test of, 16
Reading comprehension test, 15–17
Recall, of stories, 68–75
Reed, S.K., 105, 114
Rehearsal, 25–26
Reliability, of tests, 20
Resnick, L.B., 37, 39, 46, 58, 59, 110, 113, 115
Restaurant script, 75–78
Rewrite rules
  for sentences, 63
  for stories, 66–67
Rules. *See* Procedural knowledge
Rumelhart, D.E., 66–67, 72, 76, 80, 113

Scandura, J.M., 58, 109, 113
Schank, R.C., 75–76, 81, 113
Schema, 78
Scholastic Aptitude Test, 15
Scripts, 75–78
Search processes
  individual differences, in, 27–30, 35–36
  in long-term memory, 25–26
  in problem space, 90–104
Series-completion problems, 37–38, 88
Shaw, J.C., 7, 112
Short-term memory
  definition of, 24–25
  individual differences in, 28, 30–36

Short-term sensory store, 24–25
Simon, H.A., 38, 86, 91, 104–105, 107, 110, 112, 113, 114
Skill. *See* Procedural knowledge
Skinner, B.F., ix, 3, 114
Spearman, C., 18–20, 114
Spilich, G.J., 79, 114
S-R associationism. *See also* Behaviorism
    definition of, 8
    as a theory of arithmetic learning, 41–43
    as a theory of verbal learning, 60–62
Standardization, of tests, 20
Stanford–Binet test of intelligence, 19
Stein, N.L., 79, 114
Sternberg, R.J., 37, 39, 114
Sternberg, S., 32–33, 114
Story grammar, 66–75, 78–80
Strategic knowledge, 13, 82–107
Strategies, 82–107
Strategy models, 13, 82–107
Structuralism, 5–6, 10
Structure models, 12–13, 60–81
Structure of intellect theory, 20–21
Subgoals
    in problem solving, 84–85, 90–106
    in story grammars, 67–75
Subtraction
    cognitive theory of, 43–55
    example of, 40–41
    traditional theory of, 41–43

Taylor, R., 28, 113
Tests
    criteria of good tests, 20
    development of tests, 22
    future of, 36–37
    for mental ability, 15–17

Theme, in stories, 66, 68–69, 74
Thinking. *See* problem solving
Thomas, J.C., 105, 114
Thorndike, E.L., 41–43, 114
Thorndyke, P.W., 61, 66–74, 79–81, 114
Thurstone, L.L., 20, 114
Tower of Hanoi problem, 87
Trait theory, 17–23
Transfer, between stories, 74
Tree structure
    for sentences, 62–64
    for stories, 70–71
Tumor problem, 84–85
Two-factor theory of intelligence, 20

Validity, of tests, 20
van Dijk, A., 79–80, 111
Verbal ability
    cognitive theories of, 23–39
    example of tests of, 15–17
    traditional theories of, 17–23
Verbal knowledge, 12–13, 60–81
Vesonder, G.T., 79, 114
Voss, J.F., 79, 114

Wallas, G., 83, 115
Water jug problem, 87
Wickelgren, W.A., 105, 107, 115
Wolf, T.H., 17, 115
Woods, S.S., 46, 58, 115
Working backwards strategy, 83
Working forward strategy, 83
Working memory
    definition of, 24–25
    individual differences in, 28, 30–36
Writing, 79